MARKETING RESEARCH

MARKETING RESEARCH: Fundamentals and Dynamics

Gerald Zaltman
Northwestern University

Philip C. Burger
State University of New York, Binghamton

The Dryden Press
901 North Elm Street
Hinsdale, Illinois 60521

Copyright © 1975, by The Dryden Press,
A Division of Holt, Rinehart and Winston, Inc.
All rights reserved
Library of Congress Catalog Card Number: 74–80398
ISBN: 0–03–003566–X
Printed in the United States of America
4 5 6 7 8 9   071   9 8 7 6 5 4 3 2 1

To Carolyn and Marsha, G.Z.

To Virginia, P.C.B.

Contents

12   Data Analysis: The Multivariate Techniques of Linear Regression and Linear Discriminant Analysis   456

13   Data Analysis: The Multivariate Grouping of Respondents and Questions   498

Foreword

The advisory editors of The Dryden Press are pleased to publish this lucid and up-to-date marketing research text. With a conceptual foundation drawn from the philosophy of science, the authors present a rigorous yet readily understandable discussion of marketing research theory and practice. To this methodological base, Zaltman and Burger add the rigor of quantitative methods for analyzing univariate and multivariate data as well as measurement tools and concepts from the behavioral sciences. The behavioral orientation of this book provides an important substantive foundation.

The result of all of this is a workable blend of theory and application that is modern enough for the technical innovator and pragmatic enough for the marketing manager. This book has combined the proved, enduring technology of marketing research with advances of the 1970s to provide a modern, comprehensive treatment of the fundamentals and dynamics of marketing research. Thus, although this book is similar in many ways to existing texts, it is also sufficiently different in unique and important ways to represent, perhaps, a new generation of marketing research books.

In short, this straightforward book should be useful to anyone desiring to understand how one goes about the process of orderly inquiry into marketing and consumer phenomena.

Paul E. Green
Philip Kotler

Preface to the Student

The idea of writing a marketing research text first occurred to us in late 1971 as we were swapping notes on our experiences in teaching the introductory marketing research course at both the undergraduate and M.B.A. levels. Neither we nor our students were particularly satisfied with existing materials. The idea of a book simply incubated after our initial conversation. Approximately one year later we had occasion to speak with some of our former students and their immediate colleagues who were involved with marketing research—some from a doer's standpoint and others from a user's standpoint. It was quite evident from our conversation with them that both doers and users would have been better equipped for their respective first encounters with marketing research had they received a different kind of initial introduction in their courses. This rekindled our earlier interest in writing a basic marketing research text, and we started work in earnest drafting the first of several versions of our planned chapter outlines. We were carefully attentive to the expressed needs and interests of present and former students and are very indebted to them for their comments on the early expression of our ideas for this text and on various aspects of the text as it developed.

As the text began to take shape, we felt the need for additional marketing intelligence from a different market segment—the instructor. Accordingly, through the use of a mail questionnaire, we obtained the attitudes and opinions of 307 marketing research instructors. Information was obtained about the advantages and disadvantages—from both the instructors' and students' perspectives—of the text in current use, important topics most often missing or underemphasized, topics for which readings and/or cases were most useful, the use of research projects, data banks, and so forth. We feel that this first case of systematic marketing research on marketing research books and courses paid off handsomely. Many features in this book are the direct result of information provided to us by the concerned respondents in our survey. The chances are that *your* instructor was one of these respondents.

The philosophy of the book is that there is certain core material that doers and users of marketing research need in the first course and that the specialized training needs of marketing researchers on the one hand and marketing managers for whom research is performed on the other hand is best provided by advanced courses and on-the-job training. We feel the material in this book provides the basic material any marketer needs as a professional,

xvii

regardless of the degree to which he is involved in the conduct and use of marketing research. To be sure, we were constantly faced with decisions to add and delete, emphasize and deemphasize, and the net result can hardly be satisfactory to everyone. However, considerable classroom testing of the manuscript for this book gives us confidence that the reader will obtain a good grounding in the essentials of marketing research. Writing this book, which involved working closely with many practitioners, students, and faculty, was an exciting venture for us. We hope some of this excitement and the excitement of marketing research will be shared with you as you read this book.

Evanston, Ill.   '   Gerald Zaltman
Binghamton, N.Y.   Philip C. Burger
May 1974

Preface to the Instructor

Marketing research has undergone a silent but highly visible revolution during the past several years. Considered collectively, changes in the amount of research, the contexts and themes of research, and research technology (particularly in quantitative tools), have been enormous. These changes have been more or less contemporaneous with significant changes in the marketing discipline in general. While preserving well-established marketing research procedures, we have tried to introduce the more promising and, in many instances, already commonly accepted new directions in marketing research.

As we indicate in our Preface to the Student, the philosophy of this book is that there is certain core material that potential doers and users of marketing research need in the first course. The specialized needs of the researcher on the one hand and the manager on the other hand are best met by more advanced courses and practical working experience. The material we provide in this book represents what, in our judgment, is the basic material a professional marketer needs, regardless of the degree to which he is involved in the conduct and use of marketing research. To be sure, some topics are missing, and the reader may find certain topics underemphasized and others overemphasized to his liking. At the same time, the reader will find a treatment of topics missing or infrequently found in most other basic marketing research texts. These include an elementary but comprehensive discussion of the philosophy of science, which is the conceptual home of all research, a chapter on consumer behavior concepts commonly used in marketing research, a chapter on attitude research, a chapter on ethics in marketing research, three chapters presenting a basic introduction to univariate and multivariate statistics, a chapter on the preparation of research proposals and research reports, and a chapter on research utilization. We feel that strength but not complexity has been added to the usual treatment of problem definition, research design, marketing experimentation, questionnaire development and administration, marketing information systems, and sampling.

The manuscript has received extensive classroom testing in the introductory marketing research course at both the undergraduate and graduate (M.B.A.) levels. The information we received from the final round of testing was that the manuscript was very effective at either level, with differences in sophistication between the two levels readily accommodated by selective use of end-of-chapter questions and exercises and supplementary materials beyond the text. The Instructor's Manual contains guidelines for using the book with different groups of students.

A very major source of influence on virtually all aspects of this book stemmed from our own marketing research on the needs of marketing research teachers. A mail questionnaire was used to identify the problems and advantages of existing texts from the instructor's perspective and, through the instructor, from the student's perspective: the extent to which cases were used and with what topics; the use of readings; the identity of topics receiving inadequate coverage in existing books; the use of data banks; supplementary materials; and so forth. The response to our questionnaire was overwhelming: 307 usable questionnaires were returned by persons actively teaching marketing research and representing a substantial proportion of those who teach the course in the United States. Many returns were accompanied by a course outline or syllabus. The value of this information and its impact on the development of the book cannot be overestimated. It guided us in the selection and treatment of topics (particularly quantitative methods), cases, readings, and end-of-chapter questions and exercises and in the overall product positioning of the book. One particular result is the greater attention given in both the end-of-chapter material and in the Instructor's Manual to the student project approach in teaching marketing research. Another result is a more careful matching of cases and readings to topic areas.

In summary, we faced a major challenge in developing a book that contained the core mix of marketing research technology and processes required by any marketer regardless of the nature and extent of his involvement with marketing research in the real world. In meeting this challenge we were helped enormously by well over 300 colleagues in and out of academia and a very substantial number of students. We hope you will find the results satisfactory to you and your students.

Evanston, Ill.   Gerald Zaltman
Binghamton, N.Y.   Philip C. Burger
May 1974

Acknowledgments

No textbook grows into being by the lone efforts of its authors. Rather, a large number of students and faculty colleagues labor in various ways to make the effort a reality. This book is no exception. Particular indebtedness is owed to Professor Paul E. Green (University of Pennsylvania) and Professor Philip Kotler (Northwestern University) for their critical reading of different drafts of the manuscript. Professor Lawrence Feldman (University of Illinois, Chicago), Professor Philip Kuehl (University of Maryland), and Professor M. Venkatesan (University of Iowa) provided very helpful comments and advice on all chapters. Many persons gave critiques of chapters falling within their areas of special expertise. Specifically, we would like to acknowledge the invaluable insights offered by Professor Mark I. Alpert (University of Texas at Austin), Professor Ira D. Anderson (Northwestern University), Professor Richard M. Clewett (Northwestern University), Professor John Czepiel (New York University), Professor René Darmon (University of Laval), Professor Walter Henry (University of California, Riverside), Professor Sidney J. Levy (Northwestern University), Professor James Nelson (Montana State University), Professor Andrew Ruppel (University of Virginia), Professor Charles Schewe (University of Massachusetts), Professor Stanley F. Stasch (Northwestern University), and Professor Brian Sternthal (Northwestern University). These individuals have had a very significant impact on the shape and substance of this book. The more than 300 marketing research teachers who responded to our questionnaire gave us special insights into the needs of teachers and students of this subject matter. Virtually all chapters differ in some important way from what they would have looked like had no large-scale marketing research been undertaken. We appreciate the time so many people took to provide us with the information we sought and more.

Special acknowledgments are due our undergraduate and graduate students over the past few years. Without their discontent this book would not have been undertaken; without their assistance and stimulation it would have been much longer in the making; and without their critical testing as ultimate consumers the book would not be as well suited to students' interests and textbook needs as it is. Among the very large number of students, a few deserve special mention: Jean Chandon, Janice Gordon, Scott Hannah, Jack Kasulis, Eugene Schonfeld, Carol Ann Scott, and Jeff Stearman. Edith Bass and

Marion Davis performed yeoman service in typing, xeroxing, and other services which greatly facilitated the production of this book. Their efforts are very much appreciated.

MARKETING RESEARCH

Chapter 1

An Introduction to Marketing Research

Chapter 1 provides an overview of marketing research by describing what it is, its history, the reasons why it is and is not done, the people and organizations engaged in marketing research and, finally, a brief overview of a typical marketing research project. Of special importance in marketing research is the increasing emphasis on a more explicit use of scientific procedure for the purpose of a more effective implementation of the marketing concept. The reader will note that the evolution of the marketing concept is paralleled by the emergence of more scientific research work.

What Is Marketing Research?

The American Marketing Association has defined marketing research as the accurate, objective, and "systematic gathering, recording, and analyzing of data about problems relating to the marketing of goods and services."[1] However, this definition of marketing research does not include the preresearch analysis associated with marketing research that is necessary to define what information should be gathered, recorded, and analyzed. Therefore, a new definition is necessary. This new definition which assumes that the marketing organization is concerned with its environment is as follows: *Marketing research involves the diagnosis of information needs and the selection of relevant interrelated variables about which valid and reliable information is gathered, recorded, and analyzed.* The added emphasis in this definition is the diagnosis of an *information need* concerning the relationship a marketing institution has with its markets. Marketing research also includes the analysis and evaluation of action taken on the basis of information. The latter part of Chapter 2 discusses the logic of research in marketing, and so elaboration upon this definition is deferred until then. However, it should be pointed out here that the above definition and the more detailed discussion of research in the next chapter reflect changes in the scope and nature of marketing research as reflected by the contemporary practice of marketing research.

The marketing concept is a key part of the rationale for the importance of marketing research. The marketing concept states that:

> a customer orientation is backed by integrated marketing aimed at generating customer satisfaction as the key to satisfying organizational goals.[2]

The marketing concept can be contrasted to the sales concept:

> Products lead to selling and promotion, which leads to profits through sales volume.

The sales concept almost universally has been replaced by the marketing concept. The key problem embedded in the marketing concept is discovering what

---

[1] Report of a Definitions Committee of the American Marketing Association (Chicago: American Marketing Association, 1961).

[2] Philip Kotler, *Marketing Management: Analysis, Planning and Control,* 2nd ed. (Englewood Cliffs, N. J.: Prentice-Hall, 1972), p. 17.

3

customer needs are and how the company can meet these needs at a profit. This is the interface marketing research is concerned with. As will be noted shortly, this customer orientation is a particular characteristic of contemporary marketing research.

The History of Marketing Research

The history of marketing is deeply woven into the economic history of the United States. The marketing function before the Industrial Revolution of the mid-nineteenth century consisted of little more than the efforts of buyers and sellers who met at a mutually agreed upon geographic location to strike a bargain and exchange goods. As the Industrial Revolution gained momentum, the producers found that there was practically an unlimited demand for their goods since mass production had reduced the price (in real income terms) of most goods. However, as continued investment in production facilities continued, producers found that buyers would no longer clear the market as easily as before. Thus, means of competition were sought. A logical means of competition, as economic theory would suggest, is that of price. However, competitors found that overzealous price competition often resulted in lower profits. Thus, nonprice means of competition were sought. These means included competing for consumer awareness through mass media promotion, and the use of special incentives such as coupons, samples, and premium offers. Marketing research was also used to provide a competitive edge in the form of knowledge about customers which the company could use in developing marketing plans. Thus, complex marketing strategies involving variations of all the marketing tools developed.

Marketing research appears to have gone through six phases to date. These phases include (1) the industrial statistics phase: 1880–1920; (2) the random sampling, questionnaire and behavioral measurement development era: 1920–1940; (3) the management awareness phase: 1940–1950; (4) the experimentation phase (never really very strong): 1950–1960; (5) the computer analysis and quantitative methods phase: 1960–1970; and (6) the consumer theory development phase: 1970 to date. Each of these phases represents a development and refinement from the very general approaches to gathering data for solving problems to the very specific and highly relevant attempt to create theories that are meaningful and general to marketing. The six phases mentioned above are, of course, oversimplified and categorized. For example, the computer analysis and quantitative methods phase did not start suddenly in 1960 nor did it end in 1970. Rather, it was the most salient feature of marketing research during this period.

The Time-Line of Marketing Research

The chronology of the development of marketing research is shown in Figure 1.1. Before 1900, the economy of the United States was in a process of

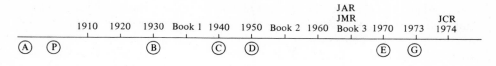

(A) Industrial Revolution — census becomes important.

(B) Government form statistical Bureaus to collect economic and commerical data regularly.

(C) Market researchers learn how to sample and measure human behavior.

(D) Market research becomes marketing research, i.e., the emphasis changes from economics to management as the central role of marketing.

(E) The computer becomes a major part of marketing research.

(G) Consumer theories become organized.

(P) Mr. Hollerith of the Census Bureau invents the paper card with holes punched, leading to mechanical tabulation of data.

Book 1 = Brown, Book 2 = Boyd and Westfall, Book 3 = Green and Tull.

JAR = *Journal of Advertising Research*

JMR = *Journal of Marketing Research*

JCR = *Journal of Consumer Research*

FIGURE 1.1 *The Chronology of Marketing Research*

conversion from an agrarian orientation to an industrial orientation. Governmental planners realized that it was important to have accurate figures concerning the level of economic activity to facilitate meaningful governmental policy to stimulate economic growth and efficiency. Thus, the census function was expanded gradually from merely counting population to measuring economic activity. This process was largely complete by the mid-1930s.[3] About 1890, an employee of the Bureau of the Census named H. Hollerith invented the paper punched card and a method for punching information on small rectangular cards which are now called "IBM" cards. This development allowed the researcher to analyze large quantities of data in an efficient, mechanical way; that is, machines were invented to sort, count, and rearrange the cards. Researchers now could make meaningful analysis and conclusions from very large samples. The punch card also made possible the later invention of the digital computer.

During the mid-1920s to about 1940, the emphasis in market analysis shifted to the individual consumer largely due to the efforts of sociologists

[3] From an interview with Ira D. Anderson, Professor of Marketing, Northwestern University, January 1973.

such as Paul Lazarsfeld.[4] The techniques of sampling, questionnaire analysis, and consumer behavior were clearly defined and developed during this period. Also, the first texts concerning marketing research as a series of coordinated activities appeared in the late 1930s. The most successful text of the period in terms of adoptions by schools was that by Brown.[5] Also, the American Marketing Association published a marketing research text in the same year when Brown's book appeared.

During the period of the 1940s, a subtle yet significant change appeared in the field of marketing. The change can be characterized as a change from market research to marketing research. Market research implied that analysis was oriented to understanding the composition and operation of specific markets. Marketing research shifted the emphasis to the management activities (marketing), which means that the firms' impacts on markets were studied. Marketing research became a significant management activity. Management decision making became the central *raison d'etre* of marketing research. One salient piece of evidence of this change was the publication of the widely used marketing research book by Harper Boyd and Ralph Westfall.[6]

In the period beginning about 1960, a new major development occurred. This development was the advent and growing availability of the large-scale digital computer. Leading marketing researchers realized that the computer extended the possibilities of marketing research markedly, especially quantitative marketing research. Two major events occurred which reflected the trend toward more quantitative marketing research. First, two major journals appeared to facilitate communication concerning the technology: the *Journal of Marketing Research* and the *Journal of Advertising Research*. Second, another text, authored by Paul Green and Donald Tull, appeared which stressed the value of information and the technology of computer-aided quantitative analysis.[7] Perhaps the most recent developments on the marketing research frontier include the development of more organized consumer behavior theories. These theories and their associated measurement systems have addressed a major task, that is, the task of developing a theory useful to marketing researchers. These theories and measurement systems are discussed in Chapters 5 and 6. One expression of this added emphasis on consumer behavior is the appearance of the *Journal of Consumer Research* in 1974. Another expression

---

[4] Lazarsfeld was a member of the American Marketing Association committee which published one of the first books on the execution of marketing research stressing consumer measurement. F. C. Wheeler, *The Technique of Marketing Research* (New York: McGraw-Hill, 1937).

[5] L. O. Brown, *Market Research and Analysis* (New York: Ronald Press, 1937).

[6] Harper Boyd and Ralph Westfall, *Marketing Research: Text and Cases* (Homewood, Ill.: Irwin, 1956).

[7] Paul Green and Donald Tull, *Research for Marketing Decisions* (Englewood Cliffs, N. J.: Prentice-Hall, 1966).

of this emphasis is the general acceptance of the marketing concept described at the very beginning of this chapter.

Thus, with the advent of theory, developing measurement technology, advanced analysis techniques, and means for dissemination of the information, marketing research seems poised for the most important step: the adoption of an integrated, *scientific* approach to marketing research blending quantitative and qualitative analysis. Marketing research appears ready to become primarily concerned with developing, for marketing management use, certified knowledge concerning customer behavior.

The Change to Science in Marketing Research

From the various early stages of marketing research, a debate has been occurring between those who would like to believe that marketing research is a science against those who say that it clearly is not. The term *science* can be tentatively defined as *the set of activities which concern studying a system which is measurable, performing studies which are reproducible, and being objective in terms of not influencing the results to fit one's own predilections.* In these terms marketing research has over time emerged as a science. It has attempted to develop measurable variables concerning human behavior; it has attempted to create reproducible experiments although it is clearly weakest in this point; and researchers have attempted to be objective in the study of human behavior related to the world of marketing.

The Importance of Being Scientific

Why is it important that marketing research be scientific? It is important because marketing research has to deal with certified knowledge, and without certified knowledge good management decisions cannot be made. The implication of this statement is that the scientist attempts to uncover objective "truth." Because management is primarily interested in making decisions based on accurate and unbiased data, it is clear that the market researcher must follow scientific procedure in order for data to be collected and analyzed properly.

This book, particularly Chapters 2 and 3, stresses the utilization of scientific methodologies; that is, it emphasizes rigorous and sound ways of thinking about marketing problems and for conducting research into their nature. As indicated earlier, with the development and merging of behavioral science oriented research and research into quantitative techniques, it has become especially important to study marketing research as a scientific process. There are several benefits resulting from this perspective:

1. Problem definition is made easier and more accurate.
2. Research questions related to the marketing problem become more focused and precise.

3. Marketing research becomes more clear and precise with regard to the statement of behavioral and marketing concepts and their measurement.
4. Marketing research is conducted in a more methodical and systematic way.
5. Ideas and hypotheses become tested under circumstances where their credibility is more readily established or desired.
6. The accuracy and completeness of description and explanation are enhanced.
7. Better marketing predictions can be made.
8. Marketers are able to intervene in the marketplace more effectively, thus increasing the likelihood of marketing objectives being attained.
9. A more constructively critical approach can be pursued in the evaluation of the overall research process.

Why Marketing Research?

The object of marketing research is to collect and analyze data concerning the interface between the firm and its market, thereby enabling the marketing decision maker to maximize the effectiveness of decisions relating to product, price, promotion, and distribution. Thus, the single most important reason for undertaking marketing research is to improve the quality of managerial decision making. Marketing research often has important implications for parts of the firm other than marketing. For example, research on the changing level of consumer demand may help production management forecast factory personnel needs for meeting the new level of demand.

The most direct impact of marketing research is, of course, felt by marketing management. *Marketing research is undertaken to guide managers in their analysis, planning, implementation, and control of programs to satisfy customer and organizational goals.* Table 1.1 presents several specific topics which are the frequent focus of marketing research. They receive attention because the understanding obtained improves marketing efficiency. Research on any of the topics shown has implications for one or more of the major functions of analysis, planning, implementation, and control of marketing programs. Research concerning customer profiles relates to the analysis function. Research concerning policy relates to the planning and control functions of management, while research on mass media effort and sales method relates to implementation processes. Thus, the very core functions of management require research for them to be carried out with maximum efficiency. However, marketing research can be both a positive and negative force in marketing decision making. Exhibit 1 is a concise commentary on the proper use and frequent abuse of marketing research.

TABLE 1.1 *Areas of Marketing Research*

Research Related to Products and Services
1. New product development
2. Improvement of present products
3. New uses for old products
4. Competitive position of company's products
5. Packaging
6. Pretesting a new product
7. Customer preferences
8. Product elimination or simplification of product line
9. Costs and profits of new products
10. Naming of products

Research Related to Markets
1. Analysis of consumer markets
2. Analysis of the wholesaler markets
3. Relative profitableness of markets
4. Analysis and interpretation of general market data
5. Estimation of potential sales
6. Estimating demand for new products
7. Market analysis by customer profiles
8. Market analysis by areas
9. Establishment of sales territories
10. Establishment of sales quotas
11. Competitive condition in the markets
12. General business forecasting
13. Analysis of business potential in new market areas

Research Related to Policy
1. Marketing policy structure
2. Sales methods or distribution policy
3. Advertising policy
4. Sales compensation
5. Wholesaler and dealer margin policy
6. Premium policy
7. Inventory policy

Research Related to Sales Method
1. Advertising and selling emphasis
2. Distribution costs
3. Choice of advertising media
4. Selection of distribution channels
5. Sales performance tests
6. Sales training effects

Analysis of Mass Media Effort
1. The testing of advertising copy
2. The testing for awareness of advertising campaigns
3. The effect of media scheduling
4. The effect of advertising on brand switching

EXHIBIT 1   *Editorial: Marketing Research—Is It Used or Abused?***

One of the surest ways to lose a friend is to be openly critical of him. Similarly, marketing research often destroys its relationship with marketing management by appearing to be critical of management's decisions. Once the relationship has deteriorated, research can easily become another sales promotion device rather than an effective marketing intelligence tool.

The failure of marketing research to maintain a meaningful, decision-oriented relationship with marketing management stems from several sources. For example, research is too often conducted after the marketing decision to explain why something "went wrong" rather than at an earlier stage when it could have aided in effective decision making. Thus, the information obtained often places decision makers in a highly defensive postion regarding their decision. Moreover, when marketing management is not securely positioned in the company structure, research may be used as the executioner by other management forces.

Marketing research is essentially a tool for reducing management decision risk and thus enhancing long-term profitability. Research does this in many ways. It can be useful in almost any kind of marketing decision provided there is some uncertainty and a sufficiently high monetary risk to justify obtaining information to reduce this risk. Yet, in few companies does research play only this role.

In fact, in many major companies the marketing research function is failing to grow because it is not being applied in a positive planning role *prior* to decision making. As a result, marketing research becomes a sales promotion tool used by top management to justify marketing decisions and to encourage members of the marketing team to be "properly optimistic." For example, some large companies today readily admit to selecting test markets on the basis of strong local sales efforts or a strong broker—hardly an objective decision input.

Once research becomes a sales promotion tool, the stress on quality and professionalism can quickly disappear. In fact, it is impossible to maintain effective professional marketing research in the company if research is not clearly used in the decision area. Thoughtful and careful research design is no longer necessary; it is avoided because what management often wants is not accurate data but control over the information. Research becomes a tool for reinforcing a position or a direction rather than for examining the merits of the position under consideration.

The building of a truly effective marketing research function in the company is a delicate task requiring professional competence, management resources, and considerable tact. Striving, ambitious members of the management team are often extremely thin-skinned and sensitive to what

* The views expressed here do not necessarily reflect those of the publisher or the editorial board.

they consider to be criticism, even though it may be valid marketing research.

Management's receptivity to research information often tends to be directly related to the extent to which the information agrees with management's prejudgments. The greater the conflict between the management's prior expectations and the research findings, the more violent is the resistance to the research and the criticism of the methodology.

Yet, ironically, this research is truly valuable to management because it suggests a *change* in direction. Research presentations are warmly received if everything presented dovetails nicely with the ideas that management had before the research. Yet, this latter kind of research is often of less value because it produces no change in management thinking.

Because of these problems and the relatively short history of the marketing research function in many major companies, acceptance of effective research faces some real challenges.

Marketing research now has the tools for making truly substantive contributions to marketing decisions and corporate profits. Refined information collection techniques, experimental designs, and Bayesian procedures provide valid decision contributions. The problem centers around management's general lack of awareness of the kinds of technical progress that have been achieved in this decade.

The problem of replacing bad research with good research is largely psychological rather than technical. At this point in time, it seems even more critical that the marketing research profession find better ways of selling research usefulness than making further technical progress. The problem of selling research is actually compounded by the fact that far too often it has been "sold out."

Contrary to legend, good research *can* drive out bad research. The problem centers on management's interest in good research, and this, in turn, depends on its applicability to marketing decision making. Marketing research, if it is to be done at all, should be done early in the decision process and done thoroughly. Far better to do one project and do it well than to cover every management question with ineffective and inadequate marketing information.

DAVID K. HARDIN

President
Market Facts, Inc.

Source: *Journal of Marketing Research*, Vol. VI (May 1969), p. 239.

Barriers to Research

Despite a very substantial increase in the proportion of firms who engage in marketing research, a surprisingly large number of firms do not undertake research of any form even though evidence suggests that such research would be financially rewarding to them. It appears that one barrier derives from a fear of loss of status. An executive may fear that research results may reflect unfavorably upon him. The research could show some of the assumptions he has been working with to be wrong or show that as, say a brand manager, he is in fact less effective than a superficial assessment may show. Also, the executive may be placed in a position where someone new (the researcher) may be telling him how to perform his function. In fact, the nature of past interpersonal experience with researchers is a major determinant of whether a businessman will encourage or support research or listen to it if it is done. Attitudes toward research are important in other ways[8]:

> . . . the alleged need for (research) seems to contradict the time honored assumption that a good business executive is primarily a born intuitive artist. True, he has to learn the business by working his way up; but once he has done this, he either has it or he doesn't. So why worry about things like decision-making processes and research?

This attitude is widely held, often with devotion.

Another barrier, related to organizational factors, is that a surprising number of companies of all sizes do not have a clear, commonly accepted definition of their goals. This makes it difficult to formulate the important questions which research should address. In such instances executives often develop their own goals which may conflict with those held by other executives in the same organization, thereby creating power struggles. In cases such as this research becomes a political tool advocated by those who feel the research would support their position and rejected by those whose position would be undermined.

Systematic marketing planning and research should accompany one another with each giving direction to the other. Where systematic planning does not take place, clear research tasks are generally lacking.

One difficulty in conducting research is the inability to use specialists. It is generally recognized among marketing practitioners that specialists in psychology, sociology, anthropology, semantics, mathematics, statistics, and so forth can help improve the practice of marketing as a result of their own research. The problem is how to use these specialists productively. Before specialists can be used effectively marketing management must learn about the resources particular specialists have to offer, how to gain the cooperation of specialists, how to develop fruitful working relationships, and how to incorporate the concepts of specialists in their own thinking.

Where marketing research departments or functions do exist, they are often isolated from top management. It is not unusual in such instances to find that the marketing research which is done is routine and concerned only with

---

[8] J. W. Newman, "Put Research into Marketing Decisions," *Harvard Business Review* (March–April 1962), pp. 105–112.

short-term problems. This further widens the gap between top management and the marketing research group. To narrow this gap many companies have developed a research generalist within the research team. The responsibilities of this generalist often include[9]:

1. Establishing a mutually satisfactory working relationship with the marketing manager, one characterized by friendliness, trust, and easy two-way communication.
2. Acquiring a thorough understanding of marketing problems and how the marketing executive thinks about them.
3. Suggesting and planning a research program which will help the executive check his operating assumptions, make his model more complete, and keep it up to date with the constantly changing environment.
4. Making sure that the most appropriate technical specialists are called into action at the right time.
5. Serving as middleman between the research technicians and the marketing manager during the conduct of the research.
6. Helping the marketing manager understand the research, its strengths, and its limitations.

Who Does Marketing Research?

The activities surrounding marketing research are carried out, in large part, by five major types of institutions. These institutions include (1) publishing companies and government agencies, (2) large companies with marketing research departments, (3) advertising agencies, (4) market research consulting agencies, and (5) academic researchers. In terms of dollars, the largest amount of marketing research is performed by publishing companies and governmental agencies. The federal government through the Department of Commerce and the Bureau of the Census acts as the marketing research arm of the federal government. Included in its activities are large consumer panels dealing with the use of medical services, and a large panel dealing with consumer spending plans. The Bureau of the Census performs periodic quarterly surveys using small samples from the U. S. population. In addition, a total survey or complete enumeration of the U. S. population is undertaken every ten years, the latest one in 1970. In addition to the government, there are several large private firms that collect large quantities of marketing data to sell to the industrial sector of our economy.

One of the largest of these is the F. W. Dodge division of McGraw-Hill

[9] *Ibid.*

Book Company. The F. W. Dodge Corporation collects data concerning the construction of houses, apartment buildings, and office buildings throughout the country. It details the amounts of fixtures and materials that go into new buildings together with listings of architectural firms which design the buildings and financial firms which supply funds for construction. Thus, F. W. Dodge performs a complete marketing research service.

Another major market research company of a slightly different kind is the Dun & Bradstreet Corporation. The Dun & Bradstreet company collects financial data from almost all the firms in the United States who wish to use credit. Based on the questionnaires that the companies fill out and independent checking which is done by Dun & Bradstreet personnel, the Dun & Bradstreet people create a financial risk rating which governs how much interest a given company will pay for its borrowing. In addition, Dun & Bradstreet supplies marketing research information commercially.

Other private companies which fall into this category are the A. C. Nielsen Company, Time Incorporated which operates the Selling Area Marketing Incorporated service (SAMI), R. R. Donnelly in Chicago which operates a mailing list service for random sampling, and numerous other service companies. Each one of these commercial enterprises collects data using the techniques to be discussed in this book and then sells the data on the open market.

The second major sector of market research activity resides in private companies' marketing research departments. Such companies as Quaker Oats, Gillette, Kraft Corporation, General Foods, General Mills, and many more, maintain large market research staffs to analyze various types of problems related to their products and services.

For example, William Fox, director of advertising, Bristol-Myers, commented in an interview that they "rely very heavily on market research. Almost all of it is done internally. We spend just about the same amount of time and money on old products as we do on new ones. Marketing research is very important to advertising people, more so than the sales promotion people because ads are more flexible than entire sales promotion campaigns. The ad people can find out where the weak areas are and aim particular ads toward that problem." Russ Bowman, promotional development manager of Bird's Eye division of General Foods commented in another interview that "The promotion development manager uses marketing research for nearly all products. We use it for testing new products, we use it in terms of monitoring sales, awareness of attitudes of the consumer—it's very important to know how a customer comes to try a product. At Bird's Eye, we have our own internal market research program as well as an outside consultant. MRCA Research Co. tells us how quickly we get people to try a new product and this is very important to a promotion manager."

In addition, many companies who are not thought of as standard users of commercial marketing research, maintain marketing research departments.

Examples of these are banks, insurance companies, the American Hospital Association, and many others.

Another major factor in the marketing research activities of this country are the large advertising agencies. Advertising agencies such as J. Walter Thompson; Batten, Barton, Durstine and Osborne; Young & Rubicam maintain large research departments to perform research related to advertising and client needs. Historically, the advertising agencies supplied marketing research as a service for their clients; however, in the mid-1960s, the advertising agencies changed this policy and began charging clients for specific research projects.

The fourth major group of marketing research companies is that of the marketing research consulting agencies. Such companies range from large companies like Elrick and Lavidge, Inc., Market Facts Inc., Management Science Associates, Market Research Corporation of America, National Family Opinion in New Jersey, down to very small companies like Management Research and Planning Inc. in Evanston, Illinois. Some of these companies specialize in the collection of data and some of these companies specialize in the design of research projects. However, all of the agencies will both design and execute a research project on demand. Often one agency will subcontract to another agency in order to get some work done. For example, a small company like Management Research and Planning will design a research project to fit a client's needs and then subcontract the actual data collection process to a company which has a large field staff such as Market Facts.

Academic researchers have provided a rich resource for the commercial marketing research world. Academic researchers have developed analysis techniques and computer programs, are testing certain consumer theories, have developed new measurement methodology, and are constantly reviewing and criticizing methods as they develop. Most marketing researchers in academia reside in schools of business or management. Prominent academic personalities have organized governmental and commercial marketing research services. Professor George Brown of the University of Chicago recently was Director of the Bureau of the Census, for example. The developments created by the academic market researchers are transmitted to the commercial world through the *Journal of Marketing Research*, the *Journal of Advertising Research*, the *Journal of Marketing*, and *Research on Consumer Behavior*, through consulting, teaching future managers, and through executive training programs conducted by such agencies as the American Management Association.

Social Marketing and Marketing Research

In the past few years there has been a discernible trend in the application of marketing expertise and experience to social problems. This practice, termed *social marketing*, involves "the design, implementation, and control of programs calculated to influence the acceptability of social ideas and involving considerations of product planning, pricing, communication, distribution, and *marketing research*."[10] Of interest here is the use of marketing research as a tool in the process of marketing social ideas, practices, and products. Increasingly, social planners and activists are seeking assistance from professional marketing research consultants and agencies. Traditionally, marketing research has been more action-and-results oriented rather than research oriented outside the business marketing area. Stated another way, the proportion of research intended to produce action guidelines is greater in marketing research than in social research. The absolute volume of action oriented marketing research measured in dollar terms is also greater than similarly oriented research in any single social context such as education, alcohol and drug abuse, family planning, and so forth. Thus, there is among marketers a great pool of expertise and experience with what has come to be called actionable research. It is this expertise that is being sought to help solve social problems.

There are numerous examples now of marketing researchers providing assistance to social agencies. In one recent 14-month period alone, professional marketing researchers were engaged in nearly three dozen social action programs receiving national attention. These included: designing consumer panels for a major educational research and development center; using techniques for developing advertising appeals to assist an international family planning agency in preparing a promotional campaign; identifying and measuring the dimensions of various market segments for a political candidate; location research for a new church; performing a cost-benefit analysis of alternative health delivery systems in the context of communicable diseases; market testing various package designs for oral contraceptives; and assessing the deal proneness of farmers in selected less developed countries in Southeast Asia.

Notice that the above examples of research involve such marketing techniques and concepts as market segmentation, deal proneness, and delivery systems, as they apply to situations outside conventional marketing. There are some distinctions to be made, however. There is a difference between the use of a concept as a research technique, as in the case where store location analysis was used to find a site for a new church building, and research into the effectiveness of a marketing technique such as determining whether special deals offered to low income farmers would increase their use of new fertilizers. Some marketers contend that only the former (the actual use of a marketing technique) constitutes social marketing while other marketers claim that evaluation of the potential impact of a marketing technique in social contexts is also social marketing. Although this difference of opinion merits attention, it is beyond the scope of this section to pursue the issue further. It must suffice to

---

[10] Philip Kotler and Gerald Zaltman, "Social Marketing: An Approach to Planned Social Change," *Journal of Marketing*, Vol. 35, No. 3 (July 1971), pp. 3–12, italics added.

say that both types of research will be used increasingly in contexts outside the conventional domain of marketing.

What Does a Typical Marketing Research Project Look Like?

A typical marketing research effort encompasses many individual steps for completion. Universal Marketing Research, Inc. has developed a detailed illustration of how to solve a typical consumer research problem. This is shown in chart form in Figure 1.2. The discussion below is based on material provided by Universal Marketing Research, Inc. The reader should be aware that there are alternative approaches to solving the same problem. These alternative approaches are treated elsewhere in this book.

Step 1 Figure 1.2 shows the steps involved in solving a typical consumer research problem. The steps begin with a statement of the marketer's problem; for example: "How can we increase the share of market now enjoyed by our frozen orange juice?" Thereafter, the job is up to the researcher. The chart shows how he should go about solving the marketer's problem.

Step 2 Discussion with the client has two purposes: (a) to obtain from the client all relevant data on the characteristics of his product and its place in the market; (b) to get some notion of his business philosophy—his business aims and the fervor with which he promotes them.

Step 3 Review of research on related problems might entail a study of products with similar marketing problems.

Step 4 Study of competitive products and markets should cover all the phases of the marketing of competitive products, including their advertising.

Step 5 Development of ideas or hunches is the next big step. This is the stage where the researcher develops his mental point of departure—the ideas or hunches that, if proved correct, will provide the basis for the development of the recommendations for the advertiser's marketing action. There are two major ways to develop ideas or hunches: steps 6 and 7.

Step 6 Researcher's observations of his own behavior, motives, attitudes, and learning processes cover why the researcher himself likes the client's product, why he came to use it if he did so, and the like.

Step 7 Researcher's observations of other people calls for formal investigations to get additional ideas. Examination of behavior means objective scrutiny of how consumers behave in purchases: their frequency and place of purchase,

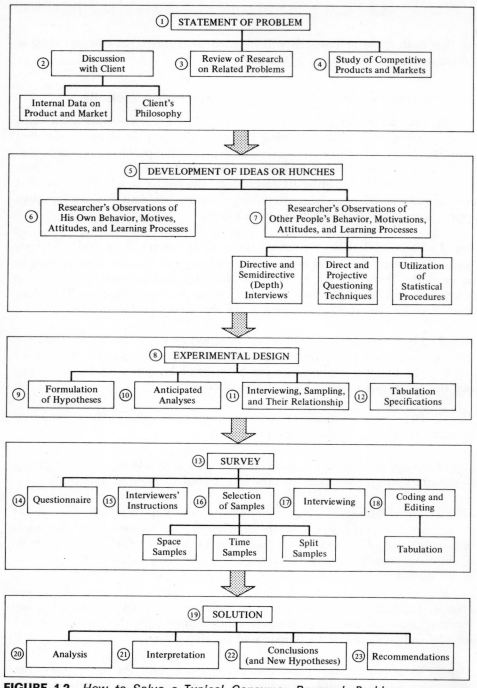

FIGURE 1.2 *How to Solve a Typical Consumer Research Problem*
Source: Universal Marketing Research, an affiliate of Alfred Politz Research.

their frequency of exposure to advertising media; in other words, the consumer's overt acts. Motivational investigations determine which motives actuating a consumer are pertinent to the product's purchase and can also be controlled by the marketer. Examination of attitudes determines whether attitudes are favorable, unfavorable, or neutral toward a product or service. Examination of learning processes provides insight into the ability of people to learn to use a new product to replace a competitive product.

The researcher may use several techniques for these formal studies. One is directive and semidirective (depth) interviews. These are generally long, rambling interviews in which the interviewer may control, to varying degrees, the area of the respondent's answers. This control may be exercised by subtly bringing the respondent back to the subject at hand. In direct and projective questions, the researcher may use clinical procedures developed in psychology and psychiatry. The projective techniques include the Rorschach (ink blot), sentence-completion, Thematic Apperception (explanation of what is happening in a picture) tests, and others. Their essential purpose is to get the person who is being interviewed to project his personality, through a process that is not apparent to him, into the answer that he gives. The idea is to catch the respondent off guard to get responses that, if properly interpreted, may give a more accurate estimate of a consumer's motives in making a particular purchase. Very often a direct question is used as a stimulus. Utilization of statistical procedures is often necessary to determine buying motives or to identify the relative importance of motives. A minor motive may be the most prevalent one and hence more significant in purchases than what seems to be a more vital motive. Very often, the motives of people with respect to the purchase or nonpurchase of a particular brand are very small and insignificant. However, the accumulation of these small motives makes one brand a leader and another a loser in the marketplace. Statistical procedures, through the accumulation of large numbers of observations, make it possible to detect these motives.

Step 8   Research study design is the third major step in investigating a consumer research problem. It implies the use of a kind of blueprint that permits the researcher to proceed to the anticipated analysis of his data. It entails the examination of all facets of a marketing problem, starting with the formulation of hypotheses based on hunches or ideas that the researcher has developed through observation, depth interviews, direct questioning, and/or statistical procedures. The researcher now must test and measure the factors that prompt a consumer to purchase a product. The researcher must test them numerically to determine the relative importance of each in the marketing situation. There are four major steps involved: steps 9 through 12.

Step 9   Formulation of hypotheses: After the researcher has accumulated various ideas and hunches, he expresses them as hypotheses to be tested.

Example: "Consumers would like to buy frozen orange juice in larger cans."

Step 10   Anticipated analysis: The researcher at this stage must anticipate the analyses that he will have to make to come up with a solution to the marketer's problem. For example, he must anticipate analyzing the proportions of consumers liking frozen orange juice in small cans, in large cans, and in both sizes so that he can determine whether the overall sale of orange juice would be greater or smaller as the result of a change in the size of the can.

Step 11   Interviewing, sampling, and their relationship: In devising the questionnaire and establishing samples, it should be remembered that one affects the other. If, for example, the researcher wants to ask questions about the degree to which consumers believe that protopectins are found in frozen orange juice and the degree to which they believe that protopectins are health-giving, it may be desirable to ask each question of a different sample of the population, because to ask both questions of a single person might be to influence her (such a process is called using a split sample).

Step 12   Tabulation specifications: The researcher who formulates a hypothesis anticipates certain types of responses and the categories into which replies may fall. He alerts tabulators to these possibilities.

Step 13   The survey is the operation in which the hypotheses are put to test the market in which the researcher is interested. It involves steps 14 to 18.

Step 14   Pretest of questionnaire in a small sample is not to test the hypotheses but to test the wording of the questionnaire, for example, is it clear and so phrased that the answers cannot be ambiguous.

Step 15   Interviewers' instructions: The interviewers on the researcher's staff are now instructed as to the nature of the survey and the purpose and design of the questionnaire.

Step 16   Selections of samples: For the frozen orange juice marketing problem, for example, it is necessary to sample the market for frozen orange juice— not only consumers who already use it, but also those who do not. It may be determined to sample only housewives, if it is known that they buy a great majority of frozen orange juice. The sample may be a probability sample, in which the probability or change of each individual housewife's being chosen is known or can be determined in space (such as geographic areas); in time (such as days of the week or seasons of the year), and split samples (see step 11) may be needed.

Step 17   Interviewing is most successful if the accuracy and reliability of the interviewers are known to the researcher.

Step 18   Coding and editing: The questionnaires are edited for legibility and meaning, and the responses are then grouped into categories for coding and tabulation. Coding is merely the translation of the text description of a category of response into a number that is possible to tabulate by machine.

Step 19   The solution implies the analysis of tabulated returns, their interpretation, the conclusions to be drawn, and the recommendations to be made to the client.

Step 20   Analysis implies the determination of the meaning of the tabulated responses.

Step 21   Interpretation is the application to the client's problem of the meaning found in the responses.

Step 22   Conclusions are the statement of the courses of action that might be taken by the client in view of the researcher's interpretation of the survey.

Step 23   Recommendations cover the course of action that the researcher thinks the client should take or should not take, plus what will happen if he takes this course of action. Thus, research is not merely the collection and evaluation of information; it can also predict the results from a course of action it recommends.

Summary

Marketing research is an essential function for any enterprise whether it be commercial or noncommercial in orientation. Accompanying the increasing use of marketing research is an increasing scientific rigor in its application. Marketing research is used for a variety of purposes and can range from very simple to very complex techniques.

Questions and Exercises

1. What limitations are inherent in the definition of marketing research suggested by the American Marketing Association? For example, it has been criticized as suggesting that marketing research be confined to commercial goods and services, that it ignores preresearch analysis, and so on. Do you agree or disagree? Is the definition offered in this text subject to these same criticisms?

2. Suppose that you are the brand manager for a new brand of spray-on floor polish and need information concerning consumers' use of this product; for example, which rooms in the house is it used for, how often is it used, and so on. Assume, furthermore, that you are chairman of the Public Park Committee in your town, a suburb of a major city, and the Committee has been asked for information about the public's use of the park system. How similar are the information needs in each instance? What kinds of questions would be asked in each situation? Is the marketing research process in the case of the floor polish any different from that in the case of the public park example?

3. How would you overcome the various sources of resistance to marketing research? In responding to this question place yourself in the role of an agency which sells marketing research services.

4. What can marketing research contribute to solving problems that an experienced marketing manager cannot? Is personal experience a type of information or data which could be used in the same way as data collected from a questionnaire or interview?

5. When is it not possible to conduct formal marketing research?

Project Related Questions

1. In which area(s) of marketing research does your project fall? (See Table 1.1 in this chapter.)

2. What is the specific marketing problem you are investigating? State this problem briefly and succinctly.

3. Why is it important to study the marketing problem you have selected? Will it help marketing management in their analysis of a program? Their planning? Their implementation? Their control?

4. Given the nature of your project, what barriers might you encounter in proposing and conducting this research? Assume you are conducting this research as a member of a middle-sized corporation, what organizational problems could arise? (See page 11.) What government restrictions might you face?

5. If you were to seek assistance from an outside source, what type of agency would you contact first?

6. Develop a time schedule for your project using the relevant activities from Figure 1.2 as the various activities to be assigned deadlines.

7. Does the data you need to complete the project exist commercially and can you purchase this information at a reasonable cost?

Chapter 2

Science in Marketing Research

Chapter 1 noted the increasing explicit role and importance of scientific activity in marketing research. Science, as a process of using proper research techniques to find a general pattern of fact or reality, is actually a part of everyday life. Every rational decision is the result of some research method in which alternative propositions are considered with respect to their relative value. Alternatives are continually eliminated until finally a decision is reached as the optimum solution to the problem presented. The reader is, in reality, constantly participating in the scientific process with varying degrees of rigorousness. A better understanding of the characteristics and processes of carefully practiced scientific activity will almost certainly improve the quality of decision making. An understanding of science is especially relevant in the field of marketing where important decisions must be made after much research. The intent of this chapter is to present to the reader, in a more systematic way than he may have encountered before, the basic qualities of science. The greater sensitivity to rigorous thinking procedure should better enable the reader to evaluate and conduct marketing research soundly.

Characteristics of Science and Scientific Knowledge

It is well at the outset to ask what we mean by the term "science." Science can be defined as a discipline using proper research techniques for the purpose of finding general patterns of fact or reality. The goal of science is the extension of certified knowledge. Thus, in marketing we are concerned with the proper use of knowledge-gathering techniques for the purpose of discovering new patterns of fact or reality. This also involves the process of certifying that a new finding is indeed a fact or at least has a high probability of being true. The basic traits of scientific knowledge are rationality and objectivity. Scientific knowledge is rational in that it consists of concepts and reasonings which constitute ideas. These ideas are combined in accordance with some set of logical rules which in turn produce ideas not previously realized. Moreover, these ideas are usually organized into sets of propositions which are statements relating ideas or concepts. Scientific knowledge is objective when it is factually true.

Why is Science Important?

Science is important because sometimes it makes desirable outcomes possible. In 1958, Sputnik was launched by the USSR and caused much consternation and embarrassment in America. The goal of reaching the moon by 1970 was agreed upon by a large segment of American society. Scientists from various disciplines, scientific methods, and many physical theories were brought together until the desired objective was attained, on schedule, in 1970 when Col. Armstrong stepped off the spacecraft onto the moon. Similarly, in the mid-1970s, society has agreed that social ills such as poverty, poor education, weak and corrupt political systems, and so on, are major problems to be corrected. As with the spacecraft, social scientists, scientific methods, and many social theories are being mobilized to achieve the objectives. Without science and its emphasis on discovering truth and using its discoveries to improve the existing order, none of the following would have been possible: the pyramids of Egypt, metallurgy, keeping time, electricity, measuring distance, the piston and other types of engines, the construction of large buildings, flight, psychiatry, and many more. Whether it was done by the ancient Egyptians, Aztecs and

Mayas of Central and South America, the Chinese, Americans, or Europeans, the process of science has been about the same. In order to create meaningful and lasting change, marketers must adopt scientific methodologies.

Since an understanding of the main features of science is essential to performing marketing research scientifically, we shall discuss here an inventory of the main features of science. These features are summarized in Table 2.1.

TABLE 2.1 *Characteristics of Science and Scientific Knowledge*

- Scientific knowledge is factual.
- Scientific knowledge goes beyond facts.
- Science is analytic.
- Scientific research is specialized.
- Scientific knowledge is clear and precise.
- Scientific knowledge is communicable.
- Scientific knowledge is verifiable.
- Scientific research is methodical.
- Scientific knowledge is systematic.
- Scientific knowledge is lawful.
- Science is explanatory.
- Scientific knowledge is predictive.
- Science is open.

Scientific Knowledge Is Factual

Science starts by establishing facts and seeks to describe and explain them. Established facts are empirical data obtained with the aid of theories and in turn help clarify theories. We use theories of buyer behavior, for example, to help us learn more about how buyers respond to point-of-purchase promotional techniques. In the process of doing this and learning about specific behavior, we can often gain new insights which modify the original theory and make it still more useful the next time it is employed.

Scientific Knowledge Goes Beyond Facts

The market researcher should not confine himself to facts which are easily observed and already in existence. He may want to create new facts such as new attitudes toward a particular product through the use of mass media; this can be done with the aid of rigorous experimentation in which the researcher determines the best communications approach for establishing a desired new attitude among consumers. New facts should be authentic. The researcher should verify new facts with experimentation and comparison with what is already known. Various methods of verification are presented throughout this book.

Going beyond facts means not only the mere description of them but also providing explanations. A theory is a set of logical propositions which explain a phenomena. A theory can answer questions such as, "How was the newly established brand image produced?" It is possible for theory to be applied to establish or *create additional facts which have favorable consequences for the producer*. The notion of explanation is discussed in more detail in the next chapter.

Science Is Analytic

The market researcher scientist tries to decompose the buying decision process into its basic parts to determine the mechanisms which account for the way the process functions. He examines the interrelationships among the component parts of the buyer decision process. For example, an "interest" stage in the decision process may precede and then be maintained along with an "evaluation" stage in the buyer decision process. The nature of the original interest, however, may influence how the potential buyer undertakes his evaluation of the product. If his original interest is one of curiosity he may evaluate the information he obtains about the product in a relatively objective way. However, if his initial interest is characterized by disbelief, he may be more sensitive to or influenced by negative information during the evaluation process. This could reinforce his original disbelief. Note that here we observed that the evaluation process influences, that is, reinforces, the original nature of the potential buyer's interest.

After analyzing the component parts separately and then in their interrelationship, the market research scientist is then able to determine how the whole decision process emerges. He thus has a better understanding of that process than he would have had by looking at the process as a whole without analysis of components of decision making.

Scientific Research Is Specialized

It should not be expected that every researcher be very familiar with or an expert in every research methodology or context. The market researcher should realize that many specialties, many perspectives, can be brought to bear on most problems. For instance, research on distribution channels may require specialists from economics, consumer behavior, geography, and demography. Moreover, field surveys, laboratory experiments, census data analysis, and so on, may be appropriate specialized data-gathering methods for research on channels of distribution, depending on the nature of the problem.

Scientific Knowledge Is Clear and Precise

Scientific knowledge strives for precision, accuracy, and reduction of errors although it is almost always impossible to achieve these completely. The researcher attempts to reach these objectives by stating questions with maximal clarity, giving unambiguous definitions to concepts and measures, and recording observations as completely and in as much detail as possible. For example, in conducting market segmentation studies, the researcher should define very specifically what the relevant criteria (for example, age, income, geographic location, personality, and so on) are for segmenting a market, and the reasons for using these criteria. The methods used or available for use to measure each segment and actually perform the segmentation should also be clearly specified.

Scientific Knowledge Is Communicable

Research must be, in principle, communicable, that is, it must be sufficiently complete in its reporting of methodologies used and sufficiently precise in the presentation of its results, to enable another independent researcher to replicate the study for independent verification or to determine whether replication is desirable. Even if reasons exist, such as potential loss of competitive advantage, for keeping research results solely within the organization, the person who is to utilize the research findings must have a basis for evaluating them. This, in turn, depends partly on his having information about the research assumptions and methodology employed so as to determine possible sources of error and bias in the data-gathering and analysis processes. If implications of the findings are very significant in terms of marketing actions and the expenditure of funds, several independent replications may be desirable before committing large scale funds. A comparison and evaluation of the replications in relation to the original study means that the results of the investigations be presented precisely and fully.

Scientific Knowledge Is Verifiable (Falsifiable)

Scientific knowledge must be testable empirically through observational or experimental experiences. This is one of the basic rules of a science. It must be possible to demonstrate that a given marketing proposition or theory is false. This may at first glance appear strange. Why "false" rather than "true"? Technically, there may be other untested theories which could account for the results we obtained in our study of a marketing proposition. At the very least, there may be a competing explanation which could be the "real" explanation for a given set of research findings. Thus, we can never be certain that our proposition or theory is *the* correct one. The scientist can only say, "I have a theory which I have objectively tested with data and the data are consistent with my theory." If the possibility of proving an idea false or wrong is not inherent in our test of an idea, then we cannot put much faith in the evidence that suggests it to be true. No other evidence was allowed to manifest itself.

Many techniques of empirical investigation are available and are treated in various parts of this book. It must suffice to say here that the various marketing research techniques discussed later are all, in one way or another, intended to show that our ideas or propositions are or are not consistent with observed and measured facts.

Scientific Research Is Methodical

Market research in a given problem area should begin with relevant current knowledge as the starting point and proceed in a carefully planned way to satisfy explicit previously defined information needs. This involves a careful definition of the specific problem(s) faced by the marketer. Determining that a problem exists is relatively easy, at least compared to the task of identifying the source and character of the problem. There are a series of steps the market researcher scientist must take in order to complete a meaningful bit of research. Among these steps are the careful preselection of the experimental design and other analytical techniques to be used in the investigation.

Scientific Knowledge Is Systematic

The scientific concepts or ideas a market researcher uses in relation to a given problem are related to one another in systematic ways. Some concepts are "causers": they cause certain outcomes to happen. This suggests a theoretical interrelatedness among independent concepts. The researcher must be sensitive to this and must study it systematically by looking at the influence each concept has alone and then again in connection with the other concepts.

Scientific Knowledge Is General

The market researcher should place individual facts into general patterns which should be applicable to a wide variety of phenomena. For example, aspects of consumer personality relative to risk-taking behavior should be considered with regard to new product contexts as well as contexts involving established products. This provides generalizations which can guide marketing strategy in both instances. Thus, scientific knowledge should be able to be generalized to two or more events. These events may constitute the same phenomenon occurring on more than one occasion in which case we are concerned with the issue of prediction. The two events may also be somewhat different phenomena which nevertheless can be compared in certain ways. Thus, we are concerned with determining what a given buyer does that is the same each time he purchases a particular product, that is, what is it that occurs in one buying instance that the marketing researcher can confidently predict will happen again in the next comparable buying instance. The marketing researcher is concerned with learning not just what one individual buyer does in a situation but rather what he does that others are also likely to do in the same situation. Can we generalize from one or a few consumers to all consumers?

Scientific Knowledge Is Lawful

Science in marketing seeks laws, that is, general enduring patterns of consumer behavior. We try to convert a particular fact into a case of a general law.

Science Is Explanatory

In scientific marketing research it is not sufficient to describe certain market phenomena; it is also necessary to explain them or to provide better explanations where possible. This enables the marketing strategist to formulate his market policies more effectively. Knowing the shape of a demand curve— having a description of it—is useful for determining price and levels of production. However, knowing why the demand curve has a particular shape, that is, having an explanation of it, enables the marketer to undertake actions that can shift the demand curve in a desirable direction and perhaps alter its elasticity in favorable ways. Presumably the explanation identifies relevant factors which can be manipulated, that is, are marketing decision variables.

Scientific Knowledge Is Predictive

In addition to explaining how market processes occur, it is also desirable, as already mentioned, to be able to say with reasonable certainty how they may occur in the future. This enables the manager to be able to plan for the future and equally importantly to be able to intervene in the market processes and influence their outcome. A major source of error in prediction is the basing of them on wrong assumptions and the research must be wary of this. Price decisions based on a wrong assumption about the elasticity of product demand may produce sales markedly different from those predicted. Correct assumptions but incorrect information may also contribute to poor predictions.

Science Is Open

Knowledge is constantly changing. All scientific statements must be susceptible to tests which make possible their refutation, otherwise we cannot have confidence in its truth. For this reason existing theories should never be accepted as unimprovable or unalterable. Existing theories will, generally, be falsified sooner or later, and new, improved theories will take their places. In physics, for example, Newton's theory of time, motion, and mass of bodies has given way to Einstein's theory. Subsequently, Einstein's theories have yielded to more refined theories.

Models, Steps, and Criteria of Scientific Processes

We have reviewed characteristics of science; perhaps the next issue to be raised is, what does a scientist do? The following answer is perhaps the most concise yet inclusive response to this question to be found in the literature.

With regard to real world phenomena, a scientist "endeavors to *describe*, to *order*, to *record* (measure) them, to *understand* and to *explain* them; in these activities he is motivated particularly by a desire to be able to *predict* new phenomena, so that their predictability shall enable him to *control* his sector by influencing the phenomena."[1] These processes accurately describe the activities of marketers although most marketers are typically engaged in only one or two of the processes. Furthermore, most marketers (practitioners at least) are interested primarily in the processes of prediction and control. However, because accurate prediction and effective control depend heavily on prior knowledge, other marketers engage in description, explanation, and so on, for the purpose of providing sound knowledge foundations for action.

The Scientific Method

A scientific method is a set of prescribed procedures for establishing and connecting general laws about events and for predicting events yet unknown. It has proved difficult to model the scientific method.[2] It is not within the purpose of this chapter to discuss the many reasons which account for this. It must suffice to say simply that controversy exists about what constitutes the appropriate procedures of a scientific method. The position adopted here is that there are alternative ways of conveying meanings of scientific methodology. Mario Bunge has suggested eight operations as being the main steps involved in the application of the scientific method.[3] These are presented in Table 2.2. A ninth step could be added: Determine the domains in which the assumptions and the techniques hold, and state the new problems raised by the research.

TABLE 2.2   *Steps in the Application of Scientific Methodology*

1. Ask well-formulated and likely fruitful questions.
2. Devise hypotheses both grounded and testable to answer the questions.
3. State assumptions.
4. Derive logical consequences of the assumptions.
5. Design techniques to test the assumptions.
6. Test the techniques for relevance and reliability.
7. Execute the tests and interpret their results.
8. Evaluate the truth claims of the assumptions and the fidelity of the techniques.

9. Determine the domains in which the assumptions and the techniques hold, and state the new problems raised by the research.

---

[1] Adriaan D. de Groot, *Methodology* (Paris: Mouton Co., 1969), pp. 18–19.
[2] David Harvey, *Explanation in Geography* (London: Edward Arnold, Ltd., 1969), p. 31.
[3] Mario Bunge, *Scientific Research*, Vol. I (New York: Springer-Verlag, 1967), p. 8.

TABLE 2.3   *Rules for Executing the Research Cycle*

1. State your problem precisely and, in the beginning, specifically.
2. Try definite and somehow grounded conjectures rather than noncommital or wild hunches; risk hypothesizing definite relations among clearcut variables.
3. Subject your assumptions to tough tests rather than to soft ones.
4. Do not pronounce true a satisfactorily confirmed hypothesis; regard it as, at best, partially true.
5. Ask why the answer should be as it is and not otherwise.

A few rules to follow for the adequate execution of research are summarized in Table 2.3 and now will be discussed.

1. *State your problem precisely and, in the beginning, specifically.* The stated problem should not be simply that sales are down or below target, but rather that market penetration is too low, consumer awareness is too low, the product does not meet consumer expectations, and so on. If sales are below target due to low consumer awareness, the problem statement should further specify, if possible or relevant, whether awareness is particularly low for certain consumer segments. In stating problems as questions, we would not ask simply why consumers purchase luxury items but rather some more precise question such as why some particular consumers have a specified rank order of preferences among luxury items. Care must be exercised to avoid stating problems too narrowly so as to preclude possible solutions.

2. *Try definite and somehow grounded conjectures rather than non-committal or wild hunches; risk hypothesizing definite relations among clearcut variables.* Do not be content with just the idea that frequency of exposure to advertising messages affects recall of their content, but hypothesize that this may only be true within a specified range of exposure and then only for particular consumer groups. Or, rather than saying the use of nonfinancial incentives such as dishware may increase the sale of supermarket items, be more specific about the type of items whose sales will be most influenced by incentives. Moreover, the marketing researcher would want to hypothesize relationships between price levels of particular products and magnitude of the incentives required to stimulate their sales.

3. *Subject assumptions to tough tests rather than to soft ones.* In the example above, don't just use simply advertising messages but vary messages according to complexity. If, in the example above involving incentives, the product under consideration were seasonal, we would want to test the effect of incentives during the favorable season as well as the unfavorable, or at a time when complimentary products were

not on special sale. In effect, the marketing researcher wants to control for other factors which may interfere with the direct impact of the incentives. He would also want to have a comparable situation in which incentives were not used. This would provide a standard of comparison for estimating what sales may have been at that time in the test store, had incentives not been used.

4. *Do not pronounce true a satisfactorily confirmed hypothesis; regard it as, at best, partially true.* Consider any finding concerning relationships among the complexity of advertising messages, a given frequency, and particular consumer groups to be modifiable by subsequent investigation. Other factors not considered during the first test may later be shown to be important and to modify our initial hypothesis.

5. *Ask why the answer should be as it is and not otherwise.* Ask what factors (for example, psychological mechanisms) account for the relationships observed among frequency of message exposure, complexity, and so on. Moreover, why should the relevant mechanism and obtained relations be operative and not others, that is, what conditions were conducive to our findings? What conditions, if present, may have led to different conclusions? How likely are these conditions to occur?

Feigl's Criteria for Scientific Activities

Feigl suggests several criteria or regulation ideals which characterize scientific inquiry in what he terms "factual" science, for example, physics.[4] It appears nevertheless (Feigl also acknowledges) that these criteria constitute good guidelines for scientific activities in the applied sciences (such as marketing).[5] These are shown in summary form in Table 2.4 and now will be discussed.

The first criterion is *objectivity*. Two elements are involved: one is the minimization of personal or cultural bias in the scientific activity. Note the use here of the term "minimization" is in lieu of "elimination." No scientific

TABLE 2.4 *Feigl's Criteria for Scientific Activities*

Objectivity
Reliability
Definiteness and precision
Coherence or systematic structure
Comprehensiveness or scope of knowledge

---

[4] Herbert Feigl, "The Scientific Outlook: Naturalism and Humanism," in Herbert Feigl and May Broadbeck (eds.), *The Philosophy of Science* (New York: Appleton-Century-Crofts, 1958), p. 11.

[5] See Harvey, *op. cit.*, p. 46.

activity, at least in the social or behavioral science, is ever value free.[6] This is especially relevant in social marketing. The marketing researcher should try to minimize biases by making explicit the types of biases he may be expressing or is assuming. He can only pursue objectivity and make known where, according to his own insight or introspection, he falls short. The use of laboratory experiments may be a research trait of a particular market researcher, that is, he tends to apply it to all problems. However, laboratory experiments are differentially effective with regard to different marketing research problems. The researcher should make clear the limitations of his approach and the biases this approach may produce.

Testability, another element of objectivity, imposes the requirement that scientific observations be amenable to empirical test.[7] Nagel is quite specific on this point: ". . . the quest for explanation in science . . . is a quest for explanatory hypotheses that are genuinely testable . . . the hypotheses sought must therefore be subject to the possibility of rejection, which will depend on the outcome of critical procedures, integral to the scientific quest, for determining what the actual facts are."[8] If the market researcher cannot test explanations or theories about the influence of word-of-mouth communication in the new product purchase decision process, he will have no solid basis for evaluating the real significance of word-of-mouth in this instance and hence he will find it difficult to influence and utilize word-of-mouth communication in a favorable way. Moreover, he will not have a basis for choosing between a marketing communication mix or strategy based largely on word-of-mouth, and a strategy based largely on formal mass communication (should such a choice be necessary because of limited resources). Testability also requires that the empirical test be capable of replication by other scientists.

A second criterion involves the distinction between opinion and well-substantiated belief. This is the criterion of *reliability* or "sufficient degree of confirmation." The first criterion of testability is relatively easy to establish. The criterion of reliability, however, involves matters of degree. Where do we draw the line between well-substantiated knowledge about communication patterns among industrial buyers, and hunches, that is, when does a given proposition or a given theory move from "hunch" to "knowledge?"[9] Here the element of probability enters the picture and we ask ourselves how likely it is that a given test result would happen by chance. In this instance the scientist

[6] See for example, Donald Warwick and Herbert Kelman, "Ethical Issues in Social Intervention," in *Processes and Phenomena of Social Change,* Gerald Zaltman (ed.) (New York: Wiley-Interscience, 1973); and Alan Guskin and Mark Chesler, "Partison Diagnosis of Social Problems," in Zaltman, *ibid.*

[7] Marx W. Wartofsky, *Conceptual Foundations of Scientific Thought* (New York: Macmillan, 1968).

[8] Ernest Nagel, *The Structure of Science* (New York: Harcourt, Brace, Jovanovich, Inc., 1961).

[9] For an excellent discussion of the related measurement problems, see Morris S. Cohen and Ernest Nagel, "Measurement" in Edward Madden (ed.) *The Structure of Scientific Thought* (New York: Houghton-Mifflin, 1960).

relies on experimental and statistical tools. Nevertheless, the criterion of reliability is difficult to meet.

Definiteness and precision is a third criterion which "requires that the concepts used in the formulation of scientific knowledge-claims be as definitely delimited as possible."[10] This requires that the theoretical nature of the units of theories, namely concepts, be clearly spelled out and the most appropriate operational measure of that concept be obtained. Operational measures should be standardized, where possible, by scientists. Marketing has not done this to a great degree. Appropriate measures of a given theoretical concept may vary from context to context, and the investigator must be wary of utilizing inappropriate operational measures, particularly when he is trying to draw inferences from one context to another as is common in marketing. For example, when considering the relationship between social class and brand image, it is necessary to be very clear on what is meant by social class and what is meant by brand image. What are their definitions? Do these definitions vary among different researchers? For example, one market researcher emphasizing education as an indicator of social class may find it has some particular relationship with an image held by consumers toward a branded product while another researcher, emphasizing income as an indicator of social class, may find different patterns of relationships between social class and brand image for the same product and consumers. (We are assuming brand image is defined and measured identically by the researchers.)

A fourth criterion suggested by Feigl is *coherence or systematic structure.* Information gathered or knowledge acquired should not be found in random relationships. Instead, items of knowledge should be grouped together in some logical way. Thus, related concepts should be grouped to form hypotheses and related hypotheses should be grouped to form theories.[11] The investigator should identify the body of knowledge he is drawing on and to which he is attempting to contribute. His activities should be addressed to filling "gaps" in knowledge or in replicating previous work where that is desired. Preferably, too, he should attempt to dispel conflicts or shed light on conflicting viewpoints in his area of endeavor.[12] For example, Franklin Evans' famous study of Ford and Chevrolet owners was an attempt to investigate in a rigorous fashion what motivation researchers were saying about brand images.[13] The resulting conflict stimulated several researchers to attempt to shed light on the differing viewpoints.

Finally, *comprehensiveness or scope of knowledge* is a desirable criterion. It is a goal of science, and ultimately unachievable in most instances, to develop

[10] Feigl, *op. cit.,* p. 12.

[11] A. Kaplan, *The Conduct of Inquiry: Methodology for Behavioral Science* (New York: Chandler Publishing Co., 1964).

[12] Arthur L. Stinchcombe, *Constructing Social Theories* (New York: Harcourt, Brace, Jovanovich, 1968).

[13] Franklin B. Evans, "Psychological and Objective Factors in the Prediction of Brand Choices," *Journal of Business,* Vol. 32, No. 4 (October 1954), pp. 340–367.

statements or laws having wide applicability. The larger the number of different contexts a given theory or subtheory can encompass the more powerful it is, that is, the more comprehensive it is. This flows from the criterion of systematic coherence whereby unifying hypotheses link previously unconnected theories or subtheories. At the same time, it is necessary to keep open the possibility of additions, alterations, and, importantly, deletions as new insights in the events or phenomena of concern are uncovered by the broadened scope of knowledge.

Thus far, discussion has focused on the characteristics of science, the importance of science, and the scientific method. In this section attention shifts to the fundamental process of marketing research. This process is presented in Figure 2.1 and involves nine basic steps. It is to be stressed that the

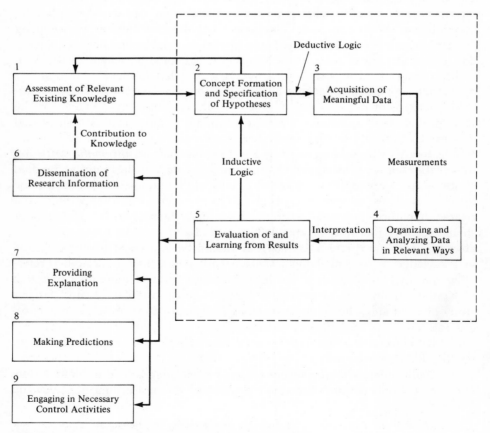

FIGURE 2.1 *A Paradigm of Research Processes*
Source: Adapted from Zaltman *et al.*, *Metatheory and Consumer Research* (New York: Holt, Rinehart and Winston, Inc., 1973).

entire preceding discussion concerning the characteristics of scientific knowledge, criteria for scientific activities, steps in the application of scientific methodology, and so forth apply equally to activity in all nine steps. The purpose here of raising some of the basic processes of research is to sensitize the reader to certain steps involved in conducting research in marketing. The value of such a sensitization is that it leaves behind a more rigorous thinking methodology. This, in turn, produces more rigorous research.

Research Defined

Scientific research may be defined as *the effort to extend certified knowledge by developing concepts and testing hypotheses, the gathering and analysis of meaningful data, and the critical evaluation of the original concepts and premises.* A representation of this process is presented in Figure 2.1. First we shall elaborate somewhat upon the process represented in the paradigm and then address the question of whether or not the term "research" can acceptably be applied to activities concerned with only one of the components in this figure.

Step 1   Assessment of Existing Relevant Knowledge   The first step or stage is to review existing information. This is assuming that the important task of defining the problem has been performed. It is neither necessary nor mandatory in research to assess existing information but it is highly desirable, since it facilitates the formation of concepts and hypotheses and the development of research designs. Furthermore, it helps avoid needless replication of research and prevents replication of mistakes.

Step 2   Concept Formation and Specification of Hypotheses   In this step, existing data and ideas are grouped together to form the basic concepts to be used in the research, to specify the relationship of the concepts, and to further specify the relationships among the hypotheses. Like the other stages, the quality of activities in this stage are of great importance. The way in which concepts are defined theoretically and operationally and the way hypotheses or propositions are stated has great bearing on the ability to confirm or refute the theory under investigation.

It is important here to distinguish two important reasoning methods, induction and deduction. Induction may be viewed as the initial part of the scientific research process and deduction the final part; they are not mutually exclusive forms of reasoning.[14] The deductive method involves going from the general to the specific. When a specific statement is inferred from a general

---

[14] For an important discussion related to this point, see C. G. Hempel, *Philosophy of Natural Science* (Englewood Cliffs, N. J.: Prentice-Hall, 1966), pp. 10–18.

statement and the general statement is true, then the specific statement is also necessarily true; that is, it is a logical certainty. For example, the statement "an innovation is any item which is perceived as new" may be a definitional law. Given the conditions that a consumer perceives a particular product as new, then we can deduce that that product is an innovation (for that consumer). As another example, consider the following:

> Statement 1: All consumers are interested in sales
> Statement 2: Ms. Jones is a consumer
> Statement 3: Ms. Jones is interested in sales

If statement 1 is true, and given statement 2, then statement 3 must be true.

Inductive inferences imply no such certainty, rather, they involve probability statements. Induction is the process by which a marketing researcher forms a theory to explain the observed facts; it involves reasoning or inference from the specific to the general. Thus, it is possible to draw false conclusions from correct premises. If we know Ms. Jones is interested in sales and that she is a consumer, it does not follow as a logical certainty that all consumers are interested in sales but it does lead to that suggestion or hypothesis. However, there is always the possibility (and in this case a good one) that there are consumers who are not interested in sales. Usually with appropriate data we can state the probability of any given consumer being interested in sales but we cannot state with absolute certainty whether any particular consumer will possess that trait.

Step 3   The Acquisition of Meaningful Data   Meaningful data are derived from specific *tests* of *deductively* derived hypotheses. Through a process of logical deduction from theory, one or more hypotheses are derived and tested empirically. Again we see the importance of intersubjective testability as the criterion of definiteness and precision. The research design employed should permit falsification of the hypotheses. The data should be collected in such a way as to constitute an empirical test which clearly allows for the possibility of the hypothesis being shown false. Ideally, the test should be so designed that if the hypothesis is supported, alternative competing theories are, at the same time, demonstrated to be false. This relates to interpretative reliability. Of course, data should also be meaningful in the conventional sense of being relevant to the problem at hand. This is the requirement of explanatory relevance. This means that "the account of some phenomenon provided by an explanation would constitute good grounds for expecting that the phenomenon would appear under the specific circumstances."[15] The importance of care-

---

[15] Gerald Zaltman, Reinhard Angelmar, and Christian Pinson, "Metatheory in Consumer Behavior Research," *Proceedings of the Second Annual Conference of the Association for Consumer Research*, David Gardner (ed.), 1971. See also Hempel, *op. cit.*, p. 48.

fully designed and tested research instruments, while not elaborated here, cannot be understated.

Step 4 Organizing and Analyzing Data in Relevant Ways This step consists of the selection and application of appropriate statistical techniques. Measurements of the basic concepts as manifest in their real world existence are undertaken at this stage. Preferably, analytical techniques relevant to causal analysis would be employed and cause-and-effect statements (causal imageries) used.[16] Causal imageries are conceptualizations of cause-and-effect among two or more variables. For example, point of purchase promotional aids are pictured as having a direct influence on the decision to buy a product, that is, they are conceived as being among the stimuli that cause the selection of a product in the first place and secondly, the selection of one brand over another.

Step 5 Evaluation Ultimately the application of technical tools is for the purpose of assessing some theory or hypothesis and learning from it. Two types of outcomes are frequently expected or desired. One outcome of the evaluation process satisfies a control function. Control is the systematic manipulation of some element related to or contained within a system so as to effect a change in one or more elements in that system.[17] Marketers are concerned with manipulating their own activities to be in accord with customer characteristics such as personality or, where possible, to intervene and alter psychosocial customer states such as attitudes. Thus, evaluation provides a basis for intervention. A second outcome is the contribution of new material for concept formation and hypothesis specification. Thus, marketers reason inductively from specific results or findings to general hypotheses which in turn are subject to testing and the start of another research cycle.

Step 6 Dissemination When marketing researchers complete their evaluation and learning experience they generally disseminate the new information in the form of written and/or oral reports to management. Frequently, too, they communicate some of the information to their professional peers through publication in journals and trade magazines and on occasion at conferences.

Steps 7 to 9 Purposes of Information Information concerning hypotheses is acquired, measured, analyzed, interpreted, and evaluated for one or more of three purposes. One purpose is to provide explanations about marketing related phenomena. Another purpose is to make predictions about these phenomena, while the third purpose, already mentioned in the discussion of step 5, is to manipulate more effectively elements of the marketing mix. These

[16] For a good source book on the measurement aspect of causal analysis see Hubert Blalock, *Causal Models in the Social Sciences* (Chicago: Aldine-Atherton), 1971.
[17] Zaltman *et al., op. cit.,* p. 485.

are very important uses of information and will be examined more closely in Chapter 3.

Types of Research in Marketing

Obviously, a considerable volume of research in and outside of marketing does not encompass the entire process shown in Figure 2.1. There are five basic types of investigation relevant to marketing, each of which is implicit or explicit in Figure 2.1.[18] The basic types of investigation are discussed briefly.

Resource Reviews

Investigations of this sort, represented by step 1 in Figure 2.1, involve the analysis and codification of existing information to be found in the written literature and in the minds of resource persons. The usual product of such investigations in marketing are review articles and case studies. The contribution to knowledge made by review articles is partly one of information dissemination and partly one of formulating new concepts and explanations. Literature reviews are also of value to the extent that they highlight areas of neglect although this is not a direct contribution to knowledge.

Hypothesis Testing

Hypothesis testing is a commonly found research activity in marketing. "Characteristically, a single or few related hypotheses, as a rule theoretically derived, are tested against empirical data . . . *in general*, an invaluable advantage of antecedent formation of (falsifiable) hypotheses, and hence of hypothesis-testing investigations, is that the investigator compels himself to be explicit and objective, to avoid contaminations, and to take a risk."[19] Hypothesis testing is a commonly found research activity in marketing.

Instrumental Investigations

Here concern is with data-gathering instruments, for example, questionnaires, psychological tests, statistical techniques, and so on. Efforts are made to validate the instrument for the purpose of minimizing the so-called operational research epistemic gap.[20] This gap refers to the lack of correspondence or isomorphism between a theoretical concept and its operationalization. The intent is to achieve a high degree of isomorphism between the data generated and the theoretical concepts involved in the research. Instrumental

[18] Zaltman *et al., op. cit.*
[19] *Ibid*, pp. 302–303.
[20] Gerald Zaltman, "Marketing Inference in the Behavioral Sciences," *Journal of Marketing* (July 1970).

investigations, while crucial to the advancement of knowledge, play an indirect role by enabling the researcher to gather more exact data in the process of concept formation and hypothesis testing. The better the instruments, the more confidence one can place in the final conclusions drawn about hypotheses. Also, the analytical techniques employed influence the amount of opportunity allowed for gaining insights into the data collected. The better the research instruments and techniques, the greater the likelihood of generating explanations not specifically conceived prior to the investigation.

Descriptive Investigations

Descriptive investigations attempt to provide profiles for a population or subgroup with respect to preselected criteria. Explanations for relationships among variables—if relations are in fact posited—are not provided. This type of study is desirable chiefly, "whenever, in preparation for explicit theory or hypothesis formation or in preparation for the instrumental realization of constructs, a survey is needed of what objects and events are on hand or are relevant . . . in a given area of the phenomenal world."[21]

Exploratory Research

Located between hypothesis testing and descriptive analysis is exploratory research.[22] This is essentially concerned with the selection and clarification of hypotheses. The researcher typically has in mind a theory or set of hypotheses and thus certain expectations about what might be found. Even so, the nature of the exploratory mission is to clarify existing ideas about relations among concepts and perhaps discover new hypotheses. This is useful when the state of available evidence is internally contradictory or insufficient to permit the statement of formal hypotheses or the detection of new concepts. Exploratory research ranges from pilot studies to laboratory experiments to statistical reanalysis (for example, factor analysis and automatic interaction detection) of existing data.

Hypothesis testing, involving as it does concept formation, the specification of hypotheses, and the acquisition of meaningful data is what is often termed pure research or "real" research by philosophers of science. In reality, all investigations discussed above have some direct or indirect special contribution to make to the development of knowledge. The major issue seems to be not which is best but rather which is most useful given the state of the art in a problem area, at a given moment in time. Different problem areas will have different optimal combinations of resource allocations among the different types of investigations.

[21] de Groot, *op. cit.*, p. 305.
[22] *Ibid.*, p. 306.

Summary

The characteristics of science and scientific knowledge have been discussed along with the importance of science. This chapter has also explored a scientific method and the logic of scientific research in marketing and the type of research in marketing. It is hoped that these topics and others in this chapter have provided the reader with a greater appreciation of the need to be scientific and an approach to being more rigorous. The next chapter will take the reader one step further in this direction.

Questions and Exercises

1. What real world processes and phenomena make it difficult to fully achieve or satisfy the various criteria established for a truly scientific approach to research in marketing contexts? Are there nonmarketing contexts where these criteria can be met more easily?
2. Is there a conflict between the statements in this chapter that "scientific knowledge is factual" and "scientific knowledge goes beyond facts"?
3. Why do scientists try to prove that a hypothesis or contention is false rather than true?
4. Consult two or three research studies reported in recent issues of the *Journal of Marketing, the Journal of Marketing Research, or Journal of Consumer Research.* Do the studies taken individually reflect all stages of the research process cited in Figure 2.1? If not, what stage or stages are involved? To what extent do the studies display the characteristics of science and scientific knowledge discussed in this chapter and summarized in Table 2.1?
5. What is the difference between deductive logic and inductive logic? Under what circumstances is each most likely to come first in a research endeavor? Provide some good examples of deductive logic and inductive logic in marketing research.
6. It is argued that "science is embedded in a particular culture and performed by individuals with various social and psychological traits which cannot be shed even in doing research. To say that scholarly research is free from such sources of bias and can be objective and neutral is false and even dangerous." Do you agree with this position? What evidence can you present to justify your own position?

Project Related Questions

1. Does your research contain hypotheses or propositions at the outset? If not, are you planning to develop hypotheses? Give an example of a possible hypothesis you might come up with.

2. What are your basic research questions?
3. Can you state your research questions in the form of hypotheses which can be tested?
4. How rigorous is your proposed test of these hypotheses?
5. Have you put in writing the major assumptions you are making?
6. Have you recognized how your initial assumptions will prevent you from thinking about alternative sources of information and alternative ways of defining the problem?
7. Have you considered Feigl's criteria for scientific activities? (See Table 2.4 and discussion on pages 33 to 36).
8. What aspect of the research process is being emphasized in your research project?
9. What aspects of the research process may pose the greatest problems for you?

Case: Cullens' Service Station

Jim Cullens operates a moderately sized service station located at the intersection of Oak and West Main Streets in a midwestern city with a population of 125,000. Jim had been in business for five years at this location and sold a nationally known brand of gasoline. He carries a full line of merchandise and offers a full line of services. Jim promoted his merchandise and services well, but despite this, his business had leveled off and remained stable for the past two years. He, therefore, decided that it was time to assess ways of improving his earnings.

Tom Windish, the oil company sales representative for Cullens' station, made weekly calls on Jim. The duties of the company representatives are to sell the company's products to the service station operators, such as Jim, who are independent businessmen. In addition, the representatives are to train or in any other way assist the service station operators in developing sound business practices and thereby improve their business operations. The next time Tom Windish arrived, Jim brought up his problem of stagnant growth.

Jim: "You know Tom, I've been in this station for five years now, but the last two haven't been as rewarding as I thought they should be. My business really hasn't grown in the last two years."

Tom: "There are many ways a guy can increase his profits. He can increase his breadth of merchandise, take advantage of discounts by buying in larger quantities, or increase his hours of operation."

Jim: "I already carry just about everything a person could want from a service station. And as far as buying in larger quantities — where would I put the merchandise? This place is just too small to do such a thing. Does the Company have any larger stations available?"

Tom: "No, not at this time. If I were you, Jim, I would be hesitant about leaving this location. You've got one of the best locations in town and you've built up a loyal group of customers. People are just not willing to patronize a new location if it's the slightest bit out of their way no matter how much they like the dealer."

Jim: "Well, I really want to stay here anyway. But how am I

going to get some additional money in my pocket?"

Tom: "Actually, Jim, I've been thinking about your situation for quite a few months. I have even discussed it with our sales manager, Art Brophy. Art's been in this business a long time. He thinks you should open your station 24 hours a day."

Jim: "I don't like that idea. With my present hours I can more or less keep my eye on the place, but I can't be available 24 hours a day."

Tom: "The more I think about it, the more I realize it's a natural. Look at all that traffic! Sure, there's not that much traffic in the late night hours, but I'll bet one-tenth of that traffic is there—after all, you're on Route 23. And you won't have any competition—you'll have a monopoly on the business! I just know it will work. You don't have to make up your mind now. Think about it for a while. In the meantime, I'll talk to Art Brophy about doing a traffic survey."

Jim Cullens was open to suggestions, but he wondered about the oil company's idea. He therefore decided to look into it further. Since Jim felt he was not financially capable of hiring a marketing research firm to study the problem, he decided to do the best he could and study the problem in what seemed to him to be an intuitively sound way.

First of all, Jim asked other gasoline dealers their opinions and experiences. Almost all of the comments were negative. Joe Geisler, the dealer across the street, had a typical reaction, "Why do you want to help out the oil company? Have they offered to subsidize the added expenses? You're crazy! If you're open 24 hours, you're going to force all of us to increase our hours!" Even Charlie Fox, an experienced operator of a 24-hour station located three miles south of Jim Cullens' on Route 23, was negative toward the idea. "You can't imagine the headaches. Don't you think I want to stop? Your customers and the oil company will never let you quit once you've started even if you're being stolen blind and losing money."

Jim also sought information from the local gasoline retailers' association. Pat Manning, the association's representative, commented: "There are many pitfalls in opening a 24-hour station. You've got to get reliable help and that isn't easy. Most people think that they are willing to work those crazy hours, but they soon find out differently. You also have to be especially careful about pilferage. In general, all of your operating costs are higher during the late night hours. In most cases, dealers don't find the additional eight hours to be profitable in themselves. However, frequently there is sufficient increased business in gasoline and the highly lucrative accessories and services during the other 16 hours to make it profitable. New customers drawn during the late hours also begin to patronize your place in the daytime. Even people that don't use your station during the late hours frequently become customers during the daytime because they perceive a 24-hour station as being dependable."

Jim Cullens thought it would also be a good idea to sample his present customers on the idea. He asked them whether or not they would favor his staying open 24 hours a day. The response was overwhelmingly positive. Many mentioned that occasionally an emergency had forced them to fill up at Charlie Fox's station.

About a week after their initial discussion, Tom Windish, the oil company representative, showed up with his boss, Art Brophy, the sales manager.

Tom: "Jim, I brought Art along today so that you would get the information from a real expert in the business."

Art: "Tom was telling me how interested you are in opening your station 24 hours."

Jim: "Well, I was considering it."

Art: "That's good thinking. I'm glad to see that we selected an individual who is smart enough and aggressive enough to be dissatisfied with his present status and is willing to expand his horizons. You know, many people are not smart enough to know that the key to this business is getting people in the door. Once their car is on the driveway, you dazzle them with service and your overall competence and you've got yourself a steady customer. That's what a 24-hour station does. It brings in new people because the other stations are closed."

Jim: "That makes sense, but are there enough people out at night to make it worthwhile financially?"

Art: "You don't have to worry about that. We've just completed a traffic survey. The results practically guarantee success."

Jim: "Nothing's guaranteed. What will the company do if I fail? It seems to me that since the company will profit from the increased business, it should share some of the risk with me."

Art: "My hands are tied as to the amount of help we can offer you, but let's sit down and discuss the particulars."

The three men discussed the details of an agreement. The Company offered to pay for the initial promotion and to somewhat subsidize the venture if Jim Cullens agreed to open 24 hours. Jim evaluated the existing, but conflicting information. He felt that he was a better than average gasoline retailer and therefore could overcome some of the problems mentioned.

He elected to conduct a carefully controlled experiment for a six-month period. He decided that he would have to make an overall profit of $400 more per month for the increased hours to be worth his trouble. He hired two reliable men to share the late night duties and had his cousin in reserve should he be needed. During the late night hours, all of the merchandise in the station was locked up except for some oil. The duties of the late night man were to only sell gasoline and oil. The new hours were promoted through handbills, signs, and even newspaper ads.

After six months, Joe evaluated the results. The gasoline retailers' association was right. The late night business in itself was unprofitable, but he had apparently picked up customers during the other hours due to the experiment. However, his profits from gasoline and oil were up only $225 per month and business had leveled off. He told his oil company representative, "I'm going back to being open 16 hours per day. It just isn't worth the extra headaches for the additional $225 profit that I made."

QUESTIONS

To what extent did any of the people involved in this case, particularly Jim Cullens, follow the rules summarized in Table 2.3? Does Cullens' own research satisfy Feigl's criteria for scientific activities? How would you approach Cullens' problem as a research task?

Chapter 3

The Structure and Function of Research Information

The latter part of Chapter 2 made repeated mention of the terms, concepts, and hypotheses or propositions and noted briefly that the results of marketing research are used for purposes of explanation, prediction, and control. Either implicitly or explicitly, consciously or not, marketing management and marketing researchers use concepts, propositions, and models for the three purposes just mentioned. For this reason it is essential for the reader to improve his understanding of how information is structured in terms of concepts, propositions, and models and how this structure functions to satisfy the needs of marketing management to explain, predict, and control marketing phenomena. Chapter 3 is intended to provide the reader with a deeper understanding and appreciation of the structure and function of information which constitute the underlying dimensions of all marketing research and, indeed, all scientific activity.

Introduction

This chapter focuses on the purposes and structure of information gathered through marketing research. The basic purposes of information are to explain market phenomena, that is, to identify the causes of an event, to predict occurrences in context of interest to marketers, and, as much as possible, to control those occurrences, that is, to manipulate some variables which cause desired changes in other variables. All three purposes or functions of information depend on adequate insight into concepts, propositions, and theories or models. This is shown in Figure 3.1. Concepts are the building blocks of theories; they are groupings of characteristics. Propositions are sequences of concepts having defined relationships with one another. A theory or model is basically a set of interrelated hypotheses or propositions. Concepts, propositions, and theories concern the structure of information. The soundness of this structure directly influences how well the information a researcher has obtained enables him to explain, predict, and control market phenomena. It is important, therefore, to look first at concepts, propositions, and theories.

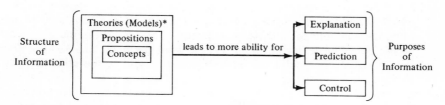

FIGURE 3.1 *The Structure and Purposes of Information*
* The term model may be more appropriate in a marketing context.

Questions or issues involving concepts, propositions, models, explanation, prediction, and control are present in most marketing situations as indicated by the recent case reported next.[1]

[1] The product and names of the persons involved have been changed.

The Case of PIX Toothpaste

A product management group for a proposed new brand of toothpaste, PIX, recently met with members of the advertising agency handling the promotion of this product. It was to be introduced for the first time in Quebec Province, Canada. The executives were primarily concerned with developing an effective advertising program. This was only the second meeting of the two groups. The information below is excerpted and condensed from tape recordings made during the meeting. The representatives of the producer were Mr. Albert Condit in charge of production and warehousing, Mr. Howard Banald, associate director for economic research and sales forecasting, and Mr. Everett Charles, brand manager of the toothpaste being introduced. Advertising agency personnel present were Mr. Jean LaPlace who was in charge of advertising copy development, Ms. Victoria Hamill, in charge of media scheduling, and Mr. James Dejeune, director of media research.

After approximately one and one-half hours of relatively nondirected discussion and steadily increasing tension in the atmosphere, Mr. LaPlace blurted, "Gentlemen! We just aren't getting anywhere in determining what it is we expect from one another and what we have to do. Frankly, I'm getting tired of this. I'll state my information needs as basically as I can." Mr. LaPlace continued by stating that he needed to know what concepts or variables in the French Canadian market were most directly related to the toothpaste in question. "Once I determine what the basic concepts are, I can then proceed to operationalize them in my advertising copy."

"Now we're getting somewhere," Mr. Dejeune added quickly. He then pointed out how once the basic concepts were identified his staff could determine relationships between the concepts to identify what themes would be most attractive to customers. "I need to know the simple relationships between the basic concepts operating in the market and the output behavior. If, for example, I know what the major market segments are and what the significant appeals would be with some statement as to the consequences of the appeals, I could set up tests in the market that would verify the simple propositions. I could test the ideas and perhaps suggest better propositions. Better propositions would lead to more effective media utilization. An example proposition would be 'a clean teeth appeal is of more interest and will lead to earlier purchase of a new toothpaste for middle income housewives than appeals based on fresh breath.' Also, some promotional themes or propositions establishing connections between concepts might be more effective in one set of media than in another and thus it is important for the most appropriate selection of media to know in advance what the relevant relationships were."

Ms. Hamill added that she needed information from the manufacturer's economic research program concerning the buying behavior of consumers for the general product class to help determine in part what sequence of media, if any, consumers follow or rely upon for information about a new product. This would facilitate scheduling of particular media and messages. Mr. Banald, already ill at ease with the discussion of consumer behavior concepts replied rather curtly, "That's what we hired you and your agency to find out. You shouldn't be asking us." He then continued to the effect that until such a model were provided for him he could not make the necessary demand forecasts or predictions needed by Mr. Condit for setting production levels, shipment schedules, and sales quotas.

The brand manager, Mr. Charles, who had been very silent up to this point spoke up and in carefully measured sentences indicated that the ultimate responsibility for the success of the product was his or at least that was how his superiors viewed the situation. He was responsible for coordinating the entire marketing program for the toothpaste in Quebec Province. His needs were to control whatever means he could to ensure the success of this marketing effort and that he was not going to permit the conversation to proceed in its present tone which could only lead to sharp divisions or conflicts among the members of the ad hoc steering committee gathered in the room. This would result in the certain failure of the toothpaste.

"What all of you are failing to see is that all of our interests and concerns are very interdependent. Mr. LaPlace needs to identify basic behavioral concepts to work with. This information I am certain can be supplied by the agency's research division. Mr. Dejeune wants to develop propositions involving these concepts so that he can derive basic messages to present to the customer through channels most appropriate for those messages. I agree fundamentally with Mr. Dejeune's assumption that effective promotional messages are best derived from behavioral propositions involving a couple or more behavioral concepts and I also agree that we need a general explanatory model of customer behavior for our product that will help us understand and predict behavior. This will be of great help to Al Condit."

He then proceeded to ask Mr. Banald and Ms. Hamill to assign a couple of people from their staffs to work together to develop such a model. "This will also be of great help to me in determining what market phenomena I can influence and what phenomena I must accept as given and adjust my overall program accordingly."

The important factors to note in the conversations just reported were that different kinds of information needs had to be satisfied for the successful launching of PIX in Quebec. Information about concepts and their interrelationships as propositions and models was considered important particularly to facilitate the explanation, prediction, and control of relevant market phenomena. These information needs and functions will be detailed more thoroughly in this chapter. As a postcript, the reader may be interested to know that the product failed. It was the opinion of the consulting agency brought in to analyze the failure that the product was poorly promoted and a major error had been made by the producer in their selection of an advertising agency.

The reason marketing managers use information gathered by marketing research is to provide a solid foundation for making decisions. The soundness of their decisions is heavily dependent on the quality of the information or data used. It is essential, then, that the marketing manager make judgments about the quality of the information given to him. The effective use of information by marketing managers involves asking key questions about the information. At the beginning of each section below a list of questions relevant to the particular section is presented. These key questions, implicit in the discussion, represent the critical approach marketing managers use to challenge the information they are provided with for decision making. If the answer to any of these questions is "no," the manager becomes more cautious in his use of the information and often requests clarification or additional information from the researcher.

Concepts

Concepts are the fundamental units which marketing researchers employ in thinking about and trying to solve marketing problems. Examples of frequently used concepts in marketing research are product positioning, market segmentation, brand loyalty, innovation, retailing, convenience goods, and loss leaders. A concept refers to certain characteristics or phenomena that can be grouped together; it is a symbol representing similarities in otherwise diverse phenomena. Likewise, the term "variable" can be defined as a measured concept. For example, the concept "consumer" as it is used in most marketing contexts identifies and groups together at least three characteristics related to (1) people, in the act of (2) consumption, of (3) ideas, goods, and services.

The market researcher must be sensitive to the fact that different concepts are often expressed by the same word. An example is provided by the term "market." In some instances, market refers to a set of potential customers while in another instance it may refer to a place where vendors congregate. For example:

> To a stockbroker, the market is the place where stocks are traded. To a produce merchant, the market is a location in the city where produce is received, sorted, and sold. To a sales manager, the market is a geographical unit, such as a city or region, for which decisions are made with respect to distributors, advertising effort, salesmen, and possibly prices. To an economist, the market is all the buyers and sellers interested or potentially interested in

a product group. Finally, to a marketer, the market is *all individuals and organizations who are actual or potential customers for a product or service.*[2]

QUESTIONS *To Be Asked by the Marketing Manager of the Information He Is Provided for Making His Decisions:* CONCEPT RELATED QUESTIONS

1. What are the basic concepts relevant to the problem?
2. What are the principal components of the concepts?
3. Are the same concepts used by different researchers? That is, do different researchers identify different concepts as being relevant?
4. Do different researchers use different terms to label the same concept? Conversely, do different concepts have the same term applied to them?
5. Is the concept specific enough to be easily operationalized and manipulated?
6. How valid is the concept for serving as a basis for making predictions about other concepts?

Another example is the concept of a reference group which is frequently employed in consumer behavior research.[3] A reference group may or may not involve a group in which the consumer (1) is a member, (2) can ever be a member, or (3) ever wants to be a member. Thus, it is necessary to be explicit in defining terms and identifying the phenomena to which they refer. This is especially important when comparing research performed by different investigators. Although different investigators may use the same term we must always ask, do they refer to the same concept?

Apart from the problem of identical terms being used to refer to different concepts, there is the problem of abstraction. Concepts may be very specific or highly general. For example, consider opinion leadership, a concept sometimes used in new product research. Reynolds and Darden note that at the very general level of abstraction we may obtain a response from a consumer to the effect that "my friends and neighbors often come to me for advice." At an intermediate level of generality or abstraction the concept of opinion leadership could be expressed by the consumer in the following way: "My friends and neighbors often ask my advice *about clothing.*" (Italics added.)

---

[2] Philip Kotler, *Marketing Management* (Englewood Cliffs, N. J.: Prentice-Hall, 1972), p. 89.

[3] Ostland Lyman, "Role Theory and Group Dynamics," in S. Ward and T. Robertson (eds.), *Consumer Behavior: Theoretical Sources* (Englewood Cliffs, N. J.: Prentice-Hall, 1973).

A more specific expression of the concept would be: "Several of my friends asked my advice about whether *the midi* would become a fashion or not."[4] (Italics added.)

There is also a question of *operationalization* which refers to the empirical expression of a theoretical concept. This is a very thorny issue. How visible or observable is the concept of opinion leadership, for example? The concept may be defined theoretically as "the degree to which an individual is able to informally influence other individuals' attitudes or overt behavior in a desired way with relative frequency."[5] But how can it be defined so as to be usable in research? With regard to opinion leadership, at least three operational definitions are possible. The researcher might collect consumer responses to the statement: "My friends or neighbors often come to me for advice." Alternatively, he might use as a stimulus the statement: "I sometimes influence what my friends buy." Still another statement would be, "People come to me more often than I go to them for information about brands." These statements are alternative but not identical operational definitions of opinion leadership. The first definition stresses particular people seeking out the respondent; the second definition stresses influence without indicating whether the information given by the respondent is solicited or unsolicited; while the third alternative stresses the ratio of giving information to seeking information. Do all three operational definitions equally reflect all aspects of the concept of opinion leadership? Obviously not. Thus, it is very important to understand the particular bias inherent in an operational definition of a concept. The bias should be evaluated in terms of what aspect of a concept it emphasizes and whether that aspect is the most relevant one for the research problem at hand.

Propositions

Propositions are sequences of concepts having specified relationships between them. In this section after a brief comment on specificity in propositions, emphasis will be placed on the various forms of relationships between concepts. This section concludes with a discussion of sources of doubt in propositions.

Specificity

Propositions involve statements of relationship between concepts. Just as concepts may be stated in varying degrees of specificity so may relation-

---

[4] Fred D. Reynolds and William Darden, "Construing Life Style and Psychographics," in William D. Wells (ed.), *Life Style and Psychographics* (American Marketing Association, in press).

[5] Everett M. Rogers and Floyd Shoemaker, *Communication of Innovations* (New York: Free Press, 1971), p. 35.

QUESTIONS *To Be Asked by the Marketing Manager of the*
Information He Is Provided for Making His Decisions:
PROPOSITION RELATED QUESTIONS

1. What propositions are implicit but not clearly stated in the research report?
2. For all propositions, how clearly stated is the nature of the relationship between concepts contained in the propositions? For example, does the stated relationship provide insight into the social, psychological, or economic mechanisms connecting the concepts in the proposition?
3. Are there clear cause-and-effect statements embodied in the proposition?
4. Is information provided which describes the condition under which cause-and-effect may actually take place?
5. Are the data collected to test the propositions based on data gathered at the ranges of the phenomena relevant to the problem at hand?
6. Does the proposition assume information which is not known or not easily interpreted?
7. Are there hidden concepts or variables in the stated propositions?

ships be stated with varying degrees of specificity. Specificity may be relevant in at least two ways. First there is specificity in terms of how explicit the mechanism connecting two variables in the proposition is. At a very general level of understanding, we have the proposition "advertising increases sales" while at a much more specific level a proposition might state that a certain level of advertising will produce a critical level of interest which in turn will yield a certain level of sales. The more understanding the researcher has of the effects of advertising on sales the more specific he can be.

Secondly, there is specificity in terms of identifying other conditions affecting the propositional relationship. What exogenous or intervening variables can we specify as being relevant to the proposition? Seasonal variations may be a mediational factor influencing the impact of advertising on sales of certain foods, types of clothing, and so forth.

Forms Relationships May Take

Among the most specific relationships are quantitative directional relationships assuming *cause-and-effect*. For example, consider the following hypothesis: "A consumer will distort (shift) his affective reaction to a specific product characteristic in the negative direction when that characteristic is linked to an unfamiliar (highly ambiguous) brand name."[6] Here degree of ambiguity is causally linked to changes in the strength of negative feelings.

The causality issue has been aptly described as an "extensive philosophical thicket."[7] Nevertheless it is important that the notion be explored. We shall present a few basic requirements for propositions of the nature "A causes B."

First, the idea of "cause" is a theoretical concept. It is *inferred* from observations. Second, A and B must be defined or operationalized independently such that the indicators involved for each are mutually exclusive. Naturally, if the same item is used in operationalizing two concepts there is bound to be some covariation between the two concepts when the item common to both varies. A third but somewhat controversial point is that A must be temporarily prior to B. This ignores, however, the fact that the anticipation of an event may bring about its own causes. In some contexts this is referred to as the self-fulfilling prophesy. Fourth, causal links cannot necessarily be inferred even with perfect correlation between A and B. Fifth, a known causal link between two concepts does not always imply correlation between them. Sometimes, other variables may interact with the independent variable of interest so as to cancel its effect on the dependent variable. For example, Jacoby *et al.* have concluded that "brand image (as mediated by brand name) does affect perception of quality, *especially for brands with strong positive images*" (emphasis added).[8] Presumably the proposition concerning brand image and quality perception is relevant primarily under conditions of strong positive images and not relevant or at least less relevant under some other circumstances. Sixth, a distinction should always be made between a particular logical statement of causality and the actual causal link or mechanism itself. Several logical causal statements, which may not agree with one another, may support an inferred causal relation. Seventh, when we say "A causes B" there are three possible situations involving condition "A": Condition A is a necessary and sufficient condition for B to occur; condition A is necessary but not sufficient for B; and A is sufficient but not necessary for event B. A *necessary condition* is a state of affairs which, if absent, would result in "B" not happening.

Thus, we always want to ask whether the particular variable or concept

---

[6] Stephen J. Miller, Michael B. Mazis, and Peter L. Wright, "The Influence of Brand Ambiguity on Brand Attitude Development," *Journal of Marketing Research*, Vol. 8 (1971), p. 456.

[7] Peter Abell, *Model Building in Sociology* (New York: Schocken Books, 1971), p. 116; see also Mario Bunge, *Causality: The Place of the Causal Principle in Modern Science* (New York: Meridian Books, 1963); Hubert M. Blalock, Jr., *Causal Inferences in Non-experimental Research* (Chapel Hill: The University of North Carolina Press, 1964); Hubert M. Blalock Jr. (ed.), *Causal Models in the Social Sciences* (Chicago: Aldine-Atherton, 1971).

[8] Jacob Jacoby *et al.*, "Brand Image and Product Quality." Working Paper, Purdue University, 1972.

viewed as the causal factor is a necessary condition. Furthermore, we would want to ask whether there are other variables whose absence or presence constitute necessary conditions for the so-called causal factor to have its impact. For example, store images may have an impact on perceived product quality only when price is high, that is, a relatively high price may be necessary before store image can have an impact on perceived product quality.[9] Second, we must consider *sufficient conditions* which are states of affairs justifying the prediction of an event: ". . . if A is a sufficient condition, then given that we have observed A we would automatically expect to observe B."[10] We shall return later to the concept of causality.

The element of *monotonicity* or linearity is another important characteristic of the relationships between variables. We must always ask whether the relationship is monotonic or nonmonotonic at least in the relevant range of operation.[11] It is particularly necessary to ask about monotonicity when "U"-shaped relationships are possible.

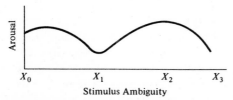

FIGURE 3.2   *The Relationship between Arousal and Stimulus Ambiguity*
Source: Howard and Sheth, 1969.

Nonmonotonicity is an especially important factor to consider for it suggests the existence of different explanations for different observed relationships between any two variables. An excellent detailed discussion of this can be found in Howard and Sheth and only the basic idea is presented here.[12] Consider a proposed relationship between arousal and stimulus ambiguity such as shown in Figure 3.2. Notice that if data gathering and measurement

[9] J. E. Stafford and B. M. Ennis, "The Price-Quality Relationship: An Extension," *Journal of Marketing Research*, Vol. 6 (1969), pp. 456–458.

[10] D. Harvey, *Explanation in Geography* (London: Edward Arnold Publishers, 1969).

[11] For a discussion of an instance where nonmonotonicity was unexpectedly found in an assumed linear relationship between prospect status and exposure to print advertising, see Alvin J. Silk and Frank P. Geiger, "Advertisement Size and the Relationship between Product Usage and Advertising Exposure," *Journal of Marketing Research*, Vol. 9 (1972), pp. 22–26.

[12] John Howard and Jagdish Sheth, *The Theory of Buyer Behavior* (New York: Wiley, 1969).

were restricted to the x_0-x_1 range, or, importantly, if the observations were made when x_0-x_1 was the relevant range, we would have a proposition to the effect that the greater the stimulus ambiguity (for example, the ambiguity of the advertising), the lower the level of consumer arousal. On the other hand, if data were collected from the x_1-x_2 range (that is, when that range was the relevant market condition or was the range of stimulation used in the laboratory experiment), we would have a proposition saying that the greater the ambiguity of the advertisement, the greater the level of consumer arousal. Conversely, as consumers learn more about a brand they have a lowered level of arousal with regard to it. (Arousal is used here in the information-seeking sense rather than in an affective sense.) In both instances the propositions would be correct interpretations but neither would fully disclose the true nature of the relationships between the two concepts of concern. It is also particularly important to note that while the propositions based on data from x_0-x_1 and x_2-x_3 are the same verbally, rather different conditions may be inherent in the two propositions. Moreover, as the consumer moves to the right on the segment of the curve between x_1 and x_2, stimulus ambiguity increases and hence arousal increases and as ambiguity decreases arousal decreases; hence, in a measurement sense these two propositions are identical, but this is very misleading. Clearly the cognitive state of the consumer is very different in the two situations. In the one case he presumably tries to structure a stimulus and in the other he has presumably already adequately structured the vague stimulus.

The notion of *threshold* is also relevant to the problem of monotonicity. Does *any* degree of change in the causal variable produce a change in the dependent variable or does a *critical threshold* of change in the causal variable have to be reached before a measurable change in the dependent variable can be brought about? Consider a proposition suggested by Rogers and Shoemaker. They propose that as the level of knowledge and adoption in a social system increases there is a cumulatively increasing pressure on the non-adopter to adopt. They refer to this as the "diffusion effect" and tie it directly to thresholds: ". . . as the rate of awareness-knowledge of the innovation increased up to about 20–30 percent, there was almost no adoption. Then once this threshold was passed, each additional percentage of awareness-knowledge in the system was associated with several percentage increases in the rate of adoption."[13]

Sources of Doubt

There are many sources of doubt in propositions. Certain questions that must be asked in evaluating propositions we now will discuss. These questions

---

[13] Rogers and Shoemaker, *op. cit.*

reflect possible problems that could make the validity of a proposition doubtful.

First, *a hypothesis may be a prediction.* For example, the prediction is commonly made that one out of five new products introduced into the market will fail. Concern here should be with the adequacy of past trends: how rigorously do they hold? Will the factors producing the past trend continue to function in the future? Second, the *proposition may be a generalization beyond known cases.* For example, the literature in the diffusion of innovations contains two widely cited generalizations—"Early adopters have a greater intelligence than later adopters," and "stimulators of collective innovation decisions are more cosmopolite than other members of the social system"—which are based on only five cases and one case, respectively. Third, *a proposition may cite an inferred variable.* The statement that "people who buy new products soon after they are placed on the market are more novelty oriented than people who adopt only after the product is on the market a long time," implies a third variable, namely, openness to communication. That is, in order to adopt early, novelty oriented people must place themselves in a situation to hear about the new product early. This is not stated in the propositions but is obviously implied. Fourth, *a proposition may state or imply a cause-effect relationship.* Here it is necessary, as discussed earlier, to determine that variable X does indeed cause Y and that the relationship between X and Y is not simply due to the fact that they are both related to some third variable Z. In this case a change in Z would cause a change in X and in Y so that it would appear that a change in X is actually the cause for a change in Y or vice versa when in fact they are not directly connected. In addition, one must also be careful of when causal relationships do hold true. For example, although it is true that social-psychological similarity between salesman and customer increases the likelihood of a sale, it is also true, at the same time, that dissimilarity may increase the likelihood of a sale. The important distinction to make in such propositions is between those variables where similarity is important (for example, racial characteristics, personality) and those where it is not (for example, expertise).

A fifth source of doubt is that the proposition *may state a necessary cause.* For example, a certain amount of information may be required before any attitude can be developed toward a product. Thus, before advertising can cause a specific attitude, a certain degree of repetition is necessary. This relates to the notion of threshold touched upon earlier. A sixth consideration is that *the hypothesis may be compound.* It may state three or more interdependent relationships. For example, the hypothesis or proposition may be that: communication exposure is associated positively with innovation adoption because of increased awareness. Here three subpropositions may be in effect involving communication exposure/adoption, communication/awareness, and adoption/awareness.

Models

Types of Models

The terms *theory* and *model* are often used synonymously with models being the somewhat more frequently employed term in marketing. For purposes here the term model will be adopted; however, the reader could quite appropriately substitute the word theory.

A model is a simplified but organized and meaningful representation of selected attributes of an actual system or process. It is a system itself which is useful for studying some other system. Alternatively, a model can be defined as sets of propositions or a system of logically related statements and ideas relating to an area of reality.

As far as marketing research is concerned, there are two major benefits of working with models. First, constructing a model of the phenomena one is concerned with (a) sensitizes the researcher to the assumptions he is making about what variables he intuitively feels are important; (b) forces the researcher to scrutinize the range of possible variables and select those he feels are most important; and (c) forces the researcher to think about relationships

---

I. Understanding Problems—Descriptive and Predictive Models
  A. Descriptive Models
    1. Transform data into more meaningful forms
    2. Indicate areas for search and experimentation
    3. Generate structural hypotheses for testing
    4. Provide a framework for measurement
    5. Aid in systematic thinking about problem
    6. Provide bases of discussion that will lead to common understanding of problem
  B. Predictive Models
    1. Make forecasts of future events
    2. Validate descriptive models
    3. Determine sensitivity of predictions to model parameters
II. Solving Problems—Normative Models
  A. Provide framework for structuring subjective feelings and determining their decision implications
  B. Provide a tool for the analysis of decisions
  C. Assess system implications of decisions
  D. Yield solutions to problems
  E. Determine sensitivity of decision to the model's characteristics
  F. Provide a basis for updating and controling decisions

FIGURE 3.3 *Uses of Management Science Models*
Source: David B. Montgomery and Glen L. Urban, *Management Science in Marketing,*
© 1969. Reprinted by permission of Prentice-Hall, Inc., Englewood Cliffs, N.J.

which may exist among the variables deemed relevant. Secondly, having a model facilitates (a) the structuring of research activity; (b) the collection of information; (c) the organization of information; and (d) the interpretation of information. Figure 3.3 is a more detailed classification of uses of management science models.

There are many kinds of models. Briefly, there are literary models sometimes called implicit models, that is, pictures of the world held in our mind. These highly abstract models may become very explicit in the form of physical models as represented by toy guns, architectural mockups, and so on. These are sometimes referred to as iconic models. They have the appearance of reality but do not behave in real ways. Somewhat more abstract physical models are analog models which display realistic behavior but do not look like the process or system of concern. A sales chart is realistic in behavior, that is, it reflects what is occurring in the market but certainly does not have characteristic features of any aspect of the market processes producing the data displayed by the chart.

QUESTIONS To Be Asked by the Marketing Manager of the Information He Is Provided for Making His Decisions:
MODEL OR THEORY RELATED QUESTIONS

1. Are all the relevant concepts and propositions included in the model? Is there some systematic exclusion of relevant ideas which may bias the results of the research?
2. Are the underlying assumptions of the model used made clear by the researcher?
3. Does the researcher state the various limitations of his model?
4. Does the model provide the necessary description of the situation being researched, if description is the goal or purpose of developing and testing a model?
5. Does the model provide the necessary predictions, if prediction is the goal?
6. Does the model provide the desired explanations, if that is the goal?
7. Are normative guidelines provided where desired?
8. If a verbal model is involved, how readily can it be quantified?
9. Is the model rich enough in terms of concepts and propositions to allow logical deductions of certain outcomes given certain hypothesized beginning conditions?

One step below implicit models in abstraction are symbolic models which employ some set of symbols to replicate the system or process of concern. Symbolic models may be verbal, schematic, or mathematical. Moreover, symbolic models may be descriptive, predictive, or normative. A descriptive model simply describes how a system functions; a predictive model attempts to describe in advance future states of variables under specified conditions; while normative models are those which present solutions, that is, they provide remedial descriptions of how a system should operate to solve a problem. All of these models may be stochastic or deterministic. In stochastic models, uncertainty is stated in the form of probability distributions, whereas uncertainty is not considered in deterministic models. Relationships between or among variables are known exactly. All of these considerations are presented in Figure 3.4.

Mathematical models may be of three types, a refinement not shown in Figure 3.4.[14] First there are substantive models, which must express the structure of consumer thought process and behavior mathematically. The structure being modeled must also contain properties believed to be inherent to consumers. These properties "could be elements of the social situation surrounding a consumer at the moment of his exposure to an ad; . . . psychological elements, such as the consumer's previous experience with the advertised brand, etc." In addition the relationship among properties in the structure should be clearly stated. Nicosia and Rosenberg regard substantive mathematical models "as devices for the translation of known and/or postulated causal relationships into structures with more clearly defined theoretical and/or empirical implications."

A second type of mathematical model is the statistically based model. This type differs from substantive models in that they do not represent substantive knowledge of hypotheses about elements of consumer thinking mechanisms and consumer behavior. They do, however, reflect uncertainty about the consequences of consumer behavior such as different brands gaining or losing market shares. Being able to predict brands' market shares is useful but does not provide behavioral insight.

A third type of mathematical model is the estimation-inference model. These are two subtypes in this model category. The first are associative statistical models which do not clearly address problems of causation. Factor-analytic models, cluster analysis, and multidimensional scaling models fall into this category. These models are used to measure psychological variables such as brand image and perceptual maps of different products. A second subgroup of the estimation-inference model is used in correlation and regression analyses.

There is an underlying dimension of desirability concerning symbolic models. The researcher should start with verbal models and translate them into schematic or logical flow models which in turn are ultimately to be con-

[14]Much of this discussion is based on Francesco M. Nicosia and Barr Rosenberg, "Substantive Modeling in Consumer Attitude Research: Some Practical Uses," in R. I. Haley (ed.), *Proceedings of the 4th Attitude Research Conference* (November 1971). Published by the American Marketing Association.

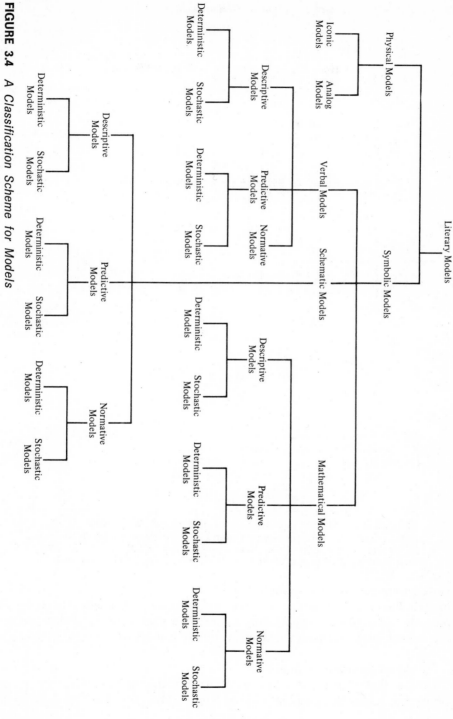

FIGURE 3.4 *A Classification Scheme for Models*
Source: Francesco M. Nicosia and Barr Rosenberg; see footnote 14.

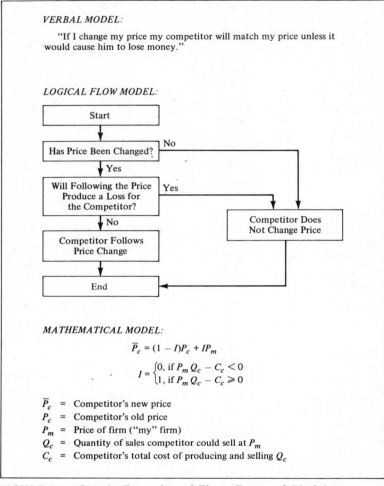

VERBAL MODEL:

"If I change my price my competitor will match my price unless it would cause him to lose money."

LOGICAL FLOW MODEL:

MATHEMATICAL MODEL:

$$\overline{P}_c = (1 - I)P_c + IP_m$$

$$I = \begin{cases} 0, & \text{if } P_m Q_c - C_c < 0 \\ 1, & \text{if } P_m Q_c - C_c \geqslant 0 \end{cases}$$

$\overline{P}_c$ = Competitor's new price
P_c = Competitor's old price
P_m = Price of firm ("my" firm)
Q_c = Quantity of sales competitor could sell at P_m
C_c = Competitor's total cost of producing and selling Q_c

FIGURE 3.5 *Simple Examples of Three Types of Models*
Source: David B. Montgomery and Glen L. Urban, *Management Science in Marketing* (Englewood Cliffs, N.J.: Prentice-Hall, 1969), p. 11. © 1969. Reprinted by permission of Prentice-Hall, Inc., Englewood Cliffs, N.J.

verted into quantitative models. An illustration of this is presented in Figure 3.5. For many marketing research problems it is often sufficient to develop only the schematic or logical flow model. We shall consider below some of the criteria and processes involved in building models.

Model Building Process

The first step is to select variables for the model. Here the market researcher selects the variables but has a justification for choosing those he did.

Moreover, it is also desirable to determine what other possible variables were omitted and why.

The next step is to determine what set of relationships exists between or among variables in the model. Also it is useful to establish what other relationships might exist but were rejected and why they were rejected. Following the specification of relationships is the determination of complexity of the variables. Are the variables complex consisting of multidimensions such as social class or are they unitary such as income? One may make models more complex or more simple by altering just a few parameters.

Models Can Be Made More

Complex by:	Simple by:
· making constants into variables	· making variables into constants
· adding variables	· eliminating variables
· using nonlinear relations	· using linear relations
· adding weaker assumptions and re-strictions	· adding stronger assumptions and re-strictions
· permitting randomness	· eliminating randomness

Explanation

Explanation, defined here as the ascription of causes to an event or type of event, plays a crucial role in the scientific process. In the area of consumer behavior, nearly all research is oriented toward the development of explanatory principles which attribute causes to instances of consumer behavior.

Scientific explanations must meet two systematic requirements. These have been labeled the requirement of explanatory relevance and the requirement of testability. Explanatory relevance means the account of some phenomenon provided by an explanation would constitute good grounds for expecting that the phenomenon would appear under the specified circumstances. Explanatory relevance is achieved when "the explanatory information adduced affords good grounds for believing that the phenomenon to be explained did, or does, indeed occur. This condition must be met if we are to be entitled to say: "That explains it—the phenomenon in question was indeed expected under the circumstances."[15]

An explanation having no test implications is devoid of empirical content; no empirical findings could support it or disconfirm it and consequently it

---

[15] C. G. Hempel, *Philosophy of Natural Science* (Englewood Cliffs, N. J.: Prentice-Hall, 1966), p. 48.

QUESTIONS To Be Asked by the Marketing Manager of the
Information He Is Provided for Making His Decisions:
EXPLANATION QUESTIONS

1. Is the explanation of a market phenomenon provided by researchers and others capable of being tested so that insight can be obtained concerning its accuracy? Can the ideas be measured in the real world?
2. Are marketing decision variables—those capable of manipulation by the marketer—clearly identified?
3. Are the variables affected by the marketing decision variables clearly identified?
4. What is the level of explanation provided? Can it be moved to a higher level of understanding?
5. What is the scope or variety of market events encompassed by the explanation?
6. How closely related are the concepts or variables used and the empirical indicators employed to describe the state of the concepts or variables? In other words, how precisely are the basic ideas in an explanation related by real world phenomena?
7. Are there possible interrelationships between the marketing decision variables or concepts and between the resultant variables? Are these possible or actual interrelationships clearly identified and described?
8. Does the explanation enable the manager to intervene in the market process effectively? Alternatively, is the information provided in such a way that the action implications for the manager are clear?
9. Is it likely that concepts other than those contained in an explanation will be active and disrupt or render useless the explanation?

---

provides little or no ground for expecting a particular phenomenon; it lacks what Hempel calls objective explanatory power. Thus, the requirement of testability is that scientific explanations must be capable of empirical test. An explanation which meets the first requirement (empirical relevance) also meets the requirement of testability whereas the converse does not hold.

Causality in Explanation

The definition of an explanation employed here relies heavily on the concept of causation which has been discussed earlier. A very brief return of our attention to the notion of "cause" will be helpful at this point. For the researcher, the object of explanation should be to provide, with as high a degree of certainty as possible, information about what variables influence, produce, or affect other variables. It is necessary to determine the nature of the marketing decision variables (causes) so that procedures can be established for manipulating them. Only when hypotheses or theoretical statements are presented in this way can they be of maximum utility in deriving marketing implications. It will be useful to formulate a causal statement in a marketing context and use this statement to discuss the properties of causal laws. This process will be illustrated by the following short case.

Case. The Salesman's Role in the Buying of a New Car.

Situation: Mr. Samuel Jones, an average middle-class person of moderate means desires to buy a new domestic car. Mr. Jones is a man who values the traditional mores of value given for value received, an honest day's work for an honest day's pay, and being fair in one's dealings.

Within a few blocks of Mr. Jones's house are two Chevrolet dealerships. Mr. Jones distinctly prefers Chevrolets and would not seriously consider buying any other brand of car. On one Saturday morning in January, Mr. Jones pays a visit to Chevrolet Dealership A. Upon entering the door to the showroom, he is approached by salesman George Brown. Mr. Brown shows the display models of Chevrolets to Mr. Jones. Mr. Jones thumps the tires, sits in the driver's seat, and looks under the hood. Mr. Brown, the salesman, then invites Mr. Jones into his tiny office to negotiate a price for the car of Mr. Jones' choice. While the two are negotiating, Mr. Brown is interrupted often by phone calls and other salesmen who stick their heads in the office door and make small jokes at the expense of a local politician. After 10 minutes or so, Mr. Jones states that he would like to look around some more and then leaves Dealership A.

Although Mr. Jones has heard equally encouraging information about Dealerships A and B and, indeed, having had good personal experiences with both dealerships, Mr. Jones decides to visit Dealership B which happens to have the same makes and models of Chevrolets on display.

On entering the door of Dealership B, Mr. Jones is met by Sam Smith, the salesman. Mr. Jones is escorted around the showroom, kicking the tires, looking under the hoods, and sitting in the seats. However, Sam Smith offers to take Mr. Jones for a test drive. Mr. Jones drives the car for ½ hour with Sam Smith sitting on the right side discussing the virtues of the new line of Chevrolets. Upon arriving back at the dealership, Sam offers Mr. Jones a cup of coffee and introduces Mr. Jones to the head of the maintenance department. Sam Smith offers to drive Mr. Jones home if he does not wish to discuss prices that same day. However, Jones says that he is interested in finding out what his favorite model costs. In about 20 minutes of uninterrupted discussion they arrive at a mutual understanding and Mr. Jones signs the purchase papers.

Managerial implications and scientific causal statement: If the customer feels that the salesman really cares about him and spends time on him which otherwise could be spent on another "prospect" the customer will feel indebted to the salesman and will want to give him some business.

Stated more scientifically: *Norms of reciprocity among customers will affect the personal selling situation.* A general analysis of Mr. Jones' situation follows.

The two variables in the case above are norms or feelings of reciprocity and the outcome of a selling effort. The connecting mechanism at the individual level might be that feelings of obligation (in turn explained by social exchange theory) develop within a consumer as he comes to perceive the salesman as investing in the selling situation resources valuable to the salesman. Because of an apparent opportunity cost incurred by the salesman (as perceived by the prospect) in his relationship with the consumer, the consumer will reciprocate by rewarding the salesman with a purchase. A number of things in the causal sentence which are properties of causal statements should be noted:

1. The statement assumes, for example, that high levels of reciprocity among customers should be found in most successful personal selling situations.
2. Changes in the level of reciprocity will produce changes in the frequency of successful personal selling.
3. Successful selling efforts by salesmen do not produce feelings of reciprocity among customers (this may at first glance seem contradictory but salesmen may only activate or stimulate this variable, not create it).
4. For a change in reciprocity to produce a change in sales, there do not have to be changes in other variables.
5. The variables involved in a given causal law may be of different classes, for example, one variable may be dichotomous and the other continuous.
6. There can be contexts where the causal law does not apply. Presumably it would not apply to "order-taking" personal selling situations but would apply to "creative" personal selling situations.
7. Other variables such as changes in level of disposable income or advertising could cause a change in sales without invalidating the causal statement.
8. Most importantly, we do not know that a given change in sales is in fact caused solely by a change in reciprocity (either among a given group or by exposure of other groups to the sales effort). Even if we hold constant the effect of advertising, income change, and other imaginable variables and still find variations in reciprocity to be associated with variations in sales, we cannot conclude with absolute certainty that the causal statement is true. There is always the chance that a variable or set of variables (including measuring errors and problems in the research design) that we have not thought of has produced the change in sales.

Levels of Explanation

There are at least four levels of explanation in the behavioral sciences.[16] These are presented in Table 3.1.

TABLE 3.1 *Levels of Explanation*

Level	Explanation
One	A certain phenomenon has an empirical existence.
Two	The phenomenon is of the nature Q and is produced by factors x_1, x_2, . . . , x_n.
Three	Factors x_1, x_2, . . . , x_n are interactive or have interacted in manner y_1, y_2, . . . , y_n to produce in some past or present time a phenomenon of the nature Q.
Four	Factors x_1, x_2, . . . x_n interact in a manner y_1, y_2, . . . , y_n for reasons w_1, w_2, ... , w_n, thus producing a phenomenon of the nature Q.

A good illustration of these four levels of explanation involving behavioral phenomena of relevance to marketing is presented by H. G. Barnett's theory of innovation as a basis for cultural change.[17] Only elements of this theory, his notion of basic wants as necessary conditions for innovation, will be treated. At level one a phenomenon, an act of innovation, that is, adoption, is observed; it is known, not just assumed, to have occurred or to be in the process of taking place.

At level two the phenomenon is observed to be of a certain nature, Q, in this instance, the purchase of an ultramodern architectural blueprint for a permanent home or possibly the actual purchase of such a home. Thus, the nature of the event, Q, consists of a purchase (a particular behavior) of an object perceived as new with "new" being defined in terms of qualitative distinction rather than in terms of time. Q, then, is composed of three factors: (1) purchase behavior, (2) perceptual processes, and (3) an object having qualitative distinction from other objects in the same general class of objects. Q may have been produced by or be a result of central subliminal wants (a type of self-want) and creative wants (a type of want that we relabel as autotelic wants). These two wants represent x_1 and x_2 in Table 3.1. Central subliminal wants are those which relate to the individual's need for self-preservation and self-definition. They influence how we structure and organize our environment. Creative wants emphasize accomplishment with the process or act of being creative being as important as and possibly more important than

[16] J. T. Doby, "Logic and Levels of Scientific Explanation," in *Sociological Methodology*, E. F. Borgatta (ed.) (San Francisco: Jossey-Bass, 1969).

[17] H. G. Barnett, *Innovation: the Basis of Cultural Change* (New York: McGraw-Hill, 1953).

the resultant innovation or objects. In general, wants of this nature result from dissatisfaction with the accepted way of doing things.

Level three is concerned with explaining how central subliminal wants (x_1) and creative wants (x_2) interact in manner y_1 to produce the adoption of the innovation in question. Explanation in this case takes the form of describing what y_1 is. In our example creative wants interact with central subliminal wants. The need to define oneself as unique, avant-garde, and so on, together with dissatisfaction of existing modes of architecture as means of achieving this self-definition, lead to the adoption of radical architectural style. But in level three the emphasis is upon the manner of interaction. It could be explained that creative wants stimulate (the manner of interaction) central subliminal wants and that for reasons of congruence or cognitive consistency the central subliminal wants are expressed in creative ways, that is, the individual establishes a self-definition of being an innovator. Being interested in doing innovative things and being dissatisfied with existing conditions brings about the idea that he is an innovator which becomes expressed in such behavior as the acquisition of a radically or at least significantly different home.

At level four explanation goes beyond the relationship of the x's to each other and attempts to account for reasons (w_1, w_2, and so on) the x factors interact in manner y_1. An explanation at this level has already been given. It was stated above that for reasons of cognitive consistency factor x_1, creative wants, cause factor x_2, central subliminal wants to express themselves in innovative, that is, creative ways. The notion of cognitive consistency in this illustration constitutes the reason, w_1.

Evaluating Explanations

There are four basic criteria for evaluating explanations. These are: scope, precision, power, and reliability. Each now will be discussed briefly.

Scope   Scope refers to the range of events to which an explanation can be applied. A number of hypotheses and theories relevant to marketing and having broad scope can be cited briefly. The two-step flow of communication hypothesis is a good example of an explanation of marketing-relevant communication behavior. Exchange theory as articulated by George Homans and Peter Blau is a theory of wide scope and relevant to marketing. E. T. Hall's theory of culture as communication is another explanation with extremely broad scope although difficult to test empirically.

Precision   "The precision of an explanation refers to the exactness with which the concepts used in explanation are related to empirical indicators, and the precision with which the rules of interaction of the variable in the system are stated."[18] Note that there are two areas of precision referred to in this quote. The first concerns the relationship between a concept and its empirical indicator. The second concerns precision in the statements concerning the relationships among concepts.

With regard to precision in the first case there is always an unavoidable gap, a lack of precision, between a concept and its empirical operationalization. "In a very real sense no theoretically defined concepts can be directly translated into operations nor can theoretical propositions be tested empirically."[19] In an article largely devoted to this problem of precision, Zaltman concludes: "Perhaps one of the greatest obstacles inhibiting the effective application of the behavioral sciences to marketing problems is that this very important quality of isomorphism (between theoretical and operational systems) can only be determined intuitively."[20]

The second aspect of precision concerns precision in the stated relationships between concepts. Blalock[21] argues vigorously for specifying relationships in the form of direct causal links stated in terms of covariations and temporal sequences for reasons of explication, testing, and measurement.

This last factor, measurement, is a key factor influencing precision. In the first case it affects the accuracy of the operationalized concept: the smaller the measurement error, the more isomorphic the relationship between theoretical concepts and their empirical indicators. In the second place measurement affects the detection of such things as interaction effects which influence the interpretation of relationships among explanatory variables.

Power   Power refers to the degree of control over the environment an explanation provides. Power depends on the precision of the description and explanation and on the completeness of the variables. An explanation encompassing all, or many, relevant variables and providing linking statements, as discussed in the preceding section on precision, is considered more powerful than an explanation which involves few variables inarticulately expressed and relies heavily on the clause, "other things being equal."

Reliability   Reliability refers to the frequency with which factors not included in the explanation interrupt the situation that the explanation concerns. It would be unusual of course to have complete reliability in marketing and the behavioral sciences in general. Reliability must be considered as a relative

[18] E. J. Meehan, *Explanation in Social Science: A System Paradigm* (Homewood, Ill.: The Dorsey Press, 1968), p. 117.
[19] H. M. Blalock, Jr., "The Measurement Problem: A Gap Between the Languages of Theory and Research" in *Methodology in Social Research*, H. M. Blalock, Jr. and A. B. Blalock (eds.) (New York: McGraw-Hill, 1968).
[20] Gerald Zaltman, "Marketing Inference in the Behavioral Sciences," *Journal of Marketing*, Vol. 34 (July 1970), p. 32.
[21] H. M. Blalock, Jr., *op. cit.*, p. 18.

thing and not in absolute terms. In some ways reliability is related to degree of precision. We can say that a certain behavior is accounted for, or explained by, the life style of the actor. This statement is rather reliable given its vague all-inclusiveness but not very precise; certainly not as precise as breaking life style down into principal component parts and explaining behavior in terms of these parts.

Prediction

Prediction is generally used in two ways. First, it is often used for making deductions from known to unknown events. An example is the use of consumer preference measures to forecast market share for a brand of toothpaste.

A second use of the term involves making assertions about future outcomes on the basis of recurring sequences of events. Sometimes, such statements are time bound, as in predicting for a given period. This is a form of prediction frequently labeled forecasting. Another form of prediction common to marketing is test marketing, which assumes that processes occurring in the test market will be "reoccurring" not only in the test market but in comparable other areas, so that the recurring sequence of events in the test market will adequately predict an outcome in the relative future in other contexts.

QUESTIONS To Be Asked by the Marketing Manager of the Information He Is Provided for Making His Decisions: PREDICTION QUESTIONS

1. Is the prediction provided by the marketing researcher sufficiently specific so that the expected future events can be identified at the time they are to appear?
2. Is the explanation from which the prediction is drawn sound?
3. What is the level of the stated or implied prediction? Alternatively, how detailed is the statement about an expected future outcome? Are reasons given as to why and how it will occur?
4. How many factors are considered in making the prediction? Are possible important factors missing from the analysis?
5. How many different market events does a given prediction contain?
6. How precisely stated, if at all, are the interrelationships between variables used to make predictions? Are offsetting effects considered?
7. Is it likely that factors not considered will cause the expected outcome not to occur thus rendering the predictive statements unreliable?

Scientific prediction is forecasting with the help of scientific or technological theories and data. It is a statement or set of statements (1) whose premises are true, (2) which contains data statements that are true but refer to times no later than the present, and (3) which relates to the relative future. All scientific prediction involves some theory from which deductions are possible and contains some factual evidence relevant to the propositions of the theory.

A good example of scientific prediction in consumer behavior is the use of attitudes, or more strictly empirical measures of attitudes, to predict buyer behavior. The general principle involved is a psychological one concerning the striving for consistency between attitudes and behavior. The empirical data statements may be past or current information describing how the attitudes and buyer behavior are related. On the basis of the general theory and data statements conclusions are drawn—deduced—about some state in the relative future. Cognitive consistency models and market data have also been used to predict brand preferences and actual buyer behavior.

Levels of Prediction

As in the case of explanation, there are also different levels in prediction. These levels correspond to those shown in Table 3.2 except that they are future oriented. Consider an example of different levels of prediction derived from theoretical models discussed by Rogers,[22] Lerner,[23] and others concerning innovation in developing societies. The basic theory involves four interrelated concepts: literacy, cosmopoliteness, empathy, and innovativeness.

At level one the simple statement is that in the relative future more innovative social units (society, group, individual) will exist. The social unit is the phenomenon of concern.

The second level of prediction is that more innovative social units, Q, will exist as a result of increases in literacy, cosmopoliteness, and empathy. These three variables are the factors x_1, x_2, and so on, referred to in Table 3.1. Q is the nature of the phenomenon.

At the third level of prediction we may say that the three factors have interacted in the past, and/or are now interacting and/or will interact in the future in such a manner as to produce a change in innovativeness. The "in such a manner" is the focus of prediction at this level. For example, we might predict the following manner or type of interaction between literacy and empathy: higher degrees of mastery over symbols in written form (literacy) widen experiences through meaningful encounters with the print media, and unlock mental abilities, allowing the social unit to encompass these new experiences. This, in turn, increases the ability to project oneself into the role or situation of another. Such identification is a direct antecedent of being innovative.[24]

---

[22] E. M. Rogers, *Modernization among Peasants* (New York: Holt, Rinehart and Winston, 1969).

[23] D. Lerner, *Passing of Traditional Society* (New York: Free Press, 1958).

[24] H. G. Barnett, *op. cit.*

At level four, emphasis is on the reasons why (w_1) literacy and empathy (and the other factor combinations, for example, literacy-cosmopoliteness, and so on) interact in the manner (y_1) just described and why empathy and the other variables may produce innovativeness directly independent of the impact of interaction effects. The reason why empathy affects innovativeness may be found in the concept of vicarious modeling. The reason for the literacy-empathy relationship may be found in contemporary theories of creativity. Thus, the prediction that Q is of a specified nature ultimately rests on the prediction that vicarious modeling, certain creative processes, and other reasons have been or will be in operation. The reasons just cited are themselves subject to analysis at each of the four levels of explanation and prediction.

Evaluating Predictions

Scope   The scope of a prediction refers to the range of events that it covers. The range of events may be viewed both longitudinally and latitudinally. If there is a long chain of events which must take place before a given phenomenon will occur and there are no other causal events capable of producing that phenomenon, then a prediction of that phenomenon must encompass or include accurate prediction of the state of events in the chain. Scope of prediction may also be viewed laterally, that is, in terms of the number of final events the predictive explanation covers.

Precision   The precision of a prediction refers to the degree of isomorphism between the concepts involved in the prediction and their empirical indicators. In addition to the important quality of isomorphism, precision is also affected by the accuracy of the empirical indicators, that is, the quality of measurements with which the prediction is made. This is a methodological problem of some concern. As with nonpredictive explanations, the precision of the statement describing the rules of interaction among system variables is also important. This is very relevant to the problem of scope. The greater the longitudinal scope of a prediction, the greater the degree of precision required in stating the relationships among the X's and between X's and Q's. As Stinchcombe[25] has observed, "the elegance and power of an explanation can only be as good as the causal connection among variables allows it to be." This is also a reminder that statements of relationships between variables should not only be precise but be causal as well.

Power   Power in precision is a function of the precision of the predictive statement and its completeness. The more precise and encompassing of vari-

    [25] A. L. Stinchcombe, *Constructing Social Theories* (New York: Harcourt Brace Jovanovich, 1968), p. 129.

ables a predictive explanation is, the more powerful it is. It is more powerful in the sense that it provides a greater opportunity to control, and to control more accurately, those variables amenable to control or external manipulation by the researcher or planner.

One problem affecting that aspect of power involving completeness is the issue of prediction as feedback: a stated prediction may affect its own fulfillment. This is largely relevant to social rather than physical contexts. A promotional campaign stressing the virtues of a new nonprescription drug may, through the power of suggestion, cause people to actually experience relief solely on the basis of the prediction that it would provide relief. Studies on placebo effects provide the scientific grounding for such a statement. However, the feedback could be negative if excessive unrealistic expectations were built in the consumer's mind which the product could not match in actual use.

Reliability Reliability in prediction concerns the frequency with which factors not included in the prediction explanation interfere with the predicted phenomenon, that is, cause it not to happen exactly as the explanation predicted. To some extent there can be a tradeoff between reliability and precision. The less precise the prediction or, alternatively, the more vague it is, the greater the degree of fluctuation allowed in the phenomenon Q. It is up to the researcher to determine the final tradeoff point.

Control

Explanation serves a twofold function: (1) to satisfy the human need to anticipate events (prediction), and (2) to be able to control future events. It is this latter phenomenon, control, which is of concern here. Many scientists claim that control is the central factor in the scientific enterprise. Even so, the philosophy of science has relatively little to say about a metatheory of applied behavioral science. Yet, the control function of scientific knowledge is of such great importance in applied activities such as marketing that it is essential to investigate the various criteria and guidelines for exercising control and evaluating control efforts.

Definition of Control

Control is the systematic manipulation of some element related to or contained within a system so as to effect a change in one or more elements in that system. "A system is an entity which is composed of at least two elements and a relation that holds between each of its elements and at least one other element in the set."[26] Control over a particular event is achieved

---

[26] R. L. Ackoff, "Toward a System of Systems Concepts," *Management Science,* 17 (1971), p. 662.

if the relations specified in the explanation may be manipulated; manipulation of relationships requires manipulation of variables. The definition of control also specifies that an external state, that is, the environment of a system, may be a source of causal forces. The environment of a system is defined as "a set of elements and their relevant properties, which elements are not part of the system but a change in any of which can produce a change in the state of the system."[27] Control over an event is achieved if endogenous and/or exogenous variables contained in an explanation are manipulated so that a desired result is obtained.

QUESTIONS To Be Asked by the Marketing Manager of the Information He Is Provided for Making His Decisions: CONTROL QUESTIONS

1. Are the manipulable factors (marketing decision variables) clearly defined?
2. Is the information presented by the researcher sufficiently clear so that the strategies and tactics to be employed for bringing about desired effects can be readily determined?
3. Is there adequate information concerning conditions when intervention will be most effective?
4. Into what theoretical issues can given marketing research problems be translated?
5. What additional insight about control can be obtained by exploring the theoretical area defined?
6. When the research is called for to provide feedback on past management action, does it provide adequate information to evaluate that action?
7. Does the research data clearly focus upon the objectives sought by management's actions?
8. Does the data indicate how management action could have been more efficient?
9. Does the data shed light on how the intervention brought about the effect? Can the data show how other mechanisms other than those believed to be operative might have brought about the desired effects?

Levels of Understanding in Control

Following the structure of Table 3.1, four different levels of understanding in the control process can be defined. At the first level there is the simple identification of the criterion variable(s) and the noting that a certain condition can be wrought by the change agent. The second level involves the identification of manipulatable causal factors (the x's) capable of bringing about the

[27] *Ibid.*, pp. 662–663.

phenomenon Q. The third level represents a still higher level of knowledge about the control situation. It identifies the strategies and tactics (the y's) to be used to alter existing relational patterns among x's and between x's and the condition out of which Q is to emerge. The final level is the specification of the reasons (w's) why strategy y, and so on, can affect the relations among x's and between x's and the criterion variables. This involves identifying facilitating factors in the system or the system's environment.

At level one the criterion variable is identified. In the illustration used here this variable will be product quality perception. It is ascertained that this is a manipulatable variable, that is, within the deliberate control of the change agent. The next level of understanding permits the marketer to say that the product will have a perceived quality Q as the result of his manipulating price and channel of distribution. At level three the marketer knows through adequate research that, for his product class and market segment, there is a certain price range within which there is a relatively high positive association between price and perceived product quality. Presumably, consumers reason that a high price is due to high workmanship and/or more durable and functional features, thus enhancing the objective quality of the product. There may also be an interaction between causal factors having an additional effect on perceived product quality. The imputed relationship between price and quality and the added causal impact of the interaction effect between price and store images would presumably lead to a strategy of relatively high price and distribution through outlets having favorable images. At a still higher level of understanding he would base this action on certain reasons ($w_1, w_2, \ldots, w_3$) such as the income level of the relevant market segment, the importance of quality, and so on.

Translating Practical Problems into Theoretical Issues

Argyris also sees merit in translating practical problems into theoretical issues.[28] The client's problems become empirical illustrations of more general theories from which the empirical problem phenomena can be deduced. By translating the client's problems into theoretical issues, that is, by induction, the problems may be analyzed using a wealth of concepts and findings in other settings which may be generalizable to the specific situation of the client. Without having first translated the particular problems into theoretical issues, the new suggestions and insights provided for control strategies might otherwise be missed. Marketing has benefited considerably from this process. For example, the translation of brand selection and loyalty problems into learning theory and small group theory issues has proved very fruitful and the recasting

[28] C. Argyris, *Intervention Theory and Methods* (Reading, Mass.: Addison-Wesley, 1970).

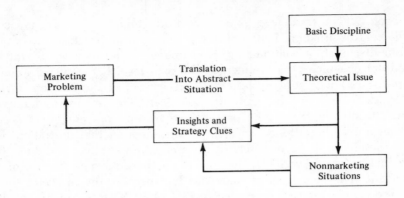

FIGURE 3.6 *Iteration between Problems and Theoretical Issues*

of salesman-prospect relations into an exchange theory issue has provided new guidelines for the recruitment, training, and assignment of salesmen.

The process involved in the iteration between practical problems and theoretical issues is shown in Figure 3.6. Given a marketing problem the first step is to translate it into a more abstract theoretical issue as defined by the current state of knowledge in the discipline(s) contributing information to the particular issue. Exploration of the theoretical issue at a theoretical level can contribute insight and marketing strategy clues directly to the marketing problem. The marketing problem is viewed simply as an explanadum, that is, as an empirical manifestation of the theoretical issue. Additional insight and guidelines may be derived by examining the implications of a theory in its application in areas traditionally considered as nonmarketing settings.

Categories of Evaluation of Control Efforts

Effort   Five categories of criteria for evaluating the success or failure of a control performance have been suggested in the literature.[29] The first category concerns effort. This involves what was done and how well it was done and uses such criteria as the quantity and quality of activity occurring. Emphasis is on input rather than output. This is one of the easiest evaluative tasks. The number of dollars invested in advertising is easy to assess in detailed ways, for example, by market segment, by media, and so on. The approximate number of consumer exposures to advertising can also be known with a high degree of accuracy.

Performance   Performance criteria relate to measuring the results of efforts rather than the effort itself. Such questions as the following are asked: What

---

[29] E. H. Suchman, *Evaluative Research* (New York: Russell Sage, 1967), pp. 60–73.

changes occurred? Were these the intended changes? Was it of the desired magnitude? Did the advertising create positive images? Did it reach the intended audience? What was the purchase response rate? Given that many programs involve a hierarchy of objectives, performance criteria can be applied at each level of the objectives.

Adequacy   The adequacy of a performance given the total need is another important criterion. A promotional campaign intended to precipitate trial of a product can hardly be adjudged adequate if it only succeeds in stimulating interest. It is less adequate still if it only stimulates awareness and is least adequate when it only reminds consumers of the product's existence. Both exposure and impact must be considered as essential elements of adequacy. Bigman notes: "We must distinguish between effectiveness and impact. By the latter term I mean the strength of the influence upon exposed individuals. A program or activity may have considerable impact, affecting markedly the thoughts and actions of those it touches; it will be necessarily judged ineffective if it is so designed that this impact is confined to a small fraction of the group it is intended to reach and influence."[30]

Efficiency   The next criterion is efficiency. It is "concerned with the evaluation of alternative paths or methods in terms of costs . . . in a sense, it represents a ratio between effort and performance—output divided by input."[31]

Process   Finally, we have the criterion of process. This involves the analysis of the means whereby a program achieves whatever effects it may have. It calls for an overview and analysis of the impact of particular sequences in the control program. It is concerned, in other words, with the overall program and with the interaction among parts of the program or elements in the system. Are particular components interacting in such a way as to produce dysfunctional effects? Are there bottlenecks in the process?

Summary

This chapter has covered the basic structure of information (concepts, propositions, and models) and the uses of information (explanation, prediction, and control). Only the surface of the topics was covered, however, and the interested reader is urged to go into the subject matter further. It should be evident to the reader that the content of this chapter, while abstract and complex in some areas, has considerable relevance to the everyday practice of marketing and marketing research.

[30] S. K. Bigman, "Evaluating the Effectiveness of Religious Programs," *Review of Religious Research*, Vol.2 (1961), p. 113.
[31] E. H. Suchman, *op. cit.*, p. 64.

Questions and Exercises

1. The brand share for product X fell 10 percent when the price of the product was raised 55¢. What kind of information is necessary to prove that the price hike *caused* the drop in market share?

2. Take a concept with which you are familiar (that is, social class, opinion leadership, personality, and so on) and discuss how you would operationalize the concept for use in a questionnaire. Criticize your concept and its operationalization in terms of its validity.

3. The following is a very general proposition regarding the relationship between selling effort and sales: Increased selling effort leads to increased sales. Discuss how the specificity of this proposition might be increased. What additional factors are likely to be relevant? Rewrite the proposition in a more specific manner.

4. The relationship between two variables may be either monotonic (ever decreasing or ever increasing) or nonmonotonic (it may change course at some point such as a U-shaped function). When the true nature of the relationship is nonmonotonic, what problems arise for the researcher and how may he overcome them?

5. You are a brand manager for a liquid detergent and are always on the lookout for ways to improve your brand's sales. You happen to read a study done by a frozen foods manufacturer which found that the use of newspaper coupons greatly increased sales of his product. While you are anxious to try this technique for your products you recognize that the proposition may not be valid in general or more specifically for your particular product. Discuss your doubts about the proposition. What additional information might increase the validity of the proposition?

6. In the case study presented in the chapter what alternatives to the causal statement given might be offered? What steps could be taken to determine what actually caused the action of interest (that is, purchasing the car)?

7. Give an example of each of the four levels of explanation discussed in the chapter.

8. Evaluate the prediction: when customers feel that a salesperson has made an investment in them (through his time) they are more likely to purchase something from him.

Project Related Questions

1. List and define all the concepts you are using in your research.

2. Apply the various questions on page 53 to your project. Be particularly sensitive to questions 3 and 5 in this figure.

3. What are the sources of doubt in the hypotheses or propositions you are concerned with in your project? What about hidden assumptions? Implied cause-and-effect relationships?

4. Which questions on page 55 are most relevant to your project? Have you concerned yourself with these questions?

5. What type of model or theory is implicit in your research assumptions and propositions or hypotheses?

6. Try stating the basic model you are working with in writing as well as in terms of a diagram where the different concepts are written down and connected by lines where relationships are believed to exist. Can you attach arrows to these lines to suggest causal relationships?

7. Using the criteria on page 65, should the model be made more (a) complex or (b) simple?

8. What level of explanation do you want to achieve? (See Table 3.1.)

9. What is the scope or variety of events you want to explain?

10. Assess your project in terms of the questions on page 66. Is prediction a goal of your project?

11. If so, assess your project in terms of the questions on page 72. Be particularly sensitive to questions 4 and 7.

12. What level of prediction if any is intended, is involved in your project?

13. Have you translated the practical problems you are concerned with into theoretical issues? List the relevant theoretical issues.

14. Assess your project in terms of the questions on page 76. Which of these questions are of greatest relevance to your project?

Chapter 4

Problem Definition and Research Design

As with all managerial activities, planning must occur to implement marketing research. The marketing researcher must plan a number of activities in order to successfully execute the research for a minimum expenditure. First, the researcher must create a method of monitoring his environment in order to build models of how the environment works. Then the manager must decide which series of methods are appropriate to his problem. In order to do this, he must understand how the internal logic of his research can be achieved. Then he must attempt to maintain the generalizability of his findings. To do this he must select one of several possible experimental designs. This chapter introduces the methodological considerations which are necessary for several following chapters.

Introduction

Research is marketing management's method for exploring problems and gaining insight into matters of concern so that remedial activity may be instituted or new opportunities exploited. The basic overall process is to define the nature of the problem. The first part of this chapter is concerned with the general aspects of this task. An important step in defining or analyzing problems is to determine what variables have what kind of impact on whatever it is that is being experienced as a marketing problem.

Various research designs are available for determining what causal variables are having particular impacts on sales, consumer attitudes, and so forth. These research designs are discussed here in some detail. However, it is also necessary to be aware of possible sources of errors in designing and conducting research. This helps minimize the possibility of making decisions on the basis of incorrect information. Consequently, prior to the discussion on research design there will be a treatment of types and sources of error in marketing research.

Problem Exploration

There is probably no activity in marketing research which is more important than the definition of the research problem. Sadly, the task of defining marketing research problems is one of the most neglected issues in marketing. The proper definition of the problem is important for several reasons. The way a problem is defined influences:

1. the selection of the population to be studied;
2. the method for selecting the sample from the population;
3. the design of the research to be conducted;
4. the kind of data to be gathered;
5. the statistical modes of analysis; and
6. the remedial action to be initiated by management.

An incorrect definition of a marketing problem can render ineffective all subsequent efforts to bring about changes intended to help remedy a problem and thus result in a waste of scarce resources and a lower level of satisfaction among buyers and users.

A marketing problem can be thought of as *a situation which is perceived by the marketing organization as a source of dissatisfaction for its members and for which preferable alternatives are considered possible*. Note there are two important aspects to this definition: first, something is considered a source of dissatisfaction; and second, improvements (preferable alternatives) are believed possible.

Defining Problems

An initial guideline for defining problems is provided by the discussion in Chapter 3 concerning levels of analysis in explanation, prediction, and control. The guideline suggests the following steps. First, the task of defining problems has been largely treated as intuitive and not performed on a vigorous basis. How, then, can the problem definition task be made more explicit? It appears that the following steps could be followed. First, there is a statement of the symptom, that is, a certain phenomenon exists. Secondly, a statement is required saying that the phenomenon is of the nature Q and is produced by factors $x_1, x_2, \ldots, x_n$. Q represents the experience of a symptom and x_1, x_2, and so on, are the causal factors whose functioning represents the real problem to be remedied. A third step, an analytical activity, is desirable as a means of increasing the likelihood that remedial efforts will be effective. This step is at a level of explanation which states that factors $x_1, x_2, \ldots, x_n$ are interactive or have interacted in manner $y_1, y_2, \ldots, y_n$ to produce in some past or present time a phenomenon of the nature Q. Finally, for the most complete understanding of the problem an analytical level is necessary which states that factors $x_1, x_2, \ldots, x_n$ interact the way they do for reasons $w_1, w_2, \ldots, w_n$, thus producing a phenomenon of the nature Q.

The experience of a drugstore chain in the Eastern United States provides an example of this process. The drugstore chain had difficulty in maintaining what it considered an optimal inventory of nonprescription antidepressant drugs. There were seemingly random fluctuations in the demand for this product resulting in oversupply at some times and undersupply at other times. Thus, the symptom experienced, Q, was an inability to maintain "adequate" stocks of a particular high-profit item. The marketing staff of the drugstore chain challenged the hypothesis offered by retail operators that the fluctuations were random. The marketing division hired a medical sociologist as a consultant to work with them on this problem. The consultant postulated the alternative hypothesis that the consumption of antidepressant drugs was associated with particular societal activities.

Sociologists had for a long time noted and studied the covariation between consumption of physician prescribed and over-the-counter antidepressant drugs on the one hand, and societal activities such as holidays and prominent events on the other hand. The relationship observed was that consumption of such drugs declined quite noticeably prior to holidays and other occasions as elections and major sporting events. Thus, covariation was found between the symptom and some other independent phenomena. These other phenomena are rationally related to drug consumption by a social theory which need not be analyzed here. The basic notion, however, was tested. First, the drugstore chain records showed that consumption did fall off markedly prior to national holidays and the Christmas-New Year seasons. Moreover, a substantial proportion of the population in the region were Jewish and, as the theory predicted, there were also sharp declines in antidepressant drug sales prior to the important Jewish holidays falling in September/October.

In this example the immediate causal variables, identified initially by observing covariation, could not be manipulated, but the drugstore chain could, and did, adapt their inventory practice by ordering smaller quantities in advance of major societal events and increasing inventory immediately afterward. Although this ended the problem exploration activities of the chain, an interesting sequel developed approximately three months later.

A manufacturer of two popular, nationally distributed over-the-counter antidepressant drugs went further in the analysis of this problem. They hired, at the suggestion of the director of research for the drugstore chain, the same medical sociologist to consult with their promotional department. The intention was that a further understanding of the theory behind the association of special events and drug consumption could provide a clue for advertising appeals. The phenomenon, Q, was shown to be affected by a societal event, x_1. Another causal factor, x_2, is also part of the theory. This is the need for association or affiliation; that is, a need to feel that one belongs to or can identify with others in society. The consultant explained that these two factors, x_1 and x_2, interacted in manner y. The interaction of the manner y was that prominent events (x_1) provided a salient reference point that individuals felt they shared with other persons, thus satisfying to some extent the need for association (x_2). The reasons (w_i) why this interaction takes place lies in a further elaboration of the general theory which cannot be undertaken here.

The promotional department, having the information that social-psychological isolation is associated with—in fact is one of the causes of—the use of antidepressant drugs, decided to utilize this information in their advertising. They also planned to advertise more heavily during periods when no major events were taking place or were about to occur. The manufacturer in cooperation with an advertising agency proceeded to conduct behavioral laboratory tests of appeals stressing loneliness and found that such appeals were far more effective (in the laboratory setting) than any of their other advertising when it was pretested. Thus, the further analysis by the manufacturer of the theory employed by the drugstore chain was apparently success-ful. The word "apparent" is used deliberately. The reader might be interested to know that the appeal was never used. The legal staff of the company learned through informal channels outside the firm that the Federal Trade Commission was aware of the promotional plans and was prepared to intervene if the plans were put into effect. The company decided not to spend additional funds on developing the campaign in light of the possible injunction against using the appeals. They did, however, adjust their scheduling of advertising.

Let us introduce a more refined version of the four-step procedure just mentioned.

Step 1   Identify indicators of marketing problems. A marketing indicator is a measurement of a marketing phenomena whose movements indicate whether a particular marketing situation is improving or worsening in terms of some goal.

Step 2   Monitor indicators of marketing problems.

Step 3   Determine whether the measurement of the indicator has exceeded a threshold or level signifying a danger.

Step 4   Determine what variable or set of variables covary with the indicator variables. These covarying variables are the potential causes of or explanation for the problem.

SUBSTEP 4(a)   Determine whether there are possible explanatory variables which function in time periods considerably removed from the period when symptoms are first noted.

SUBSTEP 4(b)   Determine whether there are possible explanatory or causal variables related to the symptoms at certain times and not at others.

Step 5   Select the most plausible explanatory variables. Plausibility is estab-lished by virtue of logic, past experience, past research, and soundness of the underlying theory or model.

Step 6   Determine whether variables among the most plausible set are (a) sufficient but not necessary; (b) necessary but not sufficient; (c) neither necessary nor sufficient; and (d) both necessary and sufficient.

Step 7   Determine what is the structure of relationships among the causal or explanatory variables and between these variables and the problem symp-toms. Possible relationships are shown below. Q's represent symptoms, x's represent explanatory variables.

Serial relations, single effect:

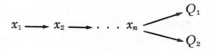

Serial relations, multiple effects:

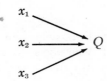

Independent relations, single effect:

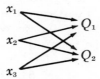

Independent relations, multiple effects:

Independent serial relations:

$$x_1$$
$$\downarrow$$
$$x_2 \longrightarrow Q$$
$$\uparrow$$
$$x_3$$

Step 8 Identify marketing decision variables, that is, those endogenous variables which marketing management can manipulate and influence, and exogenous variables, that is, those variables to which management can only adjust.

Step 9 Identify and match appropriate management actions with regard to endogenous and exogenous variables.

The recent experience of one of the five largest oil companies provides a concrete example of this nine-step procedure for exploring problems. The particular context of this example involves gas stations in the Detroit metropolitan area. The oil company purchased land, built the gas station, and then leased the station to operators. Periodically oil company representatives visited the stations to check on pump prices, cleanliness, and mechanical services. In addition, the company sponsored area wide promotions for their operations.

Executives of the company had selected total area sales and their market share as their most important marketing indicators. This selection of indicator is step 1. Data concerning these indicators were collected quarterly for the Detroit area. This monitoring corresponds to step 2. In the Fall of 1971 executives became very concerned when market share dropped substantially for the second consecutive quarter while total area sales remained relatively constant. Observing market share dropping below a predefined acceptable level is step 3. The company then set about step 4 by examining price and competitive advertising which might account for the declines. They noted that a major competing brand had been advertising intensively stressing station operators' concern for car care. Price was found to be relatively stable. In addition, many complaints had been received concerning cleanliness of rest rooms and lack of courtesy by pump attendants. Past experience coupled with the results of a small survey of car owners led executives to believe that the main reasons for loss of market share were a deterioration in the public's perception of the quality of services provided by their stations (step 5). This perception may have resulted in part from the competitive advertising by the other major oil company stressing the supposed superior quality of their services which implied that the company in question had *relatively* poorer services. This perception was deemed to be a necessary but not sufficient condition for the problem to arise (step 6). The situation could be described graphically as follows:

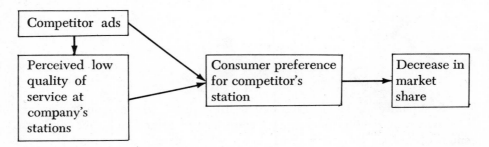

Competitor's advertising was accepted as an exogenous variable which the company could not manipulate. However, the company could manipulate the content of its own advertising. To some extent, the company could also pressure station operators to try to improve their general services in keeping with the new promotional campaign that the company was about to launch. This campaign (step 9) was to stress general customer service and expertise in car maintenance offered by the company's stations.

Sources of Marketing Problems

Marketing problems may stem from one or more sources. First there may be a marketing *policy problem*, that is, a difficulty concerning a general orientation or operating philosophy of marketing management. A major marketing consulting agency in the new product field has found numerous instances where new product failures were a result of management attitudes toward introducing new products. For example, they found, among technologically oriented firms, a high profit expectation of the new product. This expectation is often expressed in terms of a policy to the effect that a new product should demonstrate success very early. When this expectation was not met soon after market introduction the new product tended to be withdrawn and labeled a failure. Typically in such cases the consulting company is called upon by top management to evaluate the R & D departments where top management often feels the problem to be. Experience, however, also leads the consultant to study management attitudes toward keeping a new product on the market. The problem of insufficient new product "successes" often lies in the policy of withdrawing products from the market too soon rather than the quality of product generated by the R & D group. Policy problems are also found in the general strategies management pursues in marketing its product lines.

The *organizational structure* of a firm or its marketing division may be a source of problems inhibiting agency effectiveness. This is a general type and source of problems which has been underresearched in marketing. For example, a producer and marketer of educational products at one time had its product promotion department divided into two independent groups, salesforce and mass media advertising. Each group formulated its own promotional strategies independently of the other with no communication mechanisms, formal or informal, available to coordinate their activities. The managers of the respective groups did not report to a common person. Consequently, the advantages of coordinating personal and impersonal promotional strategies were seldom realized. Often the company found the two groups pursuing somewhat incompatible approaches which confused customers. Based on research conducted within the organization by a management consulting firm, the company reorganized, keeping the separation but having the two groups report to the same person who would coordinate the two basic promotional methods. As part of the reorganization, semiannual workshops were conducted where members of the two groups met for a formal brainstorming session.[1]

Related to organizational structure problems are *person problems*. Marketing management may lack expertise in a new product area or the salesforce may lack the necessary technical skills to describe or demonstrate a product

[1] See Chapter 15 for discussion of the method and reasons for its use.

or to match the product with client needs. People problems are often solved by training programs or special seminars, sometimes by firing employees and pirating employees of other organizations. Person problems are most likely to occur when a firm adds a new product line and/or when it enters a particular market for the first time.

On another dimension, person problems may be found among the roles of the influencer, decision maker, buyer, or user of the product or services offered by a firm. In fact, this is the area where most marketing research occurs. Research focuses on the knowledge, attitudes, and behavior of various market segments and examines their needs and preferences. As indicated in Chapter 3 marketing is concerned with explaining, predicting, and controlling person-related marketing phenomena. Much of this book, as with all existing marketing research texts, is concerned with person problems as they occur in the marketplace in conjunction with product and channel problems to be discussed shortly.

The *production process* is another source of difficulty in marketing although typically not one the marketing manager can do much about. Production process problems, when they result in shipping delays, for example, create ill will among the firm's customers who in turn direct their displeasure toward the salesman. Also, when quality control is inadequate or certain product specifications cannot be met, customers or potential customers become dissatisfied. Problems may also be of a *channel* nature. Problems in this area may be expressed as questions. Given the nature of the product, what are the available channels for its distribution? Once the problem of identifying the alternative channels is completed, the next issue is which channels or what combination of channels are optimal in terms of time and cost? Given the intended buyers, what channels are available? What channels are optimal in terms of time and cost? Is there resistance among brokers, jobbers, wholesalers, and retailers to carrying the product line?

There are also *product or service problems*. Considerable marketing research effort concerns demand forecasting for new or existing products. Will the market grow by the addition of new users? Will existing users consume still more? New product or service problems often encountered include: incompatibility of the new product with present products; incompatibility with existing media; incompatibility with current merchandising techniques; lack of packaging uniqueness; no pride of ownership engendered; the product not being susceptible to segmentation; lack of distributor acceptance; legal complications; and no communication uniqueness.

Still another type of problem is the *communication process problem*. The basic character of this problem is a lack of shared meaning between the marketing organization and some other unit with whom there is an attempted exchange or transaction. A lack of shared meaning or understanding does not necessarily cause a problem. A given product, for instance, may do well although management's views of the product differ from those of the buyer and user. Often, however, a product or service will not achieve its full potential because information about its existence or proper use is insufficiently disseminated. Also, the wrong information and negative attitudes may be held by potential users. Communication process problems usually entail modifying the promotional program of a product or service based on information collected from consumers.

Categories of Problems

There appear to be five possible categories for each of the problems just mentioned. These five categories are recurrent problems, rerecognized problems, current problems, refashioned problems, and unrecognized problems.[2]

A *recurrent problem* is defined as one which is persistent and visible. The high failure rate of new products is an example. The likelihood of a new product failing has been consistently high over time resulting in considerable resource loss. A *rerecognized marketing problem* is one which has received new attention but has always been present. For example, despite their widespread use, our understanding of why and how incentives or "deals" influence consumers is quite poor and only recently has research attention again been devoted to this topic. A *current problem* is one which has recently been labeled, generally acknowledged as existing, and receiving attention. An example of this is the current concern in marketing research with discrepancies between attitudes consumers hold toward particular products and their actual purchase behavior. Another problem concerns the use of standardized psychological and personality tests to explain consumer behavior. The particular problem is that these tests were developed for purposes other than the study of consumer behavior and hence may not be appropriate for the study of various consumer behaviors. A *refashioned problem* is simply one of long standing which has been given a new definition. For example, problems in the relationship between manufacturers and distributors have been redefined in terms of conflict theory. An *unrecognized marketing problem* is one which has not received substantial attention due to low visibility.

The various categories are not mutually exclusive or necessarily exhaustive. For example, a channel-related problem such as conflict between producers and distributors may be both a current problem and a redefined problem. Moreover, this channel-related problem may also be classified as a communication problem to the extent that the conflict is a result of different understandings of what constitutes an appropriate distribution strategy. Thus, a marketing

---

[2] E. O. Smigel, "Introduction," *Handbook on the Study of Social Problems* (Chicago: Rand McNally, 1971), p. xii.

problem grid analysis might be useful in analyzing research problems. Such a grid is shown below:

Product

Categories	Basic Types of Problems						
	Policy	Organiza- zation	Person	Produc- tion	Channel	Product	Communi- cation
Recurrent							
Rerecognized							
Current							
Refashioned							
Unrecognized							

Types and Sources of Error in Marketing Research

Before introducing specific data-gathering designs which produce information to help the marketing researcher to understand and solve problems, it will be useful just to sensitize the reader to various types and sources of error in marketing research.

The aim of research is to obtain data by some means short of a total enumeration which accurately reflect the "true" state of the whole population of interest. If 50 percent of the population likes a brand of Scotch whiskey because of its taste, it is expected that approximately 50 percent of those responding in a properly designed and executed research project would show that same preference. The extent to which the research results deviate from that true 50 percent is called *research error* or the research effect.

Error in research can come from many sources. It may be intentional (in which case it is neither ethical nor research) or unintentional. Potential sources of error, shown in Table 4.1, include the researcher and respondent, the research design, sampling procedures, and the controls used in the execution of the study. These now will be considered.

Researcher/Experimenter Effects

Although it has been known for some time that interviewers may bias survey results, a complete documentation of the ways in which they and even

TABLE 4.1 *Types and Sources of Error in Marketing Research*

Researcher/Experimenter Effects
Expectancy
Evaluation apprehension
Demand characteristics

Sources of Internal Invalidity
History as a source of error
Nonstandard measures as a source of error
Interviewer cheating
Maturation effects
Testing effects
Instrumentation decay
Mortality as a source of bias

Sampling Errors

---

the researcher himself may do so has only recently been offered.[3, 4] These effects or sources of error are due to the fact that research is almost always "intrusive" in some manner. The very act of responding to an interviewer's question, for example, affects the thoughts that the respondent holds about the topic. It is not the same as if the researcher used a ruler to determine the length of some object. Furthermore, the research act is a social situation and respondents "react" to the situation.

Researcher/experimenter effects can be classified into three categories: expectancy, evaluation apprehension, and demand characteristics.[5]

Expectancy Researchers in any field seldom enter into a study without an idea of what their results are likely to be. In fact, the scientific method itself suggests that hypotheses be formulated. These are expectations about potential outcomes. These expectancies may be expressed by the client to the researcher or may be formulated by the researcher himself and are what a study is to test. Expectancies about outcomes are a powerful source of biased error in research;

[3] Early studies in the field concerning interviewers include Daniel Katz, "Do Interviewers Bias Poll Results?" *Public Opinion Quarterly*, Vol. 6 (Summer 1942), pp. 248–268; H. L. Smith and H. Hyman, "The Biasing Effect of Interviewer Expectations on Survey Results," *Public Opinion Quarterly*, Vol. 14 (Fall 1950), pp. 491–506; and R. H. Hansen and E. S. Marks, "Influence of the Interviewer on the Accuracy of Survey Results," *Journal of the American Statistical Association*, Vol. 53 (September 1958).

[4] Much of the work done on these problems has been done in the field of experimental social psychology. See, for example, Rosenthal, *op. cit.*, 1966, and the volume of invited essays edited by R. Rosenthal and R. L. Rosnow, *Artifact in Behavioral Research* (New York: Academic Press, 1969).

[5] This classification is suggested in the organization of the volume edited by Rosenthal and Rosnow, *op. cit.*

bias in the direction of the expected outcome. Difficulties arise in that the researcher communicates in some manner the response he expects the respondent to provide. For example, in one experiment, all children in an elementary school were given an intelligence test disguised as a test to predict academic "blooming."[6] A table of random numbers were then used to select 20 percent of the children who their teachers were told "would show unusual academic development" during the coming school year. As a result of the teachers' expectations, these randomly selected children did show statistically significant IQ gains at the end of the year. In some manner, the teachers affected the behavior of their students by virtue of their expectations of what that behavior would be.

It might be noted that expectancy effects extend even to the task of computation. There is some reason to believe that computational errors may tend to favor the direction of the expectancy, that is, the hypothesis. In marketing research, these expectations are transmitted primarily through the interviewer. To control for these effects, therefore, one of the basic strategies is to keep interviewers "blind" as to the purpose of the research. Otherwise, the interviewers will attempt to influence their respondents to answer in a way consistent with the interviewer's view of the purpose of the research. Table 4.2 summarizes ways in which expectancy can be minimized. The intent of these techniques is to minimize the personal influence that an individual researcher can have on his researchers. It also controls overly curious interviewers who may try to determine the exact research hypotheses.

All of the above sources of error depend on forms of communication to produce the effect. As Table 4.2 suggests, restricting communication between researcher and respondent can minimize some types of error. This is not as easily done in survey research as it is in experimental studies,[7] however, and for obvious reasons. It will be useful to discuss briefly some of the types of unintended communications which bias responses.

Shifts of posture, eye movements, gestures, and tone of voice are some of the ways in which cues are transmitted. People communicate not only through the use of words, but also through the use of paralinguistic, kinetic, tactile, and other channels.[8] "Most of the time, words express only a portion of our meaning when we interact with other persons. Even with the audio-aural channel, people may reveal *how they feel about what they say* by such cues as speaking style, tone of voice, degree of vehemence, and so on."[9]

---

[6] *Ibid.*, p. 410.

[7] Survey research generally involves administering questionnaires to consumers in their natural environment (the field) while experimental studies often involve isolating consumers at some location in order to clearly administer some manipulation.

[8] R. L. Birdwhistell, *Kinetics and Contexts: Essays on Body Motion Communication* (Philadelphia: University of Pennsylvania Press, 1970).

[9] D. L. Phillips and K. J. Clancy, "Modeling Effects in Survey Research," *Public Opinion Quarterly*, Vol. 36 (Summer 1972), pp. 246–253, at p. 248.

TABLE 4.2   *Minimized Contact as a Control for Expectancy Effects*

A. *Automated Data Collection Systems*
1. Written instructions
2. Tape-recorded instructions
3. Filmed instructions
4. Televised instructions
5. Telephoned instructions

B. *Restricting Unintended Cues to Subjects and Experimenters*
1. Interposing screen between subject and experimenter
2. Contacting fewer subjects per experimenter
3. Having subjects or machines record responses

Source: Robert Rosenthal, *Experimenter Effects in Behavioral Research* (New York: Reprinted by permission of Naiburg Publishing Corp., 1966), p. 403.

TABLE 4.3   *Differential Reinforcers of Desired and Undesired Responses*

Reinforcers	
Positive	Negative
Smiling	Head shaking
Head nodding	Raising eyebrows
Looking happier	Looking surprised
Looking more interested	Looking disappointed
Recording response more vigorously	Repeating response
	Pencil tapping
	Holding photo up longer
	Tilting photo forward
	"Throwing" photo down

Source: Robert Rosenthal, *Experimenter Effects in Behavioral Research* (New York: Reprinted by permission of Naiburg Publishing Corp., 1966), p. 284.

In experiments where subjects were to rate photos held by an experimenter, the actions shown in Table 4.3 were found to "increase the likelihood of desired responses and decrease the likelihood of undesired responses.[10] In a study of telephone interviewers, it was found that nonvisual voice cues were sufficient to demonstrate bias.[11] The study concluded: "If, as has been found here, interviewers systematically bias respondents' reports on a variety of measures even when they are not in one another's presence, biasing effects may be much greater when interviewer and respondent actually confront one another."[12]

[10] Rosenthal, *op. cit.*, p. 284.
[11] Phillips and Clancy, *op. cit.*
[12] *Ibid.*, p. 253.

Evaluation Apprehension   The problem of expectancy focuses on the researcher. What about the respondent or subject, however? There seem to be indications that there are factors related to respondents which systematically operate to bias research. One of these is termed evaluation apprehension: a tendency of the respondent to "put his best foot forward."[13] A respondent looks at an interview or experiment as an evaluation, after which he desires to win a positive evaluation from the interviewer. It is a feeling all have experienced at one time or another. For example, there are probably few persons who can say, after completing a personality or intelligence test, that they have *not* wondered, or even asked aloud, "How did I do?" One of the authors, for example, had the following experience. After completing individual interviews with different managers and the president of a firm, he was sitting in his car making notes on some of the interviews when the plant manager literally came running around the corner of the building. When he reached the car, he asked, with a worried look on his face, how he had done—how his answers compared to those of the firm's president! After the plant manager left, the author wondered to what extent the plant manager's answers had been affected by his apprehension.

The most common form of evaluation apprehension is that known as social desirability.[14] This is the tendency to respond in the manner which is generally accepted by society. The effect of social desirability may be due to differences in status, for example. The distance between the social classes of interviewer and respondent strongly affect this tendency. A large distance, as when an upper middle-class white professional interviews a lower-class black, will tend to produce socially desirable responses. Too small a difference and the interviewer is seen as personally involved resulting in similar biases.[15]

Evaluation apprehension, like expectancy effect, is aroused by the researcher and the situation. General strategies for reducing evaluation apprehension are similar to those noted above. For one, any cues to the respondent as to the goodness or badness of particular responses should be suppressed. The interviewer or researcher should be as nearly neutral as possible in the sense that he or she may be able to reward or punish good responses. One would never expect, for example, to receive unbiased responses from a subject if it were his boss who was doing the interviewing.

The following example illustrates the extent to which evaluation appre-

---

[13] H. W. Riecken, "A Program for Research on Experiments in Social Psychology," in N. F. Washburne (ed.), *Decisions, Values, and Groups*, Vol. 2 (New York: Pergamon Press, 1962).

[14] D. P. Crowne and D. Marlowe, *The Approval Motive* (New York: Wiley, 1964). See also A. L. Edwards, *The Social Desirability Variable in Personality Assessment and Research* (New York: Dryden, 1957).

[15] B. S. Dohrenwend, J. Colombotos, and B. P. Dohrenwend, "Social Differences and Interviewer Effects," *Public Opinion Quarterly*, Vol. 32 (Fall 1968), pp. 410–422.

hension may bias research. Local police in Los Angeles conducted a study on pornography.[16] Their findings were that 98 percent of the public favored restrictions on nude night club acts and on films and publications depicting sex or nudity. Another study conducted by a local college found that only 36 percent wanted such legislation, and among a young age group the figure was as low as 12.9 percent. The difference was attributed to the use of police as interviewers. The director of the college survey noted that the reason he did his survey "is that when police do a survey they identify themselves as police officers."[17] He felt this to be a source of bias.

Demand Characteristics An interview or experiment is not a nonevent. It is a certain type of social situation. The respondent, therefore, assumes the role of one "taking part in an interview." The questions and his answers are not isolated events but part of the total situation.

One of the most well-known studies in which the results could be attributed to demand characteristic is the famous Hawthorne study.[18] No matter what changes the researchers made, work output increased. The workers had guessed the purpose of the study or were reacting to the attention they were receiving from the experimenters and hence reacted in a helpful manner. One of the first ideas that occurs to an interview respondent is "why is he asking me these questions? What is he getting at?" Depending on the answers the respondent formulates to those questions, his answers and responses are directed toward "helping" the researcher.[19]

One may consider the placebo effect a form of demand characteristic. Patients reporting improved health when taking chemically inert pills are responding to the situation and not to any real effect of a drug. Demand characteristics are particularly likely in studies of attitudes and attitude change.[20] Respondents easily guess the meaning and purposes of the investigation and behave accordingly. Volunteer respondents or subjects may also be

---

[16] "The Naked Truth," *Playboy*, Vol. 19 (June 1972), p. 66.

[17] *Ibid*.

[18] The "Hawthorne Study" is one of the first organization behavior studies reported. It occurred in the late 1930s when a group of behavioral scientists visited the Hawthorne works of Western Electric Corporation on the west side of Chicago. The major hypothesis of the study was that workers would perform better under improved lighting in certain sections of the plant. No matter whether lighting levels were increased or decreased, production levels improved.

[19] Not always, of course. One respondent in a study on family planning matters mentioned to a friend who, unknown to the respondent, was also a friend of the researcher that she was going to try to "screw up" the study by giving unusual answers. Obviously the problem may work both ways, although typically it is in the direction of helping the researcher once the respondent has guessed the correct direction.

[20] M. T. Orne, "Demand Characteristics and the Concept of Quasi-Controls," in Rosenthal and Rosnow, *op. cit.*, pp. 143–179, at p. 156.

particularly prone to demand characteristics. There is evidence which suggests that those who volunteer are more likely to exhibit helping behaviors.[21]

Sources of Internal Invalidity

Research results can be threatened (attacked as invalid) in two ways: (1) the logic of the research can be such that the results can be explained by some phenomenon other than the hypothesized model under test and (2) that the results of the test cannot be generalized to anything beyond the time, place, and persons who were studied. To solve these problems, the researcher must carefully understand the problems and then select designs and methods which minimize the probability of invalidity arising.

In designing research, there are several major sources of unintended hypotheses that can lead to invalidation of the research findings. It is essential that the research designer keep the sources of invalidity clearly in mind when designing and executing his research. Table 4.4 shows two major types of invalidity.[22] Internal invalidity refers to the errors existing within the research procedures which weakens the logic of the research conclusions. External invalidity is defined as those artifacts which prevent the research findings from being generalized beyond the immediate research circumstances. Sources of internal invalidity will be discussed below.

History as a Source of Error   Research projects take time. A large-scale survey may take several weeks or considerably more to complete. The field work for even small studies is seldom completed in less than a week. In the time it takes to complete the study many things may happen in the environment that could bias the results of the study. The world is not the same on the day the field work is completed as it was on the day the field work started.

Competitors may test market a new product in one or more of the study's sampling areas, or a strike or breakdown may have kept the product off the shelves. These are events outside the control of the researcher that can seriously bias results if not totally ruin the investment in the study. One research group, for example, found it necessary to purchase their product on the open market in a nearby city to maintain desired stock levels in a study city when a strike prevented normal deliveries.

Several strategies are available to minimize the potentially biasing effects of history. The first and most obvious strategy is to keep the field work portion of the study as short as possible. Two factors are generally in opposition to

---

[21] R. Rosenthal and R. Rosnow, "The Volunteer Subject," in Rosenthal and Rosnow, *op. cit.*, pp. 59–118.

[22] Drawn and extended from the original formulation of D. Campbell and J. Stanley, *Experimental and Quasi-Experimental Designs for Research* (New York: Rand McNally, 1963), p. 5, and Philip Emmert and William D. Brooks, *Methods of Research in Communication* (Boston: Houghton-Mifflin, 1970), p. 131.

TABLE 4.4 *Sources of Invalidity in Marketing Research*

Sources of Internal Invalidity	Sources of External Invalidity
History	Ecological relevance
Maturation	Problems in defining variables
Testing (sensitizing)	Inadequate statistics
Instrument decay	Poor theory
Selection	Misguided scientism
Mortality	Interaction effects
Nonstandard measures	
Interviewer cheating	

this, however. The first is that there is a very real tradeoff between costs and time. More interviewers mean a great increase in training costs and interviewer compensation. It may be necessary, for example, to pay better than the going rate in order to attract sufficient interviewers in a given period.

A second reason in opposition to shortening the study period has to do with the basic study design. Studies of product movement, attitude change, and the like are basically *longitudinal* in nature. Shortening the study period reduces the probability that the research will be able to observe changes in independent and dependent variables necessary to reach conclusions concerning the process being studied. That is, the differences in attitude in response to a new advertising campaign might be measurable over a two-week period, but four weeks may mean the difference between obtaining significant rather than nonsignificant differences.

The second strategy for minimizing the effects of history is one of planning and control. Thorough planning in advance of field work can assure that stocks are available and cannot be tied up by outside events. Prior planning can avoid scheduling studies into the final weeks of a political campaign when normal media schedules and advertising are preempted. Control means the complete monitoring of all potentially biasing events. The level of competitive advertising or trade dealing, stock levels, and unusual weather conditions are the kinds of indicators that must be watched for unusual variances. If such should occur, then it may be possible to adjust the data accordingly or even eliminate the affected area or region from the study. The whole thrust of this strategy is to identify potentially biasing external sources of bias and to prepare strategies to cope with or to allow for the partialling out of their effects.

Nonstandard Measures as a Source of Error   Much error in market research can be attributed to the use of nonstandard measures. Whether the problem is one of an interviewer rephrasing questions or the use of product from differing production batches in a taste test, the effect is the same. Both produce biased data.

As an example of the extent to which this is an important everyday problem, consider the following case. One major food products company regularly conducts taste comparisons between its products and those of competitors. In these tests, it uses its own product selected from brokers' open warehouse stocks, which, according to coding, has been in the distribution channel the average amount of time a regular case would be before reaching the store. It is also a requirement that all of the product be from the same production batch. By a careful analysis of competitive coding systems, the firm is able to select competitive product samples which meet the same requirements. Only then can they be assured that the stimulus pairs, theirs and their competitors' products, are standardized in the taste tests. It is not unusual for this firm to spend a thousand dollars locating several cases of their competitors' products which meet the requirements.

Physical requirements are relatively easy to standardize compared to data collection, however. A number of examples have already been presented which demonstrate the ability of interviewers to bias results. The use of nonstandard techniques is the most prevalent source of these problems. Interviewers may deviate from written instructions, rush through certain questions, or even restate them in different words. They may follow rules to the letter in the first three interviews of the day only to complete the last two in one-third of the normal time. Obviously each of these deviations from the standard methodology produce differing answers from respondents. This general problem is discussed in more detail in Chapter 8.

Interviewer Cheating   The data collector in primary research is generally the interviewer. It must be noted, however, that, while the interviewer is a critical element in the research program, he is also generally poorly paid and subject to the least control. Because of this, there is great opportunity and incentive for the interviewer to be less than honest. More details of this phenomenon can be found in Chapter 8.

Maturation Effects   Maturation is directly analogous to history except that maturation refers to changes in the experimental units themselves. Similarly, the greater the span of time between experimental events, the greater the opportunity for maturation to occur. Often, changes in the experimental units is related to the biological life processes of human test subjects. If a test takes place over a period of years, such as a manufacturer of birth control devices might conduct or the testing of a fluoride toothpaste additive might require, the individual test subjects themselves might change by growing old, improving their educational and socioeconomic status, getting sick, and so on. The real difficulty with history and maturation is not that they operate in some research designs, but with how to control them by selecting the most appropriate time interval between experimental events. At first glance, one might think that invalidity can be eliminated by merely shortening the time interval between experimental events. The shorter the time interval, the less possibility for history or maturation is true enough. But eliminating them entirely might create a problem of external invalidity.

For example, in the case of testing a television commercial, the external validity of a testing procedure is improved by allowing some time between exposure and response measurement. The marketing researcher must think in terms of optimum time intervals between events. And, he must think in terms of relative time intervals between events: what is a long span of time in one test is a short span of time in another test.

Testing Effects   Testing invalidity, which is sometimes referred to as sensitizing respondents, occurs when the testing procedure provides respondents with cues about what to pay attention to, encourages prestige biases, and otherwise provides an abnormal frame of reference for respondents. For example, a packaging test procedure might start out with a questionnaire on packaging materials, shapes and features, then expose respondents to a series of proposed new packages, followed by another questionnaire on the same materials, shapes, and features. The first questionnaire would sensitize the respondents to pay attention to certain details they might not ordinarily notice in the store. Thus, by providing the respondents with an unnatural (to them) frame of reference for perceiving the attributes of the test packages, selective attention and selective perception would not operate in a normal way and the testing procedure would introduce a source of invalidity.

Prestige biases operate in many different ways. People tend to overclaim their viewership of documentary television programs and their readership of "high class" magazines such as *Atlantic Monthly* and *Harpers*. They also tend to "underclaim" consumption of products for which they believe there are societal sanctions: liquor, beer, cigarettes, wine, and in some parts of the country, coffee. A researcher can get around these biases in many different ways. For example, in a study of the consumption of alcoholic beverages, the National Institute of Mental Health used exaggerated scales so that the heaviest drinkers would actually answer in the middle of the scale and thus, would not perceive their consumption as being abnormally high or socially unacceptable. The long scale reassured heavy drinkers that there were still other people who consumed more alcohol than they did.

Testing effects can also cause other types of biases such as development of expertise by the test subjects and artificial media exposure. For example, a panel of consumers might be organized as a professional testing panel for testing food products. As the panel operates over time, maturation might occur as the panel members change their body chemistry such as through menopause in the case of maturation and some members might stop smoking in the case of history. They may also learn to improve their discrimination between different batches of product or among different product formulations. This learning is often desirable because it can increase the sensitivity of the research procedure. However, all members of the panel may not learn equally well or at the same rate. In other situations, the researcher may not want test subjects to develop expertise since this might cause them to play the role of expert and respond as they think other people would respond rather than as they would normally act or answer on their own account.

The media exposure effect of a test procedure is less widely recognized as a problem in marketing research. This effect occurs in many panel studies where the same respondents are asked detailed questions about a product class at regular intervals over time. For example, in a study of birth control usage and the utilization of birth control devices, a researcher might ask respondents to fill out a questionnaire after each time they are involved in sexual activity. The reading and filling out of these questionnaires would generate more "media exposure" to birth control concepts than the respondents would be exposed to through the normal channels of communication such as magazines, word-of-mouth, and personal contacts with their doctors. The questionnaire is seen then as a form of "ad" or "media vehicle" which preempts the natural marketing communication process.

Instrumentation Decay   Instrumentation decay refers to the fact that the actual measurement instrument itself may change over time. In personal interviewing, *the interviewer together with the questionnaire* is the testing instrument. The interviewer may do a better job of accurately recording answers and probing for more information after doing the first 10 to 20 interviews. If a lot of interviewing is being done in a day, the interviewer may get fatigued as the day wears on or get bored after doing 80 or 90 interviews with the same questionnaire.

Instrumentation decay may also result from not selecting test subjects the same way each time the test is run. Similarly, the test variable or stimulus may not be universally applied to all test subjects or equally each time it is applied to the same subject. The intervals between experimental events may not be equal for all subjects or equal for the same subject each time the stimulus is applied. For example, in the case of testing trademarks using pupil dilation measures, it is essential that light intensity be held constant from trademark to trademark for the same subject and from subject to subject throughout the test. In a test of packaging also using pupil dilation response, the researcher may vary the light intensity for each package so that he may discover which package is most likely to be seen and recognized at low light levels such as might occur if the product were put on the bottom shelf in the supermarket aisle. However, he would attempt to vary the light intensity equally for all packages and for all subjects. The principal way to avoid the confounding effects of instrumentation problems is to standardize the research procedures. Interviewers must practice before beginning interviewing. The questionnaire must be pretested and retested.

Mortality as a Source of Bias Mortality refers to the fact that subjects may not complete the experiment. For example, mortality is especially likely to occur in time series using panels of households. Some of the households may grow tired of repeated questioning or filling out diaries or may move and drop out of the panel. If the experiment extends over an extensive period of time, subjects may literally die. If an experiment is unpleasant, such as testing the product quality of sunburn lotions, subjects will be especially motivated not to go through with the complete testing procedure. Mortality is often measured in its own right and used as an experimental variable. The researcher may want to know when a person will drop out of an experiment or how much stimulation of the experimental variables can be withstood by the test subjects. Large marketing research companies which operate panels of households are particularly interested in minimizing and controlling mortality. For example, since certain demographic classes have different mortality rates in large panel operations, the marketing research firm may overrecruit households in those high mortality classes. This insures that at the end of the study, there will be enough households included in the sample to make it representative.

External Invalidity

External invalidity is defined as the lack of ability to generalize the results of an experiment to the larger world. In particular, if a researcher performs a laboratory experiment which has many artificial assumptions about consumer behavior, the experiment can be said to be externally invalid. Typically, laboratory experiments have most difficulty with external invalidity while field experiments which have no controls have trouble with internal invalidity. However, field studies can also suffer from external invalidity if certain things happen.

An example of external invalidity occurs occasionally in test marketing. One large soap company is reputed to have become aware of a competitor's test market in a medium size U.S. city. The marketing group of the nontest company purposefully bought extra advertising and undertook a coupon campaign for an existing brand of soap in order to make the test market invalid. Such practices, while not widespread, are cause for serious ethical concern (see Chapter 16). The phenomenon involved by such practice is called *ecological relevance*.

Another problem that can affect external validity is the *definition of variables.* A given attitude, for example, may have a different meaning and importance from one group in a population to another. A detailed description of measurement problems concerned with attitudes is found in Chapter 8.

Inadequate *statistical procedures* may lead the researcher to reach conclusions that are not generalizable. The researcher may have uncovered statistical anomalies of a specific data set. His conclusions, then, cannot truly be generalized to any sample outside his own. This problem is extremely common in social research. Chapters 11 through 13 discuss the common statistical models. The reader should carefully assess the fit of the statistical models to real world behavior.

Poor theory can be a major problem related to external invalidity. If a researcher's theory is "bad," he will not have a model that is rich enough in detail to encompass the range of marketing behaviors which exist. Hence, if the researcher replicated a study with the same theory but a different sample setting, he would get different answers. Chapter 5 stresses the key models and variables used in developing "good" models.

The researcher may ruin his generalizability because of *misguided scientism.* If the social scientist takes a stance that requires that he divorce himself from his experiment to the point of not being aware of the dynamics truly occurring in the behavioral process, he will miss key details that help him to solve the four previous problems mentioned. Thus, the researcher should be vigilant and observant.

Interaction effects can also threaten external validity. When the testing method influences the system being tested, generalizability is brought into question. In consumer panels, for example, the mere fact that a family is brought into the panel may cause the family to change buying behavior and explore the marketplace more than might otherwise be done. Similarly, the fact that a respondent elects to participate in a given research project causes interaction between the experiment and the sample.

In sum, internal validity must be achieved in a marketing research effort to ensure that the hypotheses under study are tested properly. After solving questions of internal validity, the researcher must then ask himself if his results are specific to his sample only or can be generalized to other times, places, and persons.

Sampling Errors

Although not in the purview of this chapter (see Chapter 10), the manner in which respondents are chosen can introduce serious errors into a research effort. These errors include (1) nonrepresentativeness, (2) random sampling errors, (3) sampling process errors, and (4) self-selection errors. Each of these errors must be eliminated if at all possible.

Nonrepresentativeness is defined as creating a sample of respondents for a research project who do not adequately represent the total population under study. *Random sampling error* refers to error created by drawing a random sample where the rules of chance are somehow violated. *Sampling process errors* occur when data are lost due to improper interviewing, coding, or editing of research forms. *Self-selection* occurs when respondents are allowed to "get out" of an interview. This means that the sample may be biased toward "cooperator subjects" and thus have invalid results.

Designing Marketing Research Experiments

When a marketing researcher designs an experiment, he usually writes out the experimental design using a shorthand researchers have developed for this purpose. The letter X is used to represent the independent variable that is under the control of the researcher and manipulated during the experiment. Where there is more than one independent variable, X implies X_1, X_2, X_3, ... , X_n which is the set of independent variables. $-X$ is used to represent an independent variable which has one constant value or state determined by the researcher. This value or state does not vary during the experiment; it is said to be controlled. (X) is used to represent an independent variable which is neither controlled by the researcher nor manipulated. However, it is allowed to vary "naturally" and then measured by the researcher.

The letter Y is used to represent the dependent variable that is measured. Where there is more than one dependent variable, Y implies Y_1, Y_2, Y_3, ... , Y_n which is the set of dependent variables. In addition, Ya is used to represent the dependent variable measured *after* the independent variable has been manipulated, applied, or measured. Yb is used to represent the dependent variable measured *before* the independent variable has been manipulated, applied, or measured. The letter R is used to represent a random sample. Rs is a *s*tratified random sample. (See Chapter 10 for more detail.) The most common market research designs are shown in Table 4.5.

The Concept of Control

The purpose of carefully designed experiments which maximize internal and external validity is to allow the researcher to perform manipulations on some independent (causal) variable and describe or prove the effect of the independent variable on some dependent variable minimizing the validity of alternative explanations. The purpose of control groups is to minimize the alternative explanations. In other words, the researcher should design an experiment in which he can make the statement "If X, then Y will result" with a minimum possible chance that alternative explanations could account for Y. Control groups are used to rule out alternative explanations.

A classic case of experimentation is the famous Pascal experiment in 1648.[23] Pascal hypothesized that atmospheric pressure declined with increasing

[23] Excerpted from an article by E. G. Boring, in R. Rosenthal and R. L. Rosnow, *Artifacts in Behavioral Research* (New York: Academic Press, 1969), p. 1.

TABLE 4.5 *Common Market Research Designs*

Name of Design	Sample Group	Experimental Research Design	Marketing Application
1. One-shot case study		$\widehat{X}$ Ya	Preliminary research
2. One-shot case study with sample		Rs $\widehat{X}$ Ya	Descriptive studies
3. Simple before/after		Rs Yb X Ya	Pretesting ads, packaging, products
4. Static group comparison	Experimental control	R X Ya R $\widehat{X}$ Ya	Pretesting ads, packaging, products
5. Before/after control	Experimental control	Yb X Ya Yb $-X$ Ya	Laboratory behavioral experiments
6. Simulated before/after	Experimental control	R X Ya R Yb	Pretesting ads, packaging, concepts
7. Solomon four group	Experimental control 1 control 2 control 3	R Yb X Ya R Yb $-X$ Ya R X Ya R $-X$ Ya	Product concept testing, trademark pretesting, pricing tests, product change pretesting
8. Simple time series		Rs Yb Yb $\widehat{X}$ Ya Ya	Brand switching, ad wear-out studies
9. Times series with control	Experimental control	R Yb Yb X Ya Ya R Yb Yb $-X$ Ya Ya	Brand switching, ad wear-out studies
10. Multiple exposure time series	Experimental control	R Yb X_1 Ya_1 X_2 Ya_2 R Yb $-X_1$ Ya_1 $-X_2$ Ya_2	Brand switching, ad exposure, salesman call scheduling
11. Latin squares	Experimental 1 Experimental 2 Experimental 3	R X_1 Ya_1 X_3 Ya_2 X_2 Ya_3 R X_3 Ya_1 X_2 Ya_2 X_1 Ya_3 R X_2 Ya_1 X_1 Ya_2 X_3 Ya_3	Advertising effectiveness studies

Key: R: Random Sample (s: stratified); X: Independent variable—manipulated; $-X$: Controlled (measured) but not manipulated independent variable; $\widehat{X}$: Independent—natural (unmanipulated); Y: Dependent variable (b: before manipulation, a: after) altitude. His basic experiment was to take a barometric measurement in his village. He then carried the barometer up a 3000-foot mountain and took another measurement which showed substantially less atmospheric pressure. Was his hypothesis confirmed? Not necessarily, because a critic could argue that in the time it took to climb the mountain, the atmospheric pressure had changed at both the top and the bottom of the mountain. Thus, Pascal had to add something to the design to rule out the unintended hypothesis. He decided to place a second barometer at the bottom of the mountain and matched the first and second barometer readings at the beginning of the experiment. He then took one barometer up the mountain. When the mountain barometer was read, the village barometer was also read at precisely the same time. Thus, his readings might have appeared:

	Place	Time	Reading
Barometer 1	Village	Noon	30 inches of mercury
	Village	1 p.m.	29 inches of mercury
Barometer 2	Village	Noon	30 inches of mercury
	Mountain	1 p.m.	27 inches of mercury

While the barometric pressure in general changed in the one hour it took to climb the mountain, the mountain barometer reading is still much less than the control barometer. His hypothesis appears supported although there may still always be some possible other explanation.

The One-Shot Case Study: A Pre-experiment

Table 4.5 shows a variety of designs ranging from very simple to very complex. The first of these is the one-shot case study. This design is used for the development of questionnaires and experiments where hypothesis testing consists merely of ruling out bad wording and ineffective experimental manipulations. Typically, convenience samples of people are recruited with the only requirement being that the persons in the sample are not related or do not know the persons conducting the study. With such a design, the only logical requirement is that the sample persons act somewhat representatively of the larger population of which they are a part.

The One-Shot Case Study with Sample

$$Rs \; \textcircled{X} \; Yb$$

This second case is the common marketing research survey using a questionnaire. This is, perhaps, the most common design in marketing research because of its simplicity and low cost. A careful, stratified random sample is drawn accurately reflecting the population under study, and a carefully designed questionnaire is administered. The experimental independent variable is uncontrolled except by nature. Natural variation accounts for the manipulation. This type of study is used to measure product acceptance, forecast elections, assess attitudes, to name but a few uses. The results are projectable to the entire population under study. The major drawback of the design is that the simplicity often creates many significant competing hypotheses and thereby diminishes the value of the study done using this design. An example of the competing hypothesis problem occurs in the case where management hypothesizes that awareness (advertising) positively influences sales for one of several competing brands. A survey is undertaken to test the hypothesis which shows that people who are more aware of a brand name tend to buy the brand more. However, the critic of the study could argue that the questionnaire itself created awareness and thereby guaranteed that the finding would result (test effect) and that the independent variable was not really meaningful.

An example of the one-shot case study with sample concerns the "market audit" type of research. Recently, a large tire manufacturer wished to assess the state of the replacement tire market. Specifically, the management was concerned with which segments of the car owning public were buying the brand in question and which were not. The specific management goal was to increase the total market for replacement tires by inducing consumers to buy sooner than they otherwise might as well as increasing market share. Therefore, the management authorized the expenditure of several tens of thousands of dollars for a market study. Specifications for the study included doing a one-shot design, interviewing a large number of randomly sampled car owners of each of the major brands of cars (a sample of several thousand), analysis of preferences for tire brands, analysis of attitudes toward tires and their replacement, media reading and watching habits of the sample, analysis of who made the purchase decision for tires, tabulation of the number of miles driven, and tabulation of demographic variables such as age, income, occupation, sex, and number of children. Bids were sought for the research contract, and one large market research agency received the contract.

A questionnaire of 10 pages was constructed, approved by management, and the data were collected by female interviewers. Management was hoping (had hypothesized) that potential tire buyers could be classified into meaningful segments who watched and read specific mass media including particular TV programs and special magazines. If this hypothesis was supported, more efficient media plans could be formulated. In addition, attitudes which were unfavorable to buying replacement tires were hypothesized. It was hoped that advertising could be used to counter such attitudes. Similarly, unfavorable attitudes toward the company were also hypothesized.

The results of the study showed that several market segments existed which could be classified on the basis of brand oriented behavior. These segments could be described as the "name" brand segment, the "mass merchandiser" segment including Sears and Montgomery Ward, and the "off-brand-price oriented" segment in which brands competed according to price. The "name" brand competed through advertising and "tie in" deals (two tires for one), and the "merchandiser" brands competed through ease of purchase and low cost installation. However, all of the other major management desires (hypotheses) did not materialize, that is, advertising segments were not found, interpretable attitude patterns among consumers concerning tires in general and the company in particular were not found. No significant differences in attitudes were found among buyers and nonbuyers of replacement tires. In addition, no significant differences were found between people who bought the particular brand in question and those who did not. In addition, car ownership was not related to replacement tire brand bought.

Simple before/after

$$\boxed{Rs\ Yb\ X\ Ya}$$

The standard before/after design has been used widely in all kinds of research. Simply put, the logic is that one performs a measurement, performs an experimental manipulation, and then measures again. An example of this technique in marketing research is a special method developed by a leading research agency for evaluating the effectiveness of specific advertisements. The technique consists of recruiting a sample of persons who are told that they are to preview some new TV shows. The solicitation is done by mail to randomly selected names from a telephone directory. The subjects must travel to a centrally located theatre where the messages are projected. Upon entering the auditorium, each subject fills out a questionnaire requesting information about his likelihood of buying certain brands in several product categories, among other information. An old television serial is shown with several advertisements included, and the brand purchase intention information is collected again. The results of the before and after measurements are compared. The underlying hypothesis is that successful advertisements will change the intention of many of the subjects to purchase.

The Static Group Comparison

Experimental group	$R\ X\ Ya$
Control group	$R\ \widehat{X}\ Ya$

The static group comparison is used often in the world of medicine to test the effects of certain health programs. Currently, a large east coast medical center is studying the long-term effects of cholesterol on heart disease. Two groups of men were recruited and randomly assigned into two groups. One group was administered a low cholesterol diet while the other group maintained a normal diet. After several years, the heart disease histories of the groups will be compared. The doctors expect that the low cholesterol group will have fewer heart problems.

Before and after with Control

Experimental group	$Yb \ X \ Ya$
Control group	$Yb \ -X \ Ya$

In much behavioral research aimed at studying the fundamentals of human behavior, before and after experiments with control groups are often used. In addition, random selection of respondents is not necessary since only very general conclusions are to be reached from the research, that is, the results are not to be specifically projected to larger populations. In these research situations, convenience samples, often consisting of college students, are used.

The general methodology involves recruiting a convenience sample. Subjects are then assigned into two groups randomly: the experimental and the control groups. An initial questionnaire is given to each group. The experimental manipulation is executed and a second questionnaire is given. One artifact that is common to this method is that of subject information gathering from the first questionnaire; that is, the subject might be influenced by the questions on the first questionnaire. This can be partially controlled by the simulated before and after experiment to be mentioned shortly.

An example of the before and after with control design is the case where the marketing researcher wishes to study how people process information concerning brands, say ball-point pens, and then decide to switch brands. A researcher wishing to perform such an experiment would recruit a sample of 200 subjects. This number is enough to create two groups of 100 which will generally yield significant results at the 95 percent confidence level (a level commonly accepted in behavioral research). The researcher randomly assigns the subjects in the two groups, experimental and control. He then gives a questionnaire to each subject about past brands purchased of the product(s) in question. A small amount of money is given to each subject who can then purchase one of the brands of ball-point pens. In addition to purchase histories, likelihood of purchasing specified brands is also asked. After the initial questionnaire is completed, the control group is presented with information promoting ball-point pens but neutral with regard to any one brand. The experimental group, on the other hand, is exposed to the same promotional information with the addition of information favorable to certain brands of ball-point pens and derogatory to other brands. The key hypothesis is that information about particular brands can influence attitudes and behavior toward those brands. The alternative argument is that selective advertising does not have any effect and that only primary advertising is influential for this product. A second questionnaire is administered to see if there are changes in attitudes and purchase intentions for both groups. Another purchase is allowed. If a person already has purchased, he may trade the pen he chose for another brand. The researcher expects that the control group will show only small changes, while the experimental group will change in the desired direction. The subjects are allowed to keep the brand of pens they have chosen.

The Simulated before and after

Experimental group	R X Ya
Control group	R Yb

This case is a cross between the before and after, and the before and after with control. Two groups are recruited randomly then matched on relevant characteristics. Then, one group receives the before questionnaire. The other group receives the experimental manipulation and the final questionnaire only. Thus, the initial questionnaire cannot give the experimental subjects any information. This design assumes that the two groups are comparable because the "after" readings of the control group can be used as the "before" readings of the experimental group. In addition, no real control in the standard sense exists.

Solomon Four Group Test

Experimental	R Yb X Ya
Control 1	R Yb $-X$ Ya
Control 2	R X Ya
Control 3	R $-X$ Ya

There are cases where the researcher believes that there is a significant question as to the degree to which prior measurement Yb affects the degree to which the manipulation, X, changes Ya and is also worried about the degree of effect of the manipulation X. In this instance the researcher would choose the Solomon four group design. All groups are created by random assignment or are matched in the sampling procedure. The Solomon design can rule out the following unintended hypotheses: the groups are not comparable, the test instrument has effects on Ya, the sample has matured, and the manipulation has worked.

An example of this occurs in the world of education where students are given special reading programs. First, control group 1 and the experimental group are pretested. Then the experimental group and control group 2 go through a reading program while control groups 1 and 3 do not. Ideally, if the reading program is really effective, the following results should occur:

Test A: *Ya* (experimental reading scores) are greater than
              Ya (control 1 reading scores) and

Test B: *Ya* (experimental) are greater than *Yb* (experimental) and

Test C: *Ya* (control 1) are the same as *Ya* (control 3) and

Test D: *Ya* (experimental) are the same as *Ya* (control 2) and

Test E: *Ya* (control 1) is the same as *Yb* (control 1).

The tests performed in the reading example have the following conclusion and rule out the following hypotheses:

Test A shows that the test for reading speed was sensitive to the manipulation.

Test B shows that the students did improve as they should have.

Test C shows that the pretest did not bias the results.

Test D proves that the pretest did not bias or cause the experimental students to improve their scores unnecessarily.

Test E shows that no learning by the sample occurred between the first and last test (that is, no natural improvement occurred due to maturation of the sample).

Simple Time Series

$$\boxed{Rs \;\; Yb \;\; Yb \;\; \textcircled{X} \;\; Ya \;\; Ya}$$

In some situations, time can be a major factor in a design. Where there are "wear-out" effects such as the forgetting of advertising messages over time, special time series designs can be constructed. In the case of the simple time series, several prior measures *Yb* are taken to establish that the subjects are in a stable (unchanging) condition. Then an advertisement or some other stimulus is given to the subjects. The recall of the ad is measured (*Ya*) several times afterward. The experimenter expects that the *Ya*'s should decline the farther away they are from the exposure *X*.

An example of the simple time series method is the standard consumer panel[24] where households are recruited for a period of several years. Purchase diaries and questionnaires are administered periodically to each household. Attitude and purchase behavior are measured over time, perhaps once per month. Natural changes in *X* are noted by changes in promotion levels reported by the sample or known to exist in the communities in which the panel members live. Changes in buying behavior and attitude are noted over time. Results tend to show the following types of results as shown in Figure 4.1. A promotion occurs for brand 1 (*X* manipulation). In the case of *no change*, the experimental manipulation has no effect. The *permanent change* case shows

[24] See Chapter 8 for details on panels. A panel is defined as a series of time series measurements of the same sample of people.

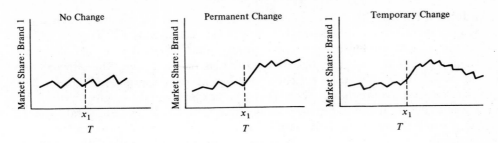

FIGURE 4.1 *Possible Time Series Outcomes*

that the manipulation causes permanent alteration in some sample attitudes and behaviors. The *temporary change* case illustrates that some change in some measured attitude and behavior eventually decays or returns back to the original level.

Time Series with Control

Experimental group	R Yb Yb X Ya Ya
Control group	R Yb Yb —X Ya Ya

Where a time series is required and the experimenter wishes to establish the validity of his manipulation X, he would then choose to add a control group.

Where there is substantial doubt about the real effect of the manipulation X, a control group is necessary. An example of this type of design is a moderate size North Carolina community which has a cable TV system. Actually, two sets of TV cables feed the TV programs to the community. These two sets of cables totally overlap so that two neighbors may be fed from two separate cables. The cable TV network plays different commercials over the cables holding the programming constant (the same programs are available on each cable). The community cable users are then surveyed several times before and after test commercials and control commercials are broadcast to test the effect of the commercials.

Multiple Exposure Time Series

Experimental group	$R \; Yb \; X_1 \; Ya_1 \; X_2 \; Ya_2$
Control group	$R \; Yb \; —X_1 \; Ya_1 \; —X_2 \; Ya_2$

It is conceivable that there is a synergism between several manipulations in that the effects of a manipulation are not merely additive but have effects that are greater than merely additive. This is often the case where two different kinds of promotion are used such as an advertisement appearing in a trade journal and the subsequent call by a salesman. The ad will help the salesman perform his function and thus make him more effective. Such a test would include recruiting a matched sample of respondents. Then a before measure Yb is administered to each group. Then an ad is sent to the experimental group and another measurement Ya_1 is taken to show the effect of the ad. A salesman then calls on each member of the experimental group. The experimental group should show that Ya_1 (experimental) is greater than Yb (experimental) if the initial ad was effective. Then Ya_2 (experimental) should be greater than Ya_1 (experimental) and Yb, Ya_1, and Ya_2 (control) should all be the same and Yb (experimental) should be the same as Yb (control). Additional controls can be added to isolate the effects of X_1 and X_2 individually.

Latin Squares, Factorial, and Randomized Block Designs

There are a series of designs called factorial designs which allow the researcher to explore several manipulations at once by using several samples and several manipulations. A variation called Latin square designs allows the researcher to test several different variables at three different levels each. As shown in the following design box, each manipulation X_1, X_2, and X_3 is administered in different order to three samples. If the results of the manipulation have no interaction, the effect of the manipulation is merely the sum $Ya_1 + Ya_2$, and so on. However, in most cases in behavioral research, interactions do exist among variables such that Latin square designs are not feasible.

Similarly, randomized block designs require that the experimental manipulations X are administered randomly to each group in time. This type of design controls the effect of sequence and sample composition on the measurement of experimental manipulation.

Experimental group 1	R Yb X_1 Ya_1 X_3 Ya_2 X_2 Ya_3
Experimental group 2	R Yb X_3 Ya_1 X_2 Ya_2 X_1 Ya_3
Experimental group 3	R Yb X_2 Ya_1 X_1 Ya_2 X_3 Ya_3

Where there are interaction effects among various manipulations, X, such as various forms of advertising that have carryover effects and differential initial impacts, a variation of factorial design is useful. For example, in testing the effects situation of three levels of advertising expenditure X_1 (high), X_2 (medium), and X_3 (low), there are three possible experiments.[25] Each possible sequence of ad spending is explored, that is, each manipulation (advertisement expenditure level) appears only once in each row and column of the square. Each row of the square represents an experimental group. Group 1 experiences a high level of ad spending (X_1) and measurement Ya_1

[25] R. J. Jessen, "A Switch-Over Experimental Design to Measure Advertising Effect," in R. Frank, A. Kuehn, and W. Massy, *Quantitative Techniques in Marketing* (Homewood, Ill.: Irwin, 1962), p. 190.

followed by a low level of expenditure (X_3) followed by Ya_2 and then the medium level (X_2) followed by Ya_3. Similarly, experimental groups 2 and 3 experience the manipulations X in different orders. One can analyze the initial readings (Ya_1) for each of the three groups to assess the initial effects of each of the three advertisements. The results showed a high Ya_1 for X_1 and a relatively lower Ya_1 for X_3.

Assuming that the groups are randomly assigned or matched on relevant characteristics, one would expect that if the same treatment were given to each group (X_1, X_2, X_3), the final measurement (Ya_3) would be the same for all of the groups. With this assumption, the carryover effects of the manipulations X can be studied. One can test the hypothesis that a carryover exists by examining group 1 and group 2. Group 1 experiences a high level of expenditure (X_1) followed by a low level (X_3). Group 2 experiences a low level of ad expenditure. If there is no carryover, the measurement Ya_2 for group 1 will not be significantly different from Ya_1 from group 2. If there is carryover from the high level of spending in group 1, the measurement Ya_2 should reflect this by being higher than the noncarryover case experienced by group 2. In addition to testing the carryover hypothesis, the degree to which carryover exists can be deduced by computing the magnitudes of the differences between the carryover conditions and the noncarryover conditions.

This design is also useful in determining optimal sequencing of the manipulations X. This means that if the experiment examined the last reading (Ya_3) of group 1 versus the last measurement (Ya_3) of group 2, he would find that the group 2 reading would be larger. This would occur because a larger dose of ad spending occurred closer in time to the last reading for group 2 than occurred for group 1. Figure 4.2 illustrates this condition. The histogram in Figure 4.2 represents the reading that would occur if no carryover existed while the circle and line show the actual readings. For group 1, the initial high spending level improves the second time period reading by quite a bit (around 50 percent). In addition, the second time period reading improves the third reading but only by a small amount (about 16 percent). However,

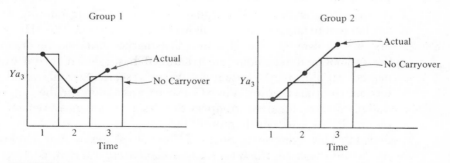

FIGURE 4.2 *Latin Square Results Showing Carryover*

in the case of group 2, the low first reading improves the second reading by 20 percent or so which in turn improves the third reading by 30 percent. Thus, in terms of improvement due to carryover, the sequence of manipulations X_3, X_2, X_1 yields a better final result than X_3, X_1, X_2. These results are hypothetical but illustrate the nature of the analysis needed to isolate the effects uncovered by the Latin square design.

Summary

This chapter has explored three different problems of marketing research and laid the groundwork for the following chapters which explain marketing research methodology. Specifically, this chapter explored recognition of marketing problems as they affect the marketing research process. Major problems of research validity were examined and then research designs which are designed to counter or solve validity questions were shown. Although many designs are possible, only those designs which are commonly used in marketing research were shown.

Questions and Exercises

1. Develop a list of criteria to use in evaluating a definition of a marketing problem.
2. How might a sales promotion manager determine that the basic problem involving a decline in sales is more related to inadequate sales force management as opposed to inadequate advertising management? Design an experiment which could help determine whether the problem is rooted more in the sales force area or in the advertising area. What sources of bias or error might be present in your research design?
3. What types and sources of error in marketing research are especially likely to be present with the individual research design discussed in this chapter?
4. A manufacturer of power lawnmowers is considering offering a free garden tool to anyone buying a mower in the month of May. He would first like to evaluate the idea in a test market situation before using the promotional technique on a national basis. What is the experimental variable in this situation? What research design would you recommend that he use? Why? Construct a diagram for the suggested design to show for each group in the design what measurements are required and into which groups the experimental variable is introduced. (This exercise is adapted from Venkatesan and Holloway, *An Introduction to Marketing Experimentation*, 1971, p. 64.)

5. As the head of a large marketing research firm, you are in charge of designing a large advertising campaign to be launched by a federal government agency to reduce gasoline consumption.

   Before working on any specific recommendation, you have decided to create two research teams, respectively, in charge of problem definition and research design.

   You are now in the process of providing the general guidelines under which the two teams will work.

   (a) Provide a check list of questions to be investigated by the problem definition team. [*Hint*: Construct the list which, in your judgment, minimizes the risk of problem misidentification. Be specific.]

   (b) Provide a check list of questions to be investigated by the research design team. [*Hint*: Be sure that upon answering these questions the research design team will have on hand all the information necessary to choose the right experimental design.]

   (c) As the head of the problem definition team, you are in charge of uniting a report summarizing the team position for each question in the check list submitted to your team by the research director. [*Hint*: Answer each question separately. Describe supplementary areas of the problems that have been investigated by the team outside of the general guideline questions. Define what the problem is not. Come out with a clear, concise definition of what the problem is.]

   (d) As the head of the research design team, you are in charge of reporting the kind of experimental design that, in the team's judgment, will produce the information necessary to choose the most efficient advertising theme for the campaign. [*Hint*: List the explanatory variables that are regarded by the team as the most plausible in explaining individual gasoline consumption. Graph the structure of the relationships that link explanatory variables and gasoline consumption. Determine which variables are controllable and which are not. Distinguish between short and long term. Determine which research design is best given the various sources of error likely to affect the measurement of the explanatory variables as well as the measurement of gasoline consumption. Discuss the inclusion or exclusion of interaction effects that are reflected by the proposed research design. Discuss the internal and external validity of the proposed design. Explain the reasons that motivate the particular tradeoff between internal and external validity that is reflected by your experimental design.]

Project Related Questions

1. Have you developed a step-by-step procedure similar to that discussed on pages 86 to 88 for defining your research problem? Be particularly careful about steps 4 to 7.
2. What is the general source of the marketing problem?
3. What general category of problem is being addressed by your project?
4. Consult Table 4.1. Which types and sources of error are you most likely to encounter?
5. Have you adequately considered ways of minimizing the errors you could encounter?
6. Ideally, which research design should you use for your project? Being realistic, how readily can you implement this design? What compromises are necessary? What effect does this have on the validity of your study?
7. Have you considered the dollar costs of your research design if you were to pursue it on a large scale? Is this cost justified in terms of the value of the information obtained?
8. What special skills or expertise are required for the successful implementation of the most preferred research design?

Lawson & Worthingham, Inc.

Lawson & Worthingham, Inc., was an old and well-known producer of sauces used in flavoring meats and in other household cooking. The company's products were of high quality and were widely imitated by other firms, many of whom sold their brands at substantially lower prices than those charged by Lawson & Worthingham. To offset this competition, the company supported its excellent reputation by a modest expenditure for advertising in national magazines, and by a series of cooking school promotions. These demonstrations were held in a leading department store in each of several cities.

It was the impression of executives that this type of promotion was successful in increasing sales, but they believed that more objective evidence should be gathered regarding the plan's effectiveness before funds were appropriated for the expansion of the program. The problem was presented to A. J. Nichols, a sales consultant with whom one of the executives was acquainted. He agreed to conduct a sales test of the demonstration plan. The sales test he planned was to be a store audit procedure in which sales information on meat sauces would be obtained by checking the inventories and purchases of a sample of food stores.

The city of Fort Worth, Texas was selected as the locale for the experiment, principally because the company's demonstration school "team" was next scheduled to appear there, but also because this city was sufficiently large to be fairly representative of most cities.

Mr. Nichols went to Fort Worth and obtained the cooperation of the national advertising manager of the *Star-Telegram,* who introduced him to division managers of chain stores represented in the city and to many of the larger independent grocers. A sample of 37 stores was selected as an adequate cross section of the grocery retailers serving middle- and upper-class consumers. The cooperation of these store owners was obtained and a practice inventory count was taken in each store by an experienced investigator. Care was taken to make certain that the investigator knew the location of reserve stocks as well as those on the shelf, and that she was acquainted with the invoice records of each store so that she could compute receipts of merchandise.

The test began officially on February 10, the week before the opening

SOURCE: Reprinted with permission from H. Boyd and R. Westfall, *Marketing Research: Text and Cases,* 3rd ed. (Homewood, Ill.: Richard D. Irwin, Inc., 1972), pp. 123–125.

of the cooking school promotion in a Fort Worth department store. Inventories of the test stores were taken on that day and at the end of each of the four succeeding weeks. From these data and information on purchases each week, Mr. Nichols computed weekly sales of Lawson & Worthingham sauces (see Exhibit 1) and prepared the following summary:

Sales of Lawson & Worthingham Sauces before, during, and after the Cooking School Promotion

Test week	Bottles sold in 35 stores*	Index of sales relative to base week
Feb. 10–Feb. 17 before school	240	100.0 (base)
Feb. 17–Feb. 24 week of school	275	114.7
Feb. 24–Mar. 3 week after school	292	121.7
Mar. 3–Mar. 10 2nd week after school	301	125.4

* Questions about the accuracy of the invoice and purchase records of two stores caused Mr. Nichols to omit them from the test.

On March 24, Mr. Nichols submitted a report to the executives of Lawson & Worthingham in which he presented the above table along with certain comments and conclusions, among them the following:

"The evidence indicates clearly that the cooking school promotion stimulated a sales increase of approximately 25 percent for each of the two weeks following the promotion.

"It seems likely that this increase in sales can be attributed almost entirely to the stimulation from the cooking school. This conclusion is based on the fact that improvement in display, as observed in the stores checked, would appear to be of little influence.

"Some idea of the competitive situation in Fort Worth . . . can be gained from the following description of the stock and display of sauce in . . . store during the test. . . . On a large six-shelf self-help display case,

only seven bottles of Lawson & Worthingham sauces were displayed. These bottles, marked 25¢, were placed so that the customer saw only two of them. . . . Other sauces, three of which were displayed in two-dozen lots, included:

Brand A at 14¢
Brand B at 10¢
Brand C at 22¢
Brand D at 10¢
Brand E in two sizes at 10¢ and 19¢

The obvious conclusion is that less expensive sauces were being given dominant display in this store. In other stores checked, Lawson & Worthingham was given a better break on display, but in few stores was it given dominant display."

1. Were Mr. Nichols conclusions justified?
2. Could the test be designed more effectively?

EXHIBIT 1 *Complete Tabulation of Sales of Lawson & Worthingham Sauces in 35 Fort Worth Stores—February 10 to March 10**

Store no.	Week Ending February 17	Week Ending February 24	Week Ending March 3	Week Ending March 10
1	5	0	9	0
2	3	15	3	13
3	4	12	6	4
4	44	42	18	20
5	55	28	48	77
6	1	0	2	2
7	6	8	14	7
8	5	16	8	13
9	5	5	8	6
10	4	3	3	1
11	3	18	4	12
12	20	21	5	8
13	4	1	3	3
14	1	3	1	2
15	7	7	22	18
16	1	1	13	1
17	2	5	4	2
18	2	4	2	2
19	1	1	3	1
20	2	1	2	1
21	2	16	16	10
22	1	3	3	3
23	3	10	6	6
24	3	2	4	2
25	3	2	9	9
26	12	14	27	27
27	0	2	1	1
28	6	6	12	4
29	2	4	5	9
30	5	5	9	7
31	8	6	8	6
32	1	0	1	2
33	5	4	5	9
34	4	2	3	3
35	10	8	5	10
Total	240	275	292	301

* Two stores were eliminated from the total because of doubtful accuracy of the data.

Falstaff Brewing Corporation
Taste and Image Research

Falstaff Brewing Corporation, a large St. Louis, Missouri brewer with one of its eight plants located in San Jose, California, had been unable to improve its sales performance in California despite strong retail distribution and heavy promotional efforts there. Falstaff sales were roughly 5 percent of total beer sales in Southern California and 10 percent in Northern California, but both figures were well below Falstaff's average share of 16 percent for all of its sales districts, which covered half the United States.

Mr. Alvin Griesedieck, Jr., vice president and director of marketing turned to Mr. Willard Evans, the director of market research, for help in determining why Falstaff's California performance was not better. Mr. Evans reasoned that consumer awareness of the Falstaff brand was not a factor. Previous studies showed that many Californians had recently moved from the East and Midwest, often from areas where Falstaff was well established.

While Mr. Evans was considering the California problem, Mr. Hugh Schwartz, executive director of the Institute for Design Analysis in San Francisco, paid him a visit. Mr. Schwartz brought with him a copy of a report on an experimental taste test of eight brands of beer he recently had conducted in the San Francisco Bay Area. The test had been designed to determine the influence of label design on the perceived flavor and difference for certain brands of beer. Mr. Schwartz could not divulge the data in a form which would relate them to specific brands.

Mr. Schwartz proposed that a consumer taste test between the Falstaff brand and two or three of its leading competing brands be conducted in California. His proposal was accepted and the test was conducted during the spring of 1962.

PLANNING THE TEST

In talking about the test, Mr. Evans commented: "We want to know first whether California beer drinkers actually could taste and logically define differences between certain brands. Secondly, we wanted to learn what they thought an 'ideal' beer should be and how this image compared with the image they had of Falstaff."

With these goals in mind, Mr.

SOURCE: Reprinted with permission from Joseph W. Newman, *Marketing Management and Information: A New Case Approach* (Homewood, Ill.: Richard D. Irwin, Inc., 1967), pp, 123–142.

Schwartz designed a test to accomplish three objectives:

1. To determine the extent to which consumers can perceive taste differences between Falstaff, Brand A beer, and Brand B beer in a "blind" test in which the brands would be unidentified. Both competitive brands were classified by laboratory technical personnel as having characteristics which differed.
2. To determine consumer impressions or "images" of the taste of the above three brands, plus Brand C and Brand D.
3. To relate the blind taste-test results and the brand taste images to the consumer conception of the characteristics of an ideal beer.

TEST PROCEDURE

The Institute for Design Analysis rented a store in an area of high pedestrian traffic of Oakland, California, in which to conduct the study. It took three weeks to obtain the desired sample of 800 male respondents from pedestrians passing by the store. Mr. Evans had decided that one test location in California was adequate at that stage for Falstaff's purpose. Only male beer drinkers were interviewed, since previously published surveys estimated that they drank 78 percent of the beer sold.

The testing procedure was outlined to the test staff as follows:

In the study we are going to interview 800 male beer drinkers. One of you will be assigned the job of recruiting beer drinkers. Screen out those who drink less than one glass or bottle of beer per week. As the test progresses, you will be required to recruit definite kinds of people. In the beginning, however, all male drinkers will be acceptable.

Under no conditions will we interview anyone under 21 years of age. If there is any question whatsoever, you must request identification in the form of either a driver's license or draft card. Further, we will not interview anyone who is in the slightest bit intoxicated. In this case, let him fill out the background information sheet and then tell him that the quota for his brand is filled. Give him one of our premiums and thank him for stopping in.

There will be four different test locations within the store: the first is a general waiting area; the second where the consumer fills out the background information and ideal beer sheets; the third where the taste test is conducted; and the fourth where the brand-image profiles are administered.

The receptionist will give the letter and the attached background information sheet to the consumer. It will be the receptionist's responsibility to see that the consumer fills out the form correctly and completely. (See Appendix A.)

The background information was used as the basis for assigning 25 percent of the respondents to each of four taste groups so that the groups were similar in such characteristics as race, occupation, age, weekly beer consumption, and brand preference. (See Exhibit 1.)[1]

---

[1] Exhibits follow study questions at end of reading.

Taste Group I	Falstaff v. Falstaff
Taste Group II	Falstaff v. Brand A
Taste Group III	Falstaff v. Brand B
Taste Group IV	Brand A v. Brand B

The taste test actually was made with 900 respondents, representing an oversample of 100. The extra represented an allowance for unusable responses sufficient to assure that 800 qualified responses had been obtained during the test.

"Ideal" Beer

The second part of the questionnaire presented an open-end question which asked the respondent to describe in his own words the taste attributes of an ideal beer.

The respondent then was asked to describe the ideal beer by placing an X in one of seven boxes appearing between each of eight "paired opposite" descriptive phrases. (See below.) The position of an X between the two extremes indicated his feeling as to what the ideal beer should be in regard to the quality concerned.

From previous taste tests, Mr. Schwartz had concluded that certain descriptive phrases were regarded positively, while their opposite phrases were regarded negatively. The rating form was designed so that the "positive" phrases were distributed evenly between the left- and right-hand sides.

Bitter beer	☐ ☐ ☐ ☐ ☐ ☐ ☐	Not bitter beer
Good-quality beer	☐ ☐ ☐ ☐ ☐ ☐ ☐	Poor-quality beer
Strong alcoholic content	☐ ☐ ☐ ☐ ☐ ☐ ☐	Weak alcoholic content
Watery beer	☐ ☐ ☐ ☐ ☐ ☐ ☐	Full-bodied beer
Good flavor	☐ ☐ ☐ ☐ ☐ ☐ ☐	Poor flavor
Sweet beer	☐ ☐ ☐ ☐ ☐ ☐ ☐	Not sweet beer
Has no bad aftertaste	☐ ☐ ☐ ☐ ☐ ☐ ☐	Has a bad aftertaste
Light beer	☐ ☐ ☐ ☐ ☐ ☐ ☐	Heavy beer

Blind Taste Test

For the next part of the test, the respondent was directed to the tasting area in the store. The instructions given to the testing staff for the blind taste test follow:

Ask the consumer to sit down. Then explain to him what he is expected to do while tasting the beer. Please read the instructions on top of Form III to the consumer and ask if he has any questions about it. (See Appendix A.)

Then serve him one of the beers. In all cases fill the glass completely and in the manner in which you have been instructed. The consumer must fill out the form completely. Do not let him make more than one X for any of the pairs of phrases.

The consumer will never be told the brand name of the beer he is testing. He will never see the bottle from which the beer is poured.

The tester will place the glass in front of a number on the table, indicating that the consumer is rating number 24. The tester will not tell the consumer anything about the beer except, if questioned, to say that the beer is made by a reputable brewery. No other information about the beer will be told to the consumer.

During each test there will be only two numbers on the table. After the consumer has ranked one beer, he will then taste and rank the second. Remember that the respondent must not cross-taste, but must rate each beer by itself. After he has drunk the first beer and rated it, please remove it.

The tester will permit the consumer to drink as much or as little of the glass of beer as the consumer wishes.

The taste test was carefully supervised to control sequence rotation in any pairing of number codes, the freshness of the beer, the temperature at which it was served, and the consistency of pouring methods. The test staff had purchased the beer from a high-volume retail outlet and a reading of the code indicated that the beer was fresh.

The respondent was served a full glass of one of two unidentified brands. He was asked to taste the beer and then describe it by placing X's appropriately between each of the same paired opposite phrases used to obtain descriptions of the ideal beer. The procedure then was repeated for the second unidentified brand.

The respondent then was asked to indicate by code number which of the two beers he preferred. Following this the respondent was asked to explain

in his own words the reasons why he preferred the coded brand. (See Appendix A.)

Taste Impression

Upon completion of the blind taste test, the respondent was asked to describe his impression of the taste of Falstaff and each of four well-known competitive brands of beer sold in California by using the same pairs of descriptive phrases used earlier. He was given a separate form for each of the five brands. The testing staff was instructed as follows:

> By this time the consumer will be familiar with the taste-rating procedure. However, it is important to ask him to rate even those brands which he might not have tasted, based on his impressions of the beer. Before the consumer leaves, make sure that he has checked one box for each of the five forms. You will also give him the notebook which is his gift and our way of saying thanks for his cooperation.

The entire testing procedure required approximately 20 minutes.

Tabulation of Responses

A taste profile was developed for each of the five brands by combining the descriptions given by all respondents. To facilitate the compilation, a number was assigned to each box on the eight-phrase rating forms as follows:

$$1 \quad 2 \quad 3 \quad 4 \quad 5 \quad 6 \quad 7$$

Bitter ☐ ☐ ☐ ☐ ☐ ☐ ☐ Not bitter

The frequency of response for each box was tabulated and an average was computed for each pair of descriptive phrases. The standard deviation for each average was also computed for use in determining statistical significance.

Brand profiles were computed for the entire sample and for each of the four test groups. The results from each test group were broken down for subgroups based on age, occupation, consumption pattern, and "usual brand." In the report, the data were summarized using averages of all scores for each item or pair of phrases.

FINDINGS
The Ideal Beer

Responses given most frequently when respondents were asked (in an open-end question) to describe the taste of an ideal beer were "not bitter," "smooth and mellow," "somewhat light," and "very light." (See Exhibit 2.)

The profile of an ideal beer, determined by use of the eight pairs of descriptive phrases, was described by the Institute for Design Analysis as follows (see Exhibit 3):

It was most desired that the ideal beer have good flavor and be of good quality.

It should not be too sweet or bitter . . . nor have a discernible aftertaste.

It should promise some "alcoholic content," but a great amount was not thought desirable.

While the ideal beer was on the light side of the heavy-light continuum, the ideal beer should be full-bodied, not watery.

The ideal-beer profile did not vary significantly among light, medium, heavy, and very heavy drinkers. There also were no significant differences between white- and blue-collar workers or between those under and over 40 years of age.

While reviewing the test results, Mr. Schwartz and Mr. Evans questioned the advisability of having required all respondents to describe their ideal beer as the first step of the test. They wondered whether this might have influenced responses obtained later by the use of the same descriptive phrases in the rating forms. In other words, the effect might have been to minimize scaling differences for the beers subsequently tasted in the blind taste test. Also, if a respondent liked the taste of a beer in the blind taste test, it was possible that he might tend to describe it in the same terms he used to describe his ideal beer.

The Blind Taste Test

Taste Group I unknowingly compared Falstaff and Falstaff. No respondent recognized that the two servings were of the same beer. Forty-three percent said they preferred the beer when it was served under one of the codes used and 52 percent said they preferred it when served under the other code. The blind-taste profiles of the two servings were almost identical. (See Exhibit 4.) Mr. Schwartz considered that the difference between scores for "light beer" and "heavy beer" was not significant.

The taste profiles for the beers used

in Test Groups II, III, and IV also varied only in minor respects, as follows:

> *Group II, Falstaff v. Brand A—* Falstaff was considered a lighter beer, less bitter and with less aftertaste than A. However, these differences were not statistically significant.
>
> *Group III, Falstaff v. Brand B—* the latter was perceived as a lighter beer, Falstaff as more full-bodied. Again, these and related differences were not statistically significant.

A combining of the results obtained in each blind taste-test group resulted in profiles for the three brands which were almost identical. There were no statistically significant differences.

Blind Taste Profiles v. the Ideal Beer Since the profiles for the three brands tasted were so similar, they deviated from the ideal-beer profile on the same taste characteristics to about the same degree. (See Exhibit 5.)

Preference in Blind Taste Comparisons Additional evidence that the respondents were unable to distinguish taste differences among the beers tested was the fact that no one brand was significantly preferred to the others and the widest range in preference was illustrated by Falstaff v. Falstaff. (See Exhibit 6.)

There were no significant differences in preferences by age, occupation, or consumption pattern of respondent.

Reasons for Preferences After indicating which brand they preferred in the blind taste test, respondents were asked the reasons for their preference. (See Appendix A.) Mr. Schwartz noted in the report that ". . . the consumers used the words selected from the various phrases that they had been rating." (See Exhibit 7.)

The reason most frequently mentioned for preference was that of better taste or flavor. Next was that the beer was full-bodied rather than watery.

The report pointed out that in Test Group III there were some interesting and significant taste differences mentioned. For example, Falstaff was preferred over B, although B was thought to be lighter, smoother, and of better quality than Falstaff in the image section that follows.

Taste Images This section reported beer drinkers' taste images for Falstaff, Brand A, Brand B, Brand C, and Brand D. The images were obtained from a test in which the brand names were made known to the respondents.

Mr. Schwartz reported the following differences in taste-image profiles (see Exhibits 8A and 8B):

> *Not bitter beer/bitter beer:* B was thought the least bitter beer, with D second. Falstaff, A, and C were clustered in the middle of the continuum.
>
> *Good - quality beer / poor - quality beer:* B and D were regarded as being the closest to a good-quality beer. Falstaff was in the middle.
>
> *Strong alcoholic content/weak alcoholic content:* The image of all five beers was much the same here.

There was some indication that B was thought to have the weakest alcoholic content. (Impressions of a stronger or weaker alcoholic content are definitely a function of image only.)

Full-bodied beer/watery beer: All five brands were seen to be in the middle of the range.

Good flavor/poor flavor; not sweet beer/sweet beer: All five brands were close to the middle on both attributes.

Has no bad aftertaste/has a bad aftertaste: B was thought to have the least bad aftertaste, followed by D and Falstaff.

Light beer/heavy beer: B was seen as being lighter than the other four brands.

Interpretation of Taste Results Mr. Schwartz interpreted the brand taste-image results as follows (see Exhibits 8A and 8B):

The image of all five brands was remarkably close. Only B clearly differentiated itself from the other brands. D did this somewhat by paralleling the image of B, yet not with the same image clarity.

The image of Falstaff was much less clear than that of several brands. Falstaff ranked third among the brands on each pair of phrases. Falstaff's taste image was stable and did not vary among different types of beer drinkers.

A and C had almost identical taste images—somewhat heavier, stronger alcoholic beers.

Falstaff Blind Taste v. Brand Taste Image v. Ideal Falstaff's blind taste-test profile was compared with its brand taste image and the taste profile for the beer. The results of the comparisons as reported by the Institute for Design Analysis follow (see Exhibits 9A and 9B).

First, Falstaff's blind taste profile and its brand taste image were well matched on most of the eight characteristics. In four instances, differences were noted illustrative of contrasts or conflicts between taste impression and image impressions:

Not bitter/bitter beer: The brand taste image was more bitter than the blind taste rating.

Strong alcoholic content/weak alcoholic content: In the taste test the beer was rated as stronger in alcoholic content than it was in the brand taste image.

Has no bad aftertaste/has a bad aftertaste: In the blind taste test the beer's "less aftertaste" rating was higher than in the brand taste image.

Light beer/heavy beer: In the blind taste test it was considered a lighter beer than in its brand image.

Secondly, on four of the image attributes, Falstaff differed significantly from the ideal profile. It was seen as being poorer in quality, more watery, poorer in flavor, and more likely to leave a bad aftertaste than the ideal beer. This, however, was illustrated to an almost identical degree by the other brands.

SUMMARY AND CONCLUSIONS

Mr. Schwartz summarized the results as follows:

The ideal beer was flavorful, full-bodied, not bitter, and of good quality. Falstaff and its two competitors varied from this ideal in the actual taste test.

The blind taste profiles of Falstaff, A, and B were identical. Each beer was preferred by about half the beer drinkers in the four test groups, including the control group of Falstaff v. Falstaff (which had the widest range in preference).

Falstaff did not have a distinct taste image which separated it from the other four brands rated. B had the clearest taste-impression profile—it was distinguished as a light beer with a mild aftertaste. D had a similar if somewhat less distinct taste image.

Mr. Schwartz came to the following conclusions:

Most consumers could not discern taste differences among the three beers tested. The findings could be interpreted to mean that all three beers tasted identical to these consumers.

Beer drinkers did have, however, an image of the ideal beer in their minds. The significance of this ideal taste image should be further studied from the following angles:

1. To determine what consumers mean when they seek "good flavor" and a "full-bodied" beer.
2. To determine if these concepts could be translated into useful marketing devices.

WHAT RECOMMENDATIONS FOR MANAGEMENT?

Mr. Evans reviewed the research report in his effort to determine what recommendation he should make to the marketing vice president as to what should be done to increase Falstaff's share of the California beer market.

QUESTIONS

1. What were the main elements of the research approach?
2. Was the research well designed to accomplish the stated objectives?
3. Evaluate the taste test from the standpoint of experimental design.
4. What alternative research designs might have been used?
5. Develop a design which you feel is as good as or better than that used in this case. Might the data obtained be different in any significant way?

EXHIBIT 1   *Description of Sample*

Sample	I *Falstaff* *and* *Falstaff*	II *Falstaff* *and* *Brand A*	III *Falstaff* *and* *Brand B*	IV *Brand A* *and* *Brand B*	*Total*
Total interviews	198	201	202	199	800
Race: white	75.3%	75.1%	76.2%	74.9%	75.4%
Occupation: white collar	49	47.5	47.1	47.7	47.9
Age: 40 and over	48	49.8	48.1	45.8	47.9
Consumption: 10 and under					
(bottles, cans, glasses)	57.6	56.6	61.4	64.2	60
Usual brand					
Falstaff	10.6	9.5	10.4	10.5	10.4
Brand A	12.1	12.9	12.9	11.6	12.4
Brand B	11.6	11.9	11.9	12.6	12

EXHIBIT 2   *Beer Drinkers' Descriptions of the Characteristics of an Ideal Beer**
(Total Interviews: 634)

An Ideal Beer Is:	Percent Mentioning†
Not bitter	23.5
Smooth, mellow	21
Somewhat light	17.5
Very light	16.6
Distinct malt or hop taste	9.9
Somewhat bitter	6.9
Very tangy	6
Slight malt or hop taste	4.7
No aftertaste	4.7
Somewhat heavy	5
Somewhat tangy	4.6
Somewhat sweet	2.8
Some aftertaste	2.7
Aged	2.1
Very heavy	1.9
Very sweet	1.7
Very bitter	0.6
Miscellaneous taste attributes	17.7
Nontaste attributes	21.6

* Of 800 selected interviews, only 634 respondents actually referred to taste attributes in answering this question.

† 166, or 21 percent of the respondents, did not know or did not answer this question.

EXHIBIT 3 *A Profile of the Taste Attributes of the Ideal Beer*

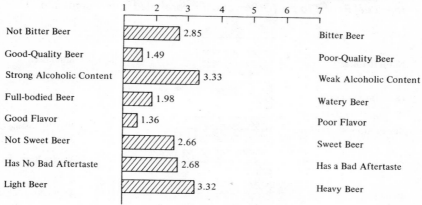

Not Bitter Beer	2.85	Bitter Beer
Good-Quality Beer	1.49	Poor-Quality Beer
Strong Alcoholic Content	3.33	Weak Alcoholic Content
Full-bodied Beer	1.98	Watery Beer
Good Flavor	1.36	Poor Flavor
Not Sweet Beer	2.66	Sweet Beer
Has No Bad Aftertaste	2.68	Has a Bad Aftertaste
Light Beer	3.32	Heavy Beer

Base: 800 Northern California beer drinkers.

EXHIBIT 4 *A Comparison of the Blind-Taste Profiles of Falstaff (Code 16) and Falstaff (Code 18)*

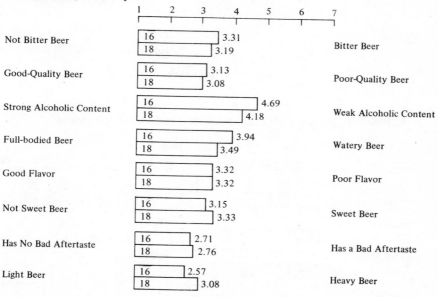

	16	18	
Not Bitter Beer	3.31	3.19	Bitter Beer
Good-Quality Beer	3.13	3.08	Poor-Quality Beer
Strong Alcoholic Content	4.69	4.18	Weak Alcoholic Content
Full-bodied Beer	3.94	3.49	Watery Beer
Good Flavor	3.32	3.32	Poor Flavor
Not Sweet Beer	3.15	3.33	Sweet Beer
Has No Bad Aftertaste	2.71	2.76	Has a Bad Aftertaste
Light Beer	2.57	3.08	Heavy Beer

Base: 198 Northern California beer drinkers.

EXHIBIT 5 *A Comparison of Falstaff's Cumulated Blind-Taste Profile with the Ideal-Beer Profile (Other brands paralleled this comparison.)*

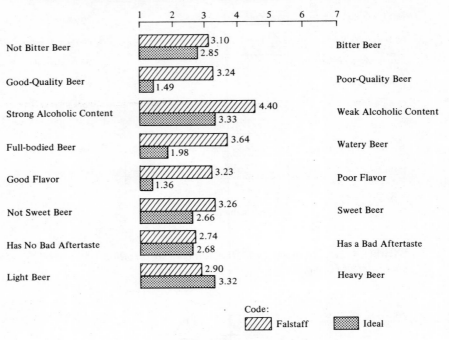

	Falstaff	Ideal	
Not Bitter Beer	3.10	2.85	Bitter Beer
Good-Quality Beer	3.24	1.49	Poor-Quality Beer
Strong Alcoholic Content	4.40	3.33	Weak Alcoholic Content
Full-bodied Beer	3.64	1.98	Watery Beer
Good Flavor	3.23	1.36	Poor Flavor
Not Sweet Beer	3.26	2.66	Sweet Beer
Has No Bad Aftertaste	2.74	2.68	Has a Bad Aftertaste
Light Beer	2.90	3.32	Heavy Beer

Code: ///// Falstaff   ▒▒▒ Ideal

Base: 799 Northern California beer drinkers.

EXHIBIT 6 *Blind-Taste Test: Percent Choosing Each Brand*

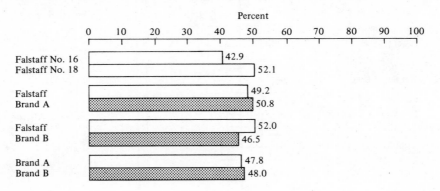

	Percent
Falstaff No. 16	42.9
Falstaff No. 18	52.1
Falstaff	49.2
Brand A	50.8
Falstaff	52.0
Brand B	46.5
Brand A	47.8
Brand B	48.0

EXHIBIT 7 *Reasons for Preferring One Brand over Another**

Reasons for Preference	Test I (198)		Test II (201)		Test III (202)		Test IV (199)	
	Falstaff #16 (%)	Falstaff #18 (%)	Falstaff (%)	Brand A (%)	Falstaff (%)	Brand B (%)	Brand A (%)	Brand B (%)
Better taste, flavor	26.3	32.3	27.4	28.9	31.0	27.7	27.2	19.1
Full-bodied, not watery	12.6	18.7	11	16.4	19.8	9.4	13.1	15.1
No aftertaste	9.1	6.6	8.5	6.5	5	5.9	6	8.6
Not bitter	8.1	7.6	11.5	6.5	7.4	6.4	6	11.1
Light	8.1	7.6	8	5	1.9	11.9	7	5.5
Smoother	6.6	2.5	5.5	3	3.5	14.4	2.5	7
Not sweet	4.5	3.1	9	8.5	7.9	3.5	4.5	2
Stronger, heavier	2.5	5.1	5.5	5.5	12.9	5.9	7.5	1.5
Good quality	5	3	5	2.5	2.5	12.4	6	4
Sweet	2	1.5	1	1.5	1.5	3.5	2	2
Mild	2.5	1.5	5	3.5	1	0.5	2	3
Heavy alcohol content	1.5	7.1	4	2.5	1.5	1.5	2.5	4
Some aftertaste	1	3	1.5	1	1	2.5	1.5	1
Somewhat tangy	1	2.5	3	5.5	2	1	1.5	. . .
Light alcohol content	1	1.5	2.5	2.5	1.9	1.9	3	2
Miscellaneous	1	2	1.5	2	1	1	1.5	2
No answer or don't know	26.4	27.9	21.5	26.3	19.9	15.5	21.6	18.5

* Multiple mentions cause totals of more than 100 percent.

EXHIBIT 8A   *A Comparison of the Taste-Image Impression Profile of Fal-staff and Four Other Brands*

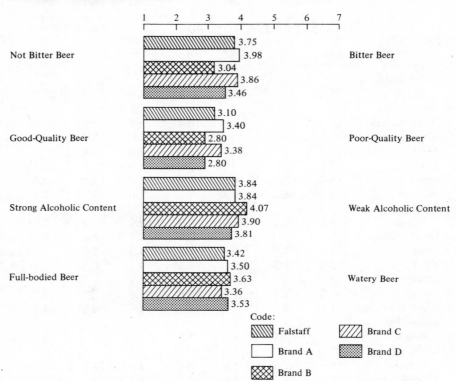

Code:

Base: 800 Northern California beer drinkers.

EXHIBIT 8B   *A Comparison of the Taste-Image Impression Profile of Falstaff and Four Other Brands*

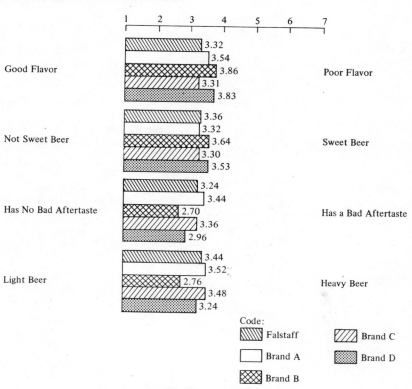

Good Flavor — 3.32, 3.54, 3.86, 3.31, 3.83 — Poor Flavor

Not Sweet Beer — 3.36, 3.32, 3.64, 3.30, 3.53 — Sweet Beer

Has No Bad Aftertaste — 3.24, 3.44, 2.70, 3.36, 2.96 — Has a Bad Aftertaste

Light Beer — 3.44, 3.52, 2.76, 3.48, 3.24 — Heavy Beer

Code:
Falstaff   Brand C
Brand A   Brand D
Brand B

Base: 800 Northern California beer drinkers.

EXHIBIT 9A *A Comparison of Falstaff Cumulated Blind-Taste, Image-Impression Profile, and Ideal-Beer Profile**

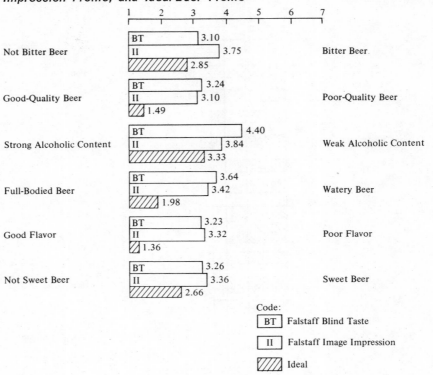

Not Bitter Beer	Bitter Beer
BT 3.10 / II 3.75 / Ideal 2.85	
Good-Quality Beer	Poor-Quality Beer
BT 3.24 / II 3.10 / Ideal 1.49	
Strong Alcoholic Content	Weak Alcoholic Content
BT 4.40 / II 3.84 / Ideal 3.33	
Full-Bodied Beer	Watery Beer
BT 3.64 / II 3.42 / Ideal 1.98	
Good Flavor	Poor Flavor
BT 3.23 / II 3.32 / Ideal 1.36	
Not Sweet Beer	Sweet Beer
BT 3.26 / II 3.36 / Ideal 2.66	

Code:

BT	Falstaff Blind Taste
II	Falstaff Image Impression
////	Ideal

*Other brands differed similarly from the ideal.

EXHIBIT 9B *A Comparison of Falstaff Cumulated Blind-Taste, Image-Impression Profile, and Ideal-Beer Profile*

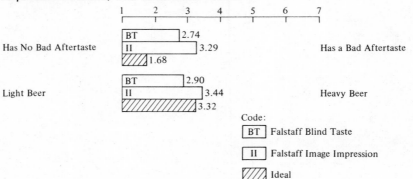

Has No Bad Aftertaste	Has a Bad Aftertaste
BT 2.74 / II 3.29 / Ideal 1.68	
Light Beer	Heavy Beer
BT 2.90 / II 3.44 / Ideal 3.32	

Code:

BT	Falstaff Blind Taste
II	Falstaff Image Impression
////	Ideal

Base: Falstaff blind taste: 799 Northern California beer drinkers.
Falstaff image impression: 800 Northern California beer drinkers.
Ideal: 800 Northern California beer drinkers.

Interview Number _____ 1–
                          2–
                          3–
                      R4–1
                       –3
                       –5

APPENDIX A:
QUESTIONNAIRE
AND RATING FORMS
Taste-Testing Background Information

In order to help us make the best of your opinions, we would like to have the answers to the following questions. It is not necessary for you to sign your name to any of these forms. In that way your answers remain *strictly confidential* and are used only for research purposes.

1. What is your occupation? What kind of firm do you work at? And exactly what kind of work do you do there?

   _____ 5–1
                             –3
   _____ –5
                             –7

2. In which of the following age groups do you belong?
   Check one:

   50 or over _____ 6–1
   40 to 49   _____ –3
   30 to 39   _____ –5
   21 to 29   _____ –7

3. About how many glasses, bottles, or cans of beer do you generally drink during a week?

   _____ 7–

4. What is your usual brand of beer, that is, which *one* beer do you most often purchase?

   _____ 8–

5. What is your favorite brand of beer, that is, the beer that you *prefer* to drink?

   _____ 9–

6. What other brands of beer do you consider *good* beers, that is, beers that you like drinking?

   _____ 10–
   _____

7. What other brands of beer do you consider *bad* beers, that is, beers that you dislike drinking?

   _____ 11–
   _____

8. Now we'd like your ideas on what an *ideal* beer would taste like. How would you describe the taste of an *ideal* beer? In particular, what taste and other qualities would make it an *ideal* beer?

   _____ 12–
   _____ 13–
   _____
   _____
   _____
   _____

——————————————————
——————————————————
——————————————————
——————————————————
——————————————————
——————————————————

FINISHED THIS BACKGROUND
INFORMATION   QUESTION-
NAIRE.

Please do not write below this line

Receptionist —————— t/a ——————

——————————
——————————
——————————

PLEASE LET THE RECEPTION-
IST KNOW WHEN YOU HAVE

Ideal Beer Rating Form
Form II   Interview Number ————

Note below the eight pair of opposite phrases which are often used to describe differences in beer tastes.

For each pair of opposite phrases, tell us how close you feel the *ideal* beer should be to either of the opposites.

Please place an X in the box which *comes closest* to describing where the *ideal* beer should be on each pair of opposite phrases.

Bitter beer	□ □ □ □ □ □ □	Not bitter beer	14—
Good-quality beer	□ □ □ □ □ □ □	Poor-quality beer	15—
Strong alcoholic content	□ □ □ □ □ □ □	Weak alcoholic content	16—
Watery beer	□ □ □ □ □ □ □	Full-bodied beer	17—
Good flavor	□ □ □ □ □ □ □	Poor flavor	18—
Sweet beer	□ □ □ □ □ □ □	Not sweet beer	19—
Has no bad aftertaste	□ □ □ □ □ □ □	Has a bad aftertaste	20—
Light beer	□ □ □ □ □ □ □	Heavy beer	21—

Blind Taste-Test Rating Form (A)
Form III   Interview Number ————
                                           Beer Tasted ————|
                                                  t/a   31—

After tasting as much of this beer as you'd like, we want your reactions to it. While making your evaluation, if you feel that you'd like to taste it again, please do so.

For each of the eight opposite phrases listed below, place an X in the box which comes closest to how you would describe the taste of this beer.

Bitter beer	□ □ □ □ □ □ □	Not bitter beer	32—
Good-quality beer	□ □ □ □ □ □ □	Poor-quality beer	33—
Strong alcoholic content	□ □ □ □ □ □ □	Weak alcoholic content	34—
Watery beer	□ □ □ □ □ □ □	Full-bodied beer	35—
Good flavor	□ □ □ □ □ □ □	Poor flavor	36—
Sweet beer	□ □ □ □ □ □ □	Not sweet beer	37—
Has no bad aftertaste	□ □ □ □ □ □ □	Has a bad aftertaste	38—
Light beer	□ □ □ □ □ □ □	Heavy beer	39—

Blind Taste-Test Rating Form (B)

Of the two beers that you just tasted, which one did you prefer? Please write the number of the one you preferred.

———— 80—

Why did you prefer this beer? What did you particularly like about it? How did it compare with the other beer?

———————————————————————————————————

———————————————————————————————————

———————————————————————————————————

———————————————————————————————————

———————————————————————————————————

———————————————————————————————————

———————————————————————————————————

Chapter 5

Consumer Behavior
and Marketing Research

Marketing research is about people. It concerns people as they act as individuals or together as groups. Marketing research is one of the most important mechanisms customers have for communicating their desires to marketers, and because of this it is the major tool marketers have for learning how to improve their marketing mix. It is essential, then, for the reader to be familiar with some of the more commonly used concepts about customers.

Introduction

A substantial proportion of all marketing research involves the direct study of people. The kinds of people studied are extremely varied including such individuals as housewives, children, executives of large corporations, and managers of small businesses. Similarly, a very wide range of variables have been studied with regard to all the possible people marketing managers are anxious to understand. Included among these variables or concepts are personality, self-images, feelings about how one ought to behave, attitudes toward salesmen, products, and corporations, feelings about the honesty of particular mass media, collective decision-making processes in companies and families, and potential buyers' perceptions of new products.

For example, a major producer of breakfast cereals recently initiated a study of the interaction between mothers and their children to determine whether there are particular patterns of interaction which are associated with different degrees of influence exerted by the child on the choice of cereals to be purchased. If there are distinct patterns, the market may be segmented accordingly and different appeals may be developed for each segment. As a way of both characterizing the different patterns of mother-child interaction and determining effective promotional appeals, questions are asked which are designed to reveal (1) the images mothers have of themselves as "nutritionists" for their children, (2) personality traits associated with exertive children and mothers, (3) the most influential media for mothers and children on matters pertaining to food, and (4) general attitudes toward cereal and toward breakfast as a daily event.

It is important to notice in the case of the cereal manufacturer that there is a desire to learn through marketing research whether the mother or child exerts more influence on the choice of cereals. Or, more precisely, the manufacturer wants to know under what conditions the child is more likely to be influential and vice versa. The manufacturer had already defined the relevant units of analysis and wanted to determine the most frequent patterns of relationships among them. Identifying the relevant units of analysis is an important early step in the marketing research process. The first part of this chapter will address this issue. Following this the chapter will examine some of the many important behavioral science concepts studied in both industrial and consumer market research. Examples of frequently asked research questions involving these concepts will be presented.

Determining the Proper Unit of Analysis

The first step in implementing the research plan is to determine the proper unit of analysis. By unit of analysis we mean the type or category of person, group, or firm on which the study will focus. For example, it is possible to study individuals, families, buying committees, or even entire firms and communities. On the other hand, it may be fruitful to study children as consumers of breakfast cereals or to study their mothers as buyers of breakfast cereals. The first example can be thought of as the problem of choosing the correct level of aggregation. The second example involves choosing the relevant role for analysis.

Relevant Roles of Analysis

Whether the research focuses on consumer or industrial products or services, four distinct role types can be discerned: (a) users, (b) buyers, (c) decision makers, and (d) influencers. Although the roles are distinct it is possible for the same person to perform several roles. (See Table 5.1.) In the example above, the child may be both a user and an influencer. If the research project involved the taste of a new breakfast food, for example, the child as user might be a more important respondent to study than the mother. If, on the other hand, the project involved the effect of nutritional information labeling, obviously the mother would be a more important respondent in her roles as decision maker and buyer. Similarly, a survey study of industrial buying in the oil equipment industry suggests that boards of directors are more likely to decide on major capital purchasing while special buying committees implement the decision.

TABLE 5.1 *Relevant Roles for Research Analysis*

Role	Characteristic
User	The person most directly involved in the consumption (or use) of the product or service of interest
Buyer	The individual who actually makes the purchase
Decision maker	The person who decides that the satisfaction of needs requires a purchase and has the authority to direct the expenditure of funds
Influencer	A person who, by word or action, deliberately or not, exerts some influence on the decision to buy, the actual purchase, and the use of some product or service

The user is the person most directly involved in the consumption (or use) of the product or service of interest. The child who eats breakfast cereal is one example; a secretary who uses paper and typewriter ribbons is another. As simple as the concept of user may seem, there are some difficulties with the classification. Take the case of pet foods. Is the dog or cat the user or is it the person who feeds the pet? The answer is—it depends. It depends on the type of research being done. Babies, pets, lawns, and plants all consume prodigious amounts of nutrients, yet few researchers would presume to question them about their attitudes toward a new brand.

The buyer is the individual who actually makes the purchase. This has been the focus of most so-called consumer studies. Again, the mother buys breakfast cereal or the purchasing agent completes and sends out a purchase order for typewriter ribbon. Buyers are important because frequently they are the ones who can choose among the various sources of supply in a given product category. The purchasing agent may order a different brand of toner powder for the office copying machine than that made by the machine's manufacturer.

Although the buyer is given latitude in the actual purchase, it is important to note that he may not decide on his own to buy or not to buy. This is the province of the *decision maker*. The decision maker is that person who decides that the satisfaction of needs requires a purchase and has the authority to direct the expenditure of funds. In the terms of marginal utility theory,[1] a mother may decide that the expenditure of 29¢ for a squirt gun is offset by the marginal utility of a happy child. A decision maker may be a child with a penny, a newly married couple in a furniture store, or the U.S. Senate debating an appropriations bill.

The roles of user, buyer, and decision maker have one thing in common which separates them from the last role to be discussed, that of influencer, and that is that they are conscious roles. Buyers, users, and decision makers are generally aware of their actions in these roles. An influencer, however, may not be aware that he is influencing a purchase decision. A conscious influencer might be a neighbor who is knowledgeable about washing machines or the information systems expert in the firm who gives advice on the selection of accounting machines. Both are aware that they are influencing a purchase decision. Unconscious influencers are typified by the "guy on the next street" who just bought a new Mercedes or the picture in the woman's pages of the newspaper of a smiling couple dressed in the latest fashions in Acapulco. As a result of these unconscious influencers, our perceptions of Mercedes and Acapulco may be enhanced and indeed affect our choice of cars and vacation

---

[1] Marginal utility theory assumes that a person makes decisions concerning the trading of a resource (like money) to improve his satisfaction. Thus, if a child is crying in a food store, it may be worth the expenditure of 15¢ to buy a candy bar to make him be quiet and prevent embarrassment.

spots. *Influencers,* then, are those persons or groups who, by their words or actions, whether conscious or not, exert some influence on the direction of a purchase decision.

Influence agents are many and varied. Individuals have already been identified as influencers. Reference group theory[2] suggests a far greater number. There are informal reference groups of which the individual may or may not be a member, and to which he may or may not aspire to belong. These include such things as the country club set, the fellows at the corner bar, or a group of scientist colleagues. Purchase decisions are influenced by the individual's reference to what members of these groups might think of the intended purchase or whether they already sanction the possession of the good in question.

Similarly, there are formal reference groups such as churches, unions, clubs, companies, and others. The fact that the individual is a member of the engineering department in his firm is one thing; but he may also base his decisions on what members of another department or company may do. For example, in a study in the steel industry, one respondent remarked that the members of management in his company watched closely what another company did in terms of new processes, and often took similar actions themselves. In this instance, the members of the firm were using another firm as a reference group.[3]

Models of Buyer and Consumer Behavior

Because people are no less human in one situation than in another and because the variety of situations of interest to marketers are great, it is not surprising that most concepts in the behavioral sciences are investigated by marketing researchers. Because it is not possible to thoroughly review the consumer behavior literature here, only some of the behavioral concepts most frequently employed will be briefly presented. First, however, it will be useful to look at some general models of buyer behavior which incorporate the behavioral concepts to be discussed.

Recently, some marketing researchers have attempted to construct models of buyer and consumer behavior. These models have included a wide array of behavioral variables including all those discussed in this chapter. The models attempt to interrelate these variables showing how they all work together to affect marketing relevant behavior. The models are quite complex. Moreover, their implications are not fully tested and understood. However, a few paragraphs about these models will give the reader at least some feeling of their character and perhaps entice him to consult the original works.

---

[2] Reference group theory states that individuals are influenced through stimuli expressed by certain types of other people.

[3] John A. Czepiel, "The Diffusion of Major Technological Innovation in the American Steel Industry: An Analysis of Social Processes in a Complex Industrial Community," in the *Proceedings of the Second Annual Albert Haring Symposium on Doctoral Research in Marketing* (Indiana University Graduate School of Business, April 1972), pp. 66–86.

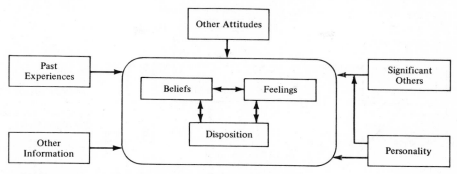

FIGURE 5.1 *A Model of Static Customer Choice*
Source: Alan R. Andreason, "Attitude and Consumer Behavior: A Decision Model"
in Lee Preston (ed.), *New Research in Marketing* (The Institute of Business and
Economic Research, University of California at Berkeley, 1966), p. 4.

One of the first models was developed by Alan Andreasen.[4] The basic
structure of his model (shown in Figure 5.1) involves as preliminary influence
factors, information about intrinsic and extrinsic features of products, their
price and availability. Also important are existing attitudes toward the sources
of information. These factors are filtered by the individual; that is, they are
reduced and distorted as a result of various perceptual processes operating
within the individual. The filtered information may result in new beliefs,
feelings, and dispositions or may simply reinforce those that already exist.
Perceived social norms, values held by reference groups, and personality traits
of the individual both influence and are influenced by the individual's filtration
processes. The resulting disposition of the individual may be to buy or use a
product or to discontinue consideration of the product. Constraints such as
income and the relative importance of other needs to be satisfied by other
products influence whether a favorable disposition to act actually is expressed
by a purchase or by use of the product.

Francesco M. Nicosia has developed a model of consumer decision
processes which is presented as a summary flow chart structure of consumer
behavior.[5] (See Figure 5.2.) The model consists of *four fields* of activity. In
the *first field* there is a flow of messages from the firm which, together with
attributes of the product and environmental factors, constitute a stimulus.
When the consumer is exposed to this stimulus he processes the data to produce
an attitude. Many physiological, social, and psychological factors influence
the consumer's processing of the stimulus. The consumer's attitude and his

[4] Alan R. Andreason, "Attitude and Consumer Behavior: A Decision Model," in Lee
Preston (ed.), *New Research in Marketing* (Berkeley, Calif.: The Institute of Business and
Economic Research, University of California, 1966), p. 4.

[5] Francesco Nicosia, *Consumer Decision Processes* (Englewood Cliffs, N. J.:
Prentice-Hall), 1966.

Field One: From the Source of a Message to the Consumer's Attitude

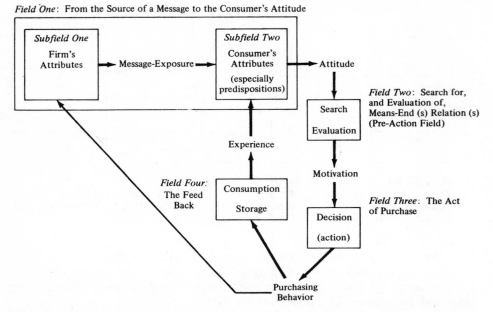

FIGURE 5.2   *The Comprehensive Scheme: A Summary Flow Chart*
Source: Francesco Nicosia, *Consumer Decision Processes*, p. 156, © 1966. Reprinted by permission of Prentice-Hall, Inc., Englewood Cliffs, N.J.

other attributes serve as an input into *field two.* This area consists of the evaluation of the attitude toward the advertised brand or product and alternatives and the consideration of the product's ability to satisfy needs. Factors relevant to this evaluation process include talking with other people, the product and brand attributes, one's personal situation and prior shopping experience. If the advertised product is considered a good means for satisfying some end, then a favorable motivation develops toward this product.

Field three consists of the transformation of the motivation into an act of purchase. Various constraints such as availability may operate to make the act of purchase difficult to carry out. *Field four* involves the use or consumption of the product. As a result of use new motivations may result which modify processes in field three. New attitudes or the reinforcement of existing attitudes may also be a consequence of consumption, thus modifying future experiences in area two. Finally, new predispositions may result which modify or influence subsequent activities in field one.

In 1969, John A. Howard and Jagdish Sheth published their theory of buyer behavior.[6] (See Figure 5.3.) Most briefly, their model consists of certain

---

[6] John A. Howard and Jagdish Sheth, *The Theory of Buyer Behavior* (New York: Wiley, 1969).

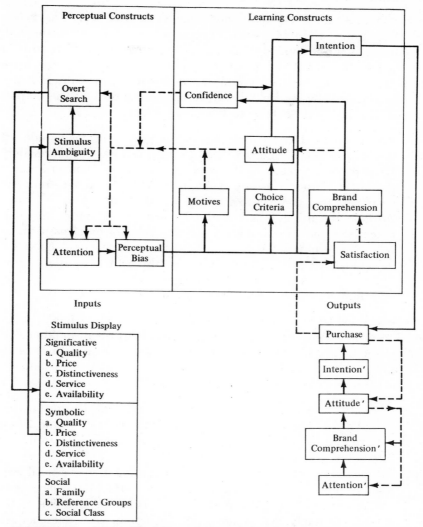

FIGURE 5.3 *A Simplified Description of the Theory of Buyer Behavior (Solid lines indicate flow of information; dashed lines, feedback effects.)*

Source: J. A. Howard and J. Sheth, *The Theory of Buyer Behavior*, p. 30. Copyright © 1969 John Wiley & Sons, Inc. Reprinted by permission of John Wiley & Sons, Inc.

inputs which influence perception of products and services. Inputs can be transmitted through three channels. The first is called significative and includes such product characteristics as quality, price, and distinctiveness. If the input is communicated not by the product itself so much as by mass media and catalogs, they are considered as coming from symbolic (that is, word or picture) channels. Alternatively, information may come from social channels such as reference groups and social class. The various inputs from the three channels influence how the individual perceives the product which in turn influences his learning about the product. Important elements in the learning process include motives, choice criteria, confidence, and attitudes. Stimuli which are processed by perceptual and learning processes result in outputs or responses. Howard and Sheth note five such outputs:

1. *Attention* is a buyer's response that indicates the magnitude of his information intake and is related to his sensitivity to information.
2. *Comprehension* refers to the store of knowledge about a brand that the buyer possesses at any point in time. It can range from simple awareness to a complete knowledge of its attributes.
3. *Attitude* toward a brand is the buyer's evaluation of the brand's potential to satisfy his motives and is related to predisposition.
4. *Intention* to buy is the buyer's forecast of which brand he will buy; it includes not only predisposition but also a forecast of inhibitors.
5. *Purchase behavior* is the overt manifestation of predisposition together with inhibitors; it is actual behavior.

The final model to be discussed is the one suggested by James F. Engel, David T. Kollat, and Roger D. Blackwell.[7] Theirs is called a "multimediation" model by which they mean that many processes intervene or mediate between exposure to a stimulus and the final outcomes of behavior. This model contains four basic modules or units (See Figure 5.4).

1. *Central control unit.* This contains the psychological command center including *information* and *experience, evaluative criteria,* and *attitudes.* All are affected by *personality* and together interact to form a filter through which stimuli are processed.
2. *Information processing.* Stimuli passing through the central control unit are processed in four phases: *exposure, attention, comprehension,* and *retention.* Although exposure is necessary for attention to occur, it does not imply that it must, since comprehension does not necessarily flow from attention, and so on.
3. *The decision process.* This includes *problem recognition* and flows through *internal search and alternative evaluation, external search and alternative evaluation, purchasing processes,* and *outcomes.* Every stage need not be present in every purchase decision.
4. *Environmental influences.* These are constraints on the decision process and include *income, culture, family, social class, physical,* and other

---

[7] James F. Engel, David T. Kollat, and Roger D. Blackwell, *Consumer Behavior,* 2nd ed. (New York: Holt, Rinehart and Winston, 1973).

factors. These may operate to facilitate the process or to introduce a *hold* in the process.

An important concept, common to the four models discussed, is the concept of attitude. Attitudes have become one of the most frequently and seriously studied variables by marketing researchers. Attitudes are important to study because they may influence the behavior of the person holding them or the behavior of others who are influenced by the person having the clear attitude. Behavior, of course, will not always correspond with attitude. Favorable attitudes toward a product may not result in its actual purchase because the product may not be compatible with other machinery used by the firm, the product may be too expensive for the housewife's budget, or it may simply not be easily obtained. Reasons for discrepancies between attitudes and be-

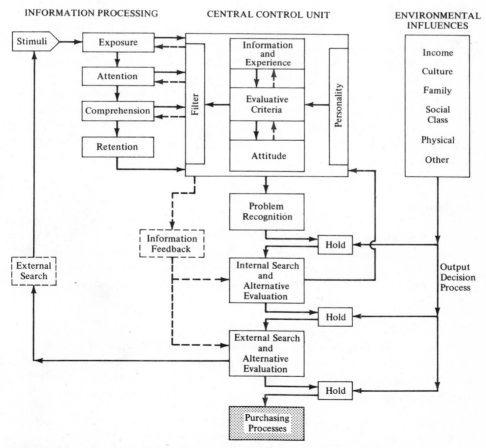

FIGURE 5.4 *A Model of Purchasing Processes*

havior are many and are of concern to marketers. Nevertheless, attitudes often do influence behavior in the marketplace. Because of the importance of attitudes in contemporary marketing research the next chapter is devoted to this topic.

Behavioral Concepts Used in Marketing Research

Culture   Culture is ". . . that complex whole which includes knowledge, belief, art, law, morals, custom, and any other capabilities and habits acquired by man as a member of society."[8] The study of culture is of obvious value in international marketing where the marketer is crossing the boundary between cultures. Table 5.2 presents the numerous questions asked in cross-cultural marketing research. The very same questions apply in *subculture* research. A subculture is a way of behaving peculiar to a particular group within a larger society. It is possible to simultaneously live in and be affected by more than one subculture. For example, within the United States it is possible to speak of the urban black subculture, the Appalachian subculture, age-specific subculture, or even a drug subculture.

There are several methodologies available for conducting culture research. One method is the field study where the investigators enter the culture setting and gather data intensively through observation, participation in daily activities, and perhaps administering tests. A method which does not necessarily involve physical entry into a culture by a researcher is the content analysis approach. This approach involves monitoring verbal or written communication for repeated expressions about values, norms, concerns, and so forth. In preparation for a massive nutrition improvement advertising campaign in Central America researchers from the advertising agency spent days analyzing unstructured interviews which were recorded by tape. Several specific beliefs were identified and advertising appeals were developed which were consistent with these beliefs. Another method for analyzing cultures or subcultures involves the systematic sampling of a representative cross section of the group under study. CBS News has used this approach in studying the values of youths and parents. Table 5.3 contains examples of the type of questions that can be asked in this approach.

Roles and Status   The expression *role* and *status* must be defined in terms of each other. The term *role* refers to the expectations that group members have in common concerning the behavior of a person who occupies some position within the group.[9] On the other hand, the position occupied by the individual within a group relative to the other members is termed his *status* level. Role,

[8] Edward B. Tylor, quoted in A. L. Kroeber and C. Kluckholm, *Culture: A Critical Review of Concepts and Definitions* (New York: Random House, 1963), p. 81.

[9] A. Paul Hare, *Handbook of Small Group Research* (New York: Free Press of Glencoe, 1962), p. 122.

TABLE 5.2 *Marketing Questions in Cross-Cultural Research*

1. *Determine relevant motivations in the culture.* What needs are fulfilled with this product in the minds of members of the culture? How are these needs presently fulfilled? Do members of this culture readily recognize these needs?
2. *Determine characteristic behavior patterns.* What behaviors are characteristic of purchasing behavior? What forms of division of labor exist within the family structure? How frequently are products of this type purchased? Do any of these characteristic behaviors conflict with behavior expected for this product? How strongly ingrained are the behavior patterns that conflict with those needed for distribution of this product?
3. *Determine what broad cultural values are relevant to this product.* Are there strong values about work, morality, family relations, and so on, that relate to this product? Does this product connote attributes that are in conflict with these cultural values? Can conflicts with values be avoided by changing the product? Are there positive values in this culture with which the product may be identified?
4. *Determine characteristic forms of decision making.* Do members of the culture display a studied approach to decisions concerning innovations or an impulsive approach? What is the form of the decision process? Upon what information sources do members of the culture rely? Do members of the culture tend to be rigid or flexible in the acceptance of new ideas? What criteria do they use in evaluating alternatives?
5. *Evaluate promotion methods appropriate to the culture.* What role does advertising occupy in the culture? What themes, words, or illustrations are taboo? What language problems exist in promoting the product? Can the name and major selling claims used in present markets be translated into this culture? What types of salesmen are accepted by members of the culture? Are such salesmen available?
6. *Determine appropriate marketing institutions for this product in the minds of consumers.* What types of retailers and intermediary institutions are available? What services do these institutions offer that are expected by the consumer? What alternatives are available for obtaining services needed for the product but not offered by existing institutions? How are various types of retailers regarded by consumers? Will consumers readily accept changes in the distribution structure?

Source: From *Consumer Behavior*, Second Edition, by James F. Engel, David T. Kollat and Roger D. Blackwell. Copyright © 1968, 1973 by Holt, Rinehart and Winston, Inc. Reprinted by permission of Holt, Rinehart and Winston, Inc.

then, is simply the expected behavior pattern of a given status or position. Thus, an individual *occupies* a status level and *performs* a role peculiar to that status level. His actions as a member of the group compose his role behavior. It should be noted that the individual performs the role, while it is the group that determines the expectations of a given role and the status level that the role has in terms of prestige and deference.

TABLE 5.3 *CBS Cross-Sectional Study of Youth and Parents (Selected Questions and Responses)*

(1) The following statements represent some traditional American values. Which of them do you *personally believe in* and which do you *not believe in*?

	Youth			Parents		
	Total Youth (%)	College (%)	Non-college (%)	Total Parents (%)	Parents College Youth (%)	Parents Non-college Youth (%)
(a) Hard work will always pay off						
Believe in	74	56	79	83	76	85
Do not believe in	26	43	21	17	24	15
(b) Everyone should save as much as he can regularly and not have to lean on family and friends the minute he runs into financial problems						
Believe in	86	76	88	96	90	98
Do not believe in	14	24	11	3	10	2
(c) Depending on how much strength and character a person has, he can pretty well control what happens to him						
Believe in	74	62	77	74	71	75
Do not believe in	26	38	23	24	28	23
(d) Belonging to some organized religion is important in a person's life						
Believe in	66	42	71	89	81	91
Do not believe in	34	57	28	11	17	9

(2) Many people feel that we are undergoing a period of rapid social change in this country today, and that people's values are changing at the same time. Which of the following changes would you *welcome*, which would you *reject*, and which would *leave you indifferent*?

TABLE 5.3 *(continued)*

	Youth			Parents		
	Total Youth (%)	College (%)	Non-college (%)	Total Parents (%)	Parents College Youth (%)	Parents Non-college Youth (%)
(a) Less emphasis on money						
Would welcome	57	72	54	Not asked of		
Would reject	13	11	13	parents		
Leave indifferent	30	17	33			
(b) Less emphasis on working hard						
Would welcome	30	24	32			
Would reject	46	48	45			
Leave indifferent	23	28	22			
(c) More emphasis on law and order						
Would welcome	76	57	81			
Would reject	10	23	7			
Leave indifferent	12	19	11			
(f) More sexual freedom						
Would welcome	27	43	22			
Would reject	39	24	43			
Leave indifferent	34	33	34			
(g) More vigorous protests by blacks and other minority groups						
Would welcome	12	23	9			
Would reject	73	56	77			
Leave indifferent	15	20	14			

(18) Which of the following considerations will have a relatively strong influence on your choice of career?

Your family	35	31	36	Not asked of		
The money that you can earn	47	41	49	parents		
The prestige or status of the job	21	23	20			
The security of the job	45	42	46			

153

TABLE 5.3   *(continued)*

	Youth			Parents		
	Total Youth (%)	College (%)	Non-college (%)	Total Parents (%)	Parents College Youth (%)	Parents Non-college Youth (%)
The ability to express yourself	47	66	43			
The challenge of the job	52	71	47			
The opportunity to make a meaningful contribution	60	76	56			

(24) For each of the following, please tell me whether you feel it needs no substantial change, needs moderate change, needs fundamental reform, or should be done away with.

Big business						
No substantial change	20	10	23	Not asked of		
Moderate change	52	52	52	parents		
Fundamental reform	24	34	21			
Done away with	3	3	3			
The military						
No substantial change	20	10	23			
Moderate change	43	29	46			
Fundamental reform	29	49	25			
Done away with	7	11	6			
The universities						
No substantial change	20	11	23			
Moderate change	50	56	49			
Fundamental reform	28	32	27			
Done away with	1	—	1			

CBS News, *Generations Apart* (New York: Columbia Broadcasting System, 1969), pp. 2–3. [Note: Question numbers and letters correspond to source.]
Source: From *Consumer Behavior*, Second Edition, by James F. Engel, David T. Kollat and Roger D. Blackwell. Copyright © 1968, 1973 by Holt, Rinehart and Winston, Inc. Reprinted by permission of Holt, Rinehart and Winston, Inc.

Research questions related to roles and status are varied. An East Coast firm which designs and manufactures women's clothing asked a sample of women working outside the home to identify the various roles they perform and to describe the most preferred style of clothing for each role. For example, they asked the women to describe how their dresswear for business lunches differed, if at all, from what they might wear for a luncheon sponsored by a women's social club. The intention was to determine whether two different markets existed for noon lunch dresswear. Although the results of this study have been kept confidential for competitive reasons, it is known that differences in dress were found by the research.

Roles are also important in the study of decision making. What, for example, is the relative importance of the roles of husbands and wives relative to one another in making decisions? One method for studying this is to ask questions such as those shown in Exhibit 1. In addition to asking how the decision would be made ideally, subjects are also asked how decisions are in fact made, how important they are, and how often they are made. Responses are then analyzed from the perspective of personality variables, social class, and other social and psychological variables. The kinds of questions that are raised in analyzing these data include the following: Are there differences between husbands and wives on individual items or in their overall response? If so, are these differences related to social class, that is, is there more or less consensus among couples having high social class compared to low social class placement?

Norms   Norms are standardized modes or rules of behavior which establish a range of tolerable activities for the individual in his relationship with other people. Among other things, norms establish what are acceptable and unacceptable products to buy and consume in specific situations. Thus, a very basic research question, particularly when dealing with new products, is whether the good or service is compatible with existing norms among the target consumers. Research is often conducted to determine whether specific promotional approaches are consistent with existing norms. Existing norms are also analyzed to identify and select possible promotional messages. A major midwest advertising agency, for instance, has recently conducted an extensive content analysis of social norms among adolescents in order to find clues for advertising appeals for a campaign to introduce a new soft drink.

Delbert Miller has developed a set of scales measuring norms and patterns of national cultures.[10] This particular set of scales is being used in a study in progress concerning the role of the commercial sector in family planning. The complete instrument covers 20 different patterns or norms. A few are presented in Exhibit 2.

[10] Delbert C. Miller, "The Measurement of International Patterns and Norms: A Tool for Comparative Research," *Southwestern Social Science Quarterly*, Vol. 48 (March 1968), pp. 531–547.

EXHIBIT 1 *Husband-Wife Decision Making*

Each of us has some idea of what a marriage relationship *should* be like. We have a notion of how things *ought* to be; who, for example, has what rights in the marriage. We'd like your opinion this time about who SHOULD make the decisions in a marriage. It's understandable that on any matter, husband and wife might very well discuss the question briefly or at length. Yet, the *final* decision, the *last* word on the subject, may be the right of only *one* of the marriage partners. On the other hand, some questions, you may believe, should be resolved only by compromise or joint decision where both husband and wife would have equal rights in the matter. (Remember, we're interested in how you think things *should* be, not necessarily how they really are in most relationships.)

The rating scale here, once again, has five points. Unlike the previous scales, the numbers have nothing to do with "more or less." The rating asks simply: Who, in your opinion, should have the final say in this decision?

Wife always or nearly always	1
Wife most of the time	2
Husband and/or wife—equally, by compromise, or in a joint decision	3
Husband most of the time	4
Husband always or nearly always	5

Rate each item quickly after studying the rating scale.

1 2 ③ 4 5	When to try to have children
1 2 ③ 4 5	When and how to punish children for misbehavior
1 2 ③ 4 5	How many children to have
1 2 ③ 4 5	Where to go for an evening's entertainment
1 2 ③ 4 5	Buying an electrical appliance
1 2 ③ 4 5	Buying household furnishings
1 2 ③ 4 5	Which school a child should attend
1 2 ③ 4 5	Choice of radio or TV program
1 2 ③ 4 5	What birth control procedures should be used
1 2 ③ 4 5	When to have sexual intercourse
1 2 ③ 4 5	Where to go on a vacation
1 2 ③ 4 5	What doctor to go to if someone is sick
1 2 ③ 4 5	Whether or not the wife should work
1 2 ③ 4 5	Whether or not to buy life insurance
1 2 ③ 4 5	What car to get
1 2 ③ 4 5	When a child must be home at night
1 2 ③ 4 5	When a child must be in bed at night

A commercial health clinic specializing in surgical contraception was recently concerned with how the norms of reference groups as perceived by potential patients or clients influenced the potential clients' behavior. One task was to determine whether various reference groups were perceived as

EXHIBIT 2 *Miller's Scale Battery of International Patterns and Norms*

Delbert C. Miller
Indiana University

Respondent: Kindly check if you are male or female and indicate years lived in native country and in other countries. Sign your name and give your address if you wish a final report. Read the accompanying directions carefully before you begin. Thank you.

Check: Male_____ Female_____

Years lived in:
Native Country _____
Other Countries _____

(Optional)
Name: _____
Address: _____

1. SOCIAL ACCEPTANCE

1	2	3	4	5	6
High social acceptance. Social contacts open and non-restrictive. Introductions not needed for social contacts. Short acquaintance provides entry into the home and social organizations.		Medium social acceptance. Ready acceptance in neighborhood and in community organizations but not in family and social life. Friendly in business and other public contacts.		Low social acceptance. Acceptance in specifically designated groups in which membership has been validated. Sponsored introduction is needed for social contacts in all parts of community life.	

2. STANDARDS OF PERSONAL AND COMMUNITY HEALTH

1	2	3	4	5	6
High standards of personal and community health valued in all parts of society. Hygienic habits valued		Varied. High community standards for water and sewage. Personal habits and community standards for cleanliness and hygiene vary widely across the community.		Personal and community standards of hygiene are not valued highly.	

157

EXHIBIT 2 *(continued)*

3. CONCERN FOR AND TRUST OF OTHERS

1	2	3	4	5	6
High concern for others. Respect for the motives and integrity of others. Mutual trust prevails.		Moderate or uneven pattern of concern for and trust of others.		Lack of concern for others and lack of trust.	

4. CONFIDENCE IN PERSONAL SECURITY AND PROTECTION OF PROPERTY

1	2	3	4	5	6
High confidence in personal security. Free movement, night and day, for both sexes. High sense of security of property. Locking of homes is optional.		Moderate confidence in personal security. Confidence of men is high in personal security but women are warned to take precautions. Movements of women restricted to daytime. Simple property precautions essential.		'Low confidence in both personal security and protection of property. Men and women restrict all movement at night to predetermined precautions. Many property precautions obligatory. Extensive use of locks, dogs, and guards.	

5. FAMILY SOLIDARITY

1	2	3	4	5	6
High solidarity with many obligations of kinship relations within large, extended family system.		Relations of solidarity within a limited kinship circle with specified obligations only.		Small, loosely integrated, independent family with highly specific individual relations.	

6. INDEPENDENCE OF THE CHILD

1	2	3	4	5	6
Child is raised to be self-reliant and independent in both thought and action.		Child is given specified areas of independence only.		Child is raised to be highly dependent and docile.	

7. MORAL CODE AND ROLE DEFINITIONS OF MEN AND WOMEN

1	2	3	4	5	6
Single code of morality prevails for men and women. Separate occupational and social roles are not defined for men and women. Similar amounts and standards of education prevail.		Variations between moral definitions for men and women exist for certain specified behaviors. Occupational and social role definitions vary in degree. Varying educational provisions for the sexes.		Double code of morality prevails. Separate occupational and social roles for men and women exist and are sharply defined. Amount and standards of education vary widely between the sexes.	

8. DEFINITION OF RELIGION AND MORAL CONDUCT

1	2	3	4	5	6
Belief in the sacred interpretation of life as primary explanation of purpose of life and role of death. Emphasis is placed on importance of worshiper role in fulfilling spiritual obligations and duties.		Belief in supreme being a sacred purpose for life. Emphasis is placed on secular interpretation of moral values and importance of applying them to daily conduct.		Belief in secular interpretation of life. Emphasis on importance of achieving the good society for achieving the good life. Moral values prescribed by social and scientific definitions of human well being in the society. Emphasis on social conduct as moral conduct.	

9. CLASS STRUCTURE AND CLASS CONSCIOUSNESS

1	2	3	4	5	6
Highly conscious of class differences. Extensive use of status symbols. Social classes and social circles rigidly defined. Very small upward class movement. Contacts between classes limited by social distinctions. Private schools predominate for upper social groups.		Class consciousness prevails moderately. Upward class movement occurs but definite characteristics mark off and limit contact between classes.		Class consciousness low. Class differences devalued. Minimal use of status symbols. Considerable upward class movement. Relatively free social contacts between social classes. Public schools dominate for all social classes.	

EXHIBIT 2 *(continued)*

10. CONSENSUS OVER GENERAL PHILOSOPHY AND OBJECTIVES OF THE SOCIETY

1 2	3 4	5 6
High concensus over philosophy and objectives of the society as achieved either through evolution or revolution. Competition and conflict between parties takes place within generally accepted goals of the society. Stable governments usually prevail.	Consensus is partial. Differing ideological systems conflict. Stable government may be maintained but under threat of overthrow.	Absence of consensus (or very low) over philosophy and objectives of the society. Conflicting and splinter parties may represent the divergent ideologies and cleavages. Unstable governments prevail.

11. LABOR'S ORIENTATION TO THE PREVAILING ECONOMIC AND SOCIAL SYSTEM

1 2	3 4	5 6
Highly alienated. Ideologically opposed to the prevailing economic and social system. Revolutionary in orientation.	Antagonistic. Partly alienated with some unions ideologically in support and some in opposition to prevailing economic and social system.	Highly assimilated. Ideologically in agreement with prevailing economic and social system: Labor disputes over distribution shares of goods and services to working people but accepts on-going system.

12. BELIEF IN DEMOCRATIC POLITICAL SYSTEM

1 2	3 4	5 6
Strongly committed. Deep and persistent belief in the democratic processes regardless of problems or crisis.	Reserved commitment. Belief in democracy as process requiring careful control against mass abuse. Accepts necessity of dictatorial intervention in crisis situations or special safeguard such as one-party systems, relinquishing freedoms in internal crises, etc.	Lack of belief in democracy as political system. Regarded as weak and ineffectual in the solving of problems and improving the lot of the average man. Generally regarded as dangerous because it exposes government to mob psychology.

13. DEFINITION OF WORK AND INDIVIDUAL ACHIEVEMENT

1	2	3	4	5	6
A belief in hard work as obligation to self, employer, and God. Efficiency values accepted. Individual is expected to progress in his work life.		Work is important to the advancement of self and family. Efficiency values accepted. Achievement expectations vary.		Lack of belief in hard work. Work is regarded as necessary, but involves no obligation beyond delivery of minimum services. Efficiency values rejected. Individual is expected only to maintain family status at his inherited level.	

14. CIVIC PARTICIPATION AND VOLUNTARY ACTIVITY

1	2	3	4	5	6
High civic activity. People work together to get things done for the community. High identity with volunteer groups. Civic participation and volunteer activity in groups is an important source of social prestige. Moral and altruistic motives are important sources of motivation.		Moderate activity in special areas. Organized participation exists for economic or political self-interest but often is lacking for a general community need.		Low civic activity, often deliberately avoided with no social sanctions. Low identity with volunteer groups. Civic participation is not an important source of prestige. Mistrust of motives is common since self-interest is generally assumed as the principal motivation for all persons.	

15. DEFINITION OF THE ROLE OF PRIVATE AND PUBLIC OWNERSHIP OF PROPERTY

1	2	3	4	5	6
Strong belief in the right of private property for all persons in all types of goods. Private ownership and control of means of production is accepted for all industries and services except for a few natural monopolies (i.e. water, post office, etc.)		Belief in the wide mixture of private ownership and public ownership in all industries and services. Public ownership of large basic industries (steel, coal, electricity, etc.) and services (transport and communication) is especially common.		Strong belief in the public ownership and governmental controls of all industries and services except for small enterprises. Private ownership accepted in the ownership of personal goods.	

161

EXHIBIT 2 *(continued)*

16. STANDARDS OF HONESTY AND INTEGRITY OF GOVERNMENT OFFICIALS

1	2	3	4	5	6
Government officials at all levels have a high standard of honesty and integrity. Violations are prosecuted vigorously and punished with appropriate penalties.		Government officials are generally honest but there are differences in the honesty of officials at different levels. Violations do occur and are prosecuted. The certainty of detection and the severity of penalty varies according to differing practices.		Government officials at all levels commonly engage in various kinds of corrupt practices. Most violations are seldom prosecuted. Occasionally token prosecutions are made when abuse becomes excessive.	

17. POLITICAL INFLUENCE OF FOREIGN ENTERPRISE ON HOST GOVERNMENT

1	2	3	4	5	6
Foreign enterprise has marked political influence on major economic and political policies of the nation. It can resist attempted nationalization of its own enterprises and enforce favorable trade and political relations.		Foreign enterprise does have significant political influence over certain economic conditions of its special concern, but it has no real influence over political policy and process within the host country.		Foreign enterprise has no real influence over national policies—economic or political. Host government may enforce strict control over all foreign enterprise but often permits foreign enterprise to operate within same set of guidelines as domestic firms.	

18. ENCOURAGEMENT OF FOREIGN ENTERPRISE

1	2	3	4	5	6
All foreign enterprise is strongly encouraged to invest and operate businesses of all kinds throughout the country.		Selected forms of foreign investment are encouraged. Use of foreign management personnel may be discouraged.		Foreign investment and operation of enterprise is discouraged by official and unofficial means.	

19. DEGREE OF NEPOTISM IN ORGANIZATIONAL LIFE

1	2	3	4	5	6
	Family members of owners, managers, clerical, and manual workers are given preferential and sometimes privileged opportunities for employment in all types of organizations.			Merit and training is the sole basis for selection of all persons in all types of organizations.	

Family members of owners, managers, and professionals are given priority within organizations owned or managed by their relatives.

20. DEGREE OF EXPECTED RECIPROCITY IN FAVORS AND REWARDS

1	2	3	4	5	6
	Pattern of expected reciprocity in favors prevails in regard to economic or political support given to individual or political support given to individual or group. Personal basis of contact is encouraged and reciprocity is expected by a returned favor (or gift) in near future.	Reciprocity is expected only in specific situations when both parties have a written or oral agreement to exchange political and social support for services rendered.		No pattern of expected reciprocity prevails in economic or political life. Favors or special gifts for service and business rendered is regarded as self-serving and "wrong."	

Source: Delbert C. Miller, *Handbook of Research Design and Social Measurement*, 2nd ed. (New York: David McKay Company, 1970), pp. 333–338.

having favorable or unfavorable norms. A sample of the questions used to determine this is presented in Exhibit 3.

EXHIBIT 3 *How would you expect your decision to have a vasectomy to be looked upon by your:*

	Very Approving	Approve	Don't Care	Dis-approve	Very Dis-approving
(a) Parents and inlaws	1	2	3	4	5
(b) Siblings	1	2	3	4	5
(c) Other relatives	1	2	3	4	5
(d) Friends	1	2	3	4	5

Social Class A social class is a category—a situation of people with roughly similar status ranking in a particular community or society. It is important to note that there exists no single class structure in the United States which is accepted as completely valid. Many systems of social stratification exist simultaneously. Social class structure has been determined in several ways: *reputationally*, by asking many respondents to rank people they know in the community in which they live; *sociometrically*, through asking people about and observing those with whom they associate; *subjectively*, by asking individuals to rate themselves on social class; and *objectively*, rating them on the basis of one or another variable used as criteria for stratification. These last include income, education, and occupation. The so-called objective method is used most frequently in applied research.

Social class influences are pervasive. Social class influences the probability of being born at all and in the end, the type of funeral a person is given by his survivors. Social class has been found to be associated with the purchase of particular foods, the use of credit cards, and preferences in clothing to mention just a few. A major Chicago suburban bank found that compared to the community as a whole, a disproportionately large number of users of a special checking account plan consisted of upper-middle-class people. The same research determined that the media reading and listening habits of this group were very similar, thus enabling the bank to place its advertisements more selectively and reach more of this particularly responsive group. The basic questions in the research, then, were "What is the social class distribution among users of the special plan?" and "What is the communication behavior of the various social class groupings?" Questions of this nature are commonly asked in consumer research.

One reason social class has been researched in marketing is that it is considered to be a determinant of life style, particularly leisure-time activities. Leisure-time activities express themselves in the consumption of many goods and services and account for an ever increasing proportion of individual and family income. One instrument used in marketing to measure the use of and enjoyment of leisure time is presented in Exhibit 4.

EXHIBIT 4   *Your Leisure-Time Activities*

The use of leisure time is supposed to be an increasingly important social problem. We want to know how people usually spend their leisure time. Here is a list of activities. On the left side of the page put a circle around the number that tells how often you do these things now, using the key at the top of the column. On the right side of the page put a circle around the number that tells how well you like these things, using the key at the top of the column. If you never do the activity mentioned, circle number one in the left column to indicate no participation, and circle no number on the right side of the page. Try not to skip any item.

How Often Do You Do These Things
1. Never
2. Rarely
3. Occasionally
4. Fairly often
5. Frequently

How Well Do You Like These Things
1. Dislike very much
2. Dislike
3. Indifferent
4. Like
5. Like very much

How Often Do You Do These Things
1. Never
2. Rarely
3. Occasionally
4. Fairly often
5. Frequently

How Well Do You Like These Things
1. Dislike very much
2. Dislike
3. Indifferent
4. Like
5. Like very much

How Often Do You Do These Things
1. Never
2. Rarely
3. Occasionally
4. Fairly often
5. Frequently

How Well Do You Like These Things
1. Dislike very much
2. Dislike
3. Indifferent
4. Like
5. Like very much

---

1 2 3 4 5	1. Amateur dramatics	1 2 3 4 5
1 2 3 4 5	2. Amusement parks and halls	1 2 3 4 5
1 2 3 4 5	3. Art work (individual)	1 2 3 4 5
1 2 3 4 5	4. Attending large social functions (balls, benefit bridge, etc.)	1 2 3 4 5
1 2 3 4 5	5. Attending small social entertainments (dinner parties, etc.)	1 2 3 4 5
1 2 3 4 5	6. Book reading for pleasure	1 2 3 4 5
1 2 3 4 5	7. Conventions	1 2 3 4 5
1 2 3 4 5	8. Conversation with family	1 2 3 4 5
1 2 3 4 5	9. Card playing	1 2 3 4 5
1 2 3 4 5	10. Church and related organizations	1 2 3 4 5

EXHIBIT 4 *(continued)*

1 2 3 4 5	11. Dancing	1 2 3 4 5
1 2 3 4 5	12. Dates	1 2 3 4 5
1 2 3 4 5	13. Entertaining at home	1 2 3 4 5
1 2 3 4 5	14. Fairs, exhibitions, etc.	1 2 3 4 5
1 2 3 4 5	15. Informal contacts with friends	1 2 3 4 5
1 2 3 4 5	16. Informal discussions, e.g., "bull sessions"	1 2 3 4 5
1 2 3 4 5	17. Indoor team recreation or sports—basketball, volleyball	1 2 3 4 5
1 2 3 4 5	18. Indoor individual recreation or sports—bowling, gym, pool, billiards, handball	1 2 3 4 5
1 2 3 4 5	19. Knitting, sewing, crocheting, etc.	1 2 3 4 5
1 2 3 4 5	20. Lectures (not class)	1 2 3 4 5
1 2 3 4 5	21. Listening to radio or TV	1 2 3 4 5
1 2 3 4 5	22. Literary writing—poetry, essays, stories, etc.	1 2 3 4 5
1 2 3 4 5	23. Magazine reading (for pleasure)	1 2 3 4 5
1 2 3 4 5	24. Movies	1 2 3 4 5
1 2 3 4 5	25. Newspaper reading	1 2 3 4 5
1 2 3 4 5	26. Odd jobs at home	1 2 3 4 5
1 2 3 4 5	27. Organizations or club meetings as a member	1 2 3 4 5
1 2 3 4 5	28. Organizations or club meetings as a leader (as for younger groups)	1 2 3 4 5
1 2 3 4 5	29. Outdoor individual sports—golf, riding, skating, hiking, tennis	1 2 3 4 5
1 2 3 4 5	30. Outdoor team sports—hockey, baseball, etc.	1 2 3 4 5
1 2 3 4 5	31. Picnics	1 2 3 4 5
1 2 3 4 5	32. Playing musical instrument or singing	1 2 3 4 5
1 2 3 4 5	33. Shopping	1 2 3 4 5
1 2 3 4 5	34. Sitting and thinking	1 2 3 4 5
1 2 3 4 5	35. Spectator of sports	1 2 3 4 5
1 2 3 4 5	36. Symphony or concerts	1 2 3 4 5
1 2 3 4 5	37. Telephone visiting	1 2 3 4 5
1 2 3 4 5	38. Theater attendance	1 2 3 4 5
1 2 3 4 5	39. Traveling or touring	1 2 3 4 5
1 2 3 4 5	40. Using public library	1 2 3 4 5
1 2 3 4 5	41. Visiting museums, art galleries, etc.	1 2 3 4 5
1 2 3 4 5	42. Volunteer work—social service, etc.	1 2 3 4 5
1 2 3 4 5	43. Writing personal letters	1 2 3 4 5
1 2 3 4 5	44. Special hobbies—stamps, photography, shop work, gardening, and others not included above	1 2 3 4 5
1 2 3 4 5	45. Fishing or hunting	1 2 3 4 5
1 2 3 4 5	46. Camping	1 2 3 4 5
1 2 3 4 5	47. Developing and printing pictures	1 2 3 4 5

Source: Delbert C. Miller, *Handbook of Research Design and Social Measurement*, 2nd ed. (New York: David McKay Company, 1970), pp. 295–297.

Decision-Making Processes   It is frequently desirable to measure or monitor the various phases of buyer decision making. Decision making may be defined as "a conscious and human process, involving both individual and social phenomena, based upon factual and value premises, which concludes with a choice of one behavioral activity from among one or more alternatives with the intention of moving toward some desired state of affairs."[11] A decision is, then, an outcome of a mental process which itself cannot be measured directly. Various stages in decision models such as the one presented in Figure 5.3 are abstractions. They are abstractions of some set of mental processes by which the individual recognizes some need or desire, locates alternatives which promise to satisfy the desire, learns more about those alternatives, forms some criteria for evaluation, and on the basis of those criteria, chooses some course of action.

An interesting decision model has been developed by Rogers and Shoemaker emphasizing individual consumer response to innovation. This is presented in Figure 5.5. It consists of knowledge, persuasion, decision, and confirmation. In the first stage the individual is exposed to the innovation's existence and gains some understanding of how it functions. At the persuasion stage he forms favorable or unfavorable attitudes toward the innovation. In the decision stage the individual chooses to adopt or reject the innovation and at the confirmation stage he seeks reinforcement for the decision he has made and may even reverse his decision if exposed to conflicting messages.

This model, as elaborated upon by Rogers and Shoemaker, is especially valuable for new product marketing. It indicates the relative importance of different sources of information at different decision stages, when the product attributes are most likely to become salient, and so forth. Research questions often asked with the guidance of such models include the following: At what decision stages are the various market segments? What sources and types of information are used disproportionately more at particular stages? What are the most relevant attributes of the product or service as perceived by the different consumer groups of concern? At what stage are each of these attributes likely to be most salient? Do individuals with different social and psychological characteristics use different kinds of information? Answers to these research questions provide guidelines for developing the total marketing mix for the particular product and intended market segments. Table 5.4 shows how information collection and purchasing behavior can be mediated by situational, product, personal characteristics, and environmental factors.

Decision-making models also exist for formal organizations. These models are useful as guidelines in formulating research questions for industrial and institutional marketing situations. Examples of research questions often raised

[11] F. A. Shull, A. L. Delbecq, and L. L. Cummings, *Organizational Decision Making* (New York: McGraw-Hill, 1970), p. 31.

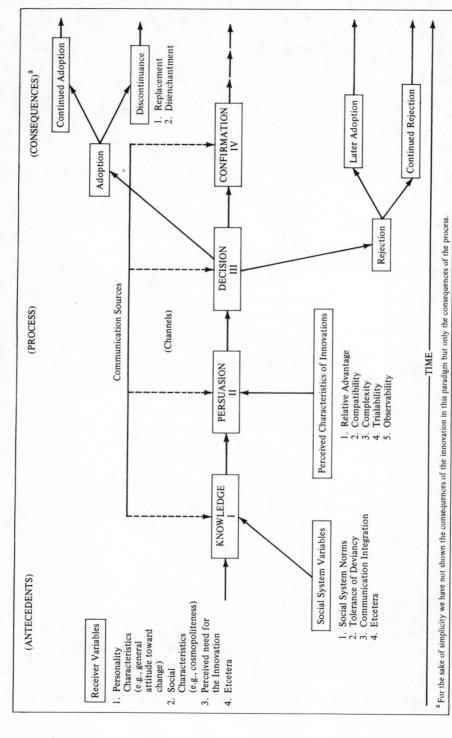

FIGURE 5.5 *A Paradigm of the Innovation-Decision Process*

Source: Everett M. Rogers and F. Floyd Shoemaker, *Communication of Innovations: A Cross-Cultural Approach*, 2d ed., p. 102. Copyright © 1971 by The Free Press, A Division of The Macmillan Company. Reprinted with permission of The Macmillan Company.

[a] For the sake of simplicity we have not shown the consequences of the innovation in this paradigm but only the consequences of the process.

TABLE 5.4 *Determinants of the Type of Decision Process: The Case of the Habitual Decision*

(1) *Situational variable.* Consumers have a higher probability of engaging in extended decision-process behavior when:
   (a) There has been little or no relevant experience because an individual has never purchased the product.
   (b) There is no past experience because the product is new.
   (c) Past experience is perceived as obsolete because the product is purchased infrequently.
   (d) Past experience with the product has been unsatisfactory.
   (e) The purchase is considered to be discretionary rather than necessary.
   (f) The purchase is considered to be particularly important; for example, a gift.
   (g) The purchase is socially "visible."

(2) *Product characteristics.* Extended decision-process behavior is more likely to occur when:
   (a) The consumer feels committed to the product for an extended period of time, so that future needs and/or product performance are difficult to forecast.
   (b) The consumer perceives available alternatives as having both desirable and undesirable attributes.
   (c) The product is high priced relative to the consumer's income.

(3) *Consumer characteristics.* Decision-process behavior is more likely to be extended rather than limited or habitual when:
   (a) The consumer has a college education.
   (b) The consumer is in the middle-income category as opposed to high or low income. (Middle income is defined in this case as $5000–$7500.)
   (c) The consumer is under 35 years old.
   (d) The consumer's occupation falls in the white-collar class.
   (e) The consumer enjoys "shopping around."
   (f) The consumer perceives no urgent or immediate need for the product.

(4) *Environmental factors.* Consumers have a higher probability of engaging in extended decision-process behavior when:
   (a) A difference is perceived between an individual's customary behavior and that of a group to which he belongs and/or an important reference group.
   (b) There is disagreement among family members about requirements and/or the relative desirability of alternatives.
   (c) Strong new stimuli or precipitating circumstances exist. These may consist of general news (threat of war, inflation, and so on) or of news regarding specific products that may be transmitted by advertisers.

Source: From *Consumer Behavior*, Second Edition, by James F. Engel, David T. Kollat and Roger D. Blackwell, Copyright © 1968, 1973 by Holt, Rinehart and Winston, Inc. Reprinted by permission of Holt, Rinehart and Winston, Inc.

in industrial marketing with the assistance of organization decision-making models are: How complex is the organization in terms of the number of different roles? What is the hierarchy of roles in terms of their influence on company decisions? What special approaches are necessary for salesmen to follow when contacting specific role occupants? Does the buying committee, if one exists, make decisions to purchase or primarily function to implement decisions? For example, not long ago a producer of refrigeration equipment asked a marketing research firm to conduct an analysis of the decision-making processes of two of the major types of companies using their products. It was found that in both instances when companies were small, buying committees played the role of information gatherers for top executives who made the decision as to which equipment was to be purchased. When the companies were large, buying committees played a substantially more important role. This information was used to develop more effective selling strategies for salesmen.

Communication   Communications research is a rich source of knowledge for marketers. Especially fruitful has been research in persuasion: "the act of manipulating symbols so as to produce changes in the evaluative or approach-avoidance behavior of those who interpret the symbols."[12] Symbols are words, packages, pictures, all of the various elements of communication which the firm may use to communicate to the consumer. This research tradition is, therefore, of great interest to salesman, researcher, and manager alike.

Research in persuasion can be grouped into several recognized categories. One such can be termed the organization of the persuasive argument: how to present the issues. Another focus is on the persuader: the primary question here is on the credibility level of the communicator and its impact on persuasion. A third focus is on the characteristics of the audience: do personality or sex differences affect the ability of the message to persuade? A fourth category concerns research into the effect of group membership: what is the effect of others on the persuasive message? One last category is concerned with the persistence of effects: if the message changes an attitude, how long will the change remain? These five categories of research are presented in Table 5.5 together with an expanded list of questions with which they are typically concerned.

It is obvious how the study of consumers' behavior to the mass media is related to real marketing problems. Advertising and sales promotion budgets and media buying depend on the knowledge of how many and what kind of people read, watch, or listen to various printed and audio-visual media. But interpersonal influence is just as important. Table 5.6 presents data which

---

[12] Gary Cronkite, *Persuasion: Speech and Behavioral Change* (Indianapolis, Ind.: Bobbs-Merrill, 1969), p. 15.

TABLE 5.5   *Categories of Research in Persuasive Communication*

Organization of the Persuasive Argument

How can you best use fear to influence people?

Do you tell your audience what to think, or do you present the evidence but let them draw their own conclusions?

When should the most important arguments be presented in a persuasive appeal?

Does information change attitudes?

Are emotional appeals more powerful than factual ones?

Is humor an effective persuasive technique?

The Persuader

Does a man have to believe in the persuader before he believes in his message?

Are there ways to enhance the persuasiveness of the low-credibility communicator?

Should a persuader try for a maximum of opinion change or just a little opinion change?

Is a persuasive appeal more readily accepted by listeners who share certain similarities with the communicator?

Characteristics of the Audience

Who is more persuasible, a man or a woman?

Does knowing about someone's personality help you to determine his susceptibility to persuasive appeals?

In order to change someone's opinion, what must you know about his reasons for holding that opinion?

The Influence of Others

How important are such groups as neighbors, family, fellow workers, and friends in molding opinion?

Which members of a group are most easy to persuade?

Is it easier to change an opinion that has been stated publicly, or one that a person keeps to himself?

What kinds of control does the group exercise over its members' opinions?

The Persistence of Opinion Change

Is opinion change at its highest point right after the persuasive communication has ended?

Are there any ways to make the impact of persuasive appeal last longer?

Source: Marvin Karlins and Herbert I. Abelson, *Persuasion: How Opinions and Attitudes Are Changed*, 2nd ed., pp. 5, 41, 69, 83, and 107. Copyright © 1970 by Springer Publishing Company, Inc.

show the usage and importance of various channels in three types of purchase decisions: those concerning small appliances, clothing, and food. Although marketer-controlled communications were most important in bringing items to the respondents' attention, the most important sources of information in the decision process were those which were consumer controlled, primarily interpersonal communications.

TABLE 5.6 *Usage of Information Channels in the Purchase Decision Process*

Channels	Small Appliances			Clothing			Food		
	First	Else	Most Impor-tant	First	Else	Most Impor-tant	First	Else	Most Impor-tant
Marketer-controlled									
Advertising	48	23	8	35	27	16	45	25	19
Salesmen	1	1	1	4	1	6	0	0	0
Sales Promotion*	9	7	9	19	14	32	26	16	27
Nonmarketer-controlled									
Personal influence									
Friends, neigh-bors, relatives†	23	41	53	27	29	33	16	19	29
Immediate family	8	7	11	2	4	0	12	12	21
Professional advice	6	8	13	0	0	0	1	0	0
Editorial and news material‡	1	0	1	6	6	6	0	0	1
No mentions	4	13	4	7	19	7	0	28	3
Total (*N* = 99)	100%	100%	100%	100%	100%	100%	100%	100%	100%

Note: Three questions were asked:
"Could you tell me how this product came to your attention for the *very first time?*"
"How *else* did you hear about this product before you bought it?"
"Which *one* of these ways was your *most important* source of information in your decision to buy this product?"
* Includes sampling, displays, in-store shopping, packaging.
† Includes actual discussions as well as noticing the item or trying the item, for example, in the home of a friend.
‡ Includes *Consumer Reports.*
Source: From *Innovative Behavior and Communication* by Thomas S. Robertson. Copyright © 1971 by Holt, Rinehart and Winston, Inc. Reprinted by permission of Holt, Rinehart and Winston, Inc.

A common research question both in consumer and industrial marketing involves identifying opinion leaders. Opinion leaders are persons who influence the thoughts and behaviors of other individuals through interpersonal communication. Opinion leaders may be actively sought for advice or may actually seek out persons whom he can influence. Also, neither the leader nor follower may be explicitly aware of the influence process occurring. Opinion leaders for specific product or service categories are known to share common social-psychological traits and behaviors and hence, once identified, can be approached through strategies which take advantage of this information. A nationally known clothing apparel manufacturer has just launched a research program to determine first whether fashion leaders exist for clothing apparel among male college students and, if so, what types of communication media such students use to keep informed of developments in men's fashions. They intend to use this information for planning their next year's advertising strategies.

Motivation　Motives are inner striving conditions or energizers described as wishes, desires, or drives which activate behavior toward particular goals. The drives that constitute motivation are of two basic types: *biogenic* and *sociogenic*. Biogenic motives include hunger, sex, and survival needs, while sociogenic motives include hopes, fears, and opinions. There is of course a relationship between both types of motives; each type in some ways conditions some motives in the other category.

Maslow suggests a more comprehensive classification.[13] Instead of speaking of two distinct classes of motives, he hypothesized that motives were ordered hierarchically in terms of the importance of their being satisfied. His classification proceeds from lowest to highest as shown in Figure 5.6. Maslow theorized that the lower needs (hunger, thirst, and so on) must be fulfilled before the higher needs become operative.

Traditional marketing literature has distinguished motives on a somewhat different basis.[14] It has spoken of (a) primary and selective; (b) rational and emotional; (c) patronage; and (d) conscious and dormant motives.

1. *Primary buying motives*: Those that lead to the purchase of a class of article or service.
   Selective buying motives: Those that determine choice within the product class.
2. *Rational motives*: Those in which external and measurable product features are reasons for purchase (economy, durability, and so on).
   Emotional motives: Those which are psychological, sociological, or cultural in nature (conformity, pride, and so on).
3. *Patronage motives*: Those which determine the source from which a purchase will be made.
4. *Conscious motives*: Those which are felt and experienced by the buyer without intervention by the marketer.
   Dormant motives: Those which are unrecognized and must be brought to the buyer's attention.

Engel stated that the role of "the motivation researcher is to discover with a useful degree of accuracy the *balance* of objective performance factors and subjective emotional factors underlying a consumer's purchase decision."[15]

---

[13] A. H. Maslow, *Motivation and Personality* (New York: Harper & Row, 1954).

[14] James F. Engel, David T. Kollat, and Roger D. Blackwell, *Consumer Behavior* (Holt, Rinehart and Winston, 1968), chap. 4, pp. 59–61.

[15] James F. Engel, "Motivation Research—Magic or Menace?" *Michigan Business Review*, Vol. 13 (March 1961), p. 29.

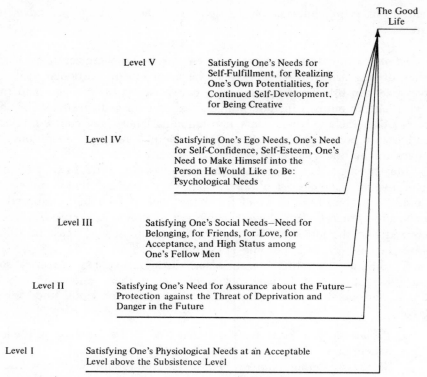

The Good
Life

Level V   Satisfying One's Needs for
Self-Fulfillment, for Realizing
One's Own Potentialities, for
Continued Self-Development,
for Being Creative

Level IV   Satisfying One's Ego Needs, One's Need
for Self-Confidence, Self-Esteem, One's
Need to Make Himself into the
Person He Would Like to Be:
Psychological Needs

Level III   Satisfying One's Social Needs—Need for
Belonging, for Friends, for Love, for
Acceptance, and High Status among
One's Fellow Men

Level II   Satisfying One's Need for Assurance about the Future—
Protection against the Threat of Deprivation and
Danger in the Future

Level I   Satisfying One's Physiological Needs at an Acceptable
Level above the Subsistence Level

FIGURE 5.6 *Maslow's Five-Level Need Hierarchy*
Source: Diagram by M. H. Jones, *Marketing Process*, Data on "Hierarchy of Needs"
from *Motivation and Personality*, 2nd Edition, by Abraham H. Maslow (Harper &
Row, 1970).

Some examples of the use of research into consumer motivations are those
which have related self-concept and self-confidence in automobile purchases.
These are both related to what Maslow referred to as the *need for self-esteem*
and the *need for self-actualization*. Grubbs and Hupp[16] found rather clear-cut
relationships between self-concept and the make of car purchased. Bell[17] was
concerned with the methods used by buyers to protect themselves from being
persuaded to make a purchase in instances where they lacked self-confidence.
He found that those with high general self-confidence and low specific self-
confidence were motivated to seek help in purchasing. These buyers used
"purchase pals" to lend support in their negotiations.

In general, market researchers have not found research in motivation

[16] Edward L. Grubbs and Gregg Hupp, "Perception of Self, Generalized Stereotypes,
and Brand Selection," *Journal of Marketing*, Vol. V, No. 1 (February 1968), pp. 58–63.
[17] Gerald D. Bell, "Self-Confidence and Persuasion in Car Buying," *Journal of Marketing*, Vol. IV, No. 1 (February 1967)), pp. 46–53.

to be very rewarding in terms of using motivations to predict consumer purchases. Research in motivation has been useful for generating ideas.

Personality   Personality theory has been in a process of reevaluation in both marketing and psychology since the early 1960s. This is not to say that personality is not useful to marketers. More accurately, personality is too complex a concept to be used as an inexpensive, quick, and reliable predictor of mass consumer behavior. Its role lies in aiding the one who will put in the effort to *understand better* the complex nature of human behavior.

Personality is defined as "the configuration of individual characteristics and ways of behaving which determines an individual's unique adjustments to his environment."[18] In describing or appraising personality, many schemes have been advanced. A sample from one test, the California Psychological Inventory, is presented in Figure 5.7. This test measures some 18 traits. Individuals respond to each statement indicating with an "X" on a special answer sheet whether they feel it is true or not true of them. A special "mask" is then placed over the answer sheet allowing only those responses which indicate a dominance orientation to show. The number of X's are then tallied

46. I think I would like the work of a school teacher.

47. Women should not be allowed to drink in cocktail bars.

48. Most people would tell a lie if they could gain by it.

49. When someone does me a wrong I feel I should pay him back if I can, just for the principle of the thing.

50. I seem to be about as capable and smart as most others around me.

51. Every family owes it to the city to keep their sidewalks cleared in the winter and their lawn mowed in the summer.

52. I usually take an active part in the entertainment at parties.

68. I am embarrassed by dirty stories.

69. I would disapprove of anyone's drinking to the point of intoxication at a party.

70. Sometimes I cross the street just to avoid meeting someone.

71. I get excited very easily.

72. I used to keep a diary.

73. Maybe some minority groups do get rough treatment, but it's no business of mine.

74. It is very hard for me to tell anyone about myself.

75. We ought to worry about our own country and let the rest of the world take care of itself.

76. I often feel as if the world was just passing me by.

X	X		X		X					X	X	X	X		X		X	X								X	X		X
31	32	33	34	35	36	37	38	39	40	41	42	43	44	45	46	47	48	49	50	51	52	53	54	55	56	57	58	59	60
		X	X		X												X		X	X		X	X	X	X			X	

X	X		X				X		X								X	X		X	X				X	X		X	
61	62	63	64	65	66	67	68	69	70	71	72	73	74	75	76	77	78	79	80	81	82	83	84	85	86	87	88	89	90
		X		X	X	X			X		X	X	X	X	X			X	X			X			X		X		X

FIGURE 5.7
Source: California Psychological Inventory

[18] Ernest R. Hilgard, *Introduction to Personality*, 3rd ed. (New York: Harcourt Brace Jovanovich, 1962), p. 447.

TABLE 5.7   *Properties Commonly Used to Describe or Assess Personality*

1. Physique or Temperament
Physical endowments of bodily size, grace, strength, appearance because these affect the manner in which the individual affects and interacts with others and in the way they affect his image of himself. Temperament, an individual characteristic mood, because it is thought to be influenced by inherited physiological patterns.

2. Intellectual and Other Abilities
Intellectual and skill abilities (musical, for example) because they influence what the individual is capable of doing and responding to.

3. Interests and Values
The kinds of things any individual likes to do, enjoys, or appreciates are a reflection of personality.

4. Social Attitudes
Attitudes toward aspects of contemporary culture reveal aspects of the individual's personality such as authoritarianism, dogmatism, and so on.

5. Motivational Dispositions
Motivational dispositions (need for achievement, for example), whether conscious or not, reveal facets of personality.

6. Expressive and Stylistic Traits
Many expressive and stylistic traits (politeness, talkativeness, hesitancy, sociability) seem somewhat independent of content or situation (that is, are exhibited at home, in the office, at social gatherings) and are used to characterize individuals.

7. Pathological Trends
A method of describing a normal person by the extent to which he differs from others in the direction of one or another mental illness.

Source: Adapted from Ernest R. Hilgard, *Introduction to Personality*, 3rd ed. (New York: Harcourt Brace Jovanovich, 1962), pp. 452–453; 1967, pp. 487–488.

to determine the raw score on this trait. Table 5.7 summarizes some common properties of individuals often used to assess personality.

The concept of personality and the availability of short, pencil and paper personality inventories early sent marketers into the field ready to correlate purchasing behavior with personality types and traits.[19] Intuitively, it seemed that there were ready relationships between the traits such as "impulsiveness" or "sociability" and the buying behavior of consumers, or so it seemed. Those early studies showed otherwise. Franklin Evans[20] used the Edwards Personal

[19] For a complete review of the role of personality in marketing, see Harold H. Kassarjian, "Personality and Consumer Behavior: A Review," *Journal of Marketing Research*, Vol. 8 (November 1971).

Preference Schedule to test for personality differences between Ford and Chevrolet owners but found that he could account for only 63 percent of the variance, barely better than chance (50 percent). Demographics, on the other hand, predicted correctly in 70 percent of the cases. Later, however, Westfall[21] was able to differentiate between standard, compact, and convertible car owners, using the Thurstone Temperament Schedule. Koponen[22] in a large-scale study using the J. Walter Thompson consumer panel and the Edwards personality profile was able to account for less than 10 percent of the variance in purchase behavior. More recent studies by Sparks and Tucker[23] and Alpert[24] have been more sophisticated and have yielded more satisfactory results.

Alpert, somewhat like Westfall earlier, hypothesized that the important relationship was not that which existed between personality and the brand but between personality and "the relative importance a buyer places upon various product attributes."[25] Moreover, both he and Sparks and Tucker recognized that there are complex interactions among traits and products.

Using cluster analysis, a sophisticated multivariate statistical technique, Sparks and Tucker found that males who used shampoo, alcoholic beverages, cigarettes, and were fashion adopters were best described as sociable, emotionally stable, and irresponsible. A second cluster was composed of users of headache remedies, mouthwash, late fashion adoption, and infrequent use of after-shave lotion. These were described as sociability, cautiousness, and emotional instability. They summarized as follows:

> This seems to be exactly the kind of relationship personality theory implies; not a simple connection between sociability and fashion adoption, but a more complex one in which sociability combined with emotional stability and irresponsibility is oriented toward one sort of action while sociability combined with emotional instability and cautiousness is oriented toward its opposite.[26]

[20] Franklin B. Evans, "Psychological and Objective Factors in the Prediction of Brand Choice: Ford vs. Chevrolet," *Journal of Business,* Vol. 32 (1959), pp. 340–369.

[21] Ralph Westfall, "Psychological Factors in Predicting Product Choice," *Journal of Marketing,* Vol. 26 (April 1962), pp. 34–40.

[22] A. Koponen, "Personality Characteristics of Purchasers," *Journal of Advertising Research,* Vol. 1 (1960), pp. 6–12.

[23] David L. Sparks and W. T. Tucker, "A Multivariate Analysis of Personality and Product Use," *Journal of Marketing,* Vol. VIII (February 1971) pp. 67–70.

[24] Mark I. Alpert, "Personality and the Determinants of Product Choice," *Journal of Marketing,* Vol. IX (1972), pp. 89–92.

[25] *Ibid.,* p. 88.

[26] James F. Engel, Henry F. Fiorillo, and Murray A. Cayley, *Market Segmentation: Concepts and Application* (New York: Holt, Rinehart and Winston, 1972), p. 181.

For other examples of the use of attitudes see Harper W. Boyd, Jr., Michael L. Ray, and Edward C. Strong, "An Attitudinal Framework for Advertising Strategy," *Journal of Marketing,* Vol. 36 (April 1972), pp. 27–33; Dik Warren Twedt, "How Does Brand Awareness-Attitude Affect Marketing Strategy," *Journal of Marketing,* Vol. 31 (October 1967), pp. 64–66; Frank M. Bass and W. Wayne Talarzyk, "An Attitude Model for the Study of Brand Preference," *Journal of Marketing Research,* Vol. IX (February 1972), pp. 93–96.

Summary

Consumer behavior research is one of the most challenging and difficult of all marketing tasks to perform in an effective manner. Many of the basic approaches, concepts, and processes used in consumer research have been presented. It is to be stressed, however, that these topics have only been touched on the surface and many other important topics could not be addressed at all.

Questions and Exercises

1. A national chain of department stores has been faced with an increasing decline in its share of the market. Management believes it is because changes are occurring among consumers that are not being evaluated adequately by the firm. The management has hired you to head a major research project studying consumer behavior. Describe how the decision process models presented in this chapter might be used to guide the research project.
2. Select one of the behavioral concepts presented in the chapter and suggest how information about this concept would be collected and used for a specific product.
3. Briefly discuss the relative importance of each of the four relevant roles of analysis in the following situations: purchase of toothpaste for a family, purchase of office furniture for a firm. Who is likely to play each role?
4. Looking at the models of consumer behavior presented in the chapter, which variables seem to be of particular importance in the decision-making process?
5. Develop a model of consumer behavior for a purchase decision that you are interested in investigating. In the model indicate how the variables which you plan to measure (such as demographics, past experience, personality, and so on) relate to each other and to the stages in the consumer decision process. (Refer to the consumer behavior models presented in this chapter.)
6. Give an example of how and why culture may influence clothing styles. How can marketers use knowledge of cultural variables?
7. How are the concepts of roles and status related to the relevant roles of analysis? For example, does the *status* of a *user* influence the importance of that role in the decision-making process? Give examples.
8. Social class has been suggested as a determinant of life style. How does this concept relate to the purchase of a car? How might you measure social class without using the traditional demographic indi-

cators such as income, education, and occupation? Could you accurately guess an individual's social class simply by observation?

9. Give examples of products which require habitual decision making and extended decision making.

10. How would a questionnaire designed to measure consumer behavior for a habitually purchased product differ from one for a product requiring extended decision making? Would the relevant variables differ?

11. What are audience characteristics? Discuss how these characteristics might influence consumer response to a particular product.

12. Why are opinion leaders an important focus in marketing research? How can such persons be identified? Who are relevant opinion leaders for clothing purchases?

13. List the motives which should be considered in investigating consumer behavior in the purchase of a new car, a box of cereal, a television set. Why are these motives important?

Project Related Questions

1. What is the most important unit of analysis in your study or project? The individual consumer? The family? A buying committee in a large firm? An industry? And so forth.

2. What are the important roles for you to study in your project? How important is the buyer compared to the decision maker?

3. Are different roles performed by the same or different persons?

4. Of what value to your project are the different models of buyer behavior which can be found in the literature?

5. List the various behavioral concepts or variables which you are using in your project. Have you defined these well enough?

6. How do the various behavioral concepts relate to one another?

7. Do you anticipate problems in measuring these concepts?

8. What behavioral concepts have you explicitly excluded from your study?

Maria Buys a Mustang[*]

The case reported below concerns the purchase of automobiles. What are the particular psychological and sociological factors affecting Maria's decision and general behavior? Develop a behavioral model of the buying process reported here. How does your model resemble those mentioned in this chapter?

"M" is a 23-year-old social studies high school teacher who is leaving the Chicago Public School System to take a teaching position in a suburban, DuPage County school with a proposed salary of $10,000 commencing fall of 1974. She presently rooms with a friend on the Near North side of Chicago. Faced with the alternatives of staying in Chicago and commuting to work or moving to DuPage, she decided to buy a car.

> We had just renewed our lease and I couldn't pick up and go leaving my roommate with all that rent to pay by herself, and I hate to move—crating and hauling stuff all over, and professional movers just cost too much. The last time we moved I rented one of those U-Haul vans and drove it myself—I was a nervous wreck. . . . Besides, who wants to live out THERE—there's nothing going on at night. . . . I hate to even ride buses, much less a train, and with a car I could drive on vacations and save all kinds of money. . . .

Her first step was to get copies of the *Consumer Reports* issues that had articles about cars. Her parents had been getting this magazine, and she remembered having seen issues comparing popular models in established classes: compact, midsize, luxury, and so on. She borrowed two copies, one that compared the compacts—Vega, Pinto, Datsun, and so on—and the other dealing with sporty models—Firebird, Nova, Mustang and, so on.

> The articles in the CU journals were very pessimistic—they had little good to say about any of the models tested. Performance-wise they all have their faults, I guess it's service that counts. . . .

Admittedly, M's preference in automobiles tended toward the sporty, slightly-larger-than-compact models. Pontiac Firebirds had been her long-time favorites, although she had never ridden in nor driven one. A friend had a Pontiac Grand Prix, she liked its ride and assumed that the two were similar:

* Prepared by Kathleen M. Byborny.

After all, they're made by the same people.

Her decision to "buy a car" was made just prior to the running of the Auto Show in McCormick Place. At the show, M toured the floor gathering pamphlets and brochures and did not hesitate, when reaching the Pontiac exhibit, to get into the driver's seat of the Firebird model.

> The seats were too low to the ground and the console was really ugly—it looked like cheap plastic and stuck out between the buckets like a sore thumb. And the sticker price was high—I hadn't been thinking realistically about price— just looks—and I loved the way it looked, really sleek and sexy. What I liked about it the most was the front bumper—all rubber and no chrome—chrome can really look bad after a while.

M had gone to the Auto Show with her sister, "A," who made it a point of telling M how much she didn't like Firebirds.

> She kept telling me how nice a Mustang was—that was only be- cause the guy she had just broken up with drove a '68 yellow one. A hadn't really gotten over breaking up with him yet.

They did, however, "in deference to A" go to the Mustang model:

> It was okay—they showed a Mach I. I didn't like the sports roof, I thought it would be hard to see out the rear window with such a slant.

They looked at all the cars and ex- hibits at the Show; M wasn't actively comparing models because at that stage, although with an admitted mini- mum of thought on the subject, she figured that when she finally walked into an automobile showroom to com- plete a sale, it would be for a Firebird.

In the following weeks, she told her fellow workers of her decision to buy a car. "Great—what kind?" they would ask, to which she generally re- plied "A Firebird, I guess," until she started getting bad feedback from pre- vious Firebird owners.

> All of a sudden it was open season on Firebirds—everyone was telling me how they kept breaking down all the time—not just for minor re- pairs, but incidents when the car just gave up and wouldn't run for days, and then would start up again like nothing had happened. I fin- ally realized that maybe a Fire- bird wouldn't be a good idea, with all the mileage I would be putting on. I had for so long assumed that I would get one, after that, I didn't know what to do.

At that time, A came back into the picture with news that her friend "P" had just bought a used 1971 Mustang hardtop.

> I went to see it—there was nothing spectacular about it. It was an ugly sea green color with black interior and roof. I mean, it was okay, but not my idea of a great looking car. Besides it was used—I'd never get a used car—why put up with other people's cast-offs?

As it happened, M went bowling with her sister A and sister's girlfriend P a short time later. Upon leaving the alleys, walking through the parking lot to P's "ugly green" car, M's eye caught:

> this great looking Mustang. A told me that it was a '71 Mach I—it really looked different than the one at the (Auto) Show. It was a bright lime green color, it was dark outside so I couldn't see the interior. The front end was something like the Firebird, all rubber and no chrome. I still didn't like the back (sports roof) but other than that it was real sporty—I must have walked around it five times. Finally I got into P's car and we left.

After continued badgering and reminders from A about how much M liked that car that night, M went, one Sunday afternoon, with her parents to a large Ford dealership to look at and price the 1973 Mustang models. In the showroom they had a "USA Special" model, white with blue and red trimmings.

> That car (USA Special) was really pretty—but white cars get old-looking fast. They had a yellow green Mach I there, the finish wasn't metallic and it didn't look as nice as the one I saw in the parking lot. I asked the salesman and he told me that they discontinued the color in the '73 line.

In considering alternatives, she faced a dilemma; she didn't want the Mach I because it cost too much and she didn't like the sports roof; but she didn't like the hardtop either, although it was in the proper price range, because it had the chrome front end (not rubber like the Mach I). After looking

around, she picked up a brochure and went home.

She set aside thoughts about cars until later that week when she paged through the Mustang pamphlet she got from the dealer and found an interesting option that could be gotten with the hardtop model.

> They called it the decor group, which included the rubber bumper and honeycomb grill, the black lowerside mouldings and amber lights of the Mach I—in other words, I could get the front end of the Mach I with the back end of the hardtop!

The following Sunday she returned with her father to ask about the price of the decor group:

> The next thing I knew I was ordering a car, and my father was nowhere around—I guess he didn't want to be blamed if I was dissatisfied with my final decision. . . . When it came to a color, I decided on a medium lime metallic—I didn't like the chartreuse and remembered someone telling me that dark colors tend to fade after awhile (they offered a forest green color)—I've always been partial to green, although in a Firebird, I would have gotten the burnt orange, they didn't offer the Mustang in orange, I don't like red Mustangs. . . . I didn't get much optional equipment like air-conditioning, I did get an AM radio and, of course, the decor group.

Since M's brother was lending her the money to finance the car (so that she wouldn't have to pay exhorbitant bank interest rates) and the money was tied up in a six-month certificate which became due in a month and a half, M and her father set up a day and time that they wanted to take delivery of the car. (Customarily, the dealer will call the purchaser to tell him the car is in the lot; in this case, M assumed, with reassurances from the salesman, that the car would be delivered in three weeks to the dealer leaving it to sit in the lot three more weeks before they were ready to pay for it.)

> The reason I had my father come along is that we agreed that he'd take the title to the car in his name. Insurance rates are unreasonably high for unmarried girls under 25. With this arrangement I could save on insurance, at least, because parking at the apartment costs $40 a month and license plates, vehicle stickers, gasoline, and maintenance are really gonna take a chunk out of my salary.

Two weeks before the scheduled pick-up date, M happened by the car lot to see if it had been delivered yet.

> When I ordered the car all I had to judge the color on was a three-inch swatch, but the minute I looked in the lot (she had been driving by in her father's car) I picked it out immediately—it was so bright and shiny. . . .

On the day M had agreed to take delivery of the car, she and her father were at the lot at 9:30 A.M.:

> I saw the car sitting out in the lot and thought that it was rather strange that they didn't have it in the garage for a wash—the wheel-

covers weren't even on yet. At first I thought that it wasn't my car . . . we went into the office and found out that our salesman was on vacation and I sensed a mix-up. But the salesman told us that it would just take a few minutes to clean it up, so we waited. After fifteen minutes I saw someone go out to the lot, get into the car (the one she had thought all along was hers) and drive it into the garage. I figured that in twenty minutes I'd have my car—well, I was wrong. After an hour my father went into the garage, I stayed outside, and he came out boiling. It seemed as though the antenna hadn't been put on yet and that they were just starting to work on it. The wheelcovers hadn't been brought out yet. My father has a terrible temper, and he went storming off to the office manager who told him that it would be only a few minutes more. Well, after another forty-five minutes of smoking cigarettes, he went back into the garage. I went with him this time, to see what was happening. They were pounding on the wheelcovers, and as I walked around the car I noticed that the racing mirrors (they were to come with the car free of charge) hadn't been put on—I was afraid to mention it to my father, but he noticed it the same time I did, and he literally blew up. He got a hold of the office manager again and told him that if his daughter wasn't so set on getting this car, that he'd ask for his money back and walk out. After some apologies the manager said that I could get the mirrors put on the car when I came in for my first servicing, father agreed, very reluctantly, and in fifteen minutes the car was ready and I drove it home. Needless to say the Ford people sent out letters of apology and that 'if we can be of any further service' junk. You know, I got kinda mad through all that waiting, but, I waited so long to get a car, I wasn't gonna blow the whole thing because I had to wait a couple more hours.

To date there have been no mechanical problems with the car, the racing mirrors were installed a few weeks after delivery. "I'm pleased," were her final comments.

A Model of Industrial Buyer Behavior

*Jagdish N. Sheth**

Although industrial market research has generated large data banks on organizational buyers, very little from the existing data seems helpful to management. What is needed before more data are collected is a realistic conceptualization and understanding of the process of industrial buying decisions. This article integrates existing knowledge into a descriptive model to aid in industrial market research.

The purpose of this article is to describe a model of industrial (organizational) buyer behavior. Considerable knowledge on organizational buyer behavior already exists[1] and can be classified into three categories. The first category includes a considerable amount of systematic empirical research on the buying policies and practices of purchasing agents and other organizational buyers.[2] The second includes industry reports and

[1] For a comprehensive list of references, see Thomas A. Staudt and W. Lazer, *A Basic Bibliography on Industrial Marketing* (Chicago: American Marketing Assn., 1963); and Donald E. Vinson, "Bibliography of Industrial Marketing" (unpublished listing of references, University of Colorado, 1972).

[2] Richard M. Cyert *et al.*, "Observation of a Business Decision," *Journal of Business*, Vol. 29 (October 1956), pp. 237–248; John A. Howard and C. G. Moore, Jr., "A Descriptive Model of the Purchasing Agent" (unpublished monograph, University of Pittsburgh, 1964); George Strauss, "Work Study of Purchasing Agents," *Human Organization*, Vol. 33 (September 1964), pp. 137–149; Theodore A. Levitt, *Industrial Purchasing Behavior* (Boston: Division of Research, Graduate School of Business, Harvard University, 1965); Urban B. Ozanne and Gilbert A. Churchill, "Adoption Research: Information Sources in the Industrial

Purchasing Decision," and Richard N. Cardozo, "Segmenting the Industrial Market," in *Marketing and the New Science of Planning*, R. L. King, ed. (Chicago: American Marketing Assn., 1968), pp. 352–359 and 433–440, respectively, Richard N. Cardozo and J. W. Cagley, "Experimental Study of Industrial Buyer Behavior," *Journal of Marketing Research*, Vol. 8 (August 1971), pp. 329–334; Thomas P. Copley and F. L. Callom, "Industrial Search Behavior and Perceived Risk," in *Proceedings of the Second Annual Conference, the Association for Con-*

* ABOUT THE AUTHOR.
Jagdish N. Sheth is professor of business and research professor in the College of Commerce and Business Administration, University of Illinois, Urbana-Champaign.

SOURCE: Reprinted from the *Journal of Marketing*, Vol. 37 (October 1973), pp. 50–56. Published by the American Marketing Association.

185

observations of industrial buyers.[3] Finally, the third category consists of books, monographs, and articles which analyze, theorize, model, and sometimes report on industrial buying activities.[4] What is now needed is a

---

sumer Research, D. M. Gardner, ed. (College Park, Md.: Association for Consumer Research, 1971), pp. 208–231; and James R. McMillan, "Industrial Buying Behavior as Group Decision Making," (paper presented at the Nineteenth International Meeting of the Institute of Management Sciences, April 1972).

[3] Robert F. Shoaf, ed., *Emotional Factors Underlying Industrial Purchasing* (Cleveland, Ohio: Penton Publishing Co., 1959); G. H. Haas, B. March, and E. M. Krech, *Purchasing Department Organization and Authority*, American Management Assn. Research Study No. 45 (New York: 1960); *Evaluation of Supplier Performance* (New York: National Association of Purchasing Agents, 1963); F. A. Hays and G. A. Renard, *Evaluating Purchasing Performance*, American Management Assn. Research Study No. 66 (New York: 1964); Hugh Buckner, *How British Industry Buys* (London: Hutchison and Company, Ltd., 1967); *How Industry Buys/1970* (New York: Scientific American, 1970). In addition, numerous articles published in trade journals such as *Purchasing and Industrial Marketing* are cited in Vinson, same reference as footnote 1, and Strauss, same reference as footnote 2.

[4] Ralph S. Alexander, J. S. Cross, and R. M. Hill, *Industrial Marketing*, 3rd ed. (Homewood, Ill.: Richard D. Irwin, 1967); John H. Westing, I. V. Fine, and G. J. Zenz, *Purchasing Management* (New York: John Wiley & Sons, 1969); Patrick J. Robinson, C. W. Farris, and Y. Wind, *Industrial Buying and Creative Marketing* (Boston: Allyn & Bacon, 1967): Frederick E. Webster, Jr., "Modeling the Industrial Buying Process," *Journal of Marketing Research*, Vol. 2 (November 1965), pp. 370–376: and Frederick E. Webster, Jr., "Industrial Buying Behavior: A State-of-the-Art Appraisal," in *Marketing in a Changing World*, B. A. Morin, ed. (Chicago: American Marketing Assn., 1969), p. 256.

reconciliation and integration of existing knowledge into a realistic and comprehensive model of organizational buyer behavior.

It is hoped that the model described in this article will be useful in the following ways: first, to broaden the vision of research on organizational buyer behavior so that it includes the most salient elements and their interactions; second, to act as a catalyst for building marketing information systems from the viewpoint of the industrial buyer; and, third, to generate new hypotheses for future research on fundamental processes underlying organizational buyer behavior.

A DESCRIPTION OF INDUSTRIAL BUYER BEHAVIOR

The model of industrial buyer behavior is summarized in Figure 1. Although this illustrative presentation looks complex due to the large number of variables and complicated relationships among them, this is because it is a generic model which attempts to describe and explain all types of industrial buying decisions. One can, however, simplify the actual application of the model in a specific study in at least two ways. First, several variables are included as conditions to hold constant differences among types of products to be purchased (product-specific factors) and differences among types of purchasing organizations. These exogenous factors will not be necessary if the objective of a study is to describe the process of buying behavior for a specific product or service. Second, some of

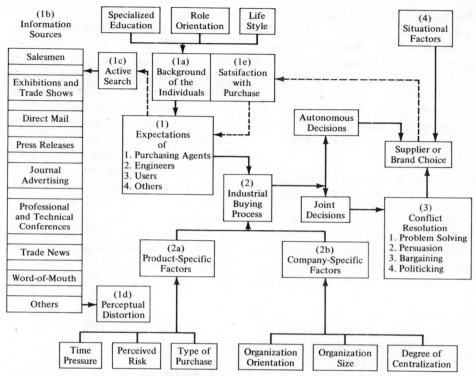

FIGURE 1 *An Integrative Model of Industrial Buyer Behavior*

the decision-process variables can also be ignored if the interest is strictly to conduct a survey of static measurement of the psychology of the organizational buyers. For example, perceptual bias and active search variables may be eliminated if the interest is not in the process of communication to the organizational buyers.

This model is similar to the Howard-Sheth model of buyer behavior in format and classification of variables.[5] However, there are several

[5] John A. Howard and J. N. Sheth, *The Theory of Buyer Behavior* (New York: John Wiley & Sons, 1969).

significant differences. First, while the Howard-Sheth model is more general and probably more useful in consumer behavior, the model described in this article is limited to organizational buying alone. Second, the Howard-Sheth model is limited to the individual decision-making process, whereas this model explicitly describes the joint decision-making process. Finally, there are fewer variables in this model than in the Howard-Sheth model of buyer behavior.

Organizational buyer behavior consists of three distinct aspects. The first aspect is the psychological world of the individuals involved in organizational buying decisions. The second aspect relates to the conditions which precipitate joint decisions among these individuals. The final aspect is the process of joint decision making with the inevitable conflict among the decision makers and its resolution by resorting to a variety of tactics.

PSYCHOLOGICAL WORLD OF THE DECISION MAKERS

Contrary to popular belief, many industrial buying decisions are not solely in the hands of purchasing agents.[6] Typically in an industrial setting, one finds that there are at least three departments whose members are continuously involved in different phases of the buying process. The most common are the personnel from the purchasing, quality control, and manufacturing departments. These individuals are identified in the model as purchasing agents, engineers, and users, respectively. Several other individuals in the organization may be, but are typically not, involved in the buying process (for example, the president of the firm or the comptroller). There is considerable interaction among the individuals in the three departments continuously involved in the buying process and often they are asked to decide jointly. It is, therefore, critical to examine the similarities and differences in the psychological worlds of these individuals.

Based on research in consumer and social psychology, several different aspects of the psychology of the decision makers are included in the model. Primary among these are the *expectations* of the decision makers about suppliers and brands [(1) in Figure 1]. The present model specifies five different processes which create differential expectations among the individuals involved in the purchasing process: (1a) the *background of the individuals*, (1b) *information sources*, (1c) *active search*, (1d) *perceptual distortion*, and (1e) *satisfaction with past purchases*. These variables must be explained and operationally defined if they are to fully represent the psychological world of the organizational buyers.

Expectations

Expectations refer to the *perceived* potential of alternative suppliers and brands to satisfy a number of explicit and implicit objectives in any particular buying decision. The most common explicit objectives include, in order of relative importance, product quality, delivery time, quantity of supply, after-sale service where appropriate, and price.[7] However, a number of studies have pointed out the critical role of several implicit criteria such as reputation, size, location, and reciprocity relationship with the supplier;

[6] Howard and Moore, same reference as footnote 2; Strauss, same reference as footnote 2; McMillan, same reference as footnote 2; *How Industry Buys/1970*, same reference as footnote 3.

[7] Howard and Moore, same reference as footnote 2; *How Industry Buys/1970*, same reference as footnote 3; Hays and Renard, same reference as footnote 3.

and personality, technical expertise, salesmanship, and even life style of the sales representative.[8] In fact, with the standardized marketing mix among the suppliers in oligopolistic markets, the implicit criteria are becoming marginally more and more significant in the industrial buyer's decisions.

Expectations can be measured by obtaining a profile of each supplier or brand as to how satisfactory it is perceived to be in enabling the decision maker to achieve his explicit and implicit objectives. Almost all studies from past research indicate that expectations will substantially differ among the purchasing agents, engineers, and product users because each considers different criteria to be salient in judging the supplier or the brand. In general, it is found that product users look for prompt delivery, proper installation, and efficient serviceability; purchasing agents look for maximum price advantage and economy in shipping and forwarding; and engineers look for excellence in quality, standardization of the product, and engineering pretesting of the product. These differences in objectives and, consequently, expectations are often the root causes for constant conflict among these three types of individuals.[9]

Why are there substantial differ-

ences in expectations? While there is considerable speculation among researchers and observers of industrial buyer behavior on the number and nature of explanations, there is relatively little consensus. The five most salient processes which determine differential expectations, as specified in the model, are discussed below.

Background of Individuals The first, and probably most significant, factor is the background and task orientation of each of the individuals involved in the buying process. The different educational backgrounds of the purchasing agents, engineers, and plant managers often generate substantially different professional goals and values. In addition, the task expectations also generate conflicting perceptions of one another's role in the organization. Finally, the personal life styles of individual decision makers play an important role in developing differential expectations.[10]

It is relatively easy to gather information on this background factor. The educational and task differences are comparable to demographics in consumer behavior, and life style differences can be assessed by psycho-

---

[8] Howard and Moore, same reference as footnote 2; Levitt, same reference as footnote 2; Westing, Fine, and Zenz, same reference as footnote 4; Shoaf, same reference as footnote 4.

[9] Strauss, same reference as footnote 2.

[10] For a general reading, see Robert T. Golembiewski, "Small Groups and Large Organizations," in *Handbook of Organizations*, J. G. March, ed. (Chicago: Rand McNally & Company, 1965), chapter 3. For field studies related to this area, see Donald E. Porter, P. B. Applewhite, and M. J. Misshauk, eds., *Studies in Organizational Behavior and Management*, 2nd ed. (Scranton, Pa.: Intext Educational Publishers, 1971).

graphic scales on the individual's interests, activities, and values as a professional.

Information Sources and Active Search
The second and third factors in creating differential expectations are the source and type of information each of the decision makers is exposed to and his participation in the active search. Purchasing agents receive disproportionately greater exposure to commercial sources, and the information is often partial and biased toward the supplier or the brand. In some companies, it is even a common practice to discourage sales representatives from talking directly to the engineering or production personnel. The engineering and production personnel, therefore, typically have less information and what they have is obtained primarily from professional meetings, trade reports, and even word-of-mouth. In addition, the active search for information is often relegated to the purchasing agents because it is presumed to be their job responsibility.

It is not too difficult to assess differences among the three types of individuals in their exposure to various sources and types of information by standard survey research methods.

Perceptual Distortion   A fourth factor is the selective distortion and retention of available information. Each individual strives to make the objective information consistent with his own prior knowledge and expectations by systematically distorting it. For

example, since there are substantial differences in the goals and values of purchasing agents, engineers, and production personnel, one should expect different interpretations of the same information among them. Although no specific research has been done on this tendency to perceptually distort information in the area of industrial buyer behavior, a large body of research does exist on cognitive consistency to explain its presence as a natural human tendency.[11]

Perceptual distortion is probably the most difficult variable to quantify by standard survey research methods. One possible approach is experimentation, but this is costly. A more realistic alternative is to utilize perceptual mapping techniques such as multidimensional scaling or factor analysis and compare differences in the judgments of the purchasing agents, engineers, and production personnel to a common list of suppliers or brands.

Satisfaction with Past Purchases   The fifth factor which creates differential expectations among the various individuals involved in the purchasing process is the satisfaction with past buying experiences with a supplier or brand. Often it is not possible for a supplier or brand to provide equal satisfaction to the three parties because each one has different goals or criteria. For example, a supplier may be lower in price but his delivery schedule may not be satisfactory.

[11] Robert P. Abelson *et al., Theories of Cognitive Consistency: A Source Book* (Chicago: Rand McNally & Company, 1968).

Similarly, a product's quality may be excellent but its price may be higher than others. The organization typically rewards each individual for excellent performance in his specialized skills, so the purchasing agent is rewarded for economy, the engineer for quality control, and the production personnel for efficient scheduling. This often results in a different level of satisfaction for each of the parties involved even though the chosen supplier or brand may be the best feasible alternative in terms of overall corporate goals.

Past experiences with a supplier or brand, summarized in the satisfaction variable, directly influence the person's expectations toward that supplier or brand. It is relatively easy to measure the satisfaction variable by obtaining information on how the supplier or brand is perceived by each of the three parties.

DETERMINANTS OF JOINT VS. AUTONOMOUS DECISIONS

Not all industrial buying decisions are made jointly by the various individuals involved in the purchasing process. Sometimes the buying decisions are delegated to one party, which is not necessarily the purchasing agent. It is, therefore, important for the supplier to know whether a buying decision is joint or autonomous and, if it is the latter, to which party it is delegated. There are six primary factors which determine whether a specific buying decision will be joint or autonomous. Three of these factors are related to the characteristics of

the product or service (2a) and the other three are related to the characteristics of the buyer company (2b).

Product-Specific Factors

The first product-specific variable is what Bauer calls *perceived risk* in buying decisions.[12] Perceived risk refers to the magnitude of adverse consequences felt by the decision maker if he makes a wrong choice, and the uncertainty under which he must decide. The greater the uncertainty in a buying situation, the greater the perceived risk. Although there is very little direct evidence, it is logical to hypothesize that the greater the perceived risk in a specific buying decision, the more likely it is that the purchase will be decided jointly by all parties concerned. The second product-specific factor is *type of purchase*. If it is the first purchase or a once-in-a-lifetime capital expenditure, one would expect greater joint decision making. On the other hand, if the purchase decision is repetitive and routine or is limited to maintenance products or services, the buying decision is likely to be delegated to one party. The third factor is *time pressure*. If the buying decision has to be made under a great deal of time pressure or

[12] Raymond A. Bauer, "Consumer Behavior as Risk Taking," in *Dynamic Marketing for a Changing World*, R. L. Hancock, ed. (Chicago: American Marketing Assn., 1960), pp. 389–400. Applications of perceived risk in industrial buying can be found in Levitt, same reference as footnote 2; Copley and Callom, same reference as footnote 2; McMillan, same reference as footnote 2.

on an emergency basis, it is likely to be delegated to one party rather than decided jointly.

Company-Specific Factors

The three organization-specific factors are *company orientation, company size,* and *degree of centralization.* If the company is technology oriented, it is likely to be dominated by the engineering people and the buying decisions will, in essence, be made by them. Similarly, if the company is production oriented, the buying decisions will be made by the production personnel.[13] Second, if the company is a large corporation, decision making will tend to be joint. Finally, the greater the degree of centralization, the less likely it is that the decisions will be joint. Thus, a privately owned small company with technology or production orientation will tend toward autonomous decision making and a large-scale public corporation with considerable decentralization will tend to have greater joint decision making.

Even though there is considerable research evidence in organization behavior in general to support these six factors, empirical evidence in industrial buying decisions in particular is

sketchy on them. Perhaps with more research it will be possible to verify the generalizations and deductive logic utilized in this aspect of the model.

PROCESS OF JOINT DECISION MAKING

The major thrust of the present model of industrial buying decisions is to investigate the process of joint decision making. This includes initiation of the decision to buy, gathering of information, evaluating alternative suppliers, and resolving conflict among the parties who must jointly decide.

The decision to buy is usually initiated by a continued need of supply or is the outcome of long-range planning. The formal initiation in the first case is typically from the production personnel by way of a requisition slip. The latter usually is a formal recommendation from the planning unit to an ad hoc committee consisting of the purchasing agent, the engineer, and the plant manager. The information-gathering function is typically relegated to the purchasing agent. If the purchase is a repetitive decision for standard items, there is very little information gathering. Usually the purchasing agent contacts the preferred supplier and orders the items on the requisition slip. However, considerable active search effort is manifested for capital expenditure items, especially those which are entirely new purchase experiences for the organization.[14]

The most important aspect of the

---

[13] For some indirect evidence, see Strauss, same reference as footnote 2. For a more general study, see Victor A. Thompson, "Hierarchy, Specialization and Organizational Conflict," *Administrative Science Quarterly,* Vol. 5 (March 1961), p. 513; and Henry A. Landsberger, "The Horizontal Dimension in Bureaucracy," *Administration Science Quarterly,* Vol. 6 (December 1961), pp. 299–332, for a thorough review of numerous theories.

[14] Strauss, same reference as footnote 2.

joint decision-making process, however, is the assimilation of information, deliberations on it, and the consequent conflict which most joint decisions entail. According to March and Simon, conflict is present when there is a need to decide jointly among a group of people who have, at the same time, different goals and perceptions.[15] In view of the fact that the latter is invariably present among the various parties to industrial buying decisions, conflict becomes a common consequence of the joint decision-making process; the buying motives and expectations about brands and suppliers are considerably different for the engineer, the user, and the purchasing agent, partly due to different educational backgrounds and partly due to company policy of reward for specialized skills and viewpoints.

Interdepartmental conflict in itself is not necessarily bad. What matters most from the organization's viewpoint is *how* the conflict is resolved (3). If it is resolved in a rational manner, one very much hopes that the final joint decision will also tend to be rational. If, on the other hand, conflict resolution degenerates to what Strauss calls "tactics of lateral relationship,"[16] the organization will suffer from inefficiency and the joint decisions may be reduced to bargaining and politicking among the parties involved. Not

only will the decision be based on irrational criteria, but the choice of a supplier may be to the detriment of the buying organization.

What types of conflict can be expected in industrial buying decisions? How are they likely to be resolved? These are some of the key questions in an understanding of industrial buyer behavior. If the inter-party conflict is largely due to disagreements on expectations about the suppliers or their brands, it is likely that the conflict will be resolved in the *problem-solving* manner. The immediate consequence of this type of conflict is to actively search for more information, deliberate more on available information, and often to seek out other suppliers not seriously considered before. The additional information is then presented in a problem-solving fashion so that conflict tends to be minimized.

If the conflict among the parties is primarily due to disagreement on some specific criteria with which to evaluate suppliers—although there is an agreement on the buying goals or objectives at a more fundamental level —it is likely to be resolved by *persuasion*. An attempt is made, under this type of resolution, to persuade the dissenting member by pointing out the importance of overall corporate objectives and how his criterion is not likely to attain these objectives. There is no attempt to gather more information. However, there results greater interaction and communication among the parties, and sometimes an outsider is brought in to reconcile the differences.

Both problem solving and persua-

[15] James G. March and H. A. Simon, *Organizations* (New York: John Wiley & Sons, 1958), chapter 5; and Landsberger, same reference as footnote 13.

[16] George Strauss, "Tactics of Lateral Relationship: The Purchasing Agent," *Administrative Science Quarterly*, Vol. 7 (September 1962), pp. 161–186.

sion are useful and rational methods of conflict resolution. The resulting joint decisions, therefore, also tend to be more rational. Thus, conflicts produced due to disagreements on expectations about the suppliers or on a specific criterion are healthy from the organization's viewpoint even though they may be time consuming. One is likely to find, however, that a more typical situation in which conflict arises is due to fundamental differences in buying goals or objectives among the various parties. This is especially true with respect to unique or new buying decisions related to capital expenditure items. The conflict is resolved not by changing the differences in relative importance of the buying goals or objectives of the individuals involved, but by the process of *bargaining*. The fundamental differences among the parties are implicitly conceded by all the members and the concept of distributive justice (tit for tat) is invoked as a part of bargaining. The most common outcome is to allow a single party to decide autonomously in this specific situation in return for some favor or promise of reciprocity in future decisions.

Finally, if the disagreement is not simply with respect to buying goals or objectives but also with respect to *style of decision making*, the conflict tends to be grave and borders on the mutual dislike of personalities among the individual decision makers. The resolution of this type of conflict is usually by *politicking* and back-stabbing tactics. Such methods of conflict resolution are common in industrial

buying decisions. The reader is referred to the sobering research of Strauss for further discussion.[17]

Both bargaining and politicking are nonrational and inefficient methods of conflict resolution; the buying organization suffers from these conflicts. Furthermore, the decision makers find themselves sinking below their professional, managerial role. The decisions are not only delayed but tend to be governed by factors other than achievement of corporate objectives.

CRITICAL ROLE OF SITUATIONAL FACTORS

The model described so far presumes that the choice of a supplier or brand is the outcome of a systematic decision-making process in the organizational setting. However, there is ample empirical evidence in the literature to suggest that at least some of the industrial buying decisions are determined by ad hoc *situational factors* (4) and not by any systematic decision-making process. In other words, similar to consumer behavior, the industrial buyers often decide on factors other than rational or realistic criteria.

It is difficult to prepare a list of ad hoc conditions which determine industrial buyer behavior without decision making. However, a number of situational factors which often intervene between the actual choice and any prior decision-making process can be isolated. These include: temporary economic conditions such as price controls, recession, or foreign trade; inter-

[17] Same reference as footnote 16.

nal strikes, walkouts, machine break-downs, and other production-related events; organizational changes such as merger or acquisition; and ad hoc changes in the market place, such as promotional efforts, new product introduction, price changes, and so on, in the supplier industries.

IMPLICATIONS FOR INDUSTRIAL MARKETING RESEARCH

The model of industrial buyer behavior described above suggests the following implications for marketing research.

First, in order to explain and predict supplier or brand choice in industrial buyer behavior, it is necessary to conduct research on the psychology of other individuals in the organization in addition to the purchasing agents. It is, perhaps, the unique nature of organizational structure and behavior which leads to a distinct separation of the consumer, the buyer, and the procurement agent, as well as others possibly involved in the decision-making process. In fact, it may not be an exaggeration to suggest that the purchasing agent is often a less critical member of the decision-making process in industrial buyer behavior.

Second, it is possible to operationalize and quantify most of the variables included as part of the model. While some are more difficult and indirect, sufficient psychometric skill in marketing research is currently available to quantify the psychology of the individuals.

Third, although considerable research has been done on the demo-graphics of organizations in industrial market research—for example, on the turnover and size of the company, workflows, standard industrial classification, and profit ratios—demographic and life-style information on the individuals involved in industrial buying decisions is also needed.

Fourth, a systematic examination of the power positions of various individuals involved in industrial buying decisions is a necessary condition of the model. The sufficient condition is to examine trade-offs among various objectives, both explicit and implicit, in order to create a satisfied customer.

Fifth, it is essential in building any market research information system for industrial goods and services that the process of conflict resolution among the parties and its impact on supplier or brand choice behavior is carefully included and simulated.

Finally, it is important to realize that not all industrial decisions are the outcomes of a systematic decision-making process. There are some industrial buying decisions which are based strictly on a set of situational factors for which theorizing or model building will not be relevant or useful. What is needed in these cases is a checklist of empirical observations of the ad hoc events which vitiate the neat relationship between the theory or the model and a specific buying decision.

QUESTIONS

How appropriate is the model in this article for describing the purchase of a major piece of equipment such as a tractor? For office supplies? What are the major strengths and limitations of the model as you interpret it? Does it permit explanation, prediction, and control? Are the concepts and their interrelationships clearly defined? How, if at all, does the model Sheth presents differ from models of consumer behavior? Are there different assumptions and different factors involved?

Three Depth Interviews on Cottage Cheese

TECHNICAL NOTE

The function of Motivation Research is to seek new insights into the consumer's behavior. It endeavors to reveal motivations at three levels of the individual's personality: (1) what he shows to the world, (2) what he really thinks, (3) what he subconsciously believes. It assumes that a person responds to non-rational considerations and is primarily motivated by his self ideal, the person he would like to be. The individual is dominated not only by what he says his interests are, but also by hidden hopes, prejudices, and emotions. Advertising is effective only as it creates desirable images in the consumer's mind, images that coincide with his real thoughts, not those he outwardly expresses. The purpose of the unstructured, or depth, interview is to get behind the person's rationalization of his motives and to discover why he behaves as he does. In this respect the depth interview may be more valuable in uncovering advertising appeals than the formal type of questionnaire set up on preconceived ideas of how the consumer might react to product appeals.

FIRST INTERVIEW

Examples of Motivation Research

INTERVIEWER: For the next few minutes, I would like you to just settle back and take it easy and tell me everything you can about your impressions of cottage cheese—what you think about it, and any reactions that come to your mind. When I mention *cottage cheese*, what do you think about?

HOUSEWIFE: Small curd, large curd, creamed, country style, low calorie content.

INTERVIEWER: Anything else?

HOUSEWIFE: Yes; half pint, chives, then pineapple, and—I don't like pineapple—it's too "icky" sweet. I like chives—it tastes good. The next thing I think of is the uses of cottage cheese for salads, particularly with gelatin. Cottage cheese as a diet control. Then the packaging of it. Cottage cheese in plastic containers versus waxed paper containers.

SOURCE: David E. Faville, *Selected Cases in Marketing Management* (Englewood Cliffs, N. J.: Prentice-Hall, 1972).

197

INTERVIEWER: Which do you prefer?

HOUSEWIFE: If I can get them, I take the plastic containers because I can use them afterward for refrigerator dishes for left-overs.

INTERVIEWER: Have you ever seen cottage cheese advertised?

HOUSEWIFE: Only for salads.

INTERVIEWER: Can you name me any brands of cottage cheese?

HOUSEWIFE: Yes, Tuttle's—"Tut, tut, eat nothing but, Tuttle's Cottage Cheese."

INTERVIEWER: Where did you see that?

HOUSEWIFE: I heard it over the radio, but I can't see any difference between it and the brands I use.

INTERVIEWER: What brands do you use?

HOUSEWIFE: New Forest, Angel Clear, or Durbeyfield Creamery[1]—I prefer the dry type.

INTERVIEWER: Why do you prefer the dry type?

HOUSEWIFE: I connect the dry type with having fewer calories, but I'm sure that has nothing to do with it.

INTERWIEWER: Why do you say that?

HOUSEWIFE: I don't know enough about it to say, but I just don't think it does.

INTERVIEWER: You think that the creamed type then, has more calories than the country style dry type?

HOUSEWIFE: Well, it stands to reason the creamed style has more calories or they wouldn't call it *creamed.*

INTERVIEWER: Have you seen any advertising of cottage cheese?

HOUSEWIFE: Yes, in magazines in connection with salads. They all contain recipes for using cottage cheese.

INTERVIEWER: What magazines?

HOUSEWIFE: Oh, *Ladies' Home Journal, Good Housekeeping*—women's magazines.

INTERVIEWER: What women's magazines do you read regularly?

HOUSEWIFE: *Vogue* and *Harper's Bazaar,* but I occasionally see *The Ladies' Home Journal, House Beautiful,* and *Good Housekeeping* at the beauty parlor.

INTERVIEWER: You mentioned pineapple and chives in cottage cheese. Is there anything else you would like to see with cottage cheese?

HOUSEWIFE: No, it is too easy to make up some combination yourself. When I fix it with pineapple myself, then it isn't so sweet. I use it with all sorts of things, vegetables or fruits and cottage cheese. I make cottage cheese and lime Jell-O salad.

INTERVIEWER: Where do you buy your cottage cheese?

HOUSEWIFE: Most of the time I get it from the milkman—Durbeyfield Creamery. He comes at eleven o'clock when I'm thinking about lunch. I prefer New Forest, because theirs is drier than the others. Angel Clear is next, and Durbeyfield next—but they may all come from the same outfit so far as I know.

INTERVIEWER: What makes you think they might come from the same outfit?

HOUSEWIFE: Because they all taste pretty much alike. I think when you get it from the milkman, though, you can always be sure it's fresh because it comes straight from the dairy.

[1] Names fictitious.

Sometimes it sets around in the stores and gets sour.

INTERVIEWER: Do you serve cottage cheese to guests?

HOUSEWIFE: Not straight cottage cheese. That is something you use for your own diet. If you have guests, you doctor it up.

INTERVIEWER: How do you mean, "doctor it up?"

HOUSEWIFE: I mean putting it in recipes—salads, lime Jell-O, cottage cheese and pineapple. If I use it with lemon Jell-O, I use a vegetable combination like cucumbers and celery and carrots.

INTERVIEWER: Do you think cottage cheese should be advertised more?

HOUSEWIFE: I don't think cottage cheese needs to be advertised. It's in too much demand already, like eggs and milk.

INTERVIEWER: If cottage cheese were to be advertised more, what form of advertising do you think should be used?

HOUSEWIFE: Oh, I don't know. I suppose it could only be advertised in connection with recipes or diets. I usually buy it from the milkman, but if I happen to be shopping, I buy it at New Forest. But there isn't enough difference that I'm going to quibble about it.

INTERVIEWER: You mentioned cottage cheese as suitable for diets. Can you tell me more about that?

HOUSEWIFE: For reducing diets. I see it in magazines. It seems to sustain you while you are dieting. Cottage cheese is derived from milk. It sustains you better than a fruit or a vegetable. I just have a feeling it is more sustaining.

INTERVIEWER: What do you think cottage cheese is made of?

HOUSEWIFE: I don't know. I've often wondered. Other than milk I just don't know; I'm very curious. Nobody knows. I just go along asking but nobody tells me anything. I suppose it is cheese that in the early days could be made right in the home by whipping it up. That's where it gets the name *cottage*. But I don't really know; it's a good question.

INTERVIEWER: What might induce you to eat more cottage cheese?

HOUSEWIFE: Nothing. I eat cottage cheese every noon since I've been dieting. I like it, but I don't want any more of it. It's the most satisfying thing I know of if you are trying to lose weight.

INTERVIEWER: This has been most interesting. Thank you for your time and patience.

SECOND INTERVIEW

INTERVIEWER: Would you be willing to just sit down and relax and for the next few minutes tell me everything that comes to mind about cottage cheese, your thoughts and impressions?

HOUSEWIFE: O.K. Go ahead. What do you want to know?

INTERVIEWER: I don't want to know any particular thing. Just tell me what you can about your reactions to cottage cheese.

HOUSEWIFE: I like it. I never can get enough of it. When I'm hungry, I take it out of the refrigerator and eat two or three spoonfuls. . . . I have it with every meal except breakfast. I like the creamed cottage cheese and the small curd. I eat it with avocado and lemon juice. I like it with steak and salt and pepper. I buy it by the quart. I've always liked it all my life. I used to make it myself before they had it in the stores.

INTERVIEWER: Any brand preference?

HOUSEWIFE: Well, yes and no. The brand that New Forest carries has the best flavor. All the milk companies have it. I don't like Hardy's.[2] It has a peculiar flavor—sort of bitter. Angel Clear is too flat—doesn't taste like cottage cheese, too innocuous.

INTERVIEWER: Do you ever serve it to guests?

HOUSEWIFE: If they want it. I ask them. Sometimes with pineapple and then with the avocado and lemon juice I mentioned. I learned to eat it that way at Schrafft's in New York. It used to be my favorite lunch: avocado, cottage cheese, lemon juice, and a roll. It is quite good with grapefruit, too. You can pour the grapefruit juice over it.

INTERVIEWER: Anything else?

HOUSEWIFE: You asked me about guests. I sometimes put it on the table right in the box. It is usually gone by the end of the meal, but some people don't like it. Some people like it with tomato. That's a good combination— stuffed tomato with cottage cheese. It is indispensable for cheese cake.

INTERVIEWER: What about diet?

HOUSEWIFE: I don't have to worry about diet. I'm not eating cottage cheese to keep my weight down. It contains something that satisfies your appetite. You can eat a lot of it and not feel stuffy afterward. Some of the companies have been putting it out in plastic containers. I used to get it in colored containers. I used them for left-overs in the refrigerator, but now I have so many they just sit in the cupboard, and I have to give them away. I avoid getting cottage cheese in plastics now and just get the stuff in cardboard boxes. I hate to throw away the plastics and I get too cluttered up with them.

INTERVIEWER: What would make you eat more cottage cheese?

HOUSEWIFE: Only hunger. When I get faint I eat cottage cheese in between meals. It helps stop that empty feeling like nothing else does. Buttermilk does it too, but you can't always have that around. I'm not brand conscious, except I know the ones I don't like. Snow Rose[3] is too rich.

INTERVIEWER: Anything else?

HOUSEWIFE: Cottage cheese used to be called curded cheese. It is just another way of saying *curded cheese— cottage cheese*. It comes from skimmed milk; it has no butter fat at all. After the cream has been through the separator, the skimmed milk is left. My mother used to make it on the back of the stove—the range, remember the old kitchen range? We used to take big shallow pans of skimmed milk that was starting to get sour and whey off. Then we cooked it until the little curds hardened. Then we put it through a strainer and drained off the liquid. Just the curds remained. We put that in a bowl and ate it with salt

---

[2] Name fictitious.

[3] Name fictitious.

and pepper and cream. It was quite chewy. I just loved it.

INTERVIEWER: Do you pay any attention to cottage cheese recipes?

HOUSEWIFE: No, because I don't do much cooking any more now that I'm living alone. I look at the recipes and think how nice that would be, but I don't make them. There is a very nice recipe with lime Jell-O and cottage cheese. Cottage cheese gives a nice body to a salad, but it needs a sharp contrast like lemon or lime.

INTERVIEWER: Anything more?

HOUSEWIFE: No, I guess not.

INTERVIEWER: Thank you very much.

THIRD INTERVIEW

INTERVIEWER: I would like you to just sit back and tell me all you can about cottage cheese, your reactions to it, what you think about it, how you use it—just anything that comes to mind.

HOUSEWIFE: It is the thing I practically always get when I go to the city. I go to Manning's for lunch and I have cottage cheese and fruit salad. I think it is something you can get tired of, though.

INTERVIEWER: Why?

HOUSEWIFE: I think you'd get tired of it if you ate too much of it, but I feel there is a lot of nourishment in it. Actually, we practically always have some on hand. We use it a great deal as a side salad for our dinner and along with all kinds of things.

INTERVIEWER: Such as?

HOUSEWIFE: Oh, tomato—tomato and pineapple. We use it a lot with a mound of cottage cheese and a few prunes around it, or any old thing. Any of the fruits seem to go with it. I don't see how you can go into a restaurant and just get an order of cottage cheese without anything with it. I see people doing that. I don't see how they can get it down.

INTERVIEWER: Any brand preference?

HOUSEWIFE: Heavens, we use several different kinds. We used always to use Tuttle's. It was the one that attracted me first. I liked the taste of it better than others. It seemed to be creamier or something. Some of it is kind of watery. I usually get it at Safeway or New Forest. They have their own brands. But when we look for brands, we always get either Tuttle's or Angel Clear. . . . One other thing we like is cottage cheese with chives in it, for a certain kind of dinner, a meat dinner.

INTERVIEWER: Anything else?

HOUSEWIFE: I don't know how I can expand on the subject. We don't diet. We eat it because we like it. Of course, what I don't know about calories, you could write a book on. When I learned to cook, calories were going out and vitamins were coming in. I'm sure cottage cheese has vitamins but I don't know what kind. There isn't anything I can't eat.

INTERVIEWER: Do you ever notice advertisements of cottage cheese?

HOUSEWIFE: No, I don't read ads and the ads on T.V. drive me nuts.

INTERVIEWER: Anything else?

HOUSEWIFE: My mother used to make it forty years ago. It wasn't on the market then. Then you had raw milk and you had sour milk. I don't remember how she made it, but we felt it was quite a delicacy.

INTERVIEWER: Anything else?

HOUSEWIFE: Personally I don't think there is an awful lot of difference in the brands. I just like small curd better—country style, they call it. Dairy-Maid[4] is what you get at New Forest. The package says *creamed, country style,* and *small curd*—all on that one package. I don't know what all that means. We use pineapple and grated carrots with it and jam. We make sandwiches with it sometimes. We put jam on it. That makes it look pretty. Sometimes we just put paprika on it if the whole thing is white, to give it a little carrot top. We use cottage

[4] Name fictitious.

cheese in lime Jell-O with pineapple or grapefruit. Sometimes we put nuts and horseradish in it and sometimes I put cottage cheese in the center of a gelatin mold. I use unflavored gelatin with it in a surrounding ring and I put pickle juice and maraschino and pineapple juice in the gelatin ring. This is something I made up myself.

INTERVIEWER: Anything more you can say?

HOUSEWIFE: No, I'm all rundown. Isn't that enough?

INTERVIEWER: Thank you very much.

QUESTIONS

What use might a cottage cheese producer make of the preceding interviews and others similar to them?

Chapter 6

The Measurement of Consumer Attitudes and Preferences

Consumer attitudes and preferences form one of the foundation stones for marketing research. There are varying methods for measuring and predicting the attitudes of consumers. These methods are discussed and evaluated in this chapter.

Attitudes are among the most complex, least understood, but most used social-psychological concepts in marketing. One of the reasons for this is that at its core, the idea of an attitude seems to be simple. An attitude is a behavioral disposition which is part of the structure of human perception. Triandis offers the following definition:

> An attitude is an idea charged with emotion which predisposes a class of actions to a particular class of social situations.[1]

These definitions are saying that, for most things that a person will have contact with, he already has some response which will "come out automatically." For example, we all possess attitudes toward the members of other races, makes of automobiles, and even sex.

The definitions of attitude use the terms "social objects" and "consistencies in response" to the objects. Defining what these terms mean will help us to understand better what attitudes are. "Any person, product or creation of a person or social event can function as a social object."[2] This means that an individual can possess attitudes toward Tide detergent, a Cincinnati milling machine, dances at country clubs, and modern painting. Response consistency means, first of all, that social objects are associated with other social objects in consistent ways. An individual is more likely to associate laundry bleach with Tide detergent than clothing with milling machines. There is a consistency in the way he "thinks about" social objects. Secondly, people "feel" consistently about attitude objects. A person who admires Cincinnati milling machines is more likely to also think that they are durable, sturdy, economical, accurate, and so on. Lastly, we tend to act consistently toward the attitude object. If we find modern art stimulating, we are more likely to go to see an exhibition of modern art or even to own some than we would if we found it decadent or uninteresting.

[1] Harry C. Triandis, *Attitude and Attitude Change* (New York: Wiley, 1971), p. 2.
[2] *Ibid.*, p. 7.

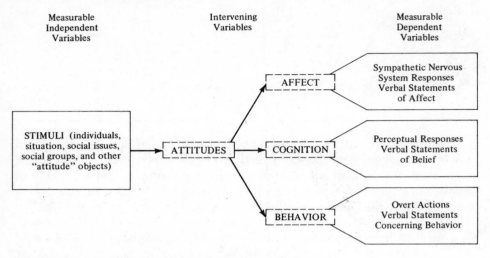

FIGURE 6.1   *A Schematic Conception of Attitudes*

Components of Attitude

Attitudes are generally considered to have three components: cognitive, affective, and behavioral, as shown in Figure 6.1.[3]

Cognitive

The cognitive component of an attitude is sometimes called the belief component; under it are subsumed the beliefs a person holds about an object. In a sense, they are what he knows about the object. This component is expressed, "I believe that . . ." or "I know it does . . ."

Affective

The affective component is that part of the attitude which says "I like or dislike it" on the other hand. It is the emotional component which refers to the feelings about the object. Here the emphasis is on the individual in relation to the object, whereas in the cognitive component the emphasis is on the object.

Behavioral

The behavioral component is the action tendency component. It is a predisposition to action. It says, given the object, what is the individual's most likely course of action?

---

[3] Or "cognitive," "emotional," and "action tendency." See Gene F. Summers (ed.) *Attitude Measurement* (Chicago: Rand McNally, 1970), p. 2; Blair J. Kolasa, *Introduction to Behavioral Science for Business* (New York: Wiley, 1969), p. 386, might refer to these three as "belief," "opinion," and "attitude."

Attitudes are generally thought to operate as a set of intervening variables. Figure 6.1 depicts the relationship between the attitude object (stimulus), attitudes (intervening variable), and actions or statements about the attitude object (response).

Most important in the cognitive organization of attitude is the idea of *centrality*. Those beliefs which deal with the individual and for which there is unanimous social support such as the statement "I am a man" are very central to the holder. We can talk further about beliefs which are *less central, peripheral,* or *inconsequential.* Another term for centrality is *ego-involvement.* Beliefs which have a high degree of centrality or ego-involvement are those around which the cognitive system is organized. These are more difficult to change than peripheral (or uninvolving) beliefs.

Attitudes or their components can be said to be affective (involve emotion or feeling) or normative (contain an idea about correct behavior to the attitude object). The affective component is the way a person feels about an attitude object. It is often determined by previous association of the object with pleasant or unpleasant experiences. We can speak about *positive* or *negative affect.* The normative dimension speaks of *seeking* or *avoiding contact.* Figure 6.2 demonstrates some behaviors in this conceptualization. According to this scheme, behavior can be described as going *toward, against,* or *away* from the attitude object.

Behavioral intentions, that is, what would be done toward an attitude

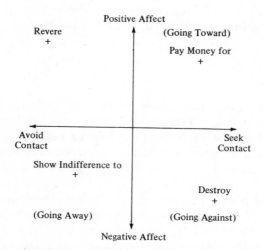

FIGURE 6.2 *The Two Basic Dimensions of Behavior toward Attitude Objects* Source: Harry C. Triandis, *Attitude and Attitude Change* (New York: John Wiley & Sons, 1971), p. 13.

object, are closely related to norms of behavior. The relationship between attitudes and behavior, however, is not direct. As Triandis noted: "Attitudes involve what people *think* about, *feel* about, and how they would *like* to *behave* toward an attitude object. Behavior is not only determined by what people *would like* to do but also by what they think they should do, that is, social *norms*, by what they have done, that is, *habits*, and by the *expected consequences of the behavior.*"[4]

Determinants of Attitude State

Attitudes are being formed and altered constantly. There seem to be at least five factors which determine the state of a person's attitude system: (1) information and feelings gathered from past want-satisfaction experiences; (2) information gathered in the past but unrelated to immediate want-satisfying effort; (3) group affiliations (especially the individual's perception of the beliefs, norms, and values of "significant others"); (4) attitudes toward related objects in the relevant attitude cluster; and (5) the individual's personality.[5]

One of the features of attitudes in which there is substantial agreement is that attitude is persistent over time. The extent to which an attitude can be changed is a function of its centrality in the individual's attitude structure and the degree to which it engenders highly favorable or unfavorable affect states. Attitude change may be brought about by (a) different want-satisfaction experiences, (b) exposure to new information, (c) changes in group membership, (d) changes in attitudes to related attitude objects, and (e) changes in personality.

Attitudes and Marketing

This section will give some examples of the place that attitudes and attitude research hold in marketing today. Three broad areas in which attitudes are used in marketing are (a) in the modeling of consumer behavior, (b) as an aid to identifying and reaching specific market segments, and (c) to determine probable customer response to new or existing products, services, or companies.

Attitudes occupy a central place in buyer behavior models. Andreason's basic model (Figure 5.1) of static customer choice is centered around attitudes. (The center box containing beliefs, feelings, and disposition are the three components of attitude described here as cognitive, affective, and behavioral.) As he describes it, "Within the attitude subsystem, the disposition to act is

---

[4] Harry C. Triandis, *op. cit.*, p. 14.
[5] Alan R. Andreason, "Attitudes and Consumer Behavior: A Decision Model," in Lee Preston (ed.) *New Research in Marketing* (The Institute of Business and Economic Research, University of California at Berkeley, 1966), pp. 2–3.

also affected by the attitude's belief and feeling components. Thus, a static *customer choice* model assumes the relationships shown . . . , with the disposition valence fixed somewhere between −1, decision to act negatively (reject, destroy), to +1, decision to act positively."[6]

It would seem inconceivable today that any buyer behavior model would be constructed without making explicit reference to attitudes.[7] In a recent study in the steel industry, Czepiel formulated a model of the industrial adoption process (the purchase of an industrial innovation) which postulated that the firm's attitude toward technological innovation would be related to the time of adoption. Results showed that earlier adopting firms did indeed have a more positive attitude toward technological innovation.[8]

As an example of the use of attitudes in identifying market segments consider the following quotation:

> Another segmentation in this market (the computer market) involves differences in prospects' attitudes toward the inevitability of progress. Although this factor has been widely ignored, it is a significant method for qualifying prospects. People who believe that progress is inevitable (i.e., that change is good and that new business methods are constantly evolving) make far better prospects for computers than those who have a less optimistic attitude toward progress in the world of business.[9]

Lastly, marketers conduct research on attitudes in order to determine consumer response to some attitude object. It may be a new or existing product, the company itself, or even advertising. For example, while consumers are thought to have a relatively stable attitude with respect to a given product class, it is expected that within this framework competing brands are evaluated differently. Furthermore, it is expected that the consumer has some ideal type within that class. Attitude research is frequently used to determine the

---

[6] Alan R. Andreason, *op. cit.*, pp. 4–5.

[7] Determining *which* attitudes are relevant in buying behavior, however, is very important. See, for example, James H. Myers and Mark I. Alpert, "Determinant Buying Attitudes' Meaning and Measurement," *Journal of Marketing*, Vol. 32 (October 1968), pp. 13–20. Also, Joel M. Axelrod, "Attitude Measures that Predict Purchase," *Journal of Advertising Research*, Vol. 8 (March 1968), pp. 3–18.

[8] John A. Czepiel, "The Diffusion of Major Technological Innovation in the American Steel Industry: An Analysis of Social Processes in a Complex Industrial Community," in the *Proceedings of the Second Annual Albert Haring Symposium on Doctoral Research in Marketing* (Indiana University Graduate School of Business, April 1972), pp. 66–86.

[9] James F. Engel, Henry F. Fiorillo, and Murray A. Cayley, *Market Segmentation: Concepts and Application* (1972), p. 181. See Article 26, p. 435, "Market Segment Identification through Consumer Buying Behavior and Personal Characteristics."

For other examples of the use of attitudes see Harper W. Boyd, Jr., Michael L. Ray, and Edward C. Strong, "An Attitudinal Framework for Advertising Strategy," *Journal of Marketing*, Vol. 36 (April 1972), pp. 27–33; Dik Warren Twedt, "How Does Brand Awareness-Attitude Affect Marketing Strategy," *Journal of Marketing*, Vol. 31 (October 1967), pp. 64–66; Frank M. Bass and W. Wayne Talarzyk, "An Attitude Model for the Study of Brand Preference," *Journal of Marketing Research*, Vol. IX (February 1972), pp. 93–96.

attitude profile of the ideal product as well as the other brands. Given this knowledge, the marketer can alter product characteristics to conform to that ideal and/or change advertising in an attempt to shift consumers' attitudes toward his product. It is very important, however, to note that consumer attitudes and behavior are not always consistent with one another. Attitudes are not the sole determinants of overt behavior. Frequently other factors are more important. Also, certain factors can occur between the time an attitude is measured and the time behavior takes place. These intervening factors can disrupt what would otherwise be a good prediction of behavior from attitudes. There is also the issue of whether attitude changes necessarily precede behavior change. An article at the end of this chapter focuses on this.

Attitude Scaling Methods

People may judge a brand of toothpaste on its taste, smell, color, consistency, and so forth. A brand's rating on each item can somehow be combined into a total or composite attitude toward the brand. Although attitudes can be measured for individual persons only, marketing research is most interested in predicting the choices of large groups of people; thus, methods of aggregating and generalizing across individuals are extremely important. Attitudes and their components should be efficiently measurable. The instruments and methods of collecting data should not be cumbersome, slow, and subject to error.

Scaling is usually accomplished using paper and pencil methods. Attitude information is interspersed in questionnaires among other information. Attitude measures can be described as falling in two separate categories: aggregative and disaggregative. Aggregative methods are defined as those methods where each component of attitude is measured separately, then combined together to form some aggregative "score." Disaggregative methods typically start with an evaluation of the object or brand and then attempt to "explain" differences due to inferred components of attitudes. This "unfolding" of attitude components is the heart of a group of methods known as *multi*dimensional *s*caling (MDS).

Aggregative Scaling Methods

The simplest aggregative scaling method is that of the *one-dimensional preference scale* such as:

Brand	Dislike	Neither Like nor Dislike			Like
A	1 . . . 2	. . . 3	. . . 4	. . . 5
B	1 . . . 2	. . . 3	. . . 4	. . . 5
etc.				

Other forms for collecting information are possible but are not discussed here.[10] The relative preference of each brand is computed by taking each respondent's vote for brand A and dividing by the sum of all his brand ratings:

$$\text{Pref}_j = \frac{\text{Rating}_j}{\sum\limits_{j} \text{Rating}_j} \tag{1}$$

The method of asking the question (the 1 to 5 scale) is generally known as the Likert scale or may be a version of the semantic differential. The reduction of the preference numbers to a 0 to 1 basis through the computation allows all brands to be compared on a common basis and hence aggregated. If a subject votes 5 on brand A and 3 on brand B, the two brands can be arranged on a common scale pictorially as:

$$\underline{0 \qquad\qquad B \quad A \qquad\qquad 1.0}$$

where A has the value ⅝ and B has the value ⅜.

A variation of this scaling method occurs when a list of brands is presented to a subject who is asked which is his most preferred brand. A value of 1.0 is assigned to the brand he designates and 0 to all of the rest. Although this method of scaling is appealing, it suffers from two major drawbacks. First, it gives no indication of what components of the brand attitude are good or bad, important or unimportant. The second drawback is that the Likert type scale is not necessarily cardinal; that is, people may not view the 3 on the scale as being three times the value of 1 but rather a number that is merely larger than 1. *Cardinality is necessary to interpret how much better brand A is compared to brand B.* It is also a prerequisite to doing statistical analysis, to be discussed in Chapter 12.

Another major method of aggregative scaling is called *Guttman scaling.* This method is used when a researcher is searching for a unidimensional scale describing an attitude structure concerning some object. The Guttman method requires an ordered set of statements about a brand such as:

Brand A tastes good	yes	no
Brand A has a pretty package	yes	no
Brand A smells nice	yes	no
etc.		

The statements are arbitrarily ordered as to importance of the statement (item). Often several orderings are investigated. The first statement is most important, the last is least. This ordering and list of statements is usually obtained in informal interviews with users of the brands in question. The brand rating is computed by examining the "yes" responses to questions. A "yes"

[10] A good summary appears in G. D. Hughes, *Attitude Measurement and Marketing Strategies* (Glenview, Ill.: Scott-Foresman, 1971).

is counted as 1 and a 0 as no. The preference score is computed by examining the questions in order. If the first question is answered "yes," 1 is added to the total score and the next question is examined. The second question is then examined and if "yes," 1 is added to the total and the next question is examined. When a "no" is encountered, the process stops. For each brand, a rating is created which is the total number of "yesses." To find the relative brand preference, the computation in Equation (1) is performed for each subject. However, the ordering of the original statements is very important and subject to controversy because a different ordering of questions will produce different brand preference scores.

A third method of scaling that is one step more complex is a variation of the *Fishbein-Rosenberg* method of scaling. This method involves the answers to two sets of questions by respondents. The first set of questions determines the importance (cognitions) of a set of general attributes of the product class such as:

In evaluating toothpaste in general, how important are the following attributes:

	Not Important At All	Very Important
Minty taste	1 . . . 2 . . . 3 . . . 4 . . . 5
Colorful package	1 . . . 2 . . . 3 . . . 4 . . . 5
etc.		

Each subject then evaluates his or her own set of evaluative criteria. Then the subject rates each brand (affective component) on the same criteria:[11]

For brand A, do the following attributes describe the brand or not:

	Does Not Describe Brand	Describes Brand
Brand A has minty taste	1 . . . 2 . . . 3 . . . 4 . . . 5
Brand A has colorful package	1 . . . 2 . . . 3 . . . 4 . . . 5
etc.		

The exact attributes are determined by prior informal interviews with the subjects in question. There is no ordering of attributes necessary. The preference scores for one subject are normalized by the following computation:

$$\text{Pref}_j = \frac{\sum\limits_{k} A_{kj} \cdot B_{kj}}{\sum\limits_{j} \sum\limits_{k} A_{kj} \cdot B_{kj}}$$

where A is each rating of importance of the general attributes, k and B is the rating of each brand j on each attribute k. For example, if a person voted 5 on taste and 3 on colorful package on the importance of the general attri-

[11] *Ibid.*

butes and 5,5 respectively on the same two attributes for brand A and 2,2 respectively for brand B, the preference scores would be:

$$\text{Pref}_A = \frac{5 \times 5 + 3 \times 5}{5 \times 5 + 3 \times 5 + 5 \times 2 + 3 \times 2} = 0.72$$

$$\text{Pref}_B = \frac{5 \times 2 + 3 \times 2}{5 \times 5 + 3 \times 5 + 5 \times 2 + 3 \times 2} = 0.28$$

The normalized method of computing attitude scores minimized the ordering problems because each subject provides item importance ratings. In addition, the method has interesting diagnostic uses by examining the importance ratings. However, the question of cardinality of the attitude score number can be raised. Table 6.1 explores the degree to which voting at different ends of the 1 to 5 scale can affect the outcome of the preference scores. The table shows a constant difference in that brand 2 is always rated one unit higher than brand 1 on the second attribute and the second attribute is rated one unit more important than the first attribute. The table clearly shows that the worst error caused by this lack of cardinality on the part of a given subject is about 10 percent (comparing the corner values in the table).

TABLE 6.1 *An Analysis of the Biases in the Fishbein-Rosenberg Scaling Method*

Brand	Rating	Preference Score		
		Att 1 = 1 Att 2 = 2	Att 1 = 3 Att 2 = 4	Att 1 = 4 Att 2 = 5
1	1,2[a]	0.417	0.423	0.424
2	1,3	0.583	0.577	0.576
1	3,4	0.458	0.463	0.464
2	3,5	0.542	0.537	0.536
1	4,4	0.462	0.467	0.468
2	4,5	0.538	0.533	0.532

[a] Reads: Respondent voted 1 for the rating of brand 1 on attribute 1 and 2 for attribute 2. This analysis is for one subject and two brands only. Att 1 means the rating of importance of attribute 1 by the respondent.

The affective-cognitive model of attitude structure can be questioned on at least six bases. These bases reflect the fundamental nature of the model and the mathematical method of combining responses together. The specific questions concerning the model[12] include:

[12] This list is drawn from P. E. Green and Y. Wind, "Recent Approaches to the Modeling of Individuals' Subjective Evaluations," paper presented at Attitude Research Conference, Madrid, Spain (December 1972). The answers are based on the authors' perception of current usage among practitioners and academicians.

1. How are the attributes rated by the respondents developed? *Answer*: Usually through small group interviews with the subjects.
2. How do the attributes relate to the "objective" rating of each brand on the attributes? *Answer*: Usually each subject is asked his perception of degree to which a brand appears to have a given attribute, that is, "objective" measurement of the brand is less important than "subjective measurement" (perception).
3. How should the attributes be presented to respondents? *Answer*: Although there is no evidential reason for one method over another, usual practice is to present a series of straightforward, simple questions as to importance of the attribute.
4. What are the scale properties of the ratings and attributes? *Answer*: The scales are only ordinal and vary between respondents and thus must be normalized by the method shown above.
5. What may be the effect of implicit correlations and halo effects on prediction based on the affective-cognitive model? *Answer*: Halo effects are minimized by normalization as shown in Table 6.1. Inter-item correlations can be minimized by factor analyzing (Chapter 13) the attributes. However, using correlated attributes amounts to measuring the same variable twice. The worst error this can cause in prediction is to bias the estimate of the attitude scale value upward by some amount.
6. Is a linear main effects model the proper one for associating the attitude score to probability of purchase? *Answer*: No, it appears that one can predict probability of purchase by taking the scale value to the ¼ power (a highly nonlinear relationship).[13]

Why Use 1 to 5 Scales?

The use of 1 to 5 scales is widespread because a scale with less choice points does not allow the respondent enough flexibility to discriminate among stimuli. Scales with 7 or more choice points typically provide too many choices and subjects have difficulty discriminating among stimuli and hence are slow to complete questionnaires. Six-point scales provide the experimenter with the option of forcing the respondent not to make a neutral choice. The respondent is forced to pick the left or right response even if it is close to the middle value of the scale. Conversely, where a neutral vote is meaningful, the experimenter can use the 1 to 5 scale. Experimenters must also decide what to do if the subject does not follow directions and checks a point halfway between two choice numbers. Typically the number nearest the center is chosen as the intended choice point. For example:

[13] P. C. Burger, "Should the Scales Resulting from Cognitive Consistency Models Be Aggregated?" Working Paper, Graduate School of Management, Northwestern University, Evanston, Illinois (May 1973).

Circle the number that most closely expresses your feeling:

	Does Not Describe Brand					Describes Brand Well

Brand A has a pleasant smell   1 . . . 2 . . . 3 . ✓. 4 . . . 5

or

Brand A has a pleasant smell   1 . . . 2 . . . 3 . ✓. 4 . . . 5 . . . 6

In the first and second cases, the number 3 would be chosen as the intended response. However, the interpretation of the 3 response is slightly different. In the first case 3 is a neutral vote while in the second case it means "slightly does not describe" the brand.

Disaggregative Methods

Recently, a new set of techniques has been made available to researchers interested in the analysis of attitudes. The name of *multidimensional scaling* (MDS) has been attached to these methods. Unlike aggregative scaling methods, multidimensional scaling and related techniques reject the notion that customers' attitudes or images can be combined into a single number or "score." Instead, they attempt to describe the complex and multicomponent nature of these images and attitudes. To this extent, they can be called disaggregative methods.

In operational terms, multidimensional scaling can be defined as a computer-based statistical technique which transforms information provided by a consumer concerning his perceptions and preferences into a set of perceptual and preferential multidimensional spaces (called attribute spaces) in which these brands or other stimuli are expressed as points.

An Example of Multidimensional Scaling

In order to make the discussion a little more concrete, one can consider the typical output obtained through a MDS computer program. This output might look like Figure 6.3. A number of interesting features can be read from this map obtained from a single consumer.

First of all, it can be seen from Figure 6.3 that the consumer's perceptions and preference of 1968 car models can be located in a two-dimensional space made up of the two attributes of sportiness and luxuriousness. In other words, the dimensionality of the attribute space is two. Second, it can be seen that, as far as perceptions are concerned, each stimulus, that is, each car model, can be represented as a point in this space and therefore corresponds to a specific combination of the two attributes. Thus, one can see that the subject perceives the Lincoln Continental as a very luxurious car but not a very sporty one. Inversely, he sees the Mustang as somewhat more sporty but much less luxurious.

In addition to the subject's perceptions, Figure 6.3 also tells us about his

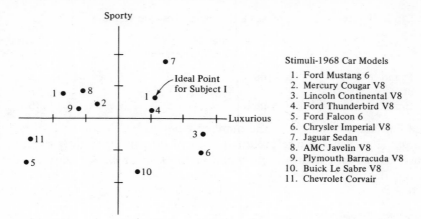

FIGURE 6.3 *An Illustration of Similarities Preference Space of Ideal Points and Stimuli*
Source: P. E. Green and F. J. Carmone, *Multidimensional Scaling and Related Techniques in Marketing Analysis,* Allyn and Bacon, Boston, Mass., p. 53.

preferences. Figure 6.3 shows the subject's ideal point which represents his perceived optimum combination of sportiness and luxuriousness as far as cars are concerned. This information is also obtained from the subject's answers. Now, one must make the basic assumption that there are geometric (Euclidean) distances lying between each of the brand-stimuli and the *ideal point* which provide indicators of the subject's respective preferences (an ideal brand of car). The car model which lies closest to the ideal point is the most preferred one, the car which comes next is the second best, and so forth. Thus, it can be seen in Figure 6.3 that the car most preferred by the subject is the Ford Thunderbird and that the car he least prefers is the Ford Falcon. Similarly, it can be seen that the subject prefers the Lincoln Continental to the Buick LeSabre, the Mercury Cougar to the Chevrolet Corvair, and so on. In fact, a complete array of preferences can be derived from Figure 6.3.

Just as distances lying between car models and the ideal point are indicators of *preferences,* distances lying between car models and other car models are indicators of *similarities.* For example, the subject perceives the Lincoln Continental and the Chrysler Imperial as very similar, that is, as having roughly the same amount of sportiness and luxuriousness. He presumably views these two cars as truly competitive. On the basis of similarities data, it can be seen that the map represented in Figure 6.3 can be "clustered" into a number of groups of cars presenting similar characteristics. The Ford Mustang, the AMC Javelin, the Mercury Cougar, and the Plymouth Barracuda would form such a group; the Chevrolet Corvair and the Ford Falcon would form another one. To a marketer, the identification of such groups can be of very real interest because it allows him to know which product is perceived as an alternative to his. If one incorporates preference data into the analysis, one can find that it is possible to order groups of cars according to their average distance from the ideal point. Thus, we can see that the subject typically prefers cars which are somewhat sporty but not very luxurious to cars which are not sporty at all and even less luxurious. Inversely, it is not clear from Figure 6.3 whether the subject prefers sporty but not luxurious cars (such as the Ford Mustang) to the luxurious but not sporty cars (such as the Chrysler Imperial). To the subject, making a choice between these two types of cars would probably be a matter of some debate.

The Process of Multidimensional Scaling

How are *maps* such as the one presented in Figure 6.3 *generated?* To illustrate the discussion, we develop an example.

The key research question is "How are the leading brands of the cola drink market perceived?" To make the discussion even more specific, the images of four brands are to be investigated: Coca-Cola, Pepsi-Cola, Royal Crown (R. C.) Cola, and Dr. Pepper. The first thing to know is how these brands are perceived relative to each other. Which brands are considered similar? What type of attributes do people use in the perception of cola drinks? In other words, one would want to collect similarities data concerning the colas.

A typical method for collecting similarities data is known as the *method of triads*. This technique consists of selecting all possible sets of three stimuli and asking the respondent to indicate those two among the three which are most similar and those two which are least similar. (This method sometimes is called a conjoint comparisons method since the subject is asked to compare only pairs which have one stimulus in common.) Accordingly, the instructions given to respondents will most probably look like this for each of the following sets of brands:

Please pick the two brands you think are most similar; next pick the two which are least similar.

	Answer
Coca-Cola, Pepsi-Cola, R. C.	. . . and . . . are most similar
	. . . and . . . are least similar
Pepsi-Cola, Dr. Pepper, R. C.	. . . and . . . are most similar
	. . . and . . . are least similar
Dr. Pepper, Coca-Cola, Pepsi-Cola	. . . and . . . are most similar
	. . . and . . . are least similar
R. C., Coca-Cola, Dr. Pepper	. . . and . . . are most similar
	. . . and . . . are least similar

The method of triads is by no means the only available method for collecting similarities data. The reader will quickly recognize that when the number of stimuli becomes large (greater than 8), the method of triads becomes laborious and inappropriate since one must ask respondents to con- sider all possible triads of stimuli.[14] Had it been decided to study the images of beer companies where the number of leading brands far exceeds 8, another method known as the *anchor point technique* would have been used. In this method each brand is selected in turn as the "anchor point." The subject is then asked to rank-order all remaining $n - 1$ stimuli according to their degree of similarity with the anchor point. Although this method is considerably faster than the method of triads, it should be recognized that it assumes a higher level of classification abilities among respondents. The anchor point method also belongs to the category of conjoint comparisons methods.

More generally, techniques such as the method of triads or the anchor point method form only one class of similarities data collection methods. This class is known as the *directly judged similarities* class. For a complete taxonomy and description of similarities data collection techniques, the reader is referred to Green and Carmone.[15]

An example of the data collection method and preparation of data for analysis assumes that a typical subject has completed the questionnaire as follows:

	Answer
Coca-Cola, Pepsi-Cola, R. C.	Coke . . . and Pepsi . . . are most similar
	Coke . . . and R. C. . . . are least similar
Pepsi-Cola, Dr. Pepper, R. C.	Dr. Pepper . . . and R. C. . . . are most similar
	Pepsi . . . and Dr. Pepper . . . are least similar
Dr. Pepper, Coca-Cola, Pepsi-Cola	Coke . . . and Pepsi . . . are most similar
	Coke . . . and Dr. Pepper . . . are least similar
R. C., Coca-Cola, Dr. Pepper	Dr. Pepper . . . and R. C. . . . are most similar
	Coke . . . and Dr. Pepper . . . are least similar

The first step in the analysis of similarities data consists in preparing the input for a MDS computer program. Most computer programs do not accept similarities data in the form just presented above but require the preparation of similarities (or dissimilarities) rank-ordered matrices.

Examining the first response, one can see that the pair Coke and Pepsi is more similar than the pair Coke and R. C. In addition, there is an implica- tion for the unstated pair Pepsi and R. C. That implication is that Pepsi and R. C. are less similar than Coke and Pepsi but more similar than Coke and R. C. The researcher examines the pairwise similarities and assigns a 0 or 1

[14] The reader with some mathematical background will recognize that the number of ways in which it is possible to form groups of 3 stimuli out of a set of n is equal to the combinational number $\left(\dfrac{n}{3}\right) = \dfrac{n!}{3!(n-3)!}$. When n exceeds 7 or 8, this number becomes large.

[15] P. E. Green and F. J. Carmone, *Multidimensional Scaling and Related Techniques in Marketing Analysis* (Boston, Mass.: Allyn and Bacon, 1970), pp. 53–57.

to the pair comparisons depending if one pair is more similar than another pair. These data are transferred to a matrix as shown in Figure 6.4.

Rows	Columns					
	Coca-Cola Pepsi-Cola	Coca-Cola R. C.	Coca-Cola Dr. Pepper	Pepsi-Cola R. C.	Pepsi-Cola Dr. Pepper	R. C. Dr. Pepper
Coca-Cola Pepsi-Cola	0	0	0	0	0	
Coca-Cola R. C.	1	0	0	1		1
Coca-Cola Dr. Pepper	1	1	0		1	1
Pepsi-Cola R. C.	1	0		0	0	1
Pepsi-Cola Dr. Pepper	1		0	1	0	1
R. C. Dr. Pepper		0	0	0	0	0

FIGURE 6.4 *Similarity/Dissimilarity Matrix Based on Example Response*

Figure 6.4 is filled in from the responses to the questionnaire by noting the stated and implied pair comparisons. First 0's are placed down the diagonal because all pairs are similar to themselves. Then the rest of the matrix is filled. Since Coke and Pepsi head the first column, looking down the column one finds the pair Coke-R. C. Since the subject has said that Coke-R. C. is less similar than Coke-Pepsi, a 1 is placed in the intersection. Conversely, a 0 is placed in the cell where the row Pepsi-Coke intersects Coke-R. C. because Pepsi-Coke is more similar than Coke-R. C. Thus, the column pairs are, by convention, rated in similarity to the row pairs with a 0 meaning more similar and a 1 meaning less similar. All of the cells are filled in the same way.

In general, Coca-Cola, Pepsi-Cola is very similar since it has only 0's in its row. It is consistently found more similar than any other pair (except "R. C., Dr. Pepper"). Inversely, it appears that Coca-Cola and Dr. Pepper are regarded by the subject as quite dissimilar brands. More generally, the row total is an indicator of dissimilarity (alternatively it can be said that the column total is an indicator of similarity). If one now reorders the matrix according to increasing row total of 1's, one obtains the matrix shown in Figure 6.5.

	Row Total	Coca-Cola Pepsi-Cola	R. C. Dr. Pepper	Pepsi-Cola R. C.	Coca-Cola R. C.	Pepsi-Cola Dr. Pepper	Coca-Cola Dr. Pepper
Coca-Cola Pepsi-Cola	0	0		0	0	0	0
R. C. Dr. Pepper	0		0	0	0	0	0
Pepsi-Cola R. C.	2	1	1	0	0	0	
Coca-Cola R. C.	3	1	1	1	0		0
Pepsi-Cola Dr. Pepper	3	1	1	1		0	0
Coca-Cola Dr. Pepper	4	1	1		1	1	0

FIGURE 6.5   *Example of Ranked Dissimilarity Matrix from Previous Example*

This matrix is said to be "completely consistent" because no 0's appear below the main diagonal (or alternatively, no 1's appear above the diagonal). In other words, the transitivity "relationship" ("if pair A is more similar than pair B and pair B is more similar than pair C, then pair A is more similar than pair C") is never violated by subject S. When the number of stimuli is small, as in the example, this result should be expected from most normal subjects. When the number of stimuli is large, it becomes difficult for a subject to respect the transitivity rule. In that case, some "0's" will begin to appear below the matrix diagonal and some "1's" will appear above it.

Finally, one must assign ranks to the pairs of brands according to their row total. In case of ties, ranks are averaged. In the sample, ranks would therefore be assigned as follows:

Coca-Cola, Pepsi-Cola	1.5
R. C., Dr. Pepper	1.5
Pepsi-Cola, R. C.	3
Coca-Cola, R. C.	4.5
Pepsi-Cola, Dr. Pepper	4.5
Coca-Cola, Dr. Pepper	6

	Coca-Cola	R. C.	Pepsi-Cola	Dr. Pepper
Coca-Cola	—	4.5	1.5	6
R. C.	—	—	3	1.5
Pepsi-Cola	—	—	—	4.5
Dr. Pepper	—	—	—	—

FIGURE 6.6 *Ranked Similarity of Individual Brands from Example as Input to Multidimensional Scaling Program (δ_{ij})*

It is clear from the data above that some brands are perceived as rather similar and others as rather dissimilar. If we rearrange this information under the form of an upper-half matrix, we obtain the basic input for MDS computer programs such as MDSCAL-V shown in Figure 6.6. Since the detailed procedure followed by the computer in generating maps is relatively complex and beyond the scope of this discussion, only the logic underlying it will be presented.

Broadly speaking, the task of the computer is to find a "configuration" of objects (brands) which, for a given number of dimensions, best expresses the original relationship shown in the dissimilarities matrix. When the number of stimuli is small, such a task is not difficult and can be done by hand.

The "one-dimensional map" (a straight line) shown below is found through a "cut and try" method which can completely satisfy all these relationships for the soft drink example.

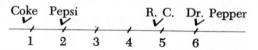

Coke is close to Pepsi yet far away from Dr. Pepper roughly in proportion to the ranked similarity. Thus, ranking has converted to a scale. The scale might be inferred to be "sweetness," with Coke most sweet and Dr. Pepper least sweet.

When the number of stimuli increases, the number of required dimensions is likely to increase too, and very soon a computer is needed. Once dimensionality structure is specified by the researcher, here is how the computer works. The computer starts with a configuration in that structure which is either provided by the researcher or generated by the computer itself. Then it "tests" the configuration against the relationships expressed in the similarities data. It accomplishes this step through the computation of the distances between stimuli (brands) as they appear in the configuration (the distances are called d_{ij}) and a set of numbers (named $\hat{d}_{ij}$) chosen to be as close as possible to the d_{ij} but constrained to be consistent with the original data ranks δ_{ij}.

The comparison between these two sets of numbers is called the *Kruskal's stress measure*. Two basic formulas have been developed for measuring the stress:

$$S_1 = \left[\frac{\sum_{i \neq j}^{n} (d_{ij} - \hat{d}_{ij})^2}{\sum_{i=j}^{n} d_{ij}} \right]^{1/2} \qquad S_2 = \left[\frac{\sum_{i \neq j}^{n} (d_{ij} - \hat{d}_{ij})^2}{\sum_{i=j}^{n} (d_{ij} - \bar{d})^2} \right]^{1/2}$$

While formula S_1 (which was the one originally developed by J. B. Kruskal) has been used in most early MDS computer program formulas S_2 now seems to be preferred by researchers.[16] Flexible MDS computer programs such as MDSCAL-V are capable of working with either formula. Most of the time, the maps obtained with the two formulas are very similar, if not identical. The value of the stress is computed and tested against standard selected values. Generally speaking, a stress of 0.05 or less is considered good. A stress of 0.01 or less is considered excellent.

If the stress computed for the original configuration happens to be unsatisfactory (that is the usual case), the computer attempts to "improve" the stress by finding a new configuration in which the ranks of the d_{ij} are closer to the original δ_{ij}. This new configuration is again tested for its stress value. If the second stress is still not satisfactory, the iterative process goes on.

Finally, a configuration $\hat{X}$ is reached for which either the stress has the minimum possible value or reaches the prespecified satisfactory level. If the value of the stress is satisfactory, the researcher might try the whole process again using a new dimensional structure (more dimensions). In fact, the problem faced by a researcher using a MDS computer program always takes the form of a tradeoff between satisfactory stress and minimum dimensionality. In practice, the solution consists in choosing the lowest dimensionality structure for which the stress is still satisfactory. In making the final decision, the researcher can always benefit from studying a graph (sometimes directly generated by the computer) which shows the value of the stress for a number of dimensionality structures. Such a graph is shown in Figure 6.7.

In the case illustrated in Figure 6.7, it is clear that the "optimum" dimensionality is 3, the number of dimensions which correspond to the "elbow" in the stress curve.

Interpreting MDS Scales

If the researcher follows all the preceding steps in submitting input data to a MDS computer program, he may very well obtain a map similar to the one presented on Figure 6.3 without labels being attached to the axes.

---

[16] It should be recognized that the difference between the first and second formula only lies in the fact that in S_2 the denominator is expressed in terms of variations from the mean rather than absolute variations. Certain theoretical advantages, not described here, are attached to this second formulation.

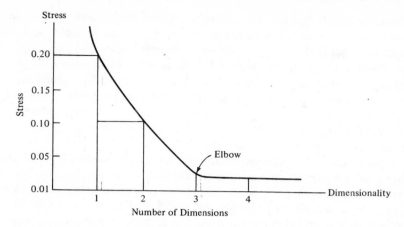

FIGURE 6.7 *Graph of Stress versus Number of Dimensions*

MDS is a numerical procedure and therefore ignores the problem of axis labeling. There are a number of ways in which the researcher can still put names on the dimensions. First, he may consider the particular pattern of stimuli (brand) projections on each axis in turn. A simple look at which stimuli (brands) fall close to the axes, which stimuli have extreme axis values, and which stimuli are in the middle, might suggest rather specific dimensions (names).

The researcher may elect to collect the labeling information from the respondents themselves. Once the maps are generated, they are submitted, unlabeled, to respondents who are asked to investigate possible labels for the corresponding dimensions once the labels are obtained, it is generally a good idea to check them again with the respondents by submitting to them the same maps as before with the axes labeled but not the stimuli (brands). Subjects are asked to "rediscover" the stimuli. Their guesses are then checked with the original points. If some convergence is achieved, confidence in the axis labeling is increased.

Finally, the researcher might ask respondents to locate the position of the brand-stimuli on a set of prespecified scales and then compare the patterns thus obtained to those derived from the multidimensional map.

Preference and MDS Scales

There are various ways in which preference data can be analyzed by MDS programs. When preference data are collected simultaneously with similarities data, a relatively easy way to analyze preferences is to make use of the concept of ideal point. The ideal point can be treated exactly as any other stimulus point and the research procedure is no different from the one used to analyze similarities data.

When the researcher is reluctant to accept the hypothesis of an explicit ideal point, another solution consists in *inferring* it from simple preference judgments. In using this approach, however, the researcher faces an important problem. There is no guarantee that the same number of dimensions are used to perceive and evaluate the stimuli (brands). Practically, some kind of compromise has to be made. A dimensionality structure has to be found which is able to represent both perceptions and preferences; or, alternatively, the rules which allow one to go from perceptual to preferential configurations have to be made explicit.

In recent years, the problem of finding adequate models able to relate preferences to geometric representations derived from similarity data has generated much research and led to the development of more sophisticated MDS type programs such as J. D. Carroll and J. J. Chang's PREF-MAP. Although relatively recent, MDS has been applied to a number of problems including image analysis, market segmentation, product life cycle analysis, ads and salesman evaluation, brand switching analysis, and attitude measurement.

MDS Problems

Current work is being developed on both computational and conceptual problems. The main problem with MDS is that (1) the interpretation of the scales require judgment and (2) the "prediction" is lacking, because the ideal points are not necessarily related to brands purchased. At the conceptual level, some of the most promising avenues for future research are (1) the attempt made to use MDS not only to analyze perceptions and preferences at a given moment, but the evolution of those perceptions and preferences over time; (2) the attempt made to incorporate stochastic instead of deterministic analysis in MDS computer programs. So far, statements of perceptions and preferences have not been subject to uncertainty measures. In the future, it might be desirable to base those perceptions and preferences on probability distributions so as to fully take into account their nondeterministic nature; (3) the attempt made to measure configuration invariance with respect to the number of stimuli considered and the data collection and data analysis techniques. What happens to a configuration if the similarities data collection, for example, is modified? Some research is currently under progress to provide at least partial solutions to such questions.

In conclusion, it thus appears that MDS is a very promising but still largely unexplored technique. Once the computational problems are solved, the application of MDS techniques will only be limited by the creative imagination of marketing researchers. To facilitate the integration of MDS tools with the already numerous set of existing techniques, researchers will increasingly have to contrast and compare results obtained with more than one analytic technique.

Summary

This chapter has attempted to discuss and define the key variables that the marketing researcher uses when he is exploring consumer behavior. Key behavioral concepts of culture, roles, status, social class, and attitudes among others are shown. Attitudes are discussed in detail together with common attitude scaling methods. In addition, consumer's role in the purchase decision is defined and illustrated. This chapter has given the groundwork for the development of the questionnaire and the laboratory form which are the most common measurement tools used in marketing research.

Questions and Exercises

1. Think about your attitudes toward a brand and model of automobile. Try to define the affective and cognitive aspects of your attitude.
2. Why is it the case that often attitudes cannot be directly linked to behavior? What intervening variables can cause problems in the linkage?
3. Find an article in the *Wall Street Journal, Harvard Business Review, Journal of Marketing,* or some other publication which discusses attitudes. What methods of measurement are implicit in the article? What uses are proposed for the attitude constructs?
4. Compute the normalized preference scores for the following persons' responses: Brand A—3 (on a 1 to 5 scale), Brand B—2, Brand C—5. Compare the result with another subject's responses of A—4, B—4, and C—5. (*Hint*: See text regarding Fishbein-Rosenberg scale.)
5. Which of the differences between the subjects in Question 4 could be due to actual preferences and which could be due to bias in responses to the scale? How might a researcher handle this problem?
6. A respondent in an interview has given the following data on a 1 to 5 scale. "In general, I feel that the following attributes have importance weighting: smell—2, taste—4, and package convenience—3." Brand A has ratings on smell, taste, and package convenience of 2, 2, and 4, respectively. (The rating is the degree to which the brand bears the trait.) Brand B has ratings of 4, 4, 2. Which brand is most preferred?
7. Some researchers have found that the general importance ratings do not add much to the explanation or prediction ability of the scaling method used in Question 6. What reasons might exist for this finding?
8. Consider some item in your experience space such as four brands of candy bars. Compare the brands using the method of triads as discussed in this chapter. Create a similarity/dissimilarity matrix.
9. Reorder the rows and columns of the similarity/dissimilarity matrix such that the lowest row totals are first and the highest are last.

10. Find the brand rankings from the ranked s/d matrix and then "by eye-ball," creating a one-dimensional scale. Try to name the scale.
11. Perform steps in Questions 8, 9, and 10 adding the ideal brand to the set. Interpret the results.

Project Related Questions

1. Have you carefully defined what you mean by "attitude?"
2. Have you carefully specified what the objects are to which the attitudes refer?
3. Are you using attitudes to predict behavior? If so, are you aware of the problems associated with this? (See, for example, the two following readings.)
4. Have you identified the factors which affect the attitudes you are concerned with?
5. How are you going to scale attitudes in your study? Will the attitude scaling mechanism give enough detail to test your hypotheses adequately? Does the respondent have enough freedom in terms of choice points, that is, will a 1–5 scale be adequate? Might a wider or narrower choice be necessary? Has this been pilot tested?

The articles that follow show how attitudes are used in marketing research. In addition, the research reported gives a representative picture of findings using existing measurement technology.

Determinant Buying Attitudes: Meaning and Measurement

James H. Myers and Mark I. Alpert

Which attitudes are related to purchasing decisions? In this article the authors argue that out of many possible attitudes only a few really relate to or "determine" buying behavior. These attitudes are defined in this article and methods of measuring them are discussed.

Although a great amount of effort is spent in measuring attitudes toward products or services, in many cases little time is devoted to determining what attitudes *mean* in terms of decision making and especially buying action. Some researchers do not even bother to ask respondents which attitudes they consider important, or which attitudes predispose them toward a particular choice in the marketplace. And even when these questions are asked, answers are often not related to *actual* buying behavior. Yet this is the really crucial information in consumer attitudinal research in most cases.

This paper will discuss *determinant attitudes*, their meaning and relevance to marketing strategy, and methods by which they can be measured. Hopefully, this discussion will encourage marketers of all types to give greater thought to the relevance of attitudes rather than to their measurement only.

MEANING OF ATTITUDE DETERMINANCE

In the wide spectrum of all of the various features of a product or brand, there are some features which predispose consumers to action (that is, to preference for the product, to actual purchase, to making recommendations to friends, etc.) and others which do not. *Attitudes toward features which are most closely related to preference or to actual purchase decisions are said to be determinant*; the remaining features or attitudes—no matter how favorable—are not determinant. Marketers obviously need to know which attitudes or features lead to—or "determine"—buying behavior, for these are the features around which marketing strategy must be built. Yet this distinction is often not clearly drawn or properly developed, even in many sophisticated consumer products or service firms.

The concept herein called attitude "determinance" is essentially the same as what Krech and Crutchfield have defined as "importance."[1] The present

[1] David Krech and Richard S. Crutchfield, *Theory and Problems of Social Psychology* (New York: McGraw-Hill Book Co., 1948).

SOURCE: Reprinted from the *Journal of Marketing*, Vol. 32 (October 1968), pp. 13–20. Published by the American Marketing Association.

authors have chosen to define a new term because "importance" has become diluted by loose usage. It usually connotes no more than a moderate relationship to decision making, while we wish to discuss attitudes which are truly *decisive*. Hence, we prefer "determinance," a term which can have more specific meaning than "importance."

For every product, brand, pattern, style, or other individual offering to the public, there are at least two "levels" of evaluation by consumers:

1. *Overall attitude* toward the item, in terms of its suitability or desirability. The relationship of overall attitude to subsequent buying action has been discussed by Palda,[2] DuBois,[3] Howard,[4] and others.
2. Attitudes toward each of the item's *component* features or characteristics. These attitudes presumably combine or summate in some way to produce an "overall attitude" toward the item.

This paper will consider primarily these latter types of attitudes; for example, *what* the important features or characteristics are and *how* they combine to affect both the overall evalua-

tion of an item and the actual purchasing decision.

Strictly speaking, then, this article will discuss "feature determinance," or "attribute determinance," rather than "attitude determinance," since the various features and attributes are what combine into the whole. However, since it is the *attitudes* toward the various features that combine into the overall evaluation or attitude, often reference will be made to determinant attitudes rather than features.

With reference to determinant attitudes, Nelson Foote, Manager of the Consumer and Public Relations Research Program for General Electric, commented:

> In the electrical appliance business, we have been impressed over and over by the way in which certain characteristics of products come to be taken for granted by consumers, especially those concerned with basic functional performance or with values like safety. If these values are missing in a product, the user is extremely offended. But if they are present, the maker or seller gets no special credit or preference, because quite logically every other maker and seller is assumed to be offering equivalent values. In other words, the values that are salient in decision-making are the values that are problematic—that are important, to be sure but also those which differentiate one offering from another.[5]

[2] Kristian S. Palda, "The Hypothesis of a Hierarchy of Effects: A Partial Evaluation," *Journal of Marketing Research*, Vol. 3 (February 1966), pp. 13–24.

[3] Cornelius DuBois, "The Story of Brand XL: How Consumer Attitudes Affected Its Market Position," *Public Opinion Quarterly*, Vol. 24, Proceedings, Fifteenth Annual Conference, American Association for Public Opinion Research (Fall 1960), pp. 479–480.

[4] John A. Howard, *Marketing: Executive and Buyer Behavior* (Columbia University Press, 1963).

[5] Nelson N. Foote, "Consumer Behavior: Household Decision-Making," Vol. 4 (New York University Press, 1961).

To further illustrate this concept, in proprietary studies asking consumers to evaluate such automobile attributes as power, comfort, economy, appearance, and safety, consumers often rank *safety* as first in importance. However, these same consumers do not see various makes of cars as differing widely with respect to safety; therefore, safety is not a determinant attitude or feature in the actual purchase decision. Without the knowledge that consumers see little difference among cars in terms of safety, it would be natural for the manufacturer to conclude that safety *is* an important motivator in terms of the purchasing decision and to stress this in promotion efforts, when the same funds might be more effectively used to stress attributes which actually determine product choice.

This is not to say, of course, that a manufacturer can get away with ignoring safety considerations. At any given time, all the various brands may have about the same level of perceived possession of an attribute (safety), and thus it will not be as important for the present as some attribute for which differences *are* the basis for current brand preferences. This should rightly lead the company to concentrate on raising its performance in features other than safety. However, if safety is totally ignored, the brand may soon be perceived as being so unsafe that its share of the market might slip. This would imply that safety could *achieve* determinance, a quality it would hold until concentration on safety by the "un-safe" company would bring its product back into line with the others. Thus, determinance is a dynamic concept, and studies relating attitudes to buying behavior need to be repeated often enough to keep informed of these possible shifts.

Non-determinant Attitudes

The concept of determinant attitudes can further be illustrated by showing results from a recent study wherein these attitudes did *not* emerge. This study was undertaken by an airline to measure its image and that of its competitors among the flying public. Passengers on each of three airlines were asked to rate that airline (the one they were traveling on) on various factors or features thought to be important, and then to give an overall evaluation of that airline. Results are shown in Table 1.

What is being sought is one or more of the rated features or services

TABLE 1 *Percentage of Passengers Rating "Excellent"*

Feature	Airline #1	Airline #2	Airline #3
Overall Service	43%	46%	49%
Baggage Check-In	42	53	48
Ticket Counter	44	49	46
Boarding Gate	45	57	47
Liquor, 1st Class	61	62	52
Liquor, Coach	39	41	37
Hostess, 1st Class	74	71	66
Hostess, Coach	61	62	55
Food, 1st Class	61	59	52
Food, Coach	42	45	36

that *relate* to the evaluation of overall service. That is, the airline rated highest on overall service should also be rated highest on at least one of the service features covered in the survey. Conversely, the lowest rated airline should also be rated lowest on this same feature. Such a feature would thus be related to the overall evaluation and would likely be a "determinant" attitude in terms of choice of airline. It is interesting to note from Table 1 that the airline receiving the highest overall evaluation (Airline #3) was not rated highest on any of the various components or features. As a matter of fact, it was rated lowest on six of the nine features! Apparently none of the features covered in this survey is related to, or "determines," the choice among airlines. What does determine choice, then? We apparently do not know, at least from the results of this survey.

The reader may protest that the criterion (overall evaluation) is attitudinal, and not behavioral. What people *say* may not be what they *do*, when it comes to actual choice among competing airlines. Yet the airline receiving the highest overall evaluation (Airline #3) was also the one showing the *greatest increase in share of market in preceding months*. Even then, however, one must be cautious in inferring *causality* from *relationships*, as in any non-experimental study. It might be, for example, that Airline #3 also increased its schedules the most during this period of time. However, when both attitudinal and behavioral criteria point in the same direction, marketers can feel more confident in drawing conclusions about determinant attitudes.

IDENTIFYING DETERMINANT ATTITUDES

In order to identify which attitudes are determinant and to discern their relative *degree* of determinance, it is necessary to go beyond the mere scaling of respondents' attitudes. The study design must also include a methodology for measuring determinance, for this will not just naturally develop in the course of scaling.

There are three major approaches to identifying determinant attitudes:

1. Direct questioning
2. Indirect questioning, including motivation research and covariate analysis
3. Observation and experiment

At the present time, it is apparently not known which of these three is most effective for any given problem or application. (A definitive study comparing these approaches under carefully controlled conditions is under way as part of a doctoral dissertation by the second author of this paper.) The purpose of this article is not to answer the question of the comparative effectiveness of the three approaches, but rather to present illustrations of each so that the techniques will be clear and can be used by future investigators.

Direct Questioning

The most obvious way to approach determinant attitudes is, of course, to ask consumers directly what factors *they consider important* in a purchasing decision. Thus, the respondent is asked to state his reasons for preferring one product or brand to another, or possibly to explain why he buys one item and not another. Or, he may be asked to rate his "ideal brand" for a given product in terms of several product attributes, so that an ideal profile may be constructed. In any event, direct questioning approaches put the respondent "on the spot" concerning his own motivations, as opposed to such indirect questioning methods as "motivation research," which infer a person's motives from what he says in response to indirect questioning or to projective stimuli.

For many years, direct questioning involved asking respondents to tell why they bought or did not buy a given product as a means of uncovering determinant attitudes. Variations of this traditional approach called for asking the respondent to name the attributes he looks for in his choice of a given product. The researcher tabulated responses according to attribute categories and presumed that frequency of naming an attribute indicated its relative importance in the buying decision.

This approach has the appeal of seeming to get directly to the issue of "Why do you buy?" However, it has unfortunately rested upon two very questionable assumptions, namely: (1) the respondent *knows* why he buys or prefers one product to another, and (2) the respondent will *willingly tell* what these reasons are. The literature of marketing research contains refutations of these assumptions; it is not necessary to go into great detail dis-

puting them here. The plain fact appears to be that consumers often do not understand their own reasons for purchasing something, and even when they do they are unwilling to admit what may make them look foolish or irrational. Consequently many answers given to traditional direct questioning approaches have often been faithfully reported, analyzed, and acted upon, only to learn later that the action taken proved to be irrelevant to the typical consumer's purchasing decision.

"Ideal" Attributes

A direct questioning approach which has been popular consists of asking respondents to describe the characteristics of the "ideal" brand or company in the product or service category being studied. By also asking for ratings on a particular brand in terms of these characteristics, one hopes to find out where "gaps" exist between his own brand image and the optimal brand image. Unfortunately, this approach shares the problems of traditional direct questioning, in that people may have difficulty in conceptualizing the "ideal" brand and also might be unwilling to admit to some of the attributes by which they really are influenced. An excellent illustration of this approach can be found in an article by Bolger.[6]

Dual Questioning

Another problem common to the above approaches is that there is little

[6] John F. Bolger, Jr., "How to Evaluate Your Company Image," *Journal of Marketing*, Vol. 24 (October 1959), pp. 7–10.

attempt by the researcher to account for the fact that certain attributes which might be seen by respondents as being important, are also seen as being possessed in *equal degree* by the competing alternative selections. Where this occurs, any approach which merely asks "What is important in choosing a ......?" will overemphasize the role of such attributes as automobile safety, for example (as mentioned earlier in this paper). For even if one elicits honest answers, the questions may not be sufficiently meaningful to allow the focus to be narrowed to attributes which truly determine consumer behavior.

This problem leads to another major direct questioning approach, one which will be called "dual questioning." This approach involves asking two questions concerning each product attribute which might be determinant. Consumers are first asked directly what factors they consider *important* in a purchasing decision, and then they are asked how they perceive these factors as *differing* among the various products or brands. As an illustration of this approach, consider Tables 2 and 3 which were developed in the process of a survey among the general public in the Los Angeles area relative to attitudes toward savings and loan associations. (The various benefits or claims are ranked in descending order in each table, so that comparisons between the tables can be made more easily.)

Notice that some items rank high in rated importance but are *not* thought to differ much among the various savings and loan associations (for

example, safety of money, interest rate earned). Thus, while safety of money was ranked first in importance, about half of all respondents felt there was *no difference* among savings and loan associations in terms of safety; therefore, safety of funds might not be the most *determinant* attitude even though it was rated the most important attitude by respondents. Conversely, some items show big differences among the various associations but are considered to be of relatively *little* importance in determining the choice of a savings and loan association (for example, years in business, parking convenience).

On the other hand, interest rate shows a very high "importance" rank-

TABLE 2 *Importance Ratings of Savings and Loan Characteristics*

Benefit or Claim	Average Ratings*
Safety of money	1.4
Interest rate earned	1.6
Government insurance	1.6
Financial strength	2.0
Ease of withdrawing money	2.0
Management ability	2.0
Attitude of personnel	2.1
Speed/efficiency of service	2.2
Compounding frequency	2.2
Branch location convenience	2.3
Time required to earn interest	2.3
Parking convenience	2.4
Years in business	2.5
Other services	3.1
Building/office attractiveness	3.4
Premiums offered	4.0

* (1—"extremely important"
   2—"very important"
   3—"fairly important"
   4—"slightly important," etc.)

TABLE 3   *Difference Rating of Savings and Loan Characteristics*

Benefit or Claim	Big Diff.	Small Diff.	No Diff.	Don't Know
Years in business	53%	31%	10%	6%
Financial strength	40	32	22	6
Parking convenience	37	35	22	6
Safety of money	36	15	47	2
Management ability	35	26	27	12
Government insurance	35	11	51	3
Branch location convenience	34	36	28	2
Attitude of personnel	34	28	33	5
Interest rate earned	33	30	35	2
Speed/efficiency of service	32	28	35	5
Ease of withdrawing money	29	18	48	5
Compounding frequency	28	36	31	5
Time required to earn interest	26	34	33	7
Building/office attractiveness	24	44	30	2
Other services offered	21	34	29	16
Premiums offered	15	36	38	11

ing and *far fewer* respondents feel there is *no* difference among the various associations relative to interest rate. Also, financial strength was somewhat lower in rated importance, but was second highest in terms of the difference among various associations. Therefore, these two—interest rate and financial strength—might be relatively determinant attitudes. In similar fashion, the researcher can proceed through an analysis of the various ratings to identify which attitudes seem to influence the choice most among various savings and loan associations and are thus presumably the most determinant.

Indirect Questioning

Another approach to identifying determinant attitudes is through indirect questioning, of which there are many forms. We will define "indirect questioning" as any interviewing approach which does not *directly* ask respondents to indicate the reasons why they bought a product or service, or which features or attributes are most important in determining choice. The most prominent form of indirect questioning is probably "motivation research," but it is by no means the only way indirect questioning can be done or used.

Motivation Research   In spite of the claims of motivation researchers that they are always uncovering the "real" reasons for buying, few carefully controlled studies can be cited in support of this position. One comparative study was done by Gerhard Wiebe,[7]

[7] Gerhard D. Wiebe, "Sampling-Motivation Research Merger: How Will It Aid Ad Men?" *Printers' Ink* (November 28, 1958), p. 23 ff.

contrasting results from "incomplete sentence" questions with results from direct questions on the same topic, in a survey of a firm which provides building maintenance services for large office buildings. The incomplete sentence approach produced, in this case at least, not only *more* information but also feelings of a different tone than were obtained from conventional direct questioning. It appears from Wiebe's results that dissatisfactions over personnel were more important than direct questioning would indicate. However, it should be noted that no attempt was made to relate these responses to any action or even to expected action on the part of customers.

Inference of "Ideal" Attributes An approach which is more quantified than most motivational research techniques, yet less quantified than the covariate and regression models discussed later, is that of *inferring* an "ideal" brand from responses which describe people's feelings about a number of competing brands or companies. These methods are similar to direct questioning; however, the respondent is not asked to expose his preferences and motives to the extent required in directly rating the "ideal" company or brand.

Louis Cohen infers the "ideal" image from the varying degree of association between certain traits and companies which are ranked at varying levels of desirability.[8] Cohen asks

respondents to associate a list of traits with several companies, and also to rank the companies on an overall basis. For each trait he then compiles a listing of the percentage of respondents associating it with their own highest rated company, and the percentage associating it with their lowest rated company. The ratio of these two percentages is called the "differentiation ratio," and traits are then ranked in descending order of the value of this ratio. The higher the ratio, the more closely a given trait is associated with high overall rating. Cohen compares this list with a list of traits said to be "most important," according to respondents, and shows that the second list, consisting mostly of cliches, does *not* separate high-rated companies from low ones, whereas there is some evidence presented to show that the first list does.

Crespi,[9] approaching the problem in a similar manner, uses the Stapel scale (a modified semantic differential scale) to compare image scores for sales leaders and sales trailers, in terms of various attributes such as "modern looking," "neat," and "masculine." The major theoretical difference between this approach and Cohen's is that Cohen's profile of the number one company is a *composite of several companies,* all rated number one by their rater, while Crespi's sales leader is the *single company,* not a composite.

Covariate Analysis Another way to discover the relative influence of vari-

[8] Louis Cohen, "The Differentiation Ratio in Corporate Image Research," *Journal of Advertising Research,* Vol. 7 (September 1967), pp. 32–36.

[9] Irving Crespi, "Use of a Scaling Technique in Surveys," *Journal of Marketing,* Vol. 25 (January 1961), pp. 69–72.

ous attitudes toward the purchasing decision is to cast the results of indirect questions into a covariate model of some sort. This method will provide a more systematic means of uncovering *relationships* between attitudes and behavior; for example, comparing attitudes of users and non-users of a product, high overall evaluations versus low overall evaluations, etc. Several illustrations of this approach are presented below.

One simplified but effective covariate approach is used by General Motors in determining which attitudes (features) should be stressed in advertisements. By comparing people who say they would consider buying a "Watusi" car with people who say they would *not* consider buying a Watusi, Smith found the two groups were very comparable on most automobile features (for example, styling, gas mileage, interior), but that there was a wide difference between those groups in terms of their perception of the trade-in value of the Watusi. This then would seem to be the "most determinant" of the features covered by the Smith survey.[10]

Another approach is to use formal correlation analysis, to develop relationships between component attitudes and overall evaluations and/or buying behavior. Seymour Banks used this approach in the study of coffee and scouring powder brands. Using linear discriminate analysis (which determines the relative importance of attitudes which can be used to divide

users from non-users of a given brand), Banks found that only three of the six rated attributes of scouring powder were related to later purchase: cleansing ability, price, and harshness on hands. For coffee, only flavor and price were important factors. Attitudes toward other product features were not found to be related either to actual purchase or to overall product preference.[11]

Another covariate model is illustrated by a regression analysis by the authors, which was designed to identify determinant attitudes for a cocktail dip mix. The mix was placed in 200 homes in the Los Angeles area that were members of the TRENDSETTERS PANEL of Haug Associates, Inc., Los Angeles. Homemakers were asked to prepare the dip according to instructions and to serve it to their families and/or friends. There was no identifying name on the cocktail dip mix. After serving the mix, housewives were asked to rate it on the following seven aspects:

> Overall opinion
> Color
> Overall appearance
> Taste
> Strength of flavor
> Spiciness
> Attitude toward buying

Each aspect except strength of flavor and spiciness was rated on a seven-point scale, from "Liked very much" to "Disliked very much." Strength of

---

[10] Gail Smith, "How GM Measures Ad Effectiveness," *Printers' Ink* (May 14, 1965), pp. 19–29.

[11] Seymour Banks, "The Relationship between Preference and Purchase of Brands," *Journal of Marketing*, Vol. 15 (October 1950), pp. 145–157.

flavor and spiciness were rated on a five-point scale from "Much too strong (spicy)" to "Much too weak (bland)." Ratings on the seven aspects were intercorrelated, this time using a "stepwise multiple regression" program written by the Health Sciences Computing Facility, U.C.L.A. "Buying intention" was designated as the dependent variable, with the remaining six variables as independent variables.

The results indicated that taste, and taste alone, is the determinant attitude or feature about this cocktail dip mix, at least among housewives in the Los Angeles area. (A similar analysis on a packaged gravy mix showed that taste again was most important, but that color was *much* more important than for the dip mix.) Another regression analysis, this time for a cat food, showed that none of the usual features identifiable by humans (for example, color, taste, odor, texture) were determinant features; rather, how much of the food the cat ate relative to how much food it usually ate at that time of day was found to be the crucial factor.

Of course, it is always possible that some feature (such as color or appearance of the dip mix, for example) might be totally unacceptable to respondents, so that these product characteristics would be rated very low and might indeed be cause for rejection of the product. This points out a major limitation of covariate analysis; namely, such analysis by itself does not indicate the *absolute level* of acceptance of the various product characteristics, and thus cannot be relied on to give the complete story. There-

fore, correlation analysis applies mainly throughout the "sensitive range" of product feature desirability among the public.

It should also be noted that both the cat food and dip mix regression analyses were done on a single brand of a product line. They did not involve either the choice among brands or the actual purchase of a product, and these might seem to be the more common and important problems. On the other hand, the single brand evaluation presented in this article is also a very common problem with consumer products manufacturers who are in the testing stage of introducing a new product. Thus, both problems (single brand and choice among brands) are very real and legitimate problems for an inquiry of this type, and methodology is basically the same for both situations.

The above covariate models have in common the *relating* of product or service component ratings with some criterion, be it product purchase, brand preference, or some overall evaluation of the product or service. Within this framework, many types of models are possible. Of course, all will suffer from the weakness of any covariate model in that *relationship* does not indicate *causality*. Experimental models are the proper way to determine causality, and these models are discussed in the next section.

Observation and Experimentation

One of the oldest techniques for attempting to identify consumer buying motives is that of direct observation of consumers in purchasing situations. A modern example of this method, as well as a clear analysis of its advantages and disadvantages, may be found in Wells's and Lo Sciuto's "Direct Observation of Purchasing Behavior."[12] The authors discuss a study in which supermarket shoppers were observed, and detailed reports were recorded of their movements and statements when interacting with certain products on display in a series of stores. The authors then drew conclusions concerning who does the shopping, the influence of children and adult males on purchasing decisions, the influence of price, and also *where* brand choices seem to be made and how much package study is involved. One of the findings of this study was that shoppers seemed to be rejecting candy packaged one way in favor of candy packaged another way. This finding would suggest that package design might be *one* determinant feature, though by no means the only one.

The *experimental* approach to attribute determinance may be viewed as an extension of the observational method, for in this approach an attempt is made to isolate the role of one or more specific features by holding all others constant, varying the factor in question, and then measuring the impact upon some operationally defined performance criterion, such as buying choice. This approach shares the advantages of the observational approach in terms of not relying

on respondent's answers, and in addition it attempts to isolate specific factors to explain why behavior occurs as well. However, where many factors must be observed, the experimental procedure is often very costly. In addition, many buying decisions take place in environments which cannot be controlled without significantly altering the relative role of the buying influences whose effects the researcher is attempting to study. However, this approach does have the major advantage of uncovering *causality*, in the sense that one or more features can be found that really "determine" buying behavior. The same cannot be said for the other approaches discussed in this article. A survey article that reports several specific findings relative to determinant attitudes is the one by Holloway and White.[13]

DISCUSSION

Each of the methods presented in this paper (direct questioning, indirect questioning, and observation and experiment) has some limitations, depending upon how each is used. In particular, any of the methods which are not used in a situation involving the actual choice among brands *must rely upon what the respondent says,* and what she says might be quite different from what she actually does in the buying situation. (Of course, some of the methods could also include the consideration of what the respondent *does* or has done.)

[12] William D. Wells and Leonard A. Lo Sciuto, "Direct Observation of Purchasing Behavior," *Journal of Marketing Research,* Vol. 3 (August 1966), pp. 227–233.

[13] Robert Holloway and Tod White, "Advancing the Experimental Method in Marketing," *Journal of Marketing Research,* Vol. 1 (February 1964), pp. 25–29.

Perhaps the major problem is that it is possible for an investigator to use many of the approaches discussed in this paper without discovering the *absolute level of acceptability* of the various product or service characteristics being considered. For example, in the case of the savings and loan illustration, respondents were not asked directly for their evaluations of each savings and loan association in terms of the various attributes being rated, nor were they asked for their evaluations of savings and loans as a whole on each attribute. Therefore, had the public been generally disenchanted with savings and loan associations in terms of one or more features or services, this fact would not have emerged from the study. (*If* motivation research does what it claims to do, it *would* uncover the absolute levels of acceptability of the various product attributes, although many times not on a quantitative basis.)

It might often be important for manufacturers to pay more attention to determinant attitudes among *products* in addition to among brands, as every product line is always vulnerable to another which improves upon some feature that may not be determinant among existing brands but could easily be determinant among products. Therefore, an investigator interested in identifying attributes which are determinant for the choice among brands should always ask for the *absolute* level of attribute acceptance for each of the brands (or for the single brand) evaluated. In this way, all brands may rank particularly low in a certain fea-

ture (for example, many of the two-thirds of the U.S. public who have never been in an airplane might consider all airlines as being equally unsafe). The research should, therefore, also ask for ratings of different products which might compete with the original product class. The methodology will remain unchanged, but the grouping of competitors, is changed. There is even the possibility that all brands of an existing product might be rated reasonably high in, for example, "ease of preparation," but some substitute product might rate even higher in this feature and thus would attract consumers on the basis of this greater convenience. This is a further reason for comparisons among various alternative products.

It should be noted that the "dual questioning" method is something like a shortcut to regression analysis, in the sense that respondents are asked to "tell" which attributes are *important* and *different* in their opinion. However, an investigator often does not know whether a given level of difference or importance is of major consequence without some set of external standards. At least regression analysis lends statistical significance tests to what direct questioning must do with a basically "eyeball" technique, and, of course, a significant correlation would not emerge unless a feature were both important (related to some criterion) and differentiated (with enough "variation" in ratings to allow "co-variation"), and thus correlation with some criterion.

There is always the danger of implying or inferring *causality* from the results of any of the methods discussed in this article—particularly covariate analysis. Results from direct or indirect questioning must be subjected to experimental or other validation for greater assurance that causal relationships do indeed exist between attitudes identified as "determinant" and the actual choice, decision, or action.

Do Attitude Changes Precede Behavior Change?

Christian Pinson and Eduardo L. Roberto

The authors show why we should rather ask,
"Under what conditions . . .

The question of whether attitude change comes before or after behavior change has been a raging controversy for many years in consumer behavior research and in the social sciences, and the subject has served as a central theme in three consecutive attitude research conferences of the American Marketing Association.

A frequent observation has been that the testing of the attitude/behavior relationship should be studied more easily in the field of consumer behavior than in any other. Noting this, Kristian Palda (1964) wrote:

> "It is one of the pleasures of advertising research that it may . . . contribute to the clarification of unresolved problems in social psychology . . . . It may do so chiefly because overt behavior in the market place is so easily ascertained by the convenient yardstick of sales. Only voting behavior approaches purchasing behavior in ease of measurement."

Why sales is such a convenient yardstick is explained by Ramond (1965): "An operational definition of sales is easier to spell out. A sale is what philosophers of science call a point-at-able event—something so obvious that we define it by the operation of pointing at it and agreeing that it has occurred, such as a housewife buying a pound of salt."

In spite of this advantage, studies linking attitude and behavior change have not gone any further than those by social psychologists in clarifying the real connection between the two variables. There is a group of consumer behaviorists who maintain that a necessary connection between attitude change and behavior change exists, or, more specifically, that behavior change must be somehow generated by an attitude change. Contesting this view is another group which holds the proposition that an attitude change is not necessary for behavior to change. Those who favor this position suggest that the only attitude change

SOURCE: Reprinted from the *Journal of Advertising Research* © Copyright (1973) Vol. 13, No. 4, by the Advertising Research Foundation.

often observed comes from an antecedent behavior change.

The following article presents an analysis of some of the theoretical and empirical arguments exchanged by these two groups. In this analysis, the propositions developed are that: (1) the theoretical basis of the controversy suffers from the fallacy of division, and (2) that the empirical arguments exchanged are obscured by terminological and methodological ambiguities, failure to take account of third factors, and the unbounded nature of the proposition empirically tested.

The belief that attitude change and behavior change are strongly related is intuitively accepted as obvious on the basis of indirect evidence from many studies showing high correlations between measures of attitudes and behavior (Bauer, 1966).

The major issue here concerns the presumption that, in a logical sense, there cannot be behavior change without attitude change. As Robertson (1971) more specifically states: "It is difficult to conceive of a change in behavior occurring without some prior change within the organism." Supporters of this view allow only one exception—the case of "coercion." For example, Roper (1966) found that ". . . some attitude change must precede behavioral change barring the circumstances of coercion. Some internal change must precede a new external act assuming that that act is voluntary." Fothergill (1968) takes the same stand: "The natural feeling of those in the advertising business that attitude changes must precede

changes in behavior must be tautologically true unless, for example, people buy things which, at least at the time of purchase, they dislike." There is the problem here of deciding what situations should be defined as coercive, but more importantly the logical basis of these statements must be questioned.

THE FALLACY OF DIVISION

Some interesting insights are gained by representing the preceding reasoning in the following syllogistic arguments: Some internal change must precede a new external act; attitude change is an internal change and behavior change is a new external act; therefore, some attitude change must precede behavior change.

While the premise is reasonable, the conclusion is not because the argument is logically fallacious.

The invalid argument involved here is what logicians call the "fallacy of division." This is found in the faulty transition from the premise that something holds true for some whole to the conclusion that the same holds true for a part of that whole (Mackie, 1967). In the present context of the attitude/behavior debate, this transition is readily seen. While it may be true that some internal change must precede a new external act, it does not necessarily follow that some attitude change must precede a behavior change, even if attitude change is a form of internal change and even if behavior change is also a form of an external act.

The real question is that of identifying the internal change. There are many plausible forms of internal changes that one can elect as possible explanatory variables. Is it, for example, a motivational variable, an opinion variable, or some other psychological factor? All too readily internal change is interpreted to be attitude change without seriously considering and screening the plausibility of these alternative internal variables.

Some may counterargue that there is not, in fact, a fallacy of division. It may be contended that the concept of attitude is broad enough to encompass any internal change. This position is best stated by Robertson (1971): "The concept of attitude as originally introduced into psychology was so broad as to refer to any intervening state of the organism that preceded and presumably accounted for a change in behavior."

The above understanding of the concept of attitude cannot be challenged on logical or theoretical grounds. After all, any definition of attitude is valid in a theoretical context. What is at stake, however, is the soundness of the controversy. If attitude is conceived as subsuming all hypothetical mediators, then there is no reason for dispute since the argument that there cannot be behavior change without attitude change is then true by definition. This holds even in the case of coercion. The conception of attitude as the set of behavior mediators must be opposed not on theoretical or logical grounds but on practical ones. For example, the assimilation of values, opinions, intentions, and cognitions all as forms of attitude will be resisted by advertising men who view these variables as fundamentally distinct from one another in terms of their observability and manipulability. Regarding attitude as a broad, hypothetical mediating variable voids the attitude concept of its practical meaning.

EMPIRICAL ARGUMENTS

For a proper, empirically grounded evaluation of the controversy, it is important to have studies dealing directly with the relationship between changes rather than between levels. Studies of change constitute the relevant evidence in the controversy.

In consumer behavior literature, there is no shortage of studies dealing with the relationship between levels of attitude and behavior. However, this is not true for studies concerning the relationship between changes in the levels of attitude and behavior, although several do exist.

Achenbaum (1968) presented data derived from a three-wave study of 4,000 women regarding their purchase behavior and attitudes toward 19 brands of packaged products. His conclusion was:

"If attitudes shift upward among non-users from June to September, the likelihood of their becoming users from September to December increases. . . . As attitudes from June to September dropped . . . the chances of a non-user becoming a user dropped too. . . . The situation is much the same among users. (Thus) . . . there is a direct relationship—a predictive one if you wish—between attitude changes and purchase behavior."

Assael and Day (1968) reported finding support for the proposition that "changes in attitudes are more closely related to subsequent behavior change, than are changes in awareness (and) that attitude change precedes rather than follows a behavioral change." Support came from the results of their analysis of time series data using a set of regression equations. The data came from Bristol-Myers' 14-month survey of brand attitude, awareness, and reported usage of deodorants and analgesics, and the Nestle Company's two-and-a-half year survey on the same variables for instant coffee.

Challenging the results of the foregoing studies are researchers who are skeptical about the empirical connection between attitude change and behavior change. The studies of Appel (1966) and Atkin (1962) represent this opposing view.

Appel reported an advertising experiment where attitude change supposedly was found not to precede a change in sales. His analysis concluded that, "The relationship between attitude and behavior is not nearly so simple as has been assumed." Atkin came to a similar interpretation after analyzing the results of a study on store patronage. He found that attitudes toward various stores changed only after shoppers bought there.

In his review of attitude research in England, Fothergill (1968) stated, "Changes in the attitude variables follow changes in the usage variable." In support of this proposition, he invoked evidence from data collected from some 250,000 interviews con-

ducted by the British Market Research Bureau, Ltd. over a five-year period (Bird and Ehrenberg, 1965; 1966).

Conflicting interpretations in the studies just reviewed prompts a closer look. Doing so reveals that major sources of disagreement of results are in the variations of terminological usages and in the measurement techniques. Achenbaum, for example, measured attitude toward a brand as the position that a person takes on a five-point rating scale from excellent to poor. Assael and Day indicated that the Bristol-Myers survey measured brand attitudes by respondent agreement with a series of statements derived from advertising themes and product characteristics, while the Nestle survey derived measures of attitudes from statements based on the relative perception of each brand. Fothergill considered "intentions to buy" and "top of the mind awareness" of a product as measures of generalized attitude.

This kind of situation is, of course, not peculiar. Use of terms with associated alternative meanings pervades the whole of social sciences. The confusing use of ambiguous terms in attitude research has even been noted by some attitude researchers themselves. For instance, Crespi (1966) comments:

> "One difficulty is the inconsistencies in the use of terminology and of techniques of measurement. These inconsistencies can easily lead to a situation in which people think they are talking about the same thing when they are not, so that they think their findings are

in conflict when they are merely different."

Remedial suggestions have been proposed but often entail problems that are as serious, if not more so. Consider, for instance, the proposal to operationalize attitude by taking more account of the behavioral component (Triandis, 1964). The measures of the behavioral component of attitude, namely intentions, have been empirically verified to be good predictors of behavior (Ajzen and Fishbein, 1970; Douglas and Wind, 1971). Thus, the more behavioral components an attitude change contains, the more likely it is to be a good predictor of behavioral change.

However, it must be realized that at the extreme this prediction could turn out to be somewhat tautological and, therefore, have almost no informational or practical value. If the measure captures a firmly crystallized intention in relation to an attitude, then it is of little interest to predict that a behavioral change will occur. For any new study seeking to establish the connection between attitude change and behavior change, it becomes too easy to obtain that relationship by operationalizing attitude into measures of behavioral intentions. The research problem is, however, not one of validating, but rather, one of testing if other attitudinal dimensions such as affect or cognitions are predictive of behavior. By reducing attitude to intentions, the researcher escapes this latter problem and lowers the discriminant validity of the attitude construct.

The different definitions of attitude can always be justified on the grounds that they merely represent what is judged by each investigator to be the most useful measure of the concept for his purposes. After all, an attitude is hypothetical construct. By definition, it can have no true expression nor a valid measure. However, it must be realized that the ambiguity of the concept of attitude greatly reduces the possibility of a given proposition's confirmation or refutation. As a consequence, the consumer behavior studies reviewed are semantically inconsistent, thereby obstructing the possibility of reaching an agreement among different observers on the meaning of the empirical evidence they obtain.

RIVAL HYPOTHESES

It is also worthwhile noting that an observed absence or presence of a relationship between an attitude change and a behavior change does not necessarily mean that the two variables are unrelated or truly related. The way attitude change and behavior change covary may, in the first place, be highly contextual as suggested by Campbell (1963), McGuire (1969), and Wicker (1969).

Moreover, several intervening variables exist which may have a suppressing or multiplier effect on the empirical connection between attitude change and behavior change. First, the threats to internal and external validity developed by Campbell and Stanley (1963) constitute a set of potential factors that can affect the degree of empirically discernible relationships between attitude and behavior change. A partial treatment of this in the marketing context is found in Lipstein (1968).

A second factor is the degree to which the consumer perceives the connection between his attitude change and the possibility of changing his future behavior. Researchers mistakenly may assume the existence of a linkage when in fact, insofar as the consumer is concerned, there are no such ties. Fishbein (1970) has strongly emphasized this aspect. This is also consistent with the often expressed hypothesis that the occurrence of behavior is a function of the perceived instrumentality of that action which brings about the desired results (Peak, 1955; Rosenberg, 1960; Rotter, 1966; and Rosen and Komorita, 1971).

A third factor is the cost of behaving relative to the cost of the act at an earlier point in time, or relative to those of other alternative forms of behaving. Krugman (1965), for example, suggested that when the individual is highly involved with an object the precedence of attitude over behavior holds. When there is low involvement, behavior precedes attitude change.

Lipstein cited "the degree of economic risk which the consumer incurs in buying a product" and "the degree of anxiety surrounding a product category" as being the important cost contingencies. He went on to say that "Attitude change does in fact precede purchase in the case of big ticket items."

From the attitude consistency school comes a fourth factor: the degree of interrelationships among different attitudes that may individually influence the same behavior. A fifth factor is the presence or absence of opportunities to perform the behavior expected. Howard and Sheth (1969) discussed this factor under the name of "inhibitory factors" and included under its rubric such variables as time pressure, lack of availability, financial constraint, and momentary price change.

Finally, a sixth factor resides in the time gap between the attitude change and the expected behavior change. The foregoing intervening factors will have a higher probability of exerting their influence as this time gap increases. As Day (1972) explained, "There is a strong likelihood that unforeseen circumstances may intervene between the attitude measurement and the actual behavior."

The implication is clear. The important question is not whether attitude precedes behavior change but rather under what conditions does attitude change precede behavior change.

EMPIRICAL TESTING

A closer look at the studies reviewed indicates still another source of ambiguity in the current controversy. Explicating this source requires reference back to the studies that have sought to test the proposition that attitude change precedes behavior change.

Logicians call this an unbounded universal general proposition. This means that all types of attitude and behavior change that have taken place in the past, are taking place at present, and will occur in the future. What is crucial to note is that, from a philosophy of science viewpoint, this proposition can never be confirmed because of its high level of spatial and temporal universality. However, a single negative instance could suffice to falsify it. This means that the proposition is refutable but unconfirmable.

In order to be refutable and confirmable, the proposition should be bounded. This means that instead of working with the proposition "attitude change precedes behavior change," we should work with its more restricted form of "all cases in x universe are such that attitude change precedes behavior change." As a research requirement, this may be attained by working with and paying more attention to singular cases under varying contexts.

REFERENCES

Achenbaum, Alvin A. Relevant Measures of Consumer Attitudes. Cited in J. Fothergill. Do Attitudes Change before Behavior? *Proceedings of the ESOMAR Congress*, Opatija, 1968, pp. 875-900.

Ajzen, I. and M. Fishbein. "Attitudinal and Normative Variables as Predictors of Specific Behaviors: A Review of Research Generated by a Theoretical Model." A paper presented at the Association for Consumer Research Workshop on Attitude Research on Consumer Behavior, University of Illinois, 1970.

Appel, W. Attitude Change: Another Dubious Method for Measuring Advertising Effectiveness. In Lee Adler and Irving Crespi (Eds.). *Attitude Research at Sea*. Chicago: American Marketing Association, 1966, pp. 141-152.

Assael, H. and George Day. Attitudes and Awareness as Predictors of Market Share. *Journal of Advertising Research*, Vol. 8, No. 4, pp. 3-10.

Atkin, K. Advertising and Store Patronage. *Journal of Advertising Research*, Vol. 2, No. 4, pp. 18-23.

Bauer, Raymond. Attitudes, Verbal Behavior and Other Behavior. In Lee Adler and Irving Crespi (Eds.). *Attitude Research at Sea*. Chicago: American Marketing Association, 1966, pp. 3-14.

Bird, M. and A.S.C. Ehrenberg. "Intentions-to-Buy and Claimed Brand Usages." A paper presented at the Ninth ESOMAR-WAPOR Congress, 1965.

Bird, M. and A.S.C. Ehrenberg. "Non-Awareness and Non-Usage." A paper presented at the ESOMAR Seminar, Deauville, 1966.

Campbell, Donald T. Social Attitudes and Other Acquired Behavioral Dispositions. In S. Koch (Ed.). *Psychology: A Study of a Science*. Vol. 6. New York: McGraw-Hill, 1963, pp. 94-172.

Campbell, D.T. and J.C. Stanley. Experimental and Quasi-Experimental Designs for Research in Teaching. In N.L. Gage (Ed.). *Handbook of Research on Teaching*. Chicago: Rand McNally, 1963, pp. 171-246.

Crespi, Irving. The Challenge to Attitude Research. In Lee Adler and

Irving Crespi (Eds.). *Attitude Research at Sea.* Chicago: American Marketing Association, 1966, pp. 187-189.

Day, George. Theories of Attitude Structure and Change. In Scott Ward and T. Robertson (Eds.). *Consumer Behavior: Theoretical Sources.* Englewood Cliffs, N.J.: Prentice-Hall, 1972.

Douglas, S.P. and Yoram Wind. Intentions to Buy as Predictors of Buying Behavior. In D. Gardner (Ed.). *Proceedings of the Second Annual Conference of the Association for Consumer Research*, 1971, pp. 331-343.

Fishbein, M. The Relationships between Beliefs, Attitudes, and Behavior. In D. Kollat, R.D. Blackwell, and J. Engel (Eds.). *Research in Consumer Behavior.* New York: Holt, Rinehart and Winston, 1970, pp. 216-235.

Fothergill, Jack. Do Attitudes Change before Behavior? *Proceedings of the ESOMAR Congress*, Opatija, 1968.

Krugman, Herbert. The Impact of Television Advertising: Learning without Involvement. *Public Opinion Quarterly*, Vol. 30, Fall 1965, pp. 583-596.

Lipstein, Benjamin. Anxiety, Risk, and Uncertainty in Advertising Effectiveness Measurements. In Lee Adler and Irving Crespi (Eds.). *Attitude Research on the Rocks.* Chicago: American Marketing Association, 1968, pp. 11-27.

Mackie, J.L. Fallacies. In Paul Edwards (Ed.). *The Encyclopedia of Philosophy.* New York: Macmillan Co., 1967, pp. 172-173.

McGuire, W.J. The Nature of Attitude and Attitude Change. In G. Lindzey and E. Aronson (Eds.). *The Handbook of Social Psychology.* Second Edition. Boston: Addison-Wesley, 1969, pp. 136-314.

Mueller, E. Effects of Consumer Attitudes on Purchases. *The American Economic Review*, Vol. 47, 1957, pp. 946-965.

Palda, Kristian. The Hypothesis of a Hierarchy of Effects: A Preliminary Evaluation. In L. Georges Smith (Ed.). *Reflections on Progress in Marketing.* Chicago: American Marketing Association, 1964, pp. 174-179.

Peak, H. Attitude and Motivation. In M. Jones (Ed.). *Nebraska Symposium on Motivations.* Lincoln, Nebraska: University of Nebraska Press, 1955.

Ramond, Charles. Must Advertising Communicate to Sell? *Harvard Business Review*, Vol. 43, 1965, pp. 146-161.

Robertson, Thomas S. *Innovative Behavior and Communication.* New York: Holt, Rinehart and Winston, 1971, pp. 66-67.

Roper, Burns. The Importance of Attitudes, the Difficulty of Measurement. In J.S. Wright and J. Goldstrucker (Eds.). *New Ideas for Successful Marketing.* Chicago: American Marketing Association, 1966.

Rosen, Benson and S.S. Komorita. Attitudes and Action: The Effects of Behavioral Intent and Perceived Effectiveness of Acts. *Journal of Personality*, Vol. 39, pp. 187-203.

Rosenberg, M.J. A Structural Theory of Attitude Dynamics. *Public Opinion Quarterly*, Vol. 24, 1960, pp. 319-340.

Rotter, J.B. Generalized Expectancies for Internal versus External Control Reinforcement. *Psychological Monographs*, Vol. 80, 1966, pp. 1-28.

Triandis, H.C. Exploratory Factor Analysis of the Behavioral Component of Social Attitudes. *Journal of Abnormal and Social Psychology*, Vol. 68, 1964, pp. 420-430.

Wicker, Allan. Attitudes versus Actions: The Relationship of Verbal and Overt Behavioral Responses to Attitude Objects. *The Journal of Social Issues*, Vol. 25, 1969, pp. 41-78.

Chapter 7

Collecting Primary Data: Constructing Questionnaires

One of the most interesting and challenging parts of performing marketing research is designing and implementing questionnaires. The researcher is forced to look deep into the process of human communication and thinking. The researcher must be able to anticipate what respondents will do and say in response to certain questions. Chapters 7 and 8 examine the problems of questionnaire design and the human interaction between interviewer and respondent, respectively.

Introduction

Frequently, the marketing researcher finds that the data he needs to solve a particular problem cannot be obtained from any existing secondary data source such as the U. S. Federal Government. The information desired may only be in the possession of individual consumers in the market. Attitudes, beliefs, opinions, feelings, past product use experiences, and future expectations are obvious examples. Census records contain much of this type of information, but the information may not be broken down into the individual consumer unit of analysis, it may be incomplete or it may be impossible to combine the existing data with data collected from other sources to get a total picture of the people whom the researcher wishes to study.

There are several means of getting this type of data. The researcher might simply observe people and their actions. Although it may be possible to infer the existence of certain attitudes or feelings from overt behavior, this process is a complex and difficult one, subject to widely varying interpretations. Moreover, it is often impossible to "observe" such things as past experiences. The personal interview and the mail or telephone questionnaire are methods frequently used by researchers to contact people and gather information relevant to the objectives of their research projects. The basic technique common to both approaches is asking questions, either directly or indirectly, to obtain the desired data. Thus, the backbone of either of these methods is the interview schedule or the questionnaire. Although both of these instruments are essentially question-asking, information-getting tools, an interview schedule is technically a list of questions that will be asked or the topic areas that will be discussed with the respondent in person by an interviewer who will also record the answers given.

Overview of Methods

The term "questionnaire" usually refers to a self-administered process whereby the respondent himself reads the question and records his answers without the assistance of an interviewer. An assumption is usually made that the self-administered questionnaire is more highly structured and more stand-

251

ardized than the interview approach. In fact, they might be visualized as existing along a continuum of flexibility:

```
|_____|_____|_____|
Unstructured          Partially          Structured          Mailed
interview             structured         interview           questionnaire
schedule              interview          schedule
                      schedule
```

An unstructured interview schedule may give the interviewer only a list of topics that he wants the respondent to discuss in his own words and from his own frame of reference. In a partially structured situation, the schedule may contain definite questions to be asked but the interviewer may be allowed to reword, rephrase, or rearrange the questions according to his own judgment. The structured interview allows even less freedom to the interviewer; he must read every question precisely as it is worded and in a standardized sequence. However, inflection, tone of voice, and visual cues can still be utilized to make the meaning clear. Such cues can also obscure the meaning of a question and cause a biased response. Mailed questionnaires by their very nature are extremely standardized, at least from the researcher's point of view. As will be seen later, different respondents will often interpret standardized questions in entirely different ways. No explication or interpretation by an interviewer is possible.

Table 7.1 presents the relative merits of the principal methods of data collection. Not all the advantages and disadvantages are present in every situation, and when a particular advantage, for example, is present it may vary in its intensity or degree of favorableness. Certainly Table 7.1 is not exhaustive; however, the pros and cons shown are the most frequently occurring ones. Table 7.2 presents a guide to preferred survey data-collection methods under varying circumstances.

One dimension not shown in Table 7.2 concerns the issue of subject sensitivity to questions. For example, a marketing research study for a commercial health clinic offering vasectomy (male sterilization) services involved asking questions of a very personal nature in order to obtain data for a promotion/education campaign. For various reasons an interview approach was indicated in lieu of a mail or telephone survey. In anticipation of possible embarrassment in using various terms associated with birth planning activities, the interviewer gave the respondent a copy of the questionnaire. This enabled the subject to respond to sensitive or anxiety-arousing questions by merely making reference to question number and precoded response. The presence of the interviewer ensured responses to the questions.

TABLE 7.1 *Relative Merits of Principal Methods of Data Collection*

Personal Interview	Mail	Telephone
Advantages		
Most flexible means of obtaining data	Wider and more representative distribution of sample possible	Representative and wider distribution of sample possible
Identity of respondent known	No field staff	No field staff
Nonresponse generally very low	Cost per questionnaire relatively low	Cost per response relatively low
Distribution of sample controllable in all respects	People may be more frank on certain issues, for example, sex	Control over interviewer bias easier; supervisor present essentially at interview
	No interviewer bias; answers in respondent's own words	Quick way of obtaining information
	Respondent can answer at his leisure, has time to "think things over"	Nonresponse generally very low
	Certain segments of population more easily approachable	Callbacks simple and economical
Disadvantages		
Likely to be most expensive of all	Bias due to nonresponse often indeterminate	Interview period not likely to exceed five minutes
Headaches of interviewer supervision and control	Control over questionnaire may be lost	Questions must be short and to the point: probes difficult to handle
Dangers of interviewer bias and cheating	Interpretation of omissions difficult	Certain types of questions cannot be used, for example, thematic apperception
	Cost per return may be high if nonresponse very large	Nontelephone owners as well as those without listed numbers cannot be reached
	Certain questions, such as extensive probes, cannot be asked	
	Only those interested in subject may reply	
	Not always clear who replies	
	Certain segments of population not approachable, for example, illiterates	
	Likely to be slowest of all	

Source: Robert Ferber and P. J. Verdoorn, *Research Methods in Economics and Business,* p. 210 © The Macmillan Company, 1962.

253

TABLE 7.2 *A Guide to Preferred Data-Collection Methods under Alternative Survey Conditions*

Conditions of Survey				Possible Data-Collection Method(s)[a]			
Funds	Time	Certain Precision Required	Type of Data	Personal Interview	Mail	Telephone	Comments on Method
Restricted	Restricted	Yes or no	Few items			X	Assuming telephone population representative
Restricted	Restricted	Yes or no	Much information	X			If funds permit
Restricted	Ample	Yes	Few items		X	X	Assuming telephone population representative
Restricted	Ample	Yes	Much information	X——X			Non-respondent follow-up needed
Restricted	Ample	No	Few items		X	X	
Restricted	Ample	No	Much information	X			
Ample	Restricted	Yes or no	Few items	X		X	Assuming telephone population representative
Ample	Restricted	Yes or no	Much information	X			
Ample	Ample	Yes	Few items	X		X	Assuming telephone population representative
Ample	Ample	Yes	Much information	X			
Ample	Ample	No	Few items	X	X	X	
Ample	Ample	No	Much information	X——X			Either joint or one method alone.

[a] A line connecting two crosses represents joint use of two data-collection methods. Otherwise, two crosses in the same line indicate that either method could be used.
Source: Robert Ferber and P. J. Verdoorn, *Research Methods in Economics and Business* © The Macmillan Company, 1962.

Key Assumptions of Questionnaire Design

By now, certain assumptions involved in the use of either the interview schedule or the questionnaire are probably clear. First, the researcher assumes that the respondent is able and willing to communicate the desired information either verbally to an interviewer or in writing on a questionnaire form. This assumption is not as easy to make as it might seem, for there are several reasons why the information is not accessible to the respondent. He may have once been in the possession of some piece of information, but has simply forgotten it. Some experiences or feelings may have been repressed because of a degree of unpleasantness or emotional stress associated with them, and they may no longer exist in the person's conscious state of mind. Still another explanation is that although the person is in possession of the information, the terms or categories in which the interviewer or questionnaire requires recollection and communication are not familiar to the respondent or are not those in which he normally codes his experiences. A more simplistic explanation, but certainly a valid one, is that the person never had the requested information. Fortunately, there are several techniques of interviewing and question asking that can be used to aid the researcher in obtaining information in some of these difficult situations.

Secondly, there is an assumption about the type of information gathered which must be kept in mind when interpreting and analyzing the data. The researcher must bear in mind that the information he gets from the interview and the questionnaire is essentially information about the respondent's verbal or written behavior. Such behavior is *one* type of actual behavior and as such expresses certain dimensions of the respondent's social or psychological reality. Although they are as real as any other type of behavior, verbal and written responses should not be considered synonymous with other types of actions.

Payne states the situation very clearly when he says[1]:

> We should keep in mind that an opinion survey does not necessarily report what the public *is* thinking. More often it reports what the public would think if asked the questions.

Constructing the Questionnaire or Schedule

The questionnaire or schedule must not merely ask the respondent for information; it must *help* him provide the correct information, in the appropriate context, and in the proper unit of measurement so that the researcher will be able to explain or predict the specific phenomena he set out to investigate. For each bit of information required, the researcher must create a means by which it can be communicated. He must decide on the specific words to be used in the question to make it precise in meaning, the form of response he wants the question to elicit, and the sequence or order of questions that will facilitate the communication of accurate and revealing information. Two overriding considerations in these decisions are (1) the objectives of the research project, and (2) the respondent's point of view. Although there may be an opportunity in a personal interview to clarify meanings or rearrange questions, the mere presence of an interviewer is no substitute for a well

[1] Stanley L. Payne, *The Art of Asking Questions* (Princeton, N. J.: Princeton University Press, 1951), p. 178.

thought-out schedule. This section will discuss some basic guidelines for question construction that apply generally to all forms of question-asking instruments. Of course, the researcher must use his own good judgment in applying and adapting these general rules to his own individual situation.

Writing a series of questions is not the first state in the development of a questionnaire. Careful planning prior to writing the first question is required if many costly mistakes are to be avoided.

Five steps in the process are[2]:

1. Deciding what information is necessary.
2. Deciding what type of questions should be used.
3. Deciding how many questions are needed and in what order they should be placed.
4. Writing the first draft of the questionnaire.
   (a) Format considerations.
   (b) Printing considerations.
5. Revision of questionnaire.

Decisions on Information Requirements

The researcher must begin by asking himself what specific pieces of information will be necessary to test the hypothesis, or investigate the relationships in which he is interested. What are the variables to be measured? What relationships between these variables are important in accomplishing the objectives of the study? One way to clarify the problem and to make explicit those assumptions that might be hidden in a general statement of the study purpose is to look ahead to the analysis stage and to try to envision what kinds of tabulation or statistical techniques will be used. By doing this, other advantages accrue to the researcher.

First, additional hypotheses may come to mind possibly requiring information not called for in the original plan. Secondly, by focusing on the ultimate means of analysis, the researcher will have a clearer idea of the unit of measurement in which the response should be expressed. A simple example is the question of age. Are categories or ranges such as 30–40 or 45 and over sufficient, or is the exact year required? Planning ahead for quantitative requirements will avoid much confusion later. Furthermore, the researcher can save not only himself, but also the respondent, a considerable amount of time by deleting unnecessary information demands. The inclusion of irrelevant or useless information will only lessen the precision of the data. After the researcher clearly identifies the information he needs, he can check to see if

---

[2] These five steps are an adaptation of the discussion by Arthur Kornhauser and Paul B. Sheatsley in C. V. Sellitz, M. Jahoda, M. Deutsch, and S. W. Cook, *Research Methods in Social Relations* (New York: Holt, Rinehart and Winston, 1959), p. 546.

his sample population has been properly selected. Do these people possess the desired information? Will they be able to communicate it to him? Is there a more reliable or economical way to get these data? This kind of detailed examination of information requirements lends precision to the researcher's statement of what he is about.

Decisions on Types of Questions

After the researcher defines his data requirements, he must decide on the type or types of questions that will best elicit each bit of information, and related to this, the type of response desired. Questions can be either direct or indirect, while responses can be categorized as open-ended, or fixed-alternative (including dichotomous and multiple choices, check lists, and so on).

Direct Questions

Direct questions are just what their name implies; they explicitly ask for the information desired. However, the directness of a question also relates to the way the response is interpreted. If, for example, the respondent is asked if he bought brand B on his last shopping trip, and the researcher is interested only in whether the purchase was made, then the question can be considered direct. If the researcher wishes to make other inferences about the respondent from this fact, such as personality type, for example, then the question is not direct. Usage of a direct question requires that the respondent possess the information, that it is readily accessible to him, that he shares a common language with the researcher, and that he is willing to reveal the information when directly asked. Often direct questions are ineffective in obtaining accurate responses to threatening or embarrassing questions. Kinsey, however, used a direct approach that seemed to penetrate these barriers.[3] His technique was to ask, "How old were you when you first . . ." rather than "Have you ever . . ." This seemed to reassure the respondent that no stigma was attached to any answer he might give. Alternately, a series of direct questions may be used to ease the respondent into a topic area, allowing him to gradually reveal his experiences.

Indirect Questions

All questions are indirect to some degree; the concept of age is not identical with asking a person how old he is. However, it is about as close as we can come to expressing the concept in words. Indirect questions, in the questionnaire sense, refer to those questions whose responses are used to indicate or suggest information, other than the actual facts given in the answer,

---

[3] Alfred C. Kinsey, W. B. Pomeroy, and C. E. Martin, *Sexual Behavior in the Human Male* (Philadelphia: Saunders, 1948).

about the respondent. When the respondent and the interviewer do not share a common language for speaking about a concept, when the content of the question is somehow threatening to the person's ego, prestige, or emotional defenses, or when the question seeks to uncover information that the respondent might perceive as revealing undesirable or socially unacceptable aspects of his personality, an indirect approach is usually called for. Three techniques are commonly used. One procedure is to phrase a question in terms of a generalized third person. If the respondent is asked, "Why do you think most people buy brand A?" he can use the generalized "other" as a vehicle for expressing his own thoughts. Or, the questions might refer to a hypothetical Mr. Jones. In this way, the question avoids a direct confrontation with psychological barriers.

A second technique is to ask seemingly direct questions that are relatively easy for the respondent to answer, but interpret these answers according to some theory about which the respondent is unaware. Many personality questionnaires use this technique. In marketing, one might ask people a series of questions on the buying patterns and combine the respondent's answers in some way to indicate his tendency to be an innovator, for example. A third indirect technique is the use of pictures, stories, or other ambiguous stimuli. Here, the researcher expects that the respondent will project his own interpretation and meaning on the situation. Motivation researchers in marketing frequently employ this tactic to gain insight into motives of which even the respondent himself may be unaware. The problem involved in the use of any indirect method is that the interpretation of the resopnses is very subjective.

Open-Ended Questions

Open-ended response questions, sometimes called free-answer questions, are those which do not provide any explicit choice of alternatives. Rather, the respondent is free to answer within his own frame of reference, and in his own words in relation to any aspect of the issue raised. Of course, questions may vary in actual degrees of openness. For example, a question such as, "How many people are there in your immediate family?" does not suggest any possible answer, but it clearly directs the thoughts of the respondent to specific channels.

Open-ended questions of various types can be used in several different ways. They are often used as an opener for discussion of a topic. For example, "When you think of dishwashing liquids, what brands come to your mind?" An answer to this type of question provides an insight into the frame of reference (number of brands perceived as salient and their identification) from which the respondent's subsequent responses will most likely be made. Or, open-end questions may be used to solicit suggestions. For instance, "What do you think this company could do to better serve the consumer?" leaves the field wide open for any comments the person wishes to make. Follow-up questions and probes often take this form. Questions asking for further clarification, for more detailed information, for reasons for a particular response, or for more extensive information can all be structured to allow maximum freedom for the respondent. Some examples might be:

"What was the result?" (follow-up)

"Why do you feel that way?" (reason why)

"Are there any others?" (probe)

Various other kinds of information can be obtained in a free-answer situation. Some examples of these are:

"What arguments do most people make for government regulation of business?"

"How many services that your bank offers can you name?"

"What brand of gasoline did you buy last?"

"How did you happen to hear of that product?"

As is readily apparent, open-ended questions are capable of eliciting a great deal of information.

Yet, free-answer questions have their limitations. When used in a personal interview, these questions provide a greater opportunity for interviewer influence to be felt. The respondent may not have thought about the question before, and his thoughts may not be organized. He may say he does not know simply because it is easier than thinking about the issue, or he may respond with the first thing that comes to mind. When used in a mail questionnaire, the open-ended question requires a high level of literacy and a greater amount of energy, motivation, and care on the part of the respondent which may discourage response. The analysis of these responses can be extremely difficult, and statistical procedures may not be applicable.

Classification categories must be set up for coding the response. When coding is done in the field by the interviewer, there will inevitably be variations in coding criteria used. Even when coding is done by a central office staff, it is often difficult to determine how to categorize a particular answer. People may use different words to describe the same phenomena, or some people may use the same word, but attach different meanings to it. These problems make data analysis a difficult task. Moreover, some researchers have suggested that, in terms of the length of the response, the usability of the information, the relevance and self-revelation of answers, and correctness of factual reporting, the open-ended question may well be more trouble than it is worth.

On the other hand, the open-ended question is better able to elicit some types of information than other types of questions, since it allows the respondent to use his own terms and his own language which contribute a degree of spontaneity and individualistic flavor to the reply. If part of the objective of the research work is to determine the respondent's level of information, the intensity of his feelings, or the structure or basis for his attitudes, the open-ended question can be highly effective. Although an ill-informed respondent may be embarrassed by his lack of knowledge or his uncertainty, the researcher will at least have some indication of whether the respondent *has* any opinion at all or whether he is merely trying to help the researcher by supplying an answer.

When there is reason to believe that the topic is outside of the respondent's range of experience, or when the researcher has little knowledge of the range of responses or terms he is likely to get, the open-ended question is generally appropriate. In the latter case, giving the respondent a list of alternatives from which to choose might mean that some valid alternatives will go unnoticed. Thus, the free-answer question is extremely useful in pilot or exploratory work. The ultimate criteria for determining the appropriateness of an open-ended question is its ability to gain the specific piece of information the research needs.

Fixed-Alternative Questions

Fixed-alternative response questions, sometimes called closed questions, are those in which the respondent is given a limited number of alternative responses from which he is to choose the one that most closely matches his opinion or attitude. Of course, one of the alternatives can be an "other" or some other notation to indicate to the respondent that he can answer in some other way if he desires. Technically, the response is still closed.

Like the open-ended question type, fixed alternative questions come in several styles. The dichotomous question is one which offers the respondent a choice between only two stated alternatives, and reduces the issue to its simplest terms. Typical response alternatives are: yes—no, approve—disapprove, true—false, agree—disagree, right—wrong, and so on. An example of a dichotomous question is presented in Figure 7.1. In situations when it might be necessary to provide the respondent with some background information, the dichotomous format can be used to set the stage for discussion. Two sides of a particular issue are given the respondent, and he is asked which position comes closest to matching his own. Payne suggests that this type of question is useful for obtaining two kinds of information: (1) factual—something either is or is not, and (2) recall knowledge—you remember or you do not. A dichotomous question, however, cannot be used in those cases where responses are apt to be qualified in some way. The issue must be clear-cut, and the alternatives directly opposed to one another. Multiple-choice questions form another group in the fixed-alternative category. Figure 7.1 contains an example of a multiple-choice question and illustrates how this type of question can be used to elaborate upon a dichotomous question.

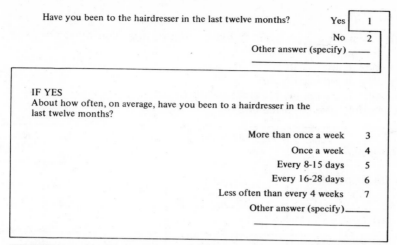

FIGURE 7.1   *An Example of a Dichotomous Question Followed by a Simple (Unprompted) Multiple-Choice Question*
Source: Joan Macfarlane Smith, *Interviewing in Marketing and Social Research*, Fig. 4 (London: Routledge & Kegan Paul, 1972).

Offering a series of possible responses, the multiple-choice question is the middle ground between the strict two-way choice of dichotomous questions and the completely open field of open-ended questions. When an issue has more than two parts, or when gradations of opinions or degrees of intensity are possible, the multiple-choice format can be used. Of course, the alternatives must be mutually exclusive and represent the appropriate range of possible replies. Check lists and rating scales are also types of multiple-choice questions. A check list is simply a statement or a problem followed by a list of answers from which the respondent can choose, while a rating scale may ask the respondent to rate a particular object along specified dimensions.

In a mail questionnaire the respondent will have an opportunity to glance over the alternatives. If this format is used in a personal interview and the length of the list exceeds four or five items, or if each item is complicated, the respondent should be given a copy of the list so that he can keep the alternatives in mind. An example of a check list is presented in Figure 7.2. The respondent might be handed the question in Figure 7.2 on a card and asked to place a check mark in the appropriate cells indicating which brands are characterized by which attributes. The question in Figure 7.3 could also serve as a rating scale where the numbers 1, 2, 3, 4 or letter x (for not applicable) could be placed across the rows to give the relative standing of each brand on the particular attribute. The same rating done vertically, that is, down each column would provide a rating describing the relative importance of each

Show Card A

(a) Which of the products listed on this card do you think are good value for money?
(b) Which are modern?
(c) Which are expensive?
(d) Which are mainly for older people?
(e) Which have cut-price offers?

Attributes \ Brands	Product W	Product K	Product M	Product T	None of them
(a) Good value for money					
(b) Modern					
(c) Expensive					
(d) Mainly for older people					
(e) Has cut-price offers					

FIGURE 7.2   *Questionnaire Design for Check List Question*
Source: Joan Macfarlane Smith, *Interviewing in Marketing and Social Research,* Fig. 5 (London: Routledge & Kegan Paul, 1972).

attribute for each brand. If the market researcher were concerned, as he often is, with the degree to which an attribute is present in a product, he would pose the quetsion in the following manner:

How would you rate brand B on cleaning ability?
Above average _____; average _____; below average _____

Another rating technique is the semantic differential approach shown in Figure 7.3. This is a commonly used technique in marketing.

Fixed-alternative questions offer several advantages to the researcher. These questions can be asked quickly and require little effort on the part of the respondent. Thus, more questions can be asked and more ground can be covered in less time. Moreover, the standardized form of the response makes coding and analysis a relatively quick and easy task. The responses are within the proper frame of reference and in a usable form. Specifying possible answers may serve to clarify the meaning of the question, or to stir the respondent's memory. In addition, the responsibility for making judgments about the

______ Brand

Bitter	:____:____:____:____:____:____:____:	Sweet
Dark	:____:____:____:____:____:____:____:	Light
Modern	:____:____:____:____:____:____:____:	Old-Fashioned
Expensive	:____:____:____:____:____:____:____:	Cheap
Unpleasant Aroma	:____:____:____:____:____ ____:____:	Pleasant Aroma

FIGURE 7.3 *A Semantic Differential Rating Scale for Coffee. (Respondent indicates point on line nearest his attitude.)*
Source: Joan Macfarlane Smith, *Interviewing in Marketing and Social Research,* Fig. 7 (London: Routledge & Kegan Paul, 1972).

respondent's attitudes is placed on the respondent himself rather than on the coder or interviewer.

As the reader has probably guessed by now, advantages in one situation are often disadvantages in another. Thus, the strengths of fixed-alternative questions, viewed from another perspective, become weaknesses. The standardized response eliminates the spontaneity and expressiveness of responses to open-ended questions. In addition, the question may force the respondent to give an opinion about an issue which is unfamiliar to him, or to make a choice between alternatives, none of which represents his true feelings. The suggested responses may remind the informant of items he may have forgotten, and may also give him an opportunity to cover his lack of information or lack of interest by selecting a response simply because it is the first one he sees or by selecting the "safe" middle response. A slight misunderstanding of a dichotomous question can result in a complete reversal of opinion.

An additional problem is encountered when the list of alternatives is incomplete. The researcher may obtain answers related to the question asked, but unrelated to the respondent's experience. For example, if the researcher asks, "Which characteristic of this product is most unattractive to you?" and then provides a list of such alternatives, there is a danger that the researcher will fail to be informed of an offensive element in the product design, simply because it was omitted from the list. Even when it can be assumed that the respondent's choice is valid, there is no way to know why he replied as he did, or from what frame of reference he replied. Of course, there may be situations where this information is irrelevant.

In short, closed or fixed-alternative questions are appropriate when the researcher has substantial information about the possible responses, and when the issues involved are clear-cut. They can be efficient instruments for data collection when there is reason to believe that the respondent's ideas are well formulated, and clearly defined choice points can be identified. The reader should not be led by this discussion to believe that there are any hard and fast rules to apply to the decision of question type. Different question formats will undoubtedly elicit different responses. However, as Payne has observed:

> Having observed different results with different types of questions on the same subject, we still cannot agree on which of the different results comes nearest the "truth." As the development of phrasing now stands, it would therefore be a disservice to imply that any type of question is generally the "best" type.[4]

Decisions on Number and Sequence of Questions

The number of questions dealing with a particular topic depends on the depth of coverage required. Will probing questions be necessary? How complex is the topic? Are there many facets of the topic that should each be dealt with separately? If problems of recall or willingness to respond are likely to be involved, a series of questions may be necessary in order to set the stage for the respondent and in order to facilitate communication. Multiple questions can also be used to repeat the same general question, but in a different context, from a different point of view, or in a different format. This helps to ensure the validity of the study by covering all bases, so to speak, and guarding against too narrow a viewpoint. For these reasons, Cannell and Kahn recommend that, in general, a battery of questions is preferable to a single question.[5]

Sequencing or ordering the questions is a two-step process. Attention must be given (1) to the sequence of questions and topics for the questionnaire or schedule, and (2) to the order of presentation of questions within each topic section. The important consideration in both cases is that the ultimate sequence reflect the topic of the respondent; the questionnaire or schedule should be respondent-centered.

The objective of the sequence of questions throughout the entire questionnaire or schedule is to make the total experience as meaningful as possible to the respondent. Giving the instrument a clearly defined beginning, middle, and end gives the respondent a logical anchor to which he can cling, and lends a sense of "completeness" to the process. What, then, should be the beginning? When trying to find a starting place, Kahn and Cannell offer the practical suggestion of starting where the respondent is, with those topics or questions that are relevant and interesting from his point of view. Opening questions that prick the curiosity and interest of the respondent, and that seem to be important enough to justify the usage of his time and energy help the

---

[4] Payne, 1951, *op. cit.*, p. 99.
[5] Charles F. Cannell and Robert L. Kahn, "Interviewing," in Gardner Lindzey and Elliott Aronson (eds.), *The Handbook of Social Psychology*, 2nd ed., Vol. 2 (Reading, Mass.: Addison-Wesley, 1968), pp. 535–536.

interviewer to build rapport and invite the participation of the receiver of a mailed questionnaire. Easy to answer opening questions serve to teach the respondent his role and to give him confidence in his ability to perform that role.

In general, it is best to delay embarrassing or threatening questions until the middle or concluding portion of the question or schedule. This is done for two reasons: (1) interest and rapport have had an opportunity to develop sufficiently to cushion the embarrassment or threat, and (2) should the respondent decide to terminate the interview, some information at least has been obtained. The latter reason may not apply to mail questionnaires, since a decision to withdraw cooperation usually means the entire questionnaire will be discarded. There is a possibility, however, that the respondent will simply leave the latter portion of the questionnaire blank, but still return the form. Personal data questions asking for information such as income, education, and so on, are sometimes placed at the end of the questionnaire or schedule for these reasons. These questions are relatively easy to answer when the respondent is willing to do so. Thus, by the time fatigue sets in, the questions are such that little effort is required. Difficult or complex questions should be asked before the respondent grows weary of the procedure. Embarrassing questions may be interspersed with other questions in the middle section. Asking them at the end of the questionnaire or schedule may leave the respondent with a feeling of uneasiness which may be upsetting or carried over into the next research experience he has. Transitional statements informing the respondent that the topic under discussion is about to change eases the respondent into a new frame of reference and facilitates the logical flow of information. Although it need not be an overriding consideration, total length and time should be kept in mind.

Within each topic section, questions should be arranged in such a way that the respondent is led in a meaningful way through the process of exploration. Thoughtful question sequencing often aids recall of information by setting the stage for discussion and reduces threat by introducing the topic gradually.

The usual bromide offered to researchers is "start with the general, then move toward the specific" questions on a particular topic. The reasoning behind this advice is that asking specific questions first may contaminate later answers by providing the respondent with information or cues as to what his answer should be by showing him the direction or drift of the questions. In other cases, however, the researcher may want to make sure certain points are considered by the respondent before he gives an answer to general evaluation questions. Thus, the specific questions should be placed before the more general ones. This decision may appear to be more important perhaps than a mail question in planning an interview schedule, since in the latter situation the researcher has no real control over the order in which questions are read and answered. However, this fact does not absolve the researcher of any responsibility for seeing that the question sequence flows logically from question to question. The questionnaire must still make sense in order to avoid possible respondent confusion and frustration.

Sequencing questions so that the general ones precede the specific is termed the *funnel* approach or sequence, so called because each question is progressively narrower in scope. This permits the researcher to gain a sense of the respondent's own frame of reference and information level, uninfluenced by cues given by other questions. The sequence begins with a number of "filter" questions designed to exclude a respondent from a particular sequence if those questions are inapplicable to him. Alternative types of filters are shown in Figure 7.4. If the purpose of the questions is to discover motivations for a particular type of behavior, it would be wise to check to see if the respondent engages in the particular activity. It would also be a good idea not to suggest possible motivations if interest lies in determining what is uppermost in the respondent's mind. For example, if we ask, "Do you feel that housewives who serve instant coffee are basically lazy?" and then ask, "Do you serve instant coffee?" or "Why do you think most people do not buy instant coffee?" the responses may be influenced, or we may have created an awkward situation. Instead, questions might begin by asking about coffee-buying habits in general.

A particular type of funnel sequence developed by George Gallop, called

Questionnaire design 93

(a) Arrow guides

Q.1 Do you yourself ever eat sweet biscuits?   Yes   1 → GO TO Q.3
                                                 No   2 → GO TO Q.2

(b) 'Branching' type (as used in programmed learning)

Q.1 Do you yourself ever eat sweet biscuits?

	Code	Route
Yes	1	3
No	2	2

(c) 'Box' type

Q.1 Do you yourself ever eat sweet biscuits?   Yes   1 → GO TO Q.3
                                                 No   2

IF NO
Q.2 Do you ever eat bars or blocks of chocolate?   Yes   1   GO TO Q.4
                                                     No   2   GO TO Q.10

FIGURE 7.4 *Types of Filter Instruction*
Source: Joan Macfarlane Smith, *Interviewing in Marketing and Social Research*, Fig. 10 (London: Routledge & Kegan Paul, 1972).

the "quintamensional plan of question design," specifies five types of questions to cover the essential aspects of an opinion.

1. Awareness of the particular topic is determined via a free-answer question.
2. Spontaneous attitudes are asked for next, again by free-answer.
3. Specific attitudes are then covered by fixed-alternative questions.
4. Fixed-alternative questions are followed by free-answer probes or reason-why questions.
5. Finally, questions designed to ascertain the intensity of feelings expressed are asked.

As the reader will note, questions begin with the general and proceed to the specific. The first question is, of course, a filter to screen out uninformed respondents, to provide a clue about the credibility of the latter responses, or to make explicit the frame of reference used by the respondent. The second question not only indicates those things which are uppermost in the respondent's mind, but also guards against investigating too narrow a range of aspects of the topic.

The inverted funnel approach is merely the reverse of the funnel design discussed above. Suppose the researcher wishes to obtain a total evaluation of a particular product. He may wish to place all respondents on an equal footing by making certain that each one has considered certain product features. Beginning the sequence with rather specific questions would be appropriate here. This technique can be useful in leading the respondent up to the total evaluation, helping him to think his answer rather than allowing him merely to answer off the top of his head.

However redundant it may seem, the fact remains that all decisions are relative. There are precious few absolutes in marketing research, and question sequencing is no different than any other area. The only absolutes stem from the purpose for which the research is intended and the requirement of a respondent-centered orientation.

Writing the First Draft: Wording the Questions

The first purpose of any question is to translate a specific objective into a form in which the researcher and the respondent can communicate, but the process by which this is done is not as easy as one might think. Whitehead once said that "Language . . . is always ambiguous as to the exact proposition which it indicates," yet language is the chief tool of the researcher. Selecting words and phrasing for questions to be used in an interview schedule or questionnaire is one of the most difficult tasks the researcher must perform.

A detailed discussion of every problem and every technique developed for question wording cannot be presented in the short space of one chapter.

Thus, the purpose of this section is to raise some of the major issues of question wording, and hopefully to sensitize the reader to problem areas and encourage him to do careful research and thinking before he actually carries out a research project.

A major fallacy in current research has been identified as "The Question Means What It Says" fallacy.[6] Clearly, in the choice of language and vocabulary, it is more important to ask, "How will the respondent interpret this?" than to ask, "What does the question mean?" It is not enough to say that the language and vocabulary used should be simple; the important point is whether the question utilizes a vocabulary that is *shared* by the researcher and the respondent and whether it is adequate for the communication of the topic. Because it is difficult to enlarge the respondent's vocabulary, the burden is on the researcher to conform to the level of understanding of the respondent. The general rule is to word the questions on a level that will be understood by the least sophisticated member of the sample population, but to avoid the appearance of oversimplification or talking down to the respondent.

Keep Meanings Clear

The problem, therefore, is not only to use familiar words and phrases, but also to use them in such a way that the number of possible meanings is reduced. If a word is used frequently, there is a high probability that it can be taken to mean many different things. For example, the word "fair" can mean just, honest, average, not bad, beautiful, courteous, and so on. Although it is usually not advisable for the researcher to use phrases and expressions that are typical of only one section of the country or of a particular group, the connotations of the words he does use may be affected by these idioms. Payne's recommendation, "don't sling slang," is tempered by a discussion of the possible double meanings that even the most seemingly innocent word can take on. At the very least, using words that have double meanings can cause a respondent to misinterpret the question. Worse than this, however, such usage may create an embarrassing situation, be offensive to the respondent, or make the respondent feel that such remarks should have been cleared by the local censor! Double meanings can be avoided by providing a clue to what is meant through proper contextual placement.

Words can have double meanings, but questions themselves can be double-barreled. It is difficult enough to obtain a meaningful response to one clearly stated issue, without confusing the respondent by asking two questions at once. Suppose the respondent were asked to agree or disagree with this statement:

[6] Charles W. King and Douglas J. Tigert (eds.), "Attitude Research Reaches New Heights," *Proceedings of the Third Annual Conference of the American Marketing Association on Attitude Research,* March 1970 (Chicago: American Marketing Association, 1970), pp. 117–118.

No return bottles are convenient to use and are more sanitary, but they are more expensive and are harmful to the environment.

What is the question? The respondent might agree or disagree with any of the propositions contained in this question. If he disagrees, what is it that he disagrees with? The general rule, therefore, is to ask one thing at a time.

Although the process is not recommended, the researcher can, with the proper choice of words and phrasing, produce what is called a loaded question or even a leading question. It is not at all difficult to do, but with due caution, these can be avoided. Leading questions are those questions which make it easier for the respondent to react in a certain way; they are not neutral. For example, the researcher could state the question this way:

Do you think it is right for the government to coddle big business by providing tax breaks?

What would you say to that question? Even the staunchest supporter of the free enterprise system may be repelled at the thought of the government "coddling" anyone, not to mention the notion of tax breaks when he is paying more and more each year to Uncle Sam. Fortunately, questions like this one are obviously leading, and careful analysis of the question prior to its actual use should point this out if the researcher is at all aware of the problem.

But what about the question:

Do you favor governmental protection of the consumer?

Implicit in the question is an alternative not explicitly stated. The assumption is made that the alternative is understood. However, it has been shown that by stating both alternatives different answers are obtained than if only one side of the issue is presented. If a "no" answer is given to this question, can it safely be assumed that the respondent does not favor governmental protection? Maybe he does not care, or maybe he does not know. The researcher cannot be sure what the respondent had in mind. Sometimes adding an "or not" at the end of the question will be enough to balance the alternatives, while in other cases the alternatives should both be spelled out in detail.

Avoid Loaded Questions

Closely related to leading questions are loaded questions, or questions containing loaded words or phrases. Loading refers to an emotional feeling attached to particular words or concepts which tends to produce automatic approval or disapproval. The danger is that respondents will react to the word or phrase rather than to the question. For example, the word "politician" may call forth different images than the phrase "elected officials." In marketing research, if the brand name is mentioned or associated with the question, the researcher may obtain far different responses, simply because of the image associated with that product. If he asks:

> Do you believe that high phosphate detergents such as brand A are harmful to the environment or not?

the respondent may react more in terms of his own image of and experiences with the particular brand or its manufacturer than to the real issue of high phosphate detergents and the environment. Loading can occur in other ways as well. If the question invokes the status quo (. . . as it is now . . . or should it be changed), responses may be influenced by the predisposition of most people to accept things as they are, or, for some groups, to accept nothing the way it is.

Questions that involve the prestige of the respondent, that are ego-threatening, or that are embarrassing may compel or prevent the respondent from answering in certain ways in order to protect their sense of dignity. Payne relates the story of a woman who reported her husband's occupation as "bank director," when his job was to "direct" bank customers to the appropriate window. Reports of magazines read, brands of beer bought, charitable contributions made, and level of education achieved may all be slightly altered to increase the respondent's prestige. Several strategies can be used to control this effect. If you must ask for the respondent's income level, allowing him to check a group figure (5,000 to 10,000, 11,000 to 15,000, and so on) may be much less threatening than a request for specific figures. A casual approach might be useful. Instead of "Do you own an air conditioner," the question might be stated, "Do you happen to own an air conditioner at the present time?" Filter questions are often helpful in obtaining accurate information. Sensitivity to the feelings of the respondents will aid the researcher in stating his question in such a way that the implication of threat is reduced and the respondent is put at ease.

Leading or loaded questions are most likely to introduce bias when the respondent has no strong opinions on the issue involved. If the respondent has thought a great deal about the issue and his feeling about it is intense, the wording of the question will probably not make too great a difference in his answer. Where people are uninformed or when their opinions are not crystalized, they are more apt to be swayed by the nuances of the question. Yet leading or loaded questions are dangerous only when they are used unintentionally. In the hands of a skilled researcher, intentionally introduced effects may achieve the objectives of the project.

Be Specific

There are many reasons why a question is ambiguous or confusing to the respondent. If the respondent is to react to a question, he must know what frame of reference to use. Free-response questions are often used to ascertain the respondent's own frame of reference, but frequently the researcher is interested in a particular reference point. For example, if the question, "Are you satisfied with the performance of your car?" is asked, the person could react in terms of his wishes ("No, I wish it were indestructible and cost nothing to run.") or in terms of what he thinks is possible ("Yes, it performs as well as present technology allows."). Or, if the question asks for the frequency of certain activities, such as "Do you go to movies frequently?," the respondent should be given some indication of the reference point to be used. Frequently in comparison to whom? How often is frequently? If a particular time period count is desired, the respondent must be told. Sometimes, the frame of reference can be made clear by tying the question to the past experiences of the respondent. This has the advantage of giving the respondent something concrete to hold onto, a peg or benchmark from which to make judgments. Providing a frame of reference simply tells the respondent what is desired, and facilitates his cooperation.

Some researchers believe that question writing is an art, not a science. In some ways, this is true. Experience can provide insights which cannot be put into hard and fast rules, while a beginner may sometimes be more alert to possible ambiguities. However, some general guidelines are available. The danger lies in ignorance or unawareness of the potential pitfalls. The researcher must not naively believe that the question says what he meant to say.

Re-examination, Revision, Pretesting

If the questionnaire or schedule has been badly constructed, the time to correct it is before it is in the hands of the respondents or interviewers. Although the re-examination, revision, and pretesting process cannot guarantee perfection, it can prevent the loss of much time, money, and effort due to poor construction of questions.

In re-examining the questions that have been written, the researcher might turn to Payne's suggestion to borrow the news reporter's five questions: Who, Why, When, Where, How.[7] If the question refers to government activity, for example, which government is referred to: the federal, state, city, county? Does the question indicate the proper time period (past, present, future, specific date?), does it indicate how the respondent is to reply (open-field, clear choice of alternatives, proper frame of reference?), and so on. Each question must be given a grueling examination and revised where necessary.

Although examination of the questions by the researcher can be useful, his interpretation is really not the most important. Therefore, it is wise to

[7] Payne, *op. cit.*, pp. 26–27.

take the questions to the people who will be asked to answer them. A panel of "experts" on question design might be asked to examine the questionnaire or schedule and give critical comments. Pretesting, however, is usually done with a small group of people who are representative of the types of people who will be used in the ultimate research project. Pretesting helps to determine whether the questions elicit responses that meet the objectives of the research, whether the questions are easily understood by the respondents, whether they are in a satisfactory order, whether they are stimulating to the respondent, and whether all important phases of the research work have been covered. Every aspect of the instrument, topic sequencing, question sequencing, ordering of alternatives, question format, and so on, must be tested as well as the instrument as a whole. A series of pretests might be conducted, with the first one being an informal personal interview-type discussion and the last one being a more formal dress rehearsal identical to the situation in the actual study.

Specific things to look for in pretesting are questions that are difficult to communicate, questions whose meanings seem to vary widely among respondents, questions whose alternatives do not seem to be realistic or clear, questions that obtain identical responses, leading questions, or any other difficulty that appears. Some specific indications of poor questions are a lack of order in the responses, all-or-none responses, or high proportion of "don't know" or "don't understand" answers, a great many qualifications or irrelevant comments, a high refusal to answer rate, or a substantial variation in answers when the order of the questions is changed. Any one of these things should cause the researcher to re-examine the questions and the situation in which they are used. After each revision, the researcher must repeat the testing process to make sure that he has not introduced a different type of complication.

As the reader has probably noted, getting an answer to a question does not prove that he has accomplished his purpose. Nor does strict adherence to the general rules of questionnaire and schedule construction and precision in question wording ensure a trouble-free instrument. In this sense, pretesting is probably the most crucial step in the process of data collection. It is in this step that the problems unique to his study can be identified and dealt with most effectively.

Finally, it is frequently useful to classify the various items in the questionnaire or interview schedule according to the scheme in Table 7.3. The main advantage of this exercise is to force the designer to think more thoroughly about each item, that is, its role, operationalization, its underlying variable or concept, and so on. It also facilitates, for third parties (people other than the designer and respondent) the processes of understanding and evaluating the questionnaire.

TABLE 7.3 *Classificatory Question Analysis*

1. Question Number
2. Question
3. Basic Concept Being Measured
4. Roles Played:
   - Independent variable
   - Dependent variable
   - Control variable
   - Index item
   - Other
5. Reliability Rating
6. Validity Rating
   - Content validity
   - Criterion validity
   - Construct validity
7. Measurement Trait (continuous, fixed interval, etc.)
8. To be Used with Question Numbers: ———, ———, etc.

Summary

Constructing a questionnaire involves making a series of decisions and compromises. The questionnaire designer must explicitly understand the problems and implications of these decisions. This chapter outlined the decisions and the impact of selection of questionnaire types, question types, wording of questions, and managing the data-collection process. Experience will quickly show the beginning researcher that not being careful in design and execution of the primary data-collection process can yield a great expense and poor (ambiguous) results.

Questions and Exercises

1. What key assumptions are implied in the use of questionnaires or interview schedules?
2. Question formats can be either direct or indirect, while response formats can be either fixed-alternative or open-ended. Construct an example of a direct, fixed-alternative question. Can your question be converted to an open-ended response format? Which format is most appropriate for gaining insight into the respondent's own frame of reference?
3. For which situations is the dichotomous question appropriate?
4. Why would a researcher include a battery of questions dealing with a particular area rather than a single question?

5. How might the sequence or order of questions affect the respondent's willingness or ability to provide information?

6. Discuss the following statement:

   Since the researcher has no control over the order in which questions in a mailed questionnaire are read, he need not be concerned about the sequence in which they are listed.

7. What is the purpose of a filter question?

8. What filter questions might precede the following question?

   What do you like most about Extran coffee?

9. In evaluating questions, it is often helpful to examine the implications of each possible alternative answer. For example, study the following questions and specify the information that would be obtained from a positive and a negative response.

   Do you favor strict governmental regulation of automobile safety features?

   Most advertisements are informative, entertaining, and honest.

10. What information can be obtained from pretesting a set of questions?

11. What factors determine the number of questions to be included in a questionnaire or interview schedule?

12. What does it mean, in practical terms, to take a "respondent-centered" approach?

13. Select a product or service that is of particular interest to you. Then hypothesize reasons for people using/not using the product or service. Construct a small questionnaire (not more than two 8½ × 11 pages) and administer the questionnaire to five persons who are not friends or relatives. Prepare a critique of your design problems including question order, question wording, hypothesis relevance, and respondent reaction.

14. Construct a three-page questionnaire to determine what consumer knowledge, attitudes, and practices are with regard to imported beers.

Project Related Questions

1. Have you considered the advantages and disadvantages of the major methods of data collection discussed in Table 7.1? Which advantages are most crucial for you to have? Which disadvantages are potentially most damaging to your project?

2. What information have you decided is necessary?

3. Have you identified the type of question most appropriate for each

type of information you need? Are you using direct questions? Indirect? Both? Others?

4. Have you made a clear decision on the number and sequencing of questions?

5. What is your plan for pretesting the questionnaire?

6. Are the questions phrased in the language of the respondents? Is there too much jargon? Vernacular?

7. Have you prepared and tested a covering letter for the questionnaire if it is to be mailed?

8. Does the format of the questionnaire minimize confusion?

9. What are the possible sources of bias in your questionnaire?

Exercise 1: Evaluating a Questionnaire
A Product Attribute Study

The following questionnaire is taken from a study which investigated the perceived attributes of innovations. One of the basic questions raised in the study (which was conducted by a national consumer products organization) was to determine whether or not certain attributes of products were particularly salient in the minds of consumers when that product is perceived to be an innovation. Questions concerning one of the various products which were studied are presented here.

What are the attributes of products that are being measured by the various questions? What hypotheses seem to be implicit in the structure of the questionnaire? What problems or weaknesses are there in this questionnaire? How would you improve upon it? Develop some alternatives or additional questions that would make the data gathered more useful to a brand manager who is concerned with launching new products.

DEAR HOMEMAKER:

We would appreciate it very much if you would take the time necessary to complete this questionnaire.

Please do not consult your husband, neighbors, friends, or any reading materials in answering this questionnaire. We are only interested in *your* opinion.

It is important that you answer *all* questions in this booklet as best as you can.

Here is how to answer:

Most of the questions have the same format. You indicate your answers by checking the box in front of the appropriate answer. For example, _____✔_____. Do not pay any attention to the figures at the right of the space where your answer is to be entered. They are for administrative use only.

If you want to justify or qualify some of your answers, by all means write your comments in the margin or the area around the questions.

The following pages will tell you what to do specifically.

Thank you *very much* for your cooperation.

Questionnaire

Please answer *all* the questions below with the following product in mind. Make sure that you remember what the product is. You may go back to the description of the product whenever you feel it necessary to refresh your memory.

PRODUCT DESCRIPTION

The product is a small piece of paper double the thickness of a paper towel. The paper, when inserted into a clothes dryer, at the start of the drying cycle, prevents wrinkles from forming in most garments. The cost is quite low.

1. Have you heard of this product before?
   (1) yes_____   (2) no_____

   1a. *If yes*, where or from whom?

Television	_____(1)
Neighbors or friends	_____(2)
Newspapers or magazines	_____(3)
Relatives (including your immediate family)	_____(4)
In the store	_____(5)
Radio	_____(6)
Other _____	(7)

   (Please specify)

   1b. Have you already tried this product?
   (1) yes_____   (2) no_____

   1c. Do you currently use or own this product?
   (1) yes_____   (2) no_____

   1d. *If you have not already tried the product*, answer the following two questions. Otherwise, go on to question 1e.

   1. I am likely to try it in the near future:

strongly agree	_____(1)	slightly disagree	_____(4)
moderately agree	_____(2)	moderately disagree	_____(5)
slightly agree	_____(3)	strongly disagree	_____(6)

277

2. I think that the claims about this product are likely to be accurate.

strongly agree _____(1)   slightly disagree _____(4)
moderately agree _____(2)   moderately disagree _____(5)
slightly agree _____(3)   strongly disagree _____(6)

1e. *If you have already tried this product*, answer the following two questions. Otherwise, go on to question 2.

1. How do you like this product?

like very much _____(1)   dislike slightly _____(4)
like moderately _____(2)   dislike moderately _____(5)
like slightly _____(3)   dislike very much _____(6)

2. In my opinion, the claims about this product are accurate.

strongly agree _____(1)   slightly disagree _____(4)
moderately agree _____(2)   moderately disagree _____(5)
slightly agree _____(3)   strongly disagree _____(6)

2. This product is not a product intended for a woman like me.

strongly agree _____(1)   slightly disagree _____(4)
moderately agree _____(2)   moderately disagree _____(5)
slightly agree _____(3)   strongly disagree _____(6)

3. If this product does not perform properly, I would not feel bad about the money which was spent on it.

strongly agree _____(1)   slightly disagree _____(4)
moderately agree _____(2)   moderately disagree _____(5)
slightly agree _____(3)   strongly disagree _____(6)

4. I do not understand how to use this product.

strongly agree _____(1)   slightly disagree _____(4)
moderately agree _____(2)   moderately disagree _____(5)
slightly agree _____(3)   strongly disagree _____(6)

5. It would not be difficult for me to evaluate the claims about this product.

strongly agree _____(1)   slightly disagree _____(4)
moderately agree _____(2)   moderately disagree _____(5)
slightly agree _____(3)   strongly disagree _____(6)

6. This is a product I would make a special effort to tell my friends about.

strongly agree _____(1)   slightly disagree _____(4)
moderately agree _____(2)   moderately disagree _____(5)
slightly agree _____(3)   strongly disagree _____(6)

7. This is the sort of product I like to try out before telling my friends about it.

strongly agree _____(1)   slightly disagree _____(4)
moderately agree _____(2)   moderately disagree _____(5)
slightly agree _____(3)   strongly disagree _____(6)

8. If a friend of mine was not familiar with this product, I would have no difficulty in describing what it is like.

strongly agree _____(1)   slightly disagree _____(4)
moderately agree _____(2)   moderately disagree _____(5)
slightly agree _____(3)   strongly disagree _____(6)

9. This product is the sort of product I usually search for all relevant information before deciding to buy it.

strongly agree _____(1) slightly disagree _____(4)
moderately agree _____(2) moderately disagree _____(5)
slightly agree _____(3) strongly disagree _____(6)

10. The product is the kind of product I generally discuss with my family before buying it.

strongly agree _____(1) slightly disagree _____(4)
moderately agree _____(2) moderately disagree _____(5)
slightly agree _____(3) strongly disagree _____(6)

11. Other people would certainly notice if I were using this product.

strongly agree _____(1) slightly disagree _____(4)
moderately agree _____(2) moderately disagree _____(5)
slightly agree _____(3) strongly disagree _____(6)

12. I would be afraid of any danger or ill effects from using this product.

strongly agree _____(1) slightly disagree _____(4)
moderately agree _____(2) moderately disagree _____(5)
slightly agree _____(3) strongly disagree _____(6)

13. Most of my friends are likely to use this product.

strongly agree _____(1) slightly disagree _____(4)
moderately agree _____(2) moderately disagree _____(5)
slightly agree _____(3) strongly disagree _____(6)

14. I am confident that such a product is based upon sound technological knowledge.

strongly agree _____(1) slightly disagree _____(4)
moderately agree _____(2) moderately disagree _____(5)
slightly agree _____(3) strongly disagree _____(6)

15. If this product does not give me full satisfaction, I can still go back *easily* to my old product.

strongly agree _____(1) slightly disagree _____(4)
moderately agree _____(2) moderately disagree _____(5)
slightly agree _____(3) strongly disagree _____(6)

16. I really do not understand what is so special about this product.

strongly agree _____(1) slightly disagree _____(4)
moderately agree _____(2) moderately disagree _____(5)
slightly agree _____(3) strongly disagree _____(6)

17. My family is likely to approve my using this product.

strongly agree _____(1) slightly disagree _____(4)
moderately agree _____(2) moderately disagree _____(5)
slightly agree _____(3) strongly disagree _____(6)

18. This product is the kind of product that could really change one's way of doing things.

strongly agree _____(1) slightly disagree _____(4)
moderately agree _____(2) moderately disagree _____(5)
slightly agree _____(3) strongly disagree _____(6)

19. How unique does this product seem *to you*?

extremely unique	_____(1)	slightly unique	_____(3)
moderately unique	_____(2)	not unique at all	_____(4)

20. How well do you feel you understand the scientific and technological basis for this product?

very well	_____(1)	not particularly well	_____(4)
well	_____(2)	not well	_____(5)
moderately well	_____(3)	not well at all	_____(6)

21. How long do you think this product has been on the market?

over 3 years	_____(1)	6 months–1 year	_____(4)
2–3 years	_____(2)	3–6 months	_____(5)
1–2 years	_____(3)	less than 3 months	_____(6)

22. To what extent do you think this product has been accepted by consumers?

widely accepted	_____(1)	slightly rejected	_____(4)
moderately accepted	_____(2)	moderately rejected	_____(5)
slightly accepted	_____(3)	widely rejected	_____(6)

SECTION: E

Now we would like to have some information about you to help us in this project.

1. Are you:

married _____(1)   single_____(2)   widowed/divorced_____(3)

2. How old are you?

21 to 25	_____(1)	41 to 45	_____(5)
26 to 30	_____(2)	46 to 50	_____(6)
31 to 35	_____(3)	51 to 55	_____(7)
36 to 40	_____(4)	over 55	_____(8)

3. How much education have you had?

some grammar school	_____(1)	some college	_____(5)
completed grammar	_____(2)	completed college	_____(6)
some high school	_____(3)	graduate school	_____(7)
completed high	_____(4)		

4. What is your family income?

Up to $3,999	_____(1)	$7,500 to 9,999	_____(5)
$4,000 to 4,999	_____(2)	$10,000 to 14,999	_____(6)
$5,000 to 5,999	_____(3)	$15,000 to 24,999	_____(7)
$6,000 to 7,499	_____(4)	$25,000 and over	_____(8)

5. What was *your* birth order in your family?

1st born	_____(1)	5th born	_____(5)
2nd born	_____(2)	6th born	_____(6)
3rd born	_____(3)	7th born	_____(7)
4th born	_____(4)	_____born	_____(8)
		please specify	

6. How large was *your* family?
    number of brother(s)
        (including deceased other than stillborn)   _____
    number of sister(s)
        (including deceased other than stillborn)   _____
    total number of brother(s) and sister(s)
        (including deceased other than stillborn)   _____

RESPONDENT'S NAME _____

ADDRESS _____

TELEPHONE NUMBER _____

Chapter 8

Collecting Primary Data: Administering the Questionnaire

After designing and pretesting a questionnaire, the next step is to administer the instrument to the respondents in the field. The process of one person asking another some prepared questions involves many interesting and complicated phenomena. This chapter examines some of these phenomena and evaluates various methods for implementing the questionnaire-interviewer-respondent communication link. This is one of the main areas where serious problems may develop and where time and cost constraints often do not permit any remedial activity when problems do occur.

The Interview as a Social Process

An interview can be viewed as a process of communication and social interaction with three variables: the interviewer, the interview schedule, and the respondent. This interaction is at once the chief advantage and the chief disadvantage of the interview as an instrument of data collection. Both the interviewer and the respondent are called upon to play roles with definite requirements. The interviewer initiates the communication, presents each area for discussion, and decides when adequate answers have been received and a new topic can be presented or the interview terminated. In addition, the interviewer must teach the respondent the role-requirements of his position as a respondent and persuade him to fulfill them.

As depicted in Figure 8.1, however, each member of the interview situation brings with him many preconceived ideas, attitudes, and stereotypes, and his own unique personality. The interaction between the interviewer and the respondent can make it possible to draw forth much information of a rich, spontaneous nature. On the other hand, both interviewer and respondent alike are apt to respond or react, consciously or unconsciously, to things other than the questions being raised. The end result or product of the interview will be a combination of all these things, and the data must be interpreted with that in mind. This interaction process must also be considered when constructing the interview schedule, when selecting and training interviewers, and when deciding what type of structure to impose on the interview situation.

Types of Interviews

The form or structure of an interview may vary widely from rigidly standardized to completely flexible in the manner in which questions are asked. Classifying according to this criteria, two major types of interviews can be identifed: (1) the structured or standardized interview, and (2) the partially structured or unstructured interview. Other types of interviews such as the clinical interview and depth interview will not be included in this discussion. These methods have been applied to marketing problems under the general name of motivation research, but the necessity of highly skilled, professional interviewers and extreme individuality limits their applicability to

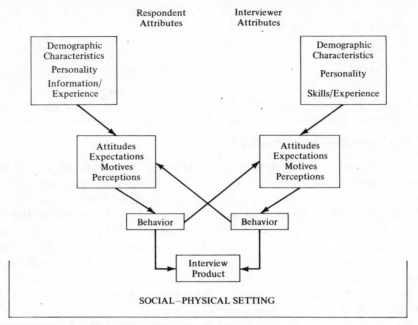

FIGURE 8.1   *The Interview as a Social Process*
Source: Adapted from Charles F. Cannell and Robert L. Kahn, "Interviewing," from *The Handbook of Social Psychology*, Volume II, Second Edition, p. 538, edited by Lindzey-Aronson, 1968, Addison-Wesley, Reading, Mass.

most marketing research projects where a fairly large sample must be contacted.[1]

Structured or Standardized Interviews

In this type of interview, interviewers are instructed to ask every question precisely as it is worded in the schedule, in the exact order, and to offer no additional explanations or interpretations. The interview schedule here resembles a questionnaire in that it attempts to present every respondent with exactly the same stimulus, and to reduce the amount of variation from one interviewer to another. As Hyman notes, however, the gains in comparability of interviews that come from standardization must be balanced against the possible loss of information due to the inflexibility of the procedure, the inability to adapt to circumstances, the limitations placed on the use of the interviewer's insight, and the formality that the standardization creates.[2]

[1] For a good discussion of types of interviews, see Claire Sellitz, Marie Jahoda, Morton Deutsch, and Stuart W. Cook, *Research Methods in Social Relations* (New York: Holt, Rinehart and Winston, 1966), pp. 264–268.
[2] Herbert H. Hyman *et al., Interviewing in Social Research* (Chicago: University of Chicago Press, 1954), p. 30.

We should note that structure in this context applies only to the manner of questioning, and not to the form of the response.

Partially Structured or Unstructured Interviews

The focused or directed interview and the nondirective or unstructured interview are examples of this category of approaches. Focused or directed interviews are guided by the interview schedule, but a great deal of freedom is allowed the interviewer. A schedule of this type may contain specific questions to be asked, or merely a list of general topics around which the interviewer will center the conversation. If specific questions must be asked, the interviewer usually is permitted to use his own judgment in the timing and sequence of questions, and may be allowed to reword or rephrase the questions in order to facilitate understanding. If given a list of topical areas, such a list will usually itemize particular aspects of the topic that must be included. The interviewer's job is to act as a catalyst to a full expression of the respondent's feelings, ideas, or attitudes on the subject, while using some directive force to keep the respondent on the subject and to elicit specific types of responses.

In the unstructured interview, however, the initiative is almost entirely in the hands of the respondent. The atmosphere is one of complete permissiveness, designed to create a completely open situation in which the respondent is free to discuss any aspect of the topic he wishes. Direction or guidance from the interviewer is held to a minimum, and is used only to aid the respondent in the full expression of his thoughts and to encourage communication.

These two types of methods can be extremely helpful in determining the respondent's frame of reference, and the psychological and sociological context of his statements. Since the conversation evolves more naturally in these situations, it is usually possible not only to obtain more information, but also information that is richer in its fullness and more revealing of the personality of the respondent. Referring back to the tradeoff process noted by Hyman, one realizes that the increase in the quality of each individual interview is obtained at the price of reduced comparability among interviews during analysis and increased inter-interviewer variation. As might be guessed, the less structured the interview, the more skilled the interviewer must be in order to carry the interview forward and to obtain relevant information. The ultimate decision as to the most appropriate method must be derived from the stated objectives of the research, the content or type of information needed, and the characteristics of the population to be interviewed. What types of quantitative analysis will be required? Is the content of the desired information highly personal or such that respondents will be reluctant to answer direct questions without the emotional support and encouragement of an interviewer in an extremely relaxed and permissive setting? What is the level of education and level of information of the respondent population? Are they likely to be inarticulate, or unable to adequately communicate verbally without specific questions being mentioned? Or do they possess so little information on the topic that one or two direct questions would be a more efficient approach? All of these considerations must be given careful thought in deciding the approach that will be most effective.

Introducing the Study to the Respondent

Although it is easy to think of a few reasons why a person would agree to be interviewed, it is easier still to name hundreds of reasons why he would not agree. Yet without the person's voluntary participation, there will be no data gathered. The introduction of the study and the interviewer's opening remarks are crucial to increasing and supporting the positive motivations of the potential respondent and playing down the negative motivations. Surprisingly, the majority of persons contacted do agree to participate, some to a degree over and above the call of duty.[3] First, then, let us look at the motives to respond to which the interviewer must appeal, and then specific techniques commonly used to introduce the project and gain respondent cooperation.

Lansing and Morgan list three groups of motivations to respond to an interviewer's request:

1. People may respond to the content or purposes of the study.
2. They may respond to the sponsorship of the study.
3. They may respond to the social interaction aspects of the interview.[4]

The topic of the interview may be intrinsically interesting to the respondent; it may appeal to some of his own special interests and activities, or it may arouse his curiosity. An interest in the chance to be of public service or help a worthy cause may be an important factor. As Sheatsley and many others have noted, people want to help.

Secondly, people may respond to the prestige or power of the agency sponsoring the research project. Perhaps the most obvious and frequently cited example of this type of influence is the extensive interviewing done in collecting census data. The request for cooperation by the census interviewer has the full weight of the federal government to rely on. While other agencies

---

[3] Sheatsley describes one project conducted by National Opinion Research in which mothers of infants were interviewed either by telephone or in person every month for 12 months, in addition to an initial interview which took 1 hour and 45 minutes. In the tenth month of the survey, 89 percent of the subjects were still cooperating. For other examples of respondent endurance, see Paul B. Sheatsley, "The Harassed Respondent: II. Interviewing Practices," in Leo Bogart, *Current Controversies in Marketing Research* (Chicago: Mackham Publishing Co., 1969), pp. 39–43.

[4] John B. Lansing and James N. Morgan, *Economic Survey Methods* (Ann Arbor, Mich.: Institute for Social Research, 1971), p. 147.

cannot depend on authority of this degree, people may know of the agency or may be impressed with the prestige of an institution identified with research.

The third group of motives, which relate to the social aspects of the interview, are perhaps the most important. Nothing is more flattering than to be asked to give your opinions by an interested, attentive listener, and that is just what an interviewer is trained to be. Some people are lonely, or just enjoy talking to people. To others, the interviewer may represent a welcome break in the day's routine. Most people find a charming stranger too curiosity arousing to resist.[5] Also, the feeling that the information one is giving will be of benefit to other people appeals to the altruistic side of people.

On the other hand, a study done by the Survey Research Center at the University of Michigan discovered three major areas of respondent concern about participating in the interview. Respondents were concerned about (1) the amount of time the interview would take, (2) the content of the questions they would be asked, and (3) the purposes for which the information would be used.[6] The introduction to a project should help to allay some of these worries and to emphasize the more pleasant aspects if the interviewer is sensitive to the feelings of the potential respondent and his situation.

The purpose of the interviewer's introductory remarks is twofold: (1) to get the respondent "in role," or to get him to cooperate, and (2) to set the stage for a successful interview. Through his opening comments the interviewer should attempt to establish his own friendliness and interest, the worth of the research project, his own professional competence, and an initial rapport with the person. A good introduction will be brief, but cover several specific points. First, the interviewer should identify himself and the agency or sponsor he represents, and present his credentials. Either a card or badge from the agency will lend credulity and legitimacy to the interviewer's request. Then, the respondent should be told something about the project and how he was chosen. Most people will not be interested in the details of the research plan or the sampling process, but a few remarks about the nature or topic of the project and the random manner of selection will reassure the respondent as to the type of information desired, and as to the chance selection of him as an informant. If the person thinks he was chosen personally, he may feel uneasy about why *he* was singled out. These pieces of information should be enough to satisfy the suspicions of most people, but a sensitive interviewer will be quick to note other doubts that the respondent may have, and adapt his technique to the situation by adding further information about the project, by providing additional assurance of confidentiality or anonymity, or by answering any questions that the person may have.

[5] See *A Guide to Survey Research for Interviewers*, Elrick and Lavidge, Inc., 1967, pp. 14–15, and *Interviewer's Manual* (Ann Arbor, Mich.: Institute for Social Research, 1969), pp. 302 and 303.

[6] Sheatsley, *op. cit.*, p. 40.

The introduction should be respondent-centered. It should not sound artificial or "canned." All comments should be phrased in terms that the respondent can understand; purposes of the study should be explained in respondent-relevant terms. Of course, the interviewer must be honest in his remarks and be careful not to "oversell" the interview. Although the information need not be complete in every detail, the interviewer is after the informed consent of the person. Otherwise, cooperation may be withdrawn during the course of the interview because of unexpected demands. At the end of the introduction, the respondent should feel that his dealings with the interviewer will be pleasant and interesting, and that he will be participating in a worthwhile project.

Conditions for a Successful Interview

In assessing the validity of the data obtained through interviews, the researcher ultimately decides that information given under particular conditions are apt to be more valid. As Hyman notes, these decisions are based on some model or conception of the nature of attitudes and on theoretical conceptualizations of the nature of interviewing procedures under which information is best elicited. Cannell and Kahn have identified three major conditions of a successful interview:

1. Accessibility of the information to the respondent.
2. Cognition or understanding by the respondent of his role in the communication process and of the questions asked.
3. Motivation of the respondent to take the role and fulfill the requirements.[7]

The interviewer, by his behavior and the techniques he employs, is the most important factor in seeing that these conditions are met.

Interviewer Techniques: Obtaining the Response

The first task that must be accomplished by the interviewer is the selection of the respondent. Often in survey research prior sampling is used to indicate the particular addresses the interviewer must visit. Even when the specific address is given, however, the interviewer may be instructed to interview a particular person, such as the head of the household, the housewife, a teenager, or the person usually responsible for a particular type of purchase.

---

[7] Charles F. Cannell and Robert L. Kahn, "Interviewing," in Gardner Lindzey and Elliott Aronson (eds.), *The Handbook of Social Psychology*, 2nd ed., Vol. 2 (Reading, Mass.: Addison-Wesley, 1968), p. 535.

In some cases, the interviewer's task is more complicated. If quota sampling is used, the interviewer may be responsible for seeing that a particular percentage of his respondents belong to a characteristic or descriptive category such as income class, ethnic background, and so on. Selecting the proper respondent is extremely important for a valid survey.

Of all the skills an interviewer must possess, the ability to establish rapport with the respondent has probably been given the most attention. The assumption, here, is that people will talk more freely and openly in an atmosphere that is warm, friendly, and permissive. However, more than friendliness is involved. As Goode and Hatt note, "A state of rapport exists between the interviewer and the respondent when the latter has accepted the research goals of the interviewer and actively seeks to help him in obtaining the necessary information."[8] The creation and maintenance of rapport with the respondent, then, will not only increase the degree to which the respondent feels free to express his opinions frankly and reduce his reluctance to discuss relevant topics, but also will motivate him to actively aid the interviewer in achieving the objectives of the interview.

The interviewer, therefore, has two roles. He is at once a human being who builds up a permissive and warm relationship with each respondent, and a technician who applies techniques that are more or less standardized. As a technician, the interviewer has several tools available to him that are helpful in obtaining adequate responses.

The interviewer must ask the questions exactly as he has been directed. In some interviews, the interviewer may be instructed to ask the questions precisely as worded and sequenced in the schedule, and in others he may be allowed to reword or rephrase a question. In either case, if the interviewer is very familiar with the schedule, he will be able to avoid the appearance of interrogation and use the schedule informally so as to create a more conversational atmosphere. Speaking clearly, repeating misunderstood questions, and using transitional phrases to help the respondent move from one topic to another will insure that the interview is carried, not dragged forward.

If the question has been clearly stated, but the response is meaningless or is incomplete, the interviewer can use several techniques to encourage the respondent to express his thoughts more clearly. A brief comment expressing interest may cause the respondent to warm to his subject and elaborate on his opinions. The interviewer may repeat the respondent's answer as he records it, and pause expectantly. If permitted, the interviewer might ask for specific kinds of additional information. More frequently, however, he is instructed to use neutral requests or probes. Such phrases as "How do you mean?" "Can you tell me what you had in mind?" and "Can you tell me more about your think-

---

[8] William J. Goode and Paul K. Hatt, *Methods in Social Research* (New York: McGraw-Hill, 1952), p. 189.

ing on that?" are all examples of requests for clarification and elaboration which are neutral in that they do not suggest to the respondent that his previous statement was wrong, or that there is some answer which is preferred over another. Probing is a useful technique in exploring the "Don't know" response. At times, this may indicate a genuine lack of an opinion or knowledge, but occasionally a respondent may use the "don't know" category in order to avoid giving a response that might be considered offensive or strange, or to avoid focusing on an issue. The respondent may not have understood the question, or his opinions may be vague so that he wants to stall for time to collect his thoughts or he may not want to make the effort to do so. Probing remarks or questions can be used to advantage in discovering the meaning attached to the "don't know." By skillfully using probes, the interviewer motivates the respondent to communicate more fully by enlarging on what he has already said, clarifying what he said, or explaining why he said it, and keeps the discussion focused on the content of the interview so that irrelevant information is kept to a minimum.

Throughout the interview, the interviewer must be alert to decreasing motivation to participate and increasing boredom or hostility. Although the respondent initially agreed to cooperate with the interviewer, there is always the possibility that he will decide at some point to terminate the conversation. The interviewer must be sensitive to critical moments or respondent redecision, and be careful to maintain interest and rapport.

Use of Visual Aids

One of the advantages of using the personal interview is that it is possible to incorporate visual as well as verbal stimuli into the process of evoking responses. Visual aids are sometimes used as an indirect technique to obtain information on subjects which tend to cause feelings of awkwardness or embarrassment when respondents are questioned directly about them. Occasionally, a researcher is interested in getting reactions to a complex stimuli that is difficult or impossible to put into words. In marketing, for instance, a firm may wish to measure response to a new advertisement, a new package, or some new or existing feature of a particular product. A simple description of the advertisement or the package is not likely to evoke the same type of response as the actual physical presentation of the object. To get reactions to product features, the respondent might need to touch or "try out" the product. In addition to these advantages, visual techniques can be used to evoke responses from which inferences about hidden motivations or feelings can be obtained. Motivation research, which was quite popular in the 1950s, made much use of these and other indirect methods, providing much insight into consumer motivations and perceptions. Mason Haire utilized a somewhat related technique to analyze consumer behavior in buying instant coffee.[9] In this case, the visual aid was a pair of shopping lists. The respondent was asked to describe the type of person most likely to have written each list. The person who included instant coffee in her list was described as sloppy, lazy, and a poor housewife. It is unlikely that direct questioning would have been able to obtain this kind of information.

Recording the Response

There are two principal methods of recording responses. If the schedule is precoded so that it provides the interviewer with a list of alternative responses, the interviewer simply circles, checks, or otherwise indicates the response that matches most closely the thought expressed by the respondent. Question A8 in Figure 8.2 is an example of this method of recording. Here, the interviewer must rely on his own judgment and his interpretation of the instructions he has been given in order to classify the response. In some situations, the choice of responses may be part of the question itself. For example, if the respondent is asked, "Which brand of detergent is the easiest to use—brand A, brand B, or brand C?," the interviewer need only check the appropriate brand. Some questions, however, are not precoded, and the interviewer is instructed to record the response verbatim. Question A10a in Figure 8.2 illustrates this procedure. Shorthand is helpful here, but other techniques such as being prepared to write as soon as the question has been asked, using common abbreviations, and crossing out errors rather than erasing can increase the interviewer's speed. After the interview is completed, the interviewer should take a few minutes to edit the schedule. Editing involves checking the schedule to make sure that all items are filled out, that the responses are clear or make sense, and that all writing is legible. At this time, the interviewer might be instructed to write a thumbnail sketch of the interview, the respondent, characteristics of the respondent's environment, or any problems encountered during the interview.

When selecting a recording procedure, the researcher should be aware of problems inherent in each method. Errors and omissions frequently occur when precoded questions are used. Because of the complexity of the interview situation and the variety of things an interviewer must do, even the best interviewer will occasionally neglect to record a response. Therefore, the editing procedure should be emphasized. If necessary, the interviewer can return and obtain the missing data. An additional problem may arise as a result of differences in coding judgment among respondents. This could

---

[9] Mason Haire, "Projective Techniques in Marketing Research," *Journal of Marketing* (April 1950), pp. 220–239.

A7. Looking further ahead - do you expect that, say, *about five years from now*, prices of the things you buy will be higher than they are at present, lower, or just about the same?

I hope they will be the same. (Yes, but what expect? RQ) Oh, they'll be higher I guess.

(IF *DON'T KNOW* OR *DEPENDS*)   A7a. On what does it depend in your opinion?

Wages go up so prices of things usually go up too.

A8. Now, turning to business conditions in the country as a whole - Do you think that *during the next twelve months* we'll have good times financially, or bad times, or what?

☐ GOOD TIMES   ☒ GOOD, WITH QUALIFICATIONS   ☐ PRO-CON

☐ BAD, WITH QUALIFICATIONS   ☐ BAD TIMES   ☐ UNCERTAIN

A8a. Why do you think that? *They'll be good if we don't have a steel strike this summer.*

A9. Would you say that *at present*, business conditions are better or worse than they were a *year ago*?

☒ BETTER NOW   ☐ ABOUT THE SAME   ☐ WORSE NOW

COMMENTS (IF ANY): *Much better!*

A10. During the *last few months*, have you heard of any favorable or unfavorable changes in business conditions?

I sure have! (R laughs)

(IF *YES*)   A10a. What did you hear? *Well, there's the steel industry*
(R talks at length about what he did when he went on strike.) *strike. The auto industry will probably be next. (Also note R's answer to Q. A25.)*

A11. How do you think the way things are going in the world today — I mean the Cold War and our relations with Russia -- are affecting business conditions here at home?

Uh .... I don't know

A11a. Do you think they make for good times, or bad times, or what?

Well, it does'nt help any (Explain?) I think the cold war doesn't help here (pause)- probably makes for bad times.

A11b. Why do you think so? *Everyone is tense over the situation. They don't want to make long-term investments.*

FIGURE 8.2 *An Example of a Completed Questionnaire Page*

seriously jeopardize the validity of the research findings. When verbatim recording is utilized, errors and omissions due to the pressure of the interview situation may be even more prevalent. As Oppenheim notes, however, some loss of information is inevitable.[10] The question to be asked is, at what point

[10] A. N. Oppenheim, *Questionnaire Design and Attitude Measurement* (New York: Basic Books, 1966), p. 44.

can we best afford to lose information? If coding is done by the interviewer in the field, information will be lost at this point. Or, if coding is done by a central office on the basis of a verbatim report, some information will be lost there. Further, loss will be realized during the ultimate statistical analysis. Careful attention to research objectives and testing of various methods are helpful in making a good selection of methods.

Nonresponse and Call-Back Procedures

Kish defines nonresponse as "failure to obtain observations (responses, measurements) on some elements selected and designated for the sample,"[11] but perhaps a better view is offered by Lansing and Morgan's definition of nonresponse as "the failure to obtain a *usable* report from an individual who properly falls into the sample of a survey" (emphasis added).[12] The problem of nonresponse is a cause for concern if the nonrespondents systematically differ in some respect from the respondents, causing a bias in the analysis and conclusions. The mere reduction in sample size due to nonresponse is fairly susceptible to corrective methods. Nonresponse bias is more difficult to recognize and correct. In addition, nonresponse refers not only to the interview as a whole, but also to particular items within the interview schedule.

Sources of nonresponse are varied. Two categories used by Kish, "temporarily unavailable" and "unobtainable," are helpful in examining possible sources of nonresponse and possible methods of boosting the response rate. The temporarily unavailable group includes the respondent who is not home, who is busy, who is too tired, and so on. Several factors such as the nature of the respondent, the timing of calls, and the interview situation are important here. Housewives, for example, are more often found at home than people who work; urban dwellers, and single and divorced people are difficult to contact. Seasonal activities and working schedules should be considered in timing calls, and advance appointments might be used to alter the interview situation. This group will be susceptible to such methods of response improvement as better interviewing techniques (greater assurance of anonymity, greater motivation and interest arousal, and so on), and repeated call-backs.

Refusals, or unobtainables, are difficult to predict, but seem to be affected by the nature of the respondent, the sponsorship of the study, and the nature of the questions. Some refusals are definite and final; repeated contacts will not be successful. Other respondents may respond to a different approach or a different interviewer, or another time. Some refusals may be due to incapacity or inability. Persons not found, and lost interview schedules also belong to the general category of unobtainables. The range of nonresponse

---

[11] Leslie Kish, *Survey Sampling* (New York: Wiley, 1965), p. 532.
[12] Lansing and Morgan, *op. cit.*, p. 157.

varies greatly. The Survey Research Center reports a nonresponse rate of 10 to 25 percent for personal surveys, while a response rate of 91 percent was obtained by other researchers on the very personal topic of contraceptive practice.

The first method the researcher should turn to in trying to boost his response rate on the overall interview is improvement of his data-collection procedures. For those people temporarily unavailable, persistence in the use of call-backs can be very effective. The decision to pursue call-back methods rests on two assumptions: (1) that the number of additional responses that will be obtained is large enough to justify the effort, and (2) that decreasing the proportion of nonresponse will reduce the effect or bias. Lansing and Morgan suggest the applicability of a cost/benefit analysis. More contacts will be made, but the probability of actually securing an interview may drop. Information about the degree to which the later interviews will produce data which differs from the earlier calls, how the cost per interview obtained increases, and how the benefit of the information secured decreases is necessary in order to determine the number of call-backs to make. After four or five calls and a response rate in the 80's, the remaining nonresponse effect is most likely widely scattered rather than systematically biased, the data will be costly to obtain, and the data will probably be of significantly lower quality.[13]

For those effects due to complete refusal, or to the impossibility of location, other methods are available which will aid in correcting for bias. Subsampling, substitution, replacement procedures, or statistical tools are all possible techniques. Subsampling the call-backs may be economical if the repeated calls are likely to be more expensive than the first contact. Substitution is a possibility, but often the substitutes resemble the people who have already responded rather than the nonrespondents. However, if the characteristics of the nonrespondents are known, a replacement list can be drawn up and used effectively. Still another alternative is statistical correction of the bias by means of weighting or other devices.

Item nonresponse may be due to a number of factors. On the respondent side, sources of item omission might be incapacity to answer or refusal because of the personal or threatening nature of the question. On the interviewer's side, neglect, carelessness, or recording of invalid or meaningless answers may be the cause of gaps in the data. If a respondent happens to be hostile or uncooperative, the interviewer may be tempted to skip questions or to just write anything down. Some respondents are more prone to leave items unanswered. For example, older respondents and those of low-income status tend to make more omissions. In the analysis of the data, the researcher can ignore the gaps and analyze only the information he has. Or, he may assume that the response would be similar to those given by similar people. If item non-

[13] Lansing and Morgan, *op. cit.*, pp. 161–162.

response is particularly frequent, the researcher may look for ways of restructuring and improving the questionnaire design.

Selection and Training of Interviewers

Attempts to identify a particular "interviewing personality" have met with little success. Research done in this area lends little credence to the hypothesis that generally speaking, members of certain social groups or persons with a particular personality type make better interviewers than others. In other words, prediction of success in interviewing on the basis of particular characteristics or of combinations of characteristics has not proved to be reliable. Of course, minimum standards of education, intelligence, and social skills must be met. Much has been written about the interviewer's ability to operate in social situations, emphasizing qualities of sensitivity and empathy. On the other hand, it has been suggested by some researchers that, although some degree of social skill is required, an excessive social orientation hinders superior performance of the interviewer role. Hyman hypothesized and discussed at great length the importance of a professional task orientation for the successful accomplishment of interviewing objectives.[14]

Although no *general* predictors have been identified, research indicates that the combination of interviewer and respondent characteristics in *specific* interview situations is an important determinant of successful interviewing. For example, discrepancies in the class or status of the interviewer and respondent may inhibit certain types of responses. Race, religion, age, and sex differences have all been found to affect responses, especially when the respondent holds critical views of a group to which the interviewer obviously belongs.

These findings imply that interviewers should be selected or assigned to a particular project after giving careful consideration to the characteristics of the respondents and the subject of the interview. Interviewers should be within the "range of communication" of the respondents. If the interviewer is below this range, his competence may be questioned; if he is too far above this range, certain responses may be withheld because the respondent is somehow inhibited by the interviewer's projected personality. In selecting interviewers, one must consider possible interactions of characteristics of both parties to the interview. Precisely matching characteristics is not required. For example, it is not feasible to have highly trained technicians interviewed by persons with the same degree of knowledge. It is important, however, that the interviewer be sufficiently able to communicate with the respondent on the particular topic.

After selection of interviewers has been made, some form of training is

[14] Hyman *et al., op. cit.,* pp. 282–283.

necessary. Training is not a substitute for a good selection procedure; obvious deficiencies in personality or social behavior cannot be overcome within the budget of most studies. Yet there is much about interviewing that can be taught. Training complements the selection process by teaching the new interviewer how best to use his capabilities to accomplish research objectives. It attempts to minimize errors and achieve some standardization of interviewer performance.

Cannell and Kahn[15] suggested four major areas which should be covered in any training program:

1. Provide the new interviewer with the principles of measurement, give them an intellectual grasp of the data-collecting function and a basis for evaluating interviewing behavior.
2. Teach the techniques of interviewing.
3. Provide an opportunity for practice and evaluation by actually conducting interviews under controlled conditions.
4. Offer careful evaluation of interviews, especially at the beginning of actual data collection. Such evaluation should include review protocols.

The interviewer must understand the total research process, and the part his efforts will play in the successful execution of that process. He cannot be expected to strive to achieve research objectives if he does not fully understand how his particular activities relate to them. For example, training manuals often include information about the purposes of research, sampling design and aims, schedule construction, and data analysis.[16] This background information also serves to motivate the interviewer to perform his function well. He should feel that he is a significant part of an important undertaking. Many marketing researchers feel that the "hired hand mentality," avoidance of difficult tasks, and so on, extensively studied in the context of factory production, is also typical of interviewers. No amount of training can hope to instill in the interviewer the same degree of dedication that characterizes the researcher who conceives and plans the project. However, a feeling of importance and involvement helps the interviewer feel that he has a stake in seeing that the research is done properly.

A certain amount of technical knowledge can be acquired through written and verbal instructions, but "learning by doing" provides the interviewer with the opportunity to try out these procedures and to gain confidence and skill in using them. Role-playing can be used effectively in training. Playing the role of a respondent as well as an interviewer allows the new

---

[15] Cannell and Kahn, 1968, *op. cit.*, pp. 584–585.
[16] See, for example, *Interviewer's Manual, op. cit.*, and *A Guide to Survey Research for Interviewers, op. cit.*

interviewer to see both sides of the situation. Demonstrations by supervisors, trial interviews of family members, friends, or strangers, tape or phonographic recording of interviews can also be used to aid the interviewer in mastering the proper techniques. Continuing supervision and prompt correction of errors in interviewing insure that interview quality is maintained.

Although there is a general consensus about the importance of the goals and objectives, there is little evidence to indicate clearly which method is best, or how much time should be spent in training. Research findings indicate, however, that training does make a difference. Although large professional agencies can afford a permanent staff to handle this function, other researchers must seek to create an adequate training program in line with research objectives and within time and budget constraints.

At this point we would like to refer the reader to the somewhat lengthy but enjoyable and informative Exhibit 1. This scenario prepared by Sidney J. Levy offers considerable insight into the social and psychological aspects of personal interviewing.

EXHIBIT 1 *Musings of a Researcher: The Human Side of Interviewing*
Sidney J. Levy

The growth in volume of marketing research puts strain on the interviewing resources of the country. Recruiting, training, controlling, and evaluating interviewers are tasks that make special demands on those who handle field work. The researcher-interviewer interface is one that has not been much explored, and my purpose is to express informally some ideas stimulated by the problems of understanding the human situation in the field.

As a start, my thoughts turn in a reminiscent direction, wandering back to the early days of working on qualitative research at Social Research, Inc. Thinking idly about interviewing and interviewers, I remember Mrs. Burlun. Mrs. Burlun was a squat, cheery woman of about 60. Her daughter started interviewing for us, and then along came Mrs. Burlun. Mrs. Burlun did not know that we did "motivation research"; it wasn't called that then. She didn't fret about whether asking people questions was immoral, unethical, or intrusive. Normally, she did not even understand me when I would explain a project to the interviewers. Afterwards, her daughter would explain more clearly what I wanted. But Mrs. Burlun had hold of certain basic ideas very well. She met her quotas, usually on time; she asked the questions as they were written and wrote down the answers as they were given, briefly or fully and with characteristic idiomatic expressions. There was never any worry as to whether Mrs. Burlun asked all the questions, or interviewed the people she had said she did. Validation was no problem with Mrs. Burlun because she wanted to do what was right.

After Mrs. Burlun I remember Mrs. Smith. A quick, vigorous woman, she said she liked interviewing because she came from the Western mountains and wanted outdoor air. When Mrs. Smith interviewed a housewife, she went after her like a terrier, exploring remarkably a richness of personal anecdotes. Rarely was there a remark that might arouse an unanswered speculation in the mind of a frustrated research analyst, since the remark would also arouse questions in Mrs. Smith's mind and she pursued them inquisitively. We felt we knew Mrs. Smith's respondents like intimates and relatives; and they may well have found the experience therapeutic. Mrs. Smith didn't need to be told to Probe, because she wanted to know, too.

A third great lady of the interviewing trade was Madge Miller. She was a big, round woman and candid about it; and a very moral person—maybe not the best one to send out on a liquor study. She baffled me because when she came into the office I had the impression she never stopped talking, making me wonder how her informants ever got a word in edgewise. Nevertheless, her interviews were voluminous records of detailed discussions of the research topics. Somehow, she rarely found respondents who had very little to say because her desire to tell us what they had said was so great that most of her interviews were like herself, plump with words. There was no need to tell Madge Miller to Report Verbatim; she knew no other way. We should honor the memory of Madge Miller.

I think about these women and the many other interviewers I have known over the years. Their handwriting ranges from crystal clear to interviews that go unread and wasted—and bless those who type. Interviewers come in every conceivable size, shape, hairdo, and education. It is apparent that there is no one kind of good interviewer. Of course, one may set up optimally desirable qualifications. The field director I rely on the most, Leone Phillips, recently listed the following qualifications for an interviewer:

> She should be healthy, active, energetic, intelligent, have a sense of humor, be tactful, persistent, adaptable, tolerant, interested in people, with a sense of responsibility, careful attention to details, etc. She should be 25 to 55 years, have 20 hours available including A.M., P.M., and weekends, have High School or better, a car, legible handwriting, stenographic skills, membership in organizations. She should be willing to work on demand for a relatively low hourly rate.

Frankly, I have met such a woman only once in my life, and I married her.

In addition to marveling at the diversity of interviewers, I also think about the goals of marketing research organizations. These include serving clients and associates by gathering information and processing it either into tables or verbal conclusions. The wish and hope are to do these things competently, efficiently, accurately, and economically, as well as imaginatively and insightfully. The trouble is that involved in the enterprises are two groups known as interviewers and researchers.

A great deal of energy goes into the relationship between researchers and interviewers, and often there is much tension in this relationship. As we all recognize, dimly or sharply, this tension comes about because researchers are very eager to impress upon interviewers that they should be honest, careful, precise, closely attentive to instructions and the wording of questions; while interviewers are very eager to impress upon researchers that interviewing is in general impossible, that the questions are poorly worded, and that any new techniques included are an insult to human intelligence. The researcher is restlessly anxious because "God knows what is going on out in the Field"; while the interviewer is inclined to agree with Nancy Cooley that complex questionnaires developed by brilliant analysts without actual interviewing experience are the biggest problems in market research interviewing today. The interviewer doubts that such long lists of repetitive items are really essential; while the researcher thinks "I've got troubles of my own explaining to the client why the study is going to be late, why one city looks as though the interviewers must have tipped the respondents to the sponsor's brand name—and why are so many respondents always being interrupted by babies and telephone calls?"

In short, the interviewer wonders why researchers must be so demanding and unreasonable; and the researcher wonders why this array of individuals, with all their individuality, have to intervene themselves between those lovely respondents and the research report. My favorite field director recently commented, "I am continuously amazed at the little awareness and tolerance research people have for the problems interviewers face in the field."

I mention these issues without offering any solution, since I don't think the situation is going to change readily. I think interviewers must reconcile themselves to the facts that the demands are going to become greater, and that they are just going to become more skillful. That is, I believe they are going to continue to develop as they have in the past. Years ago, we decided to show people pictures during the interview and have them tell stories. Back came the interviewers, agonizing about how it couldn't be done. Back came the sterile, uncooperative little stories told to the pictures. But the second time and the third time the stories got better and better, fuller and more individually expressive. The interviewers found more people willing to tell the tale. Then we tried incomplete sentences, and went through the phase when hardly anyone would behave as though it was a sensible task. Nowadays, thousands of interviews are rapidly and (almost) casually gathered with such picture stories and rounded off sentences.

We have gone through the same thing with devices called Comparimeters, Q-Sorts, Semantic Differentials, and numerous other approaches, all testifying to the fact that interviewers have unusual capacity to grow, given the appropriate stimulation. I doubt that much can be done to adapt the researchers, although I do counsel them to try to understand what can and cannot be accomplished in the Field. Still, knowing how well interviewers can rise to a challenge, it would be a pity to underestimate them.

This brief look at the individuality of a few interviewers, and this mention of the complex but inevitable tensions in the researcher-interviewer relationship suggest something of the psychological background to the interviewing situation. Clearly, it is a very human situation, fraught with some sense of struggle to accomplish the ever-pressing deadlines, to think on your feet, to be systematic without being barren.

Turning from this background to the interviewing situation itself raises some interesting questions. Why is interviewing so hard? Perhaps we mght take a deeper look at the psychology of interviewing, to try to discern what lies at the heart of what goes on in the interviewing situation.

Interviewing is a special kind of social situation. It usually seems apparent to noninterviewers that it is hard to do, while they simultaneously exaggerate the pleasure they suppose must be in it. Clients are often surprised that people even allow themselves to be interviewed. They are astonished at how long an interview can be, and that people will cooperate without being paid to respond. Also, many who try interviewing are unable to do it. They cannot make a contact; or having made one, they cannot gain cooperation; or they are unable to sustain an interviewing conversation.

The reasons why interviewing is hard for any given person are varied. Energy may be lacking, or verbal fluency, or the capacity to talk and write simultaneously. Some people find it difficult to keep in mind what they are being told. Individual reasons for failure are as miscellaneous as people and their abilities or disabilities.

Beyond such reasons are larger meanings that make the interviewing situation potentially (and actually) difficult. An interview is a human encounter, burdened by several facts. One fact is that the people are usually strangers to each other—or should be. The encounter of strangers is generally a troublesome one. To be approached by a stranger makes one wary. We wonder, what do you want of me? There is a fearfulness about being interrupted in the pursuit of one's own activities. This atmosphere is well-expressed in the first stanza of "The Rime of the Ancient Mariner."

> It is an ancient Mariner,
> and he stoppeth one of three
>   (the other two did not fit his sample).
> "By thy long grey beard and glittering eye,
> Now wherefore stopp'st thou me? . . ."

The psyche is jarred by the novel elements; many hasty decisions have to be made. How much of the new stimulations can be taken in, how should the other person be judged to decide whether to continue further? People may look poised, but inside they are full of wonderment, questioning, trying to learn quickly, to figure out what is going on—all is in flux. The quota calls for a young mother, and can that be a lamp in the living room, and must the dog bark so, and we're doing a study, does she look like she's turning away, who's that coming down the stairs, oh, I almost dropped my clipboard; while on the other side is a disrupted quiet moment at the ironing board, or I was upstairs doing my hair and I thought it was Thelma, do you smell something burning, Oops, you've let the cat get out, who me, you want to interview me, how silly, I don't know anything!

Names just heard may be promptly forgotten—"who'd you say you represent?" Slips of the tongue are common, demonstrating the confusion and lessening of self-control at the moment. One interviewer on a study of Kotex introduced herself as "Mrs. Jones of Sicial Resooch, doing a study of Katz."

Even after things settle down and the people in the situation are able to focus their attention at the appropriate rhythm and level, puting distractions enough aside, many problems remain. Why is there the oft-mentioned problem of rapport? Being questioned seems to be intrinsically a negative affair. It means one is expected to be in a compliant, obedient frame of mind. Traditionally, the words and situations associated with questioning have negative implications. An interview is a form of interrogation, possibly a cross-examination. Carried far enough it is an Inquisition. The situation harks back to childhood, to giving an accounting for oneself to Authority, of defending oneself against accusations of wrongdoing.

In the interview situation this parental authority often becomes the mysterious They and Them. The interviewer may say apologetically, "*They* want to know the silly question," and implies *They* will punish me if I don't get an answer. And the respondent can shift hostility away by asserting, "You can tell *Them* for me that the product or the advertising or the questionnaire is no good."

Tucked away here is the fear of saying the wrong thing or of not knowing the right answer. One of the earliest versions of the dangers of being questioned comes down to us from many centuries ago—about 400 B. C. A Field Supervisor named the Goddess Hera sent an interviewer named the Sphinx to the city of Thebes. This interviewer is described as a monster with the face of a maiden and the body of a winged lion. "What is the creature which is two-footed, three-footed, and four-footed; and weakest when it has most feet?" Every failure to find the answer cost the Thebans a life. Finally, the best respondent turned out to be a wandering stranger named Oedipus. He answered the question with the word *Man*. This got rid of the Sphinx and as a premium Oedipus was awarded the throne of Thebes.

This story may exaggerate the hazards of interviewing, but it symbolizes the fact that it has always been regarded as dangerous to expose oneself to inquisitive strangers; and helps us understand why even some modern citizens may refuse to do so.

It is fortunate for us all that these negative features of interviewing—the fear of trespassing on someone's privacy, the resentment at having one's secrets or one's ignorance exposed—are more than offset by those factors that answer the question, Why is interviewing easy?

The first plain fact is that most people are willing to be interviewed, regardless of anything. Being interviewed does at least four important things for a person. For one, it relieves loneliness and boredom. It does this in the casual sense for someone alone at home or stuck all day with the conversation of a four year old. And it relieves loneliness in the deeper sense for all people with the basic urge for contact with others. Therefore it is no wonder that the wariness on the doorstep turns to cordiality at the kitchen table, that "I'm busy with the laundry and have only a few minutes" turns into "have another cup of coffee" an hour later.

Another motive that facilitates interviewing is the urge to confess. Most people carry a sufficient load of guilt about a variety of large and small acts and wishes in their lives that they are glad to have someone— especially a stranger—who will listen and allow some relief of their feelings. The extreme examples of people who confess to murders they didn't commit make us cautious about the overly cooperative respondent who will confess to anything to feel a sense of justification in how she treats her husband or serves broccoli souffle or uses substitutes for coffee, orange juice, or butter.

The quest for any kind of knowledge can be a challenging enterprise, containing in it the seeds of revelation of the mysteries of life. We are all detectives at heart. Participating in a research implies sharing in this search for knowledge; it means being a witness giving evidence to prove one thing or another, contributing one part to the puzzle, what do people think, why do they behave one way or another? Sometimes respondents want to know how other people have answered the questions; and they take satisfaction in the part they have played.

In all these instances, whether seeking contact, expiation, or knowledge, there is a larger aim at work: the wish to demonstrate or to affirm one's worth as a person. When the interviewer arrives and says in effect, I need you, your views are important to me, tell me more, your opinion is sought by vast sponsoring institutions, the respondent feels a sense of enlargement. Here is testimony from the outside world that one is a chosen person singled out by fate from the multitudinous anonymity of modern life. The respondent feels wooed and inwardly preens with pleasure even while making complaining noises. Rapport comes about and blossoms when for a time, in its own peculiar way, the interview means that one has worth. When we see at times the ardor of the response, the way the respondent may cling to the interviewer reluctant to end the interaction, clearly for the moment it is a situation of love.

This brings me full circle because I am reminded again of our friends, Mesdames Burlun, Smith, and Miller. I think each in her way was an excellent interviewer because she did value her respondents, and was able to communicate to them that they—with us—are involved in an intriguing kind of work, one that thinks people and knowledge of their states of mind are central to carrying on the work of our world.

Sources of Interviewer Bias

During the analysis phase of the research project, the researcher typically wishes to compare and contrast responses across interviews. Implicit in such a procedure is that identical stimuli were presented to all respondents, and that differences in responses can be attributed to differences between respondents. Therefore, the degree of standardization of the interview situation achieved is an area of great concern. The interviewer is an invaluable aid in obtaining information, but he may also be a source of considerable bias; the interviewer, himself, is part of the stimuli which is presented to the respondent. Figure 8.1 emphasizes the transactional nature of the interview. Each participant will be influenced to some degree by the other. To the extent that a respondent's reaction derives from a social or interpersonal involvement, we may expect it to result in bias, since under such conditions, the response will be primarily a function of the relationship between the respondent and the interviewer, instead of a response to the task. Obviously, there will be variations in interview situations and differences among interviewers, since each social communication and each individual is, in some way, unique. Clearly, the interviewer is always an active participant in the process of data generation. Problems arise only when the interviewer's presence or participation operates to cause inaccurate or invalid information to be given, and thus to bias the results, impairing the ability of the researcher to predict or explain phenomena on the basis of the data. The subject of interviewer bias is extremely complex, and has received a great deal of attention in the literature. A detailed examination of the nature and scope of the problem would be impossible within the confines of this chapter. However, an attempt will be made to identify the major sources of interviewer effects. Two major classifications will be used. First, error or bias may be due to the attitudes or perceptions of the interviewer. Secondly, bias may result from the respondent's perception of the interviewer.

Interviewers can be characterized by age, race, sex, physical appearance, and behavioral mannerisms. These characteristics operate as cues to provide the respondent with information about the interviewer such as economic status, educational background, or group memberships. Wide disparities between interviewer and respondent on these characteristics may make communication on some topics difficult.[17] For example, a respondent may be embarrassed by his improper grammar or his lack of knowledge if he perceives the interviewer to be highly educated.

More subtle, though, is what Rosenberg terms evaluation apprehension. Although Rosenberg's discussion is made in the context of experimental designs, the concept is applicable to the interview situation. He suggests that respondents feel that they are being evaluated · according to some hidden criteria, and that under certain conditions they become apprehensive or worried that they will be judged to be unacceptable in some way. In order to gain a positive evaluation, respondents may adjust their responses so as

[17] See Milton J. Rosenberg, "The Conditions and Consequences of Evaluation Apprehension," in Robert Rosenthal and Ralph L. Rosnow (eds.), *Artifact in Behavioral Research* (New York: Academic Press, 1969), pp. 279–349.

to correspond with what they perceive will be acceptable or "correct" in the eyes of the interviewer. This may occur when the respondent perceives the interviewer to be a member of a particular group or class that would disapprove of or be offended by some responses. For example, Hyman found that when black and white interviewers were used to collect data from blacks on discrimination problems, black interviewers obtained more information concerning resentment of discrimination than did white interviewers.[18] Other studies have been conducted which demonstrate this effect, but the reader need only consult his own imagination to discover that many situations may be conducive to such behavior. Williams concluded that bias becomes significant when the disparity between interviewer and respondent is great and the content or subject matter is controversial.[19] Hyman, however, felt that bias would occur when a state of "over-rapport" had been created. In this case, the respondent finds the interviewer so friendly and nice that he says what he thinks the interviewer wants to hear.

Interviewer attitudes and perceptions may also cause a bias to appear in the data. A great deal of attention has been focused on studies which examine the interviewer's own attitudes or opinions on the topic under investigation in relation to the type of responses he reports. In a study on opinions about prefabricated housing, it was found that interviewers who were themselves favorable to such housing reported more favorable responses.[20] When writing down long answers to questions, it is possible that interviewers, consciously or unconsciously, sometimes record selectively according to their own views. Situational factors such as time pressure and ambiguity of the response may be a contributing factor here. Under these conditions, the opportunity and temptation to slant or bias answers is increased. Of course, most training programs and instruction booklets warn the interviewer against stating the question using facial expressions, or acting in any other manner so as to lead or pressure the respondent to react in a particular way, or to communicate to the respondent that one response is more correct than another.

Another source of bias that can be attributed to the interviewer concerns his opinions about the respondent, rather than about the topic of the interview. Hyman felt that this type of bias occurred more frequently than did the ideological bias. An interviewer may expect that a respondent will answer in a certain way on the basis of the respondent's role, his previous responses, or his personal characteristics. If a respondent can be identified with a particular role such as a mother, a housewife, a business executive,

[18] Hyman *et al., op. cit.,* p. 159.

[19] J. Allen Williams, Jr., "Interviewer-Respondent Interaction: A Study of Bias in the Information Interview," *Sociometry,* Vol. 27 (April 1964), pp. 338–352.

[20] R. Ferber and H. Wales, "Detection and Correction of Interview Bias," *Public Opinion Quarterly,* Vol. 16 (March 1952), pp. 107–127.

or divorcee, the interviewer may expect that the informant will know more about role-related activities than others. The interviewer may skip questions that do not *seem* to apply to a person in that role. Thus, the warning to new interviewers to ask *every* question! After the interview has progressed beyond the first few questions, a pattern of response may become noticeable. When a reply is ambiguous or especially long, the temptation is that the interviewer will interpret or selectively record the response so that it is consistent with his perception of the respondent's attitude structure. In addition, the interviewer may expect that people with particular characteristics or members of a particular group are more likely to respond in a certain way.

Although training programs attempt to establish a uniform role or pattern of behavior in interviewing, each research project should be examined for possible situational factors that will increase the probability of bias. Group membership reactions on the part of the respondent are dependent on question content and the social situation. Restriction of the interviewer's activities will lessen the opportunity to introduce bias, while demoralizing demands, complex or antagonizing questions, apparent repetition in the schedule or other factors which create a conflict between the demands of the job and those of the actual field situation will increase the probability that bias will occur. In imposing a tighter structure on the interview, however, the researcher must be alert to any *constant* bias created by the structure and to the loss of information that may result. Interviewers can be assigned in a manner that will minimize the undesirable interaction, or statistical procedures can be used to correct or at least measure the effects of bias.

The ability of the interviewer to influence responses is sometimes overestimated. In some cases, the interviewer's presence may serve to inhibit any tendency on the part of the respondent to embellish or otherwise distort the data for the sake of prestige or ego-enhancement. In other cases, either the respondent may be completely detached from the social aspects of the interview, or the interviewer shows amazing control. In one reported incident, the interviewer characterized the respondent as a creep whom she didn't trust. The respondent, on the other hand, said that the interviewer was pleasant and polite and that he had the feeling that the interviewer liked him.

Advantages and Disadvantages of Interviewing

The personal interview is a powerful tool in the data-collection arsenal of researchers. However, the decision to use this instrument should not be haphazard. Interviewing has inherent strengths and weaknesses which should be carefully weighed against the research objectives and the resources available to the researcher.

Interviews are likely to be expensive in terms of time, energy, and money.

Interviewer cost per interview alone may be substantial if the sample population is geographically dispersed, if the interview itself is lengthy, or if the
complexity of the investigation requires highly skilled interviewers. Sudman,
for example, noted that only about 35 percent of the interviewer's time is
spent on actual interviewing. Traveling time, locating the respondent took
40 percent of his time, editing and clerical tasks took 15 percent, and studying
materials and attending to administrative matters took the remainder. Sudman,
though, has also been active in devising ways to reduce interviewer costs.[21]
Contacting large numbers of people may take a great deal of time and require a large, complex staff organization.

The human side of the interview presents special problems. First, it is
difficult to assume that the stimuli presented to each respondent is identical.
Secondly, in order to encourage frank, honest discussion, the interviewer often
assures the respondent of anonymity. However, the physical presence of the
interviewer may cast suspicion on this guarantee. Psychological anonymity is
more difficult to establish. The interviewer may be recording only the subject's public conduct. In addition, the information obtained is subject to distortion by human factors. The data may be inaccurate or incomplete if the
interviewer's work is often difficult or impossible. A highly structured interview
situation may be criticized for imposing responses on the informant, while
unstructured interviews may be too subjective and it may be impossible to
subject the data to statistical analysis.

On the other hand, personal interviews offer several distinct advantages. All types of people can be reached by this method, and the rate of
return is usually good. Literacy is not necessary, and even where verbal
articulation is difficult for the respondent, the interviewer can offer emotional
support and encouragement. Verbal behavior may be more spontaneous than
formal, written communication, and delicate or personal matters can be
handled more pleasantly since the interviewer can adapt his technique to
reassure the respondent and to build up a permissive, warm atmosphere.
Furthermore, a wealth of information can be obtained. More intensive coverage
of the subject is possible, and probing questions, adapted to specific responses,
can be used. The interviewer can make notations about characteristics of the
respondent and his environment to round out the picture that the interview
creates. Use of visual aids or stimuli increase the scope of items which can be
covered. Although the interviewer can be a source of error, he can be valuable
in clarifying the meaning of questions by adapting his language to a level
within the range of communication of the respondent, in checking the accuracy of the information given, in controlling the selection of the respondent,

---

[21] Seymour Sudman, *Reducing the Cost of Surveys* (Chicago: Aldine Press, 1967),
and "New Approaches to Control of Interviewing Costs," *Journal of Marketing Research,*
Vol. 3 (February 1966), pp. 56–61.

and in providing the researcher with feedback on problems encountered with the interview schedule or research design. In short, the flexibility and adaptability of the interview makes it possible to gain information that is impossible to get by any other method.

If there is any reason to believe that interviewing might be useful for a particular situation, then all possible effort should be made to do so. Researchers should not be blinded to alternative data-collection methods, however. Frequently he can get the data he needs from existing sources in a more economical way, and thus save many hours of his time as well as that of the respondent.

Mailed Questionnaires

A mailed questionnaire, like the interview schedule, is an instrument for measurement and for collection of data. Like the interview schedule, it must be designed to achieve a particular objective, to be used on a specific group of respondents, and to be compatible with the subject matter. Because the questionnaire is self-administered, however, a few specialized techniques have been developed to ensure success in its use.

Goode and Hatt have identified four considerations that must be taken into account in determining the appropriateness of a mailed questionnaire for a research project. These are:

1. The type of information required.
2. The type of respondent reached.
3. The accessibility of respondents.
4. The precision of the hypotheses.[22]

Mailed questionnaires are not well suited for those situations where in-depth or intensive coverage of a topic is required. A question with eight possible answers, each of which is followed by three probes, would require a series of 24 questions. This kind of in-depth questioning would most likely cause the questionnaire to be carefully filed in the wastepaper basket. Even if the person attempts to fill it out, he may have difficulty understanding how to proceed through the tangle of questions. In order to encourage completion of the questionnaire, the form should be relatively brief.

Obviously, the respondent must be able to read and write. It has been estimated that, for purposes of filling out relatively simple questionnaires, at least 10 percent of the adult population must be considered illiterate. Any complexity introduced into the questionnaire design would most likely raise this percentage substantially. However, Cannell and Fowler found that level of education was more highly correlated in a positive direction with the ac-

---

[22] Goode and Hatt, *op. cit.*, pp. 170–175.

curacy of report in personal interviews than in self-administered procedures. They suggest that perhaps the less educated group needed more time to express their ideas.[23] Unfortunately, one could speculate that someone else filled the form out for them. In any event, the respondent is not a professional at this task. Your questionnaire could be the first one he has ever seen. The researcher should keep the complexity of the task to a minimum for most general population studies.

The mailed questionnaire can be used effectively as an economical means of reaching a geographically dispersed sample population. For reasons of time and money, this procedure may be the only feasible alternative. The researcher should be warned, however, that returns of the initial questionnaire are usually low. Therefore, costs of various methods should be compared on the basis of how much usable data is likely to be secured.

Because a mail questionnaire is so standardized and inflexible, revisions in midstream are difficult or impossible to make. The researcher is not likely to pick up any extra information or additional insight that an interviewer might provide. Therefore, a mailed questionnaire is more appropriate to situations where a great deal of exploratory work has been done, and the hypotheses and relevant variables are sharply in focus. A good procedure would be to conduct a few interviews to test the adequacy of the content and format of the questionnaire prior to final construction and mailing.

Two serious problems exist in the use of a mailed qustionnaire: lack of response, and inaccurate or incomplete information. Questionnaire construction and techniques in its usage should be developed with these problems in mind.

The Appeal for Response

The importance of good introductory remarks for obtaining an interview was discussed earlier in this chapter. When a mail questionnaire is used, a cover letter accompanying the form must accomplish the same purpose. Identification of the organization sponsoring the study, the topic of investigation, the purposes for which the information is intended, and usually a guarantee of anonymity or confidentiality should be included as well as an appeal for the respondent's aid. A personal touch and an appeal to altruistic motives are often effective in encouraging the respondent to fill out the questionnaire. Above all, instructions on how to complete the form and how to return it to the sender should be as simple and concise as possible. The questionnaire and cover letter must stand alone; no one is present to coax a person to respond. One can well imagine what would happen if the respondent was confronted with five pages of technically worded instructions, an unsigned form cover letter, and a questionnaire to be returned in person! The cover letter

[23] Charles F. Cannell and Floyd J. Fowler, "Comparison of a Self-Enumerative Procedure and a Personal Interview: A Validity Study," *Public Opinion Quarterly*, Vol. 27 (Summer 1963), pp. 250–264.

must "sell" the questionnaire to the respondent, and convince him that filling it out will be neither time-consuming nor difficult. Such factors as interest in the subject, prestige of the sponsoring agency, the appeal of the particular questionnaire, and strongly held opinions about the topic are related to the percentage of responses obtained. Like the interviewer's introduction, the cover letter should seek to activate respondent motivation.

The appearance of the questionnaire itself is often a factor in gaining respondent cooperation. First impressions formed by a quick glance at the form may be the deciding factor in the respondent's decision to comply with the researcher's request. The layout and design of the questionnaire can also be used to build rapport. The amount of space provided for answers may influence the length of the respondent's replies; sufficient space can prevent respondent frustration and an appearance of overcrowding. Type faces, styles, and colors can be used effectively to facilitate comprehension and completion of the form. Different colors of paper, in a size that is easy to handle contribute to an attractive questionnaire design.

Special Wording Problems

In constructing a questionnaire that will be sent through the mail, a double emphasis should be placed on clarity. Each question must be able to stand on its own. In addition, the sequence of the questions should be carefully analyzed. In a personal interview it is possible to structure the schedule questions to produce special effects, or to delay some questions so that they will not affect others. In self-administered procedures, there is no guarantee that the respondent will not read through the entire form before answering any question, skip randomly, from one section to another, or edit earlier answers in light of other answers. One advantage of the mailed questionnaire, however, is that the respondent can check records or get information that he himself does not possess, but that another member of the family does. This kind of information may not be available in an interview situation.

Special attention should be given to the way questions are asked and the order in which they are asked to make certain that no patterns exist which might lead the respondent to think that some answers are more desirable than others. The claim is often made that since no interviewer is present, there will be no interviewer bias. However, respondents are conscious that someone will eventually read their replies, and may take this into account in recording their answers. Guarantees of anonymity and no requirement of a signature on the form may ease this problem somewhat and encourage respondents to give honest opinions, even on personal matters.

Response and Nonresponse Bias in Mail Questionnaires

Several problems of bias occur in the use of mail questionnaires, the majority of which arise from the inability to control or sometimes even identify the sample population. Of the responses the researcher receives, many may have been filled out by someone other than the person to whom the questionnaire was addressed. Even assuming that the form was completed by the person for whom it was intended, the resulting sample is self-selected by the respondents and there is evidence to indicate that those people who do respond differ from those who do not. Respondents are usually less mobile, more interested, and more partisan, and are of different socioeconomic groups than nonrespondents. If the questionnaire is completely anonymous, there is no way for the researcher to know what type of people are represented by his data.

Thus, low returns, often typical of mail questionnaires, usually indicate a biased sample, and even a high response rate cannot guarantee that no bias exists if the questionnaires are returned only by certain groups. Several things can be done to ascertain and try to correct this bias. One procedure is to ask the respondent to mail the questionnaire anonymously, and to mail separately a post card with his name on it and stating that he has returned the questionnaire. This protects the informant's anonymity, but provides the researcher with valuable information and the ability to check for bias. Another alternative is to send out blanket reminders, or contact known nonrespondents by phone or in person. These methods can be very effective in boosting return rates. Stafford used preliminary contact rather than follow-up efforts to increase mail returns with some success,[24] and Ford found that advance letters, while not speeding reply or causing improvement of data supplied, did contribute to a higher response rate.[25] Special inducements to respond, such as monetary reward have also been used. Wotruba reported a study comparing three approaches: (1) a cover letter with a quarter attached to the questionnaire, (2) the same cover letter, but including the promise of 50¢ for those responding, and (3) a cover letter with no inducement or promise. Significant response rate differences were noted between the first and second approaches, with the first approach producing the fewest incomplete replies. Wotruba theorized that the psychological, rather than the monetary effect was greatest because it created a feeling of obligation.[26] For some reason, self-addressed, stamped envelopes seem to produce higher response percentages than business-reply type envelopes.[27] Special delivery stamps are especially effective in producing a response from those individuals to whom a second request is sent. In any event, the problem of nonresponse is serious enough to warrant a great deal of attention. As Parten states, "unless the surveyor intends to see that insofar

[24] James E. Stafford, "Influence of Preliminary Contact on Mail Returns," *Journal of Marketing Research,* Vol. 3 (November 1966), pp. 410–411.

[25] Neil M. Ford, "The Advance Letter in Mail Surveys," *Journal of Marketing Research,* Vol. 3 (November 1966), pp. 398–400.

[26] Thomas R. Wotruba, "Monetary Inducements and Mail Questionnaire Response," *Journal of Marketing Research,* Vol. 3 (November 1966), pp. 398–400.

[27] Mildred Parten, *Surveys, Polls and Samples* (New York: Harper & Row, 1950), p. 388.

as possible every person to whom a questionnaire is mailed responds either by mail, telephone, or personal interview, or that a small sample of nonrespondents is covered by some means, he had better refrain from conducting the survey. The findings obtained almost certainly will be so biased that no statistical tabulation would be meaningful."[28] Picking up questionnaires at the respondent's home at a preselected date is another effective technique for increasing completed returns.

Personally delivering and picking up a questionnaire that is administered by the respondent seems to be a good way to combine the personal attention of interviews with the low-cost, short-time features of mailed questionnaires. Introductory remarks and explanations of the purpose of the study can be adapted to the individual, and the personal contact seems to increase response rates while holding interviewer bias to a minimum. Nonrespondents can be identified, and can be separated from those cases where the address is a vacant building or lot. Less skill is required of the interviewer. Still, however, respondents must be literate, and capable of expressing their thoughts in written form. Clarification of misunderstandings cannot be provided.

Advantages and Disadvantages of Mail Questionnaires

Mail questionnaires are relatively inexpensive since no interviewers, supervisors, or other related personnel must be hired. They can be used to reach widely scattered sample populations and large numbers of people. This technique is sometimes thought to be more objective than other methods, since the stimuli is standardized and identical from one respondent to another; no interviewer is present to create social pressures. If anonymous, the questionnaire method may encourage honesty and frankness. And, respondents can take their time in answering the questions, and pick the time that is most convenient for them.

On the other hand, the disadvantages of mail questionnaires are such that some researchers have despaired of using them. Most of the disadvantages result from the fact that once the questionnaire is in the mail, the researcher has little control over the data-collection process. He cannot control the identity of the respondent, the people he will consult, the order in which questions are asked, or the final sample represented. Furthermore, when the cost of inducement or follow-up efforts are counted, the cost of the mail questionnaire may be as great as personal interview in terms of the amount of usable information obtained. Some amount of "interviewer" effect may still exist, and the standardization of the stimuli may be more imagined than real. Each respondent will interpret questions in his own way. Without an interviewer present to clarify misunderstood items, the variation can be quite substantial.

[28] Parten, *op. cit.*, p. 392.

The ultimate decision to use any research instrument must be based on the research objectives, the type of respondent involved, and the nature of the questions to be asked. There is no such thing as too much emphasis on precisely stated research goals and objectives which clearly define what the researcher hopes to accomplish by his efforts.

Other Types of Questionnaires

Questionnaires can be administered through other channels, particularly by telephone. Telephone interviews as indicated in Table 7.2 are inexpensive and can usually be done in a short period of time. This method personalizes the situation somewhat, but the physical absence of the interviewer reduces the social motivation. However, the disadvantages of telephone interviewing are many. It is much easier to say "no" over the phone than to refuse to help someone standing in front of you. A person's experiences with telephone sales tactics may make the negative response almost automatic. Furthermore, the interviewer cannot use visual cues to adapt his approach to the individual. From the respondent side, credentials cannot be examined. Even if cooperation is obtained, bias may result from the use of this technique, since many people do not have listed telephone numbers. In addition, the interview must be kept quite short. Perhaps the telephone can best be utilized as a supplement to other techniques. Preliminary interviews or requests for appointments for personal interviews, reinterviews, and follow-up interviews can all be done by telephone.

Group interviews or administering questionnaires to large numbers of people at one time saves time and money. This technique provides personal contact, but reduces inter-interviewer variation since the entire group is exposed to one interviewer. Detection of a constant or systematic bias, however, may be difficult. Obviously, the audience must be carefully selected to insure that its members are the kinds of people the researcher wishes to study, and there is the danger of data contamination through copying or group interaction. Personalized attention to individual people must of course be ruled out if one wishes to assume a standardized stimuli.

Leaving questionnaires in public places is still another technique. Airlines and railroads have used this approach, relying upon stewardesses and conductors to collect the questionnaires from passengers who find them on their seats.

Consumer Panels

Another data-gathering technique involving questionnaires is the consumer panel. Consumer panels consist of individuals, households, or firms whose consumption behavior is monitored over time. Typically, panel members are randomly selected from a universe of all households in the United States. Members of a consumer panel are often asked to maintain a diary in which they record products and brands purchased, media exposure habits, retail outlets visited, and the like. Alternatively, panelists are called upon periodically to complete a telephone, mail questionnaire, and/or personal interviews. In return for their help, panel members are generally compensated with attractive gifts. The major advantage of consumer panels over other types of data-collection approaches is that they allow the researcher to monitor the same consumers on a continuing basis.

Consumer panels are sponsored by the government, universities, and industrial concerns. Best known consumer panels are those operated by A. C. Nielsen, Market Research Corporation of American (MRCA), J. Walter Thompson, and the Chicago Tribune. The majority of consumer panels may be classified into three types: media audience, purchase, and dealer panels.

Types of Consumer Panels and Their Use

Media Audience Panels

Perhaps the best known media audience panel is the one operated by A. C. Nielsen. A probability sample of 1100 households located throughout the United States is selected and "Audimeters" are placed in their homes. "Audimeters" monitor when a television is turned on, how long it remains on, and to what channel it is tuned. Nielsen also maintains a consumer panel that records media habits in a diary. The data generated include the percent of the audience attracted by each channel, the audience size, and certain characteristics of audience members.

The Nielsen consumer panel, as well as other media audience panels, provide a particularly useful input into the development of media strategy by many different types of enterprises. If the market to be reached is known, the Nielsen data may be used to select the time slot and channel which most effectively reaches the target audience.

Purchase Panels

A second type of consumer panel is one in which data associated with product purchase are gathered. Characteristic of this type is the MRCA panel, which includes over ten thousand families selected from throughout the nation. Members of the MRCA panel record in a diary information concerning the brand, quantity, price, and outlet at which products were purchased. In addition, the date on which the product was bought and whether special promotion was involved are indicated. This information is mailed to MRCA on a weekly basis.

Product purchase panels allow marketers of a wide variety of products and services to monitor the effect of their efforts. Panel data may be used to track the adoption of new products, and give the marketer some indication of his market share. It indicates the effectiveness of price strategy, and suggests what impact the promotional effort is having on consumer purchase. The responses of panel members also indicate the characteristics of purchases of various products and brands. Finally, panel data help the marketer identify the outlets which are most effectively distributing his product.

Purchase panels provide a unique opportunity for field experimentation. For example, three different product prices may be instituted for three different subsamples of the panel. This may be easily achieved if the subsamples are located in different areas of a state. The product being tested would be sold at one of the three prices in each part of the state. How consumers react to the new prices may be used to plan future price strategy. A similar approach may be used to determine the potential effectiveness of various "special promotions," and the advisability of increasing the types of outlets at which the product is sold.

Dealer Panels

Panels composed of dealers provide information about retail sales, inventory, and prices. They are often used to determine total sales of various products and the market share of different brands. Dealer panels also indicate the importance of different outlets for particular types of products and for individual brands.

Since dealer panels yield data concerning aggregate consumer purchase, caution must be exercised in developing conclusions about the effectiveness of marketing strategy. A margarine manufacturer may question the usefulness of a 300,000 dollar promotional campaign because dealer panel data reveal that his market share is 25 percent before and after the promotional effort. He concludes that the 300,000 dollar expenditure merely enabled him to maintain the customers he already had. Although this conclusion may be warranted, an alternative explanation for the stability in market share is possible. The promotional effort may have attracted a substantial number of new customers as well as helped in maintaining many of the old customers of the manufacturer's brand. That market share remained constant may be attributable to successful competitive promotional efforts in attracting the manufacturer's former customers.

Thus, dealer panels provide information about aggregate customer demand for a product and brand in various outlets. However, they may mask the extensive switching in customer brand loyalty that occurs.

Limitations of Consumer Panels

Consumer panels provide the researcher with an opportunity to monitor consumption behavior continuously. They permit a number of firms to have access to data which individual firms could not afford to collect. However, there are a number of limitations associated with the use of consumer panels. Specifically, these include biases in sample composition and biases attributable to continuous reporting.

Bias in Sample Composition

Consumer panels are randomly selected from the population which they represent. Unfortunately, it is sometimes the case that a substantial number of those selected for a panel refuse to participate, drop out after agreeing to take part, or fail to complete all required materials. Moreover, once selected, panel members may change their life style. Thus, panels may not accurately reflect the behavior of the population they purport to represent.

To check these sources of bias, the researcher should examine the accuracy of panel data as a predictor of actual consumer purchase patterns. If consumer panels yield predictions that are unfulfilled by consumers' actual behavior, the representativeness of the sample should be reviewed.

Bias Attributable to Continuous Reporting

Even if panel members are initially representative, over time they may become less so. Continued panel membership may serve to make members more sensitive to the manner in which they purchase products and services. They may accumulate more information prior to purchase than they would otherwise, or they may become more sensitive to prices paid for goods and services. The act of reporting purchases may cause panel members to act in a way that is different than they normally would.

To minimize this problem, several strategies may be used. The panel could be asked to report purchase behavior intermittently rather than on a continuing basis. Alternatively, panel membership could be turned over on some systematic basis. For example, after two years' service, panel members might be required to terminate their membership and be replaced by new panelists. Although this procedure involves considerable recurrent start-up costs, it minimizes problems associated with continuous reporting.

The Editing of Completed Questionnaires

In order to guarantee the quality of the data once it has been collected through some sampling technique, it is important that checks be done in order to make sure that the data are coded into a reasonable form for computer analysis and that the data are correctly collected. Thus, it is important that the researcher set up a series of logical checks. In addition, the experimenter must carefully think through how he has coded his data in order to minimize the cost of ensuing statistical analysis.

Real People Checks

The experimenter or market researcher must be careful to make sure that his questionnaire has been answered properly by the respondent. There are several checks that he must perform. Among them are what might be called "real people checks." These checks consist of examining the questionnaire to determine if a given subject has answered questions in a consistent manner which fit that subject's social class. The experimenter checks to make sure that age is congruent with income, education, and other demographic variables; that is, it is unlikely that a janitor would earn $50,000 per year or that an uneducated person would be a bank president. Thus, the researcher must set up a series of checks to make sure that the demographic descriptions which are in the data are consistent with those which he would expect.

In addition, fatigue in questionnaires is often a serious factor. There are two major kinds of checks to insure that fatigue has not damaged the quality of the questionnaire. The first of these checks is to make sure that the respondents have not answered a series of questions in the same way; that is, for the condition where there are perhaps 20 semantic differential questions (coded 1 to 6) in a row, the researcher should make sure that the subject has not circled the #5 for most or all of the 20 questions. If the subject has done this, that is, answered a high percentage of the 20 questions in the same way, it is likely that fatigue has set in and that the questionnaire is valueless. In addition, the researcher should create two sets of questionnaires for his data collection. One questionnaire will have the sections of the questionnaire in some particular order; then the researcher would create another questionnaire which has the order reversed. To check on consistency or fatigue, the researcher then merely checks to make sure that the average values and distributions for the answers on the two questionnaires are the same; that is, he can conclude that fatigue in answering the questions did not affect or bias the result of the questionnaire.

Consistency Checks

Consistency checks are made up of a series of questions within the questionnaire which essentially ask the same question. However, the response modes are reversed; that is, at one time a person might be asked the question "Do you favor the Republican party" at one point in the questionnaire and at another point in the questionnaire he might be asked if he does not like the Republican party. His answer should be consistent to the reverse question. In addition, there should be a minimum of five of these in any questionnaire of more than three pages. The researcher then sets up a decision rule which says that if a given subject does not pass three or more consistency checks, then the questionnaire will be discarded. This is often the case with elderly respondents in that they do not pay close attention to the questions and thus fail to pass the consistency checks. In addition, this checking screens for people with poor vision and other reasons for not answering the questions properly.

Response Mode Errors

Response mode errors are especially prevalent in mail questionnaires. These response mode errors include errors where the subject fails to answer the question in the way it is specified. An example of this is the case where a respondent is faced with a 1 to 5 scale and is supposed to circle the number that is his choice. Instead, the respondent checks a value halfway between the 3 and the 4 on the scale. The researcher is forced either to make an assumption about what response the respondent meant and then assign a code number or to discard the questionnaire. A large number of response mode errors tend to indicate that the respondent does not wish to cooperate but is merely being pressured by the situation. If many response mode errors occur, it is wise to discard the questionnaire.

Classifying Free Responses

In some cases the researcher asks questions which have uncoded or unstructured answers. These answers are often called free responses. The interviewer normally asks the question such as "What is your occupation?" The respondent then answers with a word or a series of words such as steel worker, bank clerk, accountant, truck welder, or some such response. These responses are recorded verbatim on a line in the questionnaire. It becomes incumbent upon the researcher then to develop a coding scheme for such free responses. Normally free responses can be coded in several different ways. In the case of occupation, the coding can be developed around such things as amount of technical expertise, the blue collar-white collar dichotomies, degree of education required, or a number of other coding possibilities. The researcher must look at a significant number of questionnaires to determine the range of responses which have been obtained in the questionnaire. The researcher must then create categories such that numeric codes can be assigned to the free responses. Thus, classifying free responses is an important activity of the researcher. The degree of effort and care that is used in creating the free response codings determines the value of these questions in analysis. An example of this coding procedure as it relates to occupation is a coding scheme ranging between 0 and 9 which includes 0 for "unemployed," 1 for "unskilled blue collar laborer," 2 for "skilled blue collar laborer," 3 for "minor clerical," 4 for "middle level clerical," 5 for "skilled clerical," up to 9 for "professional requiring graduate education" in college.

Other Checks

Other checks are often needed to complete the process of getting the forms from a sample of respondents ready for analysis. Such checks can include checks for missing data and specification of the codes that missing data will take (usually blanks indicate missing data), and checks for interviewer problems. Missing data must be coded differently than existing or regular data. Recoding of data (assigning arbitrary numeric values) for missing values should not be done in the raw data base but rather should be done at the various stages of analysis. In other words, if blank data exist in the data set, the blank data should be left as it is and not recoded into the average value, for example, for the variable. The researcher may be required at some later point in time to go back and reanalyze the data. If the raw data have been altered, information is lost to the researcher.

Since interviewers can bias the research, it is often wise to include a code number to identify the particular interviewer. Statistical analysis of the difference between interviewers' results can be done to determine the existence of systematic interviewer bias. In this way, one can discover any deviant interviewers.

Another check is necessary to uncover evidence of what is known as "round tabling." Round tabling is the practice of involving an interviewer and perhaps one or two of his friends. The group fills out the questionnaires fictitiously, never actually interviewing real respondents. Each "round tabler" fills out a questionnaire in a slightly different handwriting and in a slightly different way. If they are careful in this process, the phony interviews can pass the real people check and consistency checks. However, this unethical practice can be minimized by doing what are called "call backs" to the people who were supposedly interviewed. Call-back procedures are dealt with in the following section.

Form Return, Follow-Up, and Call Backs

The researcher must be careful to maximize the usable number of questionnaires and experimental forms that he collects. To maximize the cost effectiveness of a given study, the researcher should try to save all "botched-up" questionnaires when possible. A record of the name and address of each respondent in the sample is usually maintained to facilitate the correction process. Respondents can then be contacted by telephone to correct the questionnaire. It is very important for the researcher to carefully check his forms, perform his checks, and call back his subjects when necessary. In this way he will maximize the cost effectiveness of his research study.

Nonresponse Analysis

In any study involving a random sample there are bound to be some subjects who do not respond. In order to assess the bias created by nonresponse in the sampling procedure and to guarantee that the sampling procedure itself does not cause biases to enter, it is useful to contact persons who did not respond to the questionnaire and analyze the reasons for their nonresponse. Usually this is done in the form of a telephone call of a very brief nature where the respondent is asked why he did not respond to the questionnaire, if he received the questionnaire in the first place, or other reasons for not answering the questionnaire. This also gives the researcher a chance to assess the credibility of his questionnaire and the seriousness with which subjects view the questionnaire. The nonresponse analysis should be carefully documented and reported in the final written report of the research which is submitted to management.

Documenting the Quality of the Data

All of the checks that are done to estimate the quality of the data, the nonresponse errors, and all checks that are done to guarantee the quality of the data should be tabulated and reported in the management report. This gives management confidence in the marketing research. In addition, it gives management the ability to estimate credibility of the research and the degree to which findings can be questioned. In all market research projects, there is a degree to which errors enter due to clerical errors, sampling errors, and so forth. It is the researcher's primary job to keep these errors to a minimum.

Summary

There are quite a variety of ways of getting the questionnaire to the respondent. These include the personal interview, mail questionnaires, and phone questionnaires. Each method has advantages and disadvantages which must be evaluated before the method is selected. In the work-a-day world of marketing research, several methods are usually used within the same research project. The sociology and psychology of the interview situation were explored in this chapter. Costs and benefits of various interview practices were explained. Error trapping procedures are suggested to maximize the chance of obtaining accurate, unbiased information.

Questions and Exercises

1. What factors should be considered in the decision to conduct structured or unstructured interviews?
2. Write an introductory paragraph for an interview schedule which is designed to increase the probability of obtaining the cooperation of a respondent.

3. Discuss the role of the interviewer in setting the stage for the interview.
4. What kinds of information can be obtained from a verbatim recording of responses that cannot be obtained from precoded question formats? Does verbatim recording insure that no loss of information will occur?
5. Why is it important to examine the characteristics of nonrespondents? Items characterized by high nonresponse?
6. What are some of the characteristics of a good interviewer? What qualities made Mdms. Burlun, Smith, and Miller (Exhibit 1 by Levy) successful interviewers? Can training improve interviewer performance?
7. The interviewer is always an active participant in the interviewing process. How can his participation sometimes introduce a biasing effect to the data obtained? Include in your discussion the effects of both over, and under, rapport.
8. What techniques can be utilized in the design of a mail questionnaire to encourage response? Try to develop a good introductory paragraph for a questionnaire.
9. Discuss the importance of clarity, simplicity, and appearance in the design of mail questionnaires.
10. The chapter stresses the importance of gaining usable information. What makes information from questionnaires not usable?
11. Describe a research problem that could best be studied by the use of consumer panel data.
12. What is the purpose(s) of doing a "real people" check?

Project Related Questions

1. What degree of structure is best for your interviewing situation?
2. Have you tested the method for introducing the topic matter to the respondent? Will it make potential respondents curious and eager to be interviewed?
3. What are the sources of bias which could enter into the interview situation? From the interviewer? From the respondent? From the physical content of the interview?
4. What steps have you taken to ensure as high a response rate as possible if you are using the mail questionnaire approach?
5. How might nonrespondents in your study differ from respondents?
6. What alternatives to personal interviewing or mailings have you considered? Why have you selected or not selected one of these alternatives?
7. Are you using other people as interviewers? If so, what training are

you considering for them? To what extent should they know your hypotheses, general objectives, and so forth?

8. Do you have a plan for checking up on interviewers to confirm that the interviews actually took place?

9. What procedures have you used or do you plan to use for editing the completed questionnaires? What kind of checks are you considering? (See pages 315–319.)

A Tale of Two Interviewers

INTERVIEW 'A'

It is a cold January evening in Smogbury. A market research interviewer walks briskly along a road in a bleak, rain-swept council housing estate. She is wearing a waterproof trench coat and a hat to match, walking shoes, and is carrying a folder in a waterproof cover. She stops at one of the houses, and walks up the short path to the front door. She knocks on the door. There is the sound of an upstairs window being opened, and a woman shouts, 'Who is it?' The interviewer (whose name is Mrs Brown) replies, 'I should like to speak to you, would you please come down?' The woman (who, it is subsequently revealed, is a Mrs Adams) opens the front door a few inches. Her hair is in rollers.

Mrs Brown Thank you very much indeed for coming down to see me. I am from Truesurveys Limited and we are carrying out a survey . . .

Mrs Adams What do you want? Are you from the Council? If so, we haven't got no lodger now.

Mrs B. No, I'm not from the Council. It's a *survey about different kinds of drinks.*

Mrs A. We don't have much money for drinks. Are you selling them? If you are then you are wasting your time. My husband said I mustn't buy nothing any more at the door.

Mrs B. No, I'm not selling anything at all. Truesurveys do these market research surveys so that the manufacturers of different products can get to know people's tastes and preferences so that they can produce better products. May I come inside, please?

(They both move back into the hall, and the front door is closed)

Mrs B. Thank you very much. *I need to interview people in different job and age groups, so first of all, what is the occupation of the head of your household and your age last birthday, please?*

Mrs A. He's an engineer.

Mrs B. What kind of engineer? Has he served an apprenticeship or had any other special training for his job?

Mrs A. Oh yes, he's a fitter in the bicycle factory down the road.

SOURCE: Joan M. Smith, *Interviewing in Marketing and Social Research* (London: Routledge and Kegan Paul, 1972), Appendix 1.

Mrs B. Has he any men working under him?

Mrs A. Oh, no.

Mrs B. And your age last birthday, please?

Mrs A. I am forty-two but I still don't see . . .

Mrs B. You are just the person I need to interview.

Mrs A. How long will it take?

Mrs B. Oh, about ten to fifteen minutes, at the most.

Mrs A. Well, you'd better come into the living-room. My husband knows much more than me, and he'd like to hear it. I won't be on the telly, will I?

Mrs B. Definitely not. Everything you say to me is completely confidential, but I should like to talk to you alone, if possible. You see, it's your own opinions I want, and your husband might want to give me his views if he is there. I have finished all my interviews with men.

(They go into the front 'parlour' and a small electric fire is switched on)

Mrs A. Would you like a cup of tea?

Mrs B. No, thank you very much for asking me, but I really would much prefer to finish the interview now.

(Mrs Adams sits down in an easy chair, Mrs Brown sits in one immediately facing her. Mrs Brown opens her folder, takes out one questionnaire, rests it on her folder, then takes a white card out of a plastic pouch and hands it to Mrs Adams.)

Mrs B. *Would you look at this Card A and tell me . . .*

Mrs A. I'm afraid I can't read that without my reading glasses.

Mrs B. I should be glad if you would get them, it is important that you should actually read the card.

(Mrs A. goes upstairs and comes again into the room wearing spectacles)

Mrs B. Thank you for getting them —you will be able to read it all right now, won't you? *Which of these drinks do you yourself ever drink nowadays?*

(Mrs Adams takes card A, and reads it)

Mrs A. Well—a bottle of stout now and again, Brownberry stout, that's what I like—and I'll have a glass of beer sometimes if I'm in company.

Mrs B. Would that be bottled, canned or draught beer?

Mrs A. Always in a bottle—you can taste the tins, and draught seems a bit flat to me. Oh yes, and I have orange squash, but that's mostly in the summer. That's all I think.

(Mrs Brown takes back the card from Mrs Adams and replaces it in the pouch)

Q.2 Mrs B. *When did you last drink bottled stout?*

Mrs A. I have my drop of stout in the pub on a Saturday night.

Mrs B. When did you *last* drink bottled stout?

Mrs A. Oh, last week, down at the Red Lion.

Mrs B. Today is Monday. Was it

since last Monday, or before that?

Mrs A. It was the Saturday before that—the Red Lion—it's a nice, snug little pub. Do you know it?

Q.2 Mrs B. No, I'm afraid I don't know it. I don't know this area very well, you see. *When did you last drink bottled beer?*

Mrs A. It was at Christmas. We had folks in, and had a bit of a party.

Mrs B. It's now 30 January. Would that be over a month ago—that is, more than four weeks ago then?

Mrs A. Yes it would.

Q.2 Mrs B. *When did you last drink fruit squashes of any kind?*

Mrs A. Oh, yesterday. I had some lemon squash with my little boy. I have not had orange squash since my holiday last September.

Q.3 Mrs B. *Now, thinking about the last time you drank bottled stout, where were you?*

Mrs A. Oh, I'm sorry, dear, I told you it was at the Red Lion. I did drink a bottle of stout here at home last Friday: I forgot that.

Q.4 Mrs B. *What brand of bottled stout was it?*

Mrs A. Oh, yes—Whiteleys, it was. I got it from the off-licence and they give stamps there.

Q.3 Mrs B. *Thinking about the last time you drank bottled beer, where were you?*

Mrs A. At home here, at Christmas time it was.

Q.4 Mrs B. *What brand of bottled beer was it?*

Mrs A. Golden Gleam—I got a dozen bottles in for Christmas from the off-licence.

Q.3 Mrs B. *Thinking about the last time you drank fruit squash, where were you?*

Mrs A. At home here with my little boy yesterday. Lemon squash it was.

Q.4 Mrs B. *What brand of lemon squash was it?*

Mrs A. It was Frutee squash. I got that from the off-licence too. It was cut-price, as well as getting the stamps.

Q.5a Mrs B. *Have you seen any advertisements for beer lately?*

Mrs A. I don't bother much at all with advertisements.

Mrs B. Could you please think whether you have seen advertisements for beer lately?

Mrs A. Well, there's a poster near the railway station—for Blossom's Beer it is.

Mrs B. What other advertisements for beer have you seen anywhere?

Mrs A. None, only that poster.

Q.5b Mrs B. *Would you describe it to me?*

Mrs A. There is an orchard and a man with a big glass of beer.

Q.5c Mrs B. *What does it say?*

Mrs A. Something about 'Blossom's Beer is Best,' I think.

Mrs B. What else can you remember about it?

Mrs A. Just the sun shining—and it looks a hot day and he's quenching his thirst.

Mrs B. What else?

Mrs A. Nothing at all. As I said, I

don't bother with adverts, I'm sorry I can't say any more.

Mrs B. You are being most helpful, thank you very much.

(Mrs Brown takes the same card as before out of the pouch, and hands it to Mrs Adams)

Mrs B. *Which of the drinks on this card do you think young people —the under-21s—drink most often?*

Mrs A. Whatever they can get, I'd say.

Mrs B. Well, which of the ones on the card do you think they drink most often?

Mrs A. I'd say, lager and lime they seem to have.

(Mrs Brown replaces the card in the pouch, and hands another card to Mrs Adams)

Mrs B. *Now would you look at this card B and tell me which of these amounts on the card comes nearest to your* total *household income, after tax deductions. Just call out the letter after the amount.*

Mrs A. Well, I suppose it's 'Y'— but I don't see what that has got to do with drinks.

Mrs B. Well, you see, all the information we get from all the people we interview is put into a computer. It comes out as figures showing what kinds of drinks people with different incomes have. *Finally, just a few details about yourself and your family.* Are you yourself in paid employment at present?

Mrs A. Well, yes.

Mrs B. What is that?

Mrs A. I'm a cleaner down at the snack bar—it's just a little job to get some pocket money, and it's nearby.

Mrs B. Is it part time, that is eight to twenty-nine hours a week, or is it full time, that is thirty hours or more?

Mrs A. Ten hours—just mornings.

Mrs B. How many adults are there in your household, apart from your husband and yourself?

Mrs A. None.

Mrs B. And how many children up to ten years of age?

Mrs A. One boy.

Mrs B. And how many between the ages of eleven and sixteen?

Mrs A. Another boy.

Mrs B. So that means there are four of you all together?

Mrs A. Yes.

Mrs B. Is '26 Elm Way, Smogbury,' the full postal address of this house?

Mrs A. Yes, it is.

Mrs B. And your name is . . .

Mrs A. What do you want that for? I thought it was all confidential.

Mrs B. The only reason for asking your name is to prove that I have in fact interviewed you. The answers you have given me are all confidential, and they will never be associated with your name.

Mrs A. My name is Adams.

Mrs B. And your initials?

Mrs A. Mary.

Mrs B. Thank you very much indeed, I am most grateful for your help.

Mrs A. That's all right—it was

quite an experience. But you should have had my husband really, he's much more of a drinker than me, and knows more about things.

Mrs B. I do assure you that your answers were just as helpful as his would have been. It was your opinion I wanted, and you were most co-operative.

(Mrs Brown looks at her watch and records on the questionnaire the time and the duration of the interview)

INTERVIEW 'B'

It is the same cold, wet January evening in Smogbury in the same council estate. A market research interviewer is walking along the road. She is wearing a fur-trimmed coat, a headscarf and highheeled shoes. She is holding up an umbrella and carrying a large shopping-bag and a handbag. She stops at one of the houses and walks up the short path to the front door. She knocks on the door. There is the sound of an upstairs window being opened, and a woman shouts, 'Who is it?' The interviewer (whose name is Mrs Green) replies, 'Oh, I am sorry to disturb you. You hadn't gone to bed, had you? I'd just like a little word with you—just for a minute.' The woman (it is subsequently revealed) is a Mrs Adams. She opens the door a few inches. Her hair is in rollers.

Mrs Green I am really sorry to trouble you—I don't want to take up your time, but if you could just spare me a minute or two . . .

Mrs Adams What's it all about?

As you can see, I've just washed my hair. When I saw you from the window I thought you was from the Council. I can see now that you're not. We had a lodger you see, and they wanted to put our rent up because of it.

Mrs G. Oh, no; I wouldn't work for *them*—they spy on all their good tenants so as to try and get more money out of them, yet they're giving council houses to all those 'blacks' all the time without asking them any questions. I've got a friend who lives on this estate and she gets really wild about it.

Mrs A. I don't blame her—a woman in the next street, she's got one of these West Indian families— more like a tribe it is—put into the house next to her. How she puts up with it, I don't know— and their habits. . . ! You aren't selling anything are you? My husband said I mustn't buy nothing more at the door. I've got caught for a lot of H.P. payments that way and can't seem to get it paid off.

Mrs G. No, not me. I used to go round with mail order catalogues, but I packed it in—no money in it—just working on commission. This is market research—chatting to you about drinks. There's 'soft' ones too, so you'll be all right, don't worry.

Mrs A. Well, you'd better come in out of the wet. All your fur is soaking wet—I'll hang your coat up.

(They move back into the hall, and

the door is shut. Mrs Green opens her wet umbrella and places it, opened, on the hall floor)

Mrs A. Come into the living room. My husband would like to hear what you have to say.

Mrs. G. Thanks ever so much, but can I use your toilet first?

Mrs A. Yes, it's first up the stairs on the right. I'll just be telling my husband about it. I won't be on the telly will I?

Mrs G. No—they just use these surveys to help them with their advertising, you know.

(Mrs Adams goes into the living-room where her husband is sitting in front of the fire)

Mr A. What's all this about? Where's that woman gone? Not selling nothing, is she?

Mrs A. Oh no, she's just gone upstairs to the toilet—she's ever such a nice woman. She's just going to chat to me about drinks. Ever so friendly she is, but I don't think *she* drinks from the way she spoke.

Mr A. No, neither do you, mind— you don't want to tell all your business to strangers.

Mrs A. Well, I don't, want you might call, drink *really*, do I? It's not worth talking about what I do have, anyway.

Mr A. No, it isn't.

(Mrs Green enters, carrying the large shopping-bag from which she takes a rather crumpled pile of questionnaires)

Mrs G. I'll just come and sit next to you Mrs . . . ? What did you say your name was?

Mrs A. I *didn't* say, but it's Adams.

Mr A. There's a lot of writing on these forms you've got. How long will it take?

Mrs G. Well, it depends on how many of the things you drink— the more there are, the longer it'll be—it'll only take a very few minutes though I'm sure.

(Mrs Green takes a rather dirty crumpled card out of her shopping-bag)

Q.1 Mrs G. Now, would you tell me which of these drinks you drink?

Mrs A. I can't read that without my glasses and they're upstairs.

Mrs G. Don't worry about that, I'll read them out to you.

Mrs A. First, would you like a cup of tea?

Mrs G. I'll not say 'no' to that, I could just do with one.

(Mrs Adams goes into the adjoining scullery to make the tea)

Mr A. Is this a good job you've got? Waste of money it seems to me. They should make things cheaper instead of spending all that on advertising and such. Do you always have to work at night?

Mrs G. I suppose they should really make things cheaper— things are going up all the time. That's all I do this for—the money. I've got to work at night on this job and I've to write down the time I came here.

(A few minutes later, Mrs Adams returns with the tea—pours it out and they all drink it)

Mrs G. I'd better get on I suppose

or I'll never get home—I'll read these things out to you.

Mr A. She doesn't drink, so it's a waste of time, I'd say.

Mrs A. You should be asking him —he knows more about it than me.

Mrs G. Oh no—you'll do! The first one's beer.

(Mrs Adams shakes her head)

Mrs G. No—not that then. There's different sorts—bottled, canned or draught—It's 'no' to all of them, is it?

Mrs A. Yes.

Mrs G. Now the next is lager—in bottles or in cans, or draught.

Mrs A. No—I don't have any of that.

Mrs G. Now stout . . .

(Mrs Adams shakes her head)

Mr A. She's told you, she doesn't drink—there's no sense in asking her all this. You don't drink yourself, do you?

Mrs G. No, I don't. My first husband was a real drunk and that turned me right off it. So it's no to canned, bottled and draught stout, isn't it?

Mrs A. Yes, that's right.

Mrs G. Now what about fruit squashes.

Mrs A. Oh yes—I do have orange squash, but that's mostly in the summertime. I buy a lot of it then, don't I, Bill?

Mr A. Yes you do—but that's a lot of questions you're asking. I thought you said . . .

Q.2 Mrs G. I'll soon be finished. That orange squash—it was last summer you said you had it, wasn't

it? It's not worth putting it down at all then. I'll cross it out.

Mrs A. Yes, about September time. It's not worth bothering about though.

Mr A. I've to be off now to the club. Don't be telling all the family secrets, will you? You didn't tell us *your* name.

Mrs G. It's Mrs Green. I don't live on this estate but I know Mrs Grey, do you? She helps with the school meals and lives in this street.

Mrs A. We know them well—Mr Grey is always round at the club —well, goodnight all.

Mrs G. (After Mr Adams has gone)

Q.5 Now this is about advertising. Have you seen any advertisements for beer lately?

Mrs A. I don't bother much at all with advertising.

Mrs G. You must have seen some on the telly, haven't you?

Mrs A. I suppose I must have done. We have it on all the time.

Mrs G. Right—well I'll put down 'on television.' What was it about?

Mrs A. I can't remember anything about any beer one. There are so many of them commercials.

Mrs G. That's all right, don't worry,

Q.6 I'll put down 'can't remember.' Now which of the drinks on that card do you think young people —that is the under-21s—drink most often? Shall I read them out again, or can you remember them?

Mrs A. Oh, I can remember them all right but I'd say they'd have whatever they can get. It'd more likely be stronger drink and drugs and suchlike I'd think, don't you?

Mrs G. Yes, I do—it's all sex and drugs with them—and rioting all the time. So I'd better put 'none of them' for that, hadn't I?

Mrs A. Yes, do.

(Mrs Green produces another crumpled card from the shopping-bag)

Q.7 Mrs G. Here's another card I'll read out to you, Mrs Adams— I'm sorry but it's a bit personal. Which of the figures I'll read out is the nearest to your total household income after tax has been deducted? Just . . .

Mrs A. You mean, you're asking how much money we've got coming in? I can't tell you that— my husband would go mad—no I can't tell you. That really is nosey I think.

Mrs G. Yes, I know it is—if you'd rather not say I'll just put 're-fused to answer'; that's all right Mrs Adams.

Mrs A. I should think it is.

Mrs G. Now I've just got to ask what your husband's job is. I don't want to know where he works—just what his job is.

Mrs A. He's an engineer.

Mrs G. An engineer in a factory, is he?

Mrs A. Yes.

Mrs. G. And you're a housewife?

Mrs A. Yes, that's right.

Mrs G. And you'll be between forty-five and sixty-four are you, Mrs Adams?

Mrs A. Goodness *no*—do I look as old as that?—I'm not, anyway.

Mrs G. How many are there of you? You and your husband— and what about children?

Mrs A. One boy of eight and one of fourteen. They should be back by now—they went to their aunty's for their tea.

That's four of you. Now I have to write down your name and address. You won't be bothered with samples or anything. I need it because they don't trust us. They might write or come and ask you if I've interviewed you. Oh yes, and it's 8.30 now, I'll write that down. You're Mrs Adams and what number of Elm Way is this?

Mrs A. Number 26, but fancy them not trusting you—and making you ask these cheeky questions. If you're passing this way, come and have a cup of tea and another natter.

Mrs G. Right, I will—and I'll be hearing about you from Mrs Grey. I must tell her I met you. I'll just pick up my things from the hall. Goodbye.

QUESTIONS

Compare Mrs. Brown's interviewing with Mrs. Green's interviewing. How do they differ in appearance, approach, procedures on entering the house, interviewing procedure, and classification data?

Chapter 9

Marketing Experimentation[1]

Experimentation is a process where events occur in a setting at
the discretion of the experimenter, and controls are used to identify
the causes of variation in subjects' response. Experimentation
generally takes place in field settings and laboratory settings. This
research approach is becoming increasingly important in marketing.
This chapter covers the various factors involved in developing
effective experiments and the application of experimentation to
marketing problems. The reader is also particularly directed to
a reading at the end of the chapter concerning the use of
unobtrusive measures in marketing research. Unobtrusive measures
are a neglected way of gathering data and are appropriate to both
experimental and nonexperimental research.

---

[1] This chapter was authored by Brian Sternthal, Northwestern University, and
C. Samuel Craig, Ohio State University.

Introduction

Experimentation in marketing is but another tool at the disposal of the creative researcher. It does, however, possess a unique attribute that sets it apart from other research techniques. Experimentation allows the researcher to establish, with some certainty, causal relationships between variables. This is contrasted with nonexperimental techniques, which while useful, can mislead the researcher about the true nature of reality.

Marketing experimentation's virtues can best be appreciated by considering the plight of a researcher interested in the relationship between advertising and sales volume. Over a period of years, he observed that increased advertising expenditures for gasoline were invariably associated with increased sales of gasoline. On this basis, he concluded that the advertising expenditures *caused* the sales increase. Upon closer examination he discovered that major oil companies frequently budget advertising expenditures as a percentage of forecasted sales. With optimistic forecasts that were fulfilled, the advertising expenditures necessarily rose. Now the researcher concludes that the forecasted sales *caused* the increases in advertising expenditures. However, upon closer scrutiny, the researcher discovers another set of variables which appear responsible for the rise in sales. By examining consumption patterns of new car purchasers, he finds increased automobile sales, more multiple car families, more miles driven per capita, greater ownership of recreational vehicles, and more cars with high horsepower, power options, and emission control devices, all of which result in increased gasoline consumption. Thus, his presumed relationship between advertising expenditures and gasoline sales is cast into doubt.

Marketing experimentation provides a means for resolution of the researcher's dilemma. Through experimentation the researcher is able to construct a replica of the market place, manipulate variables, observe the result, and make causal inferences. For this reason experimentation is a powerful research tool. However, as with any research tool it must be used properly to result in unambiguous findings. This chapter will attempt to provide a basis for understanding marketing experimentation and hopefully serve as a first step in conducting marketing experimentation.

331

What is Marketing Experimentation?

Perhaps the best way to deal with the question of what is marketing experimentation is through an example. The example begins with a researcher interested in a marketing phenomenon called the "price-quality" relationship.[2]

He had observed that consumers frequently prefer the higher priced brand, even when it is identical to cheaper alternatives in all respects except brand name. Many consumers seem willing to pay two or three cents more per gallon for national brands of gasoline over independent brands. All aspirin is chemically the same, yet many consumers opt for Bayer aspirin rather than considerably cheaper store brands. Given these observations the researcher decided to examine the relationship between price and quality through an experiment.

For his experiment he selected a random probability sample of 60 beer drinkers. To disguise the true purpose of the study, the subjects were told that "the experiment was part of a product test of three beers for a brewer, providing an opportunity for a behavioral study of how people make purchase decisions . . ."[3]

Actually, the three brands of beer (labeled M, L, and P) were identical; they came from the same brewer and batch. Through the instructions and different label letters the subjects were led to believe that the brands were in fact different. This belief was reinforced by differential pricing of the brands. M was priced at $1.30 per six-pack, L at $1.20 per six-pack, and P at $0.99 per six-pack. During the study the experimenter visited all the beer drinkers 24 times. At each visit they were allowed to select one bottle for in-home consumption. To equalize the actual price, money was taped to the bottles of the two lower priced brands. This helped insure that the subjects would not automatically select the highest priced brand.

After the 24th consumption trial, subjects were given a list of words commonly used to describe beer. Approximately half the words on the list had favorable connotations (for example, smooth, rich-flavored, and full-bodied) while the other half had unfavorable connotations (for example, flat, bitter, and watery). From the list, subjects were asked to select three words that best characterized each brand. Subjects also rated each brand on a five-point scale.

The data were first analyzed by looking at the number of favorable versus unfavorable words used to describe each brand. The highest priced brand received the greatest number of favorable words (93) and the fewest

[2] J. Douglas McConnell, "The Price-Quality Relationship in an Experimental Setting," *Journal of Marketing Research,* Vol. 5 (August 1968), pp. 300–303.

[3] J. Douglas McConnell, "The Development of Brand Loyalty: An Experimental Study," *Journal of Marketing Research,* Vol. 5 (February 1968), pp. 13–19.

unfavorable words (71), while the lowest priced beer received the fewest favorable words (57) and the greatest number of unfavorable words (101). Subjects also gave the highest overall rating to the highest priced brand and the lowest overall rating to the lowest priced brand. Over all the consumption trials, the highest priced brand was selected over 41 percent of the time.

This experiment demonstrated rather clearly that there is a price-quality relationship. When price is the only purchase or consumption cue available, it influences the perception of quality. Subjects consistently perceived the highest priced brand to be of higher quality than the other brands when in fact all brands came from the same batch.

Marketing Experimentation Defined

The example illustrates, through description, what experimentation is. To develop a more thorough understanding of experimentation in a marketing context, a formal definition will be advanced. This definition identifies the key elements of experimentation for diverse marketing settings.

When the term *experimentation* is mentioned in a social science context the unitiated envisage a white frocked experimenter in a sterile looking laboratory filled with hidden microphones, television cameras, and one-way glass. Although this description typifies the setting in which much academic research is conducted, it is not necessarily an ingredient of experimentation. In fact, as the preceding example illustrates, many marketing experiments are conducted in quite natural settings.

In essence, *experimentation is a process where events occur in a setting at the discretion of the experimenter, and controls are used to identify the sources of variation in subjects' response.*[4] The definition indicates that the experimenter systematically manipulates some factor or factors to elicit a response from the subjects. In an experiment, the factor manipulated is referred to as the *independent variable.* In the beer study described earlier, the independent variable was price. The manipulation was achieved by simply indicating that brands M, L, and P sold for different amounts of money. This manipulation allowed the experimenter to examine the effect of different price levels on imputed quality by the variation in the subjects' perceptions of the brands. The actual variables chosen to measure the subjects' response are termed *dependent variables.* In the beer example two dependent variables were employed: number of favorable versus unfavorable words used to describe each beer, and the mean overall rating of each brand.

More generally stated, the independent variable is one that is systematically manipulated by the experimenter. Two or more levels (treatments or

---

[4] K. Weick, "Laboratory Experiments with Organizations," in J. March (ed.), *Handbook of Organizations* (Chicago: Rand McNally, 1965), pp. 194–260.

conditions) of the independent variable must be administered. For example, an experimenter may choose to study the effect of different advertising budgets on the sale of his product. Four different budgets, $50,000, $100,000, $150,000, and $200,000 are used in four different but comparable areas of the United States. The independent variable is the amount of budget allocated. Thus, four levels of the independent variable were administered: $50,000, $100,000, $150,000, and $200,000.

The dependent variable is the response given by subjects that is attributable to the independent variable. Examples of dependent variables would include paper-and-pencil measures such as an attitude scale or measures of purchase behavior employed to measure the effect of different advertising budgets.

It is important that the experimenter reduce, or if possible eliminate, the possibility that variables other than the independent variable under investigation cause the observed response. For example, to insure that price was the only causal factor in the subjects' perception of each beer's quality, several *controls* were instituted. All bottles contained the same beer. Without this control, there might have been actual differences in the taste or smell of the different beers. These *confounds* would have contributed to the subjects' perception of quality. Thus, the researcher would be unable to state unequivocally that the prices associated with the various beers caused the subjects' perception of the quality. Brand name labels were not used for the same reason.

It should be noted that in the definition of experimentation, no explicit reference was made to a specific setting. As long as measurable responses occur at the discretion and under the control of the experimenter, experimentation may be conducted in the respondents' homes, new car show rooms, shopping centers, or any other convenient setting.

From these diverse settings two general classes of settings emerge: (1) *field settings*, and (2) *laboratory settings*. Field experiments are those occurring in the real world with subjects who are typically unaware of their participation. Laboratory experiments are those which occur in contrived or artificial settings where subjects are aware that they are participating in some scientific endeavor. Of the two settings, the laboratory is probably used more often. This is attributable to the fact that it is convenient and allows for a high degree of control.

The thrust of this chapter will be an examination of experimentation in a marketing context. Initial focus will center on planning experiments. This will entail a discussion of the aspects of experimentation common to both laboratory and field research, as well as those unique to each setting. However, throughout this chapter, experimentation conducted in the laboratory will be emphasized since much of what is true of laboratory experiments applies to other settings.

Planning a Marketing Experiment: Aspects Common to Laboratory and Field Settings

Role of Experimental Participants

A distinction was made between laboratory and field experimentation on the basis of the settings in which they are performed. Laboratory research is generally conducted in a structured environment; field research is typically carried out in natural settings. However, there is a far more important, though less obvious distinction between the two, centering around the roles and interactions of the experimental participants.

Laboratory experiments are characterized by *active* involvement of both the experimenter and the subjects. In conducting an investigation, the experimenter must necessarily interact with subjects to give them instructions, administer questionnaires, answer questions, and the like. However, in performing these overt functions, the experimenter may unwittingly communicate information to subjects (for example, a nod of approval or a smile) which influences the experimental outcome.

Subjects, too, play an active role in laboratory experiments. They are aware of their participation, as they are purposively recruited and often paid for their participation. Because they are extremely conscious of their participation in a "scientific event," they are apt to behave differently than under normal circumstances. (This issue will be addressed more fully later in this chapter.)

In contrast to the single role assumed by experimental participants in laboratory experiments, two predominant types of participant activity characterize field investigations. In one, both subjects and experimenter assume active roles. Although subjects may not be aware that they are participating in a scientific inquiry, they often are told that they are cooperating in some kind of project. Their individual behavior or responses are monitored by the experimenter, in natural settings. As with laboratory experiments, there are opportunities for the subjects and the experimenter to interact. Since this type of field experiment involves procedures and issues similar to laboratory experiments, it requires no separate discussion.

The second type of field experiment is distinguished by the passive roles of experimental participants. The investigator sets up the experiment before subjects begin to participate. For example, the investigator may systematically vary the price of an item or the number of shelf-facings for a particular brand. Once these manipulations have been made, the experimenter merely returns to record the dependent variable (in this case sales), without ever having interacted with subjects. Typically, the information obtained reflects the aggregate responses of subjects rather than their individual reactions.

The subjects in this type of field experiment act without knowledge that they are participating in anything but life itself. They behave normally and freely respond to experimental stimuli. In fact, at times the experimental treatments are so unobtrusive that subjects fail to respond at all. Since this type of field experimentation is the most prevalent in marketing it will be emphasized in this chapter.

The different experimental participant roles necessitate slight alterations in the procedures followed in executing laboratory and field experiments. In the following sections the aspects common to both types of experimentation will be developed with emphasis on laboratory experiments. Then the unique aspects of each approach will be examined in greater detail.

Pre-experimental Considerations

Where do ideas for research come from? Many come from existing theory, past research, or simple observation. For example, the beer study described earlier was an outgrowth of the researcher's observation that for some products, consumers generally prefer the higher priced brands. Also, much of the research in marketing is motivated by the need to solve recurring problems; that is, what price will maximize revenue?

At the outset all research should be preceded by a statement of a problem that the researcher hopes to elucidate or solve. This problem can then be translated into specific testable hypotheses that, if confirmed, will tell the researcher what he wants to know (sometimes lack of confirmation can be an equally important finding). Once the problem has been clearly defined, specification of variables can be started.

As reasons underlying research are many and varied, it is perhaps more important to understand how problems are translated into researchable questions than to know their antecedents. If little or nothing is known about the phenomenon under investigation, a correlational approach is probably suitable. Correlational approaches involve the observation of the variation in consumers' responses as they occur in the real world (as opposed to experimental approaches where the experimenter induces the variation in response). Using a correlational approach a researcher might question shoppers' reasons for purchasing a particular brand of beer and observe the price they paid. On the basis of these data, it might be found that those shoppers who were concerned about the quality tended to pay a premium price.

In general terms, correlational studies are particularly useful to determine the important variables in a particular situation and the parameters of those variables. Given this information, the researcher may next focus on the causal relationship between price and imputed quality. In fact, the beer experiment described earlier addressed itself to this question. In turn, the experimental finding that price is an indicator of quality may then be subjected to a real world test again using a correlational approach.

Experimentation is uniquely suited to a determination of causal relationship between variables. However, there are times when other research techniques may be equally suited to the problem at hand. This is often the case when research is used as an aid to decision making.

When research is used to help management make better decisions there are a number of techniques available. These include: (1) laboratory experimentation, (2) field experimentation, (3) survey research, and (4) consumer panels. Each of these techniques present certain advantages and limitations to the researcher. It is difficult to generalize about the various tradeoffs between techniques as exceptions abound. However, at the risk of oversimplifying the relationship between the techniques, certain differences are evident.

As Figure 9.1 illustrates, the four techniques can be viewed on continua of increasing or decreasing characteristics.

Laboratory experiments are frequently low in cost and can be completed in a relatively short time period. Field experiments tend to be more costly and run for a longer duration. A high degree of control is possible with laboratory experimentation, and, to a slightly lesser degree, possible with field experiments. Because of the control achieved there are fewer confounding factors and consequently fewer alternative explanations for the observed results. With surveys and panels there is virtually no control and numerous tenable explanations for observed data. Realism tends to be lowest with laboratory experiments and highest with panels. (Later in the discussion two types of realism will be enumerated and discussed.) Finally, laboratory experiments tend to use few subjects while surveys and consumer panels frequently employ several thousand respondents.

Thus, the approach employed in research depends on the knowledge already accumulated, the needs of the investigator, and the financial constraints of the firm. When little is known about the phenomenon under investigation and the resources are available, a correlational approach may be used to determine the critical variables and their likely parameters. Given this knowledge, an experimental approach is useful to determine causal relation-

Characteristics		Laboratory Experimentation	Field Experimentation	Surveys	Consumer Panel
Cost	Low	————————————————————→			High
Time to execute	Short	————————————————————→			Long
Control	High	←————————————————————			Low
Number of subjects	Few	————————————————————→			Many
Realism	Low	————————————————————→			High
Confounding factors	Few	————————————————————→			Many

FIGURE 9.1   *Characteristics of Various Marketing Research Techniques*

ships. Finally, the applicability of experimental findings may be tested in real world situations.

The Independent Variable

Actual construction of the independent variable can be a very creative process. Consider the following fictitious example. The American Cancer Society might prepare three one-minute television commercials dealing with the dangers of smoking. Subjects are randomly assigned to conditions of high, moderate, or low threat. In each of the messages, a person introduced as the Surgeon-General of the United States indicates the dangers of smoking. In the high-threat commercial he states that smoking a pack of cigarettes a day decreases the life span by 10 years. He also notes that smoking causes cancer, emphysema, heart disease, and wrinkling of the skin. The commercial concludes with the suggestion that smokers should be sure to have a substantial amount of life insurance. The two other messages advance basically the same arguments. However, one of these, the moderate-threat commercial, uses less emotional language and is somewhat less conclusive as to the dangerous effects of smoking. The other, the low-threat commercial, is even less threatening.

These three commercials constituted three different levels of the independent variable physical threat. Subjects whose initial attitude toward smoking is known, are randomly assigned to one of the threatening communications. Subjects are then administered a questionnaire to determine the extent to which the communication changed their attitudes toward smoking. The findings indicate that people who received the moderately threatening communication are most persuaded. Those receiving a highly threatening message are persuaded somewhat less, but more than those exposed to the commercial that induced little threat (see Figure 9.2).

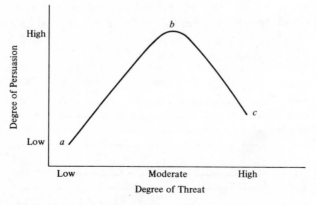

FIGURE 9.2 *Results of the Threat Study*

On the other hand, the construction of the independent variable can be a rather simple matter. The identical product could be sold at four different prices. The color of the package could be changed. A magazine advertisement could be used in black-and-white in one geographic location and in color in a comparable location. All of these represent manipulations that the experimenter makes to observe some response from his subjects.

Number of Levels   The American Cancer Society example illustrates the importance of including at least three levels of the independent variable (that is, high, moderate, and low threat). Had only two levels been manipulated, the threat persuasion relationship would have been linear and either positive or negative. As Figure 9.2 illustrates, if only low and moderate or low and high levels of threat were induced, the implication would be that the greater the threat, the greater the persuasion (curve *ab*). On the other hand, had only moderate and high threat been introduced, greater threat would have been associated with less persuasion (curve *bc*). Manipulation of three levels of the independent variable indicated that the overall relationship between threat and persuasion was an inverted U (curve *abc*). The implication from this finding is that some moderate level of threat is most persuasive.

When it is suspected that the relationship between an independent and dependent variable is not linear, at least three levels of the independent variable should be examined. If price were the independent variable a manufacturer would want to test a sufficient number of alternative prices to be reasonably certain that he found the most profitable selling price. Since there is some evidence that the lowest price is not necessarily the price at which the most units will be sold it is important to have a number of levels.[5]

Range   The American Cancer Society example also illustrates some important guidelines that should be followed in the construction of an independent variable. An attempt was made to sample the relevant range of the independent variable. Variables should be representative of the range found in the real world situations being depicted by the experiment. If only moderate and low threat had been induced, the researcher could not make a generalized statement as to the threat-persuasion relationship. The persuasive effect of very high levels of threat would be unknown.

In selecting ranges with different product prices the researcher might start with the lowest possible offering price and then work upward in equal increments or he might start with a price near his competitions' prices and try

---

[5] McConnell, *op. cit.*, August 1968; H. J. Leavitt, "A Note on Some Experimental Findings about the Meaning of Price," *Journal of Business*, Vol. 27 (July 1954), pp. 205–210; D. S. Tull, R. A. Boring, and M. H. Gonsior, "A Note on the Relationship of Price and Imputed Quality," *Journal of Business*, Vol. 38 (April 1964), pp. 186–191.

experimental prices above and below. In regard to package colors, the entire spectrum is open to the researcher. However, he may just employ those produced by the art department instead of trying all possible hues and shades. If the independent variables were advertisement type, then the entire range is defined by black-and-white and color.

Principle of Random Assignment   In the threat study, subjects were randomly assigned to the high-, moderate-, or low-threat commercial. Theoretically, this procedure should insure that individuals' characteristics such as personality, demography, and past experience do not have a systematic effect on the dependent persuasion variable. People with vastly different profiles may be exposed to each of the threatening commercials. The only systematic difference between the groups is the amount of threat to which they are exposed. Thus, the threat level should be the only cause of persuasion.

However, suppose that in the threat study not all subjects reacted to threat in the same way. In fact, a questionnaire indicated that some subjects exposed to the high-threat commercial were only moderately threatened, while some who saw the low-threat commercial were very threatened. It is tempting to recategorize subjects on the basis of the questionnaire results into high-, moderate-, and low-threat conditions and analyze the persuasion induced. In this situation the levels of the "independent variable" are not systematically manipulated by the experimenter, but rather are selected by subjects on the basis of their responses.

In essence what has happened is that the manipulation of the independent variable was ineffective. The actual threat induced, which is a dependent measure, was then considered an independent variable and its effects on persuasion measured. It should be realized that this is not an experimental approach. Events occurred at the discretion of subjects and not the experimenter. Moreover, it violates the principle of random assignment. Variables which are unknown, or at least unmeasured by the experimenter, may be responsible for the relationship between fear and persuasion. For example, the threat felt by subjects may be attributable to their self-confidence, and it is self-confidence that is systematically related to persuasion.

Researchers conducting field experiments are always faced with *de facto* violations of the principle of random assignment. There is no way to insure that people passing a certain display or shelf-facing are not systematically different along some unmeasured or unknown dimension. To take a rather extreme example, consider a test to determine whether a black-and-white or color advertisement is more effective. The ads are run in a popular men's magazine. The black-and-white ad is run in one geographic region (area A) while the color ad is run in a demographically comparable area (area B). However, the predominately male audience in area B tends to be heavily color blind due to a fairly large static population of similar ethnic background. Over the years through intermarriage and very little migration the trait became more prevalent than in the population in general. Consequently, the experiment results in no differences attributable to color or black-and-white and the conclusion is that both are equally effective. In point of fact this is not the case. If the groups were truly comparable or had somehow been randomly assigned, the true difference would have been evident.

Generality   What implications can be drawn from the threat study? In part, the answer to this question depends on how the three levels of threat were chosen. If the levels of threat were randomly selected from all possible levels, it may be concluded that in the situation studied, moderate threat is most persuasive. On the other hand, if three specific levels were chosen, it may only be concluded that the moderate level is better than the low- and high-threat commercials tested. The advertiser is probably more interested in specific levels, because they are indicative of the commercial he should actually use. Conversely, the theoretician prefers random selection of fear levels because it affords a more general statement as to the overall fear-persuasion relationship in the situation studied.

How much confidence can another advertiser, who wishes to persuade by inducing physical threat, have that moderate threat is most persuasive? To make certain that the threat-persuasion relationship is not indigenous to the smoking issue, at least one other issue should be examined. Thus, the threat experiment should be repeated using, say, drunk driving as the topic. If the results are similar in the two studies, then there is some assurance that the relationship between the independent and dependent variable is not topic specific.

Suppose that a detergent manufacturer comes across these two studies and decides to use a moderately threatening appeal. He develops an appeal in which a housewife is threatened with disapproval from her husband for not getting his shirt collars clean. To avoid this problem, she is strongly urged to use the manufacturer's detergent. Clearly this strategy does not follow from the two threat studies. They varied physical threat and not threat of social disapproval. Unless it is observed that physical and social threat are related to persuasion in the same way, the detergent's manufacturer's strategy is unfounded. To assume that physical threat and social threat have the same persuasive consequences is a tenuous generalization.

From the discussion in this section, several prescriptions emerge for the development of independent variables. At least three levels should be induced which sample the relevant range of the independent variable. Also, the independent variable should be manipulated systematically, and then practicable subjects should be randomly assigned to the various levels. Finally, the generality of the relationship between the independent and dependent variable is dependent on whether the levels of the independent variables were randomly or purposively selected, and the number and nature of issues studied.

The Dependent Variable

Dependent variables are the measured responses of subjects which are attributable to the independent variable. In the threat study, the amount of persuasion reflected the effect of different levels of threat. In performing experiments some marketers have adopted the strategy of administering only one dependent variable. It is probably more informative to take multiple measures of subjects' reactions to the independent variable. In the threat study, subjects' understanding and agreement with the arguments contained in the threatening message could have been measured when persuasiveness was examined. These dependent variables would provide a diagnostic as to why threat had the observed persuasive effect.

Multiple dependent variables can also be beneficial in field studies. Consider an experiment in which the identical product is sold in comparable stores at two different prices. The primary dependent measure would be unit sales of the product. However, it might be advisable to record unit sales by consumption unit to identify hoarders whose consumption patterns would confound the outcome. If a limited number of consumers buy vast quantities of the product, then there is only a short-term increase in sales which cannot be meaningfully extrapolated to predict sales volume in subsequent time periods. The manufacturer might price his product at the lower price predicated on a high anticipated sales volume. However, he finds out when he markets the product that initial sales are high (when the hoarders stock up) but then drop precipitously.

Multiple dependent measures may also enhance the experimenter's confidence in a particular finding. Had measures of intentions to stop smoking and actual quitting been taken in the threat study, and had these measures indicated the relative effectiveness of the moderate threat commercial, the experimenter would have been more certain that moderate threat was most effective. The experimenter should view himself as an investigator searching for clues to solve the mysteries of human behavior. Each dependent variable provides a clue which in itself contains little information. However, when several of these dependent measures are considered together, they may increase the researcher's belief in the observed finding.

The preceding discussion indicates the major reason for taking dependent measures. They allow determination of the effect of some systematic manipulation. Two other types of dependent variables are often used to enhance experimental control. A manipulation check is often taken to see if the different levels of the independent variable were in fact induced. In the threat study manipulation checks might entail subjects' self-report of how threatened or worried each commercial made them and the experimenter's observation of the overt manifestations of worry. These manipulation checks would confirm if the different communications induced truly different amounts of threat. If they did not, the experimenter should reconstruct the independent variable.

A second control measure involves measures of certain variables that are of no direct interest to the researcher but may affect the relationship between the independent and dependent variables. The best way to handle these confounds is through methodological controls, for example, random assignment of subjects to various levels of the independent variable. However, at times this is not possible. In the price study, demographic data (for example, income) might be gathered on purchasers of the experimental product as they left the store. With the additional data the researcher could statistically eliminate any systematic effect that differential income could have on price sensitivities.

Confounds may also be measured to advance understanding. In the threat study, subjects exposed to a moderately threatening commercial were most persuaded. However, the measurement of these subjects' self-confidence revealed that those of high self-confidence were significantly less persuaded than those of low self-confidence. This finding may then serve as a hypothesis in a future study which examines the effects of self-confidence on persuasion.

Developing Effective Laboratory Experiments

The Experimental Context

Since laboratory experimental approaches typically examine only some aspect of a real world situation, subjects must be informed about the setting in which independent variables are manipulated and dependent measures taken. To achieve this purpose, subjects are generally given instructions prior to their performance of an experimental task. The instructions indicate the purpose of the experiment and what tasks subjects are expected to perform.

The experimental instructions should disguise the actual purpose of the study. In some cases deception must be used to make the experiment seem real, and to keep subjects from guessing the experiment's intent. In the beer study, for example, participants were led to believe that the taste of various beers was of concern to the experimenter. If the participants knew that the true experimental purpose was to determine the extent to which price is an indicator of quality, they may have responded in a manner that confirmed this hypothesis. Alternatively, they may have thought that the study was silly or irrelevant and refused to give accurate ratings of quality. In either event, the experimental instructions help insure that the participants acted as they would in the real world, and not as "subjects."

From an ethical standpoint, deception should be used only when it is essential to the success of the experiment, and then only when it does not cause enduring psychological and physical damage to subjects. Nor is deception always necessary. For example, experiments in which physiological response to advertisements is measured require no deception. It is unlikely that subjects are able to control their heart rate, blood pressure, skin conductance, and the like.

The instructions must capture the subjects' attention and must indicate why the study is important. Otherwise, subjects may fail to observe the independent variable carefully, or may not fully comprehend their task. Attention to instructions is enhanced by having the experimenter present them personally, rather than via a tape recorder or other mechanical device. A live experimenter may also clear up any misconceptions a subject may have about the experiment. In addition, deception is usually much more effective when presented personally by a sincere and earnest experimenter.

Despite these benefits, the use of electronic devices to transmit experimental instructions has increased in recent years. These devices insure that all subjects get exactly the same instructions and eliminate another source of variability.

Realism in Laboratory Experimentation

Realism in the Setting   The term *realism* refers to the comparability of the laboratory experiment to the real world situation it depicts. Critics argue that laboratory experimentation lacks realism since an experiment typically fails to resemble the real world situation. However, it is important to distinguish between two types of realism: mundane and experimental.[6] Mundane realism refers specifically to how well the experimental setting does in fact conform to the real world analog that it purports to depict. But if an experimental setting bears a physical resemblance to its real world counterpart, it does not necessarily contain all the other relevant dimensions. Experimental realism refers to the impact the setting has on the subject, that is, the ability of the setting to elicit a response. Thus, ultimately *realism* is the extent to which experiments capture the relevant dimensions of a real world situation. Furthermore, abstracting a situation to its relevant dimensions affords the opportunity to generalize the findings of a particular experiment to a large number of situations.

An example will clarify these points. Suppose a researcher wished to study the reduction of conflict between a manufacturer and his wholesaler. If the researcher believed that realism must be achieved by having an experiment resemble the actual situation, all or a large number of employees of both firms would be studied. Not only is this an arduous task, but also it must

[6] E. Aronson, and J. M. Carlsmith, "Experimentation in Social Psychology," in G. Lindzey and E. Aronson (eds.), *Handbook of Social Psychology*, Vol. 2 (Reading, Mass.: Addison-Wesley, 1968).

often be performed at the expense of adequate control over the factors which might cause observed employee behavior.

If, however, the researcher was concerned with capturing relevant dimensions of firms, size per se would be of little interest. More important would be the manifestations of size such as division of labor and the presence of a chain of command. This philosophy might entail the use of three-member firms, since a division of labor and a chain of command could be established between three people. Although this approach fails to resemble the real world manufacturing and wholesaling firms' organizations, it captures the relevant dimensions of size and its likely effects on conflict reduction strategies. Furthermore, when relatively small groups are studied the experimenter may achieve greater control over the causes of response.[7]

Realism in Subjects   It is often claimed that laboratory experimentation lacks realism because college students most often serve as subjects. If the purpose of a study is to observe consumers' choice of brand when price is varied, this criticism may be valid. Students may have different levels of familiarity with various brands and different sensitivities to prices than other consumers. In fact, brand choice responses in this study may not be indicative of how students at other colleges might respond, let alone other segments of the population.

When the problem is more abstract, however, students may be both convenient and representative samples, at least in preliminary investigations. For example, if the objective is to study the effect of different amounts of repetition of print ads on their memorability, it is difficult to see why the mechanism underlying this relationship would vary by subject type. Of course, these differences could be tested empirically by performing the same study with several different groups of people.

It should be noted that there is nothing inherent in laboratory experimentation that requires the use of college students. Whether students or other members of the population are recruited to serve as subjects should depend on the experimental question posed. It is generally no more valid to use church groups than it is to use college sophomores when the empirical question calls for a random sample of the population. Church groups are generally older and more conservative than the population as a whole. Thus, they are likely to be as unrepresentative as college students who tend to be younger and more liberal.

A related problem is that of sample size. Theoretically, a sample of two in each experimental condition is sufficient, since it allows the observation of variance in response between subjects. In practice most experimental research-

---

[7] Louis W. Stern, Brian Sternthal, and C. Samuel Craig, "Managing Conflict in Distribution Channels: A Laboratory Study," *Journal of Marketing Research*, Vol. 10 (May 1973), pp. 169–179.

ers attempt to have at least 10 subjects randomly assigned to each experimental condition. This procedure reflects the need to satisfy the assumptions underlying statistical data analysis procedures. Researchers schooled in correlational techniques and experienced in working with large samples appear to believe that some large absolute sample size, say 400, is necessary. Such rules-of-thumb are merely wasteful. The researcher should be more concerned with satisfying the assumptions underlying his analysis technique than conforming to some rule-of-thumb.

Artificiality in Laboratory Experimentation

In exploring the issues related to laboratory realism, we have developed strategies for high *external validity*. That is, ways have been sought to increase the generalizability of laboratory experiments to real world situations and populations.[8] In this section strategies for increasing the *internal validity* of laboratory experiments are described. Internal validity refers to whether the experimental stimulus had some significant effect on the subject's response. A high degree of internal validity gives the researcher confidence that the observed response is attributable only to the independent variable being studied.

When a subject comes into a laboratory experiment, he knows that the experimenter is attempting to elicit a particular response. This knowledge may trigger certain behaviors in the subject that are quite independent of the experimental stimulus. Minimization of these extra-experimental responses enhances the researcher's confidence that subjects' responses are attributable to the experimental stimulus.

Demand Characteristics: The Compliant Subject[9]   Subjects recruited for a laboratory experiment generally have the desire to help out the experimenter. To this end, the subjects' attempt to guess the purpose of the experiment, or what is demanded of them and then give an appropriate response. Thus, subjects' responses are motivated by the demand character of the experiment's characteristics rather than by the independent variable(s) that is of primary interest to the experimenter.[10]

Consider the following experiment. Subjects are asked to rate their preference for each of three brands of catsup when the price of all three

[8] D. Campbell, "Factors Relevant to the Validity of Experiments in Social Settings," *Psychological Bulletin*, Vol. 54 (1957), pp. 297–312.

[9] This section draws on the discussion by H. Fromkin and S. Streufert, "Laboratory Experimentation," in M. Dunnette (ed.), *The Handbook of Organizational and Industrial Psychology* (Chicago: Rand McNally, in press).

[10] M. Orne, "On the Social Psychology of the Psychology Experiment: With Particular Reference to Demand Characteristics and Their Implications," *American Psychologist*, Vol. 17 (1963), pp. 776–783; M. Orne, "Demand Characteristics and Quasi-Controls," in R. Rosenthal and R. Rosnow (eds.), *Artifact in Behavioral Research* (New York: Academic Press, 1969), pp. 143–179.

brands is the same. Then the experimenter raises the price of the subjects' preferred brand one cent. It is found that most subjects switch to their next preferred brand under these circumstances.

Apparently the conclusion is that people are very sensitive to price and switch brands on the basis of minimal price changes. However, another explanation is possible. It may have been very obvious to subjects that the experimenter expected them to act like rational economic individuals and switch to less expensive brands. Their response may be attributable to their desire to conform to the researcher's expectations rather than to the manipulation of price.

The presence of alternative explanations for subjects' behavior reduces the internal validity of the experiment. To reduce demand character and thus increase control over the response of subjects, several strategies may be used. It may be possible to reformulate the experimental design so that the hypothesis being tested is not apparent to subjects. In the above experiment, subjects could be asked to participate in a simulated shopping trip after their preferences for different brands had been measured. To disguise the experiment's intent, they might be told that the experimenter was interested in how long it took them to shop for certain products. Subjects would be cautioned not to rush or go too slowly but to take the same amount of time as they normally would. In actuality, prices would be manipulated systematically so that preferred brands were available at higher prices.[11]

The effectiveness of attempts to disguise the experimenter's purpose should be checked in the debriefing session. In some cases it may be difficult to tell whether or not subjects had guessed the experiment's intent. It has been suggested that in such situations a control group should be included in which participants receive the pre-experimental instructions and are asked to complete the same post-experimental questionnaire as those who participated in the actual experiment. They do not perform the experimental task. One problem with this control is that subjects may accurately guess how they would actually react, without uncovering the purpose of the study. Another problem is that the post-experimental questionnaire may be closely related to the experimental task that the control group did not perform. In such cases the questionnaire would be meaningless to control group respondents.

The best means currently available to determine the demand character of an experiment is suggested by Greenwald.[12] A control group is run in which subjects are given cues or told about the actual purpose of the experiment in the instructions. The experimental task is then performed, and a post-experimental questionnaire is administered. This purposeful induction of demand

---

[11] C. Samuel Craig, *Consumer Reactions to Price Changes: An Experimental Investigation,* unpublished doctoral dissertation (The Ohio State University, 1971).

[12] A. Greenwald, "Behavior Change Following a Persuasive Communication," *Journal of Personality,* Vol. 33 (1965), pp. 370–391.

characteristics should result in greater conformity to the results expected by the researcher than is observed in the responses of experimental groups. If this does not occur, it is quite likely that demand characteristics are present.

Evaluation Apprehension: The Apprehensive Subject   Experimental subjects often are apprehensive about their performance in a research study. They may feel that their responses are used by the researcher to evaluate their mental health, emotional stability, and the like.[13] To win the experimenter's approval, subjects pay close attention to cues which suggest means of good performance, rather than acting as they would normally.

Subjects' apprehension may be heightened by pre-experimental procedure. In recruiting subjects, researchers often state the purpose of their study. Suppose a researcher is interested in the effects of various levels of repetition of nonsense words on subjects' liking for these words. To disguise the purpose of his study he may tell potential subjects that he wishes to investigate the effect of personality on learning foreign languages. This description is likely to cause the subject to become apprehensive. Subjects do not want the experimenter to uncover personality flaws. To limit subjects' apprehension and heightened sensitivity to ways of looking good, it is better to present the study in technical terms such as learning foreign languages. In addition, subjects' anonymity should be assured, and subjects should be told that the aggregate data of all subjects are of major concern to the researcher.

The experimental instructions may also induce evaluation apprehension. If the instructions suggest that subjects are to be evaluated, then they will attempt to guess the response most appropriate to look good. If the instructions also hint at what responses will be considered appropriate, the subject will reliably choose that alternative. When this apprehension leads to a selection of a response that is similar to that expected from an experimental manipulation, at least two alternative explanations may account for that response. When both demand character and evaluation apprehension are present and lead to different responses in a study, subjects will attempt to look good first, and then attempt to give the responses they feel conform to the researcher's expectations.

Reactivity: The Sensitized Subject   Reactivity refers to the fact that the measurement of the dependent variable causes subjects to respond in a way that they might not have otherwise responded.[14] A persuasive message about

[13] M. Rosenberg, "The Conditions and Consequences of Evaluation Apprehension," in R. Rosenthal and R. Rosnow (eds.), *Artifact in Behavioral Research* (New York: Academic Press, 1969), pp. 279–349.

[14] D. Campbell and J. Stanley, "Experimental and Quasi-Experimental Designs for Research on Teaching," in N. Gage (ed.), *Handbook of Research on Teaching* (Chicago: Rand McNally, 1963).

a new oven cleaner may have no effect on message recipients until they are given a questionnaire which forces subjects to think about the attributes of the new oven cleaner. Thus, both the message and the mere administration of the questionnaire influence subjects' response.

It should be noted that reactivity is a different problem than demand characteristics. Subjects are not attempting to guess what the experimenter wants so that they may comply with his wishes. Rather, reactivity refers to the fact that the independent variable may not have had any impact if the dependent measure had not been administered.

Several techniques may be employed to minimize reactivity. Unobtrusive dependent variables may be used to eliminate reactivity. Alternatively, the dependent variable of interest to the researcher may be buried in a battery of questions that deal with a host of topics. Finally, it is sometimes possible to observe subsequent behavior and infer the impact of the dependent variable. In the oven cleaner study, the effect of the messages on the subsequent purchase of oven cleaner may be examined without causing reactivity.

Experimenter Bias   In some instances the experimenter seems to present subtle cues to subjects which affect their response. Two major experimenter biases have been isolated. The first pertains to personal characteristics of the experimenter, such as age, sex, race, accent, and the like. This problem is best controlled by using the same experimenter throughout the study, or systematically varying the experimenter in a replication of the experiment to insure that the experimenter is not contributing to the observed response.

The second source of experimenter bias is derived from his relationship with subjects, in giving instructions, answering questions, and generally administering the study. At present, the specific experimenter actions that give rise to experimenter bias are unknown. What has been demonstrated is that in some situations the expectations of the researcher are salient factors in guiding subjects' responses toward confirmation of his hypothesis.[15] As one might expect, experimenter bias is a more critical factor when subject apprehension is high.

To minimize this problem, a double blind approach may be used. In this situation, neither the person conducting the research nor the subjects are aware of the experimental hypotheses. Alternatively, it is sometimes possible to develop experiments in which the interaction between subjects and researcher is minimal.

Experimenter bias is not indigenous to laboratory experimentation. It may be prevalent in nonlaboratory correlational studies. Interviewers in field

[15] R. Rosenthal, *Experimenter Effects in Behavioral Research* (New York: Appleton-Century-Crofts, 1966); R. Rosenthal, "Interperson Expectations: Effects of the Experimenter's Hypothesis," in R. Rosenthal and R. Rosnow (eds.), *Artifact in Behavioral Research* (New York: Academic Press, 1969), pp. 181–277.

investigations may allow their own feelings to affect the manner in which they pose questions to respondents. For example, when an interviewer approaches a question with trepidation, the respondent is more likely not to respond to that question. In correlational studies requiring personal contact between the researcher and respondent, experimenter bias is difficult to control. Procedures such as tape recorded instructions and the use of one interviewer to minimize experimenter bias in experimentation, are impractical in many correlational investigations.

Debriefing Subjects[16]

Once subjects have completed the experimental tasks, they must be informed as to the true purpose of the experiment. Perhaps the best way to start a debriefing session is to ask subjects if they had any questions about the experiment, if there was anything that they did not understand. These questions allow the experimenter to evaluate the clarity and effectiveness of his instructions and to determine whether subjects have guessed the intent of the experiment. Subjects are often hesitant to reveal that they have guessed the true purpose of the research. The experimenter must reassure them that it is permissible to know the purpose. This may require the experimenter to indicate the disservice to himself and to other members of the scientific community if the subject's true knowledge is not revealed. If the subject has guessed the experiment's intent, the data he generated should be discarded.

If he has not guessed the purpose he must be informed. This may be achieved by asking the subject if there was anything odd about the experiment, or if there was something more to it than met the eye. Couched in these terms the subject generally states that he was suspicious of the real purpose, and may then attempt to guess the real purpose. If he still does not indicate the true purpose of the study, the experimenter should gently indicate it to him.

This procedure minimizes the subject's embarrassment. When deception is used, the reasons why it was necessary must be clearly specified. From an ethical standpoint it is extremely important that subjects leave the experiment satisfied that they understand the purpose, and have contributed to scientific knowledge.

Before the subjects leave the experimental setting, they must be sworn to secrecy as to the purpose of the experiment. This is done by indicating to the subject that his time and energy, as well as that of the experimenter, will be wasted if future participants are not naive when they come to the laboratory. Experimental study of this problem has revealed that subjects usually comply with the experimenter's request to maintain secrecy.

[16] Aronson and Carlsmith, *op. cit.,* pp. 70–73.

Developing Effective Field Experiments

Field experiments, while providing a rich setting for marketing research, present a number of unique problems. Most of these problems are directly linked to the inability to exercise strict control over all elements of the experiment. In the laboratory, virtually all aspects of the experiment can be rigidly controlled. In field experiments, additional variables beyond the control of the experimenter can confound the results. Even though the potential confounds are beyond the control of the experimenter, there are methods to account for their effect in many instances.[17] The remainder of this section will be devoted to a discussion of some of the problems associated with field experiments.

Lack of Control

Subject Cooperation   Since subjects participating in field experiments are doing so unknowingly, the situation must be structured to gain their cooperation. Subjects may be inattentive and ignore the experimental stimulus. For example, a researcher might raise the price of a specific brand of toothpaste relative to competing brands. The researcher hypothesizes that sales of the higher priced brand would decrease as consumers sought cheaper alternatives. After tracking sales for two months the researcher finds that sales of the higher priced toothpaste remained relatively the same compared to a base period and to competing brands. On the basis of his data, he concludes that price level has no effect on consumption.

On closer examination, an alternative explanation might be that consumers are in a hurry and fail to perceive the price change information. Consequently, they purchased their preferred brand regardless of price levels. In a laboratory study, the subjects would be more cooperative, in less of a hurry, and attend the price information. Thus, if the price information were attended consumption of the higher priced brand would decrease. One could argue that the field experiment gave the true result. This may be, but the conclusion was incorrect. The true effect of a price increase without the confounding variable of attention would be decreased consumption.

The essential problem in gaining subject cooperation is twofold. First, there is a general tendency for subjects to be inattentive. This inattentiveness is not the result of some nefarious plot by consumers to disrupt experimental research, but rather a product of the multitude of stimuli vying for the con-

---

[17] Many of the problems associated with field experiments are methodological in nature and are best addressed through design considerations. A complete discussion of all design problems is beyond the scope of this chapter. For a more thorough treatment of this aspect of experimentation the reader is referred to S. Banks, *Experimentation in Marketing* (New York: McGraw-Hill, 1965); and K. K. Cox and Ben M. Ennis, *Experimentation for Marketing Decisions* (Scranton, Pa.: International Textbook Company, 1969).

sumers' attention. It has been estimated that the average consumer is exposed to from 300 to 2000 advertisements in any given day. If the experimental stimulus is but one of 2000 stimuli, then the probability of it being attended to is remote. In the average supermarket there are some 8000 items. If the price of one or two of these items is varied, it may be lost in the clutter.

The other part of the problem relates to the strength of the induction or manipulation. The manipulation may not be sufficiently strong to gain the subjects' attention. Alternatively, the manipulation may gain the subjects' attention but may not be strong enough to elicit a response.

Unfortunately, the first clue the researcher may have that subject inattention is a problem is lack of significant differences in that data analysis. This is particularly true in passive-field paradigms where the experimenter has little or no contact with the subjects. In these situations it is advisable to conduct a pilot run and either query subjects after they have been potentially exposed to the experimental stimulus or analyze the preliminary data to see if there was any effect. As a general rule the first strategy, questioning pilot subjects, is preferable as early data analysis can sometimes bias subsequent events.[18]

In the active-field paradigm the problem is not quite as acute. The manipulation is made as the experimenter interacts with his subjects. Both attention and impact are at high levels. To make certain that inattention is not a potential confound in the active-field situations the experimenter should run pilot trials and thoroughly debrief the subjects to ascertain whether the induction had its intended effect.

In constructing effective field experiments, the researcher should endeavor to design situations in which subject cooperation and attention are maximized.

Extraneous Events   Since field experiments take place in natural surroundings there are any number of extraneous events that can affect experimental results. These extraneous variables fall into two general categories: (1) measurable and (2) nonmeasurable. The measurable extraneous variables will be discussed in the next section as covariates. In this section the nonmeasurable extraneous events will be treated.

Often the relevant extraneous variables are not apparent or not readily measurable. A housewife with two sick children at home, in the middle of divorce proceedings, and who has just backed into a parked automobile, is not going to be a receptive subject for an in-store field experiment. Also it would be difficult to devise a questionnaire that would tactfully get at all the relevant

---

[18] R. Rosenthal *et al.*, "The Effect of Early Data Returns on Data Subsequently Obtained by Outcome-Biased Experiments," *Sociometry*, Vol. 26 (December 1963), pp. 487–498.

antecedent events. Even if the events were recorded their effect on her behavior would be difficult to determine. (In a laboratory experiment the technique of random assignment would eliminate the effect of extraneous variables.)

Thus, by their very nature, some extraneous events defy measurement. The best prescription for dealing with their effect is to design experiments that are relatively insensitive to extraneous events. Another strategy is to use more subjects and conduct multiple replicates so that the effects of extraneous events will not systematically bias the experimental outcome.

Covariates   In addition to nonmeasurable events, there are those that can be readily measured. Measurable extraneous variables can be taken into account through statistical procedures such as analysis of covariance. For example, if an experimenter is interested in the sales volume generated from certain end-of-aisle displays at different stores he might want to control for the number of shoppers at each store. If store traffic is not accounted for, the experimenter might erroneously conclude that the end-of-aisle display in the store with the heaviest traffic was the most effective. By analyzing the data while holding the effect of store traffic constant the true effect of the displays can be determined.

In any given experimental situation there can be any number of covariates that affect the outcome. If prior theory or studies indicate what variables are essential, then the only problem is measurement. However, if a priori knowledge is lacking, then it is advisable to collect information on as many variables operating in the setting as is practicable.

Carryover Effects

Field experiments tend to run for a longer time than laboratory experiments. This is because it generally costs more to set up field experiments and researchers are interested in as many different variations of the experimental stimulus as possible. Another reason is that as subjects are not actively recruited it often takes considerable time to obtain a sufficient number of participants.

Varying the treatment conditions from week to week can interject carryover effects, that is, what was done in prior weeks can exert some influence on what is presently being done. For example, in a supermarket study of cherry sales the experimenter might be interested in the differential effects of bulk versus package sales. He might begin his study by having all stores sell bulk cherries the first week. In the second week he would have all stores sell two-pound packages wrapped in cellophane. Changing from one method of selling to another introduces carryover effects that would not be present if only one method was used throughout the study. Through proper design and statistical techniques the effect of carryover can be taken into account. A discussion of these techniques is beyond the scope of this chapter. The interested reader is referred to excellent treatments of the subject by Banks.[19]

Limited Manipulations

Field settings necessarily place certain limits on the types of manipulations an experimenter can make. Perhaps the classic example of what can be done in a laboratory setting but not in the field is a compliance experiment, in which the experimenter had subjects ostensibly administer potentially lethal shocks to an experimental accomplice.[20] The issue of limited manipulations is somewhat related to limited control. In the compliance study it would have been impossible to exercise as much control over subjects in anything short of a totalitarian police state. Since the result of the subjects' actions appeared to be injurious to the experimental accomplice, it would be difficult to execute a similar experiment in the field without using "real bullets."

In addition to not being able to make certain manipulations in the field it is more difficult to keep changing conditions and they must be done for a longer period of time. In laboratory experiments, conditions may be changed frequently with little effort. Thus, field experiments are limited in the type of manipulations that can reasonably be made. There is also some difficulty encountered in making or changing manipulations. This does not pose a practical limitation as those manipulations relevant to field-type experiments can generally be made (for example, price change, end-of-aisle displays, or change in self-facings). More elaborate manipulations are better left to the laboratory where proper control and debriefing can be used.

Measurement of Dependent Variables

There is some difficulty in securing sufficient dependent measures in field experiments. The dependent variable in passive-field studies is often something unobtrusive and easy to measure, like unit sales of an item or time spent in front of a display. Whenever attitudinal or perceptual measures are needed, the experimenter must in some way obtrude into the experimental setting. This must be done carefully so as not to alert the subject to participation and bias the response.

In active-field experiments the problem is very much the same. An example will serve to illustrate the problem. Researchers were interested in studying the foot-in-the-door technique where the experimenter gains initial compliance on an insignificant request and then attempts to gain compliance on a much more significant request (for example, a clothing salesman gets you to buy a tie and then convinces you to buy a suit to go with it). In an

---

[19] Banks, *op. cit.*

[20] S. Milgram, "Behavioral Study of Obedience," *Journal of Abnormal and Social Psychology*, Vol. 67 (1963), pp. 371–378.

"active-field" experiment it was found that when initial compliance was obtained, subsequent compliance was much higher than when there was no initial compliance.[21] However, the results provide no understanding of the mechanism underlying subsequent compliance. To take additional measures would entail returning to the subjects and securing these measures under a suitable guise.

The best way to collect additional dependent measures is left to the imagination and creativity of the researcher. However, there is one simple rule-of-thumb to follow. An attempt should be made to temporally and spacially separate the response to the independent variable and the collection of the additional dependent variables. The closer the two events are to each other, the greater the chance that the subjects will associate the two. However, if too much time elapses the entire situation may change. Further, if the experimenter is physically present when the subject is exposed to the experimental stimulus, then many of the same confounds discussed earlier in regard to laboratory experiments would apply.

Application of Marketing Experimentation to Marketing Problems

The general purpose underlying marketing experimentation, the determination of causal relationships between marketing relevant variables, was advanced earlier. From this rather abstract purpose two more pragmatic purposes emerge. First, marketers use experimentation as an aid to *decision making*. When a number of alternatives appear equally viable experimentation in either the laboratory or field frequently can provide insight into the best course of action. Second, marketers use experimentation as an aid in *theory building*. If certain phenomena are suspected to be causally related, experimentation provides a method for confirmation.

In achieving this second purpose, marketing experimentation contributes heavily to an increased understanding of marketing phenomena. By being able to abstract, control, and manipulate marketing variables experimentally, researchers are able to understand them better. Further, they are able to go beyond establishing what works to why it works.

The extent to which either of these purposes underlies any given experiment depends on the motives of the experimenter. Academic researchers are generally more concerned with theory building (or very generalized decision making). Commercial researchers are generally concerned with immediate application of results and thus tend to use experimentation to provide guidance for decision making.

---

[21] J. Freedman and S. Fraser, "Compliance without Pressure: The Foot-in-the-Door Technique," *Journal of Personality and Social Psychology*, Vol. 4 (1968), pp. 195–202.

Throughout this chapter numerous examples have been developed to illustrate various aspects of marketing experimentation. To conclude the discussion of experimentation, two examples that illustrate the purposes of experimentation will be discussed.

Decision Making Through Experimentation

When introducing a new product marketers must decide on the most effective pricing strategy. Given basic economic considerations regarding cost and competitive realities it is often not too difficult to arrive at the ultimate selling price. However, there is a critical initial decision that must be made as to the introductory offering price. The crux of the decision is: Will post-introduction sales volume be greater when the product is initially priced at its final selling price or below its final selling price?

Tenable arguments can be developed for either strategy. In the first case one could argue that people would become accustomed to paying the final price and consequently convince themselves it is worth the price. Further, if one uses a lower price initially and later switches to a higher price, many customers might not be willing to pay more for the product. In the second case, one could argue that a low introductory price would result in many more trial purchases. Introducing more people to use the product initially would result in satisfaction with the product and more repeat purchases even when the price was later increased. The decision maker faced with these two sets of arguments can either intuitively select the most persuasive position or conduct an experiment to determine the best pricing strategy.

A study conducted by Doob et al.[22] very directly addresses the central issue. Identical products (mouthwash, toothpaste, aluminum foil, and light bulbs) were introduced in a number of different supermarkets at different prices. Within each product category some of the products were sold at a low introductory price while others were sold at their regular introductory price. After two weeks those products being sold at the low introductory price were increased to the price of the product in the other stores (regular introductory price).

As one would expect, when the product was offered at the low price, sales were considerably higher. However, after a few weeks the sales of products introduced at the regular price surpassed those of the same products introduced at the low price. Over the twenty-week period of the study the total sales of the products introduced at the regular price appreciably exceeded those of products initially offered at a lower price.

---

[22] A. N. Doob, J. M. Carlsmith, J. L. Freedman, T. K. Landauer, and S. Tom, Jr. "Effect of Initial Selling Price on Subsequent Sales of Personality and Social Psychology II," *Journal of Marketing Research* (1969), pp. 345–350.

The implication for decision making is obvious. However, the generality of the findings may be questioned. The results may only apply to mouthwash, toothpaste, aluminum foil, and light bulbs. If the cost of a wrong decision is high enough it is wise to conduct another experiment using the specific products in question. However, it is rather clear that in this instance and for these product categories the best strategy is to introduce the product at its final selling price.

Theory Building Through Experimentation

There can be little argument that a knowledge of what marketing strategies work is of critical importance to the practitioner. Yet, if research does not yield an understanding of why a particular strategy succeeds, the practitioner is forced to use trial-and-error investigation each time a new situation is faced. Experimentation, on the other hand, affords the researcher the opportunity to develop theoretical guidelines that may be useful in tackling a whole class of problems. The following examples illustrate this point.

Advertisers have recently adopted the "quick-cut" technique. Quick cuts involve the rapid movement from one scene to another. For example, a television commercial for a headache remedy may use quick cuts by first showing a mother scolding her children. The next scene depicts the mother at the medicine cabinet taking brand X. This is quickly followed by a scene in which the mother is cheerfully playing with her children, and then by an announcer who explains why brand X is more than twice as effective for headache pain than the leading analgesic.

The rapid movement from one scene to another is a technique borrowed from the film industry. It is employed by advertisers because it is creative and because it is an effective means of conveying information quickly. But should the quick-cut technique be used in advertising durable goods such as stoves, or a new blade razor that has two blades on one side? To answer these questions, the cautious marketing researcher must compare the effectiveness of ads using the quick-cut technique against those in which the technique is not used, for every product tested.

Laboratory experimentation allows the researcher to determine why quick cuts work. In one approach, a tape-recorded persuasive message dealing with a familiar topic is played to one group of subjects. A second group receives the same message; however, the experimenter systematically cuts out small pieces of the tape. The remainder of the tape is spliced together. The effect of this compression procedure is to reduce understanding of the message. However, it is found that both groups are equally persuaded by the message. Apparently when the topic is familiar, understanding the message completely is unnecessary for persuasion. On the other hand, when the message topic is unfamiliar to communication recipients, the message that was compressed is much less persuasive than the one that was presented in its entirety.[23]

In this case, laboratory experimentation provides insights as to why quick cuts work. The implication is that the technique is useful in situations where the issues to be addressed are familiar to the audience, as in the case in selling a stove, detergent, butter, and the like. When the topic is unfamiliar, as is the case in ads for a new two-bladed razor or a miniature camera that gives big pictures, quick cuts are probably ineffective. In such situations, understanding is critical if the audience is to be persuaded.

Summary

Laboratory experimentation and field experimentation are gaining wider use and acceptance among marketing researchers. Through experimentation researchers are able to construct replicas of the market place, manipulate variables, observe the results, and make causal inferences. In developing effective experiments, it is important to be aware of one's role as an experimenter and the role of and interactions with the subjects. The steps in the experimental process include statements of the problem, development of an appropriate context, construction of the independent variable(s), selection of the dependent variable(s), and debriefing. These steps may be performed in a wide variety of settings. The laboratory is often used because it is convenient and adequate to research the problem at hand.

Laboratory experiments may contain elements of unrealism. However, through appropriate selection of the experimental setting and subjects realism may be increased. Artificiality may be minimized by using the strategies suggested in this chapter to reduce the demand character, evaluation apprehension, reactivity, and experimenter bias present. Laboratory experiments may then be of great value in increasing the efficiency of marketing research and demonstrating the existence of particular marketing phenomena.

In executing effective field experiments one encounters many problems similar to those encountered with laboratory experiments. In addition, there is generally less control over field experiments which results in problems with subject cooperation and extraneous variables. Field experiments are also limited in the types of manipulations that can be made and there can be some difficulty in securing adequate dependent measures.

Marketing experimentation is a powerful tool that can assist researchers in establishing causal relationships between marketing relevant variables. By knowing what variables are related (for example, price and perceived quality) and how they are related (for example, positively) marketers are in a better

---

[23] L. Wheeless, "The Effects of Comprehension Loss on Persuasion," *Speech Monographs*, Vol. 38 (1971), pp. 327–330.

position to make informed decisions. Also, by controlling and manipulating variables, marketers are better able to understand the underlying relationships and use this knowledge to construct marketing theory.

Questions and Exercises

1. Define the following terms:
   - (a) experimentation
   - (b) laboratory experiment
   - (c) field experiment
   - (d) external validity
   - (e) internal validity
   - (f) demand character
   - (g) evaluation apprehension
   - (h) experimenter bias
   - (i) reactivity.

2. Critics contend that experimentation is unrealistic because it involves the use of small nonrepresentative samples and is conducted in contrived settings. Outline arguments which refute these contentions.

3. A major objective of survey research is to determine how people feel about the issue in question; intent focuses on the content of people's thought. On the other hand, experimental research centers on the structure of thought; that is, the way people go about processing and using information. Why should the marketing practitioner be interested in both the content and structure of thought?

4. Experimentation may be conducted in a variety of settings, which are usually classified as laboratory and field.
   a. What differences distinguish laboratory from field settings?
   b. What concerns should the experimenter be particularly concerned about in each setting?

5. Experimentation has several advantages relative to surveys: Costs are often lower, time to execute an experiment is shorter, fewer subjects are generally needed, and greater control is possible. Despite these factors, experimentation is not always the preferred approach. Explain.

6. In constructing an independent variable, it is important that at least three levels of the variable which cover the relevant range be induced. Enumerate the reasons underlying this prescription.

7. An experimenter wants to determine if a causal relationship exists between individuals' opinions about a product and their purchase behavior. An opinion measure is taken on the basis of which subjects are assigned to either a positive, neutral, or negative opinion condition. Analysis of the data reveal that there is a significant difference in extent of purchase attributable to differences in opinion. The experimenter concludes that opinion caused purchase behavior.
   a. Why is this conclusion invalid?
   b. What conclusion can be drawn?

c. What procedures and findings would be required in order to make the conclusion drawn by the experimenter valid?

8. Usually in laboratory experimentation several types of dependent measures are administered.

   a. What types of dependent measures are generally taken?

   b. What is the rationale for each type of dependent measure?

9. Experiments may not closely resemble the real world situation they purport to reflect and still be realistic. Outline arguments to support this statement.

10a. What is meant by demand character?

   b. Why do demand characteristics arise in experimentation?

   c. Using an example, illustrate how demand characteristics may occur in survey research.

11a. What is meant by the term debriefing?

   b. Why is it important that experimental subjects be debriefed?

12. Why is it that independent variables which are effective in laboratory experiments are much less likely to work in field experimental settings?

13. A manager of a retail supermarket has just read a study that indicates that most shoppers circle the perimeter of a supermarket, where dairy, produce, meat, and fish are located. Fewer shoppers go up and down the center isles of the store, where candy and snack foods are located. To increase the purchase of these products, the manager decides to conduct an experiment in which he repositions the meat freezer.

   a. You have been assigned to set up the experiment. Indicate how you would go about constructing the independent variable and state what dependent measures you would administer.

   b. How would you control artifacts such as demand character, evaluation apprehension, and experimenter bias?

14. For what purposes may experimentation be employed by the marketing decision maker?

15. If the causal relationship between two variables cannot be demonstrated in a laboratory experiment it is unlikely to exist in the real world. However, the demonstration of causality in a laboratory experiment does not necessarily mean that it exists in the real world. Explain these statements.

16. Why is it acceptable to employ relatively small sample sizes in laboratory experiments while most surveys require relatively large samples?

17. What are the advantages and disadvantages of marketing experimentation? Compare it to other research techniques.

18. Discuss the major sources of biased results in laboratory experiments. What can be done to minimize each?

19. Briefly describe how you might create an experiment to test the following relationships: (1) the effect of store image on perceived quality, (2) the effect of labels on perceived beer quality, (3) the effect of humor on communication effectiveness (persuasion), and (4) the effect of advertising on sales volume.
20. What are the purposes of marketing experimentation?
21. Although greater realism can generally be achieved in field experiments researchers often conduct laboratory experiments instead. What are some of the reasons behind this?
22. As director of marketing research you have been asked to determine what the demand for a new dessert product will be. Would you use a laboratory or field experiment? How would you go about setting it up?
23. Critics of social science research argue that subjects should never be deceived or misled. What do you think?

Project Related Questions

1. Rate your method (laboratory experiment, consumer panel, and so forth) in terms of the characteristics mentioned in Figure 9.1. Which characteristics are most important for your project? Does your method rate favorably in terms of these characteristics?
2. Have you allowed enough opportunity for the independent variables to fluctuate?
3. If you are using a behavioral laboratory type setting have you considered the issue of realism in the setting? Among subjects?
4. What sources of artificiality might arise which could be most damaging to your project? What steps are you taking or can you take to minimize the problem of artificiality?
5. What general problems with field experiments are most relevant to your project? Have you done everything possible and reasonable to avoid these problems?

Unobtrusive Marketing Research Techniques

Michael L. Ray, Stanford University

The search for a single ideal measure of marketing phenomena is as old as marketing research itself. In this working paper, Professor Michael L. Ray reviews the innovations in marketing measurement techniques that he characterizes as *unobtrusive*, that is, taken without respondent awareness. He argues that there is no single best type of marketing measure. If used alone, even sales measures have shortcomings both in a managerial and in a scientific sense. Ray suggests that a combination of maximally different measures should be used in each decision situation. The wide range of unobtrusive techniques should be considered.

Ray treats each of four major types of unobtrusive measures and provides extensive illustration of their actual application. He offers some specific "how to" guidelines for marketers who would like to make such applications. (He also supplies several suggestions for further reading in the field.)

Unobtrusive research is research that is done without the respondent's or consumer's awareness of its being done. In marketing this usually means research done without the use of the interview, although interviews with a disguised purpose and a combination of interview and noninterview measures also fit in the unobtrusive research category.

Marketers use unobtrusive measures because the latter are often better representations of the marketing phenomena under study, without many of the biases of the interview. Some-times they provide a check on the accuracy of interview data. In general, I believe, they are not used enough in marketing.

Sales are one very basic unobtrusive indicator of marketing success. However, there are examples of unobtrusive measures in many areas of marketing. These include observation of eye pupil dilation to indicate buyer interest, fingerprint measurement of magazine readership, analysis of so-

SOURCE: Working Paper, Marketing Science Institute, 1973.

ciety columns to determine social class of cities, timing of various types of shopping trips, pantry checks, observations of trade journals on executive desks, and license plate censuses to determine the geographic pull of athletic events in a two-team town.[1] One study used 17 measures to measure attitudes and behavior.[2]

Unobtrusive measures in marketing must meet rather serious requirements, related to the logic of their use in research. This paper first discusses the logic of multiple and unobtrusive measures. Then, the major types of unobtrusive measures are treated, along with the ways they might be used in marketing. Finally, some major implications for the field are briefly indicated.

THE LOGIC OF MULTIPLE AND UNOBTRUSIVE MEASUREMENT

When managers attempt to determine how to measure marketing phenomena, two sets of criteria dominate: the managerial and the scientific. The managerial requirements include via-

---

[1]Quintard Gregory, "Unobtrusive Methods for Gathering Marketing Information," in unpublished paper (Graduate School of Business Administration, University of California at Berkeley, June 6, 1970), pp. 24–46; Eugene J. Webb, Donald T. Campbell, Richard D. Schwartz, and Lee Sechrest, *Unobtrusive Measures: Nonreactive Research in the Social Sciences* (Chicago: Rand McNally, 1966).

[2] Michael L. Ray, "Neglected Problems (Opportunities) in Research: The Development of Multiple and Unobtrusive Measurement," in R. L. King (ed.) *Marketing and the New Science of Planning*, (Chicago: American Marketing Association, 1968), pp. 176–182.

bility, meaningfulness in terms of objectives, relationship to key decisions, and saleability within the organization. The scientific needs are reliability and validity.

Managerial Criteria for Measures

A measure is viable from the manager's point of view if it provides quick and inexpensive (relative to the timing and importance of the problem under study) indications of the variables in which he is interested. Also, it should be possible to make appropriate measurements at various points in time so that longitudinal analyses can be made. On the basis of viability, *sales* are often a good measure since sales data are collected routinely as part of marketing efforts, and continuing indications are provided.

But even sales data can vary in terms of viability and usefulness. For instance, in recent years distributor warehouse withdrawals have been used as an indicator of grocery product market share. They have advantages over store audits as a source for this information, both because they can be gathered more quickly and because they include the sales for those supermarket chains which refuse store auditing procedures. Store audits, on the other hand, provide advantages in terms of other requirements. Panel studies provide still a different set of benefits.[3]

Measures must fit the objectives they are intended to indicate. Often a readily available measure does not

---

[3] Harper W. Boyd and Ralph Westfall, *Marketing Research: Text and Cases*, 3rd ed. (Homewood, Ill.: Irwin, 1972).

quite meet this criterion. For instance, the Zippo Manufacturing Company used the volume of their cigarette lighters sent in for repair as evidence of the effectiveness of their advertising.[4] Despite the fact that the company's free repair policy was mentioned in the advertising, one might question whether this measure alone, while a truly inventive use of naturally occurring data, is enough to indicate achievement of objectives.

Responses to mail order advertising, on the other hand, can constitute exact congruence with objectives. For instance, one magazine publisher used responses to mail offers for alternative book series being considered for publication as a guide to deciding which volumes actually should be published.[5]

Many measures pass the first two requirements of viability and relationship to objectives but provide little indication as to how key decisions should be made. The magazine publisher would have to try a large number of alternatives before he could determine, on the basis of returns alone, how to lay out and present the books themselves. One insurance broker used mentions in society columns, real estate prices, percent of professional occupation, average years of schooling, and family income as indicators of the social class level of several Chicago communities.[6] But this information could not provide final decisions on which particular types of high prestige selling methods, seminars, and advertising approaches might be more effective in one type of community than in another. Another example is with sales data: although such information often indicates *how well* a company is doing, it will not clearly indicate *why,* or *what can be done* to maintain or improve performance.

Even after data have been collected successfully, they must pass the final managerial requirement of saleability within the organization. Marketing research data often serve several other purposes beyond the economic one of improving performance.[7] Managers gain *psychological* support from research data, if it can allay their uncertainties about making certain decisions. No matter what its scientific validity, research information can serve an *organizational* purpose if it can eliminate conflicts and differences of opinion. In a larger sense, the data can have *political* value if they can help in selling the ideas of one organization or group of individuals to another. In marketing this is especially important for service organizations such as consultants, advertising agencies, and research services.

---

[4] Harry Dean Wolfe, James K. Brown, and G. Clark Thompson, *Measuring Advertising Results* (New York: National Industrial Conference Board, 1962).

[5] Russell Colley, *Defining Advertising Goals for Measured Advertising Results,* (New York: Association of National Advertisers, 1961).

[6] Roger D. Blackwell, James F. Engel, and David T. Kollat, *Cases in Consumer Behavior* (New York: Holt, Rinehart and Winston, 1969).

[7] Michael L. Ray, "The Effect of Personal Interaction on the Effectiveness of Advertising Pretests," Unpublished Master's Thesis, Northwestern University (June 1962).

The psychological, organizational, and political purposes for research can sometimes make or break particular multiple and unobtrusive research techniques. Most managers are quite impressed with action measures such as purchasing. If a particular study does not include such measures, there may be lingering doubt as to the value of results.

People who use research are often more impressed when they can "see" responses. Many marketing managers and advertising agency executives now use closed circuit telecasts of group interviews. Decision makers who watch these are often strongly impressed by the sight and sound of actual buyers responding to their products.

Scientific Criteria for Measures

While managerial requirements must be met in order to use measures at all, scientific criteria are basic to the achievement of management needs. Measures must be *reliable;* that is, they must not vary unreasonably because of irrelevant factors such as the way questions are asked, fatigue, and the like. In addition, the measures must be *valid* in the sense that they must truly measure the variables they are intended to measure.

Unobtrusive and multiple *measurements have their greatest advantage in terms of the scientific criterion of validity.* This is because validation involves the question, "How do we know?" It is impossible to "know" if research is based on single, obtrusive measures which get at only part of a phenomenon and which may be inordinately affected by variables other than those of interest.

The process of validation in any kind of social science research always involves more than one measure, and the more different the measures are, the better. In marketing research, for example, one way to test an interview measure of purchase intent is to compare it with results from a separate question reporting purchase. However, the interview measure is more strongly validated when it can be compared with actual sales or purchasing responses.

Similarly, observations of shoppers are validated by being related to interviews with the same shoppers and to sales records from the stores. In industrial marketing, the potential of a product may be indicated by salesmen's reports, by sales of related products, by power usage of target industries, by general economic conditions, and by survey data.

The answer to the question, "how do we know," then, is that we know only by making comparisons, by triangulation, by *multiple* confirmation or measurement. And we are more confident of decisions if maximally different sorts of measures give essentially the same answers. This is the basic logic of unobtrusive and multiple measurement: in order to meet management requirements, measures must be reliable and valid. In order to achieve validity it is necessary to have several different measures, and this usually means at least some unobtrusive techniques.

Overdependence on the Interview

Given the reasonableness of the above approach, it may be surprising to the reader that very little unobtrusive and multiple measurement is used either in the social sciences or in marketing. In the social sciences it has been estimated that over 90 percent of research is based on the interview.[8]

A content analysis of the literature indicates a similar overdependence on the interview—even in marketing. An analysis was made of the 1969 to 1972 editions of the *Journal of Advertising Research,* the *Journal of Marketing,* and the *Journal of Marketing Research,* as well as books on evaluating and pretesting advertising and media.[9] In addition several prominent research and planning casebooks and textbooks were studied.[10] In all, approximately 700 recent marketing reports were reviewed, and fully 81

[8] E. Webb *et al., Unobtrusive Measures: Nonreactive Research in the Social Sciences* (Chicago: Rand McNally, 1966).

[9] R. Colley, *Defining Advertising Goals for Measured Advertising Results;* H. Wolfe, *et al., Measuring Advertising Results;* (New York: National Industrial Conference Board, 1962); H. Wolfe *et al., Pretesting Advertising* (New York: NLCB, 1963), *Evaluating Media* (New York: NLCB, 1966).

[10] Roger Blackwell *et al., Cases in Consumer Behavior* (New York: Holt, Rinehart and Winston, 1969); H. Boyd and R. Westfall, *Marketing Research: Text and Cases,* 3rd ed. (Homewood, Ill.: Irwin, 1972); James F. Engel, W. Wayne Talarzyk, and Carl M. Larson, *Cases in Promotional Strategy* (Homewood, Ill.: Irwin, 1969); Stephen A. Greyser, *Cases in Advertising and Communications Management* (Englewood Cliffs, N. J.: Prentice-Hall, 1972); Darrell B. Lucas and Stewart H. Britt, *Measuring Advertising Effectiveness* (New York: McGraw-Hill, 1963).

percent of them were based on some form of the interview.

Why this overdependence on the interview even in an applied field like marketing? The main reason is that interviews meet the managerial requirements better than any other single measure.

Marketers should be warned, however, that the interview, used alone, can be a highly fallible measure. Its main problems, and also advantages, can be seen in terms of the sources of research invalidity connected with it.

Sources of Research Invalidity

One way to determine which measures to use is a negative approach; that is, one can seek to avoid *invalidity.* While this is not the only strategy suggested in this paper, it is certainly a useful one.

Table 1 shows the major sources of research invalidity.[11] The advantages of interview-type measurements are found in the last two categories. That is, because interviews and questionnaires can be controlled by the researcher, they provide stable measurement of a broader range of content. And the operating ease and validity checks with the interview are somewhat greater than with unobtrusive techniques.

The real disadvantages with the interview can be seen in the first three categories of Table 1. More so then with other forms of measurement, interviews lead to biased responses, because respondents are aware they are

[11] Adapted from E. Webb *et al., op. cit.*

TABLE 1 *Sources of Research Invalidity*

I. *Reactive Measurement Effect*
    1. Awareness of being tested
    2. Role playing
    3. Measurement as change
    4. Response sets

II. *Error from Investigator*
    5. Interviewer effects
    6. Change—fatigue/practice

III. *Varieties of Sampling Error*
    7. Population restriction
    8. Population stability over time
    9. Population stability over areas

IV. *Access to Content*
    10. Restrictions on content
    11. Stability of content over time
    12. Stability of content over areas

V. *Operating Ease and Validity Checks*
    13. Dross rate
    14. Access to descriptive cues
    15. Ability replicate

being tested, may play roles, may be changed by the measurement process itself, and may answer with irrelevant response sets such as yea-saying. The interviewer or questionnaire method itself can introduce error. And samples may be biased because only certain types of people will answer questions.

In a real sense, then, interviews are so popular because they are well-known and meet the criteria of reliability. Their validity can be questioned, however, and this is why we move to unobtrusive measures.

AVAILABLE UNOBTRUSIVE TECHNIQUES

Let us now turn to an examination of the major forms of unobtrusive measures. There are four types of unobtrusive techniques: entrapment, observation, archival records, and physical trace measures.

Entrapment of Experimental Approaches

Entrapment studies are those in which the purpose of the research is disguised from the respondent. Often the studies involve experimentation with different disguises being assigned to different people. It is possible for response to be in the form of interview, observation, archival records, or physical trace measures, although entrapment is definitely a different classification. About 3 percent of the research reports surveyed for this chapter consisted of the entrapment type.

The basic idea of entrapment is like that of projective techniques.[12] The researcher assumes that people trapped in a particular situation will demonstrate their beliefs, attitudes, values, and so on, by the way they respond to that situation. Respondents are asked to react to one type of stimulus or in one type of setting, when the true phenomenon under investigation is different.

The most frequent use of entrapment studies is for evaluation of specific marketing tools. One example is the direct mail study of book offers mentioned earlier, ostensibly an advertising response study but really

[12] D. Lucas and S. H. Britt, *Measuring Advertising Effectiveness* (New York: McGraw-Hill, 1963).

used to help decide what books to publish. Another is the use of coupons or prizes in advertising copy tests.[13] The ue of the coupons or preference for prizes is evidence of the effect of the advertising. Variations in shelf space, display locations, store type, menu covers, parking lot and shopping card advertisements, product flavors and versions, and salesmen have all been used in entrapment studies.

In the "Columbia Furniture Company" case, this large retailer trapped marketers instead of consumers.[14] The store's market share was slipping. Sales volume per salesman gave no real information on whether sales techniques were developing a continuing relationship, turning browsing and ideas into sales, or what. So management hired a number of pseudo-shoppers who acted various roles. Some actors posed as a soon-to-be-married couple looking for ideas. Others continually dickered on price, became upset when a salesman tried to interject comments, asked for information on styles, argued among themselves, or just browsed. Enthusiasm, product knowledge, and selling ability—as indicated by concealed tape recorders and shopper ratings— seemed to be most importantly related to sales. Both high volume and low volume salesmen had higher ratings on these three variables than did the middle level men. The low volume salesmen seemed to be spending *too*

much time helping customers without converting them to sales. The physical appearance of salesmen was not heavily related to the other aspects of salesmanship. Also, the salesmen lost sales and future patronage by neglecting browsers. Verbatim comments from the actors supported this. For instance:

> The attitude . . . was boredom and impatience. No attempt was made to make a sale, explain the product, or get me to come back. I was furious.

> I probably never would go back again.

> Four sales personnel, a red-haired woman and three gentlemen, were standing immediately in front of the door conversing with each other.

In general, management acquired a great deal of information to attack the declining market share situation.

The advantage of entrapment studies is that by disguise they offer the potential of avoiding the reactive, "guinea pig" effects of the interview. For instance, Columbia's sales people completed a questionnaire that seemed to show they were operating exactly as management desired. The entrapment study got beyond these role-playing responses and indicated otherwise.

But this advantage is not gained without a price. Besides having all the problems of experimentation, entrapment studies may introduce new biases of their own. For instance, is the selection of a prize indicative of

[13] *Ibid.;* Wolfe *et al., op. cit.*
[14] Blackwell *et al., op. cit.*

possible *future* purchasing behavior? Further, some entrapment techniques do not easily allow identification of the persons who made the responses.

The biggest problem with these techniques, however, is the ethical one connected with whatever deception may be involved.

Observation

Observation techniques range from simple observation of physical characteristics, expressive movement, and timing, to contrived studies involving participant observation and mechanical hardware. Only about three quarters of 1 percent of the marketing studies surveyed for this report involved observation.

Observation has been used to analyze markets, test alternative programs, and evaluate effects. Bank loan officers and salesmen reportedly use observation, in slightly different ways, to assess prospects. Characteristics of houses and the artifacts in them can indicate sociodemographic and psychographic segmentation. The effects of various kinds of promotional programs have been assessed by observation of audiences and checks of in-store support. Direct observation has often been used in retail stores, usually in combination with interviews.[15] The timing of responses, even within the interview, has been taken as an indication of the strength of attitude and intent.[16]

Contrived observation can provide a validation of interviewing procedures. This has been especially true in regard to measures of audiences. Validation has been established by comparison with videotapes and observations of reading, timed photography of television and bus poster viewing, and student participant observation of family viewing behavior. One mechanical device, the Nielsen Audimeter, has been itself a continuing source of audience data.

Observation measures lose their advantage over interviews if the observation becomes apparent to respondents. This can happen with simple observation if the observer appears to be unusual, carries a clipboard, etc. When contrived observation involves equipment, even that which measures involuntary physiological responses such as pupil dilation, it can have biasing effects similar to those from obtrusive techniques.

Archival Records

Records are used more in marketing research than any of the other unobtrusive measures. The content analysis of marketing research studies showed that about 15 percent were based on some form of record.

Records are used in basic studies of markets. For instance, sales records

---

[15] R. Blackwell *et al., Cases in Consumer Behavior, op. cit.;* William D. Wells and Leonard A. Lo Sciuto, "Direct Observation of Purchasing Behavior," *Journal of Marketing Research,* Vol. 3 (August 1966), pp. 227–233.

[16] Peter N. Sherril and Michael L. Ray, "A Practical Survey Measure of the Strength of Voting Intent," Research Paper No. 24 (Graduate School of Business, Stanford University, 1971).

are used to establish adopter categories and rates of diffusion in social change studies. Content analyses of advertising and editorial material can indicate attitudes and values. Menu and shopping lists studies show potential for certain kinds of products.

The surplus of archival measures often allows multiple measures within this data class. One study involving five measures to gauge social class of cities has already been mentioned. Another examining the effects of aircraft noise proposed the utilization of real estate transactions, school records, medical records, sales records, farming records, and complaint records. Whisky consumption, flight insurance sales, and air travel volume are all outward manifestations of anxiety occurring after plane crashes. Records of water pressure, sewage flow, and long distance telephone calling have all been used to show mass interest or disinterest in particular televised events.

When sales and other records are used as measures of performance in marketing, they come in two forms: episodic and continuing. While episodic records can be used to evaluate specific efforts such as contests or offers, continuing records offer the possibility of developing indices to check for biases that creep into record-taking over time. This type of bias, as well as the lack of depth information, are the main problems with archival measures.

Physical Trace

Physical trace measures involve the recording of the natural "residue" of behavior. This is the least used class of measures in the social sciences, and the count done for this paper indicated that only about one quarter of one percent of all marketing research involves this sort of measure.

This does not mean that there are not some outstanding examples or excellent possibilities, however. One of the more ingenious applications of physical trace measures was carried out by Z-Frank, the Chicago automobile dealer.[17] When their customers' cars came in for servicing, their auto radio dialings were checked. A tabulation of these dialings provided guidance for radio advertising buys.

Sears Roebuck and Company reportedly uses a combination of erosion and contrived observation to test new flooring products.[18] Test patches of the material are put in heavily traveled areas to test wear. A photoelectric counter provides information on the level of traffic.

Several physical trace measures have been suggested for examining magazine readership. Politz used small glue spots in the gutter of each page spread of a magazine. Broken glue spots would indicate exposure. DuBois tried fingerprinting, and the use of light sensitive paper and the wear of pages have also been proposed.

Physical trace measures generate the least reactive bias of all the data classes reviewed in this chapter. On the negative side, however, they are rather gross indicators. It is usually necessary to combine physical trace

[17] E. Webb *et al.*, *op. cit.*
[18] Q. Gregory, *op. cit.*

measures with others for more sophisticated indications.

APPLYING MULTIPLE MEASUREMENT

Marketers obviously have only
started to tap the potential of unobtrusive measurement, much less
multiple measurement. How can more
applications be made?

The most important decision in
multiple measurement is just to decide
to do it, to break the mold of using a
single measure. Beyond this, a series
of successive steps can be followed.

First, the problem for measurement should be clearly stated. It
should not be stated too specifically,
however, since more ideas for measures will be generated by a general
definition. As was seen above, unobtrusive measures tend to be used in
the standard categories of research—
market analysis, testing alternatives,
and measuring results.

Once the problem is defined, it is
advisable to have a "brainstorming"
session to develop measures ideas. The
people involved should know the
problem at hand as well as the classes
of measures that are discussed in this
paper. If the accent is on ideas, it is
surprising how many measures can be
developed. In one 20-minute session
prior to a multiple measures study of
political attitudes and behavior, ideas
for 39 measures were suggested.[19]

The set of ideas that come out of
the brainstorming phase must then

be pared down, primarily on the
basis of the management criteria mentioned earlier. The researcher must
remember the needs for continuous
measurement, of sampling, and of content to be covered. The political study
mentioned above was a developmental study which in the end used
17 measures with several different
sampling bases. But in most market-
situations the list should be reduced
to about three measures in order to
avoid managerial confusion. It is key
that the measures complement each
other in terms of sources of invalidity.

The effort required to develop a
multiple and unobtrusive research
system may seem great. But the payout can be great also, in terms of a
competitive advantage in measurement.

IMPLICATIONS

A consideration of unobtrusive research techniques forces a consideration of many other issues, both within
and directly related to marketing.
Unobtrusive measures represent relatively new ways to measure marketing
variables, and to analyze, plan, test,
and control marketing programs. Multiple measurement forces utilization
of social science analysis techniques
heretofore ignored in marketing. The
ultimate outcome of this research
should be a broadening of marketing
concepts. Nowhere is this more true
than in the application of these
measurement techniques in the social
indicators movement. Unobtrusive
techniques offer the potential of differentially biased tools to add to those
which might gauge societal effects.

[19] Michael L. Ray, "Final Analysis of a
Multiple and Unobtrusive Measures Study
of Political Attitudes and Behavior," unpublished paper (Stanford University, 1969).

The main difficulties with these measures are issues of ethics, deception, and privacy. They must be used cautiously in this regard.

SUGGESTIONS FOR FURTHER READING

Raymond A. Bauer (ed.), *Social Indicators* (Cambridge, Mass: MIT Press, 1966).

Donald T. Campbell, "Methods for the Experimenting Society," *American Psychologist*, Vol. 27 (Forthcoming 1973). Presented originally at meetings of the Eastern Psychological Association (September 1971).

Roger M. Heeler and Michael L. Ray, "Measure Validation in Marketing," *Journal of Marketing Research* (November 1972).

Gene F. Summers, *Attitude Measurement* (Chicago: Rand McNally, 1970).

Eugene J. Webb, Donald T. Campbell, Richard D. Schwartz, Lee Sechrest, *Unobtrusive Measures: Nonreactive Research in the Social Sciences* (Chicago: Rand McNally, 1966).

Security Watch Company[1]

INTRODUCTION

The Security Watch Company was founded in the United States in 1817. Because of great emphasis on quality of materials and fine craftsmanship, at the turn of the century the Security watch was considered the best American-made watch on the market. With capable management and continued attention to the finest quality, the company was a leader in the industry throughout the early 1900s.

By the 1930s, the Security watch met its first crisis. The company had in the past concentrated on producing fine pocket watches. In the twenties and thirties, some of Security's competitors, along with some new establishments, began promoting small, compact wristwatches which became increasingly popular. Although slow to react to this demand, by 1940 the Security Watch Company was making what was considered the best wristwatch available and had once more

[1] The name of the company and the industry are disguised.
This case was prepared by Kenneth P. Uhl and Bertram Schoner of the University of Iowa.
SOURCE: From *Marketing Research: Information Systems and Decision Making*, by Kenneth P. Uhl and Bertram Schoner, Copyright © 1969 John Wiley & Sons, Inc. Reprinted by permission of John Wiley & Sons, Inc.

taken its position among the leading watchmakers.

Following World War II, a major change took place in the market structure of wristwatches. In the past, when one purchased a personal time piece he very often expected it to last for a lifetime. Wristwatches were a prestige item; and for those who could afford them, jeweled watches with solid-gold cases were not uncommon. But in the 1940s and 1950s the demand for expensive jeweled watches by the public abruptly changed. This yielded to a demand for functional, inexpensive watches.

The company was very slow to react to this change in the demand structure. There were two major reasons for this: First, the management was reluctant to produce a "cheap" time piece for fear that it would destroy their fine reputation for the highest of quality and craftsmanship. Second, because their watches were almost completely handmade, Security lacked the technology, personnel, and equipment necessary to compete with mass-produced watches.

THE LOW-PRICED WATCH

It was not until 1955 that the company finally introduced a line of wristwatches in the $10–$30 price range.

Security's low-priced wristwatches did not meet with immediate market success, but by 1962 the company had gained a large share of the market and was among the leaders in the $10–$30 price range. The company felt that their eventual success in the lower price range was due to their reputation for high-quality watches.

The criteria concerning TV set use and station coverage were included because television was selected as the primary advertising media. It was felt that recent data suggested that TV provided the most efficient coverage per dollar spent. Also, advertising "impact" showed better results for television than for any other medium with the type of product that Security Watch Company was marketing.

The test markets were selected in pairs. They were:

1. Baton Rouge—Des Moines
2. Flint—Austin
3. Oklahoma City—Dayton
4. Omaha—Spokane
5. Gary—Wichita.

The purpose of the experiment was to test the following variables:

1. A special distribution effort in each of four test sets of test markets.
2. The use of different levels of advertising in each of the different sets of test markets.

The sample was divided into the following pairs:

1. Baton Rouge—Des Moines—control market
2. Flint—Austin—test market #1

3. Oklahoma City—Dayton—test market #2
4. Omaha—Spokane—test market #3
5. Gary—Wichita—test market #4.

The dependent variables in the test market program were brand share and product volume exposure (PVE); which can be defined as percent of total market sales represented by all stores displaying Security watches. For instance, if PVE = 40%, the Security watch was displayed by retail outlets making 40% of the total wristwatch sales in the $10–$30 price range. Measuring the PVE provided a method of gauging the efficiency of distribution against competition.

The test marketing program ran from August 1966 to August 1967. During the test period a commercial information organization, Research Data, Inc. was retained. Research Data, Inc. was to audit over-the-counter sales and obtain brand-share figures together with PVE figures for the following brands:

> Security
> Precision
> Worthy
> Armor.

The auditing firm presented in detail the method by which they selected the audit sample, but kept the actual store names strictly confidential.

The experimental variables in Security's test markets were advertising and personal selling. Measurement of advertising pressure was an essential part of the experiment. It was decided that "gross rating points" (GRP) would be an adequate method of measuring advertising pressure.

GRP is a term which describes the number and frequency of TV homes reached by an advertising message in a particular market. For example:

> 50% of all TV homes
> reached one time = GRP
> 100% of all TV homes
> reached 1½ times = 105 GRP.

As an example, if a certain program had a GRP rating of 50 and Security wished to advertise at a rate of 150 GRP, three one-minute ads could be scheduled in the test market for three succeeding program showings.

It was further agreed that "spot" TV ads afforded the greatest degree of flexibility, particularly in view of the local nature of the test markets. One-minute spot ads were produced and scheduled for the appropriate markets. Time slots in each of the test markets were purchased. A predetermined GRP level was reached. The GRP levels of advertising for the various test markets were assigned as follows:

1. Baton Rouge—Des Moines—control markets (only normal national advertising)
2. Flint — Austin — test market #1 (special distribution)
3. Oklahoma City—Dayton—test market #2 (personal selling team + 50 GRP advertising)
4. Omaha—Spokane—test market #3 (personal selling team + 100 GRP)
5. Gary—Wichita—test market #4 (personal selling team + 150 GRP).

Teams of seven salesmen converged on each pair of test markets (but not the control market) periodically. Their duties and assignments are shown in Exhibit 1.

In 1966, the Security Watch Company again found sales lagging significantly behind its major competitors in the low-price range—Precision, Worthy, and Armor. The company estimated that very close to 50% of the total retail sales for wristwatches was contained in the $10–$30 price range. For this reason there was great incentive to capture a major share of the low-priced market.

In the forties and fifties there had also been a significant change in the channels of distribution. The leading producers of low-priced watches had very broad distribution which not only included the traditional channels, but went into such retail outlets as drugstores and variety stores. Security had continued to follow their traditional pattern of selective distribution only to jewelry stores and the larger, well-established department stores.

With respect to quality, all four brands (Security, Precision, Worthy, and Armor) were approximately equal. The primary variants among the four brands were promotional efforts and channels of distribution. It appeared that if Security were to increase its market share in the low-priced range, the optimum level and combination of promotional efforts, along with the proper channels of distribution, would have to be ascertained. With this in mind, Security management decided in favor of experimental test marketing. The objectives of the test marketing program were:

1. Determine the effect on brand share of increased advertising and distribution efforts.
2. Determine the financial risks and requirements involved in greater promotional efforts and expanding channels of distribution.

DESIGN OF THE EXPERIMENT

The test markets were selected in cooperation with Security's advertising agency, Selmore Advertising, Inc. of Chicago, Illinois. The population of subjects was defined as the entire adult population of the continental United States. It was hoped to draw a sample which would include all social classes, ranging from upper-upper to lower-lower, in cities of approximately equal demographic characteristics. The following criteria were applied in selecting the test markets which would be included:

1. Demographic characteristics to be approximately equal to the total U. S. population and approximately equal to each other.
2. The number of TV sets in use.
3. The TV station coverage.

The market test began on August 1, 1966 and ended on August 1, 1967. A bimonthly system of manipulating the experimental variables was scheduled throughout the year. The timing was as follows:

Step 1. The first two weeks of the two-month period were devoted to distribution efforts. Seven salesmen were taken from their own territories and simultaneously assigned to each test market.

Step 2. The middle four weeks of the bimonthly period were devoted to spot TV advertising at pressure levels prescribed by the GRP assignments for each test market.

Step 3. Auditing of the dependent variables (brand share and PVE) was done by Research Data, Inc. in the final two weeks of the bimonthly period.

The above cycle was repeated in each market six times throughout the year.

A variety of personal selling and advertising tactics were employed in the test markets. They are summarized as follows:

1. Advertising was concentrated on only one model (the $18.95 model) in the $10–$30 price range.
2. A regional sales manager supervised each test market distribution effort. Because two cities with test market #4 were to receive heavy advertising, the most competent regional sales managers were selected for this test market.
3. Route sheets were drawn up for each salesman, with each wholesaler or retail outlet limited on each route.
4. A "selling check list" was provided for each salesman.
5. A daily sales quota was assigned each salesman.
6. A "breakfast" sales meeting was

held three times each week to analyze distribution results and to
give assistance.

7. Special sales report forms were designed.
8. Security Watch displays were
placed with the retailer on "guaranteed sales" (consignment).

RESULTS OF THE EXPERIMENT

Security PVE and brand-share
changes over the test period are indicated below for each test market. A
complete summary for Security and its
primary competitors is shown in Exhibit 2.

Security Brand Share Change

		1966	1967
1.	Baton Rouge—Des Moines Control markets	7.1%	7.4%
2.	Flint—Austin Distribution only	6.9	8.2
3.	Oklahoma City—Dayton Dist. + 50 GRP	6.9	8.0
4.	Omaha—Spokane Dist. + 100 GRP	7.7	9.1
5.	Gary—Wichita Dist. + 150 GRP	6.9	10.5

Security PVE Change

		1966	1967
1.	Baton Rouge—Des Moines Control markets	43%	67%
2.	Flint—Austin Distribution only	56	74
3.	Oklahoma City—Dayton Dist. + 50 GRP	55	74
4.	Omaha—Spokane Dist. + 100 GRP	62	73
5.	Gary—Wichita Dist. + 150 GRP	60	68

Security Watch brand share in the
low-price range made the following
percentage increases during the test
period which ended August 1, 1967.

	Percentage Increase
1. Baton Rouge—Des Moines Control markets	4%
2. Flint—Austin Distribution only	17
3. Oklahoma City—Dayton Dist. + 50 GRP	16
4. Omaha—Spokane Dist. + 100 GRP	20
5. Gary—Wichita Dist. + 150 GRP	52

There was no obvious explanation for the increase in PVE in the control markets (Baton Rouge—Des Moines).

CONCLUSIONS DRAWN FROM THE EXPERIMENT

The management of Security Watch Company realized that the experimental test marketing program had some shortcomings, but felt the following conclusions could be safely drawn:

1. Expansion of advertising for wristwatches in the low-price range on a national basis (as projected from test market expenses) was financially unsound at all levels of advertising pressure. Brand share gained was not significant enough to justify such expenditures.

2. By concentrating on distribution (through improved sales training and manpower reorganization), improvement in brand share was possible. Growth in brand share would be slow, but less risky than resorting to heavy advertising expenditures.

3. Low-priced wristwatches, as an advertised consumer product, are generally a "low-interest" item in the consumer's mind.

QUESTIONS

1. Criticize the experimental design and suggest what you think would be a superior design.

2. What conclusions should the company have drawn from the experiment?

EXHIBIT 1   *Security Watch Company Market Test*
Salesman Outline and Procedure

Purpose:

To prove out over-the-counter sales of Security low-price range wristwatches with advertising backing.

Place:

Eight cities in pour pairs:
Flint—Austin
Oklahoma City—Dayton
Omaha—Spokane
Gary—Wichita

Primary Product Emphasis:

The $18.95 model wristwatches (men's and ladies')

Secondary Product Emphasis:

All other wristwatches in the $10–$30 price range.

Salesmen's Activity:

Salesmen and merchandising men should visit each city in their territories listed above as soon as possible, when so instructed, to push programs to do the following:

1. Pay special attention to maintaining inventories of $18.95 and other wristwatches.
2. Outline low-priced wristwatch research for that particular area.
3. Take inventory of the $18.95 model watch and make four copies; two for merchandising men for that city, one for the salesman himself, and mail one to the marketing manager at company's headquarters.
4. Solicit wholesalers' and chain headquarters' cooperation regarding research for that city as follows:
   a. In order to get distribution for Security watches we know attainable, we will grant immediately 6-month terms on all wristwatches in the $10–$30 price range, providing they will grant such terms to their retail dealers; or in the case of chain headquarters, for distribution to branches. In all cases, terms must apply to retail dealers only in those cities. Our terms to direct accounts will apply to all their retailers in the $10–$30 price range if they cannot separate out that portion going into the cities named.
   b. We would like wholesalers' salesmen covering these cities to push wristwatch sales on 6-month terms beginning at once.
   c. Salesmen and merchandising men should cover these cities

thoroughly and take turn-over orders for the low-priced watches for cooperating wholesalers; and chain branch orders if headquarters will permit.

d. Wholesalers and chain headquarters in these cities only should be asked to permit our salesmen and merchandising men to pick up any orders out of stock on memo, so that they can deliver immediately when sales are made.

e. If possible, our salesmen should arrange for sales meetings with wholesalers but if this cannot be done within a day or two at most after his first call, do not hold up the program for a meeting.

f. The salesmen should assure our wholesale accounts that we will guarantee the wholesaler against any credit losses that they may occur involving low-price range wristwatch sales in cases where our salesmen and merchandising men may write up delivered orders for retailers whom they do not ordinarily want to sell.

Salesmen Activity:

1. The men will be assigned to particular cities.
2. Each man will be assigned to certain wholesalers and chain headquarters for taking inventory and taking orders.
3. The men will present the $18.95 model first with special emphasis on additional advertising where applicable and 6-month guarantee sales terms.
4. Place special emphasis on getting our products and displays in any store which has Precision, Worthy, or Armor displays.
5. When an order is sold, the man will deliver it then and there and put it on display. He will write up a turn-over delivered order on the particular wholesaler involved. The order must be signed by the retailer. The salesman must also rubber stamp all copies of the order with the special "guaranteed sale" stamp he will have for that purpose.
6. If immediate merchandise supplies are needed, the salesman should telephone his regional manager to make arrangements for transfer of such merchandise from other accounts in the territory or elsewhere in the region. When orders are written directly to the company, they are to be air-mailed the same day to Security headquarters where they will be processed for immediate filling.
7. When a salesman is sure he has covered all possible retail outlets in his part of the city, he is to contact the other men working in the city and help them finish up. When a city is finished, salesmen return any unsold merchandise they are carrying to the wholesalers from whom it was picked up; finish writing up all reports and mail them at once; and report to their regional managers by phone for further assignment.

EXHIBIT 2 *Security Watch Company*
Summary of Overall Experiment Results

Market	Brand	Net PVE	± A*	Share	± %†
Control	Total			100.0	
	Security	67	+24.1	7.4	+0.3
	Precision	79	+11.3	16.2	+1.1
	Worthy	90	+2.3	22.0	−0.1
	Armor	82	+9.3	14.2	−1.5
Test 1	Total			100.0	
	Security	74	+17.5	8.2	+1.2
	Precision	80	+15.9	16.0	+1.4
	Worthy	84	+1.2	22.4	−0.1
	Armor	76	+7.0	14.1	−0.6
Test 2	Total			100.0	
	Security	74	+19.4	8.0	+1.1
	Precision	69	+15.0	17.0	+1.9
	Worthy	89	−1.1	21.9	−0.2
	Armor	73	+7.4	16.5	−0.6
Test 3	Total			100.0	
	Security	73	+10.6	9.1	+1.4
	Precision	69	+19.6	15.6	+0.8
	Worthy	94	+2.2	21.7	+1.5
	Armor	79	+5.3	14.3	−0.4
Test 4	Total			100.0	
	Security	68	+9.7	10.5	+3.6
	Precision	75	+1.4	17.0	N.C.‡
	Worthy	90	+9.8	23.7	+1.1
	Armor	78	N.C.‡	16.2	−1.2

* % change in PVE from August 1966 to August 1967.
† Percentage points change in brand share over the test period.
‡ No change.

Hardon and Wales, Inc.

Hardon and Wales, Inc., numbered among its advertising clients the McLaughlin Small Appliance Company. The latter produced a limited line of small kitchen appliances such as mixers, coffee makers, electric fry pans, and toasters. Annual sales of the McLaughlin Company were about $8.5 million, and approximately $450,000 was allocated for advertising. Hardon and Wales used national consumer magazines, trade publications, and newspapers to advertise the McLaughlin line. Television was not used because it was considered to be too expensive and to place the client in a poor competitive position, since the top two sellers of small appliances (General Electric and Sunbeam) used the medium extensively. Spot radio was also considered, but the client did not believe this medium suitable for promotion of its products.

At the suggestion of the McLaughlin Company's advertising manager, the medium of outdoor advertising was given consideration; however, before launching into any extensive use of billboards, the client wanted the agency to test this medium for sales effectiveness. The McLaughlin advertising manager thought that billboard advertising of his company's appliances would have several advantages. First, this type of medium permitted a "king-size" view of the products and gave a fast sales message. Second, other appliances did not use outdoor advertising, and this could give the McLaughlin campaign the advantage of being a first in the industry.

After some discussions along these lines, the marketing research director of Hardon and Wales received the following memo from the agency account supervisor on the McLaughlin account:

TO: ERNEST PACKARD,
Research Director
FROM: FRANK W. DARR,
Account Supervisor

I have just finished a lengthy phone conversation with Randell, advertising manager of McLaughlin, as to how we might "prove" or "disprove" the effectiveness of outdoor advertising as a medium for their products.

We finally agreed that the best way would be to select one of their weaker metropolitan areas in which to try a "before and after"

SOURCE: Reprinted with permission from Richard D. Irwin, Inc., 1972. H. Boyd and R. Westfall, *Marketing Research: Text and Cases*, 3rd ed. (Homewood, Ill.: Richard D. Irwin, Inc., 1972), pp. 115–116.

brand awareness test, plus measuring the sales "before and after" some adequate outdoor advertising. Randell didn't want to go into more than one market because he says we really don't know very much about the effectiveness of this medium yet.

The objective would be to test this weak market in ample time to be able to determine by spring whether we would recommend outdoor advertising in the more important markets.

Randell assures me that we can find some market where distributors sell exclusively to retailers located within the area. He also assures me that their sales department will cooperate by taking a beginning inventory at the distributor's level and, of course, there's no problem in keeping track of shipments from the factory to these distributors. At the end of the test period salesmen will take a closing inventory of the items involved in the study.

I told Randell we could prob-ably do a brand awareness study among consumers by phone—and that we'd pick up the tab on this part of the job. As I see this, we'd do a "before and after" measurement among, say, a couple of hundred housewives. We'd find out what brands of small appliances they could recall (without any reminding) and also how they would rank these brands on quality. We'd repeat the job among a different group at the end of the test period.

Randell said his company would leave the test market alone except for normal or routine activity.

Can we proceed along the lines outlined above? Let me know your reactions as soon as possible. Thanks!

QUESTIONS

1. Would this be a good test of outdoor advertising effectiveness?
2. Should the procedure outlined in the memo be accepted?
3. What changes, if any, do you recommend?

Chapter 10

Sampling
to Gather Information

After a researcher has decided on his problem, model, data-collection technique, and measurement system, he must decide how he is to select the individual observations from the world he is studying. There are several significant decisions he must make. This chapter will show the researcher the range of rules for choosing a sampling technique and indicate when each is appropriate.

Introduction

In order to test his hypotheses, the marketing researcher must decide how he is to select observations from the "world" he is studying. The method of choosing observations is called sampling. The range of methods for selecting observations encompasses very simple "convenience" rules to highly complicated schemes. The researcher must be careful to choose a rule which best fits his research design and budget.

Sampling is used commonly by industry. For example, quality control inspectors use samples when the products come off the production line. When producing bread, inspectors will select every 100th loaf. The loaves that are selected for test are cut open to see if the center of the bread is thoroughly baked. If a number of the sampled loaves begin to show up with doughy centers, the heat of the baking oven is increased. Clearly if too many loaves were sampled, too much bread would be wasted in sampling. If too few loaves were sampled the chance that a large number of defective loaves would be produced before the problem was detected would be great. The quality control researcher must make an economic decision concerning the method and size of the sample.[1]

Accountants scrutinize the debtors of their firms by selecting only a sample of the accounts because of limited time to perform the analysis. Tax auditors for the Internal Revenue Service randomly audit a number of tax returns each year. Financial services randomly select a number of New York Stock Exchange listed firms to analyze each year because the analyst's time is limited. The use of the sampling process by institutions throughout the world is very common.

Similarly, marketing research uses sampling in many ways. Marketing researchers sample a group of people to learn the attitudes of the group. Marketers often pick only certain stores in which to introduce or test market new products. The A. C. Nielsen company selects only a small number of TV viewers in order to ascertain what the entire United States is watching on television. Museums interview a small number of their patrons to find out which displays are appealing and why.

[1] E. H. Bowman and R. B. Fetter, *Analysis for Production and Operations Management* (Homewood, Ill.: Irwin, 1967), chap. 6.

This chapter examines methods of sampling that are in common use and illustrates how the question of sample size may be answered. Fundamentally there are two classes of sampling methods: deterministic and probabilistic. Deterministic sampling rules are constructed such that those persons actually performing the sample have very specific protocols which are followed. Probabilistic sampling rules are those in which some random event generator, such as a computer, picks random numbers in some manner and these numbers form the basis on which individual observations are selected. A random event is defined as an occurrence which has several possible values and occurs with some definable frequency if many repetitions are undertaken.

Basic Definitions

There are several basic definitions that are important in sampling. The first of these is the definition of *universe* or total *population*. The term *population* means the set of items which form a total group, that is, a complete list of all subjects that are relevant to a given study. Alternative terms include the *universe, total population,* and the *sampling frame.* If one were interested in describing the behavior of persons in the United States, one would ideally have a population list of each person's name who lived within the United States. Thus, a population is the complete set of all relevant items from which a *sample* is drawn.

A *sample* is merely a selected subset of the population. The means of obtaining the sample from the population is termed the *sampling method.* *Segments or strata* are defined as subsets of the population which have common (the same) values on such variables as age, income, and education.

An overview of the sampling methods is shown in Figure 10.1. The most fundamental sampling concept is the complete census. The census is the gathering of information about all elements in a population. An example is the decennial census performed by the United States government in which data on age, residence, household composition, and many issues are collected for almost every person in the population.[2] If the resources are not available for a complete census, the data-collecting organization must resort to a sample: either purposive or random. Purposive samples can be homogenous, structured, or heterogenous. A heterogenous sample is one that has many strata while a homogenous sample has only one strata. A structured sample is one in which several strata are logically connected in some way (family relationships, scientists working on the same problem, and such). Heterogenous samples can be undertaken such that only extreme cases within a strata are examined or in a manner such that the strata is representative of universe behavior.

[2] The government has great difficulty in finding many people, especially in the ghetto areas of large cities.

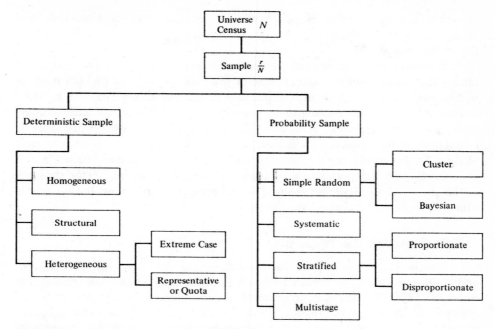

FIGURE 10.1   *A Diagram of Sampling Methods*
Source: Adapted from Johan Galtung, *Theory and Methods of Social Research* (New York: Columbia University Press, 1967), p. 56.

Probability samples can be done in several ways depending on the needs of the researcher. Using some random event generator, the researcher can use simple random samples, systematic random samples, stratified samples, or multistage samples. The exact method for performing these procedures is discussed in the following sections with examples.

Bias is defined as a methodical error that occurs in selection of respondents or measurement. Specifically, in sampling, any method which causes one element of a population to have a different probability of being selected for a sample from other elements of the population is said to cause bias. The further that a researcher deviates from a simple random sample or its logical equivalent, the more chance that the sample will be biased.

The classic example of a sample which was embarrassingly biased occurred in the 1936 election which pitted Franklin D. Roosevelt against Alfred Landon. The now defunct *Literary Digest* performed a sample drawn from the telephone directory primarily. Respondents were questioned as to voting preference. The *Digest* forecasted that Landon would win handily. As history records, Roosevelt was elected by a wide margin. Market researchers at the *Digest* forgot that people who owned phones during the economic Depression of the time were generally wealthy and tended to vote Republican (Landon).

However, a great number of people were unemployed at the time and thus could not afford telephones, that is, the phone list was a highly biased list of the population.

Sampling error is defined to be the difference between the results of taking the sample and the actual state of the total population (which is often unknown). Sampling error occurs because of the possibility that the random selection of respondents generates a sample which is accidently "off" through luck alone. For example, it is possible in a sample of six people from a population of 1000 that the six richest people in the sample are picked through chance. Such a result would be very unfortunate if the researcher desired a cross section of the population in terms of income. Sampling error declines as the size of the sample increases. (See Chapter 11 concerning the computation of means and standard deviations.)

Enumerating the Population

The researcher must examine his behavioral model or structural model and determine what definition he must operationally create concerning his universe. Typically, this is done in terms of use-characteristics of products and lifestyles of the target population. Once the universe has been defined operationally, the researcher must search his environment to see if the universe in question is listed by some agency. Thus, the researcher will see if there is a government list, magazine subscription list, credit card list, club membership list, or some such which overlaps his universe definition. Rarely, will a "perfect" list exist in the area of marketing. This is the case because the use of products and services is usually scattered across many listed groups of people.

An example of this can be seen if one attempted to create a random sample of the people who buy automobiles in Chicago. First, the researcher might try to find a list of the people who lived in Chicago. A first approximation of this list would be the Chicago telephone directory. However, many people own several telephones, many people own no telephones, and many people have unlisted numbers. Thus, the telephone book becomes an imperfect surrogate for a complete listing of the population. Another approach that the researcher might take is to examine the tax listing at the real estate office to find the owners of buildings. However, he would find that there are many multiple-family dwellings in the Chicago area and there are many people within these buildings. Thus, the sample based on tax rolls would be structured primarily toward the single family home owner, the numerically largest segment of the tax list. Another possibility of a population list would be to use the subscription list from the *Chicago Tribune* which is the largest daily newspaper in Chicago. However, since not all people read the *Chicago Tribune* and the *Chicago Tribune* has a definite editorial slant, and hence would appeal to and be read by a special audience, it appears that the *Tribune* list would also be an imperfect population list. Finally, if the researcher went to the city government to examine city auto sticker lists, he would find a very "close" approximation to the universe he needs.

In industrial research, the list of complete populations of various industries is quite good. Companies such as Dun & Bradstreet and other credit agencies maintain up-to-date lists of all companies and their officers in almost all industries. Thus, it becomes relatively easy to get an accurate list of the population of executives and companies in the industrial sector. However, even these lists are incomplete as certain small companies sometimes refuse to completely cooperate with Dun & Bradstreet.

A Review of Purposive Sampling Methods

The heart of any purposive sampling method is the set of rules used by the data gatherers for selecting the universe elements to be sampled. In most cases, these rules are devised such that the rule will not cause the information collected to be strictly a function of the rule itself. In practice, these rules are stated in terms of a place and a qualification for interviewing.

An example of a typical interviewer instruction using a Quota Sample (see Figure 10.1) would be:

> "Interview 12 Cadillac owners who appear in the parking lot of the Jewel Food Store at Fourth and Dempster Streets between 1 p.m. and 5 p.m. on July 7."

or

> "Interview every third person entering the Jewel Food Store at Fourth and Dempster Streets between 1 p.m. and 3 p.m. on July 7."

The key but not always warranted assumption underlying such rules is that there will be no effect of time or place on the respondents as they answer the questionnaire.

A variation of the deterministic sample is the extreme case sample. A sampling rule for this situation would be:

> "Interview all students in New Trier High School who scored over 130 and under 80 on the annual IQ test."

Extreme value sampling is done where there is a hypothesis that IQ (or some other variable) is the key determinant in explaining some type of behavior. Extreme value sampling causes large statistical variation.

Homogenous deterministic samples are executed using a decision rule which isolates one behavioral group. Structural deterministic samples are executed using a rule that specifies some relationship between homogenous groups. An example would be:

> "Interview atomic scientists and officials of the Atomic Energy Commission who have communicated with each other within the last six months."

Such a rule would isolate scientists and administrators who are actively exchanging information. The hypotheses related to such a study would focus on the characteristics of the communicators and the information passed.

Although deterministic samples are generally inexpensive and relatively easy to execute, the method often leads to intended and unintended structure of the data. It is difficult to argue that a set of deterministically collected data indeed represents the behavior of some wider universe. Thus, any statistical operations performed on data from such samples must be interpreted with caution. Because there is no guarantee that the sample is representative of a larger population, deterministic samples are said to be less *efficient* statistically than random samples.

A Review of Common Random Sampling Methods

There are six major methods of random sampling. Each of these is discussed with an example of how the method is used.

Simple Random Sampling

Simple random sampling is done in a manner which guarantees that any given sample of a total population has an equal probability of being drawn. For a universe containing five corporation executives (Executive A, B, C, D, E) and where the researcher wants to sample two of the five, the condition for a simple random sample is that a sample consisting of A and C has the same probability of being selected as one consisting of B and D, that is, each pair-wise combination has an equal probability of being drawn.

When it comes to samples involving tens of thousands of individuals, simple random sampling becomes more difficult. However, it may be done using the computer in the following way. If the random sample is to be drawn from a population of 10,000 persons, the list of the name and address of each member of the potential sample would be put on a computer tape. In addition, a number from 1–10,000 would be assigned to each member of the mailing list. The computer would then draw a random number between 1 and 10,000, say 475, and then search down the tape until it found that number. The person whose name and address appeared at position 475 would than be removed from the tape and put on the sample list.

The computer would then pick another number and search down the tape until it found the name and address associated with that number, remove that number from the list and post it to the sampling list, and so forth. The procedure would be repeated until a desired sample size was achieved, some 200 people. If, by chance, the computer drew a duplicate number, the computer would be alerted to disregard this and then draw another number before searching down the tape. This method of drawing without replacement of the list, that is, removing the name from the tape, approximates the simple random sample very closely for large populations.[3] However, the method is quite expensive in that much computer time is needed to search down lengthy lists of respondents. In addition, many population lists are not in machine readable form.

An example of the simple random sample is shown in Table 10.1. A list of 10,000 numbers was created using a computer and 100 numbers were randomly selected from the list. These drawn numbers are shown in Table 10.1. Then the numbers drawn were grouped into units of 1000, that is, all numbers falling between 0 and 1000, 1001 to 2000, and so on, were counted. The result is shown in Figure 10.2. The number of random picks in each group of 1000 is shown and range from 5 to 13. The average is 10 numbers in each group. The frequency of cell occurrence is shown in Table 10.2. Most of the cell frequencies cluster about the average of 10, that is, three cells had 10 numbers while only 1 cell had 11 numbers. It is interesting to note that 90 percent of the random number values fall within the range of 8 to 12 numbers in a cell. This is an example of the phenomenon called the "central limit theorem" discussed in Chapter 11 (see footnote 13 as well).

TABLE 10.1 *A Sample of 100 Numbers Drawn Randomly between 0 and 10,000*

678	7424
3987	6805
9059	4278
1780	5470
8107	6328
8764	9224
6796	63
4388	8720
9854	9060
5165	9563
4409	3849
7943	2780
3148	657
7506	4959
2825	2236
2686	9635
1248	2530
8829	8846
7880	5411
91	6224
2388	9319
8214	6612

[3] A formal proof can be found in W. Feller, *An Introduction To Probability Theory,* 2nd ed., vol. I (New York: Wiley, 1957), p. 29.

TABLE 10.1 *(continued)*

5176	3179
2472	8472
2390	408
9306	9826
9408	4756
4468	3885
4037	5214
5700	3408
3341	7085
9000	5505
7362	8651
8590	2119
3682	6479
9000	8944
3695	8400
3937	90
943	2142
7952	3459
1451	7792
505	1668
153	7752
4700	4198
1272	843
3516	7151
5590	6488
127	6431
9941	3269
5382	5724

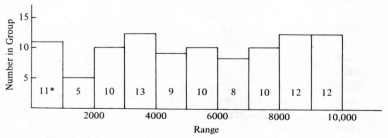

*11 numbers fell between 0 and 1000.
Average for each cell = 10.

FIGURE 10.2 *The Distribution of 100 Random Numbers Shown in Table 10.1*

TABLE 10.2 *The Number of Random Numbers Falling in Each Data Range Group*

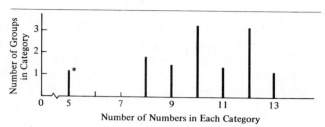

*One group consisted of 5 numbers.
Note: 90 percent of the group numbers fell between 8 and 12.

The Systematic Random Sample

The systematic random sample is similar to the pure random sample except that it requires only one pass through a large list such as the list of 10,000 that was mentioned above. The method of systematic random sampling is very simple. The first step is to simply divide the total population size, that is, 10,000, by the desired sample size, for example, 200. The division of 10,000 by 200 yields the number 50. The implication of the number 50 is that every 50th name will be picked in the sample. The second step in systematic random sampling is to randomly pick the starting point for the selection of every 50th name. Typically this number is drawn from a random number list ranging from 1–10,000 in the example shown.

Once the starting point has been chosen, then every 50th name on the list is selected, starting with the random number chosen. When the end of the list is encountered, the computer or researcher would then cycle back to the first name on the list and continue counting. Thus, the random starting point would be the first number chosen and would be the ending point of the selection procedure and a population list would be considered to be circular, that is, the last element would be the first element. Thus, the systematic random sample is relatively quick and inexpensive to do. It also can be done "by hand" quite easily. The key assumption of the systematic random sample is, of course, that the total population list is randomly ordered. If there is any intentional or unintentional order to the total population list, this ordering has to be evaluated in terms of its effect on the systematic random sampling method.

Green and Tull[4] asserted that it is possible for the systematic random sample to improve on the reliability and representativeness of the sample compared to simple random sampling in cases where there is a strict ordering

[4] P. Green and D. Tull, *Research for Marketing Decisions*, 2nd ed. (Englewood Cliffs, N. J.: Prentice-Hall, 1970).

of the total population list, that is, where the total population list is ordered by income perhaps with high income people being at the front of the list and low income people being at the bottom of the list. Thus, there is some benefit to using the systematic random sample method. The only major disadvantage of the systematic random sample occurs if there is some cycle in the list, that is, every 500th name might be a rich person. Then there is nonzero probability that one might achieve a very poor sample in terms of representativeness if one happened upon that particular cycle.

The Stratified Random Sample

Stratified random sampling is a method of segmented random sampling. Segments within a universe are defined according to one or more variables. An example would be brand usage. The marketing researcher knows that his brand share for a given product is 12 percent. The researcher wishes to compare buyers to nonbuyers for his product. He realizes that if he conducted a simple or systematic random sample of 500 subjects, he would find that about 88 percent of the subjects or 440 subjects did not use his product. Thus, he would have 60 users and 440 nonusers. Ideally he would like to have 100 of each type of user.

Thus, it becomes clear that when comparing unequal size segments or strata, a strategy of oversampling some strata and undersampling other strata is wise policy. This is the prime argument for conducting stratified random samples. The stratified random sample is executed by developing lists of members of a given strata and performing a simple or systematic random sample only within the given strata. In the example above, a simple random sample of a list of brand users would be used to achieve the sample of 100 within the user strata. A similar tactic would be used for the nonuser strata. Such user/nonuser lists are often compiled by companies using warrantee cards enclosed in the product package or advertising.

Because the stratified random sampling method does overrepresent some groups and underrepresents other groups, the result of this technique can be projected to larger populations only if the strata are aggregated and weighted to reflect their exact proportions in the real world.[5] After the weighting procedure is done, the results would be summed to form some aggregate total response function. The weighting factor causes additional sampling error, however, and the aggregate population forecasts based on stratified random sample have more error by the amount of the weighting factor squared[6] than a pure or simple random sample from the total population would.

---

[5] The Universe average $= \dfrac{w_i \text{ (user average)} + w_2 \text{ (nonuser average)}}{w_1 + w_2}$ where $w_1 =$ 12 percent and $w_2 = 88$ percent (the proportions on the actual population).

[6] If the weighting factor for strata i is w_i, the sampling error would be increased by $w_i{}^2$.

Cluster Sampling

Marketing researchers have attempted to develop strategies to get around the problem of having insufficient or improper lists of the total populations. One of these methods to alleviate the "list problem" is the cluster sample. The cluster sample is a geographically oriented sampling mechanism rather than a list oriented sampling system.

The basic method of cluster sampling is to randomly choose an area within a city, for example. First the city is mapped off into areas having roughly equal populations, that is, blocks with high density are isolated and city blocks with low density are isolated and then grouped together such that high density blocks and multiblock groups of low density have roughly the same within population. Interviewers are then sent to the randomly selected geographic areas and perform the sample based on a set of rules.

These rules typically specify that only houses or apartments in the middle of a group should be sampled and every third living unit should be sampled within this geographic area. (People who live in corner lots or apartments are usually of higher income than others.) In this way, interviewer transportation cost is minimized and in addition the number of interviews that an interviewer can do within a several-hour period is maximized. Since interviewer cost is often the largest single expense incurred in doing a data collection, this method of sampling is very commonly used in the real world. However, the cluster sampling does have biases built into it determined by the particular attitudes that are endemic in the geographic areas that are sampled.

Multistage Sampling

Multistage sampling is defined as the sampling technique where one has several random decisions to make, such as choosing a state among all the states of the United States, then choosing counties within that state and then choosing the townships within the counties for a sample. Thus, multistage indicates that one takes several random draws. This means that one randomly chooses a state, for example, and then randomly chooses a county within a state and then randomly chooses some townships within the county.

A most interesting example of this particular kind of sampling is that done by the A. C. Nielsen Company in determining those counties which are to have food stores sampled. The A. C. Nielsen Company keeps counts of the amount of goods moving through selected food stores in given geographic areas. The A. C. Nielsen Company has four major types of counties that they sample: A, B, C, D counties. The A counties are those of extremely large populations, that is, over 500,000 population; B counties are over 100,000; C counties are over 50,000, and D counties are all others. A list is constructed of all the counties in each of the A, B, C, D categories; then the geographic areas to be sampled are selected within each of the A, B, C, D classifications. Then specific stores within the geographic areas are chosen to be sampled. Since more stores are sampled in the high population counties than in the low, the A. C. Nielsen sample selection for food stores is a combination of stratified and multistage sampling. Universe estimates are done using a variation of the stratified sample correction method.[7]

Bayesian and Sequential Sampling

The concept of sequential sampling revolves around the idea that it takes time to perform a sampling procedure. Instead of having a fixed number of observations in the sample to be collected, it is possible that the marketing researcher might desire a flexible sampling rule. This rule could be based on the amount of information collected and the strength of the results, that is, one would continue the sampling process until a decision is made or his budget expires. In this way, the strength of the results influence the number of subjects who are selected into the sample. An example of this would be the situation where an executive hypothesizes that his advertising is more effective than another company's advertising. The executive wishes to be confident in results at the 90 percent confidence level.[8] He then starts collecting information. Each sample respondent contributes some information to the decision. If his advertisement is very much better than the competitor's advertising, very few individual samples have to be taken before it becomes clear that his expected result will occur. However, if his advertisement is just a "little bit better" than the competitor's advertising, he may have to take a very large sample. In fact, his research budget may be exhausted before enough examples are taken to indicate that his advertisement is better than the competitor's. Thus, the key element in sequential sampling is that a constant monitoring of the results of the sample is done as information comes in. When the decision point is reached or the budget is exhausted, the sampling is terminated. A complete discussion of Bayesian sampling is contained in Green and Tull.[9] The sequential and Bayesian method of sampling brings into clear relief the need for determining the size of the sample that one wishes to take. Determining sample size is a major problem in doing research.

The Determination of Sample Size

Determination of sample size is influenced by two major factors: (1) the economics of the data-collection process, and (2) the need to make a decision efficiently, that is, having enough observations to make a decision. The reason for being concerned with sample size is quite simple. If sample

[7] See footnote 6.
[8] See Chapter 11 for discussion.
[9] Green and Tull, *op. cit.*

size is too small, the data resulting from the sample will have a large chance of showing the wrong result through random error, that is, the chance of drawing the "wrong" decision based on the data will be unacceptable. On the other hand, if too many respondents are included in the sample, money will be wasted because unnecessary data have been collected, that is, the extra data collected from extra subjects will not have a very significant probability of altering any decision based on the sample data. There are two basic ways then of making the sample size decision. One is by rule-of-thumb and the other is by some calculated method. The rule-of-thumb measure is widely used in industry.

Because the market research data-collection process costs several dollars per interview and it is often necessary to train interviewers very carefully, the typical market research agency often will not consider a sample size less than several hundred observations. The reason for this rule-of-thumb is that it does not pay to incur the interviewer training expenses on sample sizes of less than several hundred.[10] Under 1972 prices, the typical half-hour interview concerning a questionnaire may have a direct unit cost of approximately $7 per interview. In general, a sample size of several hundred persons guarantees two major results for the experimenter. The first of these is that the experimenter can test a large number of hypotheses, especially hypotheses concerning subgroups in the sample. The second major benefit is that these hypotheses can be tested at a high level of statistical significance. Thus, the economics of the interviewing situation preclude the use of formal analysis procedures for calculating exact sample size.

Another rule-of-thumb which is often used is that in order to do a stratified analysis, minimum strata sizes have to be set. Frequently, these minimum strata sizes are established at over 30 because of the central limit theorem.[11] The normal approximation to the binomial distribution allows several simplifying assumptions to be made and allows calculations of significance to be greatly simplified. Because analysis is simplified, minimum strata sizes are often specified in commercial research. The total sample size then is determined by the aggregation of the different strata.

The Calculation of Sample Size

It is possible to compute the lower limit of sample size in a rather simple fashion. However, this calculation ignores the risk or cost of error inherent in the decision associated with the market research task being designed. This is not a serious shortcoming if the cost of error of the research

---

[10] See Chapter 7, p. 253.

[11] The central limit theorem states that a linear combination of measurements from any monotonic distribution results in a normally distributed variable which greatly simplifies statistical analysis procedures. See Chapter 11 for details.

is hard to define. This is often the case where a company is studying consumer attitudes toward its product. It is very difficult to associate a cost curve with the attitude scale which emerges from the research; that is, it is very hard to calculate how much more costly a low attitude rating is versus a high attitude rating. If management can assign potential profits and losses to a research outcome, the mathematical technique in Chapter 14 should be used to calculate the amount of money to be spent in the sampling (and total research project for that matter).

An example of the marketing researcher making the "rule-of-thumb" *sample size computation* occurs where a survey is being undertaken to assess the effects of income on size of new car purchased among car drivers in Chicago. The researcher wishes to define three categories of income: Low— 0 to $10,000; medium—$10,001 to $20,000; and high—over $20,000. In addition, three types of cars are being considered: compacts such as the Datsun and Pinto, midsize cars such as the Maverick and Chevelle, and full-size cars such as the Ford LTD and Chevrolet Impala. The researcher constructs a hypothetical table:

Sample Size by Income and Car Type

Income	Small	Midsize	Large
Low	50	50	50
Medium	50	50	50
High	50	50	50
Total	150	150	150

The researcher realizes that if he draws a sample that is either simple random or stratified along income lines, the number of persons appearing in each cell will not equal exactly 50. However, if the expected value of each cell is 50, this will allow the researcher to meaningfully test his hypotheses with a considerable level of confidence. Fifty persons per cell is regarded as a "reasonable" number because it allows the statistical procedures used in following chapters to be effectively employed without seriously discrediting or violating the underlying assumptions.

Finding the proper sample size limit through computation can be done by setting confidence limits around the findings that are associated with the research. An example of this process is illustrated by the case of the politician who wishes to take a sample prior to an election. He is running against one opponent and thus must take over 50 percent of the vote to be the winner. Since the poll will be taken three days prior to election and will be used to make a decision as to whether or not more campaigning is necessary, he wants to be 99 percent confident of winning the election to justify not campaigning any further. His statistician begins with the standard formula for a confidence interval:

$$\frac{|\overline{X} - p|}{s} \geq C$$

where $\overline{X}$ is the mean value percentage from the poll, p is the theoretical key value 50 percent, s is the standard deviation of the research results, and C is the critical value associated with 0.99 confidence in the results.[12] The politician states that he will make the following decision. If the results show a winning margin of 52 percent or more, he will stop campaigning. Similarly, if he is losing with a 48 percent margin or less, he will stop campaigning. Thus, there are two possible meaningful outcomes so that a "two-tailed" test of significance must be calculated. From the discussion in Chapter 11 and the table of normal distribution values in the back of the book, the statistician finds a critical value, C, for 0.99/2 (the confidence divided by the number of "tails") of 2.58. For the binomial distribution, the standard deviation s is given by $[p \cdot (1 - p)/n]^{1/2}$ where p is 50 percent.[13] Since s is the only item in the calculation that is a function of the sample size n, the statistician explains that larger sample sizes increase the precision of the sample. The statistician completes the calculation to find the sample size:

$$\frac{0.52 - 0.50}{[p \cdot (1 - p)/n]^{1/2}} = 2.58$$

or

$$\frac{0.02}{2.58} = \left(\frac{0.25}{n}\right)^{1/2} = \frac{0.5}{n^{1/2}}$$

or

$$n = \left[\frac{2.58 \cdot 0.5}{0.02}\right]^2 = 4160 \text{ persons}$$

Thus, the politician must obtain a sample of at least 4160 persons to get the degree of confidence needed to make his decision. The same calculation can be used for the lower 48 percent case. If the interval is not symmetrical, the smaller of the intervals is used.

Summary

Sampling is an extremely useful tactic when the cost of analyzing all individual items in a long list is not feasible. The simplest strategy in sampling

[12] See Chapter 11, p. 431.
[13] Chapter 11, p. 428.

is to assemble a list of the entire population to be sampled and then randomly select a small number of items from the list for analysis. Laymen are constantly surprised that a small sample can reliably predict the behaviors of large numbers of people. Market researchers typically select a small number of consumers to be analyzed and then project the results to a larger population. In so doing the researcher assumes that his sample is representative of the population and that systematic errors have not occurred. This chapter has attempted to outline various methods of sampling with discussion of the reasons that the researcher might choose each.

Questions and Exercises

1. You have taken a job with a TV station in Cleveland, Ohio. The station manager has decided to get an accurate count of the percentage of Cleveland TV sets which are daily tuned to his station at the following times: 9:05 A.M., 1:05 P.M., 6:05 P.M., and 8:05 P.M. Specify as exactly as you can how such a sample should be performed. Should the sample be performed in one entire week or cover an extended period of time? Should the sample be performed when the new programs are introduced on the network or some time afterward?

2. You have been hired to find out how much catsup is sold by the various chain food stores in Indianapolis, Indiana. Your boss wishes to know if there is a difference in the way each of the four chains (A, B, C, D) handle special catsup displays. Specifically, he wishes to know if any chain generates more sales through special displays than the others. If so, the other chains will be asked to adopt the same methods. Design a sampling method which specifies when and how the various chain food stores will be used for data collection concerning displays and sales.

3. How large a sample size is required to distinguish between a market share nationally of 25 percent and a sample reading of 30 percent to guarantee a result and the 90 percent confidence level?

4. How big a sample is required to distinguish a sample reading which says that housewives buy detergent 3.2 times a month from a national average of 2.7? The standard deviation of the sample is 0.8. The level of confidence is 99 percent. [*Hint*: See test in Chapter 11.]

5. Is the systematic sample the same, in mathematical terms, as the simple random sample, that is, will they result in the same probability of picking a given respondent?

6. Referring to Chapter 4, the section on research designs, and Figure 10.1, which sampling method is most suitable for each of the designs?

Make a table for your own reference which cross references both tables.

7. Referring to disproportionate or weighted samples in Figure 10.1, prove that the sampling error goes up as the square of the weighting factor.

8. Discuss the reasons why cluster sampling should be a very popular method.

9. Examine Table 10.1 and Figure 10.2. Add the first and second number together, the third and fourth, the fifth and sixth, and so on. Then create plots similar to those in Figure 10.2. Why is the resulting plot bell-shaped?

10. Does Exercise 9 suggest something about the process of taking sequential or multistage samples?

11. What is the average value of the data in Table 10.1?

12. What is the median or middle value?

Project Related Questions

1. What sampling technique have you selected? State specifically the advantages and disadvantages of this technique. Why is it best suited to your project? What biases are present? How could these biases affect the interpretation of your data?

2. How are you going to implement the chosen technique? What list of persons or organizations are you going to use? How did you find this list? What other means of locating respondents are you using?

3. What minimum sample size do you feel is necessary for generalizing to the larger population?

4. In what ways might your sample differ from the population they are supposed to represent?

Boyington Research Agency

The Boyington Research Agency serviced a substantial number of large manufacturers and advertising agencies on a variety of research inquiries. While the agency performed a great many different research activities for its clients, it specialized in national consumer surveys.

For one of these projects to determine the characteristics of users and potential users of a prepared food product, the agency drew a national probability sample of 25,000 households. A general description of this sample follows.

The sample was allocated proportionately among the four main census geographic regions. The Census of Population served as the basis for allocating the sample. The sampling universe consisted of all households within the continental United States. Thus, persons residing in quasi-households (transient hotels, institutions, military camps, etc.) were not included in this plan.

Within each region the sample was stratified by metropolitan versus nonmetropolitan counties. All metropolitan areas as defined by the census were included in the sample. Where metropolitan areas extend across state lines and into another region, the entire area was assigned to only one region. The basis of allocation was the relative amount of the area's population contained in each of the two regions. Whichever region had the largest share received credit for the entire area.

The 25,000 households were assigned on a proportionate basis to the two strata indicated above. Within each of the metropolitan counties the sample was again allocated on a proportionate basis. For example, the metropolitan Chicago area represented 5.9 percent of the population residing within all metropolitan areas and thus 5.9 percent (874 households) of this part of the sample was allocated to this area. Cook County contained 81 percent of this area's population and so 708 households were assigned to it.

Within each region it was decided to select approximately 50 nonmetropolitan counties. These 50 were selected on a probability proportionate

SOURCE: Reprinted with permission from H. Boyd and R. Westfall, *Marketing Research: Text and Cases*, 3rd ed., pp. 442–445; 436–440, Homewood, Ill.: Richard D. Irwin, Inc., 1972.

to population basis. The procedure was as follows:

1. The population for all nonmetropolitan counties was totaled for each region.
2. This total was divided by 50. Those counties which had a population greater than the resulting quotient automatically were included in the sample.
3. All nonmetropolitan counties having a population of less than 1/50 of the total were then listed by states. The sample selection was made by using 1/50 of the total as the sampling interval. The list was entered at random. A simplified example of this procedure follows:

Assume a situation in which it is desired to select five counties from the following list of thirteen Wisconsin counties.

County	Population
Washburn	11,665
Forest	9,437
Dunn	27,341
Pepin	7,462
Pierce	21,448
Sawyer	10,323
Rusk	16,790
Bayfield	13,760
Eau Claire	54,187
Price	16,344
Taylor	18,456
Clark	32,459
Ashland	19,461
Total	259,133

The sampling interval would be 259,-133 ÷ 5 or 51,826. Eau Claire County comes in with certainty since its population is larger than the sampling interval. This county is then deleted from the list and the remaining twelve counties listed and their populations cumulated as follows.

County	Population	Cumulated Population
Washburn	11,665	11,665
Forest	9,437	21,102
Dunn	27,341	48,443
Pepin	7,462	55,905
Pierce	21,448	77,353
Sawyer	10,323	87,676
Rusk	16,790	104,466
Bayfield	13,760	118,226
Price	16,344	134,570
Taylor	18,456	153,026
Clark	32,459	185,485
Ashland	19,461	204,946

This list is entered at random by selecting a random number between 1 and 51,826—say 23,121. The sampling interval of 51,826 is added to the random number start and cumulated through the rest of the list. The four counties of Dunn (23,121), Pierce (74,947), Price (126,773), and Clark (178,549) are selected in this manner.

SELECTION OF PLACES WITHIN METROPOLITAN COUNTIES

The sample size allocated to each metropolitan county was determined by the proportion of its population weight to the total U.S. metropolitan population. Within each county a total of three places was desired. These were selected with a probability proportionate to population in the same fashion as were counties. The "within-place" sampling rate was determined by the relative importance of the place. For example, assume that the following three towns were selected from DuPage County in Illinois.

| Town or City | Population | |
	Number	Percent
Downers Grove	11,900	27.8
Elmhurst	21,200	49.7
Glen Ellyn	9,500	22.5
Total	42,600	100.0

DuPage County had 2.8 percent of the population of the Chicago metropolitan area which was assigned a sample of 874 (see earlier discussion). A sample of 24 was allocated to Du-Page County (2.8 percent of 874). These 24 would be distributed among the three towns or cities in proportion to their relative population: Downers Grove would receive 7, Elmhurst 12, and Glen Ellyn 5.

SELECTION OF PLACES WITHIN NONMETROPOLITAN COUNTIES

The sample size allocated to each nonmetropolitan county is determined on the basis of the relative importance of that county in population to the total of all sample nonmetropolitan counties in the region. If a sample county had 4 percent of this population, then 4 percent of the region's nonmetropolitan sample would be allocated to that county.

The selection of the three places within each county was handled in a manner analogous to the selection of places within metropolitan counties. The "within-place" sample size was also determined in a similar fashion.

SELECTION OF BLOCKS

The average number of interviews per block for any given survey was set at two. Since the sample size for the place had already been established, the number of sample blocks was determined by dividing the sample size by two. Thus, if the sample size were one hundred, the number of blocks to be selected would be fifty.

Blocks were selected with equal probability; that is, each block had the same chance of being selected as any other block regardless of its size (number of dwelling units). A listing of all blocks within the place was obtained and each block was assigned a number. The total number of blocks was divided by the sample size desired to obtain the sampling interval. The list was entered at random through the use of a random number which identified the first sample block. The sampling interval was next added to the random number and the total identified the second sample block, and so on. For example, if there were 100 blocks within a place and 25 were to be selected for the sample, then the sampling interval would be four (100 ÷ 25). A random number between 1 and 4, taken from a table of random numbers, might be 3. Then the 3rd, 7th, 11th, 15th, 19th, 23rd, etc., blocks on the list would be included in the sample.

All households within the sample blocks were enumerated and the sample households selected by establishing a sampling interval, entering the list at random, and cumulating through the list in a manner similar to the way blocks were selected.

In order to obtain block listings it was necessary to obtain maps from any possible source such as city clerks, assessors, police departments, commercial map firms, and the Bureau of the Census. For open county segments (small rural towns and farm areas) it was not possible to obtain a block listing and, therefore, there was no alternative but to require that all dwelling units within the specified area be enumerated. From this listing the desired number to be included in the sample was obtained by using a

sampling interval after a random number start.

QUESTIONS

1. What was the reasoning behind selecting counties and cities or towns on a probability-proportionate-to-population basis?
2. Why were blocks within cities selected on an equal probability basis?
3. Did the sample design employ proper stratification?
4. Is the final sample a true probability sample, i.e., does every household in the United States have an equal and/or known chance for selection?

Haywood Company

The Haywood Company was a large meat packer which sold fresh, cured, and canned meats. The company sold its fresh meats regionally, but its cured and canned meat products were sold nationally. The sales manager of the cured meat division authorized the company's research department to undertake a national survey to determine consumer attitudes toward bacon.

After numerous conferences with personnel of the sales division, the advertising department, and the advertising agency, the research director formulated the objectives of the study as follows:

1. To provide data on the relative rankings of reasons for consuming bacon at breakfast.
2. To provide a classification of consumers into motivational types with regard to the use of bacon in general and the Haywood brand in particular.
3. To provide data on the state of consumer information and misinformation about bacon as a meat product with special reference to the direction of misinformation (i.e., is misinformation favorable or unfavorable) and the existence of fallacies.
4. To determine what stereotypes con-

sumers have of those individuals who eat bacon and those who don't.

These objectives were to be sought for the entire United States. In addition, it was planned to analyze several subgroups such as those who eat various quantities of bacon, different sexes, geographic regions, city size, type of work done, presence of children in the home, and income. Where appropriate further analyses would be made, for example, consumption groups might be analyzed *within* age groups or city size groups.

The problem of designing the sample was assigned to the department's statistician. Working from the above stated objectives, he recommended the use of a disproportionate quota sample in which interviewers would be restricted to areas selected on a probability basis. He decided that a total of 96 cells would be required as follows: three age groups within two sex groups within four city size groups within four geographic regions. He estimated that a total sample size of about 2,400 would be required and that this number of interviews should

SOURCE: Reprinted with permission from Boyd and Westfall's *Marketing Research: Text and Cases*, Third Edition, Homewood, Ill.: Richard D. Irwin, Inc., 1972, p. 436–440.

406

EXHIBIT 1

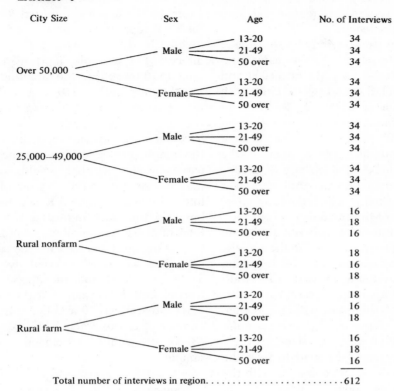

City Size	Sex	Age	No. of Interviews
Over 50,000	Male	13-20	34
		21-49	34
		50 over	34
	Female	13-20	34
		21-49	34
		50 over	34
25,000–49,000	Male	13-20	34
		21-49	34
		50 over	34
	Female	13-20	34
		21-49	34
		50 over	34
Rural nonfarm	Male	13-20	16
		21-49	18
		50 over	16
	Female	13-20	18
		21-49	16
		50 over	18
Rural farm	Male	13-20	18
		21-49	16
		50 over	18
	Female	13-20	16
		21-49	18
		50 over	16

Total number of interviews in region. 612

be divided equally among the four regions. The breakdown within a typical region would, therefore, be as shown in Exhibit 1.

The statistician stated this number of cells and the number of interviews assigned to each would permit an analysis of the following major groups:

I. Age
  1. Unmarried—13–20 years of age living at home
  2. Head of household—21–49 years of age
  3. Head of household—50 years and over

II. Sex
  1. Male
  2. Female

III. City size
  1. 50,000 and over
  2. 2,500–49,999
  3. Rural nonfarm
  4. Rural farm

IV. Region
  1. Northeast
  2. North central
  3. South
  4. West

In addition, the sample was designed to permit analyses such as age within sex, city size and region; sex within city size and region; and city size within region.

Within each region the statistician planned to select eighteen major sampling points—six cities of 50,000 and over population and twelve cities with population of 2,500–49,999. Close to each of the latter cities a town of less than 2,500 was to be selected as a minor sampling point. Also in the neighborhood of each city of 2,500–49,999 population, a rural area was to be selected in which the farm interviews were to be made.

The statistician did not designate the cities to be included in the sample. He recommended that the following selection criteria be used: (1) availability of a good interviewer, (2) dispersion of the cities within a region, and (3) dispersion by size (population) within the city size class. He stated he would be glad to pick the sample cities after conferring with the interviewing agency chosen to do the field work.

The within-place sampling plan for cities of 50,000 and over population called for a selection of census tracts, then a selection of blocks within tracts, and finally a selection of dwelling units within blocks. Since 34 interviews were required in each of these cities and no more than two persons per block were to be interviewed, 17 blocks were to be chosen. The selection procedure was as follows.

Census Tracts

All tracts within a single city were to be listed and numbered consecutively. Since one block and only one block was to be chosen within a tract, a total of 17 tracts was required. Thus, the total number of tracts was to be divided by 17 to provide a sampling interval. For example, if a city contained 170 tracts then the sampling interval would be 10 (170 ÷ 17). The list of tracts would be entered with the use of a random number chosen between one and the upper limit of the sampling interval. The tract designated by this number would come into the sample. Next, the sampling interval would be added to this number and the tract indicated by the total of these two numbers would be the second tract selected for the sample. The sampling interval would again be added and the applicable tract chosen. For example, if the sampling interval was 10 and the random number 3, census tracts 3, 13, 23, 33, 43, 53, etc. would be included in the sample.

Blocks

Within each sample tract it would be necessary to select one block. This was to be accomplished in a manner somewhat similar to that used to select the census tracts, that is, all blocks would be listed and a random number selected between one and the upper limit of the blocks present. This number would identify the sample block. For example, if there were 100 blocks then a random number between 1 and 100 would be chosen.

Commercial blocks were excluded from the block listings. For each block chosen for the sample, the statistician recommended that two contiguous alternate blocks be selected. If the number of interviews assigned to a specific block could not be accomplished, the interviewer would be instructed to go to the first alternate block to complete her work and, if this failed, to proceed to the second alternate. Interviewers were to be told to start at the northwest corner of the block and travel around the block in a clockwise fashion. The starting point within the block was to be determined by selecting a random number between the total number of dwelling units (from the Census of Population) divided by two. For example, if 60 dwelling units were located on the block, a random number between 1 and 30 would be selected—say 12. Starting from the northwest corner the interviewer would count off 11 dwelling units and attempt to interview the 12th, 13th, 14th, etc., until the necessary two respondents had been interviewed.

Each interviewer was to be assigned a quota. The quota would call for half the interviews to be conducted with men and half with women. Within each of these cells the interviews were to be divided equally between the three age groups. Interviewers were not given a quota within any specific block, but rather for their entire assignment.

In cities of 2,500–49,999 population, block statistics were not available and the plan called for obtaining block maps from each city. These were to be "gridded" and the sections so indicated to be treated as census tracts. The procedure from this point on was identical to that recommended for use

in the 50,000 and over population cities.

For the rural nonfarm towns (those of 2,500 and under), it would again be necessary to obtain maps. From the map of each city four blocks would be selected at random. The interviewer would call on all households in these blocks until she obtained her quota. No limit was to be set on the number obtained in any one block.

To select the rural farm quota, maps would again be used. Routes would be drawn on this map and a starting point indicated. All farms on both sides of the route were to be interviewed until the quota was obtained.

The statistician stated that, if this sample design were acceptable, he would work with the interviewing agency to implement it and would be responsible for assigning the quotas to the individual interviewers as well as for drawing up the applicable interviewer instructions.

QUESTIONS

1. How was the sample size determined? Could any improvements be made?
2. Do you agree with the way in which the sample was allocated among the various cells? Discuss.
3. Would the results from this sample give an accurate picture of the entire United States? If not, could the results be adjusted to provide an accurate measure?
4. Would the method of selecting the sample result in any biases?

State Farm Mutual Automobile Insurance Company
Sampling from a Listed Population

After the State Farm Company had located and opened its first claims drive-in stations in the Chicago area, policyholders' reactions and the efficiency and cost of station operation were observed. Immediate results were so favorable that the company determined to establish drive-in stations in other metropolises. A top-priority area was the Metropolitan San Francisco division, with headquarters in Berkeley.

In order to provide the Pacific region with the benefit of the Chicago experience, an operations man of the Metropolitan Illinois division was transferred to Berkeley. To conduct the underlying research, Milton Walz of the central operations control staff in Bloomington was also dispatched to devote a few weeks to arranging the San Francisco area study. One of his tasks was administering the sampling of policyholders.

POPULATION AND FRAME

The portion of the study relating to policyholders had two initial purposes: (1) to map the numbers of policyholders located in various areas within the total division; (2) to conduct a telephone survey of policyholders to test alternative locations that might be convenient to a maximum of those submitting claims. These alternatives would be indicated by analyses of traffic trends, claims volume, and radii of consumers' shopping habits (similar to the Chicago studies).

The members of the population obviously would comprise all holders of State Farm automobile casualty policies on the date of sampling. The area concerned would be the entire Metropolitan San Francisco, which was coterminous with the United States Census definition of that standard metropolitan statistical area and included the five counties of Alameda, Contra Costa, Marin, San Francisco, and San Mateo. This area had just passed the 3,000,000 mark in population and was increasing around 2 per cent per year. The number of State Farm automobile policyholders exceeded 150,000, so large a number that their total inclusion in the study would be absurd. Therefore, sampling was indicated.

This entire population could be found in the division's policyholder

SOURCE: David J. Luck, Hugh G. Wales, and Donald A. Taylor, *Marketing Research*, Third edition © 1971, pp. 248–253. Reprinted by permission of Prentice-Hall, Inc., Englewood Cliffs, New Jersey.

records. Every policy was described on a card, whose data included the policyholder's post office, street and town address, name, telephone number, and the State Farm supervisory district of the agent. These cards were filed consecutively by policy number in drawers. These numbers were sequenced by the date when State Farm approved the insurance application. Agents frequently would cumulate applications to the end of a week before sending the batch to Berkeley, which meant that a dozen or more consecutive numbers might be clustered by a single agent's area.

SAMPLE DESIGN

Mr. Walz felt that stratification of the population prior to drawing the sample would have no virtues. A proportionate representation of all sorts of policyholders in the division was desired, and with the entire population equally available, there would be neither potential sampling error nor effort avoided through placing the population in strata. On the other hand, since the policies dated back over one year (a new number being assigned at each annual renewal) and were apt to be clustered by agent, any possible distortion owing to timing or clustering should be guarded against.

The selection methods considered were (1) ordinal, taking every Nth sampling unit, or (2) by random numbers. Ordinal selection would be feasible since the total population size was known and one could readily count and extract every Nth card. Yet this would be laborious and subject to error. Use of random numbers not only

was recognized as usually the most scientific method, but it would be easy to riffle through the cards to find, if 426 were a chosen number, policies whose last digits were . . . 426. The random numbers method was chosen.

SAMPLE SIZE

The selection would manifestly be random, and so the needed size could be determined from a table based on pure probabilities. First, though, the desired confidence limits must be specified. Mr. Walz and a colleague at Bloomington pondered this question and decided to choose a 95 per cent confidence level (that is, that the sample probably would not vary from the true characteristics of the population by more than a specified margin in 95 out of 100 chances). This particular confidence was becoming so widely used in sampling that it was something of a convention.

The next decision was the specified error that would be allowable (within 95 per cent certainty). This raised the question of what aspect or parameter of the population they were most concerned with measuring. This parameter was stipulated to be the home location of the policyholders. They decided that a 3 per cent reliability limit tentatively would be chosen (that is, that the sample's measurement of home locations would not vary by more than 3 per cent from the actual locations of all State Farm policyholders in each area, at a 95 per cent confidence level).

Let us digress to explain what Mr. Walz meant by "home location." These were relatively small areas within the total metropolitan area, and he wished to map the approximate number of State Farm policyholders in each. To choose these areas, he could utilize the work of the Bureau of the Census tracts, within which its facts were gathered and analyzed. The use of these recognized areas rendered possible the employment of Census data with that acquired in the survey.

The number of tracts was too large, however, as he did not need to pinpoint locations that finely. For example, there were over 120 tracts in the city of San Francisco alone, whose populations ranged from around 1,000 to 22,000. Mr. Walz, therefore, grouped these into seventeen areas in that city. For relatively small places, such as Mill Valley, he used the town as an area. Outside of towns he used the established Census county districts. Altogether he defined eighty areas within the division.

Now he could proceed to decide the sample size required. As the computed results of confidence limits of specific sample sizes were already available in published tables, he

needed only to look up the appropriate table in such a printed collection, which was in his library.

Because the total population was finite in size (150,000), the size of sample would in some degree depend on the population size. A portion of the table utilized is shown in Table 1.

This table, which relates to a 50 per cent frequency of occurrence, was used for the sake of conservatism, although other frequencies of occurrence call for smaller samples.

Note in this table that a sample size of 1,056 is indicated, for a population nearest 100,000 and a reliability of 3 per cent. Therefore, Mr. Walz chose this size. Mr. Walz also considered that a sample of approximately 1,200 had produced satisfactory measurements in the Chicago research and that the San Francisco area's population was less than half the Chicago area's.

COLLECTION OF SAMPLE

Mr. Walz now addressed the task of collecting the sample of policy-

TABLE 1   *Table of Sample Sizes Required for Finite Populations for Selected Confidence Levels and Various Sample Reliability Limits for Sampling Attributes. 95 Per Cent Confidence Level. Per Cent in Population Assumed to be 50 Per Cent Frequency*

Size of Population	Sample Size for Reliability of				
	±1%	±2%	±3%	±4%	±5%
1,000	—	—	—	375	278
2,000	—	—	696	462	322
50,000	8057	2291	1045	593	381
100,000	8763	2345	1056	597	383
500,000 to infinity	9423	2390	1065	600	384

holder's cars from the file drawers. This would be done in the evening, after the regular clerical work was over, so that none of the cards would be missing from the drawers while clerks worked on them.

The file drawers each contained approximately 1,000 policy cards, in 150 drawers. If seven were chosen from each drawer, then 1,050 would be obtained. As these were to be obtained by random number, he consulted the table of random numbers provided in the same handbook from which he had determined sample size. A portion of that table is shown in Table 2.

With this table the sample was easily chosen at random. Mr. Walz needed to use only the numbers under column 1–4. As he needed only seven selections per drawer, each with not more than 1,000 items, he used the last three digits in columns 1–4 and the first seven sets of numbers, beginning by choosing from a drawer a policy whose number ended in 315.

Some variation in the number of cards per drawer was found, but only a few slightly exceeded 1,000. Several drawers, however, had fewer than 900 cards, so the selection produced only 1,030 cards. To remedy this, the eighth number in the table (380) was used in the "short" drawers.

TEST OF SAMPLING METHOD

To be more certain that his method would have the desired sample precision, Mr. Walz decided to try it on a smaller area. Cities in the north of Santa Clara County, which adjoins the Metropolitan San Francisco district, were so convenient to population centers in San Mateo County that a drive-in claims center on the Peninsula might well serve them too. He therefore decided to add that section and use it for his test.

The test would show the practicality and cost of the technique. More importantly, in that limited area the effort of checking the obtained sample against a complete allocation of all

TABLE 2 *Table of Random Numbers (8,000 numbers), First Thousand*

	1–4	5–8	9–12	13–16	17–20	21–24	25–
1	23 15	75 48	59 01	83 72			
2	05 54	55 50	43 10				
3	14 87	16 03					
4	38 97	67 49					
5	97 31	26 17					
6	11 74						
7	43 36						
8	93 80						
9	49 54						
10	36 76						
11	07 09						

Source: H. Arkin and R. R. Colton, *Tables for Statisticians* (New York: Barnes & Noble, Inc., 1964), p. 159.

the policyholders (numbering around 6,000) would not be prohibitive. Since there would be only four groupings of Census tracts in northern Santa Clara, the job of allocating policies to tracts would be vastly simpler than for the eighty groupings in the San Francisco area.

Using the same ratio to total population expected to be used in the San Francisco area, one in 142, his clerks selected forty-two names. These were allocated to the tract groups, and the numbers recorded. Then the whole 6,000 were so allocated. As one validation, the proportion who had comprehensive coverage in their policies was compared between the sample and the full enumeration. The former turned out to be 88.1 per cent and the latter 86.1. This obviously fell within the 3 per cent allowable error.

In terms of accuracy of estimating the number of policyholders in each tract grouping, the error was relatively greater. At the worst, in the Los Altos grouping the sample had eight names (19 per cent of the sample), whereas the total count found that 15 per cent of the policyholders were in that area. Although this slightly exceeded the 3 per cent error range that has been allowable, Mr. Walz observed that in this small sample test population of only 5,000 policyholders one would not expect the precision to be found in the large sample of 1,056 to be taken from the whole San Francisco area. Indeed, he

was encouraged that the variations in the pilot sample were so small. He then ordered the main sampling work to proceed as planned.

DISCUSSION

1. When Mr. Walz was explaining how the policyholders should be selected from the files, Mrs. Blank, the office supervisor, raised this question: "Why go to all this trouble? With 150 drawers to choose from, you ought to get all the randomness you need by simply taking the first seven from each drawer." What should Mr. Walz reply?

2. The drive-in claims stations, whose location was the purpose of the study, would serve car owners who had damage claims covered by State Farm policies. In the light of this, appraise the population definition and sampling plan that Mr. Walz adopted.

3. Suppose that in the trial sampling in Santa Clara County, the sample indicated that Los Altos had 24 per cent of the test area's policyholders, whereas the actual was determined to be 15 per cent. Would this mean that probability was not operative in the sampling method?

4. If the survey was going to be conducted by personal interviews, calling at respondents' homes, would the sampling plan have been appropriate? If not, how would you have changed it?

Chapter 11

Data Analysis: The Analysis of Individual Variables and Pairs of Variables[1]

Once the researcher has collected data as shown in Chapter 10, he must do some calculations which will lead him to draw conclusions about his model and his data. This process is usually performed in three stages. First, the researcher looks at the distribution of variables in terms of how many respondents voted on each response to a question in a questionnaire. The researcher then asks questions concerning one individual variable as it relates to other individual variables. Typically, this is done by creating tables which show these two-way relationships. In addition, the researcher may explore the correlation between two variables. These first two steps are discussed in this chapter. After the researcher explores the fundamental one-way and two-way relationships in his data, he can then perform more complicated analysis discussed in following chapters.

[1] This chapter was prepared in part by Carol A. Scott of Ohio State University.

Introduction

Once the field work is completed and the data has been collected, the researcher is ready to begin to analyze the data to see what information it contains and to interpret the meaning of that information as it relates to the purpose of the research project.[2] The field of statistics provides a variety of techniques which can be brought to bear in the analysis of data that has been quantified or represented by numbers. The discussion in this chapter will be centered around the use of statistical analysis in those cases where either an individual characteristic or a pair of characteristics is the subject of investigation.

Statistical analysis serves three major purposes: to describe the data at hand, test hypotheses, and make predictions or estimates. *Descriptive statistics* are used to reduce the data at hand to a smaller set of numbers or summary measures which represent the relevant information contained in the data. If we have observed every member of the group in which we are interested, that is, the *population*, these summary numbers are called *parameters*. If, however, we observe only a portion of the members, or a *sample*, these measures are termed *statistics*.

Frequently it is impossible or at best extremely expensive to obtain data on the entire population, but the scientist still wishes to know something about the characteristics of the population that his sample represents. *Inferential statistics* allows the researcher to make estimates, predictions, or judgments about the composition of the larger population on the basis of his sample data and the statistics computed from it. A statistic is only an estimate of a parameter, however, and will be subject to *sampling error* since only a selected portion of the population members have been observed. Thus, inferential techniques provide the means of estimation, and also provide a measure of the confidence that can be placed in them, that is, a statement of the *probability* or likelihood that our results are significantly different from chance expectations and are not due solely to the random fluctuations inherent in sampling procedures.

---

[2] Of course, consideration of the type of analysis that is desired is a major part of each of the previous stages in the research process. Here, however, we will be concerned with the actual manipulation of data.

The Concept of Hypothesis (or Model) Testing

The purpose of statistics for the marketer is ultimately to let the decision maker know if his model or set of hypotheses is right or wrong. In addition to helping the marketer evaluate his model, the statistics assign some level of certainty to the decision. This means that there are two aspects to evaluating the quality of a model; the first of these is the decision whether the model is supported by data and the second is the degree of confidence that can be associated with the "support" decision.

There are two kinds of errors that a decision maker can make when deciding whether his model is supported or not. These errors are known as alpha or Type I errors. Type I error is the acceptance of a model as being "correct" when in fact it is not true. Type II or beta error is defined as rejecting a model when in fact it is "correct." Social scientists routinely set their confidence concerning Type I error as being less than 0.05. This means that the social scientist will accept an "incorrect" model about 1 in 20 times he runs a given test. Similarly, probabilities of making Type II error are specified. The researcher realizes that increasing the probability of making Type I error decreases the probability of Type II error. It is this fact which stimulates the social scientist to use 0.05. A probability of 0.05 generally tends to minimize the chance of making either Type I or Type II error.

Another major concept of hypothesis testing is the *null* hypothesis. Typically, researchers state hypotheses in negative terms. An example might be:

> People who say they like product X will not purchase any more product X than those people who do not say so.

The underlying reason for using the null hypothesis approach is that the researcher "pretends" that the group he is sampling is homogeneous until the statistics tell him differently. When the statistics support the researcher's argument, he then says that his alternative hypothesis is not rejected. The researcher acts conservatively because he is never absolutely sure that his hypothesis is the only explanation of the occurrence he observed. All that he can say, logically, is that his null hypothesis was not supported.

The following sections of the chapter describe the fundamental parts of making the decision to accept or reject a null hypothesis. In order to make the decision, one must sample a population measuring certain variables, compute some statistics using the variables, infer something about the probability distributions which exist in the population, and finally make a decision based on the chance of making Type I and II errors.

Definition of Distribution

A second major element in statistical analysis is the array or listing of the values of the variable[3] for all observations, called the *distribution*. When

---

[3] See Chapter 5 for discussion and definition of variables.

the number of observations is large, however, such a distribution is unwieldy and relationships are difficult to see. Therefore, the scientist often condenses the data into what is known as a frequency distribution.

TABLE 11.1   *Number and Percentage of Customers Shopping at XYZ on March 4, 1971 Classified by Sex*

Sex	Number of Persons	Percentage
Female	100	40%
Male	150	60
Total	250	100%

TABLE 11.2   *Frequency and Percentage Distribution of Families in Sales Territory B Classified by Number of Children*

Number of Children	Number of Families	Percentage
0	15	5
1	36	12
2	120	40
3	90	30
4	30	10
5	9	3
Total	300	100

A *frequency distribution*[4] is merely a table in which the data have been grouped into classes and the number of cases falling into each group is shown. If the data being grouped are qualitative or quantitative and discrete, the number of observations can be expressed as proportions or percentages and the table is called a "relative frequency distribution." Tables 11.1 and 11.2 illustrate frequency distributions where simply the number of observations and proportions have been presented.

For continuous data, class intervals must be created and the observations grouped in this manner (see Table 11.3). Table 11.3 shows how sales for a product are distributed across dealers. If one were to examine the ungrouped data, he would have difficulty drawing a conclusion about the size of dealer volumes. However, by appropriate grouping, the distribution and segmentation become very clear.

[4] See Chapter 10 for an example of random sample and resulting frequency distribution.

TABLE 11.3 *Gross Sales for Franchised Dealerships of XYZ Corporation, January to March 1971 (in dollars)*

Gross Sales	Number of Dealers
50,000 and under 100,000	60
100,000 and under 150,000	75
150,000 and under 200,000	102
200,000 and under 250,000	6
250,000 and under 300,000	7
Total	250

Class limits must be precisely stated so that classification of observations is clear. If we are defining intervals of from 20 up to but not including 30, and 30 up to but not including 40, one can be sure how a value of 30 should be classified. The determination of the number and size of the interval is extremely important, since if too few classes are used, too much information about the original distribution is lost, while if too many intervals are used, the purpose of summarization is defeated and the frequency distribution is unwieldy and difficult to grasp.

Somewhere between the two extremes of a frequency distribution of one observation per class and of one class containing every observation, the researcher must find a means of adequately representing his data.[5] There may be logical breaks in the data which indicate natural intervals. Although there are some advantages to having equally spaced intervals, this type of presentation may not be possible for some data, or it may not be an adequate representation. In any case, the researcher must be careful to avoid imposing a pattern upon the data; by changing class limits the data may be made to look entirely different. More general rules for classification applicable to any kind of data are suggested by Kerlinger[6]:

1. Categories should be set up according to the research problem and purpose.
2. Categories must be exhaustive.
3. Categories must be mutually exclusive and independent.
4. Each category should be derived from one classification principle.
5. Any categorization scheme must be on one level of discourse.

[5] An excellent discussion on the construction of frequency distributions, class intervals, and number of classes is presented by Morris Hamburg, *Statistical Analysis for Decision Making* (New York: Harcourt, Brace, Jovanovich, 1970), pp. 138–149.
[6] Fred N. Kerlinger, *Foundations of Behavioral Research* (New York: Holt, Rinehart and Winston, 1964), p. 606.

The classifications must embrace each item of data (exhaustiveness), and must not overlap or influence classification of other types of data (mutually exclusive and independent). For clarity, only one rule of classification should apply to an observation at one time, and the one set of observations should be classified at a time. Frequency distributions are especially useful as presentation devices. The entire analysis can be based on the frequency distribution values to simplify computation, but if high-speed computers are available, the increased time required to process each score individually is of lesser importance.

Characterizing the Distribution: Commonly Used Statistics

Constructing a frequency distribution is one way to describe the original array of scores, but we can also compute (from the ungrouped or the grouped distribution) several statistics with known properties to indicate the behavior of the distribution of values. These statistics generally fall into two categories: (1) measures of central tendency, and (2) measures of dispersion or scatter.

Measures of Central Tendency

Several statistics can be computed to give an indication of the central tendency or average of the distribution. Each statistic utilizes certain pieces of information to present a particular aspect or fact about the array of values. Since each statistic attempts to characterize an entire distribution of values by a single number, information will be lost. Used and interpreted correctly, however, these statistics provide the researcher with a quick way to grasp some features of the distribution that might not be so obvious otherwise. The choice of which statistic to use depends on the question about the distribution the researcher asks. The most common measures are the median, the mode, and the mean. Since the mean is the most commonly computed measure and is by far the most heavily used in more advanced statistical tests, it will be discussed last.

The Median   When the values of the variable have been arranged in sequence from lowest to highest or vice versa, the midmost value in the distribution is the median. This is simply a benchmark which indicates a point such that half of the values are less than this point and half are greater. In Table 11.4, for example, one can see that the median of X, ungrouped data, is 100. In this example with an odd number of observations, the median value is clear. In the case of an even number of observations, the median is, by convention, the value halfway between the two central values. Medians can be calculated for grouped data as well. Halving the total number of observations (frequencies) tells one how many observations should be above and below the median.

TABLE 11.4   *Median of Ungrouped Data*

Observation	Value of X
X_1	40
X_2	50
X_3	90
X_4	100 (Median)
X_5	110
X_6	110
X_7	500
$n = 7$	
Median $= 100$	

The process is simply to add frequencies of classes to determine the class where the median lies and computing the value within that class which is the median. Table 11.5 illustrates this process. The median will be slightly over the value of 30. In order to reach exactly half of the observations (148), one must add a portion of the observations in the fifth class. The interval of the median class is $35 - 30 = 5$, so one must weight this interval by the proportion of additional observations needed, $5 \cdot [40/161] = 1.2$. Rounding and adding this value to 30, the median is found to be 31.

The Mode   The most frequently occurring value in a distribution of ungrouped data is called the mode, while for grouped distributions, the category with the largest number of items is called the modal class. In the latter case, a crude mode can be determined by taking the midpoint of the modal class. In Table 11.6(a) (using the same data as in Table 11.4), the mode is 110,

TABLE 11.5   *Median of Grouped Data*

Age	Number f	Cumulative Number f
Under 18	25	25
18 and under 21	19	44
21 and under 25	24	68
25 and under 30	40	108
30 and under 35	53	161 (Median class)
35 and under 40	45	206
40 and under 50	60	266
50 and over	30	296
Total	296	

TABLE 11.6   *Mode of Ungrouped and Grouped Data*

(a) Ungrouped	
Observation	*Value of X*
X_1	40
X_2	50
X_3	90
X_4	100
X_5	110 ⎫ Modal Value
X_6	110 ⎭
X_7	500
$n = 7$	
Mode = 110	

(b) Grouped
*Total Annual Income of Residents of
Orange County, Missouri, 1971
(in thousands of dollars)*

Income	*Number* *f*	
Under 3000	550	
3,000 and under 6,000	675	
6,000 and under 10,000	928	
10,000 and under 15,000	1330	(Modal class)
15,000 and under 20,000	849	
20,000 and under 30,000	515	
30,000 and under 50,000	80	
50,000 and over	73	
Total	5000	

Crude mode $12,500

since that value occurs twice while the other values occur only once. In Table 11.6(b) we see that the modal class is the class from $10,000 to $15,000, and the crude mode is $12,500.

The mode is easily and quickly computed, and may easily be interpreted for qualitative data. Since it is the most frequently observed value, it may indeed be most representative of the distribution, especially in those distributions where observations are heavily clustered at one value or in one class. However, its nonmathematical quality makes it liable to the same limitation that is applicable to the median in this respect. The modal value is also not very stable, since changing the boundaries of one interval may change it entirely. In small samples, it is possible that no two values are identical, in which case there is no mode. In other samples, there may be two or more values which occur with the same frequency (bimodal distribution), and therefore neither of these values would be an indication of central tendency. However, the characteristic of bimodality may indicate that important factors unknown to the investigator are at work.[7]

The Mean   The most commonly used summary statistic is the *arithmetic mean* or average. As its name implies, this measure is merely the sum of all values of the variable divided by the number of values or observations. Thus, the formula for the arithmetic mean is

$$\overline{X} = \frac{\sum\limits_{i=1}^{n} X_i}{n}$$

The symbol $\overline{X}$ denotes a sample mean, while the Greek letter μ indicates the mean of a population. In a similar fashion, N denotes the number of observations in a population and n refers to the number of observations in a sample. X_i in the formula merely denotes the ith value of the variable X. For a population mean, we would write

$$\mu = \frac{\sum\limits_{i=1}^{N} X_i}{N}$$

Then, using grouped data, the mean is computed by

$$\overline{X} = \frac{\sum\limits_{i=1}^{n} f_i \cdot m_i}{n} \qquad \text{or} \qquad \mu = \frac{\sum\limits_{i=1}^{N} f_i \cdot m_i}{N}$$

where f_i = frequency of the ith class; m_i = the midpoint of the ith class interval; and N, n = the total number of observations in the population or sample. An example of this is shown in Table 11.7.

The most important feature of the arithmetic mean is that the sum of the differences between each observation and the mean, or the deviations from the mean, are always zero. That is, the sum of the deviations in the negative direction will always be equal to the sum of the deviations in the positive direction. In this sense, it is a measure of centrality. Since it is rigidly defined in a mathematical way, the arithmetic mean can be utilized in a number of situations, not the least of which is in more advanced statistical tests. The

---

[7] This point of view is expressed by Kerlinger, *op. cit.*, p. 612. For a complete description of the mode and its properties, however, see Hamburg, *op. cit.*, pp. 175–178.

TABLE 11.7 *Arithmetic Mean for Grouped Data; Annual Sales of Small Retail Establishments in Sales Region A, 1971*

Dollar Sales	Number f_i	Midpoint	$(f_i) \cdot Midpoint$
15,000 and under 20,000	14	17,500	245,000
20,000 and under 25,000	25	22,500	562,500
25,000 and under 30,000	30	27,500	825,000
30,000 and under 35,000	21	32,500	682,500
35,000 and under 40,000	10	37,500	375,000
Total	100		2,690,000

$$\overline{X} = 2{,}690{,}000/100 = \$26{,}900$$

arithmetic mean is suitable for analyzing cardinal data (Chapter 6 contains definitions of data types including nominal, ordinal, and cardinal).

Measures of Dispersion

Measures of dispersion indicate the scatter of the observations about an average. Some measures of scatter are characterized by the fact that the statistic computed is in the same unit of measurement as the data from which they are obtained, and are therefore termed measures of *absolute dispersion*. If the data are expressed in dollars, in ounces, in apples, or oranges, the absolute dispersion measure is in dollars, ounces, apples, or oranges. Thus, these measures cannot be used to compare distributions which differ either in size or in units. *Relative measures of dispersion,* on the other hand, indicate scatter as some percentage of the average about which they are computed and can be used to compare distributions. Measures of absolute dispersion include the range, the interquartile range, the quartile deviation, the average (mean) deviation, and the variance and standard deviation. This chapter will discuss only two of these, the range and the variance (or standard deviation) since these are the ones most commonly used. The coefficient of variation is a measure of relative dispersion, and is the only such measure discussed here.

The range is the simplest of all measures, but provides little information. This measure can be expressed in two ways: (1) as the difference between the largest and the smallest value in the distribution, or (2) as the largest and smallest values themselves. For example, if the weekly salaries of five salesmen were $200, $215, $220, $230, and $400, the range could be expressed as either $200, or as $200 to $400 per month. The difficulty with maximum-minimum difference is that it tells us nothing about what values lie between the largest and smallest figure. If the mean were also given (in this case the mean is $253), however, the range at least gives us some indication of the breadth of the values. However, the mean tends to be "pulled" in the direction of extreme values.

The variance and the standard deviation are more difficult to compute, but tell far more about the distribution especially when the empirical distribution can be related to one of the common sampling distributions to be discussed later. The variance is computed in absolute rather than relative terms. The variance is a measure of variability of a specified measure and is defined as the average of the squared deviations of the observations from the mean of the distribution.

A population variance is denoted by the letter sigma with the square notation σ^2, while the variance of a sample is denoted by the letter S^2. Thus, the general formula for the variance is

$$\sigma^2 = \frac{\sum\limits_{i=1}^{N} (X_i - \mu)^2}{N} \quad \text{or} \quad S^2 = \frac{\sum\limits_{i=1}^{n} (X_i - \overline{X})^2}{n}$$

Squaring the deviations simply removes the effect of the signs of the deviations and weights observations distant from the mean more than those which are close to the mean. Although it does indicate the extent of variability, the variance is expressed in units which are the squares of the original units. Therefore, in order to get the measure in a form which denotes variability in the original units, and is thus easier to interpret, we simply take the square root of the variance, which is called the *standard deviation*. For a simple example to demonstrate these calculations, the mean, variance, and standard deviation is computed for five salesmen and their salaries in Table 11.8. From the table it can be seen that the variance is 5496 and the standard deviation is $74.13.

TABLE 11.8   *Variance and Standard Deviation Salaries of Five Salesmen of Alpha Company*

Salesman	Salary X	$(X - \overline{X})$	$(X - \overline{X})^2$
A	200	−53	2809
B	215	−38	1444
C	220	−33	1089
D	230	−23	529
E	400	+147	21,609
Total	1265	0	27,480

$n = 5$

$\overline{X} = 253$

$S^2 = \dfrac{27,480}{5} = 5496$

$S = \sqrt{5496} = \text{approx. } \$74.13$

A convenient way to characterize scores is to express them in terms of standard deviations. For example, the salary of salesman E lies almost two standard deviations above the mean [253 + 2(74.13) = 401.26] while the other salaries all lie less than one standard deviation below the mean.

The coefficient of variation, a relative measure of dispersion denoted here by V, is obtained by expressing the standard deviation as a percentage of the arithmetic mean. The formula is

$$V = \frac{S}{\overline{X}} \quad \text{or} \quad V = \frac{\sigma}{\mu}$$

Thus, in the example of salesmen's salaries where the mean is $253 and the standard deviation is $74.13, the coefficient of variation is 0.293 or 29.3 percent. Suppose that the researcher took another sample of five salaries and found that the mean of the new sample was also $253, but that the coefficient of variation was 52.4 percent. By comparing the two relative measures, one could conclude that the salaries of the first sample were more uniform than those in the second. In the later sample, the salaries must vary more than the first group.

Now that the most commonly used statistics have been presented, we are ready to discuss some of the most frequently used sampling distributions and their properties. Some of their characteristics can be described by the behavior of their parameters.

The Analysis of One Variable

For some research purposes only one characteristic of the members of the sample may be relevant. By using the appropriate techniques of analysis, the researcher can obtain quite a bit of information about his sample along this one dimension and can compare the results of his analysis of two or more samples. This section will discuss some of the more common statistical techniques for analyzing one variable from one or two samples. The comparison of three or more samples is accomplished by using a somewhat different approach, and, therefore, this problem will be given a section of its own, namely, analysis of variance.

The Binomial Distribution

The binomial distribution, based on the concept of Bernoulli trials, is useful for the analysis of one variable, provided that the variable is discrete and dichotomous, which simply means that there are two possible values of the variable, both of which are expressed as integers. Thus, this distribution is appropriate for those cases in which interest is focused on the number, percent, a proportion of observations falling into either of two categories, such as male-female, favorable response-unfavorable response, under or equal to 35 years of age and over 35 years of age, and so on.

Several other conditions must also be met, however. The values must be mutually exclusive and independent, which means that the variable can take on *at most* one value, and the value of one element of the sample must not affect the value assigned to any other element. One must know or be able to estimate the probability of the chance occurrence of one of the values (thus, the probability of the alternative value is also known since the sum of the two must be equal to one), and this probability must remain constant from respondent to respondent. Further, sample elements must be chosen at random, that is, each element of the population has an equal chance of being selected.[8]

For simplicity of discussion, one of the alternative outcome values will be designated a "success" and the other a "failure." Further, one can denote the drawing of n elements for a sample as n trials, the probability of success in one trial by p, and the probability of failure in one trial by $1 - p$ or q. The binomial probability density function, a rule for assigning probabilities, allows one to compute the probability P of obtaining exactly r successes in n trials, for a specific p, and expressed mathematically as

$$P(r \mid n, p) = \binom{n}{r} \, p^r \cdot q^{1-r} = \left(\frac{n!}{r! \, (n-r)!} \right) \cdot p^r \cdot q^{1-r}$$

From this general formula, then, we can derive a whole family of probability distributions, one for each combination of n and p. Each probability distribution simply lists every possible number of successes, 1, 2, 3, . . . , n, and the probability of their occurrence by chance. Fortunately, one need not calculate these by hand, but can merely refer to tables of the binomial probability distribution found in almost any statistical text. For example, if it is known that 40 percent of the individuals in the total population are female and 60 percent male, then the probability of selecting exactly 10 females by drawing a pure random sample of 20 individuals is

$$P(10 \mid 20, 0.4) = \binom{20}{10} \, 0.4^{10} \cdot 0.6^{10} = \frac{20!}{10! \, 10!} \, 0.4^{10} \cdot 0.6^{10} = 0.1171$$

These calculations would be quite time consuming if we had to do them ourselves. However, the binomial table quickly gives us the answer of 0.1146. The parameters of a binomial distribution are estimated by

$$\overline{X} = \text{Mean or expected value} = n \cdot p \quad \text{or} \quad p = \frac{\overline{X}}{n}$$

$$\text{Variance } (p) = (p \cdot q)/n$$

$$\text{Standard deviation } (p) = \sqrt{\frac{p \cdot q}{n}}$$

---

[8] Technically, in order to keep the probabilities constant, and to keep the chance of being selected equal, we must sample "with replacement." If we are sampling from a fairly large population, sampling without replacement is not a serious problem. See Chapter 9.

Tables of cumulative binomial probabilities are also available. These tables indicate, for a given n and p, the probability of obtaining r or more successes. Cumulative distributions are used in determining the significance of a difference between the sample results and the mean or expected value. A quick example will illustrate this. Suppose we gave a group of housewives a test consisting of 10 true-false questions designed to measure their knowledge of our product. The results of the test were:

Housewife	Number of Correct Answers
A	5
B	8
C	9
D	4
E	7

The expected number of correct answers by chance is $n \cdot p$ or $10(0.5) = 5$. How many correct answers must a housewife get before we can assume her score is *significantly* better than chance? Let us look at the cumulative probabilities:

Number of Correct Answers	Cumulative Probability
1	0.9990
2	0.9873
3	0.9453
4	0.8281
5	0.6230
6	0.3770
7	0.1719
8	0.0547
9	0.0107
10	0.0010

Reading from the table, we note that the probability of obtaining 8 or more correct answers by chance is 0.0547. Therefore, if the housewife scored 8 correct answers, we can conclude that she is not guessing with almost 95 percent confidence ($1 - 0.0547 = 0.9453$).

The Normal Distribution

The normal distribution is appropriate for several uses:

1. To describe the empirical distribution of a variable and thereby provide information about its characteristics

2. To test an hypothesis about a population mean on the basis of sample data
3. To test the significance of the difference between two sample means in order to infer differences between populations
4. To test an hypothesis about a population (binomial) proportion when the sample size is large
5. To test the significance of the difference between two sample proportions in order to infer a difference between populations.

Many variables can be said to be normally distributed, that is, have characteristics similar to the normal distribution. This information can be extremely useful since this distribution has some interesting properties which provide a richer description of an empirical distribution. In the second and third cases, the normal distribution is used in its role as the theoretical sampling distribution of sample means, and in the fourth and fifth cases the normal distribution is used as an approximation to the technically appropriate theoretical sampling distribution of proportions, the binomial distribution. Each of these uses will be discussed in turn in the following sections. However, the primary reason for using theoretical distributions is that they allow us to determine chance probabilities and to compare our sample results with these predictions of chance.

The normal distribution, sometimes called the Gaussian distribution, is a continuous probability distribution, that is, it is appropriate for continuous (as opposed to discrete value 1, 2, 3, and so on) variables. The normal distribution is given by

$$f(X: \mu, \sigma) = \frac{\exp\left[-\frac{(X - \mu)^2}{2\sigma^2}\right]}{\sqrt{2\pi\sigma}}$$

and graphically by the familiar bell-shaped curve (Figure 11.1), symmetrical about its mean, and whose tails on either side approach zero. The formula

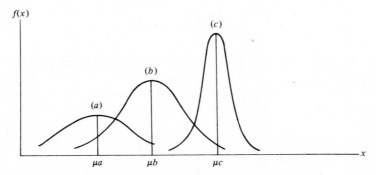

FIGURE 11.1 *A Family of Normal Curves*

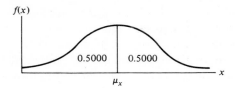

FIGURE 11.2 *Normal Distribution*

shows the fact that a normal curve is completely determined by its two parameters, μ and σ. Because each distribution is symmetrical, the mean, median, and mode are all equal.

The normal distribution is a continuous probability distribution. Since the probability of obtaining a specific number along a continuous scale is essentially zero, one must specify a range for the values of the variable and compute the probability of obtaining a value within that range. These probabilities are equal to the area under the curve between the specified limits of the range set. The total area under the curve (the sum of all probabilities) is taken to be one, and thus the probability of obtaining a value greater than the mean which divides the distribution in half is 0.5, and the probability of obtaining a value less than the mean is also 0.5 (see Figure 11.2). Furthermore, for any normal one can compute the percent of area over selected ranges as

$$\mu \pm 1\sigma = 68.27 \text{ percent}$$

$$\mu \pm 2\sigma = 95.45 \text{ percent}$$

$$\mu \pm 3\sigma = 99.73 \text{ percent}$$

Therefore, the probability of obtaining a value within the range of one standard deviation below and one standard deviation above the mean is 0.6827. These probabilities are illustrated in Figure 11.3.

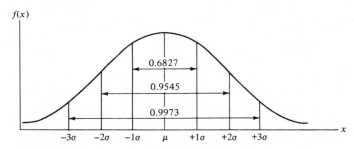

FIGURE 11.3 *The Normal Curve Areas*

For any specific range of values we could compute the probabilities by taking the integral (calculus) between the two limited values of the range. Fortunately this is not necessary, since tables have been constructed which indicate area under the curve and are available in almost any statistical text. In order to use these tables, one must transform our particular values into what are known as *standard* or *z scores*. To do this, one takes the difference between the value and the mean and divide by the standard deviation. Essentially this creates a value which is a deviation from the mean of zero in multiples or fractions of standard deviations in standard units. The general formula for this is

$$z = \frac{\overline{X} - \mu}{\sigma}$$

For example, suppose the distribution has a mean of $10,000 and a standard deviation of $2000 and one wants to know the probability of obtaining a value of the variable of between $7000 and $10,000. The z score would be

$$z = \frac{\$7000 - \$10,000}{\$2000} = \frac{-\$3000}{\$2000} = -1.5 \text{ standard deviation}$$

Note that the z score is not in the units by which the variable was measured, but in *standard units*. Then one merely looks for a z value of -1.5 in our statistical tables. A -1.5 will not appear; only positive values are recorded, but since a normal distribution is symmetrical, the area under the curve between 0 and -1.5 standard deviations is equal to that between 0 and $+1.5$ standard deviations. By adding and subtracting appropriately, one can determine the probability associated with any given range. Figure 11.4 illustrates two examples of these calculations.

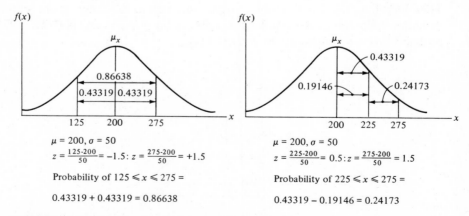

FIGURE 11.4 *Standard Normal Distribution Calculations*

Thus, if the mean and standard deviation of a distribution of values of a variable are known, and if it can be said that the values are normally distributed, a great deal is known about the appearance of that distribution. These interesting features can also be utilized in making statistical inferences (again probabilistic statements) if one views the normal distribution as the theoretical sampling distribution of sample means. Instead of computing the probability of obtaining a *value of the variable*, one will be computing the probability of obtaining a sample mean. In order to do this, however, the mean and standard deviation of the theoretical sampling distribution must be known.

The Central Limit Theorem

This information is provided by the central limit theorem which is a key concept in statistical analysis. This theorem states that

If $x_1, x_2, \ldots, x_n$ are sample observations drawn from the same distribution having mean μ and variance σ^2, and moment-generating function $M_x(t)$, then as $n \to \infty$, the limiting distribution is standard normal with $Z = (\overline{X} - \mu)/(\sigma/\sqrt{n})$.

What is important here is the generality of this statement. The reader should note that the theorem makes no assumption as to the shape of underlying distribution of the population being sampled. If a population is normal and has a moment-generating function (is not U-shaped), it can be shown that the distribution of sample means is normal even for small samples. Even if the population is not normal, however, the distribution of sample means approaches normality when the sample size is large. Furthermore, we know the mean and standard deviation of the distribution of sample means are μ and $\sigma/\sqrt{n}$, respectively, and this is precisely the information needed to compute probabilities.

The standard deviation of the distribution of sample means, $\sigma/\sqrt{n}$, is also called the *standard error of the mean* and can be interpreted as the amount by which a sample mean will differ from the true population mean. By looking at its formula, one can see that as n becomes large, the standard error of the mean ($\sigma_{\bar{x}}$) becomes small. This relationship is expressed by the *law of large numbers* which states that the distribution of sample means becomes more concentrated about the true population mean as the sample size is increased. Or, alternatively, *one might say that the larger the sample size, the better the sample mean will estimate the population mean*. Therefore, by increasing sample size one can increase the precision of his results.

Comparing a Sample to a Universe

The use of the central limit theorem in statistical inference can probably be best explained by examples. Suppose that one believes that the mean annual income of the people who buy a product is $20,000, and the standard deviation is known to be $5000. In the course of routine research on customers, a sample of 100 people who buy the product is drawn and the mean income of the sample is found to be $12,000. Is the true mean income of the sample customers really the same as the total population and the difference due to chance alone? In order to answer this question, one must examine the probability of obtaining a sample mean of $12,000 if the true population mean is $20,000. The researcher must test the significance of the difference between the sample mean and the population mean. The null hypothesis and alternate hypothesis are set up as

$$H_0 : = \$20,000$$

$$H_1 : = 12,000$$

A significance level of 0.05 will be used (arbitrarily) as our criteria of significant difference. That is, we will want to reject the null hypothesis if probability of obtaining a sample mean of $12,000 by chance is less than 5 percent when the true mean is $20,000. The z score which marks this cutoff point is 1.64 standard deviations for a one-tailed test (see Figure 11.5).[9]

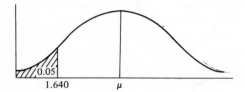

FIGURE 11.5 *One-Tailed Distribution*

Therefore, one would reject the null hypothesis if $12,000 lies more than 1.64 standard errors (the standard deviation of the distribution of sample means) away from the hypothesized population mean of $20,000. Calculating a z score for $12,000 by a generalization of our previous formula we see that

$$z = \frac{\overline{X} - \mu}{\sigma_{\overline{x}}} = \frac{\overline{X} - \mu}{\sigma/\sqrt{n}}$$

$$z = \frac{12,000 - 20,000}{5000/\sqrt{100}} = 16$$

Thus, the sample mean is quite "far" from the hypothesized mean and the null hypothesis is rejected. The researcher must conclude that the true mean of the population is not $20,000. The difference is too large to be explained by random error.

[9] If a two-tailed test were used rather than the one-tailed test shown here, the criteria z score would be 1.96. Tables of the normal as well as other distributions can be found in most introductory statistical texts including John E. Freund, *Mathematical Statistics*, 2nd ed. (Englewood Cliffs, N.J.: Prentice-Hall, 1972).

Comparing Two Samples

To illustrate a test of the significance of the difference between two sample means, one can examine the following situation. Suppose one takes a sample of 100 individuals who regularly shop at store A, and finds that the mean age is 35 years ($\overline{X}_A = 35$). A sample of 150 individuals who regularly shop at store B is taken and the mean age is found to be 28 years. The research computes the sample standard deviations σ_A to be 5 years and σ_B to be 3 years. Are these two stores drawing from two different populations? The null hypothesis is that there is no difference between the populations $\mu_A = \mu_B$. The alternate hypothesis is that the true mean of individuals shopping at store A is greater than that of store B, $\mu_B = \mu_A$. The significance level is again 0.05 and the cutoff value for z is 1.64.

To compute the z score for the sample statistics, a variation of the same formula used previously is

$$z = \frac{\overline{X} - \mu}{\sigma_{\bar{x}}}$$

In this case our statistic $\overline{X}$ is $(\overline{X}_A - \overline{X}_B)$, the difference between two sample means, and our parameter (μ) is $(\mu_A - \mu_B)$. Since we have hypothesized no difference in population means, the parameter (μ) is zero. The standard error needed is the standard error of the difference between two means which is given by

$$\sigma_{\overline{X}_A - \bar{x}_P} = \sqrt{\frac{\sigma_A^2}{n_A} + \frac{\sigma_B^2}{n_B}}$$

Therefore, our sample z score is

$$z = \frac{(\overline{X}_A - \overline{X}_B) - (\mu_A - \mu_B)}{\sigma_{\overline{X}_A - \bar{x}_B}} = \frac{\overline{X}_n - \overline{X}_B}{\sigma_{\overline{X}_A - \bar{x}_B}}$$

Since $\mu_A - \mu_B = 0$,

$$z = \frac{35 - 28}{\sqrt{\dfrac{5^2}{100} + \dfrac{3^2}{150}}}$$

$$z = \frac{7}{\sqrt{0.31}} = \frac{7}{0.557}$$

$$z = 12.56$$

Since z is greater than the critical value of 1.64, one rejects the null hypothesis and must conclude that with 95 percent confidence the two stores draw their customers from the different age populations.

Normal Approximation to the Binomial Distribution

The normal distribution can be used to approximate the binomial distribution when it is necessary to test a hypothesis about a population percent or to test the significance of the difference between two sample percentages if the sample size is large. Few statistical tables list the probabilities of the binomial for n greater than 20, since, for a sample greater than this size, the discrete binomial distribution closely approximates the normal distribution. Although the specific calculations will not be presented here, the process of testing proportions is analogous to that used for means:

$$z = \frac{X - \mu}{\sigma_x} = \frac{P_x - P_\mu}{\sqrt{\dfrac{P_x \cdot (1 - P_x)}{n}}}$$

where $P_{\bar{x}}$ is the sample proportion, n is sample size, and $P\mu$ is the total population proportion.

The chief advantage of the normal distribution is that it can be used to test hypotheses about means no matter what the underlying distribution of the variable might be as long as one is careful to use a sample size that is sufficiently large (greater than 20). The limitation is that the standard deviation of the population must be known. However, the only way the standard deviation of a population can be known with certainty is to take the value of the variable for every member of the population which is frequently impossible. If the sample size is large, an estimate of the standard deviation based on the sample data can be used with little harm done. This estimate of the standard deviation σ is given by

$$\sigma = \sqrt{\frac{\sum\limits_{i} (X_i - \bar{X})^2}{n - 1}}$$

For small samples, however, the error introduced by the process of estimation is substantial and the normal distribution is no longer the appropriate theoretical sampling distribution. In these cases, we must turn to Student's t-distribution.

t-Distribution

Student's t-distribution, developed by W. D. Gossett who wrote under the pen name of "Student," is similar to the normal distribution. The t-distribution does not require that the sample standard deviation estimate the total population standard deviation as discussed above. Like the normal distribution, the t-distribution is symmetrical, but it is slightly more scattered than the normal distribution. Unlike the normal distribution, the t-distribution changes shape with sample size, or more precisely with the number of the so-called degrees of freedom (sample size n). The number of degrees of freedom approaches 30 and the t-distribution becomes very close to normal, which explains why the normal distribution is appropriate for testing means even if the standard deviation is unknown as long as n is over 30.

One should recall that in testing the significance of the sample means with the normal distribution, a z score was computed that required knowledge of the standard error of the mean, $\sigma/\sqrt{n}$. If the standard deviation is not known, we estimate it by

$$\sigma = \sqrt{\frac{\sum_{i=1}^{n} (X_i - \overline{X})^2}{n-1}} \tag{1}$$

Substituting this value into the formula for the standard error of the mean, $\sigma/\sqrt{n}$, we find that the *estimated* standard error of the mean is the sample standard deviation divided by the square root of sample size minus one,[10]

$$\hat{\sigma}_{\overline{X}} = \frac{S}{\sqrt{n-1}}$$

The appropriate theoretical sampling distribution is now the t-distribution, and although the basic process is the same, one computes a t value which is a variation of the z value.

For testing an hypothesis about a single population mean, the t value is computed by

$$t = \frac{\overline{X} - \mu}{\hat{\sigma}_{\overline{X}}} = \frac{\overline{X} - \mu}{\dfrac{S}{\sqrt{n-1}}}$$

When testing the significance of the difference between two sample means, one needs an estimate of the standard error of the difference between two means, which is given by

$$\hat{\sigma}_{\overline{x}_1 - \overline{x}_2} = \sqrt{\frac{n_1 s_1^2 + n_2 s_2^2}{n_1 + n_2 - 2}} \sqrt{\frac{n_1 + n_2}{n_1 \cdot n_2}}$$

[10] If

$$\sigma = \sqrt{\frac{\Sigma(X - \overline{X})^2}{n-1}} \text{ and } \sigma_{\overline{x}} = \frac{\sigma}{\sqrt{n}}, \text{ then}$$

$$\sigma_{\overline{x}} = \frac{\sqrt{\dfrac{\Sigma(X - \overline{X})^2}{n-1}}}{\sqrt{n}} = \sqrt{\frac{\Sigma(X - \overline{X})^2}{n \cdot (n-1)}}$$

$$= \sqrt{\frac{\Sigma(X - \overline{X})^2}{n}} \cdot \sqrt{\frac{1}{n-1}} = \frac{S}{\sqrt{n-1}}$$

The t value will be computed in much the same way as the z score, and this formula is represented by

$$t = \frac{(\overline{X}_1 - \overline{X}_2) - (\mu_1 - \mu_2)}{\hat{\sigma}_{X_1 - \overline{X}_2}}$$

which becomes simply

$$\frac{\overline{X}_1 - \overline{X}_2}{\left(\hat{\sigma}_{\overline{X}_1 - \overline{X}_2}\right)}$$

since the null hypothesis is the difference between the two population means $(\mu_1 - \mu_2)$ which is zero. In testing one mean, the number of degrees of freedom is $n - 1$, since only one estimate is needed, while the number of degrees of freedom when two sample means are tested is the total number of sample items minus 2, or $n_1 + n_2 - 2$.

Again, the significance values are read from a table of the t-distribution widely available in statistical texts. Since there is a different curve for every sample size, however, these tables are not as complete as those for the normal distribution. For degrees of freedom from 1 through 120, the t values are listed for certain commonly used significance levels. For example, for 15 degrees of freedom and a significance level of 0.05, the t value is 2.131. Moreover, these tables are typically two-tailed, which means that the sum of the areas in the two tails is 0.05. (See Figure 11.6.)[11]

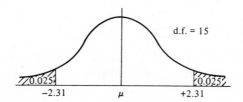

FIGURE 11.6 *Two-Tailed Test Distribution*

An example of the use of the t-distribution in analyzing the difference between two sample means is presented in Table 11.9 taken from a recent article by El-Ansary and Stern.[12] In investigating power relationships in a distribution channel, one of the relationships investigated was whether or not the self-perception of a channel member's power was significantly different

[11] For one-tailed values it is merely necessary to double the desired significance level. For example, a one-tailed test, significance level of 0.01, would utilize the t value listed for a level of 0.02.

[12] Adel I. El-Ansary and Louis W. Stern, "Power Measurement in the Distribution Channel," *Journal of Marketing Research*, Vol. 9 (February 1972), pp. 47–52.

TABLE 11.9   *Means and Simple Correlations of Power Perceptions and Attributions by Wholesalers and Dealers*[13]

Relationship	Raw Power Scores			Weighted Power Scores		
	Mean Score[a]	*t*	*r*	Mean Score[b]	*t*	*r*[c]
Wholesaler's self-perceived power: power attributed to wholesaler by the dealer	29.90 45.36	−4.21[d]	−0.02	99.73 171.91	−4.24	0.01
Dealer's self-perceived power: power attributed to the dealer by the wholesaler	26.91 34.86	−2.50	−0.32	111.32 143.77	−2.33	−0.32

[a] Maximum 85, minimum 17.
[b] Maximum 425, minimum 17.
[c] All are not significant at 0.05 level ($p = 0.42$; d.f. $= 20$).
[d] All *t* scores significant at the 0.05 level ($p = 1.96$; d.f. $= 42$). The minus signs show that the mean of the second set of perceptions is greater than that of the first.

from the amount of power attributed to him by others. Self-perception scores and attribution scores both raw and weighted were gathered, and the means were tested for significance. As the table indicated, the *t* test showed significant differences. Two things are of interest in this table. First, footnotes a and b give the range of values that power score could take on which gives the reader more information about the measurement process, and facilitates interpretation of means, since these are the means of scores taken from a Likert-type scale[14] rather than the means of values measured in some common unit such as dollars, years, inches, and so on. Secondly, footnote d tells us that all of the *t* values are significant at the 0.05 level for which the critical *t* value is 1.96 when the number of the degrees of freedom is 42. The authors concluded that there was a lack of agreement between self-perceptions of power and attributions of power and therefore no specific power structure existed.

Summary: Single Variable Analysis

Thus far we have discussed the uses of three distributions in statistical analysis of one variable for cases involving one or two samples. These uses

---

[13] From Adel I. El-Ansary & Louis W. Stern, "Power Measurement in the Distribution Channel," *Journal of Marketing Research*, Volume 9 (February 1972), pp. 47–52. Published by the American Marketing Association.
[14] See Chapter 6.

TABLE 11.10   *Tests of Significance: One Variable, One or Two Samples*

Number of Samples	Means (Continuous-Cardinal)		Percents (Qualitative Discrete-Nominal-Ordinal)	
	σ is known	σ is not known	n is small	n is large
1	Normal distribution $Z = \dfrac{\bar{X} - \mu}{\sigma_{\bar{X}}}$	t-distribution $t = \dfrac{\bar{X} - \mu}{\sigma_X}$ d.f. $= n - 1$	Binomial distribution	Normal distribution (as approximation to binomial)
2	Normal distribution $Z = \dfrac{\bar{X}_1 - \bar{X}_2}{\sigma_{\bar{X}_1 - \bar{X}_2}}$	t-distribution $t = \dfrac{\bar{X}_1 - \bar{X}_2}{\sigma_{\bar{X}_1 - \bar{X}_2}}$ d.f. $= n_1 + n_2 - 2$	[(not discussed this chapter)]	Normal distribution

are summarized in Table 11.10. A distribution does exist to determine the "goodness of fit" between empirical data and these and other theoretical distributions. This distribution is the chi-square distribution. Since chi-square is more often used in the simultaneous analysis of two or more variables, however, it will be discussed in the next section. In comparing differences between three or more samples, an analysis of variance test (*F* distribution) is most commonly used. This test of analysis deserves a section of its own, and thus will be examined in a later section.

Analysis of Two Variables

The analysis of one variable is helpful in those situations where the researcher is fairly sure that only one factor at a time is relevant to his problem. Marketing situations have been found to be notoriously complex, however, and it is more likely that the market phenomena which the researcher wishes to investigate will be caused or affected by the interaction of several variables working simultaneously. As was seen in Chapter 5, consumers can be classified in a variety of ways. In investigating the kinds of people who exhibit a particular pattern of buying behavior, one might want to determine the income levels of particular groups. However, one might be interested in the combined effects of income level and personality characteristics on buying behavior. Or, one might want to investigate the possibility that two variables are related in some manner, such that a knowledge of the value of one variable enables us to predict the value of another variable. For example, does social class indicate the kind of car a person buys? For these cases, statistical tests are needed to see if a relationship exists between two or more variables, and the strength of the relationship. In this chapter we will discuss the analysis of only two variables by the methods of cross tabulation, contingency tests, and simple correlation.

As in the analysis of one variable, the first step in examining relationships between variables[15] is to set up a frequency table, which in the case of two or more variables is called a contingency table. Contingency tables can be of almost any size, from a simple two-row, two-column (2×2) table to the general r by c table, where r indicates the number of rows and c indicates the number of columns. The construction of the table requires the recording of the number of cases falling into each cell. Frequencies, rather than percentages, should be recorded if further analysis is to be done since most statistical procedures require this information. For the presentation of data, it is nice to include percentages alongside the frequencies to facilitate comparison. The total number of elements in the sample should, of course, be clearly stated, but the number of elements in each subgroup of the sample should also be included. If one was relating size of city lived in to awareness of a new product and found that 50 percent of those people in our sample living in towns of 500 or less were classified as being aware we might be amazed at the ability of our advertising campaign to spread the word. If one knew that only two people from such towns were included in the sample, however, our conclusions might be different. Table 11.11 illustrates a very simple example of a 2×2 contingency table showing the relationship between income level and shopping center preference based on a sample of 300 residents of a city.

To ease comparison of the data, one would wish to show percentages rather than frequencies. In which direction should the percentages be computed? Table 11.12 illustrates the two possibilities, each of which answer different research questions. Table 11.11 shows the *distribution of incomes* within each preference class, which would be the appropriate table if one wanted to look at the incomes of people who preferred one or the other shopping centers. Categories may, of course, be subdivided into as many gradations as desired. For example, income levels could be split into intervals of $10,000, $5000, and so on. However, as the number of classifications increase, more observations will be needed if empty intervals are to be avoided.

Thus far only observed differences have been discussed, and no mention has been made concerning inference or statistical significance tests. Contingency tables or, equivalently, cross tabulations tell us only about our sample; without further analysis, one is powerless to make generalizations to

---

[15] The variables must be categorized in some manner as discussed on p. 420.

TABLE 11.11   *Relationship of Income Level to Preference for Shopping Centers A and B*

Income Level	Preference					
	Center A		Center B		Total	
	Number	Percent	Number	Percent	Number	Percent
High	60	40	40	26.6	100	33.3
Low	90	60	110	73.4	200	66.7
Total	150	100	150	100.0	300	100.0

TABLE 11.12   *Number of People Preferring to Shop A or B Versus Income Level*

Income Level	Center A	Center B	Total
High	60	40	100
Low	90	110	200
Total	150	150	300

larger populations or to determine the significance of differences observed. Two types of tests are available for use in the analysis. The first type of statistical test is that which determines whether a significant relationship exists, while the second type measures the degree or strength of the relationship if one exists.

The Chi-Square Distribution

The most commonly used test to determine the existence of a relationship between two variables in a table, inferred from sample data, is the test of independence of classification which utilizes the chi-square distribution. The *null hypothesis* of such a test is that there is no relationship between the variables in the given table, that is, the two variables are not contingent upon one another. In our previous example, this would mean that shopping center preference is unrelated to income level. The test involves computing the statistic χ^2 (chi-square) from the sample data and comparing this value with the values (or probabilities) given in the table for its theoretical sampling distribution, chi-square.

The chi-square test is nonparametric: it makes no assumptions as to the underlying distribution of the population, and the chi-square distribution has no parameters except degrees of freedom. Like the *t*-distribution, its shape varies with the number of degrees of freedom which are in this case defined as the number of observations that are allowed to vary. In the 2×2 table, for example, once a value is placed in one cell, the others are completely determined by the totals for the rows and columns. In general, the number of degrees of freedom will be $(r - 1)(c - 1)$ where r is the number of rows and c is the number of columns.

The computation of the statistic χ^2 involves computing an expected frequency for each cell, and taking the sum of the squared differences between the observed and expected frequencies for each, all divided by the expected frequency for each cell. The formula is

$$\chi^2 = \sum_{i=1}^{n} \frac{(f_{oi} - f_{ei})^2}{f_{oi}}$$

where f_o is the observed frequency for the *i*th cell and f_e is the expected frequency for that cell.

The contingency table (Table 11.12) will be used to determine, by means of the χ^2 test, whether income and shopping center preference are independent, or unrelated.

The expected frequency of a given cell is computed by multiplying the row total (100 in the example) in which the cell appears times the column total (150) in which the cell appears and dividing by the total number of observations in the entire table (300):

For cell *i*: $f_e = \dfrac{\text{Row total } i \times \text{Column total } i}{\text{Grand total}} = \dfrac{100 \cdot 150}{300} = 50$ for cell 1

The other frequencies are calculated in a similar fashion and are shown in Table 11.13.

TABLE 11.13 *Actual and Expected Frequencies*

Income Level		Center A	Center B	Total
High	Expected	50	50	100
	Actual	60	40	100
Low	Expected	100	100	200
	Actual	90	110	200
Total		150	150	300

TABLE 11.14   *Computation of χ^2*

Cell						
Row	Column	f_o	f_e	$\|f_o - f_e\| - \frac{1}{2}$	$(\|f_o - f_e\| - \frac{1}{2})^2$	$(\|f_o - f_e\| - \frac{1}{2})^2 / f_e$
1	1	60	50	9.5	90.25	1.8050
1	2	40	50	9.5	90.25	1.8050
2	1	90	100	9.5	90.25	0.9025
2	2	110	100	9.5	90.25	0.9025

Total $\chi^2 = 5.4150$
Degrees of freedom $= 1$

In the case of a 2×2 table, the chi-square distribution has only one degree of freedom. For this special case of one degree of freedom (d.f.), we must include a correction for continuity in our computation of χ^2. The reason for this is that chi-square is a continuous distribution while it is being used to analyze discrete cell data. For more than one degree of freedom the difference is so small that it can be ignored, but for only one d.f., a correction must be made. The standard procedure is to use Yates' correction for continuity, which transforms our formula of χ^2 into

$$\chi^2 = \sum_{i=1}^{4} \frac{(f_{oi} - f_{ei} - \frac{1}{2})^2}{f_{ei}}$$

The computation of χ^2 for our example is shown in Table 11.14. The value given in a table of chi-square of one degree of freedom and for a significance level of 0.05 is 3.841. Since the value of χ^2 computed from our sample is larger than this value, we conclude the difference between our sample and chance expectations is too large to be attributed to random error and that, therefore, income and preference are not independent and a significant relationship does exist. We do not know the degree or strength of the relationship, but only that it is significant.

Even though there are no assumptions as to the underlying distribution of the population, there are restrictions on the use of chi-square. Chi-square should generally not be used with small samples.[16] Furthermore, the expected frequency of each cell should be at least 5.[17] If this requirement is not met, classes should be combined until each cell has an expected frequency of at

[16] It is recommended that n be at least 50 since the 42 is an approximation to the underlying multinomial distribution.

[17] Some researchers qualify this requirement by stating that if d.f. is greater than one, not more than 20 percent of the cells should have expected frequencies of less than 5. For the 2 x 2 table, χ^2 is not recommended for $n < 20$. See S. Siegal, *Nonparametric Statistics* (New York: McGraw-Hill, 1962), p. 178.

least 5. In some situations combining classes would render the data meaningless, and another test must be used. One such alternative test is Fisher's exact test.

The use of Fisher's exact probability test is restricted to data which can be placed in a 2×2 contingency table. That is, we are allowed to analyze observations falling into one or the other of two mutually exclusive categories taken from two independent groups. The results of a Fisher's exact test is the exact probability of observing a particular set of frequencies, which differs from chi-square results which give us the probability of obtaining the particular frequencies or more deviant ones (χ^2 gives value in the right-hand tail).

For simplicity, the cells of a 2×2 contingency table are labeled in the following way:

	Yes	No	
Group I	A	B	$A + B$
Group II	C	D	$C + D$
	$A + C$	$B + D$	N

The exact probability of obtaining these frequencies, when the marginal totals are fixed, is

$$p = \frac{(A+B)! \; (C+D)! \; (A+C)! \; (B+D)!}{N! \; A! \; B! \; C! \; D!}$$

If one wishes to know the probability of obtaining these frequencies plus the probability of finding more extreme findings (given fixed marginal totals), one computes the sum of the exact probabilities of each alternative extreme. Such computations can become extremely tedious. Fortunately, this can be done by a computer and at least one commonly available statistical package has a Fisher's exact probability test option.

The Concept of Correlation

Both chi-square and Fisher's exact probability tests indicate whether one variable is associated with another. They are measures of joint occurrence of two variables. However, one often wishes to describe the degree to which two variables are related and the direction of that relationship. One might also want to make estimates or predictions about the change in value of one variable on the basis of knowledge about the value of another variable. In the first case, we turn to the techniques correlation analysis, which is designed to indicate the degree of mutual variation of variables, and the direction of variation.

Two variables, x and y, for example, may have a positive correlation, that is, an increase in x accompanies an increase in y. Or, they may have a negative correlation if increase in y is accompanied by a decrease in x. Finally, x and y may vary independently, in which case there is no correlation. Measures of correlation indicate the amount of variation in one variable that can be associated with the variation in another. Most of these measures take on values ranging from -1.0 to $+1.0$. A perfect positive correlation is indicated by 1.0. In addition, most of the measures discussed are sensitive only to *linear* relationships. Thus, a correlation of zero for these measures does not imply that no relationship exists; but merely that no linear relationship was found.

The most commonly used measure of association for two continuous ratio scaled[18] variables is the product-moment correlation coefficient r, sometimes referred to as Pearson's r. The observations of each of the two variables are not independent. That is, for each individual element in the sample, measurements of each of the two variables is taken. Further, it must be assumed that the variables have a bivariate normal population distribution. This simply means that, for two variables x and y, the distribution of the values of x obtained for a particular y value must be normally distributed, and that the distribution of y values obtained for any particular x value must also be normally distributed.

The correlation coefficient is a measure of the goodness of fit to a linear, "least squares" line. Although the concepts of least squares and regression lines will be treated more thoroughly in the following chapter, a general notion of the concept will be given here. For two variables x and y, we might plot the values of these variables observed from each element of the population on a sheet of graph paper and we might obtain Figure 11.7.
Line a in Figure 11.7 might have been sketched by hand to follow the general direction of the plotted values, but a more precise method is to draw the line so that the sum of the squared deviations of each of the plotted values from the line is at a minimum. This "least square" line is analogous to a mean, in that it represents an average relationship, and in that the deviations of the data from the line take on a minimum value. The coefficient r indicates how well the data fit the line.

The formula for computing r is

$$r = \sqrt{\frac{\sum\limits_{i=1}^{n} (X_i - \overline{X}) \cdot (Y_i - \overline{Y})}{\sqrt{\sum\limits_{i=1}^{n} \left[(X_i - \overline{X})^2 \right] \left[\sum\limits_{i=1}^{n} (Y_i - \overline{Y})^2 \right]}}}$$

An interpretation of the degree of correlation can be obtained from r^2, which is called the "coefficient of multiple determination." The r^2 indicates the

[18] See Chapter 6, p. 211.

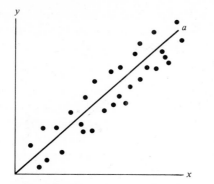

FIGURE 11.7 *An Example of Correlated Variables*

proportion of the total variation in one variable that is explained by one or more other variables. Therefore, an r^2 of 0.60 means that 60 percent of the total variation of either X or Y can be explained by or associated with the relationship between the two variables. And, $1 - r^2$ simply indicates the proportion of unexplained variation.

An example of the use of correlation occurs when the researcher wishes to express the degree to which a causal hypothesis is verified. If the marketing researcher has hypothesized that awareness of advertising for *Crest* toothpaste is directly related (and precedes) the act of purchasing, the research staff then interviews five persons asking the degree of awareness (how many advertising points remembered) and the degree of purchasing (how many units purchased in the last six months). The data collected are reported to be:

Respondent	Aware (x)	Bought (y)
1	4	6
2	2	3
3	0	1
4	3	4
5	3	2
Total	12	16

$$r = \sqrt{\frac{\sum_{i=1}^{5}\left(X_i - \frac{12}{5}\right)\cdot\left(y_i - \frac{16}{5}\right)}{\sqrt{\sum_{i=1}^{5}\left(X_i - \frac{12}{5}\right)^2 \cdot \sum_{i=1}^{5}\left(y_i - \frac{16}{5}\right)^2}}}$$

$$r = +94, \qquad r^2 = 0.88$$

The researcher would report a correlation in the positive direction of 0.94 and an explained variation of 88 percent. The marketing researcher would then argue that the statistics indicate that he believed that his hypothesis was strongly supported. Correlation analysis assumes that all measures are cardinal (purely metric; see Chapter 6).

Rank Order Correlations

The final group of correlation measures deals with rank order data. Two groups of consumers might be asked to rank, in order of preference, the brands of a product class. The researcher, then, wishes to determine the agreement or correlation between the two groups. Two possible statistics can be computed to accomplish this purpose: the Spearman rank order correlation coefficient, (r_s), and the Kendall rank correlation coefficient, τ (tau). The Spearman rank coefficient is computed by

$$r_s = 1 - \frac{6 \sum\limits_{i=1}^{n} d_i^2}{n^3 - n}$$

where d_i is the difference between the ranks given to the ith brand by each group. Thus, if brand B were ranked first by group 1 and sixth by group 2, d_b^2 would be equal to $(1 - 6)^2$ or 25. In some cases, two brands may be given equal scores by a group, or be tied for a certain rank. If the number of ties is not large, their effect is small, and we simply assign the average of the ranks which would have been assigned had no ties occurred to each brand. We then calculate r_s as before. If the number of ties is large, however, a correction factor can be introduced to offset their effect on r_s.

Kendall's tau is useful for the same type of situation as is appropriate for the Spearman coefficient, but its computation is not quite as straightforward and may best be explained by an example. Suppose two groups have ranked brands A, B, C, and D in the following way:

Brand	A	B	C	D
Group I	3	4	2	1
Group II	3	1	4	2

Rearranging the items so that group I's ranks appear in order, we see the following diagram:

Brand	D	C	A	B
Group I	1	2	3	4
Group II	2	4	3	1

To determine the degree of consistency between the two rankings, we examine group II's rankings to see how many are in the correct order, vis-à-vis one another. The first pair, D and C, are in natural order, that is, 2 (D) comes before 4 (C), and we assign a score of +1 to this pair. We proceed to compare the rank for brand D with the ranks of the other brands. The second pair, D and A, is assigned a +1, while D and B is assigned a —1. The total so far is +1. Each rank in turn is compared similarly, with the resulting final total of —2.[19] The next step is to compare this actual total with maximum possible total. A maximum value would occur if group II rankings were identical to those of group I, which is found by taking 4 things, 2 at a time, or

$$\binom{N}{2} = \binom{4}{2} = \frac{4!}{2! \; (4-2)!} = 6$$

Tau is therefore equal to the ratio of the actual total over the maximum possible total,

$$\tau = \frac{\text{Score}}{\binom{N}{2}} = \frac{-2}{6} = -0.33$$

and is the measure of correlation between the two ranks. Tied observations are treated in the same way as for the Spearman coefficient. Values obtained for r_s and τ from the same data will not be equal, and are not comparable to one another.

Most measures of correlation can be subjected to tests of significance to determine whether the correlations are sufficiently different from chance expectations and thus are not due to sampling error alone. However, the types of tests to be utilized and the rules governing their use are of such a magnitude as to be beyond the scope of a single chapter. The reader should refer to specialized statistical texts for the appropriate tests.[20]

Analysis of Variance

Although analysis of variance is perhaps best known for its use in the context of experimentation, it can also be used in those cases where no experimental manipulation or control has been exercised. This procedure is used to test an hypothesis about the equality of three or more population means on the basis of sample data. For example, suppose one takes a random sample of 30 people, 10 of which are shown advertisement A, 10 are shown advertisement B, and 10 are shown advertisement C. During the showing of each

---

[19] Rank of C versus A = —1, C versus B = —1, A versus B = —1, yielding a final total of —2. The value of +1 is scored when group I and II agree and —1 when they don't.

[20] For more detail, see Siegel, *op. cit.*, and A. M. Mood and F. A. Graybill, *Introduction to the Theory of Statistics*, 2nd ed. (New York: McGraw-Hill, 1963).

advertisement, a measure of perception (such as pupil dilation, or galvanic skin response) is taken for each individual. The question we wish to answer is whether the advertisements are equal in their ability to affect perception. Stated another way, our problem is to determine where the means of the perception scores for the three groups differ significantly.

Of course, all of the scores will vary, but the total amount of variation can be attributed to two sources. First, there will be variation of scores within each group due simply to individual differences. Secondly, there will be variation of scores between the groups due to the difference in stimuli to which they are exposed. The greater the differential effect of the advertisements, the more homogeneous will be the scores within each group, and the more hetero-geneous will be the means of the groups. Thus, one attempts to determine the equality or inequality of means by examining the variation exhibited by each group in relation to the variation observed between groups.

Several restrictions are placed on the use of analysis of variance. First, one must assume that the population distribution of values for each variable is normally distributed. Secondly, population variances must be assumed to be equal, and finally, each observation must be independent. This last assumption means that all of the samples compared must be independent and random. In some forms of analysis of variance, the assumption of independence of observations can be relaxed.

The statistic computed in the analysis of variance is an F value or F ratio whose sampling distribution is called the Fisher or F distribution. This value is simply the ratio of the variance between groups to the variance within groups. Variance in this test is referred to as the mean sum of squares or simply the mean square, which derives its name from the method of calculation. Perhaps the best way to illustrate this is by giving an example. Suppose one took a random sample of 15 individuals, divided them into three groups of five each, and showed each group a different advertisement. Table 11.15 shows the measures of perception obtained for each group. The mean of each

TABLE 11.15 *Perception Scores for Three Advertisements*

Advertisement A	Advertisement B	Advertisement C
5	2	5
6	10	6
3	9	4
8	6	2
5	5	5

Total 27	32	22	
$\overline{X}_A = 5.4$	$\overline{X}_B = 6.4$	$\overline{X}_C = 4.4$	$\overline{\overline{X}} = 5.4$

group of scores is given, as well as the mean of all 15 scores taken together, denoted by $\overline{\overline{X}}$, and termed the grand mean.

In computing a variance, one begins by taking the sum of the squared deviations of the values from the mean. Our procedure here follows this pattern. The total sum of squares can be found by squaring the deviation of each value from the grand mean and summing these squares. Mathematically, this is given by

$$\text{Total sum of squares} = \underset{j}{\Sigma}\ \underset{i}{\Sigma}\ (X_{ij} - \overline{\overline{X}})^2 = 73.6$$

where X_{ij} is the value in the ith row and the jth column. In the example, this would be $(5 - 5.4)^2 + (6 - 5.4)^2 + (e - 5.4)^2 + \cdots + (5 - 5.4)^2$. Next, one computes to total *within group* sum of squares which is found by taking the sum of the squared deviations of each observation from its own group mean, or

$$\text{Within group sum of squares} = \underset{i}{\Sigma}\ (X_{ij} - \overline{X}_j)^2 = 63.6 \qquad \text{for all } j$$

In the example, we would take the sum of the squared deviations of each value in group A from its mean of 5.4 plus the sum of the squared deviations of each value in group 3 from its mean of 6.4, plus the sum of the squared deviations of each value in group C from its mean of 4.4. Finally, the *between group* sum of squares will be needed. This is found by treating each group mean as a score. One simply takes the sum of the squared deviations of each group mean from the grand mean, or

$$\text{Between group sum of squares} = \underset{j}{\Sigma}\ (\overline{X}_j - \overline{\overline{X}})^2 = 10$$

where $\overline{X}_j$ is the mean of the jth group or column and n_j is the number of observations in the jth group. It can be shown that the total sum of squares is equal to the sum of the between group squares plus the within group sum of squares:

Total sum of squares = Between group sum of squares +

Within group sum of squares.

For the example, one therefore obtains

$$73.6 = 10.0 + 63.6$$

The estimate of the variation between groups, or the *mean square* for columns, is the between groups sum of squares divided by the number of degrees of freedom, which is defined as $C - 1$, where C is the number of columns. For example, therefore, the mean square for columns (MSC) is

$$\text{MSC} = \frac{\text{SSC}}{\text{d.f.}_{.1}} = \frac{10}{2} = 5$$

The estimate of the variation within groups, or *mean square error*, is the within group sum of squares divided by the number of degrees of freedom defined as $N - C$, where N is the total number of observations. For our example, we have

$$\text{MSE} = \frac{\text{SSE}}{\text{d.f.}_2} = \frac{\text{SSE}}{N - L} = \frac{63.6}{12} = 5.3$$

Our F value which tests the hypothesis that the advertising experiment is effective (have differing means) is the ratio of these two variances.

$$F = \frac{\text{MSC}}{\text{MSE}}$$

$$= \frac{5.0}{5.3}$$

$$= 0.934$$

These relationships are summarized in Table 11.16.

TABLE 11.16   *Table for Analysis of Variance for a One-Way Classification*

Source of Variation	Sum of Squares	d.f.	Mean Square	Variance Ration
Between samples (column means)	$\text{SSC} = \Sigma n_j (\overline{X}_j - \overline{\overline{X}})^2$	$\text{d.f.}_1 = C - 1$	$\text{MSC} = \dfrac{\text{SSC}}{\text{d.f.}_1}$	
Within samples	$\text{SSE} = (X_{ij} - \overline{X}_j)^2$	$\text{d.f.}_2 = N - C$	$\text{MS} = \dfrac{\text{SS}}{\text{d.f.}_2}$	$F = \dfrac{\text{MSC}}{\text{MSE}}$
Total	$\text{SST} = \Sigma (X_{ij} - \overline{\overline{X}})^2$	$N - 1$	. . .	. . .

To determine whether the F value is significant, one compares it with the value found in an F table for d.f._1 (numerator) of 2 and d.f._2 (denominator) of 12 under the significance level desired. For a 0.05 level, this table value is 3.89. Thus, the value is not significant at this level, and we conclude that the population means for the three groups are equal, and that the advertisements did not differ in the perception level elicited.

Summary

In this chapter, various statistical procedures designed to describe and analyze empirical distributions of one or two variables have been discussed. Methods of analysis, such as statistics, however, do not in themselves create information or tell us how to use it. They do help the researcher to pull out information from his data and to systematically present each piece in a clear way. Kaplan once stated that:

> Whatever the techniques employed, it is not the study of man which is embarrassing, but the behavior which the study discloses. The behavioral scientist must acknowledge his share of responsibility for human folly, but let him rest content with his own share![21]

His remarks, directed at behavioral scientists in general, are no less applicable to market researchers. A brilliant statistical technique cannot substitute for good planning, good data, and intelligent use of the methods of analysis.

Questions and Exercises

1. Under what conditions will the mean value of a data distribution be different from the mode?
2. Which is always smaller, the standard deviation or the standard error of the mean?
3. Compute the mean, the standard deviation, and the standard error of the mean for the data set: 3, 5, 4, 7, 4, 2, 8, 10.
4. What is the purpose of using the "t test"? Describe the conditions for which it is suitable.
5. Compute the t statistic for the data series 33, 45, 66, 35, 60. Is the process generating these data significantly different from a process which has a true mean of 37? At what level of confidence?
6. What is the meaning of the data summarized in the following table:

Age of Respondent in Years	Smokes Cigarettes		
	Yes	No	Number
0 to 15	15%	85%	200
16 to 24	30	70	100
25 to 40	50	50	150
41 to 54	45	55	70
55+	30	70	130
Number of respondents			650

7. Repercentage the data such that all of the Yes votes add up to 100 percent, and make sure that the No votes and the Total columns add up to 100 percent also. Can you draw different information from the table now? If so, what do you conclude?
8. By examining the data in the table for Exercise 6, could you state a probability that given a person between 0 and 15, he would smoke?
9. What does the chi-square test of contingency tell you about a table such as the one in Exercise 6?

[21] Abraham Kaplan, *The Conduct of Inquiry* (Scranton, Pa.: Chandler Publishing Co., 1964).

10. Compute the chi-square value for the table in Exercise 6 and the conclusion that results from it.
11. What is the chief purpose of the Spearman rank order correlation?
12. What is the chief purpose of the Pearson r correlation?
13. What is the correlation between variable A and variable B?

Variable A	Variable B
21	47
35	65
30	55

14. Supposing that an advertiser maintained advertising programs of differing levels of expenditure with the same theme in several isolated cities, is there a way that the advertiser could use experimental designs of Chapter 4 and the analysis of variance to understand the impact of the advertising?

Project Related Questions

1. Have you chosen statistics which adequately describe your distribution of sample responses?
2. Which variables are correlated with other variables?
3. Should you use parametric or nonparametric methods?
4. Have you planned the cross-tabulation analysis? Which pairs of variables would it be wise to examine?
5. Have your variables been broken down into "sensible" categories? Have you partitioned your variables in a meaningful way or should you recode them?
6. What results do you expect to see from the statistics?
7. What assumptions are made by the statistics you selected?

Chapter 12

Data Analysis: The Multivariate Techniques of Linear Regression and Linear Discriminant Analysis

Often, the researcher wishes to explore the interrelations among dependent and independent variables. The means for doing this is found in a set of methods known as multivariate techniques. This chapter discusses two of the most common such techniques: linear regression and linear discriminant analysis.

Introduction

In many cases, a researcher realizes that there are many variables which interact to predict a given behavioral outcome. Using simple statistics, he cannot isolate and study the impact of many variables acting simultaneously. Thus, he is forced to look for more "rich" and complicated methods of explaining the variance in the system he is studying. Such methods are called "multivariate methods" because they isolate the effects of many variables contributing to the explanation of human behavior. Since most human behavior has many causes and roots, multivariate techniques are essential to the market researcher. An article describing the range of techniques and uses of multivariate analysis is in an appendix to this chapter.

Linear regression and linear discriminant analysis are two common multivariate analysis techniques. Both techniques operate in a similar way and have similar sets of underlying assumptions. In addition, there are two fine computer programs available to allow the nonexpert computer user to utilize the techniques. The purpose of linear regression is to bring information concerning a group of variables to bear to predict the value of some desired variable. An example of this is the case where a manufacturer of television sets wishes to forecast the level of TV sales next year. The manufacturer knows that TV sales depend on some "independent" variables working together. Such variables include income of families, number of football games broadcast, and the amount of advertising done by TV manufacturers. To forecast, the TV manufacturer measures or obtains government forecasts concerning the "independent" variables and then performs a simple computation to find what TV sales will be.

Similarly, linear discriminant analysis is also a "forecasting oriented" statistical tool. It is not designed to predict a given value such as sales, but is rather aimed at predicting a probability that some event will occur. For example, the hypothetical TV manufacturer may wish to predict if a given person will buy a TV or not. The manufacturer knows that if a person has a high income, watches a lot of football games, and sees a lot of advertising for TV sets, he will have a high probability of buying a TV set. If the TV manufacturer comes upon a person with unknown probability of buying a TV, the manufacturer can measure the person's income, ads seen for TV, and

457

the number of football games watched and then compute the probability that the given person will buy a TV.

Some History

The tool of linear regression analysis was devised by statisticians and mathematical economists known as econometricians. The technique has been used extensively to provide reliable forecasts of economic activity among the sectors of U. S. commerce and industry and for the total U. S. economy. Thus, projections of the number of cars to be sold next year in the United States, the output of the chemical industry, and many other figures that appear in publications such as the *Wall Street Journal* are the results of economists working with linear regression analysis. In addition, individual companies often use regression analysis to predict market share and sales.

Linear discriminant analysis has a different root than regression. Discriminant analysis comes from anthropology and medicine. Anthropologists desired a method of statistically typing bone fragments into sexes, species, and so on, with certain probabilities attached. Thus, the anthropologist can measure the size, shape, and age of bone and then perform a simple calculation to calculate the probability that the bone falls into a given class. Medical doctors have attempted to use discriminant analysis to diagnose an individual's health problems. For example, a doctor can measure a person's blood pressure, weight, and blood cholesterol level, and then predict the probability that the given patient will have a heart attack.

What Does "Linear" Mean?

The "linear" in linear regression and discriminant analysis refers to the way the independent variables are combined together to form a prediction. The general form is

$$Y = A + B_1 \cdot X_1 + B_2 \cdot X_2 + \cdots + U$$

where the X's represent the independent measures such as income, number of football games watched, and advertising expenditures from the previous examples. The A is some scale constant (just a number) that brings the units of measurement of the X's into the same scale as Y. The different B's represent the slope or degree of relationship between the X's and the Y. Y is the variable to be predicted. U represents uncertainty or randomness. Every prediction made through the use of regression and discriminant analysis has some error, U. The larger the U becomes, the more potential for error there is in the predictions.

Linear Regression Analysis

This section presents a brief discussion of the multiple regression technique in general, and the Biomedical Computer Program BMD02R, "Stepwise Regression," in particular. The BMD procedure has been adapted into many other computer programs including the Statistical Package for the Social Sciences (SPSS). The presentation is arranged into the format: mechanics of regression hypotheses, statistical assumptions, and discussion of two variations of the regression tool. A discussion of the computer output, the statistic used, and tips on use of the technique are included in Technical Appendix 1.

Mechanics of Regression

Regression is frequently employed in the analysis of empirical data. In this context, regression analysis is generally referred to as a procedure of fitting a line to a given set of data (usually observations on two variables). This line, called a regression line, has properties that:

> It has become customary in correlation analysis to fit a *regression line* to the data mathematically by the *least-squares method*. As the name might indicate, the line is fitted to the data in such a way that the sum of the squared differences of the observed *Y* (the dependent variable) values from the corresponding line values is a minimum.[1]

The most explicit and formal example of this context comes from "the two-variable linear model" in economic theory, $Y = A + BX + U$, where Y is the dependent or predicted variable, A and B are unknown parameters indicating the intercept and slope of the function, U is the error or disturbance term, and X is the independent or predictor variable. A and B represent constants. "The constant A represents the value of the Y intercept when X is zero." The B constant is generally known as the "coefficient of regression."

> It represents the slope of the curve [or line, in this case] and thus will be a positive value for positive correlation, and a negative value for a negative relationship. More specifically, the constant B shows the amount of change in the dependent variable (Y) which is associated with a one-unit change in the independent variable (X).[2]

An example of the fundamentals of regression analysis is shown in Figure 12.1. A market researcher has interviewed six families and obtained the data shown in the figure. Family 1 has an income of $5000 and two TV sets. The data for each family are plotted as shown in the figure. Family 1 appears as a "1" at the intersection of $5000 and 2 TV's. Similarly, all the

[1] B. Parl, *Basic Statistics*, (Garden City, N. Y.: Doubleday & Co., 1967), p. 226.
[2] *Ibid.*, p. 227.

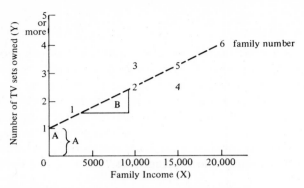

FIGURE 12.1   *An Example of a Regression Analysis*

families are plotted. A line is drawn such that the squared difference between the line and all of the data points is a minimum. This line has slope B and intersects the origin at the 1 TV set point. The slope B can be seen to be 1/5000. There is some error U with regard to the prediction of number of TV's as a function of income because two of the family data points fall off of the regression line by a total of 2 units. Thus, linear regression analysis gives the researcher a summary of the relationship of X to Y. In addition, the analysis shows how "good" the prediction of Y due to X is through reports of statistics concerned with the magnitude of U.

Typical Hypotheses

The multiple regression technique is most frequently employed in hypotheses pertaining to *prediction*. The general objective is to predict the values that the dependent variables will take, for various values of the independent variables (the predictor variables).

Multiple regression has also been employed, to a lesser extent, however, in theory construction and theory verification as a basis for *establishing control over a phenomenon*. As an example of this second usage of multiple regression, Bass notes that "one may wish to know the relationship between advertising and sales in order to control advertising."[3]

Statistical Assumptions of Regression

In order for the processes of linear regression to be meaningful, several important assumptions must be met. The *first* of these which underlies the

[3] Frank Bass, "Application of Regression Models in Marketing: Testing Versus Forecasting, *Workshop on Multivariate Methods* (University of Chicago, January 1970).

rest is that the measurement system is fully metric, that is, the numbers generated by the measuring system are perfectly related to each other. This implies that two is twice one (or binary–0,1 variables are used). Means of dealing with this issue are found in Chapter 6 in the discussion of attitude scaling in marketing research.

A second basic assumption is that the regression error term be *randomly distributed* or equivalently, that (for each observation *i*) $E(u_i) = 0$, or that the measurement of *Y*, the dependent variable, is unbiased. However, failure of this assumption will affect only the estimate of the mean of *Y*, but will not affect the estimate of the regression slope parameter (*B*).

The third assumption states that the *variance* of the error term must be *uniform* (that is, homoscedastic).[4] Heteroscedasticity does not imply, however, that the regression estimates are biased, but that the estimates will be less efficient, that is, the least squares method may not be appropriate.

The fourth assumption is that the *U*'s must be statistically independent of each other (that is, not autocorrelated) so that knowledge of U_i will not add information about another *U*. The effect of autocorrelation is to bias estimates of forecast variance and variance of the regression slope parameter *downward*—a dangerous result since no means of correction exist. One thus could be led to believe he has more information (that is, an estimate of *lower* variance) than he actually has. Typically, autocorrelation problems occur when time series data such as Gross National Product figures between 1958 and 1972 are regressed the same period's sales of U.S. Steel Corporation. This problem is usually solved by taking the first differences between observations. This amounts to regressing the change of GNP from year *t* to *t* + 1 against the change in U. S. Steel's sales in the same period. The statistic which measures the degree of autocorrelation is called the Durbin-Watson statistic.[5] The statistic is of the form

$$d = \frac{\sum_{T=2}^{n} (U_T - U_{T-1})^2}{\sum_{T=1}^{n} U_T^2}$$

and if $1 < d < 4$, the hypothesis that autocorrelation exists is rejected.

Fifth, for theory construction purposes (but not forecasting), the *U*'s must be uncorrelated with the independent variable in the regression equation. Failure to meet this assumption can lead to serious bias in the estimate of *B*.

---

[4] Homoscedasticity is defined as having constant variance across all observations. Heteroscedasticity is defined as not having constant variance.

[5] See J. Johnston, *Econometrics Methods*, 2nd ed. (New York: McGraw-Hill, 1972).

Sixth, if the true relationship between the independent and dependent variables is *not* linear (as is assumed), then the *range* over which forecasts and theoretical relationships can be accurately estimated is restricted.

The seventh assumption involves extending these assumptions to *multiple* regression analysis; one must also consider the problem of multicollinearity (where the independent variables are highly correlated among themselves). The presence of multicollinearity

> . . . reduces the efficiency of estimates of the regression slope parameters. Consequently, it is desirable to design experiments or use observations whose values of X [independent variables] exhibit as low a correlation among themselves as is possible. Observational data often exhibit high multi-collinearity, but sometimes a careful selection of variables or observations can minimize the damage.[6]

The stepwise regression procedure accomplishes this same result but by a different method. With the stepwise procedure, at every step in the regression process or iteration an independent variable having the least *multicollinearity* is selected and added to the regression equation. Multicollinearity in the BMD02R regression computer program is measured by the F statistic. Generally speaking, the higher the F score, the less multicollinearity is present. The procedure is described in the "General Description" of the program.

> This program computes a sequence of multiple linear regression equations in a stepwise manner. At each step one variable is added to the regression equation. The variable added is the one which makes the greatest reduction in the error sum of squares. Equivalently, it is the variable which has highest partial correlation with the dependent variable partialed on the variables which have already been added; and equivalently it is the variable which, if it were added, would have the highest F value.[7]

Definition of Stepwise versus Total Regression

The difference between total regression and stepwise regression centers around when and how the independent variables X are entered into the regression equation. The stepwise procedure assumes that no variables are entered in the regression equation at the beginning of the process. The computer program examines certain statistics describing the hypothesized independent variables. The variable which has the best explanation of dependent variable Y is then entered into the regression equation. The statistics for the "out" variables are recomputed after subtracting the effect of the correlation

---

[6] William F. Massy, "Statistical Analysis of Relations between Variables," in R. E. Frank, A. A. Kuehn, and W. F. Massy, *Quantitative Techniques in Marketing Analysis* (Homewood, Ill.: Irwin, 1962), p. 93.

[7] W. J. Dixon, *BMD: Biomedical Computing Programs*, 2nd ed. (Berkeley, Calif.: U. of California Press, 1970), p. 233.

of the "in" variable. Thus, the stepwise technique guarantees, in a sense, that only variables with the most independent "explanation" enter the regression.

Total regression, however, takes all of the hypothesized variables as being "in" the equation. No tests discriminating between the explanatory qualities of each variable are made. Thus, the independent variables may indeed explain the same variance of Y and may be correlated among themselves. When using this variation of the regression technique, one must examine the F statistic significance tests for each variable. The whole regression equation can be said to fail if one variable fails to meet the significant F criteria (assumption seven is violated).

Researchers have debated using the stepwise procedure arguing that the following scenario might occur. A researcher analyzes a set of 10 variables X to predict one variable Y. The set of readings X is the result of a given sample (sample number 1). The results show, using the stepwise procedure, that variables $X1$ and $X2$ are the only ones that enter the regression equation. Then the researcher replicates his sample (sample number 2). He then performs the same regression analysis. However, variables $X3$ and $X4$ now enter the regression equation as a result of the stepwise procedure. He then faces a quandary as to what the statistical "truth" is. This problem typically occurs when sample size is small (small in this sense means that the number of observations is less than two or three times the number of variables). A conservative rule-of-thumb to minimize the occurrence of the scenario states that the number of observations should be at least 10 times the number of variables.

Parsimony

The principle of parsimony is important to model builders as it implies that a researcher should strive to develop and test models which are as simple as possible while maintaining a high degree of explanation. Judging in terms of parsimony, the stepwise procedure is superior to total regression. The reason for this statement lies in the fact that the researcher can specify that only variables with a specified minimum degree of independent explanation will enter his regression equation.

Hypotheses to Be Tested with Each Regression Run

When using regression, several specific hypotheses must be tested which are subjects of the general linear hypothesis:

$$f(X, B, U) = Y$$

The specific hypotheses to be treated in any given regression involve the following test conditions:

1. The total reduction of variance from the included X variables must be significant relative to the total variance of U. This implies the use of an F statistic of the form (this tests the hypothesis that the total linear regression hypothesis is correct):

$$F = \frac{\text{Variance reduced by all } X(\text{in})/\text{d.f.}^8}{\text{Variance due to } U/\text{d.f.}}$$

2. The total variance reduced by any single variable should be significant in the manner of statement 1. This implies (this tests to make sure each independent variable is independent—assumption seven):

$$F = \frac{\text{Variance reduced by a single } X(\text{in})/\text{d.f.}}{\text{Variance due to } U/\text{d.f.}}$$

3. All of the individual b coefficients in B should be nonzero (another test of assumption seven):

$$t = \frac{b_i}{\text{std. error } (b_i)}$$

4. $E(U) = 0$ and $E(U'U) = s^2I$ implies that the residuals should be plotted and checked for homoscedasticity, that is, e is uniformly distributed for all values of a given X and have mean zero. The Durbin-Watson statistic checking autocorrelation may also be used.

The operational hypotheses involved with stepwise regression state that some subset of the hypothesized independent variables will predict the dependent variable Y. In other words, the researcher explicitly is taking into account that some of the independent variables may be correlated and not independent. The stepwise procedure used by the BMD02R or its modifications gives the user all test conditions. Variables are added to the regression equation until there is no further statistically significant reduction of variance due entering a new variable.

An Illustrative Test

A test is performed which shows the difference in results when stepwise regression and total regression are used to test the same linear hypotheses using the same data set. Demographics and interest in jams and jellies are hypothesized to predict a number of different brands of jam and jelly on hand in a given household. The predictor variables are shown in Table 12.1. The names of the variables are paraphrased from the actual questionnaire questions.

---

[8] d.f. means degree of freedom which is the number of variables—1 in the numerator and number of observations—in the denominator.

TABLE 12.1 *List of Independent Variables*

Variable Name

1   Number of boys in family between 0 and 6 years old
2   Number of boys in family between 6 and 12 years old
3   Number of boys in family between 12 and 19 years old
4   Number of girls in family between 0 and 6 years old
5   Number of girls in family between 6 and 12 years old
6   Number of girls in family between 12 and 19 years old
7   Total number of children under 18 living in your home
8   Family income
9   Income from outside regular employment
10 Rooms in home
11 Different homes have you lived in during last 15 years
12 Rent or own a house
13 Live in house, apartment, duplex
14 Degree of use—jam or jelly
15 Certain that jelly brand preferences are satisfactory
16 Willingness to try new jelly brands
17 Seriousness of jelly product failure
18 Willingness to spend time shopping for jelly

The data were generated from the Lafayette, Indiana Consumer Behavior Research Project (CBRP). This project was sponsored in part by Batten, Barton, Durstine and Osborne—a large advertising agency, the Ford Foundation, and the Krannert Graduate School of Industrial Administration of Purdue University.

The data reported here consist of a subset of the 540 housewives selected to participate in the CBRP. The sample was given systematically from phone directories of Lafayette, Indiana and vicinity. Data collection for the CBRP consisted of two questionnaires: one at the beginning of the project and one at the end of the project. In addition, laboratory and field experiments were done and a purchase diary was maintained by each of the 540 participants.

Three hundred subjects were used to test the differences between total regression and stepwise regression. The experiment was *not* "cooked up" but rather a straightforward test of the hypotheses. The same subjects, computer program, and list of independent variables were used. Table 12.2 shows the results of the comparison. The total regression has "failed" because 15 of its variables proved insignificant according to t tests of the B coefficients. The total regression is said to fail because the B coefficients of significant variables have been altered due to the effects of inclusion of insignificant variables. This effect can be clearly seen by comparing the number of children living at home variable. B value for the total regression is 0.40 versus 0.72 for the

TABLE 12.2   *Parameters and F Levels of Stepwise Versus Total Regression Independent Variables Predicting Number of Brands of Jelly Currently Owned for 300 Subjects*

	Stepwise		Total Regression	
Variable Entered	Coef. (std. error)	F Level	Coef. (std. error)	F Level
1 Number of children living at home[a] (7)	0.73 (0.08)	81.0	0.40 (0.20)	4.06
2 Use jam regularly[a] (14)	1.23 (0.15)	68.3	1.17 (0.16)	55.1
3 Jam product failure is serious[a] (18)	−0.72 (0.14)	25.4	−0.72 (0.15)	24.0
4 Other 15 variables	Not analyzed	Not analyzed	NS	NS
intercept	2.37		4.06	
Total regression F level	61.8		12.3	
Total R	0.62		0.64	
Standard error of estimation	2.298		2.302	

[a] Residual tests for homoscedasticity satisfied.
Note: All reported variables and F statistics are significant at 0.05 confidence level unless otherwise noted by NS. If the total regression had been rerun without the insignificant variables, the results would be the same as the stepwise approach.

stepwise method. One must also note that the F level in the stepwise regression is higher and thus one can have more confidence in his results. Also, the correlation (R) of the set of independent variables with the dependent variable for both methods is virtually the same. Lastly, the standard error of the estimate of the total regression is slightly larger than the stepwise regression.

How Does One Compute the Cutoff F Level in Stepwise Regression?

Computing the stopping F level for the stepwise regression involves specifying the degrees of freedom for the numerator and denominator and then consulting an F table. The degree of freedom of the numerator is the number of variables which are expected to enter into the regression equation. For a confidence level of 0.05, this number is 0.05 times the number of variables in the independent variable list. In the case illustrated in Table 12.1, this means that one variable (0.05×18) is expected to enter by chance alone. The degrees of freedom of the denominator is the number of observations (300) minus the number of degrees of freedom in the numerator (1) minus one which totals 298. One consults an F table for F (0.05, 1, 298) which is 3.84. If more variables actually enter, the level of confidence becomes greater, that is, F $(0.05, 1, 298) < F$ $(0.05, 2, 297)$. Thus, this method of computing the cutoff F level is conservative.

Discriminant Analysis

Discriminant analysis was apparently first used by R. A. Fisher (1936) for the purpose of classifying observations into the best fitting populations. This technique determines differences between populations on the basis of random samples drawn from each of the populations. The group differences are evaluated considering several variables simultaneously.

Multiple discriminant analysis (MDA) finds increasing application in marketing: it has been used to detect differences between sales territories, credit risks, early and late brand adopters (Frank & Massy), early and late buyers of a new product (Burger), Ford and Chevrolet owners (Evans), and so on. MDA also has been used to predict group membership by comparing the individual measures with the group profiles.

Discriminant Analysis Theory

There are several major assumptions central to linear discriminant analysis. Violation of the assumptions can cause serious difficulty in interpretation of results:

1. The observations are grouped, and each observation in each group involves at least two variables.
2. The populations from which the samples are obtained are multivariate normal (for statistical inference purposes) with *different means*, and all populations have *identical covariance* among variables.
3. Each population distribution is determined by the same variables.
4. The variables are independently normally distributed (this can be relaxed with new *BMD* computer programs).
5. The populations are exclusive and exhaustive.

The statistical process of linear discriminant analysis can be shown by examining an "ideal" type of experiment. A discriminant function is defined as a probability statement such as

$$\text{Likelihood } [ij] = A_j + B_j \cdot X_i$$

which states the likelihood that person i belongs to group j is a linear function of measure X. An example of this proposition is shown in Figure 12.2. A researcher has surveyed 100 college students and 100 noncollege students. The researcher has plotted the frequency of answers to the question "What is your parents' total income from all sources?" The mean value for the noncollege group was $7000 while the college groups had a mean value of $16,000. Clearly there was overlap in the groups in the $8000 to $14,000 range.

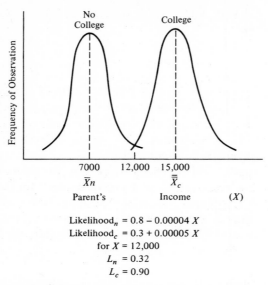

FIGURE 12.2 *An Ideal Discriminant Analysis Result*

The researcher submitted the data for analysis by the computer. The results are shown in Figure 12.2. Two functions were found by the computer. One function is for the noncollege groups while the other is for the college groups. The noncollege likelihood grows smaller as income increases while the reverse is true for the college function. The researcher is asked to classify an unknown young person into one or the other group. The researcher asks the young man what his parents' income is and he replies $12,000. The researcher computes that there is a 0.32 likelihood of him being noncollege and a 0.9 of being college. Without further information, the researcher guesses "college" knowing he has three of four chances of being correct [0.9/(0.9 + 0.3)].

An Example of a Discriminant Experiment

The program used in this analysis is the BMD07M, a stepwise procedure. It is capable of handling up to 80 variables and 80 groups. At each step in the procedure, one variable is entered into the set of discriminating variables. The variable entered is selected by one of the following equivalent criteria:

1. The variable with the largest F value
2. The variable which has the highest multiple correlation with the groups

3. The variable which gives the greatest decrease in the ratio of within to total generalized variances.

A variable can be deleted if its *F* value becomes too low.

The most important statistic provided by the BMD07M are those which help answer the following related questions:

1. *Which* independent variables are good discriminators?
2. How *well* do they discriminate?
3. What *decision rule* should be used for classifying individuals into the groups under study?

The *problem in this example* application of discriminant analysis was to determine if a set of variables existed which would adequately discriminate between readers and nonreaders of *Reader's Digest* magazine. Nineteen independent variables were chosen for inclusion in the analysis (see Table 12.3); some of these were demographic, and others were psychological variables. A total sample of 90 known readers and 90 known nonreaders was selected for analysis.

In the experiments shown here, groups were further split into two equal groups yielding four equal groups in all. One group of readers and another equal group of nonreaders is referred to as the validation sample. This group

TABLE 12.3 *Variables in Discriminant Analysis*

Number	
1.	Age: Boys under 6 years
2.	Age: Boys 6–12 years
3.	Age: Boys 12–19 years
4.	Age: Girls under 6 years
5.	Age: Girls 6–12 years
6.	Age: Girls 12–19 years
7.	Total family income group
8.	Number different houses lived in—last 15 years
9.	I am very active
10.	I am very friendly
11.	Scales: I am very intelligent
12.	I am very tense
13.	I am very interested in getting things done
14.	I very much want people to do what I tell them
15.	Husband's age group
16.	Education of husband
17.	Husband's occupation
18.	Religious denomination
19.	Average status of household (Bureau of Census status scored computed from income occupation and education of head of household)

will be used for classification only. This procedure was followed to lessen the likelihood of bias due to sampling error and search. Since the peculiar characteristics of the sample are used in calculation of the discriminant function using the analysis sample, it is expected that the proportion of cases correctly classified in the analysis sample will be biased upward to some degree. The bias is due to sampling errors in estimating the means of the populations. The direction of the bias is to show greater predictive power in classification than actually exists. The magnitude of the bias will decrease as the sample size becomes large.

The procedure used for eliminating these biases is the following: Estimate parameters using only some of the respondents (the analysis sample) available for a given study and compare predictions obtained by using these parameters to classify the remainder of the respondents. Control for bias due to sampling error is effected by performing the predictive test only on the validation sample results. The test for prediction significance is

$$T = \frac{Q - P}{\sqrt{P(1 - P)/n}} \tag{1}$$

where Q is the proportion of sample observations correctly classified by the discriminant analysis; P is the proportion one expects by chance (assuming equal group sizes, $P = 0.5$).

This T statistic is judged to be significant by examining a standard student's T table. This methodology was used to classify readers and nonreaders of *Reader's Digest* magazine for the validation sample. Three crucial points of analysis in discriminant analysis will be examined: (1) which variables entered significantly, (2) the classification results for the analysis sample, and (3) the classification results for the validation sample. The data base used is the same as the previous regression concerning jam and jelly brands.

The final list of variables is determined by examining the F ratios for each of the variables included at the final step in the output. At the final step (in the case where the F level for inclusion was specified to be 2.0), only five variables were included in the discriminant functions. Setting these F levels guarantees that only statistically significant variables will be included in the results. This means all the remaining variables (14 out of a total of 19) at this final step had F values of less than 2.0. The F levels for the above five variables are shown in Table 12.4.

Since the F values of variable 15 (husband's age group) and variable 16 (occupation of husband) are higher than the other discriminatory variables, it would appear that these two variables contribute more to the discriminatory power of the functions relative to the other variables. All are significant at the 0.05 level.

The next problem is to determine how well the final included variables discriminate subject in the analysis sample on the basis of the transformed

TABLE 12.4 *F Level for Discriminating Readers of Reader's Digest Magazine Versus Nonreaders*

Variable		F Value
Number	Name	
4.	Number of female children under 6	3.98
8.	Number of houses lived in	3.68
10.	"I am friendly"	3.06
15.	Husband's age	15.06
16.	Husband's occupation	4.08
	Total discrimination	4.51

U statistic printed on the output at the final step and a F ratio calculated in the manner indicated earlier (using the normal distribution for sample size n, greater than 30).[9] In the example, the transformed U statistic (the approximate F ratio) was calculated at 4.51 which is significant at the 0.01 level.

Lastly, it is desirable to perform another test of discrimination referred to as the "hard test" of predictive efficacy. A T ratio is calculated using Equation (1) to test the significance of the predictive accuracy of the functions for the validation sample. It was found that 66 percent of the validation respondents were correctly classified by the discriminant functions. The resulting T ratio[10] is significant at the 0.01 level since it was calculated as 3.08. So it is fair to conclude that the particular functions predict well above chance levels.

To summarize the results of the example which attempted to discriminate between readers and nonreaders of *Reader's Digest*, the results showed that one could discriminate. The final hypothesis showed that if the husband were older, the family contained fewer female children under 6 years, husband was blue collar, few houses had been lived in, and the person perceived herself as more friendly, there was considerable chance that the family would be readers of *Reader's Digest*. The "hard" test of discrimination where unknown cases were classified according to the discriminant rule and found to be 60 percent correct also showed the validity of the analysis. Thus, discriminant analysis tells the researcher if he can create meaningful distinctions among groups of respondents. Other measures that are calculated by the specific computer programs are shown in the attached appendixes. A detailed review of the mathematical underpinnings of discriminant analysis are appended for

[9] The U statistic is defined as the ratio between the determinant of the within group variance—covariance matrix to determinant of the total data variance—covariance matrix.

[10] $$T = \frac{0.50 - 0.66}{\sqrt{\dfrac{(0.5) \times (0.5)}{90}}} = 3.08$$

reference purposes. Additional technical theory and suggestions for use are found in Technical Appendix 1.

Summary

This chapter is designed to introduce the student to the linear methods commonly used by marketing researchers. These methods are linear regression and linear discriminant analysis. Both of these methods generally rely on a series of independent variables which "cause" or predict some behavior. Although causality is not implied through any of the statistical processes, generally, the scientist has created a structure of causal statements. These causal statements are tested by means of the linear statistical methods. Although these methods do not prove causality, they can defeat a causal hypothesis. In addition, these methods are used to forecast future events. Using past events, the linear methods are used to create prediction equations. These equations are then used to forecast future events using the assumption that the basic linear hypotheses hold true into the future.

Questions and Exercises

1. What is the chief purpose of multiple linear regression techniques? What does the word "multiple" refer to? What makes linear regression "linear"?
2. What does the term "least squares" refer to?
3. What is the relationship between the Pearson r correlation and the technique of multiple linear regression?
4. A famous auto parts company once used multiple regression to forecast sales for one of its products. The research analyst scoured the company files and found quite a bit of information on a year-by-year basis. The dependent variable was sales in Omaha, Nebraska dating from 1962 to 1973. The analyst discovered much data concerning Omaha and the national economy for the same period of time. The data consisted of 51 predictor variables including sales of cars in Omaha, sales of mufflers, population growth, economic growth statistics, rainfall, highway construction, and many other statistics for Omaha. In addition, he used governmental Gross National Product, Disposable Income, and Bank Reserves for the United States in general for the same period. He carefully punched the data onto computer cards with each year representing one observation for each of the independent variables. He performed a "total" regression and found that almost ½ of his variables predicted the dependent variable with a R^2 of 0.98. He was of course delighted to see that his model appeared to be supported.

Is there anything wrong with this approach to regression as a tool? What assumptions of the technique did the analyst violate, if any? Write a detailed critique of the scientific and technical problems of this analyst's approach.

5. What is the prime purpose of multiple discriminant analysis? Why is it not used too often in the "real world" of business? What serious practical limitations does it have? [*Hint*: See Chapter 6 regarding measurement.]

6. Examine Table 12.2. Assume that you were working for a jam or jelly manufacturer. Interpret the table and discuss the managerial implications of the findings reported. Are any advertising points suggested by the table?

7. Examine Table 12.4. Assume that you were working for *Reader's Digest*. Do the discriminant results suggest any management strategies?

8. In the Technical Appendix, examine the output of the BMD02R program. Specifically, look at the changes in the "F to Enter" column. Why do you suppose that the F to Enter changes as it does for the variables which are out and stay out of the regression equation? Notice how the F to Enter changes for variable 1. What could cause the changes, especially the big drop in the last step?

9. Similarly, notice the F to Enter in the Discriminant program, the BMD07M. Note how variable 7 drops in terms of F to Enter. What reasons could cause the drop?

10. Create some research designs that would effectively use the tool of regression.

11. Create some research designs that would use the tool of discriminant analysis.

12. Can regression be used with either dependent or independent variables being 0 or 1 with no other values being allowed? Is regression analysis equivalent to analysis of variance when 0 or 1 variables are used?

Project Related Questions

1. Do you have hypotheses which lend themselves to regression or discriminant test?

2. Are the variables metric or nonmetric?

3. Have you instituted proper checks to see that the analysis meets the statistical assumptions?

4. Are the independent variables "independent"? How can you check?

5. What results do you expect to see from this analysis?

The Multivariate Revolution in Marketing Research

Jagdish N. Sheth

Can the current multivariate methods revolution in marketing research be explained? What is the role of computer technology in the rapid diffusion of multivariate methods? This article defines multivariate analysis and discusses the reasons for the probable continuing increase in its use in marketing research.

Many would agree with the statement that the computer has produced significant advances in the natural and social sciences. However, this general observation overlooks the fact that these two areas have applied computer technology in different ways.

The current diffusion of computer technology is occurring at a time when most of the natural sciences possess several well-developed and invariant laws based on deductive reasoning. Under these circumstances the computer has provided opportunities for model building and for programming a complex network of constructs which enables large-scale testing of physical laws. The most outstanding example of these applications has been provided by the successful exploration of outer space.

However, the social sciences, including marketing, have yet to develop invariant laws. The result is that most of the research in this area is empirical. Attempts are made to explore realities in order to understand the basic nature of the disciplines. Thus, since much of marketing research is empirical and exploratory, the computer has been primarily used to analyze, sort, process, and compact standard commercial data into manageable data banks.

Perhaps computer utilization for model building in the natural sciences and for data analysis in the social sciences provides the best indication of the anticipated rapid adoption of multivariate methods in marketing research. In addition, two facilitating conditions have emerged which ensure large-scale diffusion of multivariate methods in the future.

SOURCE: Reprinted from the *Journal of Marketing*, Volume 35, (January 1971) p. 13–19. Published by the American Marketing Association.

474

The first condition refers to the fact that after three decades of systematic data-gathering, marketing research has learned the art of data collection. For example, procedures exist for drawing accurate samples from populations, training interviewers and respondents, receiving cooperation from respondents, designing structured questionnaires, and coding and tabulating collected data. In this respect, the marketing discipline may be more advanced than some of the other social sciences such as political science. In fact, the increasing accumulation and storage of market research reflects the validity and usefulness of the information collected. Today it is difficult to find a large-scale enterprise which has not been affected by the information explosion.

Second, the market place is a complex phenomenon. A multitude of factors intervene between the marketing activities of companies and market responses. A simple input-output approach does not seem to provide satisfactory answers to marketing problems. Therefore, attempts are constantly made to examine intervening factors and how they mediate between marketing activities and market responses. This has resulted in the collection of information which corresponds to the complexity of the phenomenon.

The capability of the computer to process these complex, large-scale data banks has resulted in the increased use of multivariate methods in marketing research. The extent of this "multivariate revolution" in marketing research is indicated by several factors. For example, a vast number of canned computer programs for these techniques are already developed and available.[1] In addition, several reviews on the usages of multivariate methods in marketing have been written.[2] A third indication is provided by the increasing number of articles in such journals as the *Journal of Marketing, Journal of Marketing Research,* and *Journal of Advertising Research* which treat applications of multivariate methods to marketing problems.

Inevitably, some questions may be raised about this revolution: How long will it last? Is it not just another fad which will fade away as soon as a new one is introduced? What will be the consequences on future marketing research if multivariate methods are here to stay? Which techniques will be the most relevant and important? However, before these questions can be answered, existing multivariate methods should be understood and classified.

[1] Kenneth M. Warwick, "Computerized Multivariate Methods," paper presented at AMA Workshop on Multivariate Methods in Marketing, Chicago, January 21–23, 1970.

[2] Jagdish N. Sheth, "Multivariate Analysis in Marketing," *Journal of Advertising Research,* Vol. 10 (February, 1970), pp. 29–39; Ronald E. Frank and Paul E. Green, "Numerical Taxonomy in Marketing Analysis: A Review Article," *Journal of Marketing Research,* Vol. 5 (February, 1968), pp. 83–98; and Paul E. Green, Frank J. Carmone, and Patrick J. Robinson, "Nonmetric Scaling Methods: An Exposition and Overview," *Wharton Quarterly,* Vol. 2 (Winter-Spring, 1968), pp. 159–173.

WHAT IS MULTIVARIATE ANALYSIS?

Although Kendall gives a more technical definition,[3] it is possible to characterize multivariate analysis as all statistical methods which simultaneously analyze more than two variables on a sample of observations. As such these methods are extensions of univariate analysis (all known distributions including binomial, poisson, and normal distribution as well as probability system and Bayesian approaches to the analysis of one variable), and bivariate analysis (including cross-classification, correlation, and simple regression used to analyze two variables).

Figure 1 presents a classification of most of the multivariate methods. It is based on three judgments the marketing researcher must make about the nature and utilization of his data: (1) Are some of the variables dependent upon others, thereby requiring special treatment? (2) If yes, how many are to be treated as dependent in a single analysis? and (3) What are the presumed properties of the data? Specifically, are the data *qualitative* (nonmetric) in that the marketing reality is scaled on nominal or ordinal scales, or *quantitative* (metric) and scaled on interval or ratio scales? The technique to be utilized will depend upon the answers to these three questions.

Multiple regression, including several of its variants such as stepwise regression and simultaneous regres-

[3] Maurice G. Kendall, *A Course in Multivariate Analysis* (London: Charles Grifflin & Company, 1957).

sion, is the appropriate method of analysis when the researcher has a single, metric dependent variable which is presumed to be a function of other independent variables. The objective of multiple regression is to predict the variability in the dependent variable based on its covariance with all the independent variables. This objective is then achieved by the statistical rule of least squares.

Whenever the researcher is interested in predicting the level of the dependent phenomenon, he would find multiple regression useful. For example, sales are predicted from the knowledge of their past relationship (covariance) with marketing efforts; market shares have been predicted based on consumer preference, retail structure, and point-of-purchase advertising and promotion; and consumer buying behavior is predicted from the knowledge of personality and socioeconomic profiles.

If the single dependent variable is dichotomous (e.g., male-female) or multichotomous (e.g., high-medium-low), and therefore nonmetric, the multivariate method of *multiple discriminant analysis* is appropriate. The primary objective of discriminant analysis is to *predict* an entity's likelihood of belonging to a particular class or group based on several predictor variables. For example, discriminant analysis has been widely used in marketing to predict whether (1) a person is a good or poor credit risk based on his socioeconomic and demographic profile, (2) innovators can be distinguished from noninnovators ac-

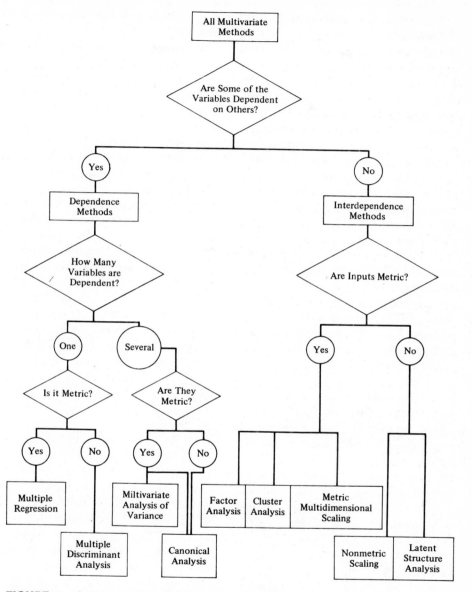

FIGURE 1 *A Classification of Multivariate Methods*

cording to their psychological and socioeconomic profiles, and (3) private label buyers can be separated from national brand buyers based on socioeconomic and purchasing differences.[4]

[4] Sheth, same reference as footnote 2.

The primary objective of multiple discriminant analysis is to correctly classify entities into mutually exclusive and exhaustive classes or groups. This objective is achieved by the statistical decision rule of maximizing the ratio of among-group to within-group variance-covariances on the profile of discriminating (predictor) variables. In addition to the prediction of class membership based on the profile, discriminant analysis reveals which specific variables in the profile account for the largest proportion of intergroup differences.

Multivariate analysis of variance (multi-ANOVA) is an extension of bivariate analysis of variance in which the ratio of among-groups variance to within-groups variance is calculated on a *set* of variables instead of a *single* variable. As such, multi-ANOVA is useful whenever the researcher is testing hypotheses concerning multivariate differences in group responses to experimental manipulations. For example, he may be interested in using one test market and one control market to examine the effect of an advertising campaign on sales as well as awareness, knowledge, and attitudes.

The objective in *canonical analysis* is to simultaneously predict a *set* of dependent variables from their joint covariance with a *set* of independent variables. Both metric and nonmetric data are acceptable in canonical analysis. The procedure followed is to obtain a set of weights for the dependent and independent variables which provides the maximum simple correlation between the composite dependent variable and the composite independent variable.

Canonical analysis appears very useful in marketing because the multitude of marketing and environmental factors tend to produce a variety of market responses. The writer, for example, is currently investigating the "hierarchy of effects" (awareness-interest-attitude-conviction-action) as multiple consequences of advertising and promotion.

Thus far the discussion has focused on multivariate methods applied to data which contain both dependent and independent variables. However, if the researcher is investigating the interrelations, and therefore the interdependence, among all the variables, several other multivariate methods are appropriate. These include factor analysis, cluster analysis, and metric multidimensional scaling if the variables are presumed to be metric, and nonmetric multidimensional scaling and latent structure analysis if they are presumed to be nonmetric.

Factor analysis is based on this proposition: If there is systematic interdependence among a set of observed (manifest) variables, it must be due to something more fundamental (latent) which creates this commonality. One can even consider all the manifest variables as simply *indicators* of this fundamental factor. What is this factor? Can it be extracted from the observed data and their relationships? Is it unidimensional or multidimensional? For example, can an individual's income, education, occupation, and dwelling area be considered as indicators of his social class? How can this factor be extracted? Conversely, factor analysis is also used as a data-reduction method which summarizes the commonality of all the manifest variables into a few factors.

The statistical approach utilized in factor analysis is to maximally summarize all of the variance (information), including the covariance (interdependence), in as few factors as possible, while retaining the flexibility of reproducing the original relationship among the manifest variables.

Factor analysis has been widely used in marketing. It has been used to (1) extract latent dimensions of relative liquor preferences such as sweetness, price, and regional popularity; (2) cluster a series of nighttime television programs or magazines based on their relative viewership and readership; and (3) systematically search for powerful predictors of a phenomenon under investigation.[5]

In *cluster analysis*, the objective is to classify a population of entities into a small number of mutually exclusive and exhaustive groups based on the similarities of profiles among entities. Unlike discriminant analysis, the groups are not predefined. In fact, two major objectives are to determine *how many* groups really exist in the population, and what is their composition.

Cluster analysis seems useful for market segmentation on personality, socioeconomic and demographic, psychological, and purchasing character-

istics of the consumers. However, several other applications have been made in marketing. Examples include the clustering of test market cities in order that they may be selected and controlled for experimentation, and grouping a variety of computers based on their objective performance characteristics.[6] Most of the clustering methods are judgmental, however, and devoid of statistical inferences. In fact, judgment is needed in selecting and coding attributes, in obtaining indices of resemblance or similarity, in choosing among various clustering algorithms, and in naming and testing derived clusters.

Both *metric* and *nonmetric multidimensional scaling* methods, unlike all other multivariate methods, start with a single piece of information. This information relates to perceived relative similarities among a set of objects, such as products, from a sample of respondents. The basic assumption in both metric and nonmetric multidimensional scaling methods is that people perceive a set of objects as being more or less similar to one another on a number of dimensions (usually uncorrelated with one another) instead of only one. However, it may be impossible to directly obtain this multidimensional map from the respondents. One reason for this difficulty is that the respondent may not be consciously aware that he is judging similarities among objects based on these dimensions. A second reason

---

[5] Sheth, same reference as footnote 2.

[6] Frank and Green, same reference as footnote 2.

is that he is unwilling to reveal factors (dimensions) that enter into his judgment on similarities. Given this impossibility of directly obtaining the dimensions, reliance is placed on statistical methods of multidimensional scaling to infer the number and types of dimensions that presumably underlie the expressed relative similarities among objects. Therefore, multidimensional scaling methods are applicable in those areas of marketing research where *motivation research* is currently used.

In both metric and nonmetric multidimensional scaling, the judged similarities among a set of objects (e.g., products, suppliers) are statistically transformed into distances by placing those objects in a multidimensional space of some dimensionality. For example, if objects A and B are perceived by the respondent as being most similar compared to all other possible pairs of objects, these techniques will position objects A and B in such a way that the distance between them in multidimensional space is shorter than that between any two other objects.

Despite the similarities between metric and nonmetric multidimensional scaling, there are two important differences. First, metric multidimensional scaling extracts the dimensionality of metric similarity data, whereas the input to nonmetric multidimensional scaling is nonmetric (ordinal) similarities. The metric similarities are often obtained on a bipolar similarity scale on which pairs of objects are rated one at a time. The nonmetric similarities are obtained by asking respondents to rank order (on the basis of similarity) all possible pairs that can be obtained from a set of objects. Various procedures such as dyadic or triadic combinations or rating scales can be used. Second, metric multidimensional scaling attempts to reduce the observed similarities to be represented in a space of minimum dimensions, from the trivial representation in n-1 dimensions, where n is the number of objects. In nonmetric multidimensional scaling, the objective is to metricize the nonmetric data by transforming nonmetric data into a metric space, and then by reducing the dimensionality. This is done by a decision rule of monotone transformation in which the observed rank orderings of pairs of objects are reproduced as closely as possible in an arbitrary metric space of some specified dimensions. This metric space is usually Euclidian, although non-Euclidian spaces can be created by the computer.

Although metric multidimensional scaling has not been applied to any large extent in marketing, nonmetric multidimensional scaling has become very popular in the last three years under the pioneering efforts of Paul Green. It has been applied to the dimensionality of similarities among automobiles, magazines, graduate schools, and several other sets of objects.[7]

Latent structure analysis shares both of the objectives of factor analysis: to extract latent factors and

[7] Green, Carmone, and Robinson, same reference as footnote 2.

express relationship of manifest variables with these factors as their indicators, and to classify a population of respondents into pure types. Traditionally, nonmetric data have been the input to latent structure analysis, although recently metric data have also been used. In marketing, the only applications of this method have been by Myers and Nicosia.[8] One of the main reasons for this has been the lack of computer programs to handle the tedious calculations inherent in this method.

IS MULTIVARIATE REVOLUTION A FAD?

A number of compelling reasons suggest that the rapid use of multivariate methods in marketing is not a fad. Instead, these methods are so important that they will be used more frequently in the future.

First, let us examine the anatomy of several behavioral and operations research methods (e.g., pupil dilation, Markov chains) that degenerated into fads. This was due to three factors. First, some operations research methods clearly proved to be ahead of their times. They presumed (through model building) considerable knowledge about the response functions to marketing efforts at a time when no one actually understood how the marketing mix is related to market reactions.

These research methods may prove useful once some laws of market behavior have been established. Second, other behavioral and operations research methods took a normative posture of how markets may or should behave at a time when the empirical inductive approach of descriptive research was considered more appropriate. Third, some methods, particularly in the behavioral area, proved to be genuine fads because they created the illusion that market complexity can be easily described by simple "buzz word" models.

None of these factors seems to be present in multivariate methods. Multivariate methods are largely empirical, deal with the market reality by working backward from reality to conceptualization, and easily handle the complexity presumed to be inherent in marketing research.

Second, multivariate methods as "innovative methods" seem to be consistent with modern marketing concepts of focusing on marketing research needs. And the most pressing need of marketing research is the ability to analyze complex data. This is clearly indicated by the following statement: "For the purposes of marketing research or any other applied field, most of our tools are, or should be, multivariate. One is pushed to a conclusion that unless a marketing problem is treated as a multivariate problem, it is treated superficially."[9]

As discussed earlier, this need for

---

[8] John G. Myers and Francesco M. Nicosia, "New Empirical Directions in Market Segmentation: Latent Structure Models," in *Changing Marketing Systems: Consumer, Corporate and Government Interfaces,* Reed Moyer (ed.) (Chicago: American Marketing Association, 1967).

[9] Ronald Gatty, "Multivariate Analysis for Marketing Research: An Evaluation," *Applied Statistics,* Vol. 15 (November, 1966), p. 158.

complex analysis is manifested today since data collection is a well-developed and standardized art, and computer capabilities are easily accessible.

Finally, a number of multivariate methods are simply extensions of univariate and bivariate analysis of data. Also, there exist a great variety of multivariate methods. Both of these factors contribute toward inhibiting their degeneration to fadism, because fads generally involve highly specialized research tools. However, some specific multivariate techniques may become fads due to overselling. In addition, we should expect the usual problems of coordinating the man-machine interface which are inevitable in the use of multivariate methods.

However, none of these factors is likely to deter the progress of the multivariate revolution primarily because all the facilitating conditions are present today.

ROLE OF THE COMPUTER IN MULTIVARIATE REVOLUTION

Perhaps the most important factor in the rapid diffusion of multivariate methods in marketing research is the availability of computer programs. In fact, we can assert that the lack of computer programs has been a major factor in the imbalance between the extensive data banks in existence today and their weak statistical analysis in most marketing research activities. It would seem that a union between multivariate methods and the computer will provide excellent opportunities for more scientific approaches to marketing problems.

What are the effects of this union on the development of marketing information systems? At present, marketing information systems in most companies basically consist of large data banks. However, a truly useful marketing information system requires an integrated approach between data banks and their retrieval and analysis in accordance with the needs of marketing management. Since most management decisions are complex, a truly multivariate analysis is needed that can be undertaken only if computer facilities are readily available. For example, a recurring decision in marketing management will involve budget allocation among several marketing forces, including advertising, direct mail, promotion, and personal selling. Ramond and Sheth have developed a marketing information system for budget allocation in which time-series audit data on market responses and marketing activities are analyzed by multivariate regression.[10] In essence, changes in shares of market responses such as sales are regressed on changes in shares of several marketing forces including advertising, direct mail, and promotion. Their relative weights and signs are then used by the marketing manager to choose one of the following alternatives given that his objective is to increase the profitability of marketing forces: (1) Maintain the present budget allocation policy. (2) Increase

---

[10] Charles Ramond and Jagdish Sheth, "Controlling Marketing Performance: Two Case Examples," paper presented to the Workshop on Marketing Information Systems, Association of National Advertisers, August 20, 1970.

the total budget by a certain amount to reach the optimum level of profitability. (3) Reallocate the budget among marketing forces proportionate to their relative weights. (4) Reduce the total budget by a certain amount to bring expenditures to the optimum level. (5) Phase out the product. This type of marketing information system could not be achieved without a complete interface between the computer and some multivariate method.

A second area benefiting from this interface is testing and estimating parameters of complex and comprehensive theories of the market place. Two specific examples may illuminate this point. First, in the area of advertising effectiveness, a number of researchers[11] have conceptualized a "hierarchy of effects" of advertising and promotion. This hierarchy usually begins with awareness and ends with purchase behavior; in between, several other effects such as interest, knowledge, preference, liking, and conviction are sequentially arranged. It is also presumed that advertising will have, in general, less impact as we move from awareness to action. It would seem that despite numerous empirical studies, no study has as yet attempted to validate the hierarchy by using an appropriate multivariate method.[12] Since the theory presumes a number of effects, canonical analysis appears most appropriate to test the theory and estimate parameters of relative relationships between the hierarchy of effects and a set of advertising variables such as media and copy. Unless such a complex multivariate analysis is done, it is not possible to either support or reject the theory of multiple advertising effectiveness. Much of the inconclusive support currently found in the research literature is perhaps due to this lack of multivariate analysis. Such multivariate analysis, however, was impossible without the appropriate computer capabilities.

Another example comes from an outstanding effort by Farley and Ring to fully test the Howard-Sheth theory of buyer behavior through the use of simultaneous linear equations and the computer.[13] Howard and Sheth have developed a comprehensive and complex theory of buyer behavior in which a large number of psychological constructs, such as attention, overt search, attitude, motives, and satisfaction, intervene between the marketing stimuli and the buyer's responses. In addition, a number of exogenous factors, such as social class, culture, and reference groups, also determine a buyer's responses via their influence on the psychological constructs. Finally, several of the constructs are dynamically interdependent on one another because of the theory's information processing

[11] Robert C. Lavidge and Gary A. Steiner, "A Model for Predictive Measurement of Advertising Effectiveness," *Journal of Marketing,* Vol. 25 (October, 1961), pp. 59–62.

[12] Kristian S. Palda, "The Hypothesis of a Hierarchy of Effects: A Partial Evaluation," *Journal of Marketing Research,* Vol. 3 (February, 1966), pp. 13–24.

[13] John V. Farley and L. Winston Ring, "Deriving an Empirically Testable Version of the Howard-Sheth Theory of Buyer Behavior," paper presented at the Third Annual Buyer Behavior Conference, Columbia University, May, 1969.

framework. Farley and Ring operationally defined these interdependencies in terms of a set of eleven simultaneous equations; then, using the panel data collected as part of the Columbia Buyer Behavior Project on a sample of more than 900 respondents, they tested the theory. Although they were only moderately successful in validating the theory, their effort represents one of the best examples of how the union between the computer and multivariate methods facilitates the testing of complex theories.

There are several areas of marketing research in which only univariate data have been collected, although the phenomenon is recognized to be complex. In these areas, the combination of multivariate methods and the computer may be most beneficial in furthering systematic and scientific analysis to possibly generate some invariant laws. An example is the research on durable appliances, particularly related to purchasing plans of households. Despite the recognition that purchasing plans are determined by a composite of several important factors, most attempts at measuring them have remained univariate. A single scale is used on which the degree of certainty of buying intentions within a specified time period is obtained from the respondents. It is very probable that this univariate scale is used as a surrogate for more complex factors and has not represented the construct well enough to either predict or explain subsequent purchasing behavior. With the use of multivariate methods such as factor analysis, it is conceivable that buying intentions may indeed prove to be a multidimensional concept.

CONCLUSION

A number of facilitating factors suggest that multivariate methods may rapidly diffuse in marketing research, and may become a way of life in the statistical analysis of marketing data. These include (1) the empirical, inductive tendency in conducting marketing research due to lack of discovery of marketing laws; (2) collection of large-scale data on marketing problems; (3) confidence in data banks in terms of their reliability and validity; and (4) availability of computers and canned computer programs. The last factor is certainly the most important one in enhancing the diffusion of multivariate methods.

The role of the computer in furthering the maturity of the marketing discipline is thus immense. By diffusing multivariate methods, it is likely to enable marketing researchers to attempt large-scale marketing information systems in which an integrated marketing approach can be undertaken. It will enable researchers to test and estimate parameters of complex generalized theories and models. With the use of multivariate methods, the computer is likely to generate a sudden increase in in-depth scientific empirical research on well-known issues in marketing.

Technical Appendix 1

Computer Output Interpretation SPSS: Stepwise Regression

This appendix is designed to be a reference manual for users of regression computer programs. This discussion is designed to help the user of SPSS and other programs to understand each item in the computer printout. Since many other computer programs are based on the original BMD02R, this exposition may be used to understand a wide variety of regression outputs. Figure 12.3 is taken directly from SPSS output. The F levels for inclusion and deletion have been set for proper levels and a plot of residuals is not included. The example is a rerun of the experiment in the chapter with a 30 percent larger sample size. Each section below is a discussion of a specific section of the computer output starting with the section on means and standard deviations.

1. *Univariate Analysis of Variables*   The means and standard deviations are shown in Figure 12.3 for each of the variables. All variables, whether used as dependent or independent, are listed.

2. *Labeling*   An optional step in the SPSS is the opportunity to name each variable (or as many variables as one wishes) used in the program. This step allows the analyst to more easily and readily comprehend the output.

3. *Correlation Coefficient Matrix*   These are all the simple coefficients representing the relationship for each possible pair of variables. Note that the coefficients are all 1's in the principal diagonal, the logical result of correlating a variable with itself. These coefficients can vary from -1 to 1. A coefficient of -1.00 means perfect negative or inverse relationship, a coefficient of $+1.00$ means perfect positive correlation, and a coefficient of 0 means no relationship. It is important to note the following in interpreting these coefficients:

   a. These coefficients are unadjusted for degrees of freedom lost in measuring the estimating equation. Thus, they are larger ·than they should be and should be adjusted by multiplying them by $N - 1/N$, with N being the sample size.

   b. It is preferable that the correlations between the independent variables be low. Otherwise, the independent variables tend to

VARIABLE	MEAN	STANDARD DEV	CASES
VAR001	0.3426	0.6152	394
VAR002	0.2893	0.5774	394
VAR003	0.21C7	0.5182	394
VAR004	0.5812	0.5912	394
VAR005	0.3122	C.5939	394
VAR006	0.2843	0.5929	394
VAR007	1.7157	1.5776	394
VAR008	3.5279	1.6253	394
VAR009	2.6751	0.7247	394
VAR010	3.C27%	1.2218	394
VAR011	4.C660	2.4424	394
VAR012	1.6218	C.4855	394
VAR013	1.3579	0.5674	394
VAR014	1.7183	C.8586	394
VAR015	1.5178	0.9113	394
VAR031	1.9492	0.9342	354
VAR032	2.5152	0.6738	354
VAR033	3.0508	0.5989	394
VAR034	2.5406	0.9244	394

CORRELATION COEFFICIENTS

A VALUE OF 99.00000 IS PRINTED
IF A COEFFICIENT CANNOT BE COMPUTED.

	VAR001	VAR002	VAR003	VAR004	VAR005	VAR006	VAR007	VAR008	VAR009	VAR010	VAR011	VAR012
VAR001	1.CCC00	0.C9269	-0.C9929	0.C7815	0.03382	-0.16306	0.32345	-0.15846	0.10192	0.00755	0.19152	-0.07621
VAR002	0.C9269	1.C0000	0.13595	0.C8821	0.16631	0.13077	0.53747	0.10254	0.08535	0.25543	0.10913	0.19162
VAR003	-0.09929	0.13595	1.C0000	-0.07752	0.27361	0.21670	0.41564	0.18183	0.00654	0.30418	-C.11758	0.14552
VAR004	0.07815	C.C8821	-0.C7752	1.CC0C0	0.05782	-0.06920	0.37796	-0.10325	0.07489	0.06521	0.14055	0.02900
VAR005	0.03382	0.16631	0.27361	0.05782	1.00000	0.24595	0.60554	0.09771	0.05257	0.27551	0.13312	0.18986
VAR006	-0.16306	0.13C77	0.21870	-0.C6920	0.24595	1.CC000	0.44839	0.27162	0.04966	0.31567	-0.05867	0.25946
VAR007	0.32345	C.53747	0.41564	0.37796	0.60554	0.44839	1.C0000	0.15195	0.12822	0.44370	0.16865	0.29113
VAR008	-0.15846	0.10254	0.18183	-0.1C325	0.09771	0.27162	0.15195	1.C000C	0.04012	0.61272	-0.06200	0.52124
VAR009	0.10192	0.08535	0.00654	0.07489	0.05257	0.04966	0.12822	0.04012	1.00000	0.00740	0.07827	-0.00294
VAR010	0.00755	0.25543	0.30418	0.06521	0.27551	0.31567	0.44370	0.61272	0.00740	1.00000	-0.06969	0.69123
VAR011	0.19152	0.10913	-0.11758	0.14055	0.13312	-0.05867	0.16865	-0.06200	C.C7827	-0.06969	1.00000	-0.18274
VAR012	-0.07621	0.19162	0.14552	0.02900	0.18986	0.25946	0.29113	0.52124	-0.00294	0.69123	-0.18274	1.00000
VAR013	0.C7061	-0.23518	-C.23109	-0.07383	-0.22666	-0.26532	-0.36075	-0.43436	-0.00119	-C.66039	0.10226	-0.66197
VAR014	-0.10100	-0.16878	-0.09504	-0.00894	-0.06661	-0.05221	-0.15076	0.01933	-0.08612	-0.01189	-0.08576	-0.03038
VAR015	-0.C767C	0.04340	-C.C1064	-0.06953	-0.11606	0.07069	-0.05665	0.14558	-0.02206	0.11039	-0.06112	0.06410
VAR031	-0.02722	-0.01588	-C.C6722	0.13060	0.00112	-0.00145	0.01781	0.05121	-0.03569	0.09933	0.10184	0.02489
VAR032	-0.02183	-0.03752	0.04545	-0.00258	0.01035	-0.10640	-0.02943	0.06467	-0.02111	0.05357	-0.12586	0.09932
VAR033	0.02864	-0.02786	0.05564	-0.02404	0.01256	-0.01208	-0.00623	-0.01453	-0.06157	0.01544	-0.03535	-0.00382
VAR034	0.12068	-0.026e4	-C.C0462	0.01594	0.07186	-0.03504	0.04457	-0.03124	-0.02583	-0.01114	0.05178	-0.01955

	VAR013	VAR014	VAR015	VAR031	VAR032	VAR033	VAR034
VAR001	0.C7061	-0.10100	-0.C7670	-0.02722	-0.02183	0.02864	0.12008
VAR002	-0.23918	-C.16878	C.04340	-0.C1588	-0.03752	-0.02786	-0.02694
VAR003	-0.231C9	-C.C9504	-0.01064	-0.06722	0.04545	0.05564	-0.00462
VAR004	-0.07383	-0.C0894	-C.C6953	0.13060	-0.00258	-0.02404	0.01594
VAR005	-0.22666	-0.06661	-C.11606	0.00112	0.01035	0.01256	0.07186
VAR006	-0.26532	-C.05221	0.C7C69	-0.00145	-0.10640	-0.01208	-0.03504
VAR007	-0.36075	-C.15C76	-0.05665	0.C1781	-0.02943	-0.00623	0.04457
VAR008	-0.43436	0.C1533	0.14558	0.C5121	0.06467	-0.01453	-0.03124
VAR009	-0.00119	-0.C8612	-0.02206	-0.03569	-0.02111	-0.06157	-0.02583
VAR010	-0.66035	-0.01189	0.11039	0.C9933	0.05357	0.01544	-0.01114
VAR011	0.1C226	-C.08576	-0.06112	0.10184	-0.12586	-0.03535	0.05178
VAR012	-0.66157	-C.03038	C.06410	0.02489	0.09932	-0.00382	-0.01955
VAR013	1.CC0C0	0.C5600	-0.09352	0.01036	-0.11745	-0.C0866	-0.01565
VAR014	0.05600	1.00000	-C.17732	0.C3288	0.01403	0.17137	0.16352
VAR015	-0.C9352	-0.17732	1.C0000	0.13257	-0.21594	-0.15550	-0.21229
VAR031	0.01036	0.C3288	0.13257	1.C0C00	-C.31004	-0.01357	-0.C0645
VAR032	-0.11745	C.01403	-0.21594	-0.31004	1.CC0C0	0.98005	0.01739
VAR033	-0.C0866	0.17137	-C.15550	-0.01357	0.0e0C5	1.00000	0.22145
VAR034	-0.01565	0.16352	-0.21229	-0.C0645	0.01739	0.22145	1.CCC00

```
* * * * * * * * * * * * * * * * * * *   M U L T I P L E   P E G R E S S I O N  * * * * * * * * * * * * * *     VARIABLE LIST  1
                                                                                                              REGRESSICN LIST  1
```

DEPENDENT VARIABLE.. VAR015   NO DIFFERENT BRANDS IN HOUSE

VARIABLE(S) ENTERED ON STEP NUMBER 1.. VAR032   ATTITUDE TCWARD BRAND

MULTIPLE R	0.21594	ANALYSIS CF VARIANCE	DF	SUM OF SQUARES	MEAN SQUARE	F
R SQUARE	0.04663	REGRESSION	1.	15.21842	15.21842	19.17237
STANDARD ERROR	0.89094	RESIDUAL	392.	311.15721	0.79377	

---------------- VARIABLES IN THE EQUATION -----------------   ----------- VARIABLES NOT IN THE EQUATION --------------

VARIABLE	B	BETA	STD ERROR B	F	VARIABLE	BETA IN	PARTIAL	TOLERANCE	F
VAR032	-0.29206	-C.21594	0.06670	19.172	VAR001	-0.08145	-0.C8340	0.99952	2.738
(CONSTANT)	2.25237				VAR002	0.03535	0.03618	0.99859	0.512
					VAR003	-0.CCC83	-0.CCC85	0.99793	0.000
					VAR004	-0.J7C09	-0.C7178	0.99999	2.025
					VAR005	-0.11384	-0.11659	0.99989	5.388
					VAR006	0.04826	0.04914	0.98868	0.946
					VAR007	-0.06306	-0.C6456	0.99913	1.636

FIGURE 12.3 *Linear Regression: Computer Output*

VAR008	0.16464	0.16826	0.99582	11.392
VAR009	-0.02663	-0.02727	0.99955	0.291
VAR010	0.12231	0.12508	0.99713	6.215
VAR011	-0.08972	-0.09116	0.98416	3.276
VAR012	0.08640	0.08805	0.99014	3.055
VAR013	-0.12054	-0.12260	0.98621	5.967
VAR014	-0.17433	-0.17852	0.99980	12.871
VAR031	0.07260	0.07069	0.90387	1.964
VAR033	-0.13910	-0.14201	0.99359	8.047
VAR034	-0.20860	-0.21360	0.99970	18.693

DEPENDENT VARIABLE.. VAR015   NO DIFFERENT BRANDS IN HOUSE

VARIABLE(S) ENTERED ON STEP NUMBER 2.. VAR034   WILLING TO SEARCH FOR REQUIRED BRAND

MULTIPLE R	0.30021		
R SQUARE	0.09013		
STANDARD ERROR	0.87149		

ANALYSIS OF VARIANCE	DF	SUM OF SQUARES	MEAN SQUARE	F
REGRESSION	2.	29.41558	14.70779	19.36539
RESIDUAL	391.	296.96005	0.75949	

------------------ VARIABLES IN THE EQUATION ------------------

VARIABLE	B	BETA	STD ERROR B	F
VAR032	-0.28716	-0.21231	0.06526	19.364
VAR034	-0.20563	-0.20860	0.04756	18.693
(CONSTANT)	2.76247			

------------ VARIABLES NOT IN THE EQUATION --------------

VARIABLE	BETA IN	PARTIAL	TOLERANCE	F
VAR001	-0.05698	-0.05928	0.98482	1.375
VAR002	0.02990	0.03131	0.99791	0.383
VAR003	-0.00196	-0.00205	0.99790	0.002
VAR004	-0.06677	-0.06999	0.99974	1.920
VAR005	-0.09940	-0.10393	0.99475	4.259
VAR006	0.04130	0.04303	0.98758	0.723
VAR007	-0.05376	-0.05628	0.99710	1.239
VAR008	0.15802	0.16523	0.99477	10.946
VAR009	-0.03197	-0.03349	0.99891	0.438
VAR010	0.11980	0.12540	0.99698	6.231
VAR011	-0.07851	-0.08153	0.98125	2.610
VAR012	0.08196	0.08547	0.98968	2.870
VAR013	-0.12344	-0.12851	0.98602	6.548
VAR014	-0.14411	-0.14903	0.97314	8.859
VAR031	0.07236	0.07212	0.90387	2.039
VAR033	-0.09766	-0.09954	0.94515	3.903

DEPENDENT VARIABLE.. VAR015   NO DIFFERENT BRANDS IN HOUSE

VARIABLE(S) ENTERED ON STEP NUMBER 3.. VAR008   INCOME

MULTIPLE R	0.33907		
R SQUARE	0.11497		
STANDARD ERROR	0.86061		

ANALYSIS OF VARIANCE	DF	SUM OF SQUARES	MEAN SQUARE	F
REGRESSION	3.	37.52288	12.50763	16.88741
RESIDUAL	390.	288.85276	0.74065	

------------------ VARIABLES IN THE EQUATION ------------------

VARIABLE	B	BETA	STD ERROR B	F
VAR032	-0.30110	-0.22262	0.06458	21.739
VAR034	-0.20059	-0.20348	0.04659	18.221
VAR008	0.08660	0.15802	0.02678	10.946
(CONSTANT)	2.47215			

------------ VARIABLES NOT IN THE EQUATION --------------

VARIABLE	BETA IN	PARTIAL	TOLERANCE	F
VAR001	-0.03320	-0.03460	0.96125	0.466
VAR002	0.01356	0.01432	0.98701	0.080
VAR003	-0.03127	-0.03266	0.96580	0.415
VAR004	-0.05110	-0.05402	0.98916	1.138
VAR005	-0.11634	-0.12273	0.98483	5.949
VAR006	-0.00336	-0.00340	0.91020	0.005
VAR007	-0.08033	-0.08422	0.97285	2.779
VAR009	-0.03846	-0.04083	0.99724	0.650
VAR010	0.03720	0.03124	0.62432	0.380
VAR011	-0.07032	-0.07394	0.97852	2.138
VAR012	-0.00018	-0.00017	0.72397	0.000
VAR013	-0.06755	-0.06432	0.80256	1.616
VAR014	-0.14804	-0.15519	0.97257	9.600
VAR031	0.06024	0.06071	0.89877	1.439
VAR033	-0.09558	-0.09876	0.94499	3.832

DEPENDENT VARIABLE.. VAR015   NO DIFFERENT BRANDS IN HOUSE

VARIABLE(S) ENTERED ON STEP NUMBER 4.. VAR014   USE OF JAM OR JELLY

MULTIPLE R	0.36917		
R SQUARE	0.13628		
STANDARD ERROR	0.85127		

ANALYSIS OF VARIANCE	DF	SUM OF SQUARES	MEAN SQUARE	F
REGRESSION	4.	44.47952	11.11988	15.34478
RESIDUAL	389.	281.89612	0.72467	

------------------ VARIABLES IN THE EQUATION ------------------

VARIABLE	B	BETA	STD ERROR B	F
VAR032	-0.29917	-0.22119	0.06388	21.932
VAR034	-0.17664	-0.17919	0.04712	14.053
VAR008	0.09056	0.16155	0.02650	11.686
VAR014	-0.15712	-0.14804	0.05071	9.600
(CONSTANT)	2.66946			

------------ VARIABLES NOT IN THE EQUATION --------------

VARIABLE	BETA IN	PARTIAL	TOLERANCE	F
VAR001	-0.05196	-0.05441	0.94721	1.152
VAR002	-0.01175	-0.01237	0.95852	0.059
VAR003	-0.04694	-0.04938	0.95571	0.948
VAR004	-0.05246	-0.05614	0.98908	1.227
VAR005	-0.12938	-0.13768	0.97811	7.497
VAR006	-0.01183	-0.01213	0.90743	0.057
VAR007	-0.11595	-0.12039	0.93114	5.706
VAR009	-0.05109	-0.05470	0.99022	1.165
VAR010	0.03126	0.02657	0.62367	0.274
VAR011	-0.08492	-0.08998	0.96990	3.167
VAR012	-0.00840	-0.00777	0.72228	0.023
VAR013	-0.05497	-0.05282	0.79751	1.086
VAR031	0.06622	0.06750	0.89746	1.776
VAR033	-0.07599	-0.07870	0.92636	2.418

487

DEPENDENT VARIABLE.. VAR015   NO DIFFERENT BRANDS IN HOUSE

VARIABLE(S) ENTERED ON STEP NUMBER 5..   VAR005   NO FEMALE CHILDREN GT6 BUT LT 12

		ANALYSIS OF VARIANCE	DF	SUM OF SQUARES	MEAN SQUARE	F
MULTIPLE R	C.39071	REGRESSION	5.	49.82284	9.96457	13.98016
R SQUARE	0.15265	RESIDUAL	388.	276.55279	0.71276	
STANDARD ERROR	0.84425					

--------------- VARIABLES IN THE EQUATION ------------------ | ------------ VARIABLES NOT IN THE EQUATION -------------

VARIABLE	B	BETA	STD ERROR B	F	VARIABLE	BETA IN	PARTIAL	TOLERANCE	F
VAR032	-0.29858	-C.22075	0.06335	22.210	VAR001	-0.04778	-0.05050	0.94623	0.989
VAR034	-0.16535	-0.16773	0.04691	12.422	VAR002	0.00791	0.0C832	0.93722	0.027
VAR008	0.09797	C.17473	0.02642	13.754	VAR003	-0.01438	-0.01477	0.89311	0.084
VAR014	-0.16854	-0.15879	0.05047	11.153	VAR004	-0.04400	-0.04743	0.98460	0.873
VAR005	-0.19853	-0.12938	0.07251	7.497	VAR006	0.02024	0.02038	0.85911	0.161
(CONSTANT)	2.69478				VAR007	-0.05709	-0.04798	0.59854	0.893
					VAR009	-0.04542	-0.04905	0.98824	0.933
					VAR010	0.08149	0.C6726	0.57732	1.759
					VAR011	-0.06902	-0.C7320	0.95310	2.085
					VAR012	0.01622	0.01478	0.70347	0.085
					VAR013	-0.08697	-0.C8268	0.76585	2.664
					VAR031	0.06626	·0.06819	0.89746	1.808
					VAR033	-0.07482	-0.C7823	0.92629	2.383

F-LEVEL OR TOLERANCE-LEVEL INSUFFICIENT FOR FURTHER COMPUTATION

DEPENDENT VARIABLE.. VAR015   NO DIFFERENT BRANDS IN HOUSE

SUMMARY TABLE

VARIABLE		MULTIPLE R	R SQUARE	RSQ CHANGE	SIMPLE R	B	BETA
VAR032	ATTITUDE TOWARD BRAND	0.21594	0.04663	0.04663	-0.21594	-0.29858	-0.22075
VAR034	WILLING TO SEARCH FOR REQUIRED BRAND	0.30021	0.09013	0.04350	-0.21229	-0.16535	-0.16773
VAR008	INCOME	C.33907	0.11497	0.02484	0.14958	0.09797	0.17473
VAR014	USE OF JAM OR JELLY	0.36917	0.13628	0.02131	-0.17732	-0.16854	-0.15879
VAR005	NO FEMALE CHILDREN GT6 BUT LT 12	0.39071	0.15265	0.01637	-0.11606	-0.19853	-0.12938
(CONSTANT)						2.69478	

FIGURE 12.3 *(continued)*

duplicate each other and, hence, contribute little more in combination than they do separately.

c. Although it seems logical to prefer the relationship between an independent variable and a dependent variable to be high because this seems to indicate good error reduction even when the other variables are included, this is not a necessary condition. It is entirely possible for independent variables with low sample correlation to show high *partial* correlation and vice versa.

4. *Dependent Variable*   The number refers to the variable designated the dependent variable in the regression run.

5. *Variable Entered*   This tells the number of the variable that is entered into the equation on this step.

6. *Multiple R*   This number is the *coefficient of correlation*. This refers to the proportion of the variance in the dependent variable that is explained by the total number of variables in the equation. Each successive step will increase this number but the contributions of successive additions will generally be smaller and smaller. This num-

ber is not to be confused with the *coefficient of multiple determination* which is R squared (R^2).

7. *Standard Error of the Estimate*   The regression line represents only a measure of the average relationship between the dependent and the independent variable(s). Usually this average relationship will not provide completely accurate estimates for individual observations. The standard error of the estimate is a measure of the standard deviation of the observations about the estimating line. The greater the dispersion, or scatter, of the observations around the regression line, the greater the estimating error.

The standard error of the estimate is a measure expressed in absolute terms, that is, in the same units as the dependent variable. Because of the use of different units and magnitudes of the dependent variable values in various correlation studies, the standard error of the estimate cannot be employed to compare the degree of relationship between variables in different kinds of studies.

8. *Analysis of Variance*   This section provides the data for a probability calculation that can be used to judge whether the observed degree of relationship should be treated as though it could have occurred by chance. The analysis of variance calculations make the following two assumptions which should be verified by the analyst before too much reliance is placed on the analysis of variance results.

a. The data generation process is such that it can fairly be treated as a random process so that the degree of variation observed in the sample data is a fair representation of the variation in the universe.

b. The universe from which the sample data came is normally distributed.

The number of *degrees of freedom* refers to the number of independent values in the sample which contribute information about the standard deviation of the universe. In each regression step, one degree of freedom is lost in the process of calculating the arithmetic mean, a necessary preliminary to the calculation of the standard deviation. In least squares regression, the number of constants in the regression equation tells us the total number of degrees of freedom that are absorbed in the calculation of the line. In the output, the regression uses K degrees of freedom which when combined with the one degree of freedom needed to calculate the arithmetic mean, leaves a residual number of degrees of freedom. The sum of these three equals the total sample size.

The *sum of squares* is shown as two numbers. The top figures refer to the sum of the squares of the deviations of the estimated values around their mean. This sum is defined as the "variation due to the regression" or the "explained variation." The bottom figure refers to the sum of the squares of the deviations of the original independent values from the estimating line. This sum is defined as "deviation about regression" or "unexplained variation."

The *F value* is obtained by dividing the "explained variance" by the "unexplained variance." Interpretation of the *F* ratio is made with reference to the appropriate *F* distribution, corresponding the existing combination of *N*, one *n* referring to the degree of freedom in the numerator of the ratio and the other to the degrees of freedom in the denominator. The *F* value can be used to test the so-called null hypothesis that the *X* and *Y* are uncorrelated. The test consists of estimating the probability, then an *F* value at least as large as that observed could have occurred by chance. Referring to a table of *F* distributions and picking the appropriate *n* values (degrees of freedom values) we find an *F* value that will occur 0.10, 0.05, 0.025, 0.01, and 0.001 of the time. These values get larger as we go from the 0.10 to the 0.001 levels of significance. The computed *F* value can be compared to these values to determine if the observed correlation could have occurred by chance alone. If our computed value is larger, say, than the table's value for 0.001, we can say that there would be about 0.001 chances that an *F* as large as this could have occurred by chance.

9. *Variables in Equation*   This section tests the variables that are included in the regression equation along with their accompanying coefficients and statistics.

   a. *Constant*: This value refers to the intercept value. It is the value of the dependent variable when the independent variables equal zero.

   b. *Column Headed "Variable"*: This identifies the particular variable at issue.

   c. *Regression Coefficient*: These refer to the *b* values in the least squares equations. Beta is B/standard deviation.

   d. *Standard Error of Regression Coefficient*: This measure is the estimated sampling error of each *b* value. As a rule-of-thumb, the *b* value should be twice the value of the standard error of regression coefficient. If not, the variable is insignificant.

   e. *F to Remove*: This value is the computed value for each variable already in the regression equation which is compared to the *F* ratio value to determine whether that variable should be removed from the equation. The addition of the variable that is included in a particular step changes the *F* values for the variables that had been included on previous steps. The *F* ratio is recomputed for each of the already included variables and is compared to the *F* ratio value predesignated by the analyst at the beginning of the program (that is, the *F* level for deletion). If the recomputed *F* value is not greater than the *F* level designated by the analyst for deletion at the beginning of the program, it is deleted from the equation.

10. *Variables Not in Equation* This section tests the variables that are *not* included in the regression equation along with their respective coefficients and statistics.

   a. *Column Headed "variable"*: This again identifies the particular variable at issue.

   b. *Partial Correlation*: Given the independent variables already in the equation, this statistic tells the amount of explanation of the variation in the dependent variable that could be added by including the independent variable at issue. It shows the relative usefulness of each of the remaining variables not included in the equation in explaining the variation in the dependent variable.

   c. *Tolerance*: The ratio of variance explained by the variable if it were divided by total variance of the variable.

   d. *F to Enter*: This value is the computed *F* ratio value for each variable *not* in the regression equation which is compared to the *F* ratio for inclusion value to determine whether that variable should be entered into the regression equation. Each step by adding a variable from the variables *not* already in the equation will change the *F* ratio value for the remaining variables not in the regression equation. This value is then compared to the *F* ratio value predesignated by the analyst at the beginning of the program (that is, the *F* level for inclusion). In general, the variable with the highest *F* ratio value will be the included variable in the regression equation in the next step. When this rule is not adhered to, it is because the programmer has designated certain variables as forced into the equation before other variables can be added.

11. *Summary Table* This table provides a quick summary of the results of the steps in the regression equation.

   a. *Step Number*: This number designates the step referred to in the summary table.

   b. *Variable Entered or Removed*: This summary gives the variable that is entered on each step and (if applicable) the variable that is removed in each step. These variables are designated by label (if given in the set up of the program) and by number.

   c. *Multiple R and RSQ*: These values relate the amount of the variation in the dependent variable that is explained by the independent variable(s) in each step. The multiple *RSQ* is simply the squared value of the multiple *R*.

d. *Increase in RSQ:* This value relates the increase in the explanation of the variation in the dependent variable attributable to the addition of the independent variable in each step.

e. *F Value to Enter or Remove:* This value relates the F ratio value that each variable had when it was included (or removed) in the equation at the step when it was included (or removed).

f. *Number of Independent Variables Included:* This is the number of independent variables included and totaled for each of the steps in succession.

12. *List of Residuals*   This list shows the residual or difference between each of the computed dependent variables and the observed dependent variable for each observation in the sample. This difference is the error term for each observation.

a. *Case:* This represents the number of the observation.

b. *Residual:* This is the difference between the computed dependent variable and the observed dependent variable in the case designated.

Output from a Linear Discriminant Analysis Program (SPSS)

The output from one of the best discriminant analysis computer programs currently available is shown in Figure 12.4. Each section of the program is discussed. The experiment is a larger sample rerun of the experiment in the chapter. Many of the output reports are interpreted in the same manner as the regression program. The parts of the output are:

1. *The Univariate Analysis*   The means and standard deviation of each variable by group is shown. The number of cases in each group is shown in the identifier section above the report of the mean values. A minus sign in front of a sample size means that the group is used only for validation and is not included in the statistical estimates. In the example in Figure 12.3, group B has a higher mean value on all variables except variable 8 than does group A. The last column is the mean value across all groups.

2. *The Beginning F Levels* (Step 0)   The raw discriminatory power of each variable is displayed before the program does any work to develop the discriminant function. Higher F values indicate greater discriminatory power. It appears that variable 6 is the strongest discriminatory variable and is thus entered into the discriminant function first.

3. *The Stepwise Building of the Discriminant Function*   At the first step the strongest variable is entered into the discriminant function. Variable 6 is entered and the remaining variables have their F values

recomputed. This recomputation amounts to removing the variance of the "out" variables which is due to covariance with the "in" variable. In general, the F levels of the "out" variables will drop toward nonsignificance as more variables are entered into the discriminant analysis. Similarly, the F levels of the "in" variables are adjusted for covariance with each other and tend to drop as more variables are entered into the discriminant function. The computer printout reports the F levels of the "in" and "out" variables, respectively. It then reports the U statistic which describes the quality of discrimination across all groups and the F level of the U statistics significance. The associated degrees of freedom for each F are reported as well. The last major report in each step is the discriminatory F between each pair of groups. In Figure 12.3, one can see that discrimination is good between groups A and B and A and C but not good between B and C. The program keeps entering explanatory variables until the cutoff level of F significance is reached. For samples greater than 100 in total, usually the F value of 2.0 is used for p less than 0.05.

4. *The Discriminant Function Coefficients*   The numbers shown in the FUNCTION report shows the coefficients which are used for calculating the conditional probability for classification of unknown cases into the groups. These figures can be interpreted as the B's are in regression. The constant also has the same meaning as it does in regression. Each function can be used to calculate a Z score for each group ($F = C + B_1X_1 + B_2X_2 \ldots$). The conditional probability is calculated by taking the antilog of Z, that is, $P_i = e^z$, where e is the base of the natural logarithms, 2.71832. . . .

5. *The Summary Table*   The summary table is the same as in the regression program.

MEANS (THE LAST COLUMN CONTAINS THE GRAND MEANS OVER THE GROUPS USED IN THE ANALYSIS).

GROUP VARIABLE VAR192   READERS DIGEST

GROUP	1.00	2.00	
VARIABLE	NEVER READ	OCCASIONALY READ IT	
VAR001	0.50980	0.31776	0.34264
VAR002	0.21569	0.30029	0.28934
VAR003	0.15608	0.21283	0.21066
VAR004	0.29412	0.32070	0.31726
VAR005	0.37255	0.30321	0.31218
VAR006	0.31373	0.27988	0.28426
VAR007	1.90196	1.68805	1.71574
VAR008	3.78431	3.48980	3.52792
VAR078	4.72549	4.71428	4.71574
VAR079	4.56039	5.10496	5.08883
VAR083	4.82353	4.76093	4.76904
VAR081	3.17647	3.16910	3.17005
VAR082	5.27451	5.22740	5.23350
VAR354	2.54902	2.72886	2.70558
VAR355	5.01961	4.20117	4.30711
VAR362	80.50980	73.37608	74.29948

STANDARD DEVIATIONS

GROUP VARIABLE VAR192   READERS DIGEST

GROUP	1.00	2.00
VARIABLE	NEVER READ	OCCASIONALY READ IT
VAR001	0.76415	0.58329
VAR002	0.46103	0.59252
VAR003	0.40098	0.53383
VAR004	0.51599	0.59412
VAR005	0.66214	0.58356
VAR006	0.61612	0.59019
VAR007	1.62636	1.56309
VAR008	1.76990	1.60197
VAR078	1.19027	1.16476
VAR079	0.88295	0.72188
VAR083	0.71067	0.74911
VAR081	1.22221	1.48891
VAR082	0.90195	0.85876
VAR354	1.17156	1.35985
VAR355	1.22458	1.57009
VAR362	13.74240	20.02458

WITHIN GROUPS COVARIANCE MATRIX (POOLED DISPERSION MATRIX)

F LEVEL FOR INCLUSION   0.0100   F LEVEL FOR DELETION   0.0050   TOLERANCE LEVEL   0.0001
CONTROL VALUES:
 1 1 1 1 1 1 1 1 1 1 1 1 1 1 1 1

****

STEP NUMBER   0

VARIABLES NOT INCLUDED AND THE F'S TO ENTER
        DEGREES OF FREEDOM   1   392

VAR001	4.3623	VAR002	0.9531	VAR003	0.0462	VAR004	0.0895	VAR005	0.6047	VAR006	0.1443
VAR007	0.8158	VAR008	1.4595	VAR078	0.0039	VAR079	1.2433	VAR080	0.2623	VAR081	0.0010
VAR082	0.1251	VAR354	0.7924	VAR355	12.6584	VAR362	6.0423			

****

STEP NUMBER   1
VARIABLE ENTERED   VAR355

VARIABLES INCLUDED AND THE F'S TO REMOVE
        DEGREES OF FREEDOM   1   392

    VAR355   12.6584

VARIABLES NOT INCLUDED AND THE F'S TO ENTER
        DEGREES OF FREEDOM   1   391

VAR001	2.2562	VAR002	0.4347	VAR003	0.0043	VAR004	0.2192	VAR005	0.7158	VAR006	0.4586
VAR007	1.0545	VAR008	1.1105	VAR078	0.0036	VAR079	1.4704	VAR080	0.0158	VAR081	0.0873
VAR082	0.3277	VAR354	0.3756	VAR362	0.0044					

U-STATISTIC   0.96862   DEGREES OF FREEDOM   1   1   392
APPROXIMATE F   12.69845   DEGREES OF FREEDOM   1   392.00

F MATRIX - DEGREES OF FREEDOM   1   392

GROUP VARIABLE   VAR192   READERS DIGEST
                          1.00
                    NEVER READ
GROUP

    2.00   12.658604
OCCASIONALY READ I

****

STEP NUMBER   2
VARIABLE ENTERED   VAR001

VARIABLES INCLUDED AND THE F'S TO REMOVE
        DEGREES OF FREEDOM   1   391

FIGURE 12.4 *Discriminant Analysis: Computer Output*

494

VAR001   3.2562   VAR355   11.5481

VARIABLES NOT INCLUDED AND THE F'S TO ENTER
          DEGREES OF FREEDOM   1   390

  VAR002   C.7220   VAR003   0.0114   VAR004   0.3665   VAR005   0.6163   VAR006   0.9503   VAR007   0.2149
  VAR008   1.8822   VAR078   0.0118   VAR079   1.3284   VAR080   0.0512   VAR081   0.0498   VAR082   0.4394
  VAR354   0.0480   VAR362   0.0004

U-STATISTIC   C.S6C62   DEGREES OF FREEDOM   2   1   392
APPROXIMATE F   8.01389   DEGREES OF FREEDOM   2   391.00

F MATRIX - DEGREES OF FREEDOM   2   391

GROUP VARIABLE   VAR192   READERS DIGEST
                                1.00
                    NEVER READ
GROUP

     2.00   8.013968
OCCASICNALY READ I

••
STEP NUMBER   3
VARIABLE ENTERED   VAR008

VARIABLES INCLUDED AND THE F'S TO REMOVE
          DEGREES OF FREEDOM   1   390

  VAR001   4.026E   VAR008   1.8822   VAR355   10.9411

VARIABLES NOT INCLUDED AND THE F'S TO ENTER
          DEGREES OF FREEDOM   1   389

  VAR002   1.0676   VAR003   0.0170   VAR004   0.2283   VAR005   0.4150   VAR006   0.4143   VAR007   0.0265
  VAR078   0.0039   VAR079   1.1538   VAR080   0.0677   VAR081   0.1098   VAR082   0.3881   VAR354   0.9415
  VAR362   1.0154

U-STATISTIC   C.55601   DEGREES OF FREEDOM   3   1   392
APPROXIMATE F   5.58209   DEGREES OF FREEDOM   3   390.00

F MATRIX - DEGREES OF FREEDOM   3   390

GROUP VARIABLE   VAR192   READERS DIGEST
                                1.00
                    NEVER READ
GROUP

     2.00   5.582138
OCCASICNALY READ I

••
VARIABLES INCLUDED AND THE F'S TO REMOVE
          DEGREES OF FREEDOM   1   389

  VAR001   3.8301   VAR008   1.7C59   VAR079   1.1540   VAR355   11.1460

VARIABLES NOT INCLUDED AND THE F'S TO ENTER
          DEGREES OF FREEDOM   1   388

  VAR002   1.0144   VAR003   C.0CC9   VAR004   0.2519   VAR005   0.3721   VAR006   0.5244   VAR007   0.0482
  VAR078   0.0150   VAR080   0.4242   VAR081   0.0507   VAR082   0.5857   VAR354   1.0156   VAR362   1.1454

U-STATISTIC   0.55518   DEGREES OF FREEDOM   4   1   392
APPROXIMATE F   4.7768C   DEGREES OF FREEDOM   4   389.00

F MATRIX - DEGREES OF FREEDOM   4   389

GROUP VARIABLE   VAR192   READERS DIGEST
                                1.00
                    NEVER READ
GROUP

     2.00   4.776847
OCCASICNALY READ I

••
STEP NUMBER   5
VARIABLE ENTERED   VAR362

VARIABLES INCLUDED AND THE F'S TO REMOVE
          DEGREES OF FREEDOM   1   388

  VAR001   4.1128   VAR008   2.8442   VAR079   1.2836   VAR355   8.7531   VAR362   1.1455

VARIABLES NOT INCLUDED AND THE F'S TO ENTER
          DEGREES OF FREEDOM   1   387

  VAR002   0.0377   VAR003   C.0203   VAR004   0.1333   VAR005   0.6072   VAR006   0.64C8   VAR007   0.2906
  VAR078   0.0048   VAR080   0.3094   VAR081   0.0718   VAR082   0.5656   VAR354   0.5319

U-STATISTIC   C.95038   DEGREES OF FREEDOM   5   1   392
APPROXIMATE F   4.05156   DEGREES OF FREEDOM   5   388.00

F MATRIX - DEGREES OF FREEDOM   5   388

GROUP VARIABLE   VAR192   READERS DIGEST
                                1.C0
                    NEVER READ
GROUP

     2.00   4.051839
OCCASICNALY READ I

495

```
STEP NUMBER          6
VARIABLE ENTERED    VAR006

VARIABLES INCLUDED AND THE F'S TO REMOVE
            DEGREES OF FREEDOM      1     387

  VAR001    4.4446  VAR006    0.6408  VAR008    2.3091  VAR079    1.4177  VAR355    9.1654  VAR362    1.2605

VARIABLE  NOT INCLUDED AND THE F'S TO ENTER
            DEGREES OF FREEDOM      1     386

  VAR002    0.7811  VAR003    0.0005  VAR004    0.1113  VAR005    0.3715  VAR007    0.0237  VAR078    0.0099
  VAR080    0.2840  VAR081    0.0648  VAR082    0.6098  VAR354    0.5997

U-STATISTIC        0.54880     DEGREES OF FREEDOM      6     1    392
APPROXIMATE F       3.48032     DEGREES OF FREEDOM      6   387.00

F MATRIX - DEGREES OF FREEDOM      6    387

GROUP VARIABLE    VAR192          READERS DIGEST
                                   1.00
                   NEVER READ
GROUP

     2.00                       3.4E0206
OCCASIONALY READ I


*********************************************************************************************************************
STEP NUMBER          7
VARIABLE ENTERED    VAR002

VARIABLES INCLUDED AND THE F'S TO REMOVE
            DEGREES OF FREEDOM      1     386

  VAR001    4.8385  VAR002    0.7811  VAR006    0.7842  VAR008    2.1989  VAR079    1.3537  VAR355    7.5794
  VAR362    0.8404

VARIABLES NOT INCLUDED AND THE F'S TO ENTER
            DEGREES OF FREEDOM      1     385

  VAR003    0.0080  VAR004    0.0658  VAR005    0.4984  VAR007    0.5143  VAR078    0.0195  VAR080    0.3023
  VAR081    0.0588  VAR082    0.5823  VAR354    0.7462

U-STATISTIC        0.54689     DEGREES OF FREEDOM      7     1    392
APPROXIMATE F       3.09303     DEGREES OF FREEDOM      7   386.00

F MATRIX - DEGREES OF FREEDOM      7    386

GROUP VARIABLE    VAR192          READERS DIGEST
                                   1.00




                   NEVER READ
GROUP

     2.00                       1.530812
OCCASIONALY READ I


F LEVEL INSUFFICIENT FOR FURTHER COMPUTATION


**********    DISCRIMINANT SCORES   **********

GROUP VARIABLE    VAR192          READERS DIGEST
                                   1.00              2.00
                   NEVER READ          OCCASIONALY READ I

VARIABLE
VAR001              1.711898            1.445614
VAR002             -0.569611           -0.405859
VAR003             -3.114631           -2.839632
VAR004              0.866104            1.264849
VAR005              0.326854            0.426080
VAR006             -1.067199           -1.010746
VAR007              0.781907            0.467517
VAR008              0.618704            0.418022
VAR079              1.144485            1.162461
VAR079              7.123677            7.418651
VAR080              4.627156            4.528386
VAR081              1.934341            1.894572
VAR082              5.134675            5.005770
VAR354              1.272506            1.403037
VAR355              0.485084            0.065805
VAR362              0.169080            0.178412

CONSTANT          -59.783585          -58.256027


**********    DISCRIMINANT FUNCTIONS   **********

GROUPS   1.00,    2.00,
         VARIABLE   COEFFICIENTS (LAMBDAS)   CHOSEN COEFFICIENT (LAMBDA/MIN. LAMBDA)
         CONSTANT      -1.5276
         VAR001         0.2663                        25.7725
         VAR002        -0.5638                       -54.5631
         VAR003        -0.2750                       -26.6159
         VAR004        -0.3987                       -38.5928
         VAR005        -0.0992                        -9.6037
         VAR006        -0.0565                        -5.4638
```

FIGURE 12.4 *(continued)*

```
          VAR007                     0.3144                          30.4284
          VAR008                     0.2007                          19.4231
          VAR078                    -0.0180                          -1.7394
          VAR079                    -0.2950                         -28.5492
          VAR080                     0.0568                           9.5595
          VAR081.                    0.0358                           3.8491
          VARC82                     0.1289                          12.4762
          VAR354                    -0.1305                         -12.6336
          VAR355                     0.4193                          40.5802
          VAR362                    -0.0103                          -1.0000
```

                    SUMMARY TABLE

STEP NUMBER	VARIABLE ENTERED REMOVED	F VALUE TO ENTER OR REMOVE	NUMBER OF VARIABLES INCLUDED	U-STATISTIC
1	VAR355	12.6584	1	0.9686
2	VAR001	3.2562	2	0.9606
3	VAR008	1.8822	3	0.9560
4	VAR079	1.1540	4	0.9532
5	VAR362	1.1455	5	0.9504
6	VAR006	0.6408	6	0.9488
7	VAR002	0.7811	7	0.9469
8	VAR354	0.7463	8	0.9451
9	VAR082	0.5995	9	0.9436
10	VAR007	0.5043	10	0.9423
11	VAR004	0.6236	11	0.9408
12	VAR003	0.3428	12	0.9400
13	VAR080	0.1900	13	0.9395
14	VAR081	0.1225	14	0.9392
15	VAR005	0.0611	15	0.9390
16	VAR078	0.0140	16	0.9390

497

Chapter 13

Data Analysis: The Multivariate Grouping of Respondents and Questions

The researcher sometimes is concerned with natural groupings or segments that exist in a given market. Several techniques exist which group persons or objects into "natural" groups. These techniques can be classified under the general terms of Cluster and Factor analysis. While the central goal of Cluster and Factor analysis is not to test hypotheses, these techniques are quite useful for understanding the structure of human behavior and the resulting data which is generated.

Introduction

The purpose of this chapter is to introduce the student to the related multivariate techniques of cluster analysis and factor analysis. These techniques are not hypothesis testing techniques in the usual sense, but rather, they are techniques which allow the investigator to examine the properties of his data and of the population which he is studying. The fundamental underlying principle of both cluster analysis and factor analysis is that of grouping. Factor analysis is designed to group certain kinds of questions into common elements called factors. Cluster analysis is designed to group people or objects which have some common underlying traits. There are many ways and many variations on the theme of factor analysis and cluster analysis. Only some very specific examples of the commonly used versions of factor analysis and cluster analysis will be treated in this chapter.

The Reasons for Analyzing Respondents and Questions

Many measures of buyer knowledge, attitudes, behavior, and other characteristics obtained within a given study are, to some degree at least, correlated in that they tend to measure the same underlying characteristic albeit in a number of different ways. Thus, the researcher would like to develop many measures of a given attitude or personality trait and then "boil down" these measures into the underlying attitude or personality trait. Factor analysis is one method of taking a large number of variables and inferring the underlying social or psychological trait using mathematical methods.

Factor analysis itself tests no specific hypotheses. Rather, it merely looks for correlated variables which work together to describe some underlying behavioral structure. An example of this is the case where a researcher believes that there are a set of beliefs that governs the consumption of a product such as a breakfast food. The researcher may believe that people judge cereal upon such traits as (1) crunchiness, (2) sweetness, (3) size of the nugget, and (4) perceived vitamin content. The researcher would then construct a questionnaire of 40 questions; ten questions or so intended to relate to each trait of thinking concerning cereal. He would then administer this questionnaire to

500 (say) adult cereal users and then perform a factor analysis to see if his questions would "boil down" to his four factors.

Cluster analysis, on the other hand, is a technique based on the presumption that a population often can be subdivided into different clusters which are internally homogeneous with respect to several characteristics. Low-income people, for example, can have different sets of priorities for community action programs and different ways of behaving than high-income people. Jewish people, Blacks, and Puerto Ricans may have very different preferences among food items. Cluster analysis is designed to group members of a sample into certain categories. Most statistical techniques such as regression, factor analysis, and discriminant analysis, assume that the population being studied has an underlying distribution of variances which are the same across the population. In addition, the multivariate techniques of regression and discriminant analysis assume that the population under study can be described by the same behavioral model. This means that if high-income people and low-income people are included in the same regression analysis problem, these people are assumed to behave in the same basic way.

Cluster analysis relaxes this assumption in that it breaks a big population into meaningful subpopulations and allows the researcher to proceed with analysis of each individual subpopulation separately. Thus, if there are major behavioral differences between subpopulations and a total population, the researcher is forced to do some form of cluster analysis to group his respondents into homogeneous subpopulations. The researcher is also deluding himself if he analyzes a total population without respect for major behavioral differences in the subpopulations.

What Is Factor Analysis?

The basic principle of factor analysis was first suggested by Charles Spearman in 1904.[1] However, the development and flowering of the use of factor analysis had to wait until the mid and late 1950s when high-speed digital computers came into being. Although the principles of factor analysis existed for a very long time and the computational ability only came recently, the use of factor analysis had to wait therefore until the early 1960s before many applications became evident in the behavioral sciences. Factor analysis originated with psychologists who wished to test for human personality and intelligence. Realizing that there were many unknown factors associated with human personality and intelligence, psychologists devised the idea of the indirect measure. The principle behind the indirect measure is that the psychologist, based on his experience, devised a set of questions, often a very

---

[1] Paul Worst, *Psychological Measurement and Prediction* (Belmont, Calif.: Wadsworth Publishing Company, 1966).

lengthy list, which was answered by many human subjects. A given human subject would evaluate the questions in terms of some structure that existed in his own mind; thus, the answers to the psychologist's questions would form a pattern. The purpose of factor analysis is to detect the pattern of the responses. A major assumption of the use of factor analysis is that when a large group of people answer the psychologist's battery of questions or battery of tests they will all use the same underlying structure (the "factor structure") in their minds to answer the questions. Therefore, the factor structure that should appear should be common to all persons in the sample.

Fundamentally, the purpose of factor analysis is to reduce a large set of variables to a smaller set of variables. Thus, a large number of variables, say 50, are reduced to a small number of factors or underlying dimensions, say 5 or perhaps 10. Basically there are two kinds of factor analysis. The first is called *R* factor analysis. The *R* factor analysis is defined as the method where the researcher examines all respondents and assumes that these respondents are using the same set of underlying behavioral structures to evaluate a large set of questions. Another type of factor analysis is called *Q* factor analysis. *Q* factor analysis examines similarities in responses across questions in a questionnaire and can be used to create clusters depending on how similarly the respondents answered the questions. Thus, *Q* factor analysis can be thought of as a form of cluster analysis. The *R* factor analysis will be discussed below.

R Factor Analysis

The mechanics of factor analysis are somewhat complex but can be reduced to a series of operational steps:

1. A special matrix is read by the computer. This matrix consists of the answers of each respondent to each question involved in the study. Thus, if there were 50 questions that each respondent or subject answered and a total of 100 persons answering all 50 questions, a matrix of data of 50 items by 100 subjects would be read by the computer. Then the program would compute the simple correlations between the pattern of response to each of the questions in the sample. The process of computing correlations is discussed in Chapter 9. The resulting correlation matrix may show that subjects are answering question x and question y in a similar way. For instance, a subject may respond to the high end of a scale on question x and also respond to the high end of a scale on question z. A similar pattern may appear for a large number of subjects in the sample. Such a result would show a high correlation between question x and question z.
2. Once the correlation matrix has been developed by the computer program, the computer program examines the pattern of the high cor-

relations and proceeds to take linear combinations[2] of the variables such that the information and the correlation is reduced to one variable. Thus, if variable x and variable z are highly correlated, then these two variables are "collapsed" together into a third variable, say w. Therefore, w is some combination of x and z. These linear combinations are called principal components. The first principal component accounts for a large proportion of the explained variance in the covariance matrix. The computer searches for another linear combination or another set of principal components which are explanatory of the residual or unexplained variation in the covariance matrix. Additional principal components are extracted until there is very little residual variance left in the covariance matrix. The principal components are constructed in such a way that each one of the linear combinations of the variables for each principal component is "orthogonal" to all the other principal components. This means that each of the principal components has no correlation or little correlation with all other principal components. The reason for this is when one derives a factor structure and wishes to use the factors for additional analysis, the analyst desires factors which are independent of each other, that is, one factor to explain the behavior of another factor. Although other forms of factor analysis exist, the description of the principal components enclosed here reflects the most commonly used type.

3. After the principal components are extracted, these principal components are rotated from their beginning position to enhance the interpretability of the factors. In other words, the principal components are tilted on their axes in one direction and another by the computer program until certain variables appear to have their effect enhanced. This enhancing feature increases the quality of interpretation of the factor.

The effect of rotation is shown pictorially in Figure 13.1. Two principal components have been created by the computer which are designated PC1 and PC2. Variables one through four are plotted in the principal component space to show their relationship to each other. V1 and V2 are highly correlated while V3 and V4 are also correlated. However, V1 and V2 are not correlated with V3 and V4. Although the principal components represent the space "well" (the variables are "bunched" nicely), inputing any meaning to the components can be difficult. The computer program can rotate the axis by a few degrees to form the rotated factors (RF) which point toward the variables. The

---

[2] A linear combination is a calculation where the original variable (measure) is multiplied by a constant and then added to a sum. This multiplication and addition to a common sum is done for all variables; thus, $z = b_1 x_1 + b_2 x_2 + \cdots + b_n x_n$ for n variables.

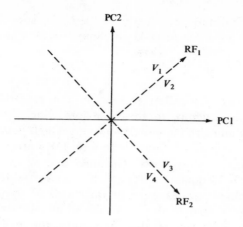

PC = Principal component.
RF = Rotated factor.
V = Variable.

FIGURE 13.1 *The Effect of Rotation on Factor Interpretation*

variables to which the rotated factor points can allow the research to name the factor.

4. The variables are then regressed against each *factor loading* and the resulting regression coefficients are used to generate what are known as factor scores for each individual person; that is, if a person has a high score on a psychological factor such as being an extrovert, he is said to bear the trait, and conversely, a person who has a low score on extroversion would be said to have an inward going personality (an introvert). Thus, factor scores are established for each factor and each individual. These factor scores are generally used in further analysis such as cross tabulation analysis and can be used as inputs to regression and discriminant analysis. Factor scores can also be used as means of market segmentation.

How Has Factor Analysis Been Used?

The multivariate technique of factor analysis has been used in the context of developing psychological tests such as IQ tests, personality tests, and other tests in the realm of psychology. Well-known tests such as the Minnesota Multiphasic Inventory (MMPI) and other personality tests have been developed using factor analysis. In the world of marketing, factor analysis has been used to look at media readership profiles of people. In a latter section of this chapter an example of this work is shown. Factor analysis has been one of the most popular exploratory analysis techniques recently devised.[3] In addition, the factor analysis programs which exist for most large computers and small computers are very easy to use.

Using Factor Analysis

When using factor analysis as a research technique, the researcher generally starts by hypothesizing a structure to the behaviors which he is exploring. He then prepares a questionnaire including questions which pertain in various way to the behaviors or attitudes of interest to him. Data are then collected from a representative sample of subjects. The data consist of the responses of these subjects to the questionnaire items. The researcher then factor analyzes his results and examines them to see if the factors which appear as a result of the factor analysis are similar to the ones that he hypothesized. If the normalized factor loadings are high, that is, above 0.4, and if the percent of variance which is explained by all the factors for the cumulative data set is greater than 40 percent,[4] he then can say that his set of factors looks to be a reasonable set. He must then prove reliability of his factors by doing successive retests of his group of factors. He then must prove validity of his factors by showing that they relate to real world behavior such as purchasing in some way.

An Example Factor Analysis Experiment

Using the data bank that was described in Chapter 12, a factor analysis exercise is illustrated in this section. The major hypothesis involved with the use of the factor analysis in this example is that people categorize magazines into groups and tend to read magazines of a similar group, that is, the magazines are stimuli in a person's environment and people tend to group magazines by the purposes the magazines serve. The sample of 398 housewives from Lafayette, Indiana, were questioned on their magazine readership. The list of magazines included fashion magazines, news magazines, newspapers, housing magazines, and some others. The responses were coded from 1, do not read at all, to 6, read almost every issue. The responses of the 398 housewives will be factored to determine whether the readership of magazines can be grouped into a pattern. A total 44 of the most popular magazines and newspapers in the country were included in the study. A computer output of a replication of this study is included as a technical appendix.

The mean readership for 8 of the magazines is shown in Table 13.1. It is particularly interesting to note that the *New York Times* (Daily), the *New York Times* (Sunday Edition), and the *Chicago Sun Times* have rela-

---

[3] See Terry G. Vavra, "Factor Analysis of Perceptual Change," *Journal of Marketing Research*, Vol. IX (May 1972), p. 193.

[4] Suggested criteria for samples of several hundred and item lists of more than 30 attitude scale questions.

TABLE 13.1 *Mean Readership of Selected Magazines in Sample*

Reader of	Mean	S. D.
N. Y. Times (Daily)	1.093[a]	0.375
N. Y. Times (Sunday)	1.215	0.748
Chicago Sun Times	1.169	0.912
Good Housekeeping	3.376	1.881
Family Circle	3.144	1.852
Ladies' Home Journal	3.343	1.929
Better Homes and Gardens	3.268	1.916
House Beautiful	2.076	1.423

[a] Coded: 1 = never read, 2 = occasionally read, 3 = read about one in every three issues, 4 = read about half the issues, 5 = read two of three issues, 6 = read almost every issue.

tively low readership but relatively high standard deviations. In addition, it is interesting to note that *Good Housekeeping, Family Circle,* and others shown in Table 13.1 have reasonably high degree of readership and fairly wide standard deviations. The mean readership of the other magazines and newspapers is not reported as they will not be dealt with in the analysis to follow.

After computing the means and the standard deviations, the computer then looks at the correlations of readership of one magazine and newspaper with another. A sample of these correlations is shown in Table 13.2. It is interesting to note again that the upper left-hand corner shows the correlations between the *New York Times* (Daily, Sunday) and the *Chicago Sun Times.* In turn, these same three newspapers have very low correlation with *Family Circle, Ladies' Home Journal,* and so on. When one looks at *Good Housekeeping, Family Circle, Ladies' Home Journal, Better Homes and Gardens,* and *House Beautiful,* it appears that they have relatively meaningful correlations among themselves. The correlations among the magazines are negative, indicating the magazines are substitutes for one another, that is, if a subject reads one, she will not read another. It is this correlation grouping that forms the basis of a factor analysis. This table is a partial reporting of the correlations to illustrate that the factor analysis process is sensitive to the correlations.

Since it appears that there are two groups of behavior working together as shown by the correlation, the factor analysis then creates or extracts the principal components which reduce the group of variables such as the *New York Times* (Sunday and Daily), and the *Chicago Sun Times* into one variable. In addition, it takes the variables *Good Housekeeping, Family Circle, Ladies' Home Journal, Better Homes and Gardens,* and *House Beautiful* and puts

TABLE 13.2 Correlation among Selected Magazines Read by the Sample

	N.Y. Times (Sunday)	Chicago Sun Times	Good House-keeping	Family Circle	Ladies' Home Journal	Better Homes & Gardens	House Beautiful
N.Y. Times (Daily)	0.63	0.18	−0.03	−0.01	−0.07	−0.03	0.07
N.Y. Times (Sunday)	1.0	−0.35	0.02	0.00	0.10	0.16	0.01
Chicago Sun Times		1.0	−0.04	0.00	−0.01	−0.01	0.01
Good Housekeeping			1.0	−0.28	−0.43	−0.19	−0.26
Family Circle				1.0	−0.18	−0.19	
Ladies' Home Journal					1.0	−0.05	−0.13
Better Homes and Gardens						1.0	−0.28

TABLE 13.3 *Selected Magazine Readership Variables Reduced to 2 Factors by Principal Components*

Readership	Factor 1	Factor 2
N. Y. Times (Daily)	0.31	0.59
N. Y. Times (Sunday)	0.40	0.64
Chicago Sun Times	0.23	0.29
Good Housekeeping	0.46	−0.39
Family Circle	0.42	−0.30
Ladies' Home Journal	0.43	−0.34
Better Homes and Gardens	0.33	−0.37
House Beautiful	0.63	−0.23

them together in an additive way to form one factor. The restriction on the principal component is that the two groups of magazine readership be independent or orthogonal from one another. Table 13.3 shows the result of the extraction of the principal components. Factor 1 shows that the *Good Housekeeping* group has a positive loading[5] of 0.63, 0.46, 0.42, and so on, and Factor 2 has a negative loading of —0.39, and so on, indicating that *Good Housekeeping* is positively related to Factor 1 and negatively related to Factor 2. This positive and negative relationship is an example of the orthogonality or independent. In addition, the *New York Times* group has high positive loading on Factor 2 and less loading on Factor 1 in the principal components analysis. If one attempted to name what Factor 1 and Factor 2 were at this stage, one would have difficulty especially if there were many other variables associated with other magazines in the analysis, that is, the interpretation of the factors is difficult when numbers appear such as are shown in Table 13.3. There is no very clear interpretation of the factors as they stand at this point in the analysis.

In order to enhance the interpretability of the two factors and possibly increase the variance explained, the factors are then rotated by a process which maximizes the variance between the factors in such a way to capture as much of the explanatory power as possible.[6] Table 13.4 shows the result of the rotation. Factor 1 very clearly becomes a house-oriented reader, that is, *Good Housekeeping* and its group loaded extremely heavily on Factor 1 while the *New York Times* group has virtually no loading on Factor 1, and similarly, the *New York Times* group loads heavily on Factor 2 and virtually has no loading on Factor 1. Because of the loading and the extreme values shown, the factors can be named in terms of their variables which load on them. For

[5] Defined as the effect or influence of the variable on the factor (see glossary).
[6] This method is called "varimax" rotation (maximizing the variance between factors).

TABLE 13.4 *Selected Magazine Readership Reduced to Two Rotated and Normalized Factors*

	Loadings	
	Factor 1	Factor 2
N. Y. Times (Daily)	−0.05	0.75
N. Y. Times (Sunday)	−0.10	0.75
Chicago Sun Times	0.04	0.24
Good Housekeeping	0.75	−0.01
Family Circle	0.50	0.00
Ladies' Home Journal	0.57	−0.10
Better Homes and Gardens	0.42	−0.02
House Beautiful	0.33	0.05

example, Factor 1 could be called house-oriented reader and Factor 2 can be the out-of-town newspaper reader. The varimax rotation reduces the communality (see glossary for definition) of the factors because it concentrates the loadings of variables on one factor and reduces the same variables effect on other factors, that is, it makes variables less common from factor to factor. When the loadings are reported on the computer output, all variables are listed for each factor. It is incumbent upon the reader of the output to determine which are the most important variables loading on a given factor. A reasonable rule-of-thumb is to report all loadings over some amount such as 0.3 or 0.4. Those variables with less than 0.3 or 0.4 loading on a factor are said not to load on that factor while those variables which load over the critical value are said to load on a factor. Thus, the varimax rotation has had the effect of enhancing the original factor structure while not substantially altering the original information. Because of this effect, varimax rotation is the most popular form of factor analysis.

The final step of this factor analysis is to plot the magazine readership factors from the previous analysis in order to see how the variables align with the factors. Figure 13.2 shows that Factor 1 clearly is the house-reader factor with the magazine related to the home lying very close to the axis of the factor and conversely Factor 2, the out-of-town newspapers, load very closely to Factor 2. Other magazines and newspapers which load on neither Factor 1 nor Factor 2 would appear as points very near the origin 0 of the plot, that is, they would load neither on Factor 1 nor on Factor 2. In this particular factor analysis only two "significant" factors were found that satisfied the criteria of factor analysis significance. These criteria[7] are:

[7] Suggested by experience, and Jagdish Sheth and D. J. Tigert, "Factor Analysis in Marketing," American Marketing Association Workshop on Multivariate Methods, 1970.

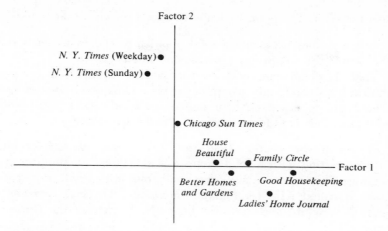

FIGURE 13.2 *A Plot of Magazine Readership Structure from Factor Analysis*

1. Each beginning eigenvalue[8] has a value greater than 1.0.
2. The loadings of the factors after varimax rotation were larger than 0.3.
3. The variance explained of all factors in the factor analysis is greater than 40 percent.
4. No variable loads significantly on more than one factor. If a factor analysis passes all these criteria and it meets the assumptions of the basic factor model in that subjects are filtering the kinds of responses of a rather homogeneous nature through themselves via questionnaire and if the variables are roughly cardinal (see Chapter 6 for definition), then the factor analysis is said to be a substantial or a significant one.

Cluster Analysis

Cluster analysis is a group of techniques which is designed to group people into some kind of meaningful classification system, that is, into some meaningful groups. There are many possible ways to create a cluster analysis and many reasons for doing cluster analysis. Cluster analysis may be necessary when subpopulations of a group are nonhomogeneous. This implies that subgroups behave differently to various inputs stimuli such as advertising, pricing, or other kinds of promotion. In addition, cluster analysis can be used as a kind of "weak" analysis of variance in that groups can be split into subgroups in order to reduce the variation among members of the group and thus infer some characteristics of the group, that is, it can be used for theory building

---

[8] The ratio of explained variance due to the linear combinations of variables and the unexplained variance.

about human behavior. There are basically two kinds of cluster analysis:

1. First is a method of taking a total population and breaking it down into meaningful subgroups ("teardown" variety).
2. An analysis which starts with each individual separately in the population and starts building groups of people adding one person at a time to each group, based on how similar each individual is to another individual. This is Q factor analysis ("build up" variety).

This discussion will center about the "tear down" variety of factor analysis, that is, starting with a total group and then forming subgroups out of the total group. The technique and computer program that will be discussed in this regard is called AID (Automatic Interaction Detector) written by Professor John A. Sonquist and Professor James N. Morgan of the University of Michigan.

AID is a procedure with some intuitive appeal because it divides a group of people using two variables as a criteria. First, the procedure asks the user to define a dependent variable to be the major part of the analysis. Figure 13.3 shows an example of AID analysis. The dependent variable is

CHART 5
PLANS TO MOVE

0. No chance of moving
1. Uncertain or depends
2. Definitely or probably will move

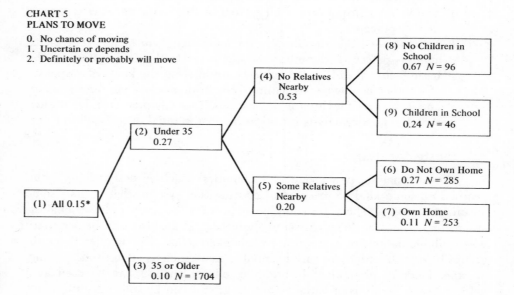

*Mean Value of Group for Dependent Variable

FIGURE 13.3

Source: ISR Proect 719, MTR 33. Sonquist and Morgan, *The Source of Interaction Effects.* Copyright 1969 by The University of Michigan; reprinted by permission of the publisher, the Institute for Social Research.

"plans to move." This means that the analysis will attempt to explain what the major segments associated with "plans to move" are. Thus, in Box (1) labeled "All" the average value for the entire sample on plans to move is 0.15. The coding is shown in the upper left-hand corner of the figure. The AID analysis then examines all of the variables and attempts to find the variables which have the largest difference in terms of mean value and sum of squares, and it picks the variable which contributes most to the splitting to be the first variable of split. In this case it happens to be age. The first split is based on people under 35 and people over 35. People under 35 have a mean value of 0.27 and the people over 35 have a different mean of 0.10. The behavioral interpretation of this is that younger people move much more readily than older people. Cell 3, the 35 or older cell, does not have any following cells indicating that there are no variables which contribute to any further explanation of that group, that is, none of the explanatory variables create meaningful differences in the mean value of "plans to move." On the other hand, cell 2, the under 35 age group, can be split further on the basis of "relatives nearby." This split shows a widely different mean of 0.53 for no relatives nearby and 0.20 for some relatives nearby.

The meaning of this split is that people who have relatives in the area in which they live are much less prone to move than those that do not. And conversely, for people having no relatives nearby. Similarly, people who own their home and have relatives nearby as shown in cell 7 are much less likely to move than those who do not own a home. And those who have children in school are much less likely to move than people with no children in school. Thus, the AID analysis is a very logical splitting procedure as illustrated in Figure 13.2 based on mean values of some dependent variables.

The AID procedure requires that discrete inputs of independent variables be used, that is, questionnaires must have votes on a variable of the nature 1, 2, 3, 4, 5, and so on, and the mean value for all persons voting 1 is compared to the mean value of all persons voting 2 on a given variable. Those groups of people voting in a similar way are then grouped together, that is, if people voting 1 on a variable are very similar in terms of mean value on the dependent variable to people who vote 2 on a given variable, then these 2 groups are lumped together. Thus, AID is a very interesting and logical way of breaking a large nonhomogeneous group into various homogeneous subgroups. It is a logical first step in doing several kinds of multivariate analysis where the homogeneity of the sample is in serious question.

A Social Marketing Example of Clustering Using AID

In this study, factors related to the accuracy of recall of campaign messages in different communication media are reported. The media include radio, television, posters, and newspapers. The messages concerned three child-feeding practices: the minimum desirable period for breast-feeding infants; feeding of the child when he is ill; and the gradual introduction into the infant's diet of food normally consumed by other members of the family. The individual messages were relatively brief and appeared in the broadcast and printed media over a period of approximately five months. The scheduling was such that messages were publicized almost daily and at varying times of the day through one or another communications media. Media time and space were donated by the stations and publishers. The form and character of the message presentations were developed by McCann-Erickson of El Salvador. The Department of Health of the Organization of Central American States selected and prepared the basic messages.

The Independent Variables   The basic dependent variable in each model is accuracy of message recall for the particular medium under consideration. When a respondent indicated he had heard or seen the health messages the interviewer asked the respondent to repeat the message. His response on recall was rated very well, well, somewhat, and not at all.

The independent variables were selected on the basis of previous research reported in the literature, a pilot study, prior work by health personnel of the Ministry of Public Health, Costa Rica, and The Organization of Central American States. The major independent variables and their role in health communication are indicated below.

1. *Level of education.* Education, apart from its impact on literacy, is believed to unlock mental abilities making it possible for individuals to attend to a greater range of stimuli and to comprehend their logical structure and significance. The higher the level of education, presumably the greater the exposure to and recall and understanding of health communications.

2. *Age.* Age has been found to be inversely related to cognitive flexibility and general openness to new ideas and practices. Consequently, older respondents in the study would be less likely than their younger counterparts to have an effective positive experience with the mass media.

3. *Cosmopoliteness.* This variable concerns the degree to which an individual is oriented toward circumstances or phenomena outside his immediate situation. This external orientation produces a more open frame of mind through exposure to a wide array of stimuli not likely to be experienced by his more localite counterpart. As in the case of education this broader perspective should have a positive impact on exposure to and recall of health messages.

4. *Perceived reliability of the medium.* The perceived reliability of a particular medium as a source of useful health-related information is an important factor affecting the attendance to and confidence

placed in a health message presented by the medium. This in turn influences recall of messages.

5. *Time of first exposure to the particular medium.* Accuracy of recall would be related to earliness of exposure because of the greater opportunity for more frequent exposure and thus more reinforcement. Alternatively, it might be argued that the recency effect would be in operation and the more recent a person's exposure, the more accurate his recall.

6. *First exposure to campaign messages through another medium.* Accuracy of recall of a message through a particular medium tan be influenced to some extent by whether or not that medium was the source of first exposure to the campaign message. The process of selective perception with regard to the particular medium is more apt to be operative—positively or negatively depending on attitudes toward the message—if prior exposure was through another medium.

7. *Exposure to any media other than the one under investigation.* The centripetal effect suggests that if an individual is exposed to one medium he is likely to be exposed to others. If this is the case, message exposure in one channel would be reinforced by message exposure in other channels, thus increasing the likelihood of recalling the message accurately.

8. *Degree of exposure.* The number of different mass media an individual exposed to will have a positive relationship with accuracy of recall of messages.

9. *Interpersonal discussion* (general model only). An indication of interest in the campaign is whether or not there is discussion of the campaign messages. The greater the degree of interest, the more likely the messages are to be recalled accurately. More importantly, this effect is accomplished through interpersonal reinforcement. Thus, we would expect the combined impact of personal and mass media channels to be more effective than mass media exposure only.

10. *Breast-feeding period.* How long the mother breast-fed her most recent child is an indicator of her knowledge of the merits of breast-feeding. Mothers who breast-fed for less than the suggested time period may have a defensive reaction to messages which are discrepant with their behavior. Accordingly, accuracy of recall of the breast-feeding message would be lower among this group.

The Data   The data consist of 545 respondents from 36 rural communities in Costa Rica. The sample was a stratified one which attempted to make the number of respondents taken from rural communities of different size categories proportional to the percentage of the rural population living in communities of those size categories. Communities of each size category were randomly selected from the 1963 National Census List of Villages, the most recent list available. Within each community the number of dwellings was obtained and the interviewers selected from every Nth dwelling a woman with a child three years old or younger. N was the number of respondents desired divided by the number of dwellings in each community. If a woman with the desired characteristics was not present in a particular dwelling, the interviewers proceeded house by house to the right until they located a woman who met the qualifications.

The Analytical Technique   In operation the sample is divided into two groups to provide the largest reduction in unexplained sums of squares of the dependent variable. All possible splits among all designated preditor variables are examined. The binary split finally selected is that which maximizes the between sums of squares for the group being split. Next, the between sum of squares for each predictor variable is divided by the total sum of squares for the group to be split (BSS_i/TSS_i). That variable with the highest ratio is selected as the first predictor variable and the sample is divided into the two groups. Each of the two subgroups are treated as separate samples and the entire process is repeated. This continues for each new split until certain predetermined conditions are encountered which stop the program.

The splitting process is stopped according to four criteria which are preselected by the researcher:

1. When the proportion of the largest total sum of squares due to any unsplit group is less than a present amount (0.00001 is suggested by Sonquist and is used in this analysis).
2. When the number of cases remaining in any unsplit group becomes less than a preset number (25 is suggested by Sonquist and is used in this analysis).
3. When the binary division of the group being split on any independent variable does not bring about a sufficient increase in the explained total sum of squares (0.006 is suggested by Sonquist and is used in this study).
4. When the number of end groups has reached a preset upper limit (50 is suggested by Sonquist and is used in this study).

General Communications Model   A general index of overall health message recall was developed on the basis of accuracy of recall for each of the separate media. The mean recall score was 2.91 (see Figure 13.4) having a range of 1 (accuracy of recall very good) to 4 (not recalled accurately at all). A total of five variables are used in the analysis and account for 44 percent of the variance in the dependent variable. The AID program examines each of the relevant preselected seven variables. The first split is based on time of first

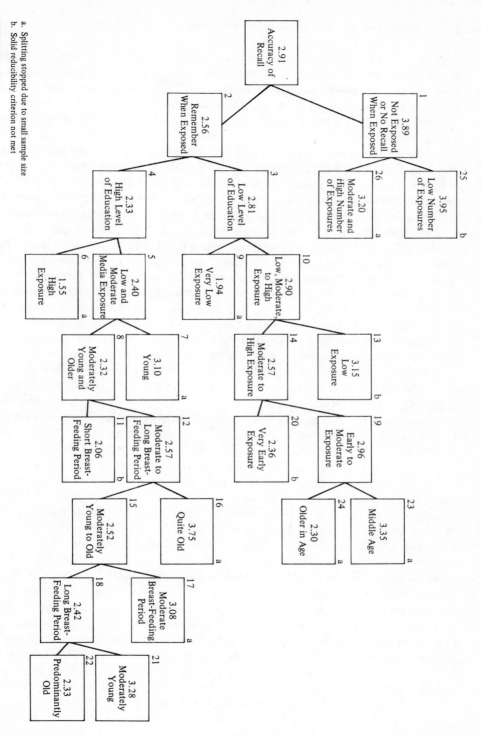

FIGURE 13.4

a. Splitting stopped due to small sample size
b. Solid reducibility criterion not met

515

exposure to the campaign messages. That is, the maximum reduction in the unexplained sums of squares is obtained by splitting the sample according to how recently respondents first encountered the campaign messages. Those respondents who were exposed only recently through any mass medium or not exposed at all had a mean recall score of 3.89 compared to 2.56 for those having moderately recent or early exposure.

The program next considers the two subgroups as separate populations and calculates the BSS/TSS ratio for all variables at their most significant dichotomous point. The variable having the highest ratio is then selected as providing the maximum reduction of unexplained variance within the preceding variable. In the case of the moderate or early exposure group this variable is education. The group with a high education has a better mean score or recall (2.33) than the low education group (2.81). Both the high and low education groups are split on the basis of the number of different media exposed to. Respondents having a high education and a low or moderate level of exposure scored 2.40 on accuracy of recall compared to 1.55 for those having high education and high exposure, that is, exposure through several channels. Thus, the population segment which has relatively early exposure to the media has a high education, and those exposed to the messages through many media have the best recall score. These are the individuals the messages register with most effectively. There is no further branching for this population group.

The next split is made on the low to moderate multiple media exposure group. The most relevant variable at this point is age which segments between the young and the moderately young and older. Age at this point appears to have a positive association with recall. The young group had a mean score of 3.10 compared to 2.32 for the middle and older age groups. This is contrary to our original expectation. The explanation, however, may be that younger mothers are more "modern" and perceive breast-feeding as a traditional rather than modern practice. Hence, younger mothers would tend to block on those messages inconsistent with their practices. The latter category is further subdivided on the basis of a behavioral variable, length of time the child of reference was breast-fed. The impact of the campaign for this population segment judged in terms of accuracy of recall seems to have had a somewhat stronger impact on mothers breast-feeding for shorter periods of time. It must be remembered that the division here is based on the moderately young or old age group who generally breast-feed longer than the young age group. This can be interpreted as a favorable indication that the campaign had an impact on those mothers (within the sample segment of this branching route) whose breast-feeding practices were most in need of some remedial treatment.

Mothers breast-feeding for a moderate to long period of time were grouped next on age. In this case the dichotomy is between those being quite old and those being moderately young to old. It will be recalled that the young group was split off earlier with no further branching. The relatively younger segment had better recall (2.52 versus 3.75 for the quite old group). Breast-feeding again enters the picture this time as before branching from age (moderately young and old). The dichotomy is between those breast-feeding for a moderate time period and those breast-feeding for a long time period. In this case those breast-feeding for a longer period had better recall. The final split in this route stems from the long breast-feeding group and is based on age. As before, the older segment (2.33 versus 3.28 for the moderately young) had the better recall score.

With regard to this first major branching it appears that the most favorable impact of the campaign occurred among those having moderately early or very early exposure to the campaign, high education, and exposure to the messages through many sources. Among the group having low exposure, recall was better if the respondents were moderately young or relatively old and breast-fed the child of reference for a relatively short period of time. Among those breast-feeding for a moderate and long period of time, message recall was better among those moderately young and old (but not very old); furthermore, recall was better for those breast-feeding for a long period as opposed to a moderate period and for predominantly old respondents as compared to the moderately young.

A second significant branch occurs among the low education group although most variables enter relatively late in the overall analysis. This group is first segmented on the basis of low to high exposure on the one hand and very low exposure on the other hand. However, the relationship with recall is inverse: the very low exposure group has a better recall than the low to high group. Yet among the latter group the moderate to high exposure group has better recall (2.57) than the low-moderate exposure group (3.15). The moderate to high exposure group is dichotomized on the basis of time of first exposure. The very early exposure group had a better recall (2.36) than did the moderate to early group (2.96). The latter group is divided between the middle age group and older age group with the latter having a better recall score (2.30 versus 3.35). In general, then, with the exception of the first entry following the low education group, those having relatively low levels of education will have better recall scores if they were first exposed to the messages very early in the campaign and if they are relatively old.

It is very important to note that neither cosmopoliteness nor interpersonal communication ever achieved a sufficiently high discriminatory value to be selected for entry into the model. At one point relatively late in the analysis cosmopoliteness was almost as important as the variable actually selected. Thus, two variables which were expected to be important did not manifest themselves as key factors.

Other Methods of Factoring and Clustering

A wide variety of factoring and clustering methods have been developed. For example, in factor analysis, a series of rotation methods have been developed which relax the assumption that the factors have to be "orthogonal" (independent) from one another. These are called oblique rotation methods and are available in the Statistical Package for the Social Sciences (SPSS). Variation in methods of extracting principal components have also been developed (the reader can find the detail of such methods in the SPSS manual).[9]

Similarly, clustering methods have been developed which have a variety of assumptions. A popular version of cluster analysis has been created called MCA (Multiple Classification Analysis).[10] This computer method examines the correlation of individual respondents across a number of variables and groups individuals together who are most correlated. The algorithm keeps adding groups and individuals together until some stopping rule is satisfied. This method is called a "build-up" method of clustering since it builds groups of similar individuals.

Stopping Rules

All of the programs which perform cluster and factor analysis have one major question involved with their use. This is: "When do you stop the factoring or clustering process?" The answer to the question usually involves pragmatic rules involved with the amount of residual variance left in the data. The user of all such programs should be particularly careful to select stopping rules which are consistent with his research objectives. If a researcher has concrete ideas about the structure of his data or sample, he should set "strict" stopping rules which cause the programs to stop as soon as most of the variance is accounted for. Conversely, if the researcher is "exploring," he may let the programs run until computer budget becomes a problem. Such "fishing" usually creates more questions than it answers, however.

Summary

This chapter has attempted to explain and analyze the common techniques of group questions and respondents into groups. The basic assumptions of the techniques and their methods of operation have been illustrated with examples. These techniques are extremely important in the development of theory and isolating groups of homogeneous subjects. The use of these techniques bears heavily on the development of market segments and the performing of accurate market research analysis. These techniques are available on both small and large computers and can be set up with a minimal degree of technical knowledge of the computer. They add a new dimension to social

---

[9] N. H. Nie, D. H. Bent, and C. H. Hull, SPSS, *The Statistical Package for the Social Sciences* (New York: McGraw-Hill, 1970).
[10] Available from the Computer Center, University of Chicago.

research and should be carefully considered as part of the design of any research project.

Questions and Exercises

1. What is the essence of the "basic factor model?" Why did the use of factor analysis begin with psychologists?
2. Briefly interpret the meanings of the correlations shown in Table 13.2. How do these relate to the principal components shown in Table 13.3?
3. How does the example in Tables 13.1 to 13.4 meet the assumptions of factor analysis? Does the example violate any assumptions of factor analysis?
4. How are names assigned to the factors? Are there other names which could be assigned to the factors shown in Table 13.4?
5. Why can't factor analysis be used for rigorous hypothesis testing based on the examples and discussion in the chapter?
6. What is the function of the eigenvalue in performing a factor analysis?
7. Why would a researcher want to perform a cluster analysis within a large sample? Describe a scenario where it might be an absolute necessity.
8. Write a one paragraph report discussing the AID results shown in Figure 13.3.
9. What key assumptions must be met to use AID? Must the data be metric (cardinal) or can some be ordinal or even nominal (see Chapters 7 and 10)?
10. Interpret the data analysis shown in Figure 13.3. How would this analysis help you to build a model of communication concerning the recall of advertising messages?
11. What is the difference between R factor analysis and Q factor analysis? Which one amounts to multivariate cluster analysis?
12. Why are clearly defined "stopping rules" necessary when using factor or cluster analysis?
13. Reviewing Chapters 11 to 13, what broad classes of models are testable using available statistical techniques? Are there any classes of models which are not easily testable using the common techniques? (Refer to Chapter 5.)

Project Related Questions

1. Is there any reason to group respondents or questions?
2. Which grouping method seems most suitable?
3. Does the data meet the assumptions of the desired techniques?
4. Have you properly set the stopping rule (so you know when to quit factoring or clustering)?
5. What results are you likely to see in using these techniques with the data?

Technical Appendix: Output from a Factor Analysis Computer Program

To illustrate how factor analysis is interpreted, the example in the chapter was rerun with a larger sample size, principal components with communality estimates in the diagonal of the correlation matrix, and varimax rotation. The results are very similar to those shown in Chapter 13. The analysis was run on the same data base as described in the example in Chapter 12. The analysis was run on the State University of New York at Binghamton IBM 370/155 using version 5.00 of SPSS available from the National Opinion Research Center of the University of Chicago as were the discriminant analysis and regression analysis. The results are shown in the sections of output shown in Figure 13.5.

1. *The variable list.* The list of factored variables are listed for later cross-reference.
2. *The univariate analysis.* Means and standard deviations are calculated for each variable. The number of valid cases are also listed. When missing values are deleted, the number of cases may be different from variable to variable.
3. *Correlation coefficients.* Same as previous examples.
4. *Inverse of correlation.* The necessary step before the extraction of eigenvalues.
5. *Variable est communality.* This section reports the results of the extraction of the eigenvectors (factors). The first eigenvector (factor) accounts for 13.7 percent of the variance and the second adds 8.4 percent. These first two will be used to construct the final two factors.
6. *Factor matrix using principal factor.* This section reports the loading (interpret-correlation) of each variable on the original extracted eigenvectors (factors). It is interesting to note that many variables load on both factors to a great degree (see variable 188 for example). This makes naming the factors next to impossible.
7. *Communality.* The communality of variables across factors is reported. If a variable loads on two factors, it is said to have high communality.

The percentage of variance explained of the 22 percent is split between the two factors and is reported.

8. *Varimax rotated.* The initial factors are rotated on their axes to enhance interpretability. The method of rotation maximizes the variance between the factors and, hence, is called varimax. It can be seen that the loading of some variables increase on one factor and decrease on the other. The factors can now be interpreted. Factor 1 is the sophisticated reader and factor 2 is the shelter magazine reader.

9. *Transformation.* This reports the angle of rotation between the initial and final factors.

10. *Factor score coefficients.* If the researcher wishes to see if a given person is a sophisticated reader, he would want to develop a score reflecting the trait. The factor scores are found by multiplying a person's answer to an answer on the questionnaire by the factor score coefficient. The coefficients are very similar to the B coefficient in regressions.

11. *The plot.* The plot shows how each variable loads on each of the two factors. However, the plot does not show degree of significance. To find these the analyst must look at the rotated factor loadings (item 8 in this presentation). The plot tends to reinforce the naming of the factors as it shows the shelter magazines along the vertical axis while the sophisticated magazines are along the horizontal.

1.VARIABLE LIST

VARIABLES..	LABELS..
VAR159	CHICAGO TRIBUNE
VAR160	CHICAGO SUN TIMES
VAR161	INDIANAPOLIS STAR WEEKDAYS
VAR162	INDIANAPOLIS STAR SUNDAYS
VAR163	N Y TIMES WEEKDAYS
VAR164	N Y TIMES SUNDAYS
VAR165	LAFAYETTE JOURNAL CARRIER
VAR166	ATLANTIC MONTHLY
VAR167	BETTER HOMES AND GARDENS
VAR168	BUSINESS WEEK
VAR169	CONSUMER BULLETIN
VAR170	CONSUMER REPORTS
VAR171	ESQUIRE
VAR172	FAMILY CIRCLE
VAR173	FIELD AND STREAM
VAR174	GLAMOUR
VAR175	GOOD HOUSEKEEPING
VAR176	HARPERS BAZAAR
VAR177	HOLIDAY
VAR178	HOUSE BEAUTIFUL
VAR179	LADIES HOME JOURNAL
VAR180	LIFE
VAR181	LOOK
VAR182	MADEMOISELLE
VAR183	MCCALLS
VAR184	MODERN ROMANCE
VAR185	MODERN SCREEN
VAR186	NATIONAL GEOGRAPHIC
VAR187	NEWSWEEK
VAR188	NEW YORKER
VAR189	PAGEANT
VAR190	PLAYBOY
VAR191	POST
VAR192	READERS DIGEST
VAR193	REDBOOK
VAR194	SATURDAY REVIEW
VAR195	SPORTS ILLUSTRATED
VAR196	TIME
VAR197	TRUE STORY
VAR198	TRUE CONFESSIONS
VAR199	T V GUIDE
VAR200	US NEWS AND WORLD REPORT
VAR201	VOGUE
VAR202	WOMANS DAY

VARIABLE	MEAN	STANDARD DEV	CASES
VAR159	1.4757	0.9140	394
VAR160	1.1701	0.5085	394
VAR161	2.4645	1.9949	394
VAR162	4.1244	2.1419	394
VAR163	1.0939	0.3759	394
VAR164	1.2157	0.7493	394
VAR165	5.3325	1.4754	394
VAR166	1.2411	0.8104	394
VAR167	3.2792	1.9137	394
VAR168	1.1580	0.5510	394
VAR169	1.3401	0.8743	394
VAR170	1.7411	1.2677	394
VAR171	1.2132	0.6013	394
VAR172	3.1472	1.8558	394
VAR173	1.1954	0.6615	394
VAR174	1.6371	1.1087	394
VAR175	3.3632	1.8828	394
VAR176	1.4543	1.0160	394
VAR177	1.3909	0.7973	394
VAR178	2.0812	1.4244	394
VAR179	3.3528	1.9287	394
VAR180	3.1701	1.8143	394
VAR181	2.7081	1.5817	394
VAR182	1.5076	0.9813	394
VAR183	3.5330	1.9770	394
VAR184	1.1218	0.6140	394
VAR185	1.1548	0.5280	394
VAR186	2.0711	1.6330	394
VAR187	2.1066	1.4668	394
VAR188	1.2741	0.7523	394
VAR189	1.1320	0.5907	394
VAR190	1.4721	1.1593	394
VAR191	2.6650	1.7545	394
VAR192	3.7107	1.9943	394
VAR193	2.2817	1.7718	394
VAR194	1.2741	0.8684	394
VAR195	1.2208	0.6416	394
VAR196	2.5152	1.8769	394
VAR197	1.1345	0.6587	394
VAR198	1.0835	0.4080	394
VAR199	2.6066	1.9975	394
VAR200	1.8580	1.2551	394
VAR201	1.6142	1.1182	394
VAR202	3.1193	1.9164	394

FIGURE 13.5 *Factor Analysis: Computer Output*

CORRELATION COEFFICIENTS..

	VAR159	VAR160	VAR161	VAR162	VAR163	VAR164	VAR165	VAR166	VAR167	VAR168
VAR159	1.CC000	0.23466	C.16218	0.02664	0.09814	0.09743	C.03049	0.07361	-0.03021	0.10513
VAR160	0.23466	1.C0000	-0.00030	-0.08021	0.18251	0.31C85	-0.04503	0.20900	-0.04107	0.02872
VAR161	C.16218	-C.CC030	1.CC000	0.40926	-0.02099	-0.00082	C.10388	0.06119	0.11125	0.10339
VAR162	0.02664	-C.C8021	0.40926	1.CC000	-0.11252	-0.09286	0.24939	-0.CC852	0.20754	0.07172
VAR163	0.09814	0.18251	-0.02099	-0.11252	1.00000	0.62352	C.03073	0.32644	-0.02947	0.00702
VAR164	0.09743	0.31C85	-0.00082	-0.09286	0.62352	1.C0000	-0.01901	0.26611	-0.08470	0.04263
VAR165	0.03049	-0.C4503	0.10388	0.24939	0.03073	-0.01901	1.C0000	-0.11404	0.20226	0.08495
VAR166	0.07361	0.20900	0.06119	-0.CC852	0.32644	0.26611	-0.11404	1.C0000	-0.08289	-0.03283
VAR167	-0.03021	-0.C4107	0.11125	0.20754	-0.02947	-0.08470	0.20226	-0.08289	1.00000	0.06377
VAR168	0.10513	C.C2872	0.10339	0.C7172	0.C0702	0.04263	C.C8495	-0.03283	0.06377	1.00000
VAR169	0.13921	0.11569	0.C9594	0.05269	0.09613	0.1867B	0.02258	0.23232	0.05412	0.10940
VAR170	0.04157	0.14347	0.11206	0.03250	0.13659	0.28663	C.05022	0.22686	0.05609	0.02834
VAR171	0.05882	0.15576	0.C5088	-0.02262	0.22642	0.23086	-0.C4856	0.28588	0.02111	0.01541
VAR172	0.05877	0.02464	0.10314	0.20728	-0.00163	0.01370	0.18189	0.00510	0.30651	0.09587
VAR173	-0.03340	0.02155	0.C3902	-0.01720	0.01810	0.C4820	0.09230	-0.01693	0.02513	0.02811
VAR174	0.117C0	0.C7365	0.C4075	0.C1156	0.02094	0.08530	-C.C8937	0.05800	0.15461	0.00814
VAR175	0.10138	C.C4338	0.17465	0.17555	-0.05098	-0.C3711	0.10790	0.05102	0.15461	0.02306
VAR176	0.16751	C.C6650	0.23082	0.10844	0.15499	0.26532	C.C4835	0.18802	0.15053	0.06757
VAR177	0.16805	C.C6042	0.22473	0.11600	0.15740	0.21627	-C.C0477	0.25153	0.08339	0.09076
VAR178	0.24361	C.C5817	0.21055	0.22103	0.06651	0.10274	0.12878	0.02267	0.32397	0.13353
VAR179	0.09140	0.02425	0.11272	0.20986	-0.07038	-0.C5456	0.12768	0.04312	0.24004	0.14283
VAR180	0.09492	C.C2314	0.C5655	0.11503	0.05115	0.08150	0.11476	0.04473	0.06617	0.03821
VAR181	0.04231	-C.C0727	0.C9740	0.12737	-0.02496	0.04606	0.114C8	0.05924	0.11078	0.12032
VAR182	0.20726	0.15243	0.11322	0.11032	0.12567	-0.C6753	-0.12419	0.13625	-0.C3754	0.08388
VAR183	0.05525	C.CC833	C.C7385	0.13914	-0.C6753	-0.04970	-0.12419	0.13625	-0.C5919	-0.02866
VAR184	0.17218	C.C6338	0.12403	0.04069	-0.04970	-0.02409	0.07677	-0.C5919	-0.00511	-0.03017
VAR185	0.16734	0.C6281	0.C7650	0.12018	0.00348	-0.02032	0.05134	0.C8100	0.00768	-0.02866
VAR186	0.08562	0.CC202	0.11325	0.07822	0.16735	0.23490	C.23490	0.15815	0.02702	0.12077
VAR187	0.17613	0.1C528	0.0326C	0.05328	0.18025	0.19201	0.05884	0.28230	0.02563	0.21767
VAR188	0.16545	0.18363	0.08450	-0.01174	0.45767	0.49520	-0.C2730	0.42975	-0.05329	0.01881
VAR189	0.02854	0.12841	0.C6555	0.C1113	-0.01012	0.1C797	0.C0791	0.16192	0.01459	0.05099
VAR190	0.08351	0.C6962	C.C7879	0.07262	0.06151	0.06C00	-0.18126	0.23604	-0.02974	-0.02300
VAR191	0.11216	0.01268	0.21832	0.20477	-0.03706	-0.02424	0.12375	0.07307	0.13175	0.09163
VAR192	-0.02614	-0.C5335	0.19164	0.18835	-0.C9265	-0.11568	0.18845	-0.C6536	0.07856	0.18143
VAR193	0.02475	0.C5356	0.01430	0.06919	-0.08185	-0.06123	0.C4195	-0.C3502	0.03378	0.06624
VAR194	0.05151	0.15424	-0.C7661	-0.15727	0.32628	0.31947	-0.10110	0.32887	-0.06760	-0.04222
VAR195	0.06190	0.C7180	0.11449	0.10958	0.27252	0.27643	0.06471	0.C8330	0.08436	0.03519
VAR196	0.11C68	0.13655	0.C7864	0.06314	0.16568	0.20482	-0.C2434	0.20921	0.08099	0.02668
VAR197	0.08596	0.C5721	0.08102	0.07210	-0.02884	-0.03127	0.07745	-0.04844	0.02703	-0.03072
VAR198	0.17064	0.C5905	0.C2310	0.C1133	-0.02236	-0.01192	0.C7055	-0.03870	0.08154	-0.04742
VAR199	0.14822	0.C4599	-0.00192	-0.02660	0.07305	0.08405	0.10926	-0.03871	0.02415	0.03461
VAR200	0.18650	C.C486 6	0.23402	0.10582	0.10682	0.22C98	0.06674	0.12432	0.11359	0.08582
VAR201	0.14170	C.C6883	0.22064	0.12739	0.08036	0.15729	0.06407	0.11134	0.21218	0.08771

INVERSE OF CORRELATION MATRIX..

	VAR159	VAR160	VAR161	VAR162	VAR163	VAR164	VAR165	VAR166	VAR167	VAR168
VAR159	1.34230	-C.25015	-0.16157	0.C9521	-0.01236	0.11680	-0.02188	C.C9223	C.17585	-0.07087
VAR160	-0.25015	1.2645	0.00231	0.06403	0.08181	-0.39039	0.01487	-0.15180	-0.02315	-0.03150
VAR161	-0.16157	0.C0231	1.48070	-0.45514	-0.02412	0.C9470	0.05567	-0.07158	0.00142	-0.09828
VAR162	C.C9521	0.06403	-0.45514	1.44592	-0.18967	-0.C4625	-0.23875	-0.C4661	-0.05915	0.03695
VAR163	-0.01236	0.C9181	-0.02412	0.18967	2.03242	-1.02604	2.31738	-0.28411	-0.11720	0.00889
VAR164	0.11680	-0.39039	0.C9470	-0.04625	-1.02604	2.31738	0.02507	0.21222	0.19888	-0.C6742
VAR165	-0.02188	0.C1487	0.05568	-0.23875	-0.14581	0.02507	1.27709	0.08695	-0.14378	-0.00408
VAR166	0.09223	-0.151BC	-0.07158	-0.04661	-0.28411	0.21223	0.08695	1.69163	0.10913	0.13271
VAR167	0.17585	-0.02315	0.00142	-0.C9015	-0.11720	0.19888	-0.14378	0.10913	1.42772	-0.02177
VAR168	-0.07087	-0.C3150	-0.C9828	0.03655	0.00889	-0.06742	-0.C04C8	0.13271	-0.02177	1.18785
VAR169	-0.08699	0.C3606	0.06010	0.C1638	0.07831	-0.07864	-0.C0928	-0.23053	0.00629	-0.14450
VAR170	0.13058	-0.C5141	-0.C9991	0.C3234	0.16311	-0.23800	-0.04538	-0.05712	-0.02022	0.08775
VAR171	0.07448	-0.C6956	0.03773	0.C7979	-0.06563	0.04508	-0.01646	-0.1C951	-0.05668	0.02053
VAR172	-0.03982	0.C9361	0.09916	-0.27913	0.05408	0.03440	-0.05253	0.16946	-0.44671	-0.27689
VAR173	0.05110	-0.04352	-0.03623	0.C8292	-0.01008	-0.02885	0.C8637	-0.C0538	0.01526	0.00198
VAR174	0.02614	0.C2965	0.10065	0.15867	0.10878	-0.18483	C.24386	0.10191	-0.09307	0.13465
VAR175	0.01939	-0.C2241	-0.14847	0.04465	0.07039	-0.04627	0.02702	-0.C4714	-0.23306	0.13723
VAR176	-0.02581	C.10030	-0.20173	-0.C0178	0.00161	-0.15040	-0.07824	-0.C9395	0.03792	-0.08315
VAR177	-0.08175	-0.C7068	-0.08797	-0.04911	-0.02673	-0.C3243	0.11719	-0.20040	-0.01758	-0.00522
VAR178	-0.25389	0.C3586	0.03248	-0.15481	-0.07283	0.03525	-0.02850	0.1B647	-0.29064	-0.07908
VAR179	-0.01863	-0.C3321	0.16426	-0.11206	0.05110	0.09876	0.01933	-0.03782	-0.06702	-0.08100
VAR180	-0.C0630	-0.C0516	-0.11068	-0.01735	-0.06425	0.04244	-0.08368	0.1C163	0.06396	0.05304
VAR181	0.03714	0.C5446	0.C4520	-0.02410	0.17264	-0.05872	-0.C2916	-0.00837	-0.05572	-0.C0483
VAR182	-0.16693	-0.12142	0.C8187	-0.17914	-0.23476	0.31224	-0.05587	-0.11082	0.05159	-0.C5454
VAR183	-0.05408	0.C1647	-0.24946	0.01306	-0.11013	0.14956	-0.04052	0.C8367	-0.10211	0.00840
VAR184	-0.C8C89	0.C3601	-0.24946	0.19854	0.06054	0.C1850	-0.05184	C.20396	0.05031	0.08975
VAR185	-0.10816	-0.C0617	0.04938	-0.20466	-0.08404	0.11290	-0.00708	-0.02409	0.04982	-0.00140
VAR186	0.01599	0.C2942	0.06418	0.C0164	-0.00600	-0.14832	-0.02158	-0.03414	0.08887	-0.07310
VAR187	-0.11380	C.C655	0.13408	-0.03712	-0.0518B	-0.05465	-0.08681	-0.33271	0.03165	-0.28414
VAR188	-0.18757	0.C5171	-0.01353	-0.C2631	-0.31219	-0.44430	0.03279	-0.34321	0.08392	0.05972
VAR189	0.09112	-0.C6611	-0.07158	0.15474	0.21077	-0.03467	-0.13085	-0.17867	0.07025	0.01244
VAR190	-0.02545	-0.C0037	-0.02985	-0.1C967	0.C0667	0.04661	0.20706	-0.17867	0.04360	0.04581
VAR191	-0.05025	0.C0923	-0.14397	-0.04695	0.04917	0.00627	-0.05999	-0.06676	-0.06120	-0.01343
VAR192	0.09774	0.C5786	-0.15891	-0.06011	-0.02908	0.19086	-0.10543	0.C3177	0.07387	-0.15040
VAR193	0.05899	-0.13466	0.07207	-0.01421	0.01957	0.05105	0.01896	0.06440	0.19200	-0.07421
VAR194	0.00183	-0.CC838	0.13915	0.13915	-0.14654	-0.06053	0.C8589	-0.28265	-0.04682	0.00581
VAR195	-0.00333	0.C1150	-0.05087	-0.07525	-0.26348	-0.22057	-0.02094	C.11327	-0.08688	0.07631
VAR196	-0.04932	-0.C818B	0.00444	-0.08547	0.00670	-0.04279	0.01294	-0.1C562	-0.08422	-0.00986
VAR197	0.13702	-0.C2333	-0.02466	-0.16191	-0.03599	0.01516	-0.02376	0.C0088	0.08297	-0.02043
VAR198	-0.11667	-0.C1080	0.15625	0.C6118	0.02968	-0.08449	0.01525	-0.12081	-0.18289	0.06038
VAR199	-0.13537	0.C3392	0.03156	0.05769	-0.07201	-0.36387	-0.C9784	0.C8713	0.01054	-0.02346
VAR200	-0.11307	0.C1523	-0.16233	0.C1389	0.12138	-0.21563	-0.C0586	0.C8397	-0.13844	0.05515
VAR201	0.08790	-0.01235	-0.15773	0.C7867	0.17332	-0.08949	-0.05667	0.04850	-0.09769	-0.04714

VARIABLE	EST COMMUNALITY	FACTOR	EIGENVALUE	PCT OF VAR	CUM PCT
VAR159	0.25501	1	6.03518	13.7	13.7
VAR160	0.21039	2	3.69344	8.4	22.1
VAR161	0.32465	3	2.56411	5.8	27.9
VAR162	0.33151	4	1.96538	4.5	32.4
VAR163	0.50758	5	1.77636	4.0	36.4
VAR164	0.56848	6	1.65078	3.8	40.2
VAR165	0.21657	7	1.40906	3.2	43.4
VAR166	0.40885	8	1.25600	2.9	46.3
VAR167	0.29958	9	1.23838	2.8	49.1
VAR168	0.15814	10	1.21664	2.8	51.8
VAR169	0.41403	11	1.14676	2.6	54.4
VAR170	0.39976	12	1.09562	2.5	56.9
VAR171	0.29763	13	1.05346	2.4	59.3
VAR172	0.75133	14	1.01478	2.3	61.6
VAR173	0.11212	15	0.96344	2.2	63.8
VAR174	0.45942	16	0.93935	2.1	66.0
VAR175	0.39705	17	0.88554	2.0	68.0
VAR176	0.49356	18	0.87574	2.0	70.0
VAR177	0.36729	19	0.81390	1.9	71.8
VAR178	0.43631	20	0.79800	1.8	73.6
VAR179	0.40942	21	0.77459	1.8	75.4
VAR180	0.25533	22	0.75065	1.7	77.1
VAR181	0.25371	23	0.70223	1.6	78.7
VAR182	0.47118	24	0.68513	1.6	80.3
VAR183	0.54158	25	0.67076	1.5	81.8
VAR184	0.63081	26	0.63019	1.4	83.2
VAR185	0.25352	27	0.60440	1.4	84.6
VAR186	0.25315	28	0.58082	1.3	85.9
VAR187	0.24436	29	0.56114	1.3	87.2
VAR188	0.48589	30	0.55436	1.3	88.4
VAR189	0.28317	31	0.54470	1.2	89.7
VAR190	0.21575	32	0.49211	1.1	90.8
VAR191	0.33146	33	0.48165	1.1	91.9
VAR192	0.31996	34	0.45777	1.0	92.9
VAR193	0.32916	35	0.41633	0.9	93.9
VAR194	0.31954	36	0.39961	0.9	94.8
VAR195	0.24456	37	0.38704	0.9	95.7
VAR196	0.19020	38	0.35508	0.8	96.5
VAR197	0.60336	39	0.33536	0.8	97.2
VAR198	0.57472	40	0.31686	0.7	98.0
VAR199	0.13582	41	0.27698	0.6	98.6
VAR200	0.29657	42	0.25359	0.6	99.2
VAR201	0.50762	43	0.23063	0.5	99.7
VAR202	0.74828	44	0.13154	0.3	100.0

% variance explained of 2 first unrotated factors

CONVERGENCE REQUIRED   5 ITERATIONS

FACTOR MATRIX USING PRINCIPAL FACTOR WITH ITERATIONS

	FACTOR 1	FACTOR 2
VAR159	-0.29701	0.04815
VAR160	-0.22195	0.23239
VAR161	-0.32944	-0.13526
VAR162	-0.26135	-0.29186
VAR163	-0.26861	0.53181
VAR164	-0.35076	0.58529
VAR165	-0.15725	-0.24566
VAR166	-0.32611	0.44250
VAR167	-0.28419	0.29680
VAR168	-0.17620	-0.06556
VAR169	-0.36872	0.13147
VAR170	-0.38453	0.19965
VAR171	-0.34536	0.25984
VAR172	-0.43150	-0.34672
VAR173	-0.07472	-0.05859
VAR174	-0.40779	-0.04448
VAR175	-0.45154	-0.38529
VAR176	-0.53513	0.12415
VAR177	-0.51663	0.13314
VAR178	-0.56826	-0.14705
VAR179	-0.47645	-0.38391
VAR180	-0.36376	-0.03209
VAR181	-0.32669	-0.11265
VAR182	-0.45683	0.05352
VAR183	-0.37412	-0.38613
VAR184	-0.12128	-0.19989
VAR185	-0.14574	-0.12860
VAR186	-0.38131	0.12053
VAR187	-0.34904	0.13373
VAR188	-0.42389	0.49191
VAR189	-0.34907	-0.01105
VAR190	-0.21690	0.13071
VAR191	-0.36943	-0.21401
VAR192	-0.20158	-0.31544
VAR193	-0.25073	-0.31399
VAR194	-0.17172	0.45025
VAR195	-0.28507	0.15179
VAR196	-0.28617	0.26180
VAR197	-0.05982	-0.20256
VAR198	-0.05971	-0.20254
VAR199	-0.13891	-0.07753
VAR200	-0.41511	0.08813
VAR201	-0.56818	0.01077
VAR202	-0.47703	-0.28900

FIGURE 13.5 *(continued)*

524

VARIABLE	COMMUNALITY		FACTOR	EIGENVALUE	PCT OF VAR	CUM PCT
VAR159	C.C9C54		1	5.27895	64.0	64.0
VAR160	0.10227		2	2.96662	36.0	100.0
VAR161	0.12682					
VAR162	0.15349					
VAR163	0.35465					
VAR164	0.46555					
VAR165	0.C8507					
VAR166	0.39216					
VAR167	0.16E86					
VAR168	0.03588					
VAR169	0.15324					
VAR170	0.18772					
VAR171	0.1867S					
VAR172	0.30E41					
VAR173	0.C0902					
VAR174	0.15627					
VAR175	0.35233					
VAR176	0.30177					
VAR177	0.28401					
VAR178	0.34448					
VAR179	C.37439					
VAR180	0.13335					
VAR181	0.11941					
VAR182	0.24975					
VAR183	0.28906					
VAR184	0.05667					
VAR185	0.03778					
VAR186	0.15992					
VAR187	0.13572					
VAR188	0.42166					
VAR189	0.12157					
VAR190	0.06413					
VAR191	0.18228					
VAR192	0.14014					
VAR193	0.16146					
VAR194	0.23221					
VAR195	0.10431					
VAR196	0.15043					
VAR197	0.04461					
VAR198	0.04455					
VAR199	0.02531					
VAR200	0.18C08					
VAR201	0.32294					
VAR202	0.31108					

VARIMAX ROTATED FACTOR MATRIX

sophisticated Reader   *Shelter mag reader* } *Factor names*

	FACTOR 1	FACTOR 2
VAR159	0.25902	0.15311
VAR160	0.31927	-0.C3649
VAR161	0.16654	C.31478
VAR162	C.01395	0.35153
VAR163 *NY Times*	0.54631	-C.23706
VAR164 *NY Times*	0.64411	-0.22519
VAR165	-0.03641	C.28939
VAR166	0.53379	-0.13125
VAR167	0.02838	0.40994
VAR168	0.09086	0.16672
VAR169	0.36745	0.13459
VAR170	0.42323	C.C9272
VAR171	0.43166	0.02141
VAR172 *Family Circle*	0.10961	0.54258
VAR173	0.01991	C.C5284
VAR174	0.28485	0.2751B
VAR175 *Good House K*	0.10032	C.54503
VAR176	0.49C62	0.24712
VAR177	0.48170	0.22499
VAR178	0.34241	0.47670
VAR179 *Ladies Home J*	0.12035	0.5959 — *high loading*
VAR180	0.25895	0.25748
VAR181	0.17890	0.29565
VAR182	0.41624	C.27657
VAR183 *Mc Calls*	0.04C30	0.53613
VAR184	-0.03476	0.23121
VAR185	0.02967	G.19209
VAR186	0.37C12	0.15145
VAR187	0.35378	0.13066
VAR188 *New Yorker*	0.64053	-C.10063
VAR189	0.26112	0.23192
VAR190	0.25031	0.03840
VAR191	0.14686	C.4CC89
VAR192	-0.04702	0.37135
VAR193	-0.00833	0.40173
VAR194	0.42013	-0.23603
VAR195	0.31619	C.06584
VAR196	0.38744	-0.01798
VAR197	-0.08368	0.19392
VAR198	-0.08376	0.19383
VAR199	0.05710	0.14848
VAR200	0.37535	0.19798
VAR201	0.44344	0.35540
VAR202	0.18154	0.52738

525

TRANSFORMATION MATRIX

	FACTOR 1	FACTOR 2
FACTOR 1	-0.76833	-0.64006
FACTOR 2	0.64006	-0.76833

FACTOR SCORE COEFFICIENTS

	FACTOR 1	FACTOR 2
VAR159	0.03892	0.01436
VAR160	0.04766	-0.01209
VAR161	0.01575	0.05819
VAR162	-0.01573	0.07816
VAR163	0.11040	-0.07643
VAR164	0.20601	-0.11482
VAR165	-0.02041	0.05877
VAR166	0.13121	-0.06533
VAR167	-0.00707	0.06815
VAR168	0.00926	0.02595
VAR169	0.05460	0.01210
VAR170	0.07486	0.00271
VAR171	0.07277	-0.00962
VAR172	-0.00903	0.13194
VAR173	-0.00105	0.01617
VAR174	0.03468	0.03872
VAR175	-0.01490	0.14607
VAR176	0.08003	0.03862
VAR177	0.09729	0.03059
VAR178	0.05927	0.10524
VAR179	-0.00637	0.15690
VAR180	0.03965	0.04102
VAR181	0.01769	0.05549
VAR182	0.08374	0.04177
VAR183	-0.01149	0.11368
VAR184	-0.00677	0.04518
VAR185	-0.00115	0.04142
VAR186	0.05476	0.01247
VAR187	0.05872	0.01232
VAR188	0.16404	-0.06910
VAR189	0.03413	0.03161
VAR190	0.04506	-0.00696
VAR191	0.01229	0.08053
VAR192	-0.01774	0.07593
VAR193	-0.01376	0.07284
VAR194	0.09091	-0.06630
VAR195	0.04505	0.00562
VAR196	0.07520	-0.02095
VAR197	-0.02388	0.04438
VAR198	-0.03217	0.04451
VAR199	0.00242	0.02905
VAR200	0.05834	0.03135
VAR201	0.08118	0.06219
VAR202	0.01312	0.10680

HORIZONTAL FACTOR 1   VERTICAL FACTOR 2

1 = VAR159	2 = VAR160
3 = VAR161	4 = VAR162
5 = VAR163	6 = VAR164
7 = VAR165	8 = VAR166
9 = VAR167	10 = VAR168
11 = VAR169	12 = VAR170
13 = VAR171	14 = VAR172
15 = VAR173	16 = VAR174
17 = VAR175	18 = VAR176
19 = VAR177	20 = VAR178
21 = VAR179	22 = VAR180
23 = VAR181	24 = VAR182
25 = VAR183	26 = VAR184
27 = VAR185	28 = VAR186
29 = VAR187	30 = VAR188
31 = VAR189	32 = VAR190
33 = VAR191	34 = VAR192
35 = VAR193	36 = VAR194
37 = VAR195	38 = VAR196
39 = VAR197	40 = VAR198
41 = VAR199	42 = VAR200
43 = VAR201	44 = VAR202

FIGURE 13.5 *(continued)*

526

Chapter 14

Marketing Information Systems: Investing in Information

The marketing researcher must decide how much to spend for a given information collection task. This chapter is designed to show that information is an investment and how the value of the investment may be computed. In addition, the researcher must understand how research is used within the organization. This chapter discusses how models are built, tested, and used by the manager.

Introduction

Information is the primary tool of the manager. All decisions are evaluated in terms of the information received by the manager, and all plans are cast into informational terms in order for them to be implemented. Information is defined as those cues which have the potential to affect managerial decisions. Therefore, the manager must develop an efficient way of collecting information from his environment, and evaluating that information. In addition, the manager must assign some value to the information to be collected.

This chapter focuses on two major tasks. First, it is necessary to understand what a marketing information system is and how its parts help the manager. Secondly, this chapter investigates the nature of the decision—whether to buy information or not. Some information is readily available in the managerial environment and requires little effort to be collected. In other situations, information must be collected with considerable effort, often involving direct and extended interaction with individuals and businesses in the marketing environment—and thus the need for marketing research develops.

The manager must decide whether it is appropriate to spend money and time to gather information. This decision is analogous to the managerial decision to invest in a security, new piece of equipment, or to complete a merger. The manager must decide how much money to invest in gathering information and he must estimate what the return on investment is going to be for each alternative information collection strategy he faces. He must then choose the alternative which yields the highest return.

How Can Information Yield Dollar Payoffs?

There are several ways in which information can yield dollar payoffs.

1. Information can be used to make a product more acceptable to consumers and thus greatly increase its ultimate market share.
2. Information can prevent the undertaking of projects which have little probability of monetary success.
3. Information can lead managers to higher levels of efficiency by using "Promotools" such as advertising, salesforce, and so on.
4. Information can suggest future products and services.

529

5. Information can monitor competitor activities and thus minimize costly "surprises."
6. Information can find new customers.

Information Is Not Perfect

Those cues which a manager receives have a credibility associated with them. This means that there is some probability, however slight, that the cues could be wrong. "Wrong" implies that the cue itself could be inaccurate or that the receiver of the cue might misinterpret it. Thus, the probability of either of these two events must be attached to the piece of information itself.

Since information has a payoff and has a probability of being right or wrong, it follows that the manager must perform some kind of *expected value analysis* when evaluating the decision to buy or not to buy research. Expected value analysis amounts to multiplying the payoff from a piece of information by its probability of being right. Similarly, the same multiplication is known as risk analysis when the potential loss from making a mistake is multiplied by the probability of the information being wrong. In either case, the most favorable alternative with the least uncertainty should be chosen by the decision maker.

How Marketing Information Flows in a Firm

The marketing manager deals in a world which requires continuous decision making regarding products and markets. Decisions concerning price, advertising, and other promotion tools, distribution of products and stock levels, monitoring of salesman activity and effectiveness, and deciding when to add or withdraw brands are all part of the daily concerns of the marketing manager. Because decisions are frequent and often very important in terms of company profit, accurate information about the state of consumers and markets is very important.

The process of obtaining and using information is pictorially described in Figure 14.1. Within the firm, there are four groups who interact with consumers. Marketing researchers ask relevant questions of consumers. In return, consumers answer the questions. The answers are analyzed and reported to marketing managers. The marketing managers help set budgets for marketing research in return. Marketing managers also create plans for promoting, distributing, and pricing the products or services of the firm. In addition, the marketing groups receive occasional consumer complaints. These complaints are consolidated and passed on to production for use in quality control. In addition, marketing management transmits distribution plans and sales predictions to production in order for production planners to set production levels. Production actually delivers the product to the consumer.

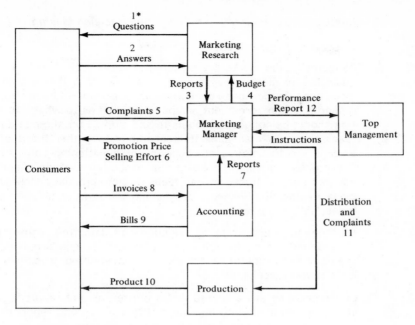

*Numbered relationship is discussed in the text.

FIGURE 14.1 *How Marketing Information Flows in a Firm*

When salesmen make a sale, an order or invoice is generated in the accounting system of the firm. When the product has been shipped by production, accounting sends a bill to the consumer. Every so often, (usually monthly or quarterly) the accounting department prepares a sales report for each salesman, product, and geographic territory based on the invoices. These reports are passed to the marketing manager. Typically, the manager compares incoming sales reports with past reports with special attention given to changes and exceptions.

Additional detail is provided for the relationships in Figure 14.2. The timing of decisions and information flows is also discussed. Thus, timeliness and quality of information are the staples of the manager's diet. Usually old information tends to be very accurate (the invoice system) while very timely information can be heavily biased (telephoning a salesman). The manager must constantly make tradeoffs as to which information collection mode is most suitable for the decision at hand. Marketing research plays a great role in the information collection and analysis process. Marketing research must attempt to provide the most accurate information as quickly as possible or face the possibility that its budget will be reduced as managers select other sources of information.

FIGURE 14.2   *Relationship of Information to Marketing Decision Making*

Relationship Number	Discussion of Relationship
1	Periodically, the marketing researchers meet with the marketing managers to discuss key management decisions that are to be made and whether these decisions can be addressed by marketing research. When agreement has been reached as to what information should be collected, models tested, and so on, the marketing research group then uses its technology to gather information through the techniques of observing or questioning consumers. The process of commissioning and executing a study can take several months. Research can focus on new product acceptance, mass media effectiveness, purchasing patterns, consumer attitudes, and much more.
2	The commissioned study is executed and data from consumers are transmitted to the firm. The data must be converted into a usable form (computer readable). This conversion process usually lasts several weeks.
3	Consumer data are analyzed and a written or oral report is presented to the marketing managers. The analysis and report preparation can take several weeks.
4	Annually each department of the firm must submit a budget for the coming year. The marketing research department must ask for enough resources to perform its function. The marketing manager has an important role in deciding whether the value of the information produced by marketing research warrants a smaller, larger, or the same operating budget.
5	From time to time, complaints about products and services are received from consumers. These are analyzed by the marketing manager and corrective action is initiated. If product quality is a problem, a meeting with production is initiated.
6	The marketing manager is continually creating, modifying, and updating marketing plans. Such plans include decisions to change prices, spend more or less on advertising, change advertising themes, hire or fire salesmen, create trade deals, create special displays, look for new products, get rid of dying products, and much more.
7	Monthly or quarterly, accounting sends the sales report to the marketing manager detailing how salesmen, territories, and products are performing. The manager realizes that, perhaps, two periods (months or quarters) have elapsed since the consumers purchased and he has seen the reports. This is due to the time

FIGURE 14.2 *(continued)*

Relationship
Number   *Discussion of Relationship*

it takes the invoice system to cycle from the sales slip to the sales report. Thus, the manager is concerned about trends and deviations. If a deviation or trend is found, the manager is forced to get on the telephone and talk to salesmen in the field to see if the deviation is still occurring and whether corrective action is warranted.

8   When the salesman "books" an order, an invoice is generated by the accounting system. Production gets one copy so the finished good can be delivered, accounts receivable gets one so that a bill can be sent when the product is delivered, and accounting keeps other copies for paying sales commissions and for marketing reports.

9   Accounts receivable sends the bill for the product after it has been delivered.

10   Production or its subsidiary, warehousing, delivers the finished good several weeks after the order is "booked."

11   The marketing manager transmits quality control problem information and sales forecasts to the production department. The production department schedules production, allocates finished product to warehouses, and plans for new capital equipment based on the information provided by the marketing manager. The information is provided each month or quarter as needed by the production group.

12   Semiannually or annually, the marketing manager meets with top management to review plans, budgets, and performance. Information is exchanged about overall company performance and the specific performance of the marketing manager.

The Marketing Information System

Marketing information systems exist in many forms and degrees among real world institutions. Some small firms have marketing information systems which consist of nothing more than a series of ringbinder notebooks. Salesmen and managers dictate memos which are placed in the ringbinders. Such memos consist of perceptions of buying motivations of customers, changes in competitive conditions, changes in economic conditions, and many more items. Periodically, these notebooks are reviewed in meetings among the marketing managers.

On the other end of the technological spectrum are the large companies which have large computer systems. These companies maintain computer files containing information about buyer behavior, competitive and economic conditions. Periodically, a computer program is run and a report is generated which is tailored to each executive's area of responsibility. Typically, small volumes of information are processed by the manual information system while large volumes are processed by the large computers. In either case, the amount of information supplied to the manager is relevant to his situation. However, the executive who has the computerized information system has a wider range of relevant information available to him. Thus, the automated information system should help the manager avoid serious mistakes and help him to make more informed decisions.

Some general specifications of an "ideal" information system can be constructed. Some of the functions of the information system can be manual and others can be automated. However, the typical current computerized information system consists only of a data bank and a statistical analyzer-report writer. However, other functions can be automated.

The general marketing information system can be viewed as six interrelating parts: the model specifier, information sorter, data bank, research designer, relationship tester, and simulator. These parts work together to help organize information and hypotheses, to retrieve significant data, to help make choices about the type and style of research, to perform statistical tests and write reports for the manager, and to help the manager make decisions by suggesting possible decisions that he can make. All six parts are shown in Figure 14.3. The figure shows that the manager interfaces directly with only

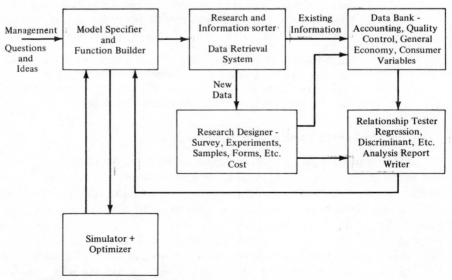

FIGURE 14.3 *The General Marketing Information System*

one section of the information system, namely, the model specifier and function builder. This also is the subsystem through which reports are displayed to him.

The Model Specifier

The model specifier and function builder is a series of operations which elicit the hypotheses of the manager. For example, if a list of variables are stored in the system, the manager can specify which variable belongs in a given model. For example, the manager states his hypotheses concerning which variables affect sales volume, which variables cause changes in market share, and so on. The model specifier and function builder can be flexible enough to allow the manager to introduce new variables as he sees fit.

The function builder is merely an interfacing mechanism by which the manager can organize his thoughts into coherent, testable models. The computer program to do this could work interactively with the man by asking him questions and structuring his responses into organized sets of variables and models.

The Research and Information Sorter

The list of variables which the manager has used in his hypotheses and their logical and arithmetic relationships are then stored. The research and information sorter interrogates the data bank to see if information concerning all of the hypothesized variables exist in the data bank. If the information does exist, it is transferred from the data bank to the relationship tester. The research and information sorter is essentially a library system which allows the data to be organized and quickly retrieved.

The Data Bank

The data bank essentially is an organized set of data from various areas from inside and outside the firm. Data in the data bank are organized into a common form such that it can be retrieved for use by the relationship tester and the report writer. Data can come from accounting, quality control in manufacturing, the general economy from the government, consumer variables from marketing research, and many more areas.

The Relationship Tester

The relationship tester and report writer is essentially a series of computer programs that will analyze the data and put them into a form that the manager can understand. These computer programs may consist of regression analysis, discriminant analysis, or any other suitable statistical technique. These techniques are discussed in Chapters 11 to 13. The report writer is a series of routines which can take the data and create standardized reports to be displayed for the manager. Different managers can have different reports, depending on their positions and their abilities to handle different kinds of information.

The Research Designer

The research designer is a series of procedures which help the manager make the decision whether it is desirable and necessary to collect new information. The dollar value of research is computed and research strategies are suggested to the manager. The research designer can also compile a questionnaire, draw a sample, and estimate the cost of research.

The research designer function can be manual. In fact, the focus of this text and the methods discussed in the purview of this text are the operations performed by the research designer. The research designer function is to decide what methods are suitable to collect the data needed to test the executive's model or to evaluate the conditions of a given market. The research designer is the mode by which new information enters the information system.

The Simulator and Optimizer

Once the manager's model has been statistically verified, the result of the statistical test can be transmitted to the simulator and optimizer for forecasting purposes. It is also possible for the subsystem to suggest alternative methods of solving a problem to the manager. For example, the manager can ask the subsystem to find the level of advertising to achieve optimum sales, or the optimum sales effort to get the best return from a given sales territory. The manager ultimately, of course, must implement the plans which are generated by the simulator and optimizer.

The primary purpose of the simulator and optimizer is to "use" the executive's model to find useful or optimal marketing plans which the executive can use to achieve his objectives.

The Status of Marketing Information

Why Don't Such Systems Exist Currently?

There are several reasons for lack of implementation of such advanced information systems. Among the reasons are institutional organization, budgetary constraints, lack of documentation habits by executives, lack of awareness of executives of methods which would be useful, and bad past experience with computer vendors.

Institutional organization is often a roadblock to marketing information system integration because various departments within the organization are unwilling to organize or share information with outside departments. One major airline has three large-scale computers in three different departments because there is no incentive for cooperation to combine information and computer facilities. The airline in question has one computer for spare parts logistics and flight scheduling, one for accounting and billing credit cards, and yet a third large computer that is solely used for flight reservations. Airline marketing executives who wish to use the computer are forced to buy time from outside vendors because the three computers are not equipped with programs to solve marketing problems. Similarly, the marketing department has great difficulty getting accounting information, reservation information, and flight scheduling information from those respective departments because those departments are "busy" with their own problems.

Budgetary constraints are often a problem in two ways: (1) the limits on the department's ability to regularly buy marketing information and (2) the unwillingness of executives to budget their own time to "tool up" to create a meaningful information system. Budgetary approval processes in many companies are "historically" oriented. This implies that past years' budgets are used as bases for future budgets. This reliance on history often works against the funding of new projects such as information systems. In addition, budget approvals often hinge on showing payback within a short period. Because rate of return of information systems is hard to quantify, payback is difficult to show. Similarly, many executives do not feel that their decision making can be improved and thus do not wish to spend their time to build an information system.

Documentation of past decisions by executives is not usually very detailed because of time pressure that most executives feel. Thus, histories of market experiments are often not well recorded and thus future generations of managers do not know of the results. New executives seldom have detailed histories of their forebearers to help keep them from making the same mistakes over again. A formalized information system can help solve this problem. In addition, those executives who are afraid of having mistakes uncovered will resist the information system.

Lack of method awareness is caused by not "retooling" often enough, if ever, by the executive. Many executives do not try to keep up with new developments in managerial style or information processing. Thus, useful new techniques are not appreciated. A part of this problem is shared by younger graduates from universities who are aware of new techniques but who are thwarted to some degree when they wish to use the new methods. This is one cause of the high turnover among younger managers.[1]

Bad past experience with computer system and equipment vendors has created a "credibility gap" concerning the performance of computers. Some large computer companies have been sued by customers and competitors because computer programs and hardware performance claims were made

---

[1] James P. Roscow, "Knocking Off the Golden Edge," *MBA*, Vol. 7, (1973), p. 20.

that were not justified. These sales practices that generated the problems have, in general, been terminated but the "burned" executives still resist new computer investments.[2]

The elements of this conceptualization of a marketing information system exists in most large and small companies. However, most of the activities occurring in this "ideal" information are not coordinated and made routinely available to the operating manager. Most of the data needed to feed such a system exists in the accounting system of the firm. In addition, governmental economic and industrial activity data are available at nominal cost. Finally, marketing research effort can generate additional data needed for the marketing information system.

The state of current managerial decision-making technology is not far advanced relative to the computing technology that is available. Currently, managers of all levels tend to rely on interpersonal contacts for the exchange of information. This method is slow, inaccurate due to selective retention of information by the manager, and subject to the vagaries of the social process in which the manager finds himself. In addition, complex analysis of alternative courses of action for major decisions is commonly done in the larger companies which have internal consulting staffs to handle such problems.[3] Because of the high cost of the analysis process, small companies are denied the opportunity to discover potentially faulty courses of action.

Current Industry Practice Concerning Information Systems

In order to analyze the state of existing marketing information systems, one must set up some criteria for evaluating such systems. Amstutz[4] has proposed five dimensions of an information system. These dimensions are:

1. Information recency
2. Management access time
3. Information aggregation
4. Analytic sophistication
5. System authority.

Management access time is defined as the time lapse between the management's request for certain information and the receipt of the desired report or display. This measures the time of response of the system to a given request. *Information recency* is defined as the time lapse between the occurrence of a given marketing event (a purchase, for example) in the real market and the time it is recorded in the management information system. This may range

---

[2] "IBM Loses Its First Anti-Trust Action," *Wall Street Journal* (Sept. 18, 1973), p. 3.

[3] General Electric is one such company that maintains an internal division for performing special analyses for all other divisions of the company.

[4] A. Amstutz, "Market Oriented Management Systems: The Current Status," *Journal of Marketing Research* (November 1969), p. 481.

from several seconds to several months. *Information aggregation* refers to the level of detail of (low aggregation means much detail) information which is stored. *Analytic sophistication* refers to the sophistication of models which exist within the information system. A very low level of sophistication would be simply a system which retrieves data and does nothing more than present the raw data to the manager who then must analyze that data by himself. As analytic sophistication increases the ability of the computer or the system to automatically handle problems increases. *System authority* refers to the ability of the management information system to make decisions. A system with low authority merely is allowed to retrieve and check data, whereas a system with high authority can perform management functions such as writing orders for certain routinely purchased items. Amstutz concluded that most companies have not fully achieved sophisticated, integrated marketing information systems.

The key problem is that companies have not integrated their marketing research activities to their marketing information system activities. Typically, a company develops an information system for accounting purposes. Accounting departments are typically reluctant to perform special analyses for marketing departments. In addition, companies have been unwilling to continually monitor changes in consumer attitudes, opinions, and advertising awareness over time. Typically marketing research is done infrequently using noncomparable methods. Another problem is that marketing research activities are usually under a different officer within the corporation than are information system activities. Thus, it is difficult to get information systems and marketing research activities together. However, it is imperative that marketing research and information systems combine together in order to use higher level and more meaningful consumer behavior models. Companies which are well known for their pioneering strides toward the full use of information systems of high level are the Pillsbury Corporation, General Mills, the Anheuser-Busch Corporation, Du Pont, and Field Enterprises.

The experience of one particular company follows. The experience of this company illustrates the nature and problems of formalizing information systems.

AAIMS: American Airlines Answers the What Ifs

Janet M. Taplin

Anyone who doubts that vice presidents can be persuaded to use terminal-based computer infosystems to solve their problems should take a look at what American Airlines has done. They've also proved that management infosystems capable of producing "bottom line" profits can be developed on time and within budget.

American Airlines (the same people whose technical competence and flair for the unusual brought you SABRE, the first successful on-line reservation system, and the in-flight piano bar) has developed an infosystem to be admired. It's called AAIMS, An Analytical Information Management System.

AAIMS can be used for information retrieval, but its primary use is as an analytical tool which easily and rapidly generates reports and/or plots. The AAIMS user need not know anything about programming. He converses with the time-sharing computer using English language commands to describe what is to be accomplished. He controls the analysis procedure just as he would a calculator. If he can state his problem, he can get his answer. He does not have to spend his time dealing with the computer's method of handling data.

American Airlines is quite proud of the system and its successful computerization of top management analyses. It's a powerful enhancement of AAL's previously implemented internal data tracking system. William Synwoldt, Director of Information Sciences, keeps his comment low key: "We were lucky. We had a definite need for a good analytical information system which would make information easily available to our top management; we had the right people, some of the best APL programmers around, at the right place, at the right time."

What he means is that AAIMS did not begin as a loudly heralded heavily staffed corporate infosystem project. Rather it was begun by only two talented and creative men, Dick Klaas, Manager of Long Range Planning in the corporate planning department and Chuck Weiss, an analyst in the operations research department.

In the spring of 1970 they began work on an econometric modeling

SOURCE: Reprinted with special permission from *Infosystems* Magazine, February 1973, Volume 20, No. 2, copyright 1973 by Hitchcock Publishing Co., Wheaton, Ill. 60187, all rights reserved.

system which was to be used by the corporate planning department. Since the model was to be used for forecasting and reporting of forecasting results, AEMS (Airline Econometric Modeling System) as the system was known in 1970, was given a time-series data orientation. Klaas set ease of use (which means ease of programming and ease of access to a data base of primary airline information) as a primary criterion for AEMS.

What the user types	*What AAIMS is doing*
/1/ USE 'A/WIDGETS' FROM 1 73 THRU 3 73	Calls a file. 'A/WIDGETS' is file name the sale of widgets in region A.
/2/ USE 'A/SKYHOOKS' FROM 1 73 THRU 3 73	Calls a file. 'A/SKYHOOKS' is file name for sale of skyhooks in region B.
/3/ USE '1' PLUS '2'	Gives the total sales of region A.
/4/ USE 'B/WIDGETS' FROM 1 73 THRU 3 73	
/5/ USE 'B/SKYHOOKS' FROM 1 73 THRU 3 73	Calculates total sales of region B.
/6/ USE '4' PLUS '5'	
/7/ USE '1' PLUS '4'	Gives total sales of widgets in regions A and B.
/8/ USE '2' PLUS '5'	Gives total sales of skyhooks in regions A and B.
/9/ USE '7' PLUS '8'	Gives total sales for all products and regions.
/10/ USE 'LABOR W'	
/11/ USE 'LABOR S'	Calculates total labor costs of widgets and skyhooks.
/12/ USE '10' PLUS '11'	
/13/ USE 'RAW MAT W'	Calculates the total costs of raw materials used to produce widgets and skyhooks.
/14/ USE 'RAW MAT S'	
/15/ USE '13' PLUS '14'	
/16/ USE 1.2 TIMES '12'	Calculates 120% overhead on total labor costs.
/17/ USE '12' PLUS '15' PLUS '16'	Calculates total manufacturing costs.
/18/ USE 'ADMIN EXPEN' FROM 1 73 THRU 3 73	
/19/ USE 'RENT' FROM 1 73 THRU 3 73	Calls files of expenses other than manufacturing expenses.
/20/ USE 'INCIDENTAL' FROM 1 73 THRU 3 73	

What the user types	What AAIMS is doing
/21/ USE '18' PLUS '19' PLUS '20'	Calculates expenses other than manufacturing.
/22/ USE '17' PLUS '21'	Calculates total expenses.
/23/ USE '9' MINUS '22'	Calculates profit or loss.
/24/ USE -0.48 TIMES '23'	Calculates tax. -0.48 is rate of income tax on earnings. The answer will appear in brackets and will be treated as a negative number. Thus final line of report is obtained by addition.
/25/ USE '23' PLUS '24'	Gives net profit or loss.
/26/ through /29/ (type in the specifications for titles to be used in the report.)	
/30/ DISPLAY ABOVE	Makes completed report available to executive.

According to Joseph Kingsley, Director of Systems Planning, who oversaw the AEMS project, valuable results were being produced in less than one month. The system's ability to adapt quickly to new needs, and its reliable production of daily reports soon gained the enthusiastic approval of senior management who came in contact with the system.

AEMS began to attract more and more attention as a succession of highly successful corporate planning projects used the system to develop analyses. Each new project seemed to make new demands on the system, and Klaas and Weiss were able to satisfy each new demand almost overnight. Senior managers began to use AEMS terminals. And they began to talk about using AEMS as a prototype of the management infosystem American Airlines had long desired. As John McCeffrey, then Assistant to the President, observed, "A management infosystem must be usable by managers. If it can be used only by technicians, isn't it defeating its purpose?"

But AEMS might have remained just a pet project of the corporate planning department had it not been for William Synwoldt. In the Spring of 1971 Synwoldt was appointed to the newly created post of Director of Management Information.

Synwoldt had no background in data processing; he was a professional manager who had been with American some fifteen years. In 1969-1970 he had been the Assistant to the President under the company's program of giving special training to its most promising managers. During that year Bill had become deeply involved in the problems of obtaining the information that management needed.

A year as manager of the task force preparing for the merger of Trans-carribean Airlines into American reinforced Synwoldt's interest in the problem of getting information to management. When he returned to American he volunteered to work on the problem of meeting management's information needs.

"Even at the presidential level you couldn't get the answers you wanted," said Bill. "It wasn't that dp wasn't trying. They were trying very hard, but they could not get the answers to management fast enough to meet the constantly changing needs."

As Director of Management Information, under the Vice President of Data Processing, Synwoldt began to look for solutions to his information needs. He felt that to undertake a full-blown MIS project, which might show results five years down the pike, would be suicide. The best business decision, he thought, would be to get a small prototype system up and running. Then he got lucky.

In looking around the airline, he discovered the new AEMS project. He knew he had his prototype. It worked; it contained the beginnings of the airline data base; it was user-oriented and easy to learn; and, because of its APL basics, it was easy to change. He also liked its philosophy: that data isn't useful unless you can do something with it.

Having found AEMS, it became necessary to adapt it to the needs of the airline as a whole. Expansion of the AEMS data base and functions were begun, and the system's name was changed to AAIMS.

AAIMS: THE PHILOSOPHY

Creating a viable management info-system requires a philosophy of information and a system of handling data that is compatible with that philosophy. It is the unique blending of system and philosophy that makes AAIMS successful.

The system as previously described, depends to a great extent on the use of APL. The underlying philosophy is *make the system user oriented.* That is, a system that the decision maker— the user—can use *directly.* No time-consuming special programming steps, and no special computer analysts. American Airlines wants its top management to use the computer directly as an analytical tool for at least two reasons.

First, some management decisions that have to be made daily, even within a matter of hours, should be made with the aid of a computer system. If the manager has to deal indirectly with the computer, decision time may arrive before all the intermediate steps have been completed.

Second, by directly using the info-system terminals, managers get a better idea of what kind of information is needed. AAIMS users, by directly exploring the analytical functions of a computer, learn new ways of looking at their problems. They learn how to redefine their information needs by experimenting with the data, and they learn new and better ways to use AAIMS.

AAIMS, the system and philosophy, has evolved as new applications have been brought to it. The specific requests of users have been generalized into general analytical functions in anticipation of other users' needs. The expansion of AAIMS, because its functions are modular and driven by the APL language, has been undertaken by both the Information Sciences and Corporate Planning Departments, with the result that more users have been served better. Not only have users been served better, but they have produced more at a lower cost. As was stated by Joe Kingsley in evaluating AAIMS: With respect to research, it has been stated that there would be no substitute for AAIMS in the analysis of corporate planning projects. Most studies could not have been done in time or with as much data manipulation. That savings in research time is 6:1. The savings in money is 3:1, considering equivalent dollars of analyst time plus computer costs.

To the management of American Airlines, the "can do" attitude which accompanies projects employing AAIMS, its low capital investment (approximately $62,500 in the first eighteen months), its low operating costs for the value produced, its high return (approximately $361,000 in cost saving and increased passenger revenues in eighteen months), all have

been compelling arguments for the AAIMS system.

AAIMS AND DP

American's management has two kinds of information needs. First, it needs information about itself and its relations with its customers. Second, it needs to analyze, compare and plan within the framework of its competition and its economic environment. The production data processing activity handles all the transactions between the airline and its customers, and produces summary reports for management. It has done this for years, but now when the information is sent to management it is no longer given to an analyst who manually turns it into meaningful competitive information. Now it is encoded into the AAIMS system for computer analysis. This relationship between AAIMS, DP and management is illustrated in the accompanying diagram. AAIMS is not a competitor to the in-house batch system, and it could never be, rather it complements the production data processing activity by extending computer power to a new class of users. Thus AAIMS fulfills a corporate need—the need for top management to use the computer as an analytical tool.

SUMMARY

Does it satisfy all the user's data processing needs?

Does it provide the user with immediate access to a wide range of information concerning many facets of our business?

	AAIMS	dp system
Does it satisfy all the user's data processing needs?	No	No
Does it provide the user with immediate access to a wide range of information concerning many facets of our business?	Yes	No

Does it provide the user with the immediate capability to add to the existing data base as new needs develop?	Yes	No
Does it enable the user to request information, generate reports, plot charts and perform detailed statistical analysis without the services of a programmer?	Yes	No
Does it provide the user with an immediate response?	Yes	No
Is it a substitute for judgement and intuition?	No	No

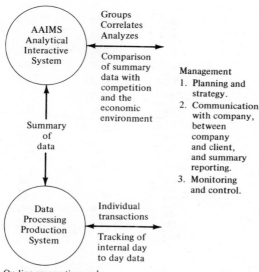

On-line reservation and
Data processing systems

FIGURE 1

From the AAIMS user manual . . .
"One does not need a comprehensive understanding of everything in this manual in order to begin using AAIMS productively. Perhaps the easiest and fastest way to gain an understanding of AAIMS is to sign-on the computer and repeat the examples of each section . . .

"AAIMS is a user oriented system. In fact, it has evolved to its present state because of an active group of contributing users . . .

"By the way, go ahead and make mistakes if you wish. Test the system, it is forgiving."

"They don't laugh when I sit down at the terminal"

When American executives learn AAIMS, they learn by sitting at a terminal. They solve practice problems. For example, Acme Corp. manufactures widgets and sky-hooks, sells them in two regions, A and B. Its products are fair-traded. Sales and costs are reported on a daily basis. The problem: assemble a projected P&L/Sales Report for the first quarter of '73.

Once you have the report, it's

The answer: Acme's first quarter projection

Line no.	Item	Jan $1000	Feb $1000	Mar $1000
(1)	Widgets	501	502	503
(2)	Skyhooks	301	302	303
(3)	Region A Total	802	804	806
(4)	Widgets	1001	1002	1003
(5)	Skyhooks	701	702	703
(6)	Region B Total	1702	1704	1706
(7)	Total Widgets	1502	1504	1506
(8)	Total Skyhooks	1002	1004	1006
(9)	Total Sales	2504	2508	2512
(10)	Labor: Widgets	301	302	303
(11)	Labor: Skyhooks	401	402	403
(12)	Total Labor W & S	702	704	706
(13)	Raw Material Costs W	201	202	203
(14)	Raw Material Costs S	301	302	303
(15)	Total Raw Material Costs	502	504	506
(16)	Overhead 120%	842	845	847
(17)	Manufacturing Costs	2046	2053	2059
(18)	Administrative Costs	200	201	202
(19)	Rent	100	101	102
(20)	Other Expenses	50	51	52
(21)	Total Expenses, nonmanufacturing	350	353	356
(22)	Total Expenses	2396	2406	2415
(23)	Profit or (Loss)	108	102	97
(24)	Federal Taxes	(52)	(49)	(47)
(25)	Net Profit or Loss	56	53	50

easy to answer the "what if" questions. For example, if the overhead can be reduced from 120% to 115%, the January pretax profit will jump from $108 thousand to $143 thousand (line 23). And so on. It's a neat way to increase awareness of the options for action an executive has—especially when the options are not always obvious.

AAIMS, APL, IBM . . . AND THE UNSAVVY USER
(Ms. Taplin comments)

As the remote access computing activity continues its evolution toward the broad marketplace of the non-computer professional . . . secretary, salesclerk, business executive . . . the lesson of AAIMS appears to be that APL has an important place in this market.

At the expense of some machine time the APL language overcomes many of the user-related limitations of existing conventional programming languages (e.g., FORTRAN, COBOL, BASIC, PL/I, etc.). These languages are machine oriented, and the true market for remote access computing is the non-computer professional. That's why this comment by American's Dick Klaas is so important:

"I saw in APL a tool which would free me from programming and release me to do my work."

APL is strongly identified with IBM. Its authors and implementors are IBM employees. Yet it should be pointed out that major APL implementations are not by IBM. IBM's APL has significant file size, security and output formatting limitations. These are not limitations of the language but of IBM's current versions of the language. Time sharing companies, like APL Services, have developed substantial enhancements. These are the enhancements which made it possible for American to build its system on a commercial service. These same enhancements make it impossible, at present, to bring the system in-house.

IBM itself has been surprised by the growing number of internal IBM users of their experimental APL system at the Philadelphia Scientific Center. These users, and they number in the thousands, have grown up in IBM without any effort on the part of IBM management to promote such usage.

All the other major computer manufacturers now offer APL. But for all this work and interest in APL, it is not currently a widely used language. Dick Klaas of American was truly a pioneer when he began, in 1970, to use APL to develop AAIMS. Of the approximately $425 million which (we estimate) were spent on remote access computer services from commercial vendors last year, APL accounted for only $5 million. However, APL usage appears to be doubling yearly; APL is growing without much help . . . because of the attributes of APL.

Up to this time (1973), IBM has not played as dominant a role in the remote access computing market as one might expect. In view of its dominance of the dp market, its share of the commercial remote computing market is surprisingly small. New machines and operating systems may improve IBM's ability to compete for the teleprocessing needs of dp centers (TSO improvements, for example). But we expect that when the potential of APL to the non-computer professional is more widely recognized, IBM may take the commanding lead in the remote access computing market that has so far eluded it.

AAIMS IN BRIEF

AAIMS is an interactive terminal-based management infosystem designed for use by the senior manager who has no background in computer programming.

AAIMS—*An Analytical Information Management System*—was developed at American Airlines corporate headquarters in New York City, using the time-sharing service of an outside vendor, APL Services, Inc., Trenton NJ.

AAIMS is implemented in AC-TION/APL, an enhanced version of IBM's APL language. ACTION/APL's extended-file and matrix-manipulation capabilities are employed to create a flexible data base structure of variable-length records and unbounded file size. The ACTION/APL interpreter itself serves as the driver (main line) program. Linked to the driver is the AAIMS system, a family of relatively small routines, each routine for an independent but cooperating function. As a result, AAIMS is easy to modify, easy to extend, easy to adapt to changing needs—critical ingredients of the successful management infosystem.

Data Environment

Data are organized in the AAIMS system on a time series* basis. The problems associated with time series data are handled automatically for the AAIMS user. Data may be stored as daily, weekly, monthly, quarterly, or yearly. Data

---

* A time series is simply a set of recordings of the values of variable quantities measured at intervals of time . . . the instant a measurement is made it becomes part of history.

may begin and end on different dates, and do not have to be of the same periodicity. AAIMS automatically adjusts for leap years and for dates occurring on different days of the week.

A complete set of data management routines is provided for data input, correction, alteration and updating. A logical name and directory structure is employed, with identification of the source and date of input of all data. Input to the public data base is restricted to those responsible for the system, and three levels of read and write file security are provided. The American Airlines AAIMS data base presently includes some 8,000 time series, each on the average consisting of monthly data for a twenty year period. On-line storage cost on the outside time-sharing service is roughly $1000 per month for the data plus an additional $30 per month for the associated directories. As Dick Klaas states, "The data base is maintained on the FISH system . . . First In, Still Here."

The data base has been designed on the basis that future data requirements cannot be predicted. The data base must be open-ended to allow expansion on an as-needed basis.

Data Base

The AAIMS data base consists of three major segments:

1) The airline industry data base includes detailed information on both American and its competitive airlines drawn from CAB reports.

2) A general economic data base—including economic, demographic, social and technological

data—currently covers the last 20 years.

3) User data bases. These are set up by users for specific projects. A data base protocol is in effect and users have access to a data base directory which identifies all private data bases available on the system. AAIMS users are encouraged to store only primary data, because derivative information is so easy to obtain (see sample terminal session). This holds down the number of derived data bases, which helps to keep non-computer-professionals from getting lost in the system while running up large storage charges.

System Capabilities

The system is designed to enable the non-programmer to selectively retrieve from the data base, perform extensive analysis, automatically produce reports and plots. AAIMS relies on simple declarative sentences and currently has a vocabulary of some 35 commands. The approach is a straight forward one which the manager can use with little attention to details extraneous to his problem. Complexities such as data dimensioning, looping and output formatting are completely eliminated. A sample command might be: DISPLAY 'REVENUE' MINUS 'EXPENSES' FROM 1 71 to 6 72. REVENUE and EXPENSES are names of time series stored in the data base. The result of the command would be to

retrieve the profit for the 18 month period stipulated.

In addition to selective retrieval, aanlytical routines are provided for:
arithmetic
time series analysis
—moving averages
—year-over-year ratios
—period-to-period ratios
—year-end totals
—exponential smoothing
statistical analysis
—correlation
—regression
—descriptive statistics
graphic analysis
—time series plots
—scatter diagrams

AAIMS qualifies as a hierarchical language. AAIMS statements may be used to define a procedure in a higher-level function. More knowledgeable users may freely intermix AAIMS commands and APL code when the limited AAIMS vocabulary does not include the desired capability. The common application of this capability is to build a routine analysis that may be run by a secretary. To run the program, the secretary merely has to type REPORT 1, a command definition, and the report would be produced.

In addition to interactively processing statements typed into the terminal, AAIMS also may be operated in a prompting mode. In this instance, the interaction helps the user to use the system. Thus users at all levels of sophistication are served by the same system.

Summary

This chapter is intended to illustrate two important points: (1) that information systems are an important part of the marketing management system, and (2) information generated by the processes of marketing research

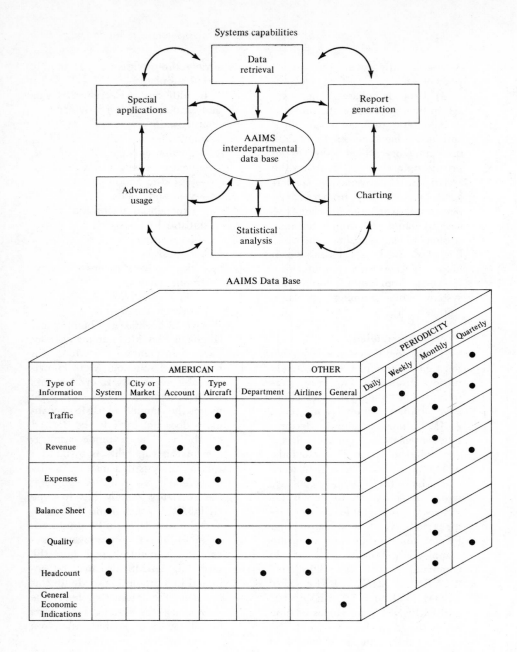

Systems capabilities

AAIMS Data Base

FIGURE 2

has dollar value. Information systems which will make the executive more efficient are still in the future. The computer technology and decision technology largely exists, but few management teams have invested the time and dollar resources to implement anything close to the "ideal" system. The reasons for this stem from the current departmentalization of most companies together with a lack of awareness by most operating managers of the potential of decision technology.

Information is an investment very much similar to stocks and bonds. There is definite dollar payout to using information. In addition, there is uncertainty or risk associated with the purchase of research. A small Bayesian analysis is shown to illustrate that the results of research can help the manager gain confidence about the outcome of his decisions.

Technical Appendix

The material that follows is designed to show the student the process for rigorously computing how much should be spent on marketing research. This section is designed to serve the student with quantitative interests. Although these computations are used in the field of Operations Research, they are not widely used in marketing to date.

The Cost and Value of Doing Research

In the management context, the primary purpose of collecting information and doing research is to reduce the uncertainty involved in making decisions. It is in this sense that the information-gathering process and the use of information become a primary management tool. Information, per se, comes in varying grades and qualities. The higher the grade of information, the more accurate it is. This implies that high grade information is less prone to being wrong than lower grades of information. Thus, the adage "you get what you pay for" applies to information. Often, but not always, high quality information has a high cost and lower quality information has a lower cost. This creates a dilemma: one must choose which relative grade of information is optimal for his particular situation. The higher the cost of being wrong, the better the quality of information which should be sought. Thus, there is a tradeoff between the cost of error and the value of information. This section will detail a mathematical plan for evaluating how much information should be bought and of what kind.

There are ten key parts to the analysis of the cost and value of information as shown in Table 14.1. The first of these parts is the forecast of cash flow based on a given market research strategy. For example, a manufacturer wishes to introduce a new product. He wants to use a certain amount and type of advertising exclusively. He knows what the amount of advertising should be over time. For example, the first month he may plan to pay $60,000, the second month $72,000, and so forth, through a number of periods of time. He also can forecast his sales over time (using his model) and thus forecast sales revenue on a period-by-period basis if his model is complete. Before he performs any kind of data collection, he has what is known as an "a priori"

TABLE 14.1 *The Steps to Evaluate the Value of Research*

1. Estimate the cash flows for the expected level of sales.
2. Estimate the cash flows for an outcome involving only one-half the expected sales.
3. Estimate the sales level for the case where double the income level results.
4. Compute the discounted cash flow rate of return for each cash flow case.
5. Assign a prior probability to each cash flow case (0.33, 0.33, and 0.34, respectively, is the most conservative possible set of values to assign for a 3 outcome case).
6. Compute the expected value outcome and the variance associated with the expected value.
7. Prepare a reliability table for various research techniques specifying the probability that the research will show the correct outcome.
8. Calculate the posterior estimates of each cash flow outcome assuming that the research shows that outcome.
9. Repeat step 8 for each possible research alternative.
10. Pick the research method that gives the most reduction in variance and least reduction of rate of return (is least costly).

notion of what his sales revenue is going to be. This notion may be approximate (have high uncertainty). Typically, there is more error associated with estimating sales revenue than with estimating costs of implementing a marketing strategy. Thus, the primary problem is one of estimating market response and subsequent sales revenue in most marketing problems. The estimates of sales revenue and total cost, no matter how rough they are, can be discounted backwards in time to give a net cash flow estimate. This discounted cash flow estimate is the basis upon which future projections are made.

The second major concept involved with evaluating information is the measure of uncertainty in sales revenues. These estimates are known as expected value and variance estimates. First, the manager creates an estimate of discount cash flow based on his expected level of sales revenue if everything goes according to plan (step 1 in Table 14.1). Then, he must generate another representing a low estimate of sales based on the assumption that things go wrong. The low estimate can be defined as representing the case where one-half of expected net sales income results (step 2 in Table 14.1). Similarly, high estimates (step 3 in Table 14.1) would be calculated for the case where the expected income curve doubles. Thus, the manager is forced to make three a priori estimates: an expected sales income estimate, one-half income estimate, and a double income estimate (these revenue levels are arbitrary).

An example of these estimates are given in Table 14.2. Table 14.2 shows estimates of sales revenue and cost over 20 periods of time which have been guessed by a manager. The income figures are simply sales revenue minus

TABLE 14.2   *Present Value Analysis for Three Different Projected Sales Levels:*
½ Expected Profit, Expected Profit, and Twice Expected Profit

For Strategy 1 Only: Expected Income

	Period						
	1	2	3	4	5	6	7 to 20[b]
Sales revenue (× 1000)	60	120	150	66	50	50	Same as 6
Total costs (× 1000)	60	72	72	43	35	35	Same as 6
Income (× 1000)	0	48	78	23	15	15	Same as 6
Investment (× 1000)	200[a]						
			One-half expected income				
Sales revenue	60	90	111	55	43	43	Same as 6
Total costs	60	72	72	43	35	35	Same as 6
Income	0	24	39	12	8	8	Same as 6
			Twice expected income				
Sales revenue	60	168	228	89	65	65	Same as 6
Total costs	60	72	72	43	35	35	Same as 6
Income	0	96	156	46	30	30	Same as 6

[a] Initial investment actually made prior to period 1.
[b] Product life estimated at 20 periods.

total direct cost. The total cost figures represent the cost of the strategy the manager is evaluating. Different marketing strategies would yield differing sales revenue and different costs. The investment figure represents the investment in creating the new product and doing its related marketing research. The one-half expected income represents the low estimates by the manager, and the twice expected income represents the high estimates by the manager. In all three cases, the total costs remain the same, and thus the income stream varies widely depending on the sales revenue situation. All of the revenue and cost estimates are made with no special information at this point in time.

Table 14.3 shows the discounted cash flow analysis (step 4 in Table 14.1) for the income stream. This particular calculation is for the expected value. A separate analysis is then done for the one-half income and double income situation. The expected income level generates a 10 percent return on investment of 200.

The next item in the analysis is the prior probability of each case (step 5 in Table 14.1), and this situation is stated to the manager as follows: "What is the probability that you achieve between zero income and the one-half expected income level?" The manager, for example, answers, "0.33." The manager is asked what is the likelihood that he achieve sales results or income

TABLE 14.3 *Present Value Calculation for One Outcome-Expected Income*

Period	Income	Present Value Factor 10%	Present Value
1	0	0.91	0.0
2	48	0.82	39.4
3	78	0.75	58.5
4	23	0.68	15.6
5	15	0.62	9.3
.			
.			
.			
20	15	0.21	3.2
		Total	200[a]

[a] If one chose a discount factor other than 10 percent, he could not recover the 200 investment in 20 periods. If the discount rate was lower, he would recover the 200 faster and more than 10 percent would not recover the 200 in 20 periods. It would take longer than 20 periods. Thus, through cut-and-dry methods it is possible to solve for the discount factor of any projected income stream.

results ranging from one-half expected income to twice expected income. Here again, he may answer, "0.33." Then the question is put to him, "How likely is it that the twice expected income, or higher, will result?" He states, "0.34." These probabilities are educated guesses on the manager's part. The 0.33, 0.33, 0.34 guesses are the most conservative possible guesses. If he feels that the "expected" likelihood is stronger than 0.33, he can make that estimate arbitrarily higher. However, the other two levels have to be adjusted so that the total probability of all the three levels adds up to 1.0.

The rate of return resulting from the income estimates are shown in Table 14.4. The values of 32 percent for the high-income estimate, 10 percent for the expected, and zero for the low estimate. After assigning the probability, the expected value and variance for all three cash flow outcomes (step 6 in Table 14.1) is done as shown in Table 14.5.

The seventh major part of the analysis (step 7 in Table 14.1) is to establish the conditional probability of being right or wrong with research. All marketing research methods have conditional probabilities which are based on the past accuracy experience of the research tool. The error probabilities are determined primarily by the sample size, and the error inherent in the research process and data-collection technique. Figure 14.4 illustrates the

TABLE 14.4   *Expected Payout before and after Performing Research*

Outcome	ROI	Probability Prior	Posterior Probabilities When Research Shows		
			Twice	Expected	½ Exp.
Twice expected and higher	25%	0.33	0.72	0.26	0.08
½ to twice expected	10	0.33	0.21	0.45	0.15
0 to half expected	0	0.34	0.07	0.29	0.77
		1.00	1.00	1.00	1.00
Expected return		11.6%	20.1%	11.0%	3.5%
Variance		213.5	67.0	86.5	52.5

TABLE 14.5   *Calculation of Variance*

$$\text{Var} = \sum_i [(X_i - \bar{X})^2 \cdot P(X_i)] \text{ and } \bar{X} = \sum_i X_i \cdot P(X_i)$$

where $\bar{X}$ = EROI = $(0.33) \cdot (32) + (0.33) \cdot (2) + 0.34 \cdot (0)$
X_i = Return on investment for each condition *i*, that is, twice expected, expected, ½ expected income, or 32%, 2%, 0% in Table 14.2
$P(X_i)$ = Probability of event X_i

so in Table 14.2
$(32\% - 11.6\%)^2 \cdot (0.33) = 137.0$
$(2\% - 11.6\%)^2 \cdot (0.33) = 30.5$
$(0 - 11.6\%)^2 \cdot (0.34) = 46.0$
___
So variance = 213.5

results of this analysis. Interpreting Figure 14.4 requires the assumption that the expected demand condition actually exists. The graph shows that 15 percent of the time research is done, the result will incorrectly yield estimates of the income or better. In addition, 75 percent of the time, the market research will correctly predict the expected income range. However, 10 percent of the one-half expected value will result.

The second graph in Figure 14.4 can be interpreted the same way. When in fact the twice the income or better exists, 30 percent of the time a research reading will result ranging from the expected value to twice the expected value. Fifteen percent of the time, one would get research results between

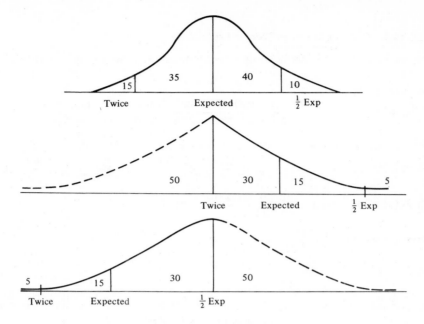

ERROR TABLE

Research Shows

Actual	Twice +	$\frac{1}{2}$ Exp-twice	Below $\frac{1}{2}$	Total
Twice Income	50	45	5	100
$\frac{1}{2}$ Exp to Twice Exp	15	75	10	100
$\frac{1}{2}$ Exp or Less	5	45	50	100
Total	70	165	65	

FIGURE 14.4   *The Assumed Real Results of Many Marketing Research Tests*

the one-half expected and expected level, and 5 percent of the time, the result would show the one-half expected level or less. The third graph can be interpreted similarly. If one knew that the twice or better demand situation was really the case, then the research would show one-half expected to twice was the case 45 percent of the time, and below one-half expected 5 percent of the time. Similarly, the second and third rows of that table can be interpreted. The expected value calculation is performed as shown in Table 14.5. The results of calculating the expected value and variance are shown in Table 14.4.

After research is done, the prior probabilities are modified, based on the results of the research (step 8 in Table 14.1). Thus, if the prior probabilities

TABLE 14.6   *Calculation of Posterior Probability*

Given research event *i* has been done and shows outcome of twice expected or better

Bayes' Theorem:

$$\text{Prob}_i \text{ (after research)} = \frac{\text{Prob}_i \text{ (prior)} \cdot \text{Prob}_i \text{ (Research}^a \text{ being right)}}{\sum_i \text{Prob}_i \text{ (prior)} \cdot \text{Prob (Research being right)}}$$

When *i* = Twice or better, expected or ½ expected

$$\text{Prob (after twice)} = \frac{(0.33) \cdot (0.50^a)}{(0.33) \cdot (0.50) + (0.33)(0.15) + 0.34(0.05)} = \frac{0.166}{0.232} = 0.72$$

$$\text{Prob (after expected)} = \frac{(0.33) \cdot (0.15)}{0.232} = 0.21$$

$$\text{Prob (after ½)} = \frac{(0.33) \cdot (0.05)}{0.232} = 0.07$$

---

[a] From Figure 14.4 error table.

were 0.33 for one event, and the research that is done shows that that event would occur, then common sense would tell us that posterior[5] probability of the event should rise. The amount of rise will depend on the quality of the research. For very accurate research, the probability will change from 0.33 to some high value. For "not so accurate" research, the probability of the event will rise from 0.33 to some lesser value. The exact calculation reflecting these changes is shown in Table 14.6. Table 14.6 assumes research has been done and it shows that the outcome will be twice the expected income level or better. Bayes' theorem is shown as the first equation in Table 14.6. Bayes' theorem is a mathematical way of modifying probabilities based on experience.

There are many real world analogs to the process. For example, a baby crawls around its playpen assuming that no toy will cause it discomfort, that is, the baby has a small prior probability that discomfort can exist in the playpen. However, if the baby comes upon a toy that pinches its finger, the infant immediately becomes more cautious. Bayes' theorem mathematically performs the same process. If information is received which has high probability of error, some relatively small change of probability belief will occur for the decision maker. However, if a very highly credible piece of information is captured by the decision maker, a large change in probability beliefs will occur, that is, in terms of the example, if highly accurate information results from some market research, indicating that the expected income level will be

---

[5] Posterior probability means the probability that results after seeing the outcome of the research.

achieved, the decision maker's prior probabilities will change a great deal. For less perfect information received, proportionately less change of probability will occur. The results of the Baynesian computations is shown in Table 14.4 under each of their potential research result columns. Thus, Table 14.4 summarizes a major part of the analysis. It is important to note that the variance drops from 213.5 to 67.0, or 86.5, or 52.5, depending on what the research actually showed. The degree of variance reduction is one of the key parts of the problem of picking the optimal research strategy. Ideally, the researcher would pick a research technique which provided the maximum reduction in variance at the lowest possible cost.

Questions and Exercises

1. When is information of very little value to the manager?
2. Why does the information collected by the accounting department often take a great amount of time to reach the marketing manager (referring to Figure 14.1)?
3. Examining Figure 14.1, is it clear why marketing managers often never know the precise impact of their pricing, promotion, and related decisions?
4. Where does the marketing manager get information about competitors' activities? (See Figure 14.1.)
5. Where might governmental pressure enter the picture shown in Figure 14.1?
6. Is a computer an absolute necessity in building an effective information system? Discuss the pros and cons.
7. Why has management resistance to high level information systems been sociological rather than technical? Are there possible effective strategies for the successful "marketing" of information systems to executives within a company?
8. Where can a high level information system "go wrong"? What kind of errors can destroy the credibility of an information system? How can these errors be avoided?
9. Examining the American Airlines information system leads one to the conclusion that the system has what primary purpose? How current are the data in the system?
10. Evaluate the system according to the Amstutz criteria.
11. Examining the Technical Appendix, are there other possible ways to define the outcomes and set the probabilities initially? Do other methods change the logic of the model? Why are such methods difficult to implement in industry? Use the model to evaluate the model.

Project Related Questions

1. In what ways will the data you are seeking yield a dollar payoff?
2. What is the cost-benefit of the information you are seeking?
3. What ways are there for minimizing the cost of gathering information of the type you seek in your project? What losses of information might be associated with these cost saving efforts?
4. Where does your project fit in Figure 14.3?
5. Can you design an information system intended to provide you with the data your project seeks on a continuing basis? What roadblocks might you face in implementing this system?

Chapter 15

Utilizing Research Information

Marketing research is primarily intended for use in analyzing, planning, implementing, and controlling programs. Curiously, very little literature exists in any field concerning the processes (excluding dissemination) whereby a research user utilizes his information. This is an especially critical process in strongly action-oriented fields such as marketing. Accordingly, attention now focuses on methods which help the marketer exact more use from his data.

Introduction

For the businessman, the major purpose for conducting research is to provide information which will enable him to make wiser decisions affecting his enterprise. Marketing research, then, is the primary means for improving the marketing function. Implicit in this view is the assumption that research results will be *used* in some effective manner. Perhaps the Achilles heel of all research lies in one special aspect of its utilization: the intuitive intellectual judgments made connecting research findings with specific marketing actions. The basic issue can be stated in question form: "How, given certain data, does the research user derive marketing strategies?" The authors, in exploring this question, conducted an exercise relevant to this issue in their marketing research class. Students were given the same recent journal article concerning a market research finding. The data or findings in the article were presented within a scenario in which the students assumed the role of a brand manager and were asked to derive brand management strategies. Faced with the same data and same situation, the students displayed some interesting phenomena. First, a large number of the strategies from different students were in direct conflict with one another although the particular strategies were vigorously defended. Second, many sound strategies and even categories of strategies generated had not even occurred to most of the other students. The same exercise was conducted with a number of middle level marketing managers having some familiarity with actual brand management and the exact same phenomena occurred. When individuals in both groups were asked to describe the process by which they arrived at their derived strategies there was considerable vagueness and uncertainty. In fact, little is known generally about the thought processes whereby people make intuitive judgments concerning the implications of data. It is not the intention of this chapter to present a theory of such judgmental processes in marketing research. Rather, we shall present an approach that will be helpful in generating a wider array of actionable implications from marketing research data.

Selection of Sources of Information

Before examining various alternatives for generating research implications it is important for the reader to realize that a substantial amount of

TABLE 15.1 *Information and Problem Sources*

	Sources of Problems					
	Market Related	Industry Related	Competitor Related	Supplier Related	Resource and Capability Related	Environment Related
Printed Sources of Data						
Professional journals[a]						
Newspapers and magazines[b]						
Trade associations						
Abstracting services						
Internal documents						
Government documents						
University Business Bureau reports						
Commercial research reports						
Other						
Interpersonal Sources						
In-house meetings						
Professional meetings						
Consultants						
Task leaders						
Other linkers[c]						
Customers						
Salesmen						

[a] For example, the *Journal of Marketing Research, Research on Consumer Research, Journal of Business, Harvard Business Review, Journal of Marketing, Journal of Advertising Research, Management Science, Public Opinion Quarterly.*
[b] *Wall Street Journal* and *Business Week.*
[c] See subsequent section in this chapter.

marketing activity is based on information not originally gathered by the marketing manager for the purpose of solving the problem at hand. Considerable data are collected on a routine basis by government agencies, industry associations, media sources, university research bureaus, and commercial research agencies. Data obtained from such sources are often very relevant to various marketing problems and tasks. In this section of the chapter attention will focus on techniques for generating research implications. This discussion is equally relevant for the use of secondary sources of data such as census data, internal data such as sales records and product pricing history, and original data gathered for the express purpose of solving the problem at hand.

The marketing manager or other users of marketing research must allocate his time and financial resources carefully in gathering data for monitoring his environment and formulating appropriate strategies for intervening in the market place. The manager can be exposed to two basic sources of research information. These are: (1) printed sources such as journals, newspapers, and special reports including those providing data from studies the manager authorized, and (2) interpersonal sources who transmit information by word-of-mouth including verbal reports of authorized studies of the problem of concern. These sources and others are presented in Table 15.1.

The manager uses Table 15.1 or some very similar table by asking, with regard to his marketing problem, which sources are most likely to be relevant to his problem needs. He may experience problems in six different areas: (1) customer's market behavior; (2) industrial-related problems, for example, inadequate channels of distribution; (3) behavior of competitors; (4) behavior of suppliers; (5) resource base and capabilities; and (6) legal and environmental conditions. These represent the columns in Table 15.1. Specific examples of each problem or challenge area are presented in Table 15.2. Of course, some sources of information are more relevant to certain problems than others. For example, trade associations may be particularly helpful in providing information relevant to changes in the industry as a whole, including competitive conditions. The *Journal of Consumer Research* may be most suited to consumer based market changes. The *Journal of Marketing Research* is especially relevant to solving problems in measuring consumer responses.

Developing Strategy from Research

There appear to be six steps involved in the overall research utilization process.

Step 1 Identification of plausible variables affecting market behavior for the situation under study.

Step 2 Systematic evaluation of each variable according to a comprehensive variable evaluation scheme.

TABLE 15.2   *Categories of Strategic Challenges*

I. Market-Related Challenges
Major changes in market structure
Major changes in the product life cycle
Major changes in demographic structure
Major changes in the types of customers served
Major changes in the price elasticity of demand
Major increases in total demand (other than above)
Stagnation of or major decreases in total demand (other than above)

II. Industry-Related Challenges
Major changes in the nature of product differentiation
Major changes in the economies of scale
Major changes in the price/cost structure
Major changes in product or process technology
Major changes in the distribution system
Major changes in barriers to entry (other than above)

III. Competitor-Related Challenges
Entry of new competitors
Exit of old competitors
Major changes in the market share of existing competitors

IV. Supplier-Related Challenges
Major changes in the availability of raw materials
Major changes in the conditions of trade
Entry of new suppliers or exit of old suppliers

V. Resource- and Capability-Related Challenges
Major excess of capital or cash flow
Major shortage of capital or inadequate cash flow
Major threat of outside takeover
Major excess of production facilities
Major inadequacy or sudden loss of production facilities
Major inadequacy or loss of top management

VI. Broader Environmental Challenges
Major changes in economic conditions
Major changes in political/legal constraints
Major changes in social/cultural values

Step 3   Establishing relationships among variables.

Step 4   Developing a theoretical paradigm.

Step 5   Systematic evaluation of each hypothesis according to a comprehensive hypothesis evaluation scheme.

Step 6   Derivation of tactic statements from hypotheses.

The main body of this chapter will focus on step 6. Various methods will be discussed for deriving marketing strategies or tactics from research. These methods are drawn from among those listed in Exhibit 1. This exhibit is certainly not exhaustive but does reflect various thinking modes as revealed to us through interviews and working experiences with many leading marketers who are very successful in making practical use of marketing research. The approach preferred or used is often based more on idiosyncratic factors such as the individual's mind set and personality than on questions related to the nature of the data or inherent features of the method. The technical appendix at the end of the chapter presents a detailed discussion of steps 1 to 6. The technical appendix builds to some extent upon some of the ideas expressed in Chapter 3 although it can be read independently of that chapter.

EXHIBIT 1   *Methods for Generating Strategies from Data*

Simulation	Schools of thought role playing
Decision trees	Reasoning from models of customer behavior
Strategic analysis	Antithetical reasoning
Brainstorming	Reasoning by analogy
Variable-hypothesis evaluation	Morphological analysis
Technological forecasting	Translating problems into theory linkers

Strategic Analysis

One approach for deriving practical implications from research involves thinking in terms of strategic challenges and strategic responses. Table 15.3 presents a list of some possible strategic responses facing business firms. In deriving strategies from research it is necessary first to identify the source of a marketing challenge or problem. As indicated in Chapter 3 this ought to be done before research is designed and conducted or, in the case where already existing data may be used, before searching for existing information. The available evidence may indicate, for example, that a major change in the product life cycle has occurred. (This evidence may or may not have been sought deliberately.) In response to this challenge the marketer should ask himself what the implications are in terms of the various possible strategic responses shown in Table 15.3. Does it mean, for instance, that there should be a change in product/market scope? Does the data suggest developing new products for existing markets? New markets for existing products?

A somewhat different organizational scheme has been suggested with regard to the standard alternative strategic responses shown in Table 15.3.[1]

---

[1] David D. Kollat *et al.*, *Strategic Marketing* (New York: Holt, Rinehart and Winston, 1972). Some of the discussion is adapted from this source: S. C. Johnson and C. Jones, "How to Organize for New Products," *Harvard Business Review*, Vol. 35 (May–June 1957), pp. 49–62.

TABLE 15.3 *Set of Strategic Responses*

I. Changes in Objectives
Growth objectives
Profitability objectives
Other objectives

II. Major Changes in Product/Market Scope
Increased penetration of existing markets with existing products
New products for existing markets
New markets for existing products
Horizontal diversification
Forward integration
Backward integration
Concentric diversification: marketing
Concentric diversification: production
Conglomerate diversification

III. Major Changes in Distinctive Competences
Marketing
Distribution
Manufacturing
R & D
Finance
Management

IV. Major Changes in Geographic Scope

V. Changes in Functional Policies
Changes in distribution channels
Changes in other marketing policies
Changes in manufacturing policies
Changes in R & D policies
Changes in financial policies
Changes in organizational and personnel policies

This is shown in Figure 15.1. Examples of each set of strategies are also presented. The research user should determine what the fundamental underlying question is which the particular strategy implies. He should then apply this question and other subquestions to the data before him. For example, for market penetration strategies the basic question might be: What should be done to gain further acceptance of our existing products? A subquestion might be, should we increase our advertising? The discussion below defines several different strategies and their fundamental question.

Products Markets	Present Products	Improvements in Present Products	New Products with Related Technology			New Products with Unrelated Technology	
			Assortment Manipulation	Expansion of the Variety of the Product Line			
Consumption markets: Same markets	(1) Market-penetration strategies	(3) Reformulation strategies	(5) Replacement strategies	(7) Product-line extension strategies		(9) Horizontal diversification strategies	
New markets	(2) Market develop-ment strategies	(4) Market extension strategies	(6) Market segmen-tation/product differentiation strategies	(8) Concentric diversification strategies		(10) Conglomerate diversification strategies	
Resource and/or distribution markets	(11) Forward and/or backward integration strategies						

FIGURE 15.1 Product-market scope and growth vector alternatives

Source: From Strategic Marketing by David T. Kollat, Roger D. Blackwell and James F. Robeson. Copyright © 1972 by Holt, Rine-hart and Winston, Inc. Reprinted by permission of Holt, Rinehart and Winston, Inc.

Market Penetration Strategies

This strategy attempts to improve the company's position with its present products in its current markets. This can be achieved by improving the efficiency and/or effectiveness of any functional area of the business. The fundamental question to be directed at data to explore their market penetration implications is: *What should be done to gain further acceptance of our existing products?* For example, does the data suggest an increase in advertising or some other specific form of sales promotion? Different promotional content? Etc.

Market Development Strategies

This alternative attempts to find new classes of customers that can use the company's present products. For example, some manufacturers of baby diapers now sell them to automobile manufacturers as polishing rags. The fundamental question here is: *What new uses and users of our present product line are uncovered by the data?* More specifically, can the product be used more intensively? Does the data uncover or suggest new uses? Etc.

Reformulation Strategies

This strategy concentrates on improving present products to increase sales to customers currently being served by the company. Detergents with bleach and enzymes are an example of this approach. The fundamental question asked of data for this type of strategy is: *What product changes are suggested?* For example, should there be changes in physical dimensions? Changes in the way the product is operated? Etc.

Market Extension Strategies

This approach is designed to reach new classes of customers by modifying the company's present products. DuPont has used this approach with many of its products, including Nylon and Teflon. *What changes in goods and services are necessary to reach nonusers?* Are economy sizes needed? Should different channels be used to reach other potential buyers? Etc.

Replacement Strategies

This strategy replaced current products with new products having better ingredients or formulations. Gillette, for example, has consistently replaced its razor blades—blue blades to super blue, to stainless steel, to platinum plus. The fundamental question here is: *What should replace present products?* Does the data suggest a need for significant improvements, alterations, substitutions of existing product lines? Should the change be to upgrade an existing product in a major way or replace it with a totally new conceptualization?

Market Segmentation/Product Differentiation Strategies

This alternative is designed to attract new customers by expanding the assortments of existing product lines. Bristol Myers, for example, offers Vitalis for men with older orientations, and Score for the youth-oriented. The fundamental question here is: *Should products be modified to appeal to different groups of buyers and/or users?* For instance, does the data identify a group of buyers not previously contemplated? Does the data suggest ways for segmenting buyers?

Product-Line Extension Strategies

This approach uses related technology to broaden the line of products offered to present customers. For example, General Electric's appliance division markets TV, radio, phonographs, refrigerators, ranges, and a broad range of small electrical appliances. The basic question here is: *Should more goods and services be made available to current consumers?* For example, what products will be attractive to each market segment?

Concentric Diversification Strategies

This strategy attracts new classes of customers by adding new products that have technological and/or marketing synergies with the existing product line. For example, in the 1960s, the Coca Cola Company, through the acquisition of the Minute Maid Corporation, diversified into the citrus-processing and coffee industries. The fundamental question for this strategy is: *Are there new products suggested by the research which will attract consumers who will also start buying existing items in the product line? What set of products are also used when customers use the product we sell?*

Horizontal Diversification Strategies

This alternative broadens the line of products offered to present customers through technology unrelated to the company's present products. The National Cash Register Company, for example, diversified from cash registers into calculating machines and computers. The fundamental question underlying this type of strategy is: *Are there product opportunities that exist relevant to the present product line but based on a different technology?*

Conglomerate Diversification Strategies

The objective of this approach is to attract new classes of customers by diversifying into products that have no relationship to the company's current technology, products, or markets. To illustrate, International Telephone and Telegraph Corporation, originally an operator of telephone systems and manufacturer of telecommunications equipment, has diversified into hotels and motor inns, rental cars, homes, and heating and air-conditioning equipment for schools. The fundamental question here is: *What product opportunities does the research suggest independently of existing company activity and skills?*

Integration Strategies

This strategy is intended to increase profitability, efficiency, and/or control by moving backward in the system to produce within the company those components which were previously purchased; or forward into additional fabrication, assembly, or distribution functions. An example of backward integration is steel companies' acquisitions of ore and transportation facilities, while the acquisition of retail outlets by clothing manufacturers is an example of forward integration. The fundamental question here is: *What opportunities exist for vertical expansion of the company's activities?*

Decision Trees

Once a general strategy has been decided upon, such as a product line extension strategy, it is helpful to construct a decision tree to assist in identifying specific alternative actions for implementing the strategy. Ideally, marketing research would permit an informed choice of the appropriate path to follow in the decision tree. Part of a simplified decision tree for product line extension is shown in Figure 15.2. Does the research indicate regional, national, international, and so on, geographical coverage? If national, what distribution strategy is most appropriate? Multiple channels? Single channels? If a multiple channel approach is best, should the approach be to use competitive or complementary channel selections? If complementary, should a push, straddle, or pull promotional effort be adopted? If a straddle approach is indicated, which media or combination of media should be used?

When constructing a decision tree the research user should describe each event or decision fork in the tree so that they are mutually exclusive. This means combinations of alternatives must be presented as a separate alternative. Also, the research user must enumerate all possible choices or events at each fork in the tree. The sequence of events or decisions do not have to be in chronological order. It is the time at which the decision maker receives information about events that counts and not the time at which they occur. For example, if research relating to push versus pull promotional strategies is received first, then this decision set may constitute the starting point for a decision tree for product line extension.

It should be clear now that the main advantage of a decision tree is to increase the number of questions asked of research data and, where answers are not readily forthcoming, to indicate areas where additional research is necessary to make informed decisions. The larger number of questions a decision tree stimulates ensures better coverage of the problem being investi-

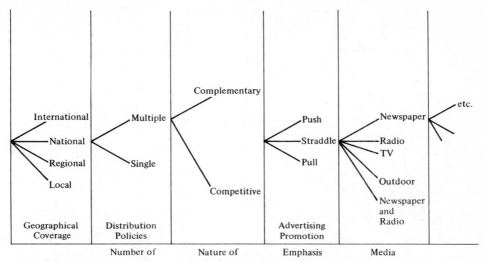

FIGURE 15.2 *A Simplified Excerpt from a Decision Tree for Product Line Extension*

gated and helps extract the maximum information a given marketing research effort can provide. An example in decision tree form of the *types* of considerations involved in formulating corporate strategy is presented in Figure 15.3.

Involving People Who Link Research to Utilization

It is often desirable for the practitioner utilizing marketing research to seek the assistance of a "linker." A linker is an intermediary between the researcher and/or research results and the practitioner. For many reasons, only one of which will be mentioned here, there are gaps in effective communication between the researcher producing data and the practitioner who must utilize the data. This gap is generally bridged, if at all, by additional persons who may be specialists in linking researchers and their data to practitioners.[2]

A linker is necessary when mutual understanding between researcher and user does not exist. There are four possible relationships between researchers and users. Following Churchman and Schainblatt[3] we can depict these relationships in the simple table on page 575.

[2] For a good discussion of this see R. Havelock *et al., The Planning of Innovation* (Survey Research Center, University of Michigan, Ann Arbor, 1971).

[3] C. W. Churchman and A. H. Schainblatt, "The Researcher and the Manager: A Dialectic of Implementation," *Management Science,* Vol. II, No. 4 (February 1965), pp. B69–87.

Generic Alternatives for Formulating Corporate Strategy

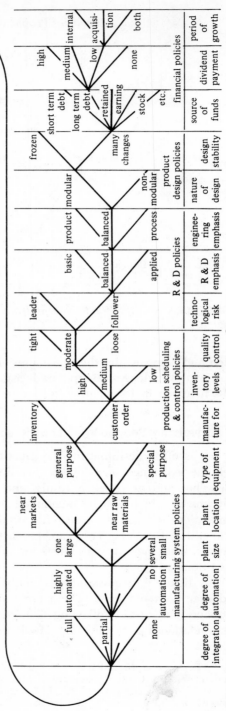

FIGURE 15.3 *The Generic Alternatives for Formulating Corporate Strategy*

Researcher Understands Manager's Needs

		Yes	No
Manager Understands Researcher and Data	Yes	Mutual Understanding	Communication
	No	Persuasion	Separate Function

Doktor and Hamilton's study suggests that a mutual understanding occurs when both the researcher and marketing manager have identical cognitive styles, that is, where they are both analytically (A) oriented or both are heuristically (H) oriented.[4] A heuristic orientation is one in which a person tends to reason by broad rules-of-thumb. Mutual understanding can also occur when the manager and researcher have different basic styles but also have an orientation or openness to the other's basic style. When the manager has an (H) cognitive style and the researcher an (A) style but with a small (H) approach, a persuader relationship is likely where the researcher tries to persuade the manager. When the manager is (H) oriented but with a slight (A) orientation and the researcher is (A) oriented, a communicator relationship is likely to occur. Finally, when the researcher is characterized as a pure (A) style of thinking and the manager characterized by a pure (H) style, a separate functionalist situation is likely.

Several different linking roles have been identified that can be helpful in shifting managers and researchers to a state of mutual understanding. These will be viewed here briefly. The marketing manager should seek and choose the type of linker whose function most closely satisfies his research utilization needs.

The Conveyor

The most elementary linker role is the conveyor who simply *passes* information from expert to nonexpert users. This passing or transfer function is often performed by salesmen, for example, from various research organizations who sell data such as credit ratings.

The Consultant

The consultant's function is to help define problems, identify existing related information, and assist in adapting existing information to the practitioner's needs. Management and marketing consulting organizations generally satisfy these needs. Academicians are also used frequently as consultants by marketing managers.

[4] R. H. Doktor and W. F. Hamilton, "Cognitive Style and the Acceptance of Management Science Recommendations," *Management Science,* Vol. 19, No. 8 (April 1973), pp. 884–894.

The Trainer

The function of the trainer is to transfer to a user an understanding of an area of knowledge or practice. For example, Advanced Management Research International, Inc., a major training agency for marketing management conducts various training programs such as pricing seminars whose purpose is "to provide an intensive learning experience on how to price, strategies for pricing, and the implementing of pricing decisions." Their trainers for this seminar involve a combination of professors and businessmen.

The Leader

The leader role functions by directing utilization efforts or by setting examples of how to utilize data. The leader exerts influence within his own group. Evidence indicates marketing managers do set for their subordinates examples of how to utilize research effectively.

The Innovator

The innovator stimulates utilization by establishing precedent and example in the use of marketing research. He is much like the leader when the leader demonstrates how to utilize research.

Reasoning from Models of Customer Behavior

One very useful technique for generating marketing strategies from existing data is to use one or more of the various models of behavior described in Chapter 5. The basic procedure involves three steps:

1. Identify variables or concepts in the model which are pertinent to the marketing problem at hand and determine the relationships between or among these variables.
2. Identify variables in the study which correspond to the concepts in the model and determine the nature of the empirical relationship between the variables.
3. Derive the marketing strategy implied by the empirical relationships.

Thus, one asks what relationships are there in the model which may correspond to and therefore suggest relationships not already considered among variables in already available data. Then comes the question, so what? What do the relationships in the data mean in terms of marketing strategy?

For purposes of illustration, the Howard-Sheth model of buyer behavior will be used here. This is shown in Figure 15.4. A data table concerning price and product choice behavior is presented in Table 15.4 and shall be used as our initial data base. Using the Howard-Sheth model we shall derive rela-

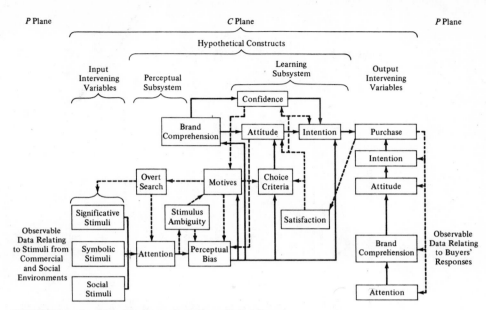

FIGURE 15.4 *The Theory of Buyer Behavior*
Source: John Howard and Jagdish Sheth, *The Theory of Buyer Behavior* (New York: Wiley, 1969), p. 54. Reprinted by permission of John Wiley & Sons, Inc.

tionships and strategies inherent in the Lambert study data but not reported. The nature of the data permit study of the relationship to be suggested. The Howard-Sheth model hypothesizes relationships between motives, perceptual bias, and stimulus ambiguity. For those products whose significative stimuli are ambiguous, the question might be raised about the relationship between motivation and perceptual bias. The corresponding concepts in Table 15.4 are difficulty of judging quality (stimulous ambiguity), sensitivity to undesirability of consequences of a bad choice (perceptual bias), and responsibility (motivation), that is, an inclination or motivation to be accountable. Thus, when it is difficult to judge the quality of a product, a buyer with a high sense of responsibility as interpreted above will be particularly sensitive to and more apt to see undesirable consequences of a bad choice. The model suggests this generalization in the existing data although the generalization was not originally allowed for or scheduled for testing. This new relationship should then be tested. The implied marketing strategy for products whose quality is difficult to judge is to stress in sales promotion that the particular brand is the choice of responsible people and that people generally never experience undesirable consequences in buying and using the product.

Another relationship suggested by the model involves the variables of

TABLE 15.4 *Directional Properties and t-Value Probabilities for Differences between Low- and High-Price Groups*

Variable	Tape Recorder	Portable Stereo	Molded Luggage	Tennis Racket	Tooth-paste	Coffee	Suntan Lotion
Perceptual variables							
Confidence in price as a predictor of quality	+ .005	+ .01	+ .005	+ .005	+ .005	+ .005	+ .005
Buying experience	+ .30	+ .005	+ .005	+ .005	+ .10	+ .20	+ .20
Difficulty of judging quality	+ .40	− .30	+ ...ᵃ	− .40	+ .10	+ .10	+ .20
Ability to judge quality	+ .025	+ .005	+ .025	+ .005	+ .10	+ .10	+ .40
Variation in quality	+ .01	+ .10	+ .10	+ .005	+ .005	+ .005	+ .025
Uncertainty	− .30	+ .40	− .025	− ...ᵃ	+ .01	+ .30	+ .01
Undesirability of consequences	+ .40	+ .10	+ .40	+ .005	+ .005	+ .025	+ .025
Social significance of brand choice	+ .20	+ ...ᵃ	+ .10	+ .025	+ .005	+ .05	+ .005
Personality traits							
Ascendancy	+ .10	+ .30	+ .20	− .30	− .30	− .30	− .30

Responsibility	+	+	+	−	−	−	−
	.40	.20	.30	.20	.20	.40	.20
Emotional stability	−	+	−	−	−	+	−
	...[a]	...[a]	.05	.05	.10	.40	.05
Sociability	+	+	+	−	−	+	−
	.10	.20	.10	.40	.40	...[a]	.20
Cautiousness	−	+	+	+	+	−	+
	...[a]	.20	...[a]	.30	.40	...[a]	...[a]
Original thinking	+	+	+	+	−	−	−
	.10	.005	.01	.20	...[a]	.20	...[a]
Personal relations	−	+	+	+	+	+	−
	.30	.40	.40	.30	...[a]	.10	...[a]
Vigor	+	+	+	−	−	−	−
	.10	...[a]	.05	...[a]	.40	.025	...[a]
Economic variables							
Father's income	+	−	+	+	−	+	+
	.10	.10	.10	.10	.40	...[a]	.20
Percentage of expenses earned personally	−	−	−	−	−	−	−
	.20	.40	.025	.30	...[a]	.01	.40

Source: Reprinted from D. V. Lambert, "Price and Choice Behavior," *Journal of Marketing Research*, Vol. IX (February 1972), p. 35. Published by the American Marketing Association.
[a] $p > .40$.

confidence, motives, attention, and social stimuli. Cautious people (an indicator of low confidence) with high sociability needs (motive) will be particularly attentive to the social significance (social stimuli from various reference groups) of their possible brand choices. Overt search is implied by virtue of having alternative brand choices.

Lambert's data, when viewed from the perspective of the Howard-Sheth model, also causes one to reflect upon the possible relationship between motive, stimulus ambiguity, and overt search: difficulty in judging quality (stimulus ambiguity) → cautiousness (in this case a motive) → overt search. Stimulus ambiguity, represented in Lambert's data by ability to judge quality and variation in quality, could be expected to cause a person high in cautiousness to go through a more intensive overt search process. Thus, a strategy could be adopted which would facilitate the consumer's overt search. Distribution of free samples or direct comparison of brands in promotional material are ways of accomplishing this.

Another example will be helpful to illustrate the use of models to derive strategies and insights not previously gleaned from the data. This time, using the same basic model, we shall consider a study on the effects of repetition of refutational and supportive advertising appeals.[5]

Looking at the graph in Figure 15.5, the question of why a refutational appeal was more successful than a supportive appeal in increasing competitive-brand users' intention to buy the test brand for the first time can be raised. Referring to the Howard-Sheth model, the factors of stimuli, attention, and perceptual bias appear as possible explanations. For example, if a negative experience (a significative stimuli) occurred with the use of a competitive brand, there will be selective attention and perception to refutational appeals. Negative statements about the competitive brand reinforce the decision not to buy it again. The more refutational appeals are perceived and attended to, the more confidence in the competitive brand is weakened, and thus the greater the propensity to switch. This argument is limited to those customers who have experienced only the competitive brand and not the test brand.

Other Data Utilization Techniques

Technological Forecasting

Technological forecasting is a series of human/computer techniques to forecast changes in technology which are likely in certain time frames. Usually a series of experts develop scenarios about changes which they feel are necessary, feasible, and desirable. Typically, an "envelope" or range of technical

---

[5] Alan G. Sawyer, "The Effects of Repetition of Refutational and Supportive Advertising Appeals," *Journal of Marketing Research*, Vol. X (February 1973), pp. 23–33. Published by the American Marketing Association.

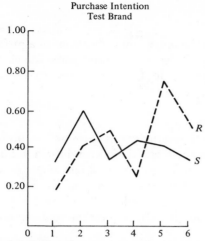

FIGURE 15.5 *The Number of Test Ad Exposures*
Source: Sawyer, see footnote 5.

specifications are produced and then probability of achieving the limits of the envelope are created by the experts. A computer than combines the envelope specifications with the probability to forecast an aggregate time to occurrence for technology. An example of this would be the forecast of the occurrence of development of ground transportation that does not use wheels, but rather uses magnetic fields to support the vehicle. The experts would assess current technology concerning magnetism and then assess what new electromagnetic developments would be needed together with the time of development with a probability. The results of a number of experts would be combined to get an aggregate forecast of time to development.

School of Thought Role Playing

This technique consists of the user asking how people with different perspectives including different theoretical orientations would interpret the data. How, for example, would an exchange-theory advocate interpret data about salesman-customer interaction? How would a motivational researcher interpret the same data?

Reasoning by Analogy

This approach essentially involves finding parallels between a process or phenomenon in one context and a process or phenomenon in another different context. The most familiar form of this is the use of behavioral laboratory work involving humans and/or rats to cast insight into real world activity.

Morphological Analysis

This technique involves identifying the important dimensions of a problem and examining their interrelationships. If there are three dimensions to a problem then a three-dimensional table would be constructed to facilitate analyzing the various interactions.

Translating Problems into Theory

This involves translating a problem into a theoretical question. A problem involving the introduction of a new product could be cast into a diffusion theory or perhaps social change theory question. The problem then becomes imbedded in a theoretical system where there may be a wealth of concepts and findings pertinent to the basic marketing problem. These concepts and findings may have been overlooked had the theoretical question not been posed.

Summary of Ingredients for Successful Marketing Research Utilization

A somewhat neglected but important issue in marketing research concerns the characteristics of research projects associated with the successful utilization of results. Effective utilization is nearly as important to the researcher as it is to the practitioner. It is important to the commercial research agency or consultant because clients who are able to use research effectively are likely to commission further research probably with the same agency. Research personnel in companies with their own research capability also have a special interest in seeing their products utilized effectively. Apart from the obvious concern of retaining one's job, there is also an issue of functional importance. The more adept researchers are in providing actionable data, the greater is their relative importance within the organization. Recently, experts on research utilization have begun to focus their attention on this issue. Some of these findings are presented below. Awareness of them can sensitize the marketing manager, especially those concerned with managing research personnel, to the kinds of settings and experiences they should foster for more effective research utilization.

1. Implementation of research findings is primarily the responsibility of the top-level administration of the sponsoring agency but the endorsement of middle-level personnel is essential.
2. The evaluation of findings which influence administrative decisions to implement or reject the findings is done largely by practitioners.
3. The involvement of practitioners in the research effort increases the likelihood that some of the findings will be of value to other prac-

titioners. It also increases the acceptability of the research by administrators and other practitioners.

4. Strategies to promote the utilization of research findings must be established early in the research planning stage. Strategies should allow for frequent review of project developments in terms of their implications for the utilization of the end product of the research. For instance, the personnel who are to act upon the research, whether they are from within the company doing the research or from another company, should be brought together with the researchers to ensure that the research efforts will yield actionable results. A single presentation of findings at the conclusion of the project is generally insufficient, that is, it does not promote maximum use of the data.

5. Research investigators should constantly seek opportunities to clarify practice implications inherent in the research. This facilitates the task of presenting results in a manner in which it is more easily consumed. For example, when a special statistical technique is used, a very simple statement should be attached to the presentation as to what the data are saying vis-à-vis that technique. This lessens resistance to reading the data and helps reduce incidents of misapplication.

6. Generally, research findings are not used in their entirety. Practitioners or other users usually employ only parts of the total research report. This can often be disappointing or frustrating to the market researcher particularly when, in his judgment, the least important findings are those selected for action.

7. Ideally, marketing research projects should, at the very outset, coopt a dissemination-utilization expert who serves as a monitor of the research project helping to keep the project moving in directions which will produce actionable results. This expert can also act as linker with the user group. Advertising account executives sometimes perform this important function.

8. Progress reports should be issued to the intended research users with specific requests for feedback. Two-way communication between the researchers and users or practitioners greatly enhances a project's success.

9. Practitioners and administrators should be involved or at least consulted in all aspects of the research including problem definition, study design, and so forth. Apart from the direct constructive contribution they may make, it instills a feeling of identification with the research project, thus establishing an openness to the results regardless of how threatening those results may be.

10. A thorough understanding of the problem, particularly as the practitioner perceives it, is necessary if the results are to have any applied

utility. Knowing how the practitioner perceives the problem even though it is not consistent with the researcher's view can be of value in two ways. First, if there is not a common perception of the problem, the researcher will have to educate the practitioner about the nature of the problem; otherwise, the practitioner is very unlikely to see the relevance of the data collected. Secondly, an understanding of the practitioner's frame of reference can aid the researcher to structure the presentation of his findings in ways that are compatible with the practitioner's perspective.

Summary

This chapter has focused on a critical aspect of management, the use of information. The processes whereby marketing managers or others reason from information to strategy are very unclear. However, several techniques for stimulating more alternative strategies have been suggested. One of the more promising techniques presented is the use of models for clues about new relationships among already existing data.

Technical Appendix: Steps for Using Data

In the discussion to follow a procedure is described for selecting plausible variables and hypotheses and deriving specific tactics for the purpose of stimulating the use of already gathered information such as may be reported in a journal article. There appear to be no existing procedures comparable to the one used here and hence the presentation suffers the drawbacks associated with work in an area having few guidelines to follow or models to build upon.

Six steps are involved:

Step 1   Identification of plausible variables affecting market behavior for the situation under study.

Step 2   Systematic evaluation of each variable according to a comprehensive variable evaluation scheme.

Step 3   Establishing relationship among variables.

Step 4   Developing a theoretical paradigm.

Step 5   Systematic evaluation of each hypothesis according to a comprehensive hypothesis evaluation scheme.

Step 6   Derivation of tactic statements from hypotheses.

It is assumed that there is an explicit statement of the situation under study before the six steps are initiated. For example, the situation might be the general phenomenon of the acceptance or rejection of innovations originating with one of the numerous commercial research and development organizations. Moreover, only those innovations may be considered which are intended for use at the elementary school level where the unit of analysis may be allowed to vary from the individual teacher to school district. The innovations may be further divided into special categories:

TABLE 15.5 *Variable Evaluation*[a]

| | Evaluation Criteria | | | | | | |
Variable Name	Observ-ability	Con-tent Valid-ity	Pre-dic-tivity	Dis-crimi-nant Power	Sys-temic Valve	Substan-tiality	Total Score
Degree of central-ization in school district	3	2	3	1	1	3	13
Risk-taking propensity	1	1	3	2	1	2	10
Etc.							

[a] 3 = good, 2 = fair, and 1 = poor.

Step 1 *Identification of plausible variables affecting market behavior for the situation under study.*

These variables are to be preliminarily screened at this stage on the basis of the investigators' experience and a literature review.

Step 2 *Systematic evaluation of each variable according to a comprehensive variable evaluation scheme.*

An evaluation scheme is presented in Table 15.5. This involves the various criteria developed in Chapter 3. Table 15.6 defines and illustrates the evaluative criteria. This scheme requires constructing a variable value index. The higher the score the more important the variable is for inclusion in the final theory. Two caveats are necessary. First, variables that would be listed in Table 15.6 would have received a preliminary screening as per step 1. Secondly, a numerical threshold would be established and all variables whose numerical index falls below that threshold would be eliminated from further analysis. The caveat implicit in this is that some exceptions should be expected. Scoring is at best only a rough indicator of probable value; expert judgment should not be suspended when examining total scores. The main reason for not adhering unwaveringly to the cutoff point established by the threshold is that the variable evaluation criteria presented in Table 15.5 are unweighted. In fact, they may be of unequal importance depending on the particular circumstances of the investigation and, ideally, the criteria should be weighted accordingly.

The example in Table 15.5 assumes for convenience that all criteria have equal weights. The variable labeled "degree of centralization," for instance, is readily observed or measured; has moderate content validity, that is, the total

TABLE 15.6 *Definitions of Evaluative Criteria*

Criteria	Definition	Examples in the Context of Innovation
Observability	The degree to which a variable is reducible to observations.	To what extent are the traits cosmopoliteness, empathy, and dogmatism observable, that is, how readily can we "see" these concepts with the best instruments currently available? Are valid concepts only those which are observable?
Content Validity	The degree to which an operationalization *represents* the variable about which generalizations are to be made.	To what degree does a self-rating scale focusing upon perceived expertise in an area actually represent the abstract concept of opinion leadership? Does time of purchase relative to other members of a social system represent the degree of innovativeness rather than venturesomeness displayed by an individual?
Predictivity	A subtype of criterion-related validity in which the criterion measure is separated in time from the predictor concept.	To what extent does time of awareness of an innovation influence time of first purchase? To what extent do initial attitudes predict time of first purchase? How adequately do the scores obtained in measuring propensity for innovative behavior predict actual purchase of innovations?
Discriminant Power	The extent to which a variable differs from other variables.	How different is innovativeness from venturesomeness? Is opinion stating the same as advice giving, that is, does the use of the term opinion leadership adequately separate itself from leadership in giving solicited advice?
Systemic Value	The degree to which a variable enables the integration of previously unconnected variables and/or the generation of a new conceptual system.	How many plausible new propositions can be established and existing propositions connected by introducing the concept of reciprocity in interpersonal selling situations involving innovations?
Substantiality	The extent to which the variable contributes to the identification of a discernible substantial market segment.	Does risk-taking propensity clearly distinguish between adopters and nonadopters of an innovation? To what extent does it classify all adopters accurately?

meaning of centrality or all its facets are reasonably but not fully represented by the operational measures; is a good predictor of innovations or other variables directly related to innovativeness; has poor discriminant power, that is, it is somewhat close to the variables of complexity and formalization; is not good at linking what appear to be otherwise unrelated variables; and does distinguish well between various market segments. It will be noted that there is a certain relatedness among the evaluative criteria. A variable rated highly on observability, for example, is unlikely to receive a low score on content validity.

Step 3   *Establishing relationship among variables.*

This step involves the construction of a matrix stating relationships among the variables remaining after step 2. The matrix in Table 15.7 will serve as an example. Variables *a, b, c,* and *d* will represent, respectively, degree of centralization of decision making in the school district, degree of exposure to innovation related information, the extent to which teachers perceive innovative behavior as being rewarded, and the innovativeness of school district. The relationships to be discussed here are logical possibilities; they are presented for illustrative purposes and may have no substantive base. By reading the matrix certain causal hypotheses become evident. For example, the greater the degree of centralization (*a*), the lower the degree of exposure to innovation related information (*b*); the more customers, in this case teachers, perceive innovative behavior as being rewarded (*c*), the more innovative the school district will be (*d*). There is reciprocal causation as well, as indicated by codes in cells falling below the diagonal: the more innovative a school district is (*d*), the more teachers will perceive innovative behavior to be rewarding (*c*).

TABLE 15.7   *Relationships among Variables*

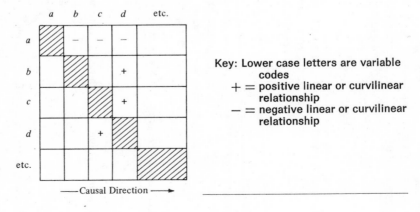

Key: Lower case letters are variable codes
+ = positive linear or curvilinear relationship
− = negative linear or curvilinear relationship

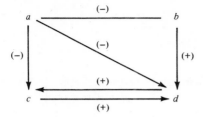

FIGURE 15.6 *A Theoretical Paradigm*

Step 4 Developing a theoretical paradigm.

A theoretical paradigm, shown in Figure 15.6, can be derived from the matrix in step 3. Variable *d*, school district innovativeness, is the dependent variable although it is also suggested as having a direct causal effect on variable *c*, teacher perceptions about innovative behavior. Standard statistical techniques, for example, path analysis, are available for studying the assumptions about causality in this theoretical paradigm or model. Obviously, the addition of even one more variable could produce a much more complex model. It is suggested that, to the extent possible without seriously violating the explanatory power of the model, only variables which have a maximum of a two-step connection with the dependent variable such as $a \to b \to d$ (ignoring in this case the direct $a \to d$ connection) be included in the model.

Step 5 Systematic evaluation of each hypothesis according to a comprehensive hypothesis evaluation scheme.

Since the number of variables and hence the number of hypotheses will be large it will be necessary to screen out the least promising hypotheses. This involves another set of criteria, this time for evaluating hypotheses. These criteria should also be reemployed for evaluating the state of the final theory after testing. Each connecting line in Figure 15.6 implies an hypothesis stating a relationship concerning at least two variables. Thus, there are a minimum of six hypotheses. This can also be derived from the matrix shown in Table 15.7. Table 15.8 provides a basis for an overall evaluation of each hypothesis. A list of evaluative criteria for hypotheses is presented in Table 15.9.

Not all criteria will be applicable to all hypotheses. The score for a particular hypothesis should be the average rating (with $3 = $ good, $2 = $ fair, and $1 = $ poor) using as *n* the number of applicable cells. As before, it may be desirable to weight each applicable criterion differently in terms of importance and the numerical threshold established as a cutoff point for discarding propositions should be viewed as a guide to be tempered by experience.

TABLE 15.8   *Hypothesis Evaluation*

Hypothesis	Evaluative Criteria					
	Internal Consistency	*Strength*	*Falsifiability*	*Scope*	*Etc.*	*Total Score*
A						
B						
C						
D						
E						
F						

Step 6   Derivation of tactic statements from hypotheses.

Each hypothesis should imply a tactic or strategy. The focus of the tactic may be to manipulate a phenomenon peculiar to the potential consumer such as the level and kind of information possessed. On the other hand, the tactic may focus on a change agent variable such as the frequency with which contacts with potential consumers are attempted. Broadly interpreted change agent variables would include such factors as selecting promotional appeals to be consistent with known personality traits of the intended market segment or adapting the nature of the innovation to be compatible with their risk-taking propensities.

Operationalizing hypotheses in the form of actionable statements is a specific instance of the so-called action level epistemic gap. Just as there is no perfect correspondence between theoretical statements and their operationalization (the "operational research epistemic gap"), there is no perfect one-to-one correspondence between the operational hypothesis and the derived tactic. This lack of correspondence is known as an epistemic gap. Only intuitive intellectual judgments may be made although guides for improving these judgments can be identified. A given hypothesis may imply more than one tactic for a given change agent or for different change agents. It is altogether possible that conflicting tactics may be derived. The criterion to be employed in making a selection in such cases concerns the compatibility of the alternative tactics with those other tactics which have been derived from other hypotheses in the same theory. The most compatible tactic is the one to be selected.

TABLE 15.9 *Criteria for Hypothesis Evaluation*[a]

Formal Criteria	
1. Well-formedness	The hypothesis obeys the rules of "formation" and "transformation" (elementary logic).
2. Internal consistency	The hypothesis contains no logical contradictions.
3. Independence	The hypothesis has primitive-concepts independence and axioms independence.
4. Strength	The hypothesis entails other theories.
Semantical Criteria	
5. Linguistic exactness	The hypothesis exhibits minimum intensional and extensional vagueness.
6. Conceptual unity	The components of the hypothesis refer to the same set of behavioral phenomena.
7. Empirical interpretability (or testability in principle)	The hypothesis is operationalizable (interpretable in empirical terms).
8. Representativeness	The hypothesis deals with deep mechanisms.
Methodological Criteria	
9. Falsifiability	The hypothesis is falsifiable—that is, confrontable with reality (facts).
10. Methodological simplicity	The hypothesis is easy to build and test.
Epistemological Criteria	
11. Confirmation	The hypothesis coheres with facts.
12. Originality	The hypothesis increases knowledge by deriving new propositions.
13. External consistency	The hypothesis is consistent with existing knowledge.
14. Unifying power	The hypothesis connects previously unconnected items.
15. Heuristic power	The hypothesis suggests new directions for research.
16. Stability	The hypothesis is able to accommodate new evidence.

[a] This table is based largely on M. Bunge, *Scientific Research*, Vols. I and II (Berlin: Springer, 1967).

Perhaps the simplest procedure for analyzing and selecting tactics is to enumerate them on the basis of intuitive yet informed judgment and then apply a set of tactic selection criteria. Consider an hypothesis adapted from Table 15.7 in step 3: the greater the degree of centralization (of authority) in a company (say a steel manufacturer) the lower the degree of exposure

TABLE 15.10   *Tactic Stimulator Grid*

	Hypothesis			
Tactic stimulator	*1*	*2*	*3*	*Etc.*
Decision stage				
Timetable				
Points of entry		a		
Mode of communication		b		
Resource availability				
Nature of innovation				
Incentive system				
Etc.				

among decision makers to innovation-related information.[6] This hypothesis has received reasonably good support in a number of different contexts. One relatively obvious actionable implication of this would seem to be the following: In a highly centralized company do not maximize the number of points in the system in which sales promotion information could be fed but concentrate initial promotional efforts at the higher management level. This may involve a second tactic, the greater use of salesmen relative to the mass media as vehicles for disseminating information.

Thus, the one hypothesis suggests two tactics each of which introduces a new consideration. The first tactic introduces the notion of points of entry into a system while the second tactic involves the interpersonal versus mass media notion. This suggests a more expedient means of formulating tactics. A number of considerations such as number of points of entry, interpersonal versus mass media, and so on, could be enumerated as tactic formulation stimulators. Table 15.10 is an example. Columns 1, 2, 3, and so on, refer to various hypotheses and the small letters within the cell refer to tactics derived from the various hypotheses on the basis of the tactic factors. Assume, for example, hypothesis 2 represents the relationship between degree of centralization with exposure to innovation information. The small letters *a* and *b* are the two tactics just mentioned above. The basic procedure for using Table 15.10

---

[6] John Czepiel, unpublished doctoral dissertation, Northwestern University, Graduate School of Management, 1972.

is to ask, for each cell, "What action, if any, does this hypothesis suggest in terms of this tactic factor?" Does, for example, our hypothesis suggest any special action depending on the particular decision-making stage the central authority is in? In the example used here this would not be relevant since the hypothesis is applicable at the awareness stage only. An exhibit would then be developed listing the various hypotheses 1, 2, 3, and so on, and indented under each hypothesis would be the various tactics, *a, b, c,* and so on.

It is likely that as the number of hypotheses examined increases, certain tactic stimulators would appear as relevant more often than other stimulators. These would constitute the core tactic stimulators for the context under study, for example, elementary school districts.

It is important to note that there is a reiterative process in step 6. Tactics generated on the basis of intuitive yet informed intellectual judgment were said to contain basic notions such as number of points of entry into a particular social system such as an industrial firm or even an industry. The points of entry idea then serves as a stimulator for other hypotheses which in turn may generate additional stimulators, and so forth.

Questions and Exercises

1. What are the relative advantages and limitations of the major techniques for developing strategy from research? Are there special types of problems and special contexts where one technique might be better than others?

2. Select an article from a recent issue of the *Journal of Marketing Research* or *Research on Consumer Behavior* which reports concepts and data from an empirical study. Conduct an analysis of the article in terms of the six steps for using data. Do the same exercise with the reading following this chapter.

3. Apply three techniques for developing strategies from research to an article in a recent marketing journal or to one of the cases you have read in this text. Which technique do you find most helpful? Are the set of strategies each method helps you generate identical or very similar?

4. Can different strategy generation techniques be used together? Try combining any two techniques and apply the combination to a set of data.

5. Assume that the study reported in Reading 15-1 was performed by an advertising agency in which you are an account executive. You must make a presentation to your client concerning the advertising strategy you plan for one of the client's major products which has considerable competition. For purposes of this example, the product is industrial floor wax which both cleans and waxes in the same

application. Based on the general findings of the study what specific promotional strategies do you recommend? How did you go about deriving your recommendations from the data?

Project Related Questions

1. Can you perform steps 1 to 6 as discussed on pages 565 to 566 using your data?
2. Evaluate your hypotheses using some of the criteria summarized in Table 15.6.
3. Develop a tactic stimulator grid using your data.
4. Develop a set of strategies from your data using some of the methods discussed in this chapter. Which methods are most suitable? Does the strategic analysis method discussed on pages 566 to 570 help?
5. What type of consultants would you seek for assistance in interpreting your data? Where would you be likely to find these consultants?
6. What problems are you encountering in interpreting your data? Describe these to a colleague with a different way of thinking and seek his assistance in interpreting your data.
7. What new hypotheses are suggested by your research project?

The Effects of Repetition of Refutational and Supportive Advertising Appeals

*Alan G. Sawyer**

A laboratory experiment compared the effects of repetition of refutational and supportive advertising appeals. When respondents were segmented on the basis of product class experience, several significant differences in the effects of the two appeals on a measure of brand purchase intention were found.

INTRODUCTION

A *refutational* approach is one which expresses or acknowledges an opposing point of view and then proceeds to refute that claim. The alternative to a refutational approach is to ignore any competitive arguments and to use a completely positive or *supportive* format. Past communication research has indicated that the particular conditions favorable to the use of a refutational appeal are somewhat complex and that the refutational appeal might benefit more than the supportive appeal from repeated exposures. This article reports the results of an experiment that compared the effects of repetition of refutational and supportive advertising appeals.

PAST RESEARCH

The refutational appeal is a subset of the more general class of two-sided communication which mentions but does not always refute the cited opposing argument. Early social psychological research found no overall difference in the persuasive effectiveness of two-sided versus one-sided messages [13]. Further analysis, however, reveals that the two-sided appeal was more effective for respondents who initially were opposed to the position of the argument and for those who

SOURCE: Reprinted from the *Journal of Marketing Research*, Vol. X (February 1973), pp. 23–33. Published by the American Marketing Association.

* Alan G. Sawyer is Assistant Professor of Marketing at the University of Massachusetts. This research was partially funded by a grant to Stanford University from the American Association of Advertising Agencies Educational Foundation. The mobile unit used in the field work was provided by Foote, Cone & Belding. The author wishes to thank Michael Ray for his many contributions to this research and to gratefully acknowledge the help of William Massy and Gerald Eskin.

had at least a high school education. Conversely, the one-sided communication was more persuasive for those who agreed with the advocated position and with less-educated persons. One-sided arguments were also less effective than two-sided when counterpropaganda was subsequently encountered [20].

The bulk of research specifically examining the relative effects of supportive and refutational communication appeals has been reported by McGuire [22]. This highly creative work resulted from an investigation of inducing resistance to persuasion. From a biological analogy which he labeled "inoculation theory," McGuire predicted that a refutational appeal would be superior to a supportive appeal in inducing resistance to a following attack on the belief in question. This prediction was upheld in a subsequent experiment using cultural truisms (e.g., "regular tooth brushing is good for your health") as the communication topics. However, when tested immediately after the defenses but before the following attack, the supportive defense was superior to the refutational. This potentially misleading greater initial effectiveness of the supportive appeal, which later experiments consistently replicated, became labeled the "paper tiger" effect.

Conventional tests of advertising effectiveness may be biased against refutational ad appeals. Copy tests which involve some measure of recall or preference for presented alternatives generally favor ads with relatively simple, straightforward product

benefit appeals. The relatively uncomplicated supportive appeal may have an unfair advantage with the simple recall or recognition measures. Similarly, since McGuire found that the motivating aspect of the refutational appeal requires some time lapse to work most effectively, the supportive appeal may benefit from tests that measure effects immediately following ad exposure. Recent research [24] has indicated that, despite the fact that respondents tended to read articles with supportive headlines over articles on the same subject with refutational headings, the refutational messages' effectiveness regarding defense to later attacking communications remained superior although somewhat muted. Copy tests which ask subjects to indicate which commercial or advertisement they prefer to watch or read overlook a more relevant criterion—the eventual persuasive effect. In addition, copy tests often neither include competitive advertisements nor present more than one exposure. Test results from such research which favor supportive-type appeals may possibly be analogous to McGuire's "paper tiger" effect.

The general reaction in the advertising trade has been similar to the negative bent of popular textbooks regarding the use of competitive or refutational appeals [6]. A common apprehension is that mentioning opposing claims or naming competitors serves only to weaken one's own claim and that such mention or admittance of the other side may even help the competitor. The potential danger of selective retention [8, 23, 33] are also cited. For example, advertising copy which states "some people prefer brand 'X', but brand 'Y' is better because . . ." may be remembered as only "some people prefer brand 'X' ". Repeated exposures could help to lessen any selective retention. Similarly, repetition might increase the persuasiveness of refutational appeals relative to that of supportive appeals by improving key aspects of the communication situation that have been isolated by researchers studying the refutational appeal. Repetition could lead to less perceived bias of the message [5, 13, 14, 20], further reduce credibility of the competitor [35], reduce psychological reactance [3, 16], as well as provide increased practice to help inoculate against attacking messages [22].

Even though effects similar to McGuire's "germ free" cultural truisms have been found with controversial issues [2, 26], it should be acknowledged that there are elements in the typical advertising situation that are quite different from the environment of social psychological experiments. These different elements include the lower overall credibility of the communication environment, the lower importance of the message to the subject, and the briefer content [31]. Despite these dissimilarities, however, the communication appeals used can be basically the same. There has been some laboratory [7] and field [12] experimental work that has demonstrated that two-sided advertising appeals can be effective.

Many advertisers [11] have decried the inapplicability of communication research to marketing and advertising. This experiment was designed to test the applicability of the research on two-sided, refutational appeals to advertising and, in addition, to test hypotheses about the relative effectiveness of repetition of refutational and supportive appeals. The need for research which combined repetition with refutational appeals was first suggested by Ray [26].

EXPERIMENTAL DESIGN, ADVERTISING STIMULI AND MEASURES

The laboratory setting used in this experiment was similar to a previous experiment [29]. Adult female shoppers in a shopping center were asked to enter a mobile testing unit in order to watch a "Shopping of the Future" demonstration. This setting helped to disguise the true purpose of the experiment. After hearing a description about a futuristic in-home shopping system in which product advertisements and descriptions were shown via closed-circuit television, the subjects watched a series of slides of print ads on a 16″ rear-view screen. These slides included either refutational or supportive advertisements for five products (test brands); these ads were exposed either 1, 2, 3, 4, 5, or 6 times. Five ads for competing products (competitor brands) were also included in the message stream; these ads were exposed two times to all subjects. All of the ads were randomly mixed in a series of 47 10-second exposures. Fourteen filler or buffer ads were randomly intermingled with the repeated ads subject to the following spacing constraints: two filler ads began and ended each series, no ad could follow itself by less than four positions, and no product class could be immediately repeated.

Each subject was randomly assigned to one of two treatments in which either refutational or supportive ads were repeated. Since the number of exposures of the test ads was varied in a Latin-Square design for each treatment block, six groups per treatment or a total of twelve groups were used in the design. Sample size per group was 20 or a total of 240 subjects.

Test advertising included both refutational and supportive forms for Parker ball-point pens, Bayer aspirin, Renault automobiles, Lava soap, and Slender diet drink. Each of the competitor brand ads used one-sided appeals and were selected for their relevance to the topic refuted by the test ads. For example, both the refutational ("Why pay $1.98 for a ball-point pen? . . .") and the supportive ("Just one could be all you ever need") test ads for the Parker "Jotter" pens deal with a price-quality appeal, and the competitor ad was for Scripto and promoted its low price ("Only 49 cents"). The main copy points of all of the ads are presented in Table 1.

After watching the advertisements, the subjects filled out a page of questions concerning the demonstration. Then they answered questions concerning unaided recall of the shown ads, brand attitudes (rated goodness on a six-point scale of various product brands), purchase intention (which

brands they might purchase if they were in the market for a particular type of product), and brand usage. Finally, they were thanked for their cooperation and given cents-off coupons which included some of the products advertised in the demonstration. The redemption rates of these coupons served as a behavior measure of advertising effect.

Several hypotheses were tested in this experiment [32], and results involved two levels of measurement— purchase intention and recall.

HYPOTHESES AND RESULTS
Purchase Intention

The refutational appeal, because of induced inoculation, less perceived bias, reduced credibility of the competitor, and/or less psychological reactance, should perform better with repetition than the repeated supportive appeal. Therefore, it was hypothesized that the relative persuasive effects measured by the purchase intention measure summed over all pairs of competing advertisements would result in a positive interaction between repetition and the refutational appeal. The exact locus of the hypothesized greater effect could not be predicted from past evidence since persuasion was always measured after both the defense and the attack. Also, the total effect of the communications in research such as McGuire's was capable of being measured by asking only one question on the concerned topic or topics. In this experiment, the total effect of repetition of the test brand ads on any brand pair was calculated by measuring the effect on

TABLE 1 *Repeated Supportive and Refutational Advertisements and Competitive Advertisements*

Repeated Ad	Supportive Appeal	Refutational Appeal	Competitive Ad
Bayer aspirin	"Bayer works wonders. Relax with Bayer . . . Bayer is 100% aspirin."	"Buffer it, square it, squeeze it, fizz it, . . . Nothing has ever improved aspirin. Bayer is 100% aspirin."	Bufferin. "Take aspirin. I did but I still have a headache. Next time take Bufferin."
Lava soap	"For real dirty hands, reach for Lava—the soap that can really clean . . ."	"Lava—world's worst bath soap! Lava users have revolted. They argue that Lava is not only a good soap for hands but for anything else too . . ."	Phase III. "Both a deodorant and a cream soap . . ."
Parker pen	"Just one could be all you ever need. At $1.98 it's the best pen value in the world. Up to 80,000 words . . ."	"Why pay $1.98 for a ball-point pen? You can get them for 49¢, 69¢, or for free. The kind that skip, stutter, etc. and run out of ink. You pay $1.98 for a Parker, but you never have to buy another."	Scripto. "Only 49¢."
Renault automobiles	"Sales are climbing. Renault's new features and fine construction are paying off . . ."	"Sure, they save money but I wouldn't want to take a long trip in one. Foreign cars are easy on the wallet but hard on everything else. Renault is changing all that."	Volvo. "The car that won't self-destruct in two years."
Slender diet drink	"The same appetite that made you fat can make you thin. Slender is a bonafide meal."	"A 225 calorie meal is easy. A good tasting 225 calorie meal is hard . . ."	Sego. "For the joy of a slender figure . . . Sego has more tasty flavors"

both brands and then subtracting the gain (or loss) of one from the other.

For each measured product class, the purchase intention measure asked a subject to assume she was on a shopping trip and to indicate which (if any) of eight brands she was most likely to purchase, which brand she was next most likely to purchase, and which ranked third in likelihood of purchase. If a brand were ranked, it received a purchase intention score of "1"; if that brand were not one of the top three in terms of purchase intention, it received a score of "0." Purchase intention scores were calculated for both the repeatedly advertised test brands and the twice-advertised competitor brands. In order to summarize the overall competitive effects of the repeated ads, a measure labeled *net purchase intention* was calculated. This measure subtracted the purchase intention score for the competitor brand from the score for the test brand. The resulting score for each subject was either —1.00, 0, or + 1.00.

There was no support for the hypothesis of greater increases in purchase intention with repetition of the refutational ad appeal as compared to the supportive ad appeal. When tested by an analysis of variance, the effects of repetition on the two appeals were nearly identical on each purchase intention measure. No measure yielded an interaction between appeal and repetition that approached statistical significance.

Although repetition of the refutational appeal did not result in the predicted greater persuasiveness compared to the repeated supportive appeal, past research has emphasized that the refutational appeal has been effective with particular segments. The next hypothesis tested in this experiment predicted that repetition of the refutational appeal would result in greater increases in purchase intention as compared to the supportive appeals for certain specified segments of the responding population.

Respondents were categorized as to their reported usage of each test brand and each competitor brand and were classified as a member of four segments: (I) non-users of either brand; (II) users of the test brand but non-users of the competitor; (III) users of the competitor brand only; and (IV) users of both brands. This grouping allowed estimation of the respondents' prior opinions toward the advertised brands and their probable reactions to the two appeals [7].

For each of the four segments interaction effects between repetition and advertising appeal were predicted for the purchase intention for both the test and competitor brands and then summed to derive the prediction for the net purchase intention score. Table 2 contains the predicted test brand repetition-appeal interactions for each segment.

These predictions used five decision rules based on insights gained from past research results. (1) If the assumed prior attitude toward the test brand were positive relative to the attitude toward the competitor brand, repetition of the supportive appeal would be more effective than repetition of the refutational appeal (Seg-

TABLE 2 *Predictive Model for Hypothesis*

	Segment			
	I	*II*	*III*	*IV*
User of test brand	No	Yes	No	Yes
User of competitor brand	No	No	Yes	Yes
Test brand: assumed relative opinion towards test brand	Neutral	Positive	Negative	Neutral
Predicted direction of repetition-appeal interaction	None	Supportive	Refutational	None
Competitor brand: assumed relative opinion towards competitor brand	Neutral	Negative	Positive	Neutral
Likely to be over-confident with present brand choice	No	Yes	Yes	No
Predicted direction of interaction	Supportive	Refutational	Refutational	Supportive
Predicted direction of interaction on net purchase intention	Supportive	None	Refutational	Supportive

ment II). (2) If the assumed prior attitude toward the test brand were negative, repetition of the refutational appeal would be more effective (Segment III). (3) If the assumed prior attitude toward the test brand were neutral, the effects of the two appeals over repetition would not differ (Segments I and IV). (4) If the assumed prior opinion toward the competitor brand were relatively positive (Segment III), or if it were possible that the respondent were overconfident about her belief in the test brand be-cause she used only one brand and tended to choose her brand with little consideration to other competing brands (Segments II and III), repetition of the refutational appeal would be more effective than the repeated supportive appeal in preventing increases in purchase intention for the competitor brand. (5) If the assumed prior opinion toward the competitor brand were neutral (Segments I and IV), the refutational appeal would be relatively less effective with repetition in controlling purchase intention for the competitor brand than the simpler, more direct, and less modest supportive appeal.

To summarize this complex hypothesis, the most important predictions were the net persuasive effects in each of the four respondent segments. A small relative superiority of the supportive appeal over repetition was predicted for non-users of either brand and for users of both brands. No overall interaction was predicted for users of only the test brand because of hypothesized offsetting interaction effects on purchase intention of the test brand and the competitor brand. Finally, a large difference in the effects of repetition in favor of the refutational appeal was predicted for the segment of users of only the competitor brand.

A linear multiple regression model was used to test the predictions of this hypothesis. For each of the four usage segments, a regression equation estimated the repetition curves for the supportive and refutational ads. Each equation included a constant term, a dummy variable term to indicate the effect of appeal, a term for the number of ad exposures, and an appeal-repetition interaction term which was the product of the second and third variables in the equation. For each dependent variable, there were 48 data points—the mean for each appeal for each of the six ad-exposure levels with each of the four usage categories. The regression model multiplied both the dependent and independent variables by the square root of the sample size of the respective cell. The result of this

manipulation was to weight each cell by the respective sample size. This method of estimation has been referred to as generalized least squares [15]. In this case, the purpose of the generalization was to correct for possible inequalities in the variance of various observations due to differences in sample size. To estimate the statistical significance of any interaction in the predicted direction, a one-tailed t-test with 8 degrees of freedom was used. Where no interactions were predicted, a two-tailed t-test was the criterion.

The exposure curves for both appeals in each of the four respondent segments are presented in Figures 1, 2, 3, and 4. Each figure graphs the mean values over the six exposure levels for three dependent variables: (1) the purchase intention scores of the test brands, (2) the purchase intention scores for the competitor brands, and (3) the net purchase intention scores.

Segment I—Non-users of Both Advertised Brands

The differences between the repetition curves of the two ad appeals were in the predicted directions (Figure 1). The interaction effects for the test brands where no significant interaction was predicted were very slight and insignificant ($t = .41$). Concerning the effects of the repeated test ads on the competitor brands, the supportive appeal demonstrated a downward trend over repetition while the effect of the refutational appeal was slightly positive; the resulting interaction between the two appeals was

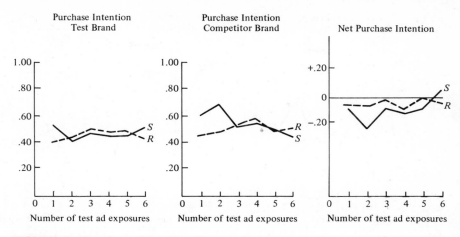

FIGURE 1 *Purchase Intention Scores for Segment I—Non-users of both brands*

significantly in favor of the supportive appeal ($t = 1.90$, $p < .05$). The net difference was, as predicted, in the direction of the supportive appeal; however, this interaction was not significant at the chosen alpha level of .05 ($t = 1.12$).

Segment II—Users of Only the Test Brand

An advantage for the supportive appeal was predicted for the test brands, but an opposite effect in favor of the refutational appeal was predicted for the competitor brands. Although the

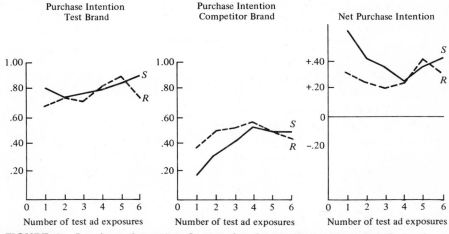

FIGURE 2 *Purchase Intention Scores for Segment II—Users of Only the Test Brand*

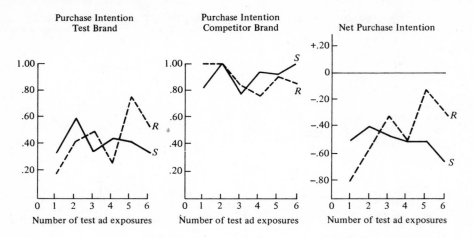

FIGURE 3 *Purchase Intention Scores for Segment III—Users of Only the Competitor Brand*

result of the first prediction was in the predicted direction, the repetition advantage of the supportive appeal was very small and insignificant ($t = .49$). The second prediction was successful and the results were especially interesting. Figure 2 shows the purchase intention scores for the twice-adver-tised competitor brands rose as the supportive ads for the test brands were repeated—an apparent "boomerang" effect. The disadvantage of the supportive appeal compared to the refutational appeal, which was significant ($t = 1.98$, $p < .05$), was predicted on the basis of McGuire's in-

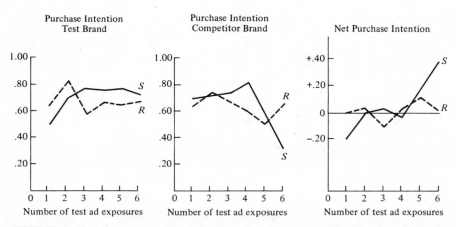

FIGURE 4 *Purchase Intention Scores for Segment IV—Users of Both Brands*

oculation theory which suggested that users of brands which advertised supportive appeals might be susceptible to ads promoting a competing brand. Concerning the net effect, the insignificance of the resulting interaction ($t = 1.60$) supported the prediction.

Segment III—Users of Only the Competitor Brand

Since a greater effect for the repeated two-sided refutational appeal was hypothesized for purchase intention of both the test brand and the competitor brand, a large advantage for the refutational appeal on the net purchase intention measure was also predicted. The results in Figure 3 indicated the superiority of the refutational appeal in this segment. Although the difference favoring the refutational appeal for the test brands was not significant ($t = .84$), the predicted advantage of the repeated refutational appeal in preventing increases in intended purchase for the competitor brands was significant ($t = 2.98$, $p < .01$). Also, the appeal-exposure interaction for the net purchase intention measure was quite pronounced and significantly in favor of the refutational appeal for this segment ($t = 3.91$, $p < .005$). The supportive appeal seemed to be ineffective in persuading people in this segment and indicated a negative effect over repetition, whereas the effects of the refutational appeal increased with added exposure. Figure 3 demonstrates, however, that even the relatively successful refutational appeal was not able to push these

negatively-oriented respondents up to or into a net positive buying attitude toward the unused brands which were repeatedly advertised.

Segment IV—Users of Both Advertised Brands

For this segment (Figure 4), the supportive ads were hypothesized to be more effective with repetition than the refutational ads. This difference was insignificant, as predicted for test brands ($t = 1.82$, $p < .20$) but, contrary to the prediction, was also not significant for the competitor brands ($t = .60$). The net purchase intention was, as predicted, significantly more positively affected by the repeated supportive appeal ($t = 2.69$, $p < .01$). In fact, the supportive appeal was able to move this apparently undecided segment from a slightly negative initial position to a decidedly positive buying attitude after six exposures.

Table 3 summarizes the results of the predictions of this final hypothesis. Concerning the effects of the repeated test brand advertising on the advertised test brands, the interactions in Segments II and III were in the predicted directions but were not significant. No interactions were predicted for Segments I and IV, and no significant differences were found. The predictions of differences in the effects of repetition of the test ads upon the reactions to the competitor ads were more accurate. All the interactions were in the predicted directions; moreover, three of the four predictions were statistically significant. Thus, the employed decision rules correctly predicted the direction of all

TABLE 3 *Summary of Results of Predicted Repetition-Appeal-Segment Interactions*

Respondent Segment	Test Brand		Competitor Brand		Net Effect	
	Predicted	Result	Predicted	Result	Predicted	Result
I	O	O(R)	S	S[a]	S	O(S)
II	S	O(S)	R	R[b]	O	O(R)
III	R	O(R)	R	R[a]	R	R[a]
IV	O	O(S)	S	O(S)	S	S[a]

Direction of non-significant interactions indicated in parentheses.
[a] $p < .01$.
[b] $p < .05$.

hypothesized interactions between appeal, repetition, and user segment. The chance probability of correctly predicting the direction of the interaction in six out of six instances was less than .02. The net persuasive effect of the repeated advertisements was defined as the induced purchase intention for the test brands minus the purchase intention for the competitor brands. Table 3 indicates that the predictions were impressively successful—three of the four predictions were statistically supported by the results, and the fourth was in the predicted direction.

Recall

The more complex refutational appeal should benefit more than the supportive appeal in terms of the extent to which the total verbal message of the ad was perceived and recalled. Repetition should also help to overcome any tendency to selectively screen the refutational communication. Therefore, it was hypothesized that repetition would interact positively with the refutational appeal on a measure of recall of the ad's copy points.

The recall question asked subjects to list each of the shown ads which they could remember and to describe as much as they could about the ad's copy and visuals. A measure labeled *recall verbal quality* measured the portion of the written advertising copy played back. The five coded categories of this variable were: no mention of any of the copy message, an incorrect recall of the message, recall of only the opposing argument in the refutational appeal, recall of most of the message (including both sides of the refutational appeal), and playback of all the main copy points.

To test this hypothesis, the recall verbal quality variable was collapsed into two categories: (1) either none or incorrect verbal recall and (2) any correct playback of copy points of the ad in question. An analysis of variance revealed that repetition of the refutational ads did result in a somewhat greater increase in recall verbal quality than did repetition of the supportive ads (see Table 4); however, the

F-value of the appeal-repetition interaction term was not statistically significant ($F = 2.13$, 5 and 20 d.f., $p < .11$). The main effects of the refutational appeal ($F = 5.95$, 1 and 4 d.f., $p < .075$) and of repetition ($F = 2.85$, 5 and 20 d.f., $p < .05$) were both significant. Thus, although repetition did appear to increase recall of the copy of the refutational ads more than that of the supportive ads, the insignificance of the result rejected the hypothesis.

TABLE 4 *Comparison of Recall Measures between Two Ad Appeals*

	Recall Verbal Quality	
Exposures	Refutational Appeal	Supportive Appeal
1	.05	.03
2	.10	.04
3	.12	.04
4	.14	.14
5	.24	.07
6	.22	.13
Mean	.145	.075

Sample size = 100 per exposure level.

Advertising folklore argues against mentioning competitive arguments because of the possibility of aiding the competitor. To test this adage, the recall scores (whether or not an ad was mentioned in free recall) of the competitor ads were examined. If this adage were true, then the recall of the competitor ads opposing the refutational ads should be greater than the recall of the same ads when confronting the supportive ads. When the recall results were examined for all of the tested ads, there was no significant defference between the two treatment conditions and, hence, no support for the advertising adage.

However, the results for one pair of test and competitor ads did support the expectation of greater recall of the competitor ad when opposing the refutational test ad. The Bayer refutational ad was the only tested ad that directly referred to a competitor. The copy of this ad stated *"Buffer it, square it, squeeze it, fizz it . . . . Nothing has ever improved aspirin, etc."* The supportive Bayer ad was completely positive ("Bayer works wonders. Bayer is 100% aspirin . . . .") and did not refer to a competitor in any way. An examination of the recall scores of the repeated Bayer refutational and supportive ads and of the competitor Bufferin ad indicated the potential danger of alluding to competition. Even though the exposure level of the Bufferin ad remained constant at two, recall of that ad increased as the Bayer refutational ad was repeated from one to six times, while the same Bufferin ad facing the supportive version of the Bayer ad did not exhibit this large increase. Figure 5 graphs the recall scores of the Bufferin ad in the two competitive situations and shows that the supportive Bayer version coincided with fewer increases in recall of the competing Bufferin ad. In fact, respondents who were exposed to the Bayer refutational ad six times and who saw the Bufferin ad only twice recalled the two ads at the same rate—70%. The F-statistics of the linear trend effects on the Bufferin recall scores of ad appeal (5.45, 1 and 222 d.f.),

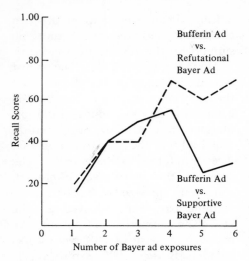

FIGURE 5 *Recall Scores of Bufferin Ad (Twenty Observations per Exposure Condition)*

repetition (9.13, 1 and 228 d.f.), and the appeal-repetition interaction (6.05, 1 and 228 d.f.) were all significant beyond the .025 level. In this particular instance, directly referring to a competitor did appear to help the competitor.

In addition to worrying about aiding a competitor by mentioning him or his arguments, advertisers worry about incomplete or selective retention of only the ad's negative copy. Recoding the recall verbal quality measure allowed a partial examination of the effects of such incomplete recall. One category of the recall verbal quality measure was where a subject recalled only the negative part of the refutational appeal (e.g., "Parker pens are too expensive" or "Renaults are uncomfortable for long trips"). Recall of this type was labeled incomplete or

negative recall and was possible only with the refutational ads. Two other recall verbal quality categories were where the subject recalled nearly all or all of the main copy points (e.g., "Parker pens are expensive, but they'll last forever" or "Renaults used to be uncomfortable and expensive to maintain, but the new models have changed all that"). This type of verbal recall quality was labeled complete or *positive recall*. Analysis of the relationships of positive and negative recall verbal quality to purchase intention offered some interesting insights.

If negative recall is a problem, then this should be reflected in lower purchase intention scores than the more complete positive recall. Table 5 presents the Pearson product-moment correlation coefficients between negative and positive recall and measures of persuasive effect. For the repeated brands, negative recall coincided with lower purchase intention scores, whereas positive recall accompanied higher purchase intention scores. The correlations of negative recall with both purchase intention for the test brands and net purchase intention were significantly negative and the correlations of each of these two variables and positive recall were significantly positive. Although these latter significant relationships were not observed for the purchase intention scores for the competitor brands and even the significant correlations were quite low, the above relationships high-lighted the potential disadvantages of the refutational appeals being incompletely learned or remembered.

TABLE 5 *Relation of Recall Verbal Quality of Repeated Test Brands with Measures of Persuasive Effect*[a]
(Pearson Product-Moment Correlation Coefficients)

	Negative Recall	Positive Recall
Purchase intention—test brand	−.104[b]	.104[b]
Purchase intention—competitor brand	.001	.008
Net purchase intention	−.069[c]	.071[c]
Number of recall responses in category	37	95

[a] Total sample size = 1200.
[b] $p < .01$.
[c] $p < .05$.

DISCUSSION

The overall goal of this experiment was to test the hypothesis that the refutational appeal would significantly interact with the number of repeated advertising exposures. The several significant three-way interactions between repetition, advertising appeal, and respondents segmented on brand usage patterns offered impressive support for this hypothesis.

The fact that the repetition function may vary with the particular advertising situation is very important for media planners. Such differences could be quite easily incorporated into many of the quantitatively sophisticated media models currently in use [1, 9, 19, 27] and should improve the usefulness of these models. Although some modelers have stated that their models' results were insensitive to small changes in the assigned frequency weights [4, 10], some of the differences indicated by this research are much larger than those which may have been considered. In fact, data based on the varying purchase intention results for different segments from this experiment were recently tested in the MEDIAC media planning system [19]. When compared to another run which employed only a single "average" repetition function, the media schedule output based on the varying repetition curves run based on the above results was considerably different in terms of reach, frequency, and total media impressions [28].

These results also may be used to formulate the content of advertising campaigns. Given the limitations of a laboratory experiment, the results demonstrated that microtheoretical notions [25] gained from social psychological research may be replicated in advertising situations. The greater effectiveness of refutational ad appeals for people who had never used the advertised brand helped to identify situations in which refutational ad appeals may be most effective. These situations might include: (1) a new product which must overcome some consumer objections (such as a rubbish compactor); (2) a brand with a low market share that wants to refute a large competitor's claims of superiority (such as the Avis vs. Hertz campaign); and (3) a high selling brand able to isolate a segment which is negatively oriented toward that brand (such as Allstate Insurance and the segment of *Consumer Reports* readers). At the very least, the results of this experiment emphasize the need to continually monitor the changing consumer market in order to be able to assess the probable existing segments and potential reactions to different advertising appeals.

When the refutational appeal is deemed appropriate, some hints can be gained from this research about a proper ad format. The unique potential disadvantage of incomplete or negative recall of the refutational appeal is very salient in advertising where exposure, attention, perception, and learning are commonly unmotivated and often selective. A common format of current refutational print ads presents the attacking statement or question in the headline and then proceeds to refute that claim or answer the question in the body copy. Such a format may be quite attention-getting and clever. However, in order to help eliminate the danger of incomplete negative recall, advertisers should perhaps sacrifice some cleverness and emphasize the refuting answer at least as much as the attack. There has been some speculation that refutational appeals might be less effective in the more intrusive (less choice) medium of television than in the less intrusive (more choice) print media [26]. However, the intrusiveness of television and other broadcast media might be more successful in completely communicating both sides of the refutational appeal. Also, advertisers should perhaps be wary of direct mention of a competitor until more research is done.

Finally, it should be noted that this experiment used a laboratory setting to expose the repeated ads and to measure their effects. Although this design and setting eliminated many shortcomings of past repetition research [29], variations in several areas could offer confidence in the reliability of the findings and further generalize the results. These changes might involve greater naturalness of the viewing environment; use of a different experimental cover (the "Shopping of the Future"); different sets of refutational and supportive ads; and wider manipulation of the exposure levels of both the test ads and competitors. Measurement improvements would involve greater probing in recall verbal quality [17, 18, 21]; rating the persuasiveness of the ads on specific product dimensions (e.g., reliability, durability, and comfort for Renaults) and on several ad dimensions (e.g., believability, defensiveness, simplicity); and a more independent and extensive usage classification (pantry audits or more extensive self-reports from another period). Given replication of the laboratory results, the findings should be tested in field experiments and in actual advertising campaigns. Some field work is now in progress [25, 30, 34].

REFERENCES

1. Aaker, David A. "On Methods: A Probabilistic Approach to Industrial Media Selection," *Journal of Advertising Research*, 8 (September 1968), 46–55.
2. Bither, Stewart W., Ira J. Dolich, and Elaine B. Nell. "The Application of Attitude Immunization Techniques in Marketing," *Journal of Marketing Research*, 8 (February 1971), 56–61.
3. Brehm, Jack W. *A Theory of Psychological Reactance*, New York: Academic Press, 1966.
4. Brown, Douglas B. "A Practical Procedure for Media Selection," *Journal of Marketing Research*, 4 (August 1967), 262–9.
5. Chu, Godman C. "Prior Familiarity, Perceived Bias, and One-Sided versus Two-Sided Communications," *Journal of Experimental Social Psychology*, 3 (July 1967), 243–54.
6. Engel, James F., Hugh G. Wales, and Martin R. Warshaw. *Promotional Strategy*. Homewood, Ill.: Irwin, 1967.
7. Faison, Edmund W. J. "Effectiveness of One-Sided and Two-Sided Mass Communications in Advertising," *Public Opinion Quarterly*, 25 (Fall 1961), 468–9.
8. Freedman, Jonathan L. and David O. Sears. "Selective Exposure," in Leonard Berkowitz, ed., *Advances in Experimental Social Psychology, Vol. 2*. New York: Academic Press, 1965, 57–97.
9. Gensch, Dennis H. "A Computer Simulation Model for Selecting Advertising Schedules," *Journal of Marketing Research*, 6 (May 1969), 203–14.
10. Gluck, Donald J. "How Many Times to Run the Same Ad?" paper presented at TIMS International Meeting, New York, 1969.
11. Greenberg, Allan. "Is Communication Research Really Worthwhile?" *Journal of Marketing*, 5 (January 1967), 48–50.
12. Haskins, Jack B. *How to Evaluate Mass Communications*. New York: Advertising Research Foundation, 1968.
13. Hovland, Carl I., Arthur A. Lumsdaine, and Fred D. Sheffield. *Experimentation on Mass Communication*. Princeton, N. J.: Princeton University Press, 1949.
14. Insko, Chester A. "One-Sided versus Two-Sided Communications and Counter-communications," *Journal of Abnormal and Social Psychology*, 65 (September 1962), 203–6.
15. Johnston, John. *Econometric Methods*. New York: McGraw-Hill, 1963.
16. Jones, Russell A. and Jack W. Brehm. "Persuasiveness of One- and Two-Sided Communications as a Function of Awareness That There Are Two Sides," *Journal of Experimental Social Psychology*, 6 (January 1970), 47–56.
17. Krugman, Herbert E. "Answering Some Unanswered Questions in Measuring Advertising Effectiveness," *Proceedings*. 12th Annual Conference, Advertising Research Foundation, 1966, 18–23.
18. Leavitt, Clark. "Structural Analysis — A Quantitative Measure,"

Journal of Advertising Research, 8 (September 1968), 3–6.

19. Little, John D. C. and Leonard M. Lodish. "A Media Planning Calculus," *Operations Research,* 17 (January–February 1969), 1–35.

20. Lumsdaine, Arthur A. and Irving L. Janis. "Resistance to Counterpropaganda Produced by a One-sided versus a Two-Sided Propaganda Presentation," *Public Opinion Quarterly,* 17 (Fall 1953), 311–318.

21. McConville, Maureen N. and Clark Leavitt. "Predicting Product Related Recall from Verbal Response," *Proceedings.* 76th Annual Convention, American Psychological Association, 1968, 677–8.

22. McGuire, William J. "Inducing Resistance to Persuasion: Some Contemporary Approaches," in Leonard Berkowitz, ed., *Advances in Experimental Social Psychology, Vol. 1.* New York: Academic Press, 1964, 191–229.

23. Mills, Judson. "Interest in Supporting and Discrepant Information," in Robert P. Abelson, et al., eds., *Theories of Cognitive Consistency: A Sourcebook.* Chicago: Rand McNally, 1968, 771–6.

24. Ray, Michael L. "Biases in Selection of Messages Designed to Induce Resistance to Persuasion," *Journal of Personality and Social Psychology,* 9 (August 1968), 335–9.

25. ———. "The Present and Potential Linkages between the Microtheoretical Notions of Behavioral Science and the Problems of Advertising: A Proposal for a Research System," in Harry Davis and Alvin Silk, eds., *The Behavioral and Management Sciences in Marketing.* New York: Ronald, in press.

26. ———. "The Refutational Approach to Advertising," paper presented at the Association for Education in Journalism Meetings, Denver, 1967.

27. ——— and Richard Clark. "Focus," unpublished paper, Graduate School of Business, Stanford University, 1970.

28. Ray, Michael L. and Alan G. Sawyer. "Behavioral Measurement for Marketing Models: Estimating the Repetition Function for Advertising Media Models." *Management Science,* 18 (December 1971), 73–89.

29. ———. "A Laboratory Technique for Estimating the Repetition Function for Advertising Media Models," *Journal of Marketing Research,* 8 (February 1971), 20–9.

30. ——— and Edward C. Strong. "Frequency Effects Revisited," *Journal of Advertising Research,* 11 (February 1971), 14–20.

31. Sawyer, Alan G. "An Application of Communication Theory to Advertising," *First Annual Proceedings of the Northeast Regional Conference of the American Institute of Decision Sciences,* in press.

32. ———. "A Laboratory Experimental Investigation of the Effects of Repetition of Advertising," unpublished doctoral dissertation, Stanford University, 1971.

33. Sears, David O. "The Paradox of

De Facto Selective Exposure without Preference for Supportive Information," in Robert P. Abelson, et al., eds., *Theories of Cognitive Consistency: A Sourcebook.* Chicago: Rand McNally, 1968, 777–87.

34. Strong, Edward C. "The Effects of Repetition in Advertising: A Field Study," unpublished doctoral dissertation, Stanford University, 1972.

35. Tannenbaum, Percy H. "The Congruity Principle Revisited: Studies in the Reduction, Induction, and Generalization of Persuasion," in Leonard Berkowitz, ed., *Advances in Experimental Social Psychology, Vol. 3.* New York: Academic Press, 1967, 271–320.

Chapter 16

Ethics in the Conduct of Marketing Research

One of the most neglected aspects of marketing research concerns
the various ethical dimensions inherent in research. The area of
ethics and value systems is a complex philosophical thicket.
The reader will have his own position, of course, whether he realizes
it or not. However, the reader should find some interesting
contrasts between his own position and those of various
professional associations relevant to marketing. A number of
ethical issues are presented in this chapter to challenge
the reader's own position.

Introduction

Ethics is that branch of philosophy concerned with morality and its problems and judgments.[1] There are two common uses of the terms ethics or morals. The first use is of a problematic nature; we simply state that something is or is not an ethical issue or problem. The second use is judgmental; the terms ethics or morals are used as the equivalent of goodness (or badness) and wrongness (or rightness). In the first usage one merely states, for example, that the stress induced in a subject during an experiment is an ethical or moral question. In the second usage, for example, we may judge that the deliberate inducement of stress or anxiety in a subject in an experiment is wrong or right. Typically, neither use of the term ethics is outwardly displayed or evidenced in the practice of marketing research, that is, neither problematic nor judgmental considerations are given explicit consideration, at least to the point where an individual not involved in the research project is able to see that one or both issues were thought over by the researcher. For that matter it is not evident in the discussion of marketing research either. (A review of nearly all marketing research texts, some eight books, considered to be important at some point in the development of marketing research did not uncover even one mention of the word ethics.)

The ethical question in marketing research has two basic facets. The first and most basic is the responsibility the researcher has to respondents or subjects. This is primary in the sense that, if the rights of respondents to ethical treatment are not respected, the field may find itself cut off from this rich source of data by both the force of law and public opinion. Secondly, the researcher has responsibilities to the client he is serving. Both facets concern the processes of marketing research. Another basic concern in marketing, generally, is the use of the results of marketing research. This particular concern will be looked at only briefly. The fundamental question raised here is whether the information gathered is used by the researcher or his client to manipulate the relevant market segments in ways which may not be compatible with the best interests of those segments (however, "best interests"

---

[1] W. K. Frankena, *Ethics*, (Princeton, N. J.: Prentice-Hall, 1963). See also P. Abelson and K. Nielsen, "History of Ethics," *Encyclopedia of Philosophy* (New York: Macmillan, 1967).

may be defined). Many social critics claim marketers do this. It is also argued, on the other hand, that the collection and use of data may not only increase the consumers' ability to make better choices but also widen the range of choices.[2] For example, marketing research can determine what information or knowledge buyers lack. Marketers can respond by supplying the appropriate information buyers need to make a wise purchase. Also, in response to learning what needs are insufficiently satisfied marketers can introduce new products targeted toward these needs thus widening the range of choices available to consumers. Thus, marketing research is one very important mechanism allowing consumers to articulate their needs and interests. This is also a criticism of marketing in two senses. First, there is an overreaction to consumer needs resulting in products having only subtle distinctions at best. Second, and more important, marketing responds to the needs of the more affluent and neglects the poor and disadvantaged who have fewer resources which are attractive to marketers. This is, of course, a matter of debate. It remains to be determined whether or not new product venture groups (or their equivalent) systematically ignore disadvantaged groups either in trying to match an existing product with an appropriate market segment or in conducting product need assessment studies to learn what products might be developed for market exploitation.

Professional Codes of Ethics

That the question of ethics in market research is real can be seen in the actions of the American Marketing Association. In June 1962, the Association adopted its first Marketing Research Code of Ethics. In 1972, that code was updated and revised and is reproduced in Table 16.1. As in any such attempt, the Code represents minimum standards. As such, it sets concrete guidelines for the practitioner. It would be well, however, for anyone involved in performing, buying, or using research to be aware of the broader issues underlying those concrete guidelines. Tables 16.2, 16.3, and 16.4 are the ethical codes of the American Sociological Association, the American Psychological Association, and the Operations Research Society, respectively. These are disciplines marketers draw heavily upon for research concepts and methodology. Also, sociologists and psychologists are often called upon to participate directly in marketing research. Therefore, it is of interest to study the codes of ethics to which they presumably subscribe. The APA code seems more strict than the ASA code, which in turn seems more strict than that of the AMA. The APA code has greater protection for the subject or respondent than either the ASA or AMA code, whereas the latter two codes favor client's protection more than does

---

[2] Herbert C. Kelman, "The Rights of the Subject in Social Research: An Analysis in Terms of Relative Power and Legitimacy," *American Psychologist*, Vol. 27, No. 11 (November 1972), pp. 989–1016.

TABLE 16.1   *American Marketing Association Marketing Research Code of Ethics*

The American Marketing Association, in furtherance of its central objective of the advancement of science in marketing and in recognition of its obligation to the public, has established these principles of ethical practice of marketing research for the guidance of its members. In an increasingly complex society, marketing management is more and more dependent upon marketing information intelligently and systematically obtained. The consumer is the source of much of this information. Seeking the cooperation of the consumer in the development of information, marketing management must acknowledge its obligation to protect the public from misrepresentation and exploitation under the guise of research.

Similarly the research practitioner has an obligation to the discipline he practices and to those who provide support for his practice—an obligation to adhere to basic and commonly accepted standards of scientific investigation as they apply to the domain of marketing research.

It is the intent of this code to define ethical standards required of marketing research in satisfying these obligations.

Adherence to this code will assure the users of marketing research that the research was done in accordance with acceptable ethical practices. Those engaged in research will find in this code an affirmation of sound and honest basic principles which have developed over the years as the profession has grown. The field interviewers who are the point of contact between the profession and the consumer will also find guidance in fulfilling their vitally important role.

FOR RESEARCH USERS, PRACTITIONERS AND INTERVIEWERS

1. No individual or organization will undertake any activity which is directly or indirectly represented to be marketing research, but which has as its real purpose the attempted sale of merchandise or services to some or all of the respondents interviewed in the course of the research.

2. If a respondent has been led to believe, directly or indirectly, that he is participating in a marketing research survey and that his anonymity will be protected, his name shall not be made known to anyone outside the research organization or research department, or used for other than research purposes.

FOR RESEARCH PRACTITIONERS

1. There will be no intentional or deliberate misrepresentation of research methods or results. An adequate description of methods employed will be made available upon request to the sponsor of the research. Evidence that field work has been completed according to specifications will, upon request,

TABLE 16.1 *(continued)*

be made available to buyers of research.

2. The identity of the survey sponsor and/or the ultimate client for whom a survey is being done will be held in confidence at all times, unless this identity is to be revealed as part of the research design. Research information shall be held in confidence by the research organization or department and not used for personal gain or made available to any outside party unless the client specifically authorizes such release.

3. A research organization shall not undertake marketing studies for competitive clients when such studies would jeopardize the confidential nature of client-agency relationships.

FOR USERS OF MARKETING RESEARCH

1. A user of research shall not knowingly disseminate conclusions from a given research project or service that are inconsistent with or not warranted by the data.

2. To the extent that there is involved in a research project a unique design involving techniques, approaches or concepts not commonly

available to research practitioners, the prospective user of research shall not solicit such a design from one practitioner and deliver it to another for execution without the approval of the design originator.

FOR FIELD INTERVIEWERS

1. Research assignments and materials received, as well as information obtained from respondents, shall be held in confidence by the interviewer and revealed to no one except the research organization conducting the marketing study.

2. No information gained through a marketing research activity shall be used directly or indirectly, for the personal gain or advantage of the interviewer.

3. Interviews shall be conducted in strict accordance with specifications and instructions received.

4. An interviewer shall not carry out two or more interviewing assignments simultaneously unless authorized by all contractors or employers concerned.

Members of the American Marketing Association will be expected to conduct themselves in accordance with the provisions of this Code in all of their marketing research activities.

---

the APA code. The ASA code focuses more on the research setting, exclusive of the subject or respondent, and emphasizes issues involved in associating with particular clients such as those who may wish to use the results of research in ways adjudged harmful. The AMA code, apart from saying that the research process should not be used as a selling opportunity, has little to say about what clients do with the research results. The Operations Research

TABLE 16.2 *American Sociological Association Code of Ethics*

PREAMBLE

Sociological inquiry is often disturbing to many persons and groups. Its results may challenge long-established beliefs and lead to change in old taboos. In consequence such findings may create demands for the suppression or control of this inquiry or for a dilution of the findings. Similarly, the results of sociological investigation may be of significant use to individuals in power—whether in government, in the private sphere, or in the universities—because such findings, suitably manipulated, may facilitate the misuse of power. Knowledge is a form of power, and in a society increasingly dependent on knowledge, the control of information creates the potential for political manipulation.

For these reasons, we affirm the autonomy of sociological inquiry. The sociologist must be responsive, first and foremost, to the truth of his investigation. Sociology must not be an instrument of any person or group who seeks to suppress or misuse knowledge. The fate of sociology as a science is dependent upon the fate of free inquiry in an open society.

At the same time this search for social truths must itself operate within constraints. Its limits arise when inquiry infringes on the rights of individuals to be treated as persons, to be considered—in the renewable phrase of Kant—as ends and not as means. Just as sociologists must not distort or manipulate truth to serve untruthful ends, so too they must not manipulate persons to serve their quest for truth. The study of society, being the study of human beings, imposes the responsibility of respecting the integrity, promoting the dignity, and maintaining the autonomy of these persons.

To fulfill these responsibilities, we, the members of the American Sociological Association, affirm the following Code of Ethics:

CODE OF ETHICS

1. Objectivity in Research

In his research the sociologist must maintain scientific objectivity.

2. Integrity in Research

The sociologist should recognize his own limitations and, when appropriate, seek more expert assistance or decline to undertake research beyond his competence. He must not misrepresent his own abilities, or the competence of his staff to conduct a particular research project.

3. Respect of the Research Subject's Rights to Privacy and Dignity

Every person is entitled to the right of privacy and dignity of treatment. The sociologist must respect these rights.

4. Protection of Subjects from Personal Harm

All research should avoid causing personal harm to subjects used in research.

TABLE 16.2 *(continued)*

5. Preservation of Confidentiality of Research Data

Confidential information provided by a research subject must be treated as such by the sociologist. Even though research information is not a privileged communication under the law, the sociologist must, as far as possible, protect subjects and informants. Any promises made to such persons must be honored. However, provided that he respects the assurances he has given his subjects, the sociologist has no obligation to withhold information of misconduct of individuals or organizations.

If an informant or other subject should wish, however, he can formally release the researcher of a promise of confidentiality. The provisions of this section apply to all members of research organizations (i.e., interviewers, coders, clerical staff, etc.), and it is the responsibility of the chief investigators to see that they are instructed in the necessity and importance of maintaining the confidentiality of the data. The obligation of the sociologist includes the use and storage of original data to which a subject's name is attached. When requested, the identity of an organization or subject must be adequately disguised in publication.

6. Presentation of Research Findings

The sociologist must present his findings honestly and without distor-

tion. There should be no omission of data from a research report which might significantly modify the interpretation of findings.

7. Misuse of Research Role

The sociologist must not use his role as a cover to obtain information for other than professional purposes.

8. Acknowledgment of Research Collaboration and Assistance

The sociologist must acknowledge the professional contributions or assistance of all persons who collaborated in the research.

9. Disclosure of the Sources of Financial Support

The sociologist must report fully all sources of financial support in his research publications and any special relations to the sponsor that might affect the interpretation of the findings.

10. Distortion of Findings by Sponsor

The sociologist is obliged to clarify publicly any distortion by a sponsor or client of the findings of a research project in which he has participated.

11. Disassociation from Unethical Research Arrangements

The sociologist must not accept such grants, contracts, or research assignments as appear likely to require violation of the principles above, and must publicly terminate the work or

TABLE 16.2 *(continued)*

formally disassociate himself from the research if he discovers such a violation and is unable to achieve its correction.

12. Interpretation of Ethical Principles

When the meaning and application of these principles are unclear, the sociologist should seek the judgment of the relevant agency or committee designated by the American Sociological Association. Such consultation, however, does not free the sociologist from his individual responsibility for decisions or from his accountability to the profession.

13. Applicability of Principles

In the conduct of research the principles enunciated above should apply to research in any area either within or outside the United States of America.

TABLE 16.3 *American Psychological Association Code of Ethics*

ETHICAL PRINCIPLES IN THE CONDUCT OF RESEARCH WITH HUMAN PARTICIPANTS

The decision to undertake research should rest upon a considered judgment by the individual psychologist about how best to contribute to psychological science and to human welfare. The responsible psychologist weighs alternative directions in which personal energies and resources might be invested. Having made the decision to conduct research, psychologists must carry out their investigations with respect for the people who participate and with concern for their dignity and welfare. The Principles that follow make explicit the investigator's ethical responsibilities toward participants over the course of research, from the initial decision to pursue a study to the steps necessary to protect the confidentiality of research data.

1. In planning a study the investigator has the personal responsibility to make a careful evaluation of its ethical acceptability, taking into account these Principles for research with human beings. To the extent that this appraisal, weighing scientific and humane values suggests a deviation from any Principle, the investigator incurs an increasingly serious obligation to seek ethical advice and to observe even more stringent safeguards to protect the rights of the human research participants.

2. Responsibility for the establishment and maintenance of acceptable ethical practice in research always remains with the individual investigator. The investigator is also responsible for the ethical treatment of research participants by collaborators, assistants, students and employees, all of whom,

TABLE 16.3 *(continued)*

however, incur parallel obligations.

3. Ethical practice requires the investigator to inform the participant of all features of the research that reasonably might be expected to influence willingness to participate, and to explain all other aspects of the research about which the participant inquires. Failure to make full disclosure gives added emphasis to the investigator's abiding responsibility to protect the welfare and dignity of the research participant.

4. Openness and honesty are essential characteristics of the relationship between investigator and research participant. When the methodological requirements of a study necessitate concealment or deception, the investigator is required to ensure the participant's understanding of the reasons for this action and to restore the quality of the relationship with the investigator.

5. Ethical research practice requires the investigator to respect the individual's freedom to decline to participate in research or to discontinue participation at any time. The obligation to protect this freedom requires special vigilance when the investigator is in a position of power over the participant. The decision to limit this freedom gives added emphasis to the investigator's abiding responsibility

to protect the participant's dignity and welfare.

6. Ethically acceptable research begins with the establishment of a clear and fair agreement between the investigator and the research participant that clarifies the responsibilities of each. The investigator has the obligation to honor all promises and commitments included in that agreement.

7. The ethical investigator protects participants from physical and mental discomfort, harm and danger. If the risk of such consequences exists, the investigator is required to inform the participant of that fact, secure consent before proceeding, and take all possible measures to minimize distress. A research procedure may not be used if it is likely to cause serious and lasting harm to participants.

8. After the data are collected, ethical practice requires the investigator to provide the participant with a full clarification of the nature of the study and to remove any misconceptions that may have arisen. Where scientific or humane values justify delaying or withholding information, the investigator acquires a special responsibility to assure that there are no damaging consequences for the participant.

9. Where research procedures may result in undesirable consequences for the participant, the investi-

TABLE 16.3 *(continued)*

gator has the responsibility to detect and remove or correct these consequences, including, where relevant, long-term aftereffects.
10. Information obtained about the research participants during the course of an investigation is confidential. When the possibility

exists that others may obtain access to such information, ethical research practice requires that this possibility, together with the plans for protecting confidentiality, be explained to the participants as a part of the procedure for obtaining informed consent.

TABLE 16.4 *Guidelines for Professional Practice in Operations Research*

GUIDELINES FOR PROFESSIONAL PRACTICE

Operations research (OR) is a science that is devoted to describing, understanding, and predicting the behavior of man-machine systems operating in organizational environments.

General

In dealing with a problem posed by an operating organization, an operations analyst should:
- Apply the scientific spirit (open, explicit, and objective) to his work.
- Take a broad and disinterested view, free of parochialism, inflexibility, or prior prejudice, that includes a lively sense of the public interest, as well as of the narrower interests of the organization involved.
- Become thoroughly familiar with all aspects of the organization's operations relevant to the problem, as well as forces outside the organization that can impact on it.
- Be responsive to the evidence adduced either as inputs or outputs of the study.

- Be equipped to bring to bear on the problem the most modern knowledge, approach, and techniques of analysis, while avoiding known pitfalls.
- Consider alternative approaches to the problem.
- Obtain access to all information that can reasonably be thought to be needed for the problem's solution, or to have a possibly significant bearing on it.
- Scrupulously observe any ground rules about confidentiality laid down by the organization being served.
- Report the study's results only to the organizational elements sponsoring the study, unless specifically directed by them to report to a wider audience.
- Keep the sponsoring elements as fully involved and informed on the work throughout its duration as is reasonable and feasible.
- Be aware of the fact that in many complex situations the study may illuminate only a portion (albeit a significant one) of the total problem.

TABLE 16.4   *(continued)*

In Beginning a Study

Experience has shown that establishing an adequate initial framework for a study is a key step that frequently plays a decisive role in its ultimate success. Therefore, *in close cooperation with the client throughout this step,* analysts should:

• Collect information and data adequate to provide the initial framework for the study.

• Take great care in formulating the problem or issue to be addressed, keeping in mind the client's needs.

• Use both imagination and meticulous attention to detail in designing alternatives for examination in the study.

• Recognize explicitly the uncertainties associated with the problem.

• Understand the subjective, as well as objective, aspects of the problem.

• Evolve appropriate criteria on the basis of which the study's results can be evaluated.

• Describe the limits of the proposed study, so that both analyst and client have a clear idea of what will *not* be done, as well as what *will* be done.

• Recognize that many of the elements involved in this step may have to be revised as the study proceeds, in the light of the knowledge the enquiry generates.

In Conducting a Study

In this step, whose activities center largely in the analytical staff, the analysts should:

• Assemble relevant information and data of verified reliability, or if not available, inputs of judiciously and suitably estimated unreliability, so that the impacts of uncertainty can be assessed in the results.

• Use (develop or choose) the best relevant models and technical tools and use them with a rigor appropriate to the problem in hand, while at the same time achieving a reasonable balance between the demands of the problem and a reasonable economy of effort.

• Employ appropriate accuracy checks, wherever possible.

• Check the sensitivity of the results to variations in assumptions and inputs, and especially to uncertainties identified in the formulation, or the input data.

• Keep in mind the need for a continuing reassessment, throughout this step, of the formulations and assumptions with which the analysis began, and of changing them and recycling the analysis when this appears to be needed.

In Reporting a Study

Recognizing that the ultimate effectiveness of a study critically depends on how well its findings are communicated, understood, and then acted upon, the analyst should:

• Insofar as possible, use the vocabulary of his client, introducing only such new concepts and terminology as are essential to understanding the findings (the jargon and technicalities of operations research should be

TABLE 16.4 *(continued)*

avoided to the greatest extent possible).

• Report clearly the problem formulation finally adopted (perhaps changed from the one with which the study began), the key assumptions used, the major alternatives considered, the essentials of the input information (and inaccuracies therein), the criteria employed (also perhaps changed from the ones with which the study began), the findings (including their sensitivity to realistic changes in assumptions, or the uncertainty in data), and their implications for policy and action.

• Delineate conscientiously what was accomplished by the study, and perhaps even more important, what was not considered or accomplished.

• Specify the limitations on methodology or conclusions that should be observed, and spell out with candor instances where definitive results are not provided by the analysis.

• Set the study in the larger context appropriate for it.

• Prepare a written report on at least two levels: one for the client following the precepts outlined above (both a short and long form of this report are frequently useful), and another fully technical report that can be examined by operations- and systems-research scientists.

• Be prepared to participate in any follow-up or implementation activities, both to assist with them and to evaluate their results.

In Reviewing a Study

In reviewing studies arising from OR practice, either one's own or someone else's, it is particularly important to keep in mind that this practice is performed in a scientific spirit. Therefore, in this role the analyst should:

• Test the work against the guidelines presented above.

• Be rigorous but fair in his thought.

• Be candid about the basis for his statements.

• Be realistic about his demands in the light of the context and scope of the study being examined.

• Avoid *ad hominem* attacks, either veiled or overt.

In Following Up Studies

In this activity, the analyst will find guidelines among those already presented. However, it is perhaps useful to add that he should be particularly conscientious in recognizing and reporting the unpredicted results and unpleasant surprises that may emerge and the possible necessity for conducting further investigations.

Society guidelines, which is of great controversy in that association, seems to be well balanced and stresses the importance of making explicit what was not done and how this affects the interpretation and utilization of data and advice.

Some insight into the ethical perspectives of directors of marketing research is available from a study by C. Merle Crawford.[3] In his study he posed a series of twenty "action" situations in which respondents were to approve or disapprove the action taken by a marketing research director in a hypothetical company. Some of the results of this study are presented in Table 16.5. In reading this table it is necessary to keep in mind, as Crawford cautions in his report, that people tend to respond in normative ways to questions about ethics. That is, responses often reflect what a person thinks is "acceptable" to society or his peers when in reality he may respond in ways considered unacceptable. Thus, while 33 percent of the people surveyed by Crawford approve of the use of hidden tape recorders, a somewhat larger percentage may actually use them if they were in a situation where such a use of tape recorders was an issue.

Rights of Respondents and Subjects

The research code specifies that respondents in research have three rights. One is that their participation in research be just that, not a distinguished sales call.[4] The second is the protection of anonymity, if that has been agreed to or promised by the research organization. The third and last is that any information given shall be held in confidence and used only for the purposes of research.

More basic questions are involved, however. These concern such topics as human dignity, privacy, and freedom from manipulation. Given the growth of experimental techniques in marketing research in addition to the survey technique, careful evaluation of this area is warranted. Some of the questions being asked about this topic are presented in Table 16.6. It should be noted that these questions are the same being asked by all of the social sciences. Psychologists, social psychologists, sociologists, political scientists—all students of human behavior, whether theoretical or applied, are concerned with these same questions.

Primary to the bulk of marketing research is the issue of privacy. As has been asked, is it merely that we as researchers have the right to ask people questions and they, in turn have the right to refuse to answer, or is there more to it? The following points have been made.[5]

1. *Not all respondents are aware of their right to refuse to participate in surveys.* It has been noted that many respondents, especially those not well

---

[3] C. M. Crawford, "Attitudes of Marketing Executives Toward Ethics in Marketing Research," *Journal of Marketing*, Vol. 34 (April 1970), pp. 46–52.

[4] For a note on phony surveys, see "Encyclofrandia," *New York*, Vol. 5 (August 21, 1972), p. 21.

[5] R. O. Carlson, "The Issue of Privacy in Public Opinion Research," *Public Opinion Quarterly*, Vol. 31 (Spring 1967), pp. 1–8. This section borrows heavily on his thinking.

TABLE 16.5 *Responses of Marketing Research Direction to Hypothetical Situations Involving Ethical Issues*

Situation	Attitude of Research Directors (n = 412)	
	Approve	*Disapprove*
Selected Research Techniques		
Ultraviolet Ink. A project director recently came in to request permission to use ultraviolet ink in precoding questionnaires on a mail survey. He pointed out that the letter referred to an anonymous survey, but he said he needed respondent identification to permit adequate cross tabulations of the data. The M. R. Director gave his approval.	29%	70%
Hidden Tape Recorders. In a study intended to probe rather deeply into the buying motivations of a group of wholesale customers by use of a semistructured personal interview form, the M. R. Director authorized the use of the department's special attache cases equipped with hidden tape recorders.	33%	67%
One-Way Mirrors. One product of the X Company is brassieres, and the firm has recently been having difficulty making some decisions on a new line. Information was critically needed concerning the manner in which women put on their brassieres. So the M. R. Director designed a study in which two local stores cooperated in putting one-way mirrors in their foundations dressing rooms. Observers behind these mirrors successfully gathered the necessary information.	20%	78%
Fake Long Distance Calls. Some of X Company's customers are busy executives, hard to reach by normal interviewing methods. Accordingly, the market research department recently conducted a study in which interviewers called "long distance" from nearby cities. They were successful in getting through to busy executives in almost every instance.	88%	10%
Fake Research Firm. In another study, this one concerning magazine reading habits, the M. R. Director decided to contact a sample of consumers under the name of Media Research Institute. This fictitious company name successfully camouflaged the identity of the sponsor of the study.	84%	13%

TABLE 16.5 *(continued)*

Situation	Attitude of Research Directors (n = 412)	
	Approve	Disapprove
Exchange of Price Data. X Company belongs to a trade association which includes an active marketing research subgroup. At the meetings of this subgroup, the M. R. Director regularly exchanges confidential price information. In turn, he gives the competitive information to the X Company sales department, but is careful not to let the marketing vice-president know about it. Profits are substantially enhanced, and top management is protected from charges of collusion.	8%	89%

Role of the Marketing Research Director

Advertising and Product Misuse. Some recent research showed that many customers of X Company are misusing Product B. There's no danger; they are simply wasting their money by using too much of it at a time. But yesterday, the M. R. Director saw final comps on Product B's new ad campaign, and the ads not only ignore the problem of misuse, but actually seem to encourage it. He quietly referred the advertising manager to the research results, well known to all people on B's advertising, and let it go at that.   41%   58%

Distortions by Marketing Vice-President. In the trial run of a major presentation to the Board of Directors, the marketing vice-president deliberately distorted some recent research findings. After some thought, the M. R. Director decided to ignore the matter, since the marketing head obviously knew what he was doing.   12%   87%

Possible Conflict of Interest. A market testing firm, to which X Company gives most of its business, recently went public. The M. R. Director had been looking for a good investment and proceeded to buy some $20,000 of their stock. The firm continues as X Company's leading supplier for testing.   40%   57%

Today's Social Concerns

General Trade Data to Ghetto Group. The marketing research department of X Company frequently makes extensive studies of their retail customers. A federally supported Negro group, working to get a shopping center in their ghetto area, wanted to know if they could have access to this trade information. But since

TABLE 16.5 *(continued)*

Situation	Attitude of Research Directors (n = 412)	
	Approve	Disapprove
the M. R. Director had always refused to share this information with trade organizations, he declined the request.	64%	34%
NMAC Request for Recent Price Study. The National Marketing Advisory Council (formed of top marketing executives and marketing educators to advise the Commerce Department) has a task force studying ghetto prices. The head of this study recently called to ask if they could have a copy of a recent X Company study which he understood showed that ghetto appliance prices are significantly higher than in suburban areas. Since X Company sells appliances to these ghetto merchants, the M. R. Director felt compelled to refuse the request.	56%	39%
Assigning Man to a Ghetto Planning Group. A local Office of Economic Opportunity group recently called to ask that the M. R. Director assign one of his men to the planning group working on the ghetto shopping center mentioned earlier. Since one result of such a center would be to force a good number of ghetto retailers out of business, and since some of these retailers were presently customers of X Company, the M. R. Director refused the request.	41%	51%
Negro Account Executive. The President of an interviewing firm which had been doing most of the field work for X Company wrote to say that a new account executive had been assigned to X. The new man was capable, personable, and black. The M. R. Director wrote back to say that there were no Negroes in the department at the moment, and that he felt it would be better all around if a different account man were assigned to X Company.	5%	94%
Hiring Jewish Marketing Analyst. When interviewing applicants for a newly created analyst position, the M. R. Director was impressed with one man in particular. But he didn't offer him the job, since the applicant referred to himself as Jewish, and it was well known that X Company wanted no Jewish marketing people.	26%	71%

TABLE 16.6   *Ethical Questions about the Respondent and Subject in Research*

Privacy

What is the right to privacy?

Should researchers inform respondents of their right to refuse?

Do psychological tests and techniques overstep the limits of normal questioning?

Do researchers have the right to ask questions about friends and neighbors?

Human Dignity

Does research view human beings as merely creatures to be studied?

What are the costs and benefits of deception?

Do research findings reveal more than people want to know?

What is the right of researchers to induce stress and anxiety in respondents and subjects?

Manipulation

Is marketing research merely a tool of mass manipulation?

Does research performed by an elitist group deny less powerful groups the right to control their own destinies?

What are the limits of meaningful manipulation of behavior in laboratory and field experiments?

Is the research interview a manipulative tool?

---

educated, are not aware of their right to refuse or are not prepared to exercise it.

Kelman[6] has noted two closely related factors which put the subject or respondent in a position where he can be manipulated to an extent considered potentially harmful and distasteful. The subject of an experiment, for instance, may feel, first, that he lacks the *capacity* to question research procedures and, secondly, that he does not have the *right* to question them. The subject often perceives the experimenter or researcher as having the knowledge of what the most appropriate research techniques are and that the researcher is using the best set of techniques. After all, the researcher is supposed to know what he is doing or he would not be in the employ of the particular university or firm. This being the case, what right does the subject have to question someone whom he perceives as being an expert? When the subject feels the inability to question the procedures placed upon him, he may even feel he does not have the right to raise questions. "At the very least it can be said that, insofar as subjects accept the investigator's legitimacy, they are reluctant to *claim* the right to question his procedures."[7] Thus, the subject is at a power

---

[6] Kelman, *op. cit.*, 1972.
[7] Kelman, *op. cit.*, 1972, p. 993.

disadvantage and is more susceptible to manipulation which could be psychologically or physically harmful.

2. *Consent to interviews is frequently gained on the basis of vague description of content.* Once the respondent has given his consent, he may find it difficult to refuse to answer when questions into more personal and sensitive areas are asked. The interview is a social situation where the interviewer is well trained in his role and where pressure of previous assent effectively prevents the respondent from breaking off questioning.

3. *Questions about others' actions and attitudes place respondents in a moral dilemma.* Respondents often feel that they are "informers" in such situations even though they may normally relish gossiping. Such questions also run the risk of "big brotherism" with all the accompanying overtones. Questions of this sort may be seen as invasion of privacy once-removed.

4. *Psychological techniques cause people to reveal things about their private lives they may be reluctant to reveal of their own free will.* Although many people are quite ready to speak to any question, even very personal ones as any experienced interviewer knows, psychological tests and projective techniques do so covertly. That is, they may be used to obtain such information without even raising the question. It can be argued that market research is using the tools of the clinical psychologist without the controls that the clinician demands.

The invasion of privacy issue can also arise in natural settings where the researcher is likely to use unobtrusive measures; that is, he observes in a systematic way some aspect of the subject's behavior without that subject being aware that the information is being obtained. Some argue that observing behavior in public places where purchases are made does not pose an invasion of privacy since the subject knows he is open to public scrutiny. It is argued that it is quite another matter when the interviewer is in the home of a subject noting, in the course of interviewing, the style preferences in home furnishings, the type of magazines and books apparently read, type of kitchen appliances, and so on. This, it is argued, is an invasion of privacy. It has been suggested, too, that simply arriving at someone's doorstep unannounced for an interview is an invasion of privacy. Furthermore, in survey research, a respondent may feel embarrassed or experience a lowering of self-esteem if he is asked questions to which he cannot supply answers either in terms of factual information or in the form of opinions. The very fact he is asked such questions implies to him that he should have responses readily available.

5. *Adequate safeguards to assure respondent confidentiality are frequently absent.* Questions with which the Bureau of the Census have great difficulty (those of age, income, religion, and political affiliation) are frequently collected by market researchers under the promise of confidentiality. Yet researchers rely only on the honesty and moral will of their employees to protect this promise instead of systems to insure it. Research offices are often filled with

uncoded questionnaires with names, addresses, and confidential data in full view of any employee or visitor. The pretext of the unsigned mail questionnaire is all too often violated through various coding techniques such as those placed in the stapling or binding areas, under the stamp, or through systematic misspellings in return addresses.[8]

6. *Research interviews may induce stress and anxiety without offering relief.* Especially as marketing research enters the social arena and even now, questions about health and other issues may cause worry without reassurance or psychic support.

Kelman[9] identifies two potentially noxious elements: (1) the degree of deception (to be discussed shortly) and (2) the probability of harmful consequences. Accurate estimates of this probability usually involve knowing a great deal more about the subject's social-psychological makeup than is generally possible in most marketing experiments. The researcher may lack the time or the capability for estimating the impact on a subject of a particular experimental manipulation. While the subject may in the normal course of his daily life be able to tolerate a particular temporary level of frustration, anxiety, or self-doubt, it is difficult to determine whether the added impact of an experiment or probing interview might be the proverbial straw that broke the camel's back.

7. *By its very nature, survey research is intrusive.* Interviewers and questionnaires take time and intrude into people's schedules without returning direct compensation. Although the personal interview gives the respondent the opportunity to at least state his views on the topic, the questionnaire only infrequently offers this compensation. Research takes from respondents and gives only very indirect returns.

8. *Subjects or respondents may be deliberately deceived.* Deception is a common practice in marketing research as in many other research contexts: the brand names of the products the subject is to compare may not be made known; the client for whom the research agency or interviewer is working is not disclosed to subject or respondents; the subject may deliberately not be informed of the uses of the information gathered; questions on a questionnaire or in an interview may be deliberately spaced to minimize the subject's grasping of the underlying hypotheses of the research; and so forth. Deception takes place in all types of research settings but is most commonly found in laboratory situations where most factors are totally under the control of the

---

[8] On the general topic of confidentiality, see R. F. Boruch, "Maintaining Confidentiality of Data in Educational Research: A Systemic Analysis," *American Psychologist,* Vol. 29 (1971), pp. 412–430; E. Manniche and D. P. Hayes, "Respondent Anonymity and Data Matching," *Public Opinion Quarterly,* Vol. 21 (1957), pp. 384–388; and J. Sawyer and H. Schecter, "Computers, Privacy, and the National Data Center: The Responsibility of Social Scientists," *American Psychologist,* Vol. 23 (1968), pp. 810–818.

[9] Kelman, *op. cit.,* 1972.

experimenter. Deception is used when the phenomenon being explored would be obscured by the subject's having certain knowledge related in some way to that phenomenon. The description given by a subject of the taste properties of a given brand of beer may differ if he is aware of the particular brand he is tasting. The respondent who knows what research hypotheses are being studied may willfully give different information than he otherwise would depending on his own feelings about the hypotheses. Thus, without some deception, it is very difficult, if not impossible, to obtain certain kinds of information.

There is little doubt the feeling "I've been had" is demoralizing, especially if the experimental manipulation has been other than trivial. Two experiments need be described in this regard. In the first a debriefing occurred. In the second, no debriefing was given.

Milgram[10] reported a study in which he was concerned with human obedience. Subjects were told, however, that they were participating in a learning experiment in which the effects of punishment were to be investigated. Each subject was paired with what he thought was another subject who was in reality an accomplice of the experimenter. Through a rigged drawing, the accomplice was strapped in a chair and electrodes attached to his body. In another room, the subject was asked to read a list of words to the victim and administer electric shocks ranging from 30 to 450 volts in increasing intensities at each mistake made by the accomplice. There was no real shock given; the accomplice victim, however, reacted by pounding on the walls and failing to give answers after the 300-volt level. Milgram reported:

> In a large number of cases, the degree of tension reached extremes that are rarely seen in sociopsychological laboratory studies. Subjects were observed to sweat, tremble, stutter, bite their lips, groan, and dig their fingernails into their flesh. These were characteristic rather than exceptional responses to the experiment.[11]

One observer's comments were as follows:

> I observed a mature and initially poised businessman enter the laboratory smiling and confident. Within 20 minutes he was reduced to a twitching, stuttering wreck, who was rapidly approaching a point of nervous collapse. He constantly pulled on his earlobe, and twisted his hands. At one point he pushed his fist into his forehead and muttered: 'Oh, God, let's stop it.' And yet he continued to respond to every word of the experimenter, and obeyed to the end.[12]

One wonders to what extent the debriefing helped the subjects. There would seem to be little doubt that at least some of the subjects "came away from

---

[10] Stanley Milgram, "Behavioral Study of Obedience," *Journal of Abnormal and Social Psychology*, Vol. 67 (1963), pp. 371–378.

[11] *Ibid.*, p. 375.

[12] *Ibid.*, p. 377.

the experiment with a lower self-esteem, having to live with the realization that they were willing to yield to destructive authority to the point of inflicting extreme pain on a fellow human being."[13] It is extremely improbable that marketing researchers would ever conduct a study like this. The next experiment, however, is one of a type that a marketing researcher might conceivably conduct.

The study was conducted by Mulder and Stemerding to examine the effects of threat on the attraction to the group and the need for strong leadership.[14] Groups of independent grocers in a number of Dutch towns were called together into group meetings. During these meetings they were told that a large organization was planning to establish a supermarket chain in the Netherlands. The experimental treatment was the probability given them that their town would be selected as a site for a store. For example, in the high threat condition, they were told that there was a high probability their town would be selected and that this would cause a measurable loss in business. The subjects were never told of the deception on the advice of the executives of the shopkeepers' organizations who had arranged the meetings. Kelman's comments on this experiment are well stated:

> I have been worried about these Dutch merchants ever since I heard about this study for the first time. Did some of them go out of business in anticipation of the heavy competition? Do some of them have an anxiety reaction every time they see a bulldozer? Chances are they soon forgot about this threat . . . and that it became just one of the many little moments of anxiety that must occur in every shopkeeper's life. Do we have a right, however, to add to life's little anxieties and to risk the possibility of more extensive anxiety purely for the purposes of our experiments, particularly since deception deprives the subject of the opportunity to choose whether or not he wishes to expose himself to the risks that might be entailed.[15]

Guidelines on the ethical usage of deception and manipulation are not easy to set. The above example is one which differs greatly from the Milgram experiment, yet in retrospect, appears to be equally questionable if not morally wrong. Obviously unusual or noxious stimuli are to be avoided. Campbell has approved of manipulations where "they constituted only experimental schedulings of harmless communications and events which were within the normal range for the arena of life involved."[16] This, however, is only one guideline as has been noted. Kelman sums up the problem of deception and manipulation as follows:

---

[13] See H. C. Kelman, "Human Uses of Human Subjects, the Problem of Deception in Social Psychological Experiments," *Psychological Bulletin,* Vol. 67 (January 1967), p. 4.

[14] M. Mulder and A. Stemerding, "Threat, Attraction to a Group, and Need for Strong Leadership," *Human Relations,* Vol. 16 (1963), pp. 317–334.

[15] Kelman, *op. cit.,* pp. 3–4.

[16] Campbell, *op. cit.,* p. 188.

The broader ethical problem brought into play by the very use of deception becomes even more important when we view it in the light of present historical forces. We are living in an age of mass societies in which the transformation of man into an object to be manipulated at will occurs on a mass scale, in a systematic way, and under the aegis of specialized institutions deliberately assigned to this task.[17]

It has been suggested that three considerations be weighted before deciding to use deception.[18] The first concerns the importance of the study. Is it significant? More specifically, does it promise a major insight into an important human problem? Is the study exploratory or final, that is, will several other studies involving deception be necessary to shed light on the particular problem being studied and will the collective deception of all the subsequent studies be offset by the insights gained? Lastly, the market researcher should ask whether there are deception-free methods available which could produce comparable data.

9. *In social marketing research there are ethical problems to be found in natural experiments.* For example, some researchers have been experimenting with the content of advertising campaign messages for the promotion of better nutrition practices and the acceptance of free immunization services. This has often been pursued by subjecting different communities to different advertising appeals including no advertising. Some workers involved in these programs and many people not involved have been quick to point out that the deliberate withholding from a community of any message or of a message believed to be ineffective relative to others is wrong. For example, in the case of immunization programs, the withholding of any special message in a (control) community prior to the arrival of the immunization team may mean that some persons, perhaps many, will not be vaccinated and are thus susceptible to the adverse consequences of not being immune to a particular illness, at least during the period of the experiment. The defense of this activity is based on the premise that the knowledge gained—knowing what communication mix is optimal—will enable all subsequent advertising campaigns to be more effective. This effectiveness is measured in terms of the added number of people showing up for inoculations. The number of people being vaccinated in the indefinite future who would *probably* not otherwise be vaccinated in the absence of having learned what advertising mix was most effective more than offsets the number not vaccinated during the experiment in those communities where the optimal mix was not used.

Despite the criticisms mentioned above it is evident that research is being

---

[17] Kelman, *op. cit.,* p. 5. See also H. C. Kelman, "Manipulation of Human Behavior: An Ethical Issue for the Social Scientist," *Journal of Social Issues,* Vol. 21 (1965), pp. 31–46.

[18] Kelman, *op. cit.,* 1972.

conducted to the mutual benefit of consumers, producers, and suppliers.[19] This is not to say that researchers should ignore the issues. Sensitivity to the issues is necessary for the conduct of research. As one researcher has noted, "Let's face it, we are able to collect our research data only because the general public continues to be willing to submit to our interviews."[20]

Rights of the Client

The researcher has ethical considerations to consider in his treatment of the client as well as the respondent or subject. Many of these resemble those of any business—basic honesty and respect for principle. Others, however, are particular to the research process.

Confidentiality

First among these is the confidential relationship which exists between client and researcher. Some of this is due to the nature of the projects upon which the researcher is likely to work. New products or store location questions are areas in which a breach of confidence may lead to quickened competitive reaction and its attendant financial losses. The evaluation of internal marketing operations and organization could likewise be the cause of unrest and instability in the firm if it were to become known. For these reasons, the researcher must maintain the confidentiality expected in his relationship with clients.

Confidentiality extends much further in the relationship between client and researcher, however. For example, the very fact that the researcher is being or has been employed by a given firm may itself be considered confidential. Although this low profile may at times be discomfiting to those who must assume it, it may not only be required but essential to the competitive posture of the client. The best role for the researcher to assume is that of a lawyer: one who makes no statement without the client's permission. It should be obvious that any information gained in the course of a project is for the exclusive use of the client and to be held in confidence.

One of the authors of this text was discussing a variety of possible research projects with the marketing research director of a major monthly magazine. A number of projects were quite obviously useful and the marketing research director was asked why the research hadn't been performed before and why it was not now being contemplated. The response was that the data would provide no competitive advantage since competition would have copies of the confidential results within a week of the time the results reached his desk. He also acknowledged that he could count on having copies of allegedly confidential research reports commissioned by his competitors. Consequently,

---

[19] E. L. Hartman, H. L. Isaacson, and C. N. Ingell, "Public Reaction to Public Opinion Surveying," *Public Opinion Quarterly,* Vol. 32 (Summer 1968), pp. 295–298.

[20] Carlson, *op. cit.,* p. 5.

the industry was in a stalemate of sorts with regard to certain types of research projects.

The AMA Marketing Research Code of Ethics adds one point which is related to confidentiality. It is that the researcher should not undertake studies for competitive clients if they should jeopardize the confidential nature of the client-researcher relationship. In one sense such a situation would be analogous to a lawyer representing both the plaintiff and defendant in a civil suit. This becomes a real problem for the larger research organizations.

Methodology and Results

The researcher is under the obligation to use adequate methodologies to obtain his data and to analyze, interpret, and report it accordingly. To misrepresent either methodology or results is no more to be condoned in research than misrepresentation is condoned elsewhere in business.

Oftentimes, however, a researcher will find himself under pressure to perform studies in a manner which would, for one reason or another, be ill-advised. He may be asked to conduct a survey when other available data may be adequate or to collect data to fit a poorly designed model. In any event, he may feel that the task will not be worth the expenditure. In this case, it is best for him to make known his thoughts to the client. Depending on the nature of the task, if the client insists, he may then either go ahead or refuse the account. On the other hand, the researcher should exercise care so as not to introduce elegancies into a project where they are not needed. It is no more ethical for a researcher to promote and perform study when something less would be adequate and appropriate than for a surgeon to perform major surgery when medication would do the job as well.

At the same time, a researcher is ethically bound to state the limitations of a study. Most common, of course, is the use of broad generalizations or forecasts made from something other than a true random sample. If a convenience sample or limited geographical samples are used, the researcher is under an obligation to state this fact and to note that any generalizations are, as a result, not necessarily valid for the population as a whole. In fact, it can be said that not only does this obligation apply to the inclusion of a disclaimer paragraph buried in the sample selection section of the report, but it also extends to demand inclusion of a positive statement to that effect. This is especially true in the case of nonsophisticated or infrequent users of research.

Similarly, possible or real sources of bias in the report should be made known to the client. This does not mean that it is necessary to overwhelm the client in a torrent of "researchese." However, if there is cause to think that question wording may have resulted in some bias, the researcher is ethically bound to point up that fact. This is especially so if the client might otherwise be led to believe that each measure is a perfect, one-to-one operationalization of the concepts in question.

These ethical obligations are more than ephemeral, moral structures designed to keep, so to speak, the researcher's reputation unsullied. They have a concrete basis in that the data the researcher provides is often used as the basis upon which major decisions or large investments are made. If he is unsure, the researcher should ask himself, "Knowing what I know about the adequacy of the methodology and techniques used given the size of the budget, am I sure enough of the data to use it?"

Obligations of the Research User

The research user or client has obligations too. The first of these is the most important. The client is bound to use the data in an ethical manner. Misstatements or misrepresentations of findings in promotion, for example, are the most common breach of this ethic. This extends to presenting results out of their context or making generalizations where such are not warranted. Most common is the "3 out of 4 doctors . . ." statement that neglects to give the exact wording of the question or to state that respondents were selected because they were heavy users in the first place. It might be added that it is unethical to ask reputable researchers to lend their name to such research. It has happened that knowingly biased customer listings, for example, have been made available to researchers without a statement of the shortcomings since they were in a direction favorable to the sponsor.

Finally, the AMA Code notes that it is unethical for users to solicit unique designs or concepts not commonly available and then to deliver it to another for execution. This, however, is not so much a breach of special research ethics as it is of commonly accepted business ethics.

Questions and Exercises

1. Is the researcher's responsibility to his client necessarily in conflict with his responsibility to his subjects? Why or why not?
2. The chapter gives the code of conduct for four different professional associations. Evaluate each of these codes and point out apparent weaknesses. Combine the better elements in each code and develop a "super" code of ethics. Feel free to include elements in your code that had not been included in the four professional association codes.
3. The value of a code of ethics in research is dependent upon the "honor system." However, those most in need of a code are the ones least likely to adhere to one. This suggests the need for compulsory compliance. Comment on the advantages and disadvantages of such a system and would such a system work?
4. In the Crawford study various hypothetical situations were evaluated as to their ethical status. The situations had varying degrees of approval and disapproval. Speculate as to why some situations were more acceptable than others.

5. A basic moral standard in our society is honesty. Do you think a researcher has the obligation to be totally honest in his research? This question not only concerns full and accurate reporting, but also disclosure of the intent of the study and questions prior to them being administered.

6. Frequently researchers place the most sensitive questions in the survey last, thus raising these issues only after a person has committed himself to responding. Do you think a researcher has an obligation to place these sensitive and personal questions first in the survey so that the respondent knows what he is getting himself into before becoming committed?

7. By definition, deception is lying, cheating, or misleading. How can anybody ever justify such behavior as being ethical?

8. The communication between researcher and subject is supposed to be confidential yet there is no legal protection for this communication. Thus, research in illegal activities and other activities may be hampered. Should confidentiality be protected by law and should the other rights of subjects and clients also be protected by the government?

9. The issue of ethics implies that there is a universal or higher moral standard that takes precedence over the implementation of a particular study. If this is true, why then should each discipline have its own code instead of a universal code applicable to all fields?

10. In reviewing nearly all marketing research texts, no mention of the word "ethics" was found. Comment on the reasons for this.

11. In all studies of human behavior, the issue of ethics is present. Comment on this statement.

12. Marketing researchers study many kinds of issues, some of which concern ways of promoting what many believe to be socially undesirable products, for example, cigarettes. Some researchers argue that they are scientists and they therefore are studying human behavior and make no judgments as to the social implications. On the other hand, others say a value judgment should be made. Comment on this issue.

13. The text comments that people's rights have to be respected or law and public opinion will interfere. Can you think of any examples where law or public opinion has addressed the issue of ethics in research?

14. If a researcher flagrantly violates a code of ethics, are there any actions or sanctions that can be used to discourage such practices?

15. Where is the line drawn between manipulation and just plain good promotion? Give examples of each type of behavior.

16. In the Crawford study, 94 percent disapproved of the discrimination

of the Negro account executive. With this in mind, how do you explain why there is still discrimination in employment?

17. By its very nature, survey research is intrusive. Research takes from respondents and gives only very indirect returns. What type of compensation should be given for cooperation?

18. This chapter concerns the ethical standards of researchers. Does the respondent also have the obligation to adhere to a set of ethical standards? If so, what would they be?

Project Related Questions

1. What rights of respondents or subjects could be violated in your project? See Table 16.6.

2. What rights of clients could be violated in your project if you were doing this project as an outside consultant for another company?

3. What steps have you taken, if any, to ensure the protection of subject and client rights?

4. What ethical issues have you encountered which are not covered by the AMA code of ethics?

5. How could the resolution of particular ethical issues affect the quality of the data you collect in your project?

In the several short cases to follow the reader should refer back to the ethical guidelines of the various professional associations and try to reach a decision as to whether the research practice in the particular case under study is ethical. The same question should be asked independently of these guidelines but using your own standard where they differ from those of the professional association.

Case 1

A psychologist in opinion research completed a study for a firm which used the findings in a case before the Federal Communications Commission. The lawyer for the adversary in the case demanded the names of the interviewees for the purported purpose of checking the evidence. The psychologist declined to comply with the request, and when the Commission charged him to show cause why he should not reveal the names, he made the following statement:

> Not only do I feel that the proposed resurvey does not constitute a sound basis for challenging the present survey, but there is also good reason to believe that if this precedent were allowed, it would endanger and eventually annihilate the proper use of surveys in which the government, industry, and academic bodies invest millions of dollars for guidance in policy-making and the advancement of knowledge. Experiments made by psychologists to explore this very point have shown that survey results vary according to whether or not the respondents believe they are speaking in anonymity.

> Perhaps the precedent for all of these protestations can be found in the Federal Government itself, which has given to the census a confidential status.

Opinion

Since the psychologist offered to make available all of his data, including the completed questionnaires for examination as long as the identity of respondents had been first removed, he was not unethical in refusing to reveal the names in connection with the answers. In fact, since he had promised anonymity for the respondents, he would have been unethical in revealing the identity of the respondents.

Question

Should the names be revealed?
Should the completed questionnaires be made available?

Case 2

A marketing research consultant making a presentation before a marketing professional association meeting gave many details of a recent study he had completed for a major beverage company. The account he gave which included references to well-known practices of his client as well as the advice they were given was sufficiently detailed that most of the audience could identify the client. The client initiated a lawsuit against the researcher and his firm claiming there was insufficient protection of their identity and they lost certain competitive advantages. However, there was never any written agreement concerning the protection of the client's identity.

Question
Is there an implied or tacit responsibility assumed by marketing researchers to protect their client's identity at all times before all types of audiences?

Case 3

The promotional material of a marketing research firm, sent to prospective industrial clients, contained the following features: (a) it cited use of its services by companies of national reputations; (b) it offered to evaluate several of the prospective client's employees without charge; and (c) it implied that its services were superior to others' and claimed the projective test used provided special insights.

In the opinion of the psychological firm involved, its literature and practices were in accord with ethical standards on the following counts: (a) its services had been and were continuing to be used by nationally known companies, apparently with satisfaction, a fact which would be important to prospective industrial clients; (b) the offer to provide some free services was intended not as a "come-on" but rather as the kind of tangible assurance business firms are in the habit of seeking when evaluating a new service; and (c) the claim to having corrected faults often found in aptitude-testing programs was justified in that the firm analyzed test data not only quantitatively but also qualitatively.

Question
Is there a difference between commercial standards and professional standards? Is it appropriate for a firm to conduct activities, for example, self-promotion, while its professional behavioral scientist employees may be limited in doing this on their own were they in private practice?

Case 4

A psychologist distributed copies of a test by mail to two different groups of psychologists with a request that the test be self-administered and returned anonymously. The true purpose of the use of the test was purposely not stated because of the experimental design of the study. Some psychologists who received the request for cooperation in taking the test complained of misuse of the test.

The American Psychological Association was asked for an advising opinion which follows:

> The risk of misunderstanding the use of a test or other technique in a study and the risk of possible harmful aftereffects should be minimized in the design of a study and the possibility of undesirable effects removed as soon as possible. In this case the investigator agreed that a statement of intent to give a complete explanation after cooperation would not interfere with the design of the experiment.

Question

What "misuse" might there be if the psychologist didn't agree to issuing a statement of intent? Does such a statement really remedy the alleged misuse? Does a statement of intent to give an explanation of the study to subject or respondent after completing the questionnaire affect response rate?

Criteria for Marketing and Advertising Research
Advertising Research Foundation

What are the basic ethical issues implicit in each of the criteria? What appears to be the position taken with regard to each issue? How does the overall position compare with that of the American Marketing Association as evidenced by its Code of Ethics?

THE CRITERIA

1. Under what conditions was the study made?

A statement of the methods employed should be made available in such detail that the study could be duplicated therefrom. In addition to the information revealed in answer to questions 2 through 8, the report should provide:

a. *Full statement of problems to be resolved by the study.*
b. *Who financed it.*
c. *Names of organizations participating in study, together with their qualifications and extent of their interest, if any, in the findings.*
d. *Exact period of time covered in collection of data, with a statement as to the representativeness of the time period regarding subjects surveyed.*
e. Date of publication of report.
f. Definition of terms used.
g. *Copies of questionnaires and instructions to interviewers.*
h. Sources of collateral data.
i. *Complete statement of methodology to be issued concurrently with the findings.*

2. Has the questionnaire been well designed?

The questions must clearly convey their meaning uniformly to all, without suggesting answers either by their context or sequence. Unreasonable demands on the memory or on the actual knowledge of the respondent should not be made. Responses to simple "why" questions are often inaccurate and to "why not" questions, more so. Diversification of subject matter trends to reduce the interest bias.

The phrasing should avoid, or compensate for, a choice of responses which would reflect such influences as prestige, embarrassment, reward or retaliation. "Usually or regularly buy or read" questions maximize such biases. Individuals should answer only for themselves.

Monotonous questioning induces

644

antagonism. Lengthy questioning may induce fatigue and cause incomplete responses. If the questionnaire was one of several completed at the same time with a single respondent, the total content of the interview must be revealed to indicate any conditioning induced by questions preceding the questions involved in the study. Limiting of space for replies limits the completeness of the answers. Repeat interviewing also may condition the response. To check on internal consistency of response, "catch" questions may be used. The questionnaire should be pilot tested.

3. Has the interviewing been adequately and reliably done?

Usually a questionnaire form will be used; the interviewer must be well acquainted with it and with the prescribed interview procedure. Where no form is used, the interviewer must have greater maturity, training and experience; where extended interviews on attitudes are involved, special reporting means such as a tape recorder may well be required. Per interview compensation usually leads to lower quality interviewing; full-time interviewers generally provide more satisfactory work than do part-time interviewers. Unsuitable, ill-trained or irresponsible interviewers are not justified by economy. Even experienced interviewers should be trained and instructed for each survey's problems. Only interviewers who can be compatible with respondents should be employed, because good rapport must be established. If the sampling plan does not specifically designate those to be interviewed, a bias often is introduced by the interviewer's picking respondents who tend to be like rather than unlike himself. The interviewer should be able to influence the progress of the interview, but must not influence the answers; it is often desirable that the interviewer not know the main purpose of the survey. The identity of the sponsor should not be known to the interviewer nor, least of all, to the respondent.

Not only should spot checks be made of the total interviews, but interviewer by interviewer comparisons should be made as well. More complete checking, to the extent of partially repeating the interview, is required if quota sampling was employed. The interviewing process should be pilot tested. On-the-scene supervisors improve interviewing quality.

4. Has the best sampling plan been followed?

The population being surveyed is most accurately represented when a random sample, in the mathematical sense, is employed. Each unit must have an equal chance or a known relative chance of being included in the sample; listing, enumerating and interviewing in every household in each defined interviewing area are tools for achieving this aim. Stratification and clustering help to make pure area sampling more economical. Disproportionate sampling may be employed to increase sampling reliability in a survey of a given size, but re-weighting must be employed in tabulating. The laws of probability, permitting calculation of error margins, only apply to truly random sampling, not to quota samples or to samples that are "random" only in an accidental or haphazard sense.

Quota sampling is preferable to accidental sampling, but still it is a matter of judgment as to how effectively various pertinent quotas have been introduced and followed in individual surveys. They should be set so as to maximize the range of coverage, especially by geographic and economic groupings. Consistency with census or other basic data is not in itself proof of sampling representativeness unless it can be proven that the subject being investigated, itself, has perfect random distribution.

Other than in the latter case, there are instances where well-constructed quota samples may be acceptable. The rate of non-cooperation in many surveys, especially of the inventory, panel or continuous type, is so high that it liquidates many of the features of random sampling in the end. Copy testing and other instances where the general, rather than the exact answer, is all that is required lend themselves to well-designed quota samples. In general, *qualitative* in contrast to *quantitative* data can be satisfactorily obtained from quota samples. Where doubt exists, random sampling should be used since this gives the maximum reliability per dollar expended.

5. Has the sampling plan been fully executed?

Substitutions for assigned units destroy a probability sample design. In personal interview surveys, refusals can frequently be overcome by repeat efforts. Not-at-homes, who have characteristics known to be different, should be brought into the sample by call-backs, or their answers should be estimated by special statistical formulas. If quotas were assigned, they should be fulfilled exactly. In quota sampling, refusals and not-at-homes are not controllable.

In mail surveys the response as well as the mail-out must be representative. To reduce biases growing out of personal interests and economic factors, which are common in mail surveys with a low rate of return, it is desirable to get as close to a 100% return as possible. In telephone surveys, refusals, not-at-homes and busy lines must not be ignored.

6. Is the sample large enough?

If a probability sample is properly designed and executed, the reliability of its results can be estimated mathematically. Breakdown data should have a large enough numerical base to keep their larger error margins within usable limits.

The desired degree of reliability should be expressed in the definition of the problem or plan of the study. Increase in sample size does not compensate for deviations from a true probability sample though it may provide a better basis for evaluating the effect of non-response.

If a probability sample is not employed, it is a matter of judgment as to what additional error is introduced as a result of using a non-random sample. The error cannot be measured statistically if the sample is non-random.

7. Was there systematic control of editing, coding and tabulating?

All editing of questionnaires should be completed before any tabulations are made, and a statement to that effect should be made a part of the report.

Editing should not involve guessing as to meaning. Where context rather than form is being edited, the same editor should handle specific related sections of all questionnaires. Local supervisors should edit for form and completeness. Directions for editing should be formulated and explained uniformly to all engaged in the process.

In machine tabulation, pre-coding not only saves time and money but catches errors and incompleteness in questionnaire design. If pre-coding is used, a pilot test should be made to develop the codes; if pre-coding is not used, a sample of the completed questionnaires should be examined to establish the codes, especially on open-end questions.

Questionnaires should be numbered serially to guarantee completeness of card punching and as a check against duplicate punching. Pattern or consistency checking of each separate column of the punched-card should be done to verify that only appropriate codes have been punched. Each column or group code should be separately counted to establish the varying bases, and to verify that different tables with the same base actually agree.

In addition in hand tabulating, spot-checking of results by individual tabulators is desired. Each step should be separately spot-checked. All transfers of data should be double-checked.

8. Is the interpretation forthright and logical?

If causal relationship is assigned to one factor, it must be proved that all other factors are held constant or allowance must be made for other variables.

The basic data which underlie percentages, ratios, weighting systems and breakdown groupings of respondents must be shown. Competitive comparisons should be made on the same bases. Since mean averages are often misleading, especially in income studies, the median should also be examined. *Any uncommon mathematical manipulation must be fully explained. Error margins and their reliability should be indicated.*

Misplaced emphasis may divert attention from weaknesses in research methods or findings. Complete answers to all questions should be uniformly reported. Interpretation, especially of responses involving memory or prediction of behavior, must not overestimate the ability of an individual to give valid responses. Small differences, considering statistical error margins, should not be over-emphasized. Charts, tables and text should not be distorted or unduly exaggerated. Simplicity and clarity should be the main objective of the analysis and presentation.

Present the results only for what they are and for what they represent.

Recommended Standards on Disclosure

The National Association of Broadcasters has developed a set of standards for agencies which conduct broadcast audience measurement research. These standards are intended to specify the kinds of information which might appropriately be disclosed about procedures used in conducting and reporting broadcast audience measurement research. What ethical issues are involved? Do you think the standards are too rigorous? Not rigorous enough? What changes would you suggest?

1. NATURE OF THE STATISTICAL INFORMATION

1.1 Type of Report and Auspices

A report on broadcast measurements should indicate whether it repsents one in a regular series of reports or whether it is a special report.

If it is one of a series, it should include information regarding the expected frequency and publication schedule of reports in the series.

The report should always specify the audience measurement service or research company that conducted the survey on which the report is based. In addition, sponsors of the report should be prominently named.

1.2 Type of Audience Measurements

In view of the fact that there are many different measurements of broadcast audiences, a research company should list and clearly define the various measures of audience that it provides in its reports.

In particular, because there are alternative criteria for counting households or individuals in television or radio audiences, each data item on the size of an audience should be accompanied by a careful explanation of the nature of that audience, covering, in particular, the following points:

a. What period of time (e.g., which particular weeks or month) the audience data refer to;

b. Whether the audience data are on the basis of households, individual persons, or some other unit of observation;

c. What rule has been used to determine whether to count a household or an individual in a television or radio audience (e.g., the rule by which a multi-set household is counted);

d. Whether the audience data represent only audiences in homes, or audiences in homes and away from home as well;

e. Whether the audience data represent certain sub-groupings of households or individuals (such as those in a particular age and/or sex group, or those with certain reported usage of product) and, in these cases, the precise definitions of the sub-groups;

f. Whether the audience data reflect the audience of a network, of a station, of a program, or of a group of stations or programs;

g. Whether the data intentionally exclude the audiences of any particular station, or group of stations, and, if so, the rules by which such exclusions are made;

h. Which particular geographic area (e.g., continental United States, a specific metropolitan area, a group of counties, a specified marketing area, or whatever) the audience data refer to;

i. Which days and which parts of the day (e.g., quarter-hours) the audience data refer to;

j. Whether the data reflect audiences at instants in time, average audience over several points in time, or an accumulation of audiences over several points in time; and

k. What definition of base has been used for measurements that are presented in the form of percentages or ratios.

1.3 Format of Reported Data

In some broadcast audience reports, captions and other headings may, because of space limitations, provide an inadequate description of the data. Therefore, where appropriate, a section referring to sample pages of the report should fully describe the contents of tables.

1.4 Supplemental Information

An audience measurement service should make available auxiliary statistical information, such as source data on population size, if it is required for interpretation of the audience measurements that it presents in a report.

Such supplemental information should be accompanied by an explanation of the nature of the data and an indication of the source from which those data were obtained.

In particular, whenever an audience measurement is expressed as a rating (i.e., in percentage terms), a precise description of the base to which the percentage can be projected should be provided, together with the numerical value of that base. This may require, for example, publication and explanation of an estimate of television households or individuals in an area.

1.5 Program Names and Broadcast Times

When audience measurements are reported by program, a research company should explain the manner in which it determines the names of programs it reports, the times at which the programs were broadcast, and whether such programs were preempted during a portion of the survey period.

The company should further explain its policy on the reporting of preemptions. It is highly desirable that any indicated programs that were pre-empted by other programs, or otherwise not broadcast during a portion of the survey period, be identified.

Similarly, the manner in which the company determines when a station is on the air, or not broadcasting, should be indicated.

The circumstances under which program names and broadcast times, as reported, may be in error should be described.

1.6 Audiences in CATV Markets

An audience measurement service should state the policy and practices it follows in crediting audiences to stations in areas where CATV systems are operative.

1.7 Satellites

A research company should, when it is relevant, fully describe its policy of reporting parent-satellite station combinations in local market reports.

1.8 AM and FM Radio Stations

A research company should, when it is relevant, fully describe its policies in reporting AM and FM radio stations in combination, and separately.

1.9 Special Promotions

A research company should state its policy of reporting special promotions and tune-in advertising which may affect broadcast audience estimates.

Moreover, the company should clearly state how it obtains information on the existence of such promotions (e.g., only on the basis of voluntary reporting by stations, or

otherwise), and, furthermore, how it determines the nature, extent, and duration of promotions.

1.10 BRC Accreditation

An audience measurement service should state if a particular report or service has received accreditation by the Broadcast Rating Council.

2. THE STATISTICAL POPULATION AND SAMPLE SELECTION

2.1 The Statistical Population

An audience measurement service should provide a description of the statistical populations for which its surveys are intended to provide estimates.

This description should state: (a) whether the elementary unit for the studies is a household, an individual person, or some other unit of observation; and (b) whether the statistical populations are restricted to a certain group of elementary units (e.g., persons 12 years of age or older).

The service should also state if the statistical population is restricted to a particular geographic area (e.g., a particular metropolitan area, or group of counties), and, if so, indicate the basis for selecting such an area.

2.2 The Frame

A research company should provide a description and evaluation of the type of frame (or frames) that is used for its surveys.

The description should provide a clear definition of the sampling unit, including any details on the formation of clusters. When multi-stage sampling is employed, information should be provided on the frames used at each stage of sampling.

The extent to which the frame is subject to various imperfections such as incompleteness, or duplication, or both should also be indicated.

When a frame is incomplete and therefore covers only a part of a statistical population, geographically or otherwise, the research company should indicate the differences between the 'target' population and the portion of the population represented by the frame, which is what is being surveyed.

The company should provide estimates of the proportion of the 'target' population that was in fact covered by a frame that is used and the proportion of the 'target' population that is excluded by the use of the frame.

The audience measurement service should make available whatever information it may have regarding differences between the characteristics of the statistical population included and excluded by the frame, and a description of the studies on which the information is based.

If no frame was used because the survey was conducted on the basis of a nonprobability sample, the report should specifically state this fact.

2.3 Sampling Plan

A research company should provide a description of the method of sample selection that it employs in the surveys on which its statistical reports are based.

If some method of probability sampling is employed in the surveys, this description of the sampling plan should indicate the manner in which sampling units are drawn from the frame for the survey. The discussion should explain any procedures that are used for stratifying the sample before or after selection, or for otherwise varying the probabilities of selecting sampling units. It should also explain any procedures that are used to select the sample in two or more stages.

In addition, the company should disclose whether the selection of the sample is done in a central office location or, wholly or in part, in the field by interviewers, and in either case, describe how it is done.

For surveys that continue over time with a continuing sample of households or individuals (a panel sample), the company should describe any procedures used to rotate sample members and to otherwise update the sample.

If the surveys are based on nonprobability samples, the company should specifically state this fact, and then describe the criteria that are, in fact, used to select the members of those samples.

3. SURVEY METHODS, OPERATIONS, AND PROCEDURES

3.1 Method of Data Collection

A research company should describe the particular method of data collection (e.g., meter, diary, personal interview, or telephone interview) that it uses in its survey work, and explain what information is collected, when it is collected, how it is collected, and how the information is recorded.

If two or more methods of data collection are employed in a survey, the service should describe each method of data collection and indicate the extent to which it is used.

If a survey upon which an audience measurement report is based obtains items of information besides those reported, the company should state this fact in its report, explain the nature of this additional information, and describe the manner in which it was obtained.

The company should make available for inspection by users a complete copy of the diary, schedule, questionnaire, or other type of reporting form used in a survey. Preferably this copy, or a facsimile, should be included with the report, or in a technical supplement.

3.2 Contacts with Sample Members

An audience measurement service should explain, in general terms, what contacts it has with members of a sample it selects for a survey, how such contacts are made, and who is responsible for making them.

When the method of data collection involves an interview, the manner in which that interview is conducted and the nature of the instructions given to interviewers should be described.

The service should state what provisions, if any, are made for contacts with non-English speaking respondents if, in fact, the population of study

has been defined to include some members who may not speak English.

Some surveys may involve preliminary contacts, prior to the actual collection of data, with members of the sample, to solicit their cooperation in participating, and to provide instruction. Similarly, some surveys may involve contacts with sample members during the course of a survey to encourage continuing cooperation. If procedures call for such contacts, the service should describe their general nature and purpose, and the means by which they are made.

If, in conducting a survey, a service employs one series of contacts for one part of the sample and a different series of contacts for other parts of the sample, it should describe each series of contacts, and the type of respondent for which each series is employed. The service should also indicate the extent to which it employs each of these procedures in conducting a survey.

The general nature of any incentives that are used in conducting the survey should be indicated.

3.3 Field Work

A research company should describe, in general terms, the nature of the field work required in its surveys, and the type of personnel responsible for that work. This description should indicate the approximate extent to which interviewers or field workers are centrally located or otherwise. It should also indicate the type of responsibilities assigned to them, the nature and the degree of supervision, the qualifications required of interviewers or field workers, the general nature and extent of training given interviewers or field workers by the research company, the basis on which interviewers or field workers are compensated (e.g., on an hourly rate, full salary, or piece-work basis), and the methods by which quality of field work is appraised by the company.

When a self-administered questionnaire or diary is used, the research company should indicate what responsibilities, and what instructions, it gives to members of the sample, and by what means such instructions are transmitted to them. The research company should report whether it verifies that basic data are, in fact, obtained from selected sample members according to survey procedures, and, if so, it should describe the nature, the extent, and the results of such verification.

3.4 Research on Accuracy of Basic Data

The research company, if possible, should indicate whether it has conducted methodological research on questions relating to the accuracy of the basic data that it collects from members of the sample. Such questions, for example, might deal with the frequency and magnitude of response or reporting errors attributable to interviewers. They might also deal with errors resulting from memory failure, deliberate mis-reporting, incomplete knowledge of the behavior of others, misunderstanding on the part of respondents, or to the breakdown of mechanical recording devices. Other questions might deal with

inherent deficiencies in the method of data collection, such as the conditioning of sample or panel members, or the reporting of sets tuned with no persions viewing. If such research has been conducted, results and conclusions from such research should be made available together with an adequate description of the nature of the research on which they are based.

3.5 Call-backs

The audience measurement service should describe the provisions it makes for call-backs or other kinds of follow-ups.

The number of call-backs allowed for and the means by which call-backs are made should be reported. In addition, it is highly desirable to describe the following: (a) under what circumstances call-backs are made—if they are only for no contacts, or for those who initially refuse as well; (b) whether special incentives are used in connection with call-backs on those who initially refuse; (c) whether call-backs on no contacts are varied by time of day and day of week and, if so, how they are varied; (d) who is responsible for making the call-backs; and (e) under what circumstances no further call-backs are made.

3.6 Rate of Response

For each of its statistical reports, an audience measurement service should provide information regarding the frequency, or the rate, of response among units predesignated for the sample.

First of all, the report should show the number of units predesignated for the sample. The predesignated sample size, as reported, may exclude any blanks in the frame that were selected as part of the predesignated sample if the number of blanks is reported separately and they are carefully described. For example, for a sample of telephone listings, selections that are determined to represent commercial establishments may be reported separately and not included in calculating the size of the predesignated sample.

Secondly, each report should show the number or the proportion of the predesignated sample units that fall into each of the following main categories:

a. Units originally selected that were not contacted in the course of the survey;
b. Units selected that were contacted, but did not participate in the survey because they refused, or for any other reason;
c. Units that did participate or at least attempted to participate, but whose information was not used because of incompleteness, illegibilities, or inconsistencies; and
d. Units that did participate and whose responses were used for the statistical report.

It should be made clear, in all cases, whether the data on the numbers of respondents or on the rates of response represent households, or individuals, or some other type of unit.

For surveys based on a continuing (panel) sample of households or individuals, it is necessary for the research company to report data on the frequency or rate of responses for each survey in which the panel is used, because at times some members of the panel will not provide information. It is not sufficient merely to report the frequency or proportion of those among the original selections who agreed to serve on the panel.

When the method of sampling employed by the survey has involved differential sampling rates among various strata, it is desirable that the aforementioned categories of responses and nonresponses be reported by strata, to enable computation of appropriately weighted rates of response. If such detail is not reported despite the existence of differential sampling rates, mention should be made of that fact.

When it is appropriate, the report should also show more detailed breakdowns of the main categories listed above. For example, in the case of a telephone coincidental study, units not participating might well be broken into sub-categories such as (a) numbers that were not telephoned at all, (b) numbers that were called, but that did not answer the telephone, (c) numbers for which the calls resulted in a busy signal, (d) refusals, (e) language difficulties, and so forth. Similarly, in the case of a diary study, units who did not participate might well be broken into sub-categories representing (a) those not contacted, (b) refusals, (c) language difficulties, and (d) sample members who promised to participate but failed to return a diary.

When a survey is designed to collect several different items of information, the rate of response may vary significantly from one item to another. In general, the proportions that the research company reports should refer to the main items of information obtained in the survey, and this should be explained in the report. In some cases, the frequency or the proportion of responses may have to be reported separately for several main items of information because there is considerable variation in the proportion from one item to another.

The research company should be careful not to imply that frequency or rate of response is the sole indicator of the accuracy of survey results. The ultimate question in judging the effects of nonresponse is whether the respondents differ from the nonrespondents with respect to the characteristics of interest in a study and, if so, by how much. Any statement on this matter by the company should be identified as being based either on opinion or on factual research, as the case may be. (Cf. section 3.7)

3.7 Effects and Treatment of Nonresponse

An audience measurement service should indicate whether it employs any special procedures or adjustments for nonresponse, after call-backs.

In particular, the company should report under what circumstances, if any, they permit substitutions for original selections. When such substitutions are permitted, the company should describe the procedures they follow in choosing the substitutes, and the extent to which the procedures are employed.

Similarly, if any system of over-

sampling, or of weighting respondents, in an attempt to adjust for nonrespondents is utilized in the survey, that system should be factually described.

The audience measurement service should indicate whether it has conducted methodological research regarding the effects of nonresponse on the accuracy of survey results. If so, the company should make available results and conclusions from such research together with an adequate description of the research on which the information is based. This discussion of the effects of nonresponse should also relate to whether special procedures or adjustments that the company employs, if any, tend to diminish the effects of nonresponse on the accuracy of the survey results.

3.8 Editing and Coding

The research company should describe, in summary form, the steps that are involved in editing and coding. This description should relate to the following:

a. In what way a basic record (such as a diary, questionnaire, schedule, or metered report) is checked for completeness;

b. Whether there are any checks on the basic data for consistency and for accuracy (such as checks on reported programs and stations) and, if so, the nature of these checks;

c. How inconsistencies (such as between a reported program and station) are reconciled;

d. Under what circumstances a basic

record is judged not usable, and discarded;

e. Under what circumstances basic records are partially utilized, if ever, and the extent of such partial utilization;

f. Whether any incomplete, inconsistent, or inaccurate records are ever completed or revised, and, if so, the nature of and the basis for such revisions, and the extent to which they are made.

In addition, a research company should indicate whether its editing and coding rules are based on the results of methodological research, and whether it has conducted research to determine the effect of these rules on the accuracy of audience estimates. The research company should also indicate whether it has conducted research concerning the frequency and magnitude of errors in the implementation of editing and coding rules. If such research has been conducted, the results and conclusions should be made available together with an adequate description of the nature of the research on which they are based.

3.9 Computation of Reported Estimates

A research company should describe how the estimates of broadcast audiences it reports are derived from the basic data obtained from the households or individual persons in the sample.

This description should indicate whether observations are weighted, and whether any other statistical adjustments to the data are made, and,

if so, the nature of all such adjustments, their rationale, and the extent to which they are applied. Also, the sources of the weights used in computations should be indicated.

It is desirable that computations be illustrated by one or more numerical examples.

There should also be some indication of the extent to which verification and quality control checks are used in the data processing operations.

3.10 Reporting Standards

If a research company has set its own standards which estimates must meet in order to be reported (such as a standard for reporting based on size of sample), it should list and explain such standards.

4. ACCURACY AND RELIABILITY OF SURVEY RESULTS

4.1 Sampling Error

A research company should give in tabular form, or provide a basis for properly calculating, standard errors of all estimates published in its statistical reports.

In any case this will necessitate reporting the actual size of sample, overall or among strata, for each of the various types of audience measurements. And, in addition, it may involve reporting effective sample sizes. In this case, there must be an explanation of how the effective sample sizes were calculated and an explanation of how to use effective sample sizes to calculate standard errors for reported survey results.

Some description of the proper interpretation of the standard error should also be included.

If a survey is conducted on the basis of a nonprobability sample, the report should specifically state that sampling errors can be inferred only on the basis of judgment, and not by the mechanical application of any standard statistical formulas.

4.2 Nonsampling Error

An audience measurement service should list and explain possible sources of nonsampling error in the estimates of broadcast audiences it publishes.

Standards already appear in several of the preceding sections (see sections 2.2, 3.4, 3.7, and 3.8) specifying that the service make available results and conclusions from methodological research to enable users to assess better the effects of certain nonsampling errors (including response errors and bias of nonresponse). The service should also make available, for the same purpose, the results of research it might have on the effects of other nonsampling errors, such as those that may occur in the processing and tabulating of basic information, together with an adequate description of the nature of the research on which the information is based.

Comparison of the demographic characteristics of sample members with available census counts may also provide some basis for assessing the magnitude of nonsampling errors in survey results, particularly the error attributable to nonresponse. When such comparisons are reported by a rating service they should be accompanied by an explanation of how the indicated figures were obtained and some interpretation of any observed discrepancies. That is, such comparisons must not be reported in vacuo, and their significance should be analyzed in light of available evidence about their impact on audience measurements. The report should also carry appropriate caveats: for example, that demographic comparisons between figures based on a government census and those based on a private research firm's sample survey are not always valid because the demographic information is obtained by different means, and usually at different points in time.

Chapter 17

Preparing the Proposal and Presenting the Results

Two important topics have been "assumed away" thus far. The first of these is the task of convincing someone in or outside of the company to approve a research project and allocate the necessary resources to carry it out. This involves the careful preparation of a research proposal. The second topic concerns the very important task of presenting the results. Although these tasks occur at opposite ends of the research continuum they both constitute part of the same problem. First, the proposal must convince the manager to support a research project. Then, the final report must be good enough to convince the manager of the value of continued research.

Introduction

In this chapter attention focuses on the initial and concluding aspects of many research projects: the research proposal and the research report. Both are instances of communication. The research proposal communicates the intention of the researcher while the research report communicates the findings of the researcher. Other aspects of research communication such as publication of results in learned journals and trade media or presentations at professional conferences are not discussed. These are of only secondary concern to most marketing managers.

The Research Proposal

The research proposal is the first significant formal written communication between a researcher and the client or audience for whom the research is intended. The formal proposal may be preceded by a letter of intent and later by an informal proposal. The letter of intent is a brief statement of an idea for research which may be of value to some agency. The purpose of the letter of intent is to receive early feedback from a potential sponsoring agency indicating that the idea is one which is or is not within the scope of projects they would be willing to fund. If the agency is interested, a frequent next step is to submit an informal preliminary proposal outlining briefly the perceived nature of the problem, the methodology to be used, and the end product of the research. Most organizations that purchase research will provide unofficial encouragement or discouragement and, if the former, may make suggestions for improving the proposal. In many cases telephone conversations will accomplish the same purposes as the letter of intent and the informal proposal. Whether it is done in writing, by telephone, or both, the experienced researcher will always make an initial contact with a potential research user before submitting a formal research proposal to that user. The preparation of a good proposal requires considerable resources which should not be wasted in "blind" proposal submissions.

Research proposals may be developed in response to a public request for proposals by government and private industry, a private solicitation, or they may be developed on the research agency's own initiative in response to a problem another organization is experiencing which the group preparing the research believes it can remedy on the basis of information provided by an appropriate investigation. Sponsoring agencies may sometimes be very explicit in terms of what research proposals on specific topics should cover. Exercise I (USAID) at the end of this chapter presents an "unofficial" statement distributed by the United States Agency for International Development describing some of the dimensions it would like to have covered by research proposals concerning the role of the private sector in family planning. The AID statement leaves little room for doubt as to what their interests are.

The task of developing effective proposals is becoming increasingly important particularly as private industry becomes more involved in government-sponsored social research. For example, the Burroughs Corporation was very involved with the Job Corps program and Westinghouse Electric and Arthur D. Little have become very active in conducting social science research in the family planning area. These and other organizations maintain a full-time professional staff whose primary tasks are to develop research proposals.

The goal of proposal presentation is to persuade a sponsor to favor a particular approach to a problem and to pay for the proposed solution. Persuasion invariably means providing the sponsor with information leading to the desired conclusion. Many knowledgeable research sponsors have established proposal guidelines for research organizations seeking funds. A summary of the typical proposal outline issued by the Department of Health, Education and Welfare is presented below. Large corporations, foundations, and other organizations sometimes have similar guidelines available to researchers interested in making proposals. Even when such guidelines are unavailable, the experienced researcher will provide adequate information to enable the sponsor to effectively evaluate the proposed project.

Typical Research Proposal Outline

1. Cover
The cover of the folder must indicate:
(a) name and address of offeror

2. Title Page
(a) the title of the research project
(b) the name, title, address, and telephone number of:
    (1) the principal investigator
    (2) the official authorizing the research proposal
    (3) the person to contact on administrative and fiscal matters, or for the purpose of negotiation

3. Table of Contents
Indicate page locations for each of the principal sections of the proposal and additional detail as appropriate. A tab index may be helpful for lengthy proposals.

4. Summary and Workscope
Provide a brief summary (not to exceed one page) which states as explicitly as possible the nature and scope of the research.

5. Research Proposal
(a) *Introduction*
>Describe the overall design of the research project.

(b) *Specific Aims*
>Provide a detailed description of the specific studies to be carried out, paying special attention to research to be conducted and results anticipated during the first contract period. Describe the study design in detail, and indicate a time schedule for completion of different phases of the proposed research.

(c) *Methods*
>Provide a detailed description of the methods to be used, with technical details and a thorough evaluation of the limitations and feasibility of the method proposed.

(d) *Previous Work in This Area*
>Describe previous work in related areas; provide appropriate citations. Indicate what preliminary studies have been carried out and the results of these pilot studies.

(e) *Review of Work of Other Investigators*
>Summarize the relevant work of others in the field, with appropriate reference to the literature.

6. Qualifications of Project Personnel
Provide biographic sketches and pertinent bibliographies for professional personnel that would be involved in the proposed project.

7. Facilities and Equipment
(a) Describe existing facilities and equipment which would be used for the proposed project.
(b) Describe any new facilities or equipment which would have to be

acquired or made available for the project and justify in terms of research needs.

8. Types of Contracts

The proposed price for performance of the work in response to this Request for Proposals shall be in accordance with one of the following contract types:

(a) Cost sharing

(b) Cost reimbursement

(c) Cost reimbursement plus a fixed fee

9. Performance Period

The Government anticipates that the proposed contracts will span a 12- to 36-month performance period, although offerors may furnish their own estimates of the time required to achieve the objectives of this research.

10. Budget

The proposed estimated costs must be presented according to the following format:

(a) Detailed breakdown of the estimated cost for the first contract period (normally 12 months or the time required to complete the work). Where applicable, detailed estimated costs should be provided for each subproject and subcontract.

(b) A detailed breakdown of estimated costs for subsequent years if more than one year will be required to complete the project.

(c) Indicate the name and address of the cognizant Government audit agency, if any.

11. Financial Capacity

The offeror should indicate if he has the necessary financial capacity, working capital, and other resources to perform the contract without assistance from any outside source. (If not, indicate the amount required and the anticipated source.)

12. Human Subjects (as applicable)

Prospective contractors being considered for award will be required to give acceptable assurance that the project described herein will be subject to initial and continuing review by an appropriate institutional committee. This review shall assure that the rights and welfare of the individuals involved are adequately protected, that the risks to an individual are outweighed by the potential benefits to him or by the importance of the knowledge to be gained, and that informed consent will be obtained by methods that are adequate and appropriate.

The proposal itself may be a written document, such as outlined above, or it may be a slide or flip chart presentation, or some other type of presentation. Regardless of the format or method of communication, the researcher wants to help the sponsor decide in his favor with confidence and with a clear understanding of the proposed research. The researcher must take great care that he does not lead his client to expect something which he will not, or cannot, deliver when the project is actually executed. When the researcher opens his concluding report with a positioning statement, the concluding positioning must match the proposed project. Many experienced researchers will incorporate part of the proposal into the final report precisely for the purpose of tying the sponsor's original expectations to the final product.

Questions Asked by Managers

A marketing manager often finds himself in one of two positions in reference to research proposals. He may be called upon to review and evaluate research proposals prepared by his staff to be submitted to outside agencies. Alternatively, he may be called upon to make a decision about supporting one research project rather than another. In either case it is necessary to apply the same criteria in evaluating the research proposal. These criteria are operationalized here in the form of several questions covering the areas of significance, design, personnel and facilities, economic efficiency, and feasibility.[1] The researcher should also realize that these criteria will be applied to his proposals and should self-evaluate his proposal accordingly.

Significance
1. Does the project focus primarily on problems of major importance?
2. In the case of public service contracts or research, will the anticipated outcome of the project produce communicable results of potential value to others on a nationwide basis?
3. Is there a clear need for accomplishing the proposed project?
4. If a research, survey, or demonstration proposal is involved, does it concern the development of new knowledge directly applicable to the problem or with the new application of existing knowledge?
5. Is the project original or can it be defended as a check on previous assumptions or conclusions?

Design or Operational Plan
1. Is the problem to be dealt with clearly defined?
2. Is there a clear delineation of the purpose and value of the project,

[1] Adapted from S. A. Johnston, "The Grant Proposal," *Grant Data Quarterly.* No date.

its plan of development, method of approach, expected outcome, and need for accomplishment?

3. Are all important aspects and consequences of the proposed project accurately conceptualized?

4. Does the proposal reflect a familiarity with the historical background of the problem, an awareness of similar projects which have been previously undertaken, and an adequate knowledge of other related activities in the field?

5. Are the questions to be answered and/or hypotheses to be tested well formulated and clearly stated?

6. Does the proposal outline fully the procedure to be followed and, whenever applicable, include information on such points as sampling techniques, controls, types of data to be gathered, and statistical analyses to be completed?

Personnel and Facilities

1. Does the proposal give evidence of there being adequate facilities for carrying out the project?

2. Is it clear that the main investigators connected with the project have the requisite skills to successfully conduct the research?

3. Is the role of all professional personnel involved in the project clearly stated?

4. Does the director or principal investigator have a history of professional experience in the project area and/or a clearly demonstrated competence for conducting work in that area?

Economic Efficiency

1. Is the suggested approach to the problem reasonable in terms of overall cost as compared with the cost of other possible approaches?

2. Is there a favorable relationship between the probable outcome of the project and the total expenditure in terms of overall value?

3. Is the period of time needed to carry out the proposal clearly stated and a general timetable provided? Are these reasonable?

4. Are the costs shown realistic with no unnecessary or padded items?

5. Are parallel requests for support from other agencies indicated?

Feasibility

1. Is the proposed project both plausible in its potential to be accomplished and substantive in its anticipated outcome?

2. Does the proposed project duplicate other projects currently being conducted?

3. Is it clear that the project cannot be funded by the originator's institu-

tion if the proposal is going to an outside agency or is coming from another department within the company?

These and other questions specific to the situation at hand are implicit if not explicit in the evaluation of research proposals. A study of 605 disapproved research grant applications submitted to a U. S. government agency turned up the following most frequent reason for a proposal not being approved: (1) the problem is of insufficient importance or is unlikely to produce any new or useful information; (2) the proposed research is based on a hypothesis that rests on insufficient evidence; (3) the proposed tests, or methods, or scientific procedures are unsuited to the stated objectives; (4) the description of the approach is too nebulous, diffuse, and lacking in clarity to permit adequate evaluation; (5) the overall design of the study has not been carefully thought out; (6) the investigator does not have adequate experience or training, or both, for this research; (7) the investigator appears to be unfamiliar with pertinent literature or methods, or both; and (8) the requirements for equipment or personnel, or both, are unrealistic.

Selecting a Contractor

One approach to selecting contractors for specific marketing research is the Contractor Evaluation Scheme (CES) used by some governmental agencies. CES is a method for selecting a contractor to perform a specific marketing research task at a specific cost. It involves a systematic method for evaluating the contractor's technical capabilities and ranking them on an interval scale, that is, contractor X may receive a total score of 70 and contractor Y a score of 85. Once the contractor's technical capabilities have been evaluated and scored, his cost estimate is taken into account.

The usual CES procedure involves the formation of an evaluation committee. The contractor's price estimates are separated from the proposal and the proposal given to the committee. The committee, using a matrix analysis, determines which contractors have the highest scores. The results of this evaluation are reviewed along with the price or cost estimates and one or two contractors are usually selected for further negotiations.

The contractor should be evaluated on the basis of technical evaluation factors. A sample of factors and their respective weighted scores are:

	Weighted Score
1. General experience in marketing research work	20
2. Experience in marketing research in area of concern	5
3. Overall quality of proposal	15
4. Grasp of the problem	20
5. Proposal approach (innovative, appropriate, realistic, etc.)	25
6. Experience and qualifications of key personnel on assignment	15
Total Possible Score	100

In reviewing these technical factors, the committee should consider the following:

1. *General Experience in Marketing Research Work*   What are past jobs? How complex? How long has a contractor been in business? What is his reputation? Who are his past clients? Does the contractor's experience qualify him for this job?

2. *Experience in Marketing Research in Area of Concern*   Does the contractor have any prior experience in the relevant product area? The consumer area of interest? Is the contractor familiar with the formal and informal dynamics of the company?

3. *Overall Quality of Proposal*   How does the proposal appear as a whole? Is it presented well? Is it logical? Is it straightforward and easy to follow? Is it overly complex and complicated? Is it complete?

4. *Grasp of the Problem*   Has the contractor clearly grasped the problem? Does the proposal state the problem as it is understood by the committee? Is the contractor's understanding of the problem complete? Has the contractor overstated the problem?

5. *Proposal Approach*   What exactly does the contractor propose to do? How relevant is it to the problem? How innovative is his approach? How realistic is the approach given the financial and time constraints? Is the approach overly simplistic or complex?

6. *Experience and Qualification of Key Personnel*   Key personnel to work on the project should be identified and biographical data should be included in the proposal. How qualified are they on the basis of education and experience?

Once the proposals have been weighted they should be paired with their costs. The contractor with the highest score generally is chosen for further negotiation. In case of a tie, the contractor submitting the lowest price should be chosen. In some cases two contractors may have close scores, but there may be a significant price difference. For example, contractor X may have scored 85 with a price of $20,000, while contractor Y scored 80 with a price of $10,000. In this case it would make sense to select contractor Y for $10,000.

A sample evaluation matrix is presented in Table 17.1 with a hypothetical rating of the contractors by factors. Figure 17.1 presents a comparison of the contractors' scores on the technical evaluation and the contractors' costs.

Figure 17.1 has the evaluation scores from Table 17.1 plotted on the vertical axis and the contractors' cost plotted on the horizontal axis. The graph is utilized for comparing evaluation scores and costs.

First a selection zone is mapped out on the graph. In this example, it has been decided that no contractor receiving a score under 70 costing less than $60,000 or more than $110,000 will be considered. The reason for setting a lower cost limit is that even though a contractor may score 85 at an extremely

TABLE 17.1   *Technical Evaluation Matrix Analysis*

Factors		Contractors			
		A	B	C	D
Factor 1	(20)	15	15	20	20
Factor 2	(20)	10	15	20	15
Factor 3	(20)	15	20	15	15
Factor 4	(25)	10	10	20	25
Factor 5	(15)	10	5	10	15
Total	100	60	75	85	90

Contractor Costs

Contractor	Costs
A	$ 40,000
B	$ 80,000
C	$ 75,000
D	$175,000

low cost, it is unlikely that he could perform well at that low price. Also, a contractor may deliberately underbid to get the job.

In the cited example, it can be seen that contractors C and B fall within the Selection Zone and should be considered for the job. Contractor C could be selected outright for the job, having scored 85 at a cost of $75,000 as opposed to contractor B who scored 75 at a cost of $80,000; or contractors C and B could be invited to discuss and refine their proposals.

An Approach to Presenting Research Information

If the end product of the research process is information, the researcher must have a "product concept," a central idea of the role information is to play in decision making. The marketing system is a communications system. The marketer produces messages through a system of specialists: product designers, attorneys, advertising agencies, public relations firms, and so on. Then he monitors market response through another system of specialists: accountants and market researchers. The researcher is a link between the marketer and the market. Obviously, the researcher must be able "to talk the language" of both consumers and business. The researcher's role in this system is to communicate, filter, simplify, and transmit information from consumers to management.

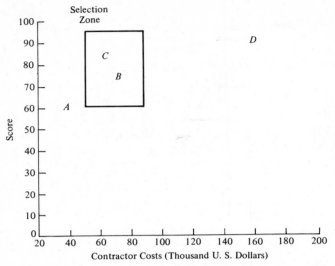

FIGURE 17.1 *Evaluation Score/Contractor Costs Analysis*

Information value is determined by four basic characteristics:

1. News content of the information
2. Organization and structure
3. Timeliness and frequency
4. Distribution.

These characteristics are directly related to the prevailing state of the audience for the research information. If the audience is already aware of the facts contained in a research report, they gain very little information from reading it. If the audience is not experienced in research methodology, technical terminology will cause misunderstanding. If the audience needed the information yesterday, but it arrived today, there may be no reason to use it. If the audience is diffused throughout the country, but the information is available only in one place, there is little possibility for it to be used effectively. If the audience's decision involves the possibility of a $15,000 gain and the research needed to make the decision costs $20,000, researching the decision will insure at least a $5000 loss.

There are many different audiences for research information. Each type has its own information needs and interests. The more common audiences are listed in Table 17.2 along with a sample of their respective interests. Many firms have adopted one of two practices involving research data they have asked to be collected. One practice is for management to first interpret the research findings and then ask the researcher to evaluate these interpretations, to the extent possible, in light of the research techniques used. A second

TABLE 17.2

Audience Type	Research Interests
Top corporate management	Corporate policy and corporate strategy implications, impact on earnings and related financial decisions, long-term strategy and corporate position
Middle management	Divisional policy and divisional strategy, brand operations and brand strategy, inter-brand profitability and market share, medium-term strategy and industry position
Operating management	Brand and product operating strategies (sales, advertising, promotion, pricing, and so on), current profitability and marketing performance, near-term future potentials, short-term marketing tactics
Other marketing researchers	Methodology (sampling techniques, research design, instrument construction, analytical procedures), differences between alternative methods, replication of new methods
Research management	New methods with higher cost-effectiveness, research communications, research budgeting, organization operations, research positioning, interstudy relationships
Government agencies	Implications for legislation and industry regulation, government intervention policy, implications for the public welfare
The public	Implications for consumer decision making, product and brand choice decisions, health and safety implications
Trade associations	Implications for preserving industry status quo, inter-industry competition and marketing performance, industry policy and lobbying strategy
Legal bodies—courts	Criteria for deciding between adversaries in legal actions, evidence in present cases, precedents in future cases, legal strategy and tactics

approach is growing out of the increasing practice of marketing research firms to offer nonresearch consulting advice. This approach is to have the researcher, with his understanding of the relevant factors impinging on his study, to interpret his own findings and make his own recommendations at the time his research report is submitted.

In order for information to have value, research must convey news to the audience. It must be something which the audience did not previously know.

For example, a research study may discover that customers for a product are really using it for different reasons than management thinks they are.

When research confirms management opinion, it may still provide information. In fact, one of the frequent uses of research is not to determine what decision alternative to choose, but how much confidence to place in the selected course of action. By reducing the risk involved in a decision, an investment in research can produce overall cost savings. For example, the decision to market a new product may require between $36 million and $44 million. The investment is such that even at the $44 million figure, the project would be profitable and the company would go ahead with the project. However, if the company could get a better fix on the cost, it could budget its funds better and save substantially. If a market research study produced a reliable estimate that the actual cost would be $40 million, the company would not have to reserve an extra $4 million for the project and could invest it elsewhere producing greater growth.

The news content of research information depends to a great extent on what the audience expects from the research study. These expectations are the direct result of how the researcher has positioned the project in the past and how he positions the project when he begins to report his findings.

The term positioning as used here refers to the benefits that the researcher promises and claims that his audience will receive. For example, the researcher might claim that his study will show how to increase market share. Or, a researcher might promise his colleagues that his study shows how to relate consumer personality types to brand preferences. From this point of view of the audience, the research may or may not support the claims made. It is obvious that the audience will evaluate the research according to what claim the researcher makes for it.

Every research communication should start out with some sort of positioning statement. Generally, a brief situation analysis, problem description, or reason-why statement will serve to tune the audience in on the research project and the context in which it was done. This setting up of the audience is especially important where the audience is not familiar with the circumstances surrounding the beginning of the research project or where there has been a significant lapse of time between the start of the project and the presentation of the findings.

For example, an advertising agency research team presented a client company president with a new marketing strategy on one of the company's brands that was declining in market share. The project was originally undertaken at the request of the vice-president of marketing and the president was totally unfamiliar with the project until two days before the presentation. By prefacing the presentation with some background remarks, the project director tuned in his audience—the president—into why the project was done and how the company should view his recommendations.

It is a fact of life that research often evaluates people as well as marketing plans, products, and environment. Whenever research is done on a subject which is heavily laden with human emotional energy or ego-involved for the audience, the audience is likely to favor research supporting current attitudes and denigrate research contradictory to existing attitudes. Often, the very managers who grasp research as a tool for managerial control rebel against research when it is used to evaluate their own performances.

The researcher must position his research findings carefully whenever his subject is controversial or sensitive to his audience. Also, there may be times when a research project produces contradictory results or findings which run counter to prevailing theory. The researcher should attempt to acknowledge these at the outset and position them in the context of the research situation. Thus, the researcher inoculates his audience against surprise contradictions.

Finally, it is necessary to understand that the good researcher avoids giving his audience all the details of his research. No matter how interesting the researcher thinks his own research is, his audience may be less interested. Too many details can cloud real issues, confuse people who are unfamiliar with research techniques, and generally overpower the audience. To this end, the researcher must tailor his communications to each individual audience. Often, the same project should be reported differently to different audiences—technical and methodological reports for technically minded researchers, brief summaries of findings and recommendations for top management, comprehensive and detailed reports for the research department's files.

Organization and Structure

The research communication must be structured to lead the audience to a logical emotional and intellectual climax—approval of the findings and adoption of the recommendations where recommendations are made. There are many ways to structure an effective message. The researcher should select the one structure that makes the most sense for the type of audience and material that he is presenting.

The two most common structures for organizing a research communication are problem-analysis-solution structure and chronological structure. Problem-analysis-solution structure boils down to establishing the problem and its significance, then analyzing the dimensions and causes of the problem, and making the logical recommendations. This particular structure parallels the scientific method itself although the researcher may omit "blind alleys" and false starts from his presentation of the project.

Chronological structure is time-oriented in that the message is communicated either as the research project proceeded from start to finish or as the problem-analysis-solution events occurred. For example, one might explain how at the start of the project in 1968, a particular phenomenon was found and how, in 1970, enough data was gathered to perform an analysis of this phenomenon. In 1971 and in 1972, the findings of this analysis were tested in four test markets. Evaluation of the test market results led to broad distribution in 1973.

Or, for example, one might explain how a sales decline was noted in every year since 1965 as a result of declining distribution and the growth of mass merchandisers in retail sales of the product. The trend shows that the sales decline is due to the company's failure to keep pace with product distribution changes.

Some forms of research communication (slide and flip chart presentation film) have two structures: video and audio. These structures should correspond. What is shown at any point in the presentation should be the same thing that is verbally explained.

Since the purpose of structure is to give the communication a wholeness of thought, the person who is to give the presentation should prepare his own material. Even when the slides or charts will be prepared by an outside studio, the presenter should prepare precise rough visuals, and organize his material before sending it out for final preparation.

If, as sometimes happens, the presentation must be cut short due to unforeseen time constraints, having a well-defined structure aids in the elimination of extraneous material without destroying the overall storyline or central idea.

Structure should not be confused with the common practice of outlining the report or presentation. Structure is concerned with the logical flow of ideas while outlining is primarily concerned with the physical organization of material and facts. It is quite possible to have a brilliant outline with the facts all neatly arranged, but to have no emotional and intellectual climax. Table 17.3 shows the general outline of the typical comprehensive marketing research report. This represents the "stand alone" or "single-shot" report in that other reports or presentations are not needed. Any audience member can read the report and find almost everything that he wants to know. Deviations from this format are common depending on the material to be reported and the audiences for the information.

Timeliness and Frequency

Increasingly, marketing research is done on a systematic basis at regular predetermined intervals. The growth of marketing information systems and syndicated research services have been particularly influential in fostering the trend toward systematic, periodic research reporting.

The general principle underlying this trend is that as markets become more dynamic, executives need regular reports over time in order to get a clear picture of the changing states of the marketing system. The more dynamic the markets, the more frequent the reports must be, and the faster each report must be produced from the time of data collection to reporting. Information

TABLE 17.3 *Research Report Outline*

I. Title Page
  (a) title
  (b) author's name
  (c) documentation numbers and project identification numbers
  (d) classification
  (e) circulation test
  (f) issue date and destroy date

II. Table of Contents
  (a) section subtitles and pages
  (b) illustration titles and pages
  (c) graph titles and pages
  (d) figure and titles and pages

III. Abstract of Report
  (a) what was attempted by research project
  (b) when
  (c) where
  (d) how and with what techniques

IV. Summary of Report
  (a) problem definition and date
  (b) what was researched
  (c) when
  (d) where
  (e) how and with what techniques
  (f) major findings
  (g) recommendations

V. Introduction
  (a) what prompted the undertaking of the project
  (b) who prompted the project
  (c) how the problem was defined

VI. Statement of Objectives
  (a) how the problem definition was resolved
  (b) what was the research objective

VII. Research Methods
  (a) research design
  (b) data instruments (questionnaire, customer records, etc.)
  (c) data-collection methods
  (d) sampling technique
  (e) field work

VIII. Methodological Limitations
  (a) weaknesses in research design
  (b) exogenous events that may have influenced findings

TABLE 17.3   *(continued)*

      (c) errors in research methods
      (d) alternative causes for findings

IX. *Analysis of Findings*
      (a) discussion of items of significance
      (b) discussion of items of insignificance
      (c) interpretations of findings

X. *Conclusions and Recommendations*
      (a) what research findings show
      (b) what actions should be taken (or not taken)

XI. *Technical Appendix*
      (a) informational tables, graphs, illustrations
      (b) technical discussion of research methodology and sample
      (c) sample validation if relevant

XII. *General Appendix*
      (a) selected portions of preliminary interviews
      (b) project diary: dates, places, names, events, etc.
      (c) copies of forms, questionnaires, records, and data instruments

XIII. *Acknowledgments*
      (a) names, titles, and affiliation of contributors
      (b) contribution of each contributor

XIV. *References and Bibliography*
      (a) names, titles, and source of related research

XV. *Index*

XVI. *Project Accounting Report (optional and placed appropriately)*
      (a) project expenses by category
      (b) project expenses by supplier
      (c) project expenses by item and date
      (d) discussion and analysis of costs

is perishable and must be used to make decisions while there is still time to effect the future state of the marketing system.

To produce reports that are timely, that is in time to make decisions before the data and findings have become obsolete, researchers have turned to computer technology. Computers are not new to marketing research. However, to date, they have been primarily used only for data tabulation and analysis. Recently, and probably more so in the future, optical scanning and time-sharing will play a major role in cutting the time between data collection and reporting.

Optical scanning uses special, standardized forms for the recording of information. These forms may be filled out using an ordinary typewriter or even hand printing. The optical scanner, a special input device for large computers, literally reads the typewriting or handwriting. Light is directed against the form and is reflected back into the machine's "retina," just as the human eye functions. The image of the characters is translated into machine readable code for tabulation. Analysis is done using standard techniques just as if the machine had read punched cards or a data tape.

In a special application using computers, the A. C. Nielsen Company has developed a system for reporting television ratings within 24 hours of air time. A special device is attached to the television sets of a sample of 1000 of all U. S. TV households. This device records the time that each set is turned on and the station to which it is tuned. Late at night, the central computer automatically dials the device and uses the household's phone line to transmit the data that it has stored. When all households have been phoned, the computer tabulates the results and prints out reports. Using these reports, a company knows exactly how many households were tuned in during their commercial message the day before.

In contrast to timeliness, where maximum speed is an objective, frequency of reporting has no simple, clear-cut objective. Too frequent reporting can swamp executives in more information than they can assimilate or constructively use. It can also "deaden the senses" by creating an atmosphere where executives feel they can never catch up to the swelling tide, so that when really important information is reported, it runs a chance of being ignored. In addition, too frequent reporting may cause "purpose tremor," the overreacting to crisis information such that each feedback reaction cycle tends to compound previous errors. Too infrequent reporting does not give a clear-cut picture of the marketing system and tends to hide the important fluctuations in time series data, making it impossible to relate marketing information to other types of information.

The crux of finding the optimum reporting frequency for a marketing information system or series of reports depends on the individuals in the audience for the information and the dynamics of the marketing system.

Different reporting frequencies may be used for different audiences. For example, in packaged goods where purchase frequency is high and attitudes can change rapidly, monthly data collection and processing may be necessary to get a clear picture of the marketing system. Reports may be furnished to brand managers monthly, while top management may receive quarterly reports.

The optimum frequency in one industry may not be the optimum frequency in another industry. It is doubtful that very frequent reporting on the state of the furniture industry would reveal significant change from report to report. In the furniture industry, quarterly or semiannual reporting may be sufficient to keep management abreast of changes in the marketing system.

Similarly, the distribution of research information exposure is important. In highly seasonal industries such as lawn and garden equipment, continuous year-round reporting is not needed nearly so much as a massive dose of information in the planning stages of preparing for a coming season.

Finally, the amount of information to be reported must also be considered in determining optimum frequency. The marketing research department of a major beer company produces an annual report on the state of the industry. The report is massive, filling 17 looseleaf bindings, and one copy is given to each department in the company. Although one annual report may sufficiently reveal the state of the industry, it is unlikely that many people are capable of assimilating such a mass of information. It might be much more effective to break the information into quarterly reports, each one dealing with a different aspect of the industry.

Distribution

Once the research project has been completed and the findings are assembled, there are three questions which must be resolved: Should the findings be distributed? Who should get them? How should they be distributed?

The question of whether or not to distribute the findings of a given project is not as clear-cut as it might first appear. Market researchers often do research that they do not want to distribute.

For example, 20 or 30 studies might be performed on various products by the marketing research department in the interest of developing a new testing procedure. The findings of these studies would obviously interest the brand managers on those products. However, the research department may not want to distribute the findings until they have all the "burrs" out of their new testing procedure. R & D in the marketing research area is one of the commonest reasons for not distributing research findings. Such research is done for the purpose of improving the company's marketing research efforts and the results of these pioneering studies are of primary interest to the research department. It is often particularly important that such R & D efforts in the marketing research area be kept confidential. If marketing researchers are to develop new techniques, their developmental work must be shielded from the scrutiny of the general corporate population. Just as a scientist in basic research or product R & D, the marketing researcher will make mistakes, run up "blind alleys," and go through a trial-and-error process in his work. If every study— both good and bad, successful and unsuccessful—is offered for distribution and criticism throughout the company or organization, the researcher can hardly be expected to take risks and try new techniques.

Sometimes, a study will be undertaken, but for one reason or another, it will fail. Such studies should not be distributed. Unfortunately, business has come to put such a stigma on failure that bad research must often be distributed despite its obvious flaws. There is no reason to believe a marketing researcher will be any more "right" all of the time than to believe every brand manager, ad agency creative director, financial executive, or attorney will always be "right."

When mistakes or catastrophies do occur, it is far better to correctly repeat the study, if there is time, and to complete the project late. As a well-known marketing consultant once remarked: "Five years from today, the client won't remember whether the project was completed on time. He'll only remember whether you were right or wrong. And that's what your reputation is based on."

Similarly, the question of who should get research findings is not necessarily clear-cut either. Many companies operate on a need-to-know basis. Thus, a brand manager may obtain information on the brand that he manages but not on other brands marketed by the company. Other companies employ a classification procedure so that only certain people have access to certain information.

The advent of computer-based information systems has made the task of enforcing corporate security doubly difficult. Most systems are equipped with elaborate systems of passwords to protect the data stored inside the computer, high technology fire protection systems to protect the hardware itself, and the conventional armed guards.

The problem of keeping marketing information secret is not without its price. Aside from the expense of maintaining classification systems, guards or whatever, the people who work in an atmosphere of tight security may not perform as well as they might in an environment of free flowing information. This is sometimes called a "chill factor," the extent to which tight security makes people modify their behavior to conform to the security standards.

For example, a junior level marketing executive may read a report and get a "hot" idea for improving his products' sales performance. He may want other information to validate his hunch. However, he finds that he is not permitted access to the information he wants. His enthusiasm for the idea is dampened and, finally, quietly abandoned. No one in the company may ever know that the idea existed. Thus, tight security takes its toll by cutting down the stimulation of an organization's people, and costs the organization the ideas that would have resulted from a high-information environment.

The research management problem is how to provide the organization with an information-rich environment without reducing security below acceptable risk levels. A stratified approach is often the best solution to such problems. The researcher may give a flip chart presentation on the results of a project to a broad spectrum of company executives from lower echelons to top management. However, only select executives may be given written reports. A lower level manager who has an idea and wants access to a written report can obtain one for a limited time by asking. Such an approach keeps everyone informed while limiting distribution of written material to those people who have an interest in the findings.

With the ever-growing population of duplicating machines and computer systems, management should be legitimately concerned about the security of marketing information. However, concern should not lead to paranoia. One major packaged goods company buys brand share data from a major syndicated research service. These data are locked in a special room. Executives may not take information out or duplicate any of the reports. The company has only four major competitors and every one of them has similar brand share data of its own. Some of them even purchase the exact same syndicated service.

In many cases, the real purpose of security systems is not to protect information from competitors. Most of the larger competitors of any given company have marketing information which is as good or better. Besides, industrial espionage is not highly common in the marketing research area since practically any study can be duplicated at a lower cost than espionage. In fact, it is common practice to research competitive products with consumers, pull copies of competitors' commercials off the air for testing, and to monitor brand shares, distribution levels, and pricing of all major competitors. Often, the simplest answer to security in the marketing area is that in highly dynamic markets, information grows old and stale quickly. If old information falls into the hands of competitors, it is generally of little value either because it is relevant only to the company which produces it or because the marketing system has changed since the report was produced.

More often, security in the marketing area is enforced because companies fear that market research information will fall into the hands of government regulatory agencies or consumer advocates, either of which could cause the company embarrassment.

As mentioned, classification systems are often used to control information distribution. The successful classification system is a set of rational decision rules which are enforced to control information flow. Emphasis on the word "rational" cannot be overstated. However, the operation of a successful classification poses several problems. Researchers and executives must be encouraged not to overclassify information. That is, they must not use the classification system as a means of gaining attention for the information and reports that they distribute. Overclassification dampens the free flow of information. Similarly, the classification system must be time-oriented so that information is systematically declassified and purged or destroyed. The system must be people-oriented so that any one can have access to the most confidential information if the situation warrants such access. Finally, the distribution of marketing information must be considered from a technological standpoint. Computer capability has increased to the point where it is now possible to have

managers in different parts of the country assess a comn.
and marketing models through a network of time-sharing
phone lines. Although such systems are extremely costly
significant impact on numerous industries such as airlines wl.
keep track of customers. Indirectly, they have also affected th
other goods and services such as the application of informatio.
banking and credit verification.

The use of portable computer terminal with time-sharing s,
also enabled many marketers to use their marketing research data \ .__ique
ways to benefit their customers. For example, a large insurance company has
developed a model for determining the amount and type of insurance a head of
house should buy given his characteristics such as income, age, number and
ages of children, occupation, and so on. A salesman can call on a customer
and use a portable terminal to input the pertinent information about the
customer. The model analyzes the data and prints out an insurance plan.

Sealtest Foods has a similar model that their salesmen can use when
calling on supermarket managers. The salesmen can input data on the supermarket such as its volume and neighborhood type. The model will print out
a planogram of the optimum ice cream cabinet for maximizing ice cream
profits and sales, complete with what type of items to put in the cabinet, how
they should be placed, how much space the store should allocate to each type
of product, where in the store the cabinet should be located, sales and profit
forecasts.

Being a Communicator

After a communications strategy has been worked out in terms of positioning, message, message structure, audience, and distribution, the research
report, presentation, or information system must be put together. It does not
follow that because one is a good researcher he is an equally good communicator. For some people, report writing and oral presentations are trying
experiences. For others, the reverse is true; a person can be an excellent
communicator, but lack the analytical strengths that mark a good researcher.

For example, a Vice-President and Management Supervisor at a leading
advertising agency presented a new campaign to a client for the coming year.
The account billed $2.5 million, but his presentation was so impressive and
persuasive that the client voluntarily added $1 million to the budget. This
addition was the equivalent to getting a new $1 million account without having
to prepare any extra ads or doing any extra work. Three weeks after his
presentation, a management consultant, hired to determine why the brand in
question was declining in sales, showed that the agency's recommendations
were 180 degrees opposite from sound, analytical, marketing planning.

The good researcher who is also an effective communicator is not commonly found. But this does not have to be the case. Communication skills can be learned just as research skills can be learned.

Writing the Research Report

Writing an effective report usually requires developing an outline or a first step. Several questions must be asked and answered in developing a good outline. A sample of such questions is presented below[2]:

1. What is the purpose of the work? Was it achieved? Why is it important?
2. Are there conclusions and recommendations?
3. Can you separate main issues from side issues?
4. Do you have enough information for an introduction that will "bring the readers on board"?
5. What information will be included and what will be omitted?

For greater ease in outlining the following guidelines have been offered.[3]

1. Keep causes and effects together.
2. Finish one topic before starting another.
3. Separate opinion from fact.
4. Use headings and subheadings to denote the relative weights of topics and subtopics.
5. Indicate in the outline where illustrations and tables will clarify and support the text.

Above all, the research report is written for the audience and several questions about the readers should be asked[4]:

1. What do they need to know about the subject?
2. What are their educational and technical levels?
3. How much detail and accuracy do they need?
4. What is their attitude toward the subject and you?
5. What is their organizational relationship to you; is it the same level, above or below?
6. What kinds of artwork, if any, will help them most?

Once the strategy has been determined and the outline has been written, the report writer knows basically what the report will do and look like. Each individual section of the report will tell its own "little story" about sampling,

---

[2] H. K. Mintz, "Business Writing Styles for the 1970's," *Business Horizons* (August 1972), pp. 83–87.
[3] *Ibid.*
[4] *Ibid.*

methodology, analysis, and so on. Therefore, each section will have its own beginning and ending. And each will be written to encourage the audience to agree with the writer in stages or subclimaxes. Thus, by the time the audience reaches the report's findings and conclusions, it will be favorably predisposed toward the research recommendations.

There are two places to begin writing the report: at the beginning with the title page or at the end with the climax and recommendations. Oddly enough, the latter is often the preferable place to start writing because that is where the report must climax. By starting at the climax, the statements and sections leading up to it are more likely to be in line with the recommendations.

Sentences and paragraphs can be either long or short; what matters is the psychological time it takes to read them. Easy reading sentences enable the reader to move along quickly even though there may be many words. Sentence structure and smooth transitional phrases are very important in speeding up the reading process. The language of the research report is simple, clear, precise, and to the point.

Marketing problems are rarely funny. Humor, along with slang and technical jargon, should be avoided. Preference should be given to understatement, brevity, and frankness. This is not to suggest that anecdotes cannot be used if they serve a legitimate purpose of illustrating a point or research finding. For example, in a report to the top management of a leading bank, a researcher quoted a few humorous responses of several bank customers to illustrate various customer attitudes.

Often, the quickest way to communicate is with tables, graphs, or illustrations. However, these communication formats should not be inserted haphazardly. Each table, graph, illustration, figure, diagram, and so on, should have a title which clearly identifies it, should be numbered so that it can be identified in the body of the report, and should be on a numbered page. Whenever possible, similar data should be graphed or tabled the same way to give the report a continuity from page to page and section to section.

Reproduction of the research report can vary widely from simply typing to actually setting the document in type, and printing it. The greater the number of copies that are needed, and the more impressive the document needs to be, the higher the quality of reproduction. The same holds true for binding the document. Bindings range from simply stapling the pages of the report together to using a full textbook binding with leather cover, embossed with gold leaf. In general, the reproduction and binding of the research report should match the ideas inside the document and the audience. The more important the ideas and audience, the more impressive the document.

Several research organizations have reproduction and binding standards depending on the audience and the material. When dealing with clients, these document standards quickly position different reports for members of the client organization and help them recognize which reports deserve the most attention.

Presenting Research

Increasingly, businesses are getting away from "the fat document" type of report and relying more on personal presentation using flip charts, slides, and so on. With the executive reading time dwindling and the ability to ask the presentor questions, group presentations are a faster, better way to communicate and reach understanding. Such stand-up presentations are a principal means of research communication by advertising agencies, large companies, syndicated research services, and other types of companies.

The stand-up presentation is usually of three types: flip chart, slide, and other. The slide presentation is well suited for groups of twenty or more people. It is generally considered a formal way to present material. It is durable; the same presentation may be given over and over, and the quality of the visual material will always be the same. A tray of slides and a slide projector are relatively compact for easy traveling.

If the charts are "homemade," a flip chart presentation tends to be less formal than slides. It is given with the lights on so that the presentor and the audience have a greater sense of being face to face, in personal conversation. For small groups of under twenty people, the personal presence of the presentor helps hold the audience's attention. Flip chart presentations are not particularly durable. After a dozen or so presentations, the charts will become worn, wrinkled, and frayed around the edges. They also tend to accumulate smudges and finger prints. Flip charts, particularly large-sized charts, do not make traveling easy. If the presentor must bring his own easel for holding the charts, transporting the easel becomes a giant headache.

Other types of presentations include: film, desk-top charts, film cassettes, telephone presentations, meetings, and so on. All of these types of presentations have their own unique features. With the exceptions of telephone presentations, letters, memos, and meetings, these forms of presentation are used for special situations.

Preparation of the visual part of either slide or flip chart presentation is relatively simple. Experienced presentors generally make up a rough draft of each slide or chart. Once the entire set of slides or charts has been completed, they rehearse two or three times with the roughs just to make sure the presentation covers what is needed, takes the right amount of time, and climaxes when it should. This is generally referred to as "tracking." The roughs themselves may be no more than sheets of lined paper with the appropriate words hand printed, and with graphs hand drawn. For slides, the roughs will be sketched sideways since slides are wider than they are high.

After rehearsing with the roughs, and debugging the presentation, the professional presentor will number the roughs, photocopy them, and turn the originals over to a graphic arts slide maker or chart maker for execution into slides or full-size charts.

Summary

It has been said that no good idea succeeds on its inherent merits alone. Good research ideas must be successfully "packaged" as proposals to compete with others either within the company or with outside agencies. The guidelines mentioned at the start of this chapter are those frequently used by persons experienced in proposal presentations. Similarly, the results of research are not automatically accepted but rather must be properly organized keeping in mind the needs, interests, and background of the audience(s) for whom the research results are intended.

Questions and Exercises

1. Comment on the differences and similarities between a letter of intent, an informal preliminary proposal, and a formal research proposal.
2. Research proposals may be developed in response to a public request, a private solicitation, or on the research agency's own initiative. Comment on how research proposals may differ depending on the source of the initiative that prompted the proposal.
3. This chapter includes a typical HEW research proposal outline. Comment on the reasons why HEW might want the information included under each of the categories listed.
4. This chapter includes criteria that can be used in evaluating a research proposal. Comment on whether or not the list is complete. Comment on reasons why each of the reasons may be important.
5. This chapter presents the CES system used by many agencies of the government. Comment on its strengths and weaknesses. This chapter also includes a sample of factors used in evaluation and their respective weights of importance. Would you include other factors, exclude any, or alter the importance weights?
6. The research proposal and the research report are two instances of information. Comment on the similarities and differences between the two concerning not only their purpose but also their techniques of presentation.
7. How is it possible that the same project can produce reports of dramatically different scope?
8. Is it possible to have too much information?
9. Two common structures for organizing research communication are problem-analysis-solution structure and chronological structure. Com-

pare and contrast the two and comment on their advantages and disadvantages.

10. It is far better to repeat a study if it was improperly done than to disseminate the results provided there is sufficient time to do so. If there is not enough time what should the researcher do and what issues should he consider in making his decision?

11. This chapter comments on how security may dampen innovativeness. Comment on measures that will not hinder innovativeness but also insure security.

12. A person may be a good researcher but a poor report writer. Comment on the skills necessary to be a good researcher and a good report writer. Comment on the similarities and differences between the two types of skills.

13. Comment on the advantages and disadvantages of hearing an oral presentation versus reading a written report on research findings.

14. Would you agree with the statement, knowledge of one's audience is a prerequisite for important research? Why?

15. Evaluate the research proposal one of your fellow students has prepared in response to Exercises 1 and/or 2 (following). Enumerate the weaknesses. Would you fund such a proposal if you were in the position of the agency requesting proposals?

16. Assume you are a member of the marketing research division of a large commercial organization and have been assigned to act as a liaison with the sales-force group. Prepare a research proposal (to be submitted to the director of marketing research) in which you suggest an investigation of social and psychological factors influencing the interaction between salesmen and their clients. [*Hint*: Review Chapters 4, 5, and 9.]

17. As the research director of a marketing consulting organization you have been asked to prepare a research proposal to be submitted to a candy manufacturer. The research to be conducted is intended to provide the manufacturer with information concerning their very high rate of failure in introducing new candy products during the past two years. It is expected that the research will guide them to more successful ways of test marketing and launching their new products.

18. What differences, if any, might there be between proposals submitted to government agencies and those submitted to commercial agencies?

19. Prepare a written or oral research report to an advertising manager using the data presented in Reading 15-1.

20. Prepare a written or oral research report for a new products manager based on Reading 17-1.

Project Related Questions

1. Have you developed a reasonable outline for your proposed project? Have you specified the aim, methodology, other related work, and so forth?
2. Have you systematically addressed the various questions asked by managers which are discussed on pages 664 to 666? Which of these questions are most pertinent to your proposed project?
3. Who is the audience for this research? What are their information needs?
4. What key questions is your audience or client interested in?
5. What form will the final report take? An oral presentation? Written?
6. Have you decided upon the proper structure of your presentation?
7. Have you considered explicitly the items mentioned in Table 17.3?

Exercise 1 (USAID)

The following information is excerpted from a "request for proposals" issued by the United States Agency for International Development (USAID). Assume you are the Director of Marketing Research for a major management consulting firm and your organization has decided to submit a proposal. Working with two or three colleagues prepare such a proposal.

ARTICLE I:
STATEMENT OF WORK

The Contractor will survey global patterns of commercial distribution of contraceptives in (1) *Pakistan*, (2) *Turkey*, (3) *Brazil*, (4) *Columbia*, (5) *Korea*, (6) *Indonesia*, (7) *Tunisia*, (8) *Ghana*.

Part One: Introduction

Although some work can be done by the Contractor in the United States (library research, interviews with pharmaceutical manufacturers, contacts with trade associations, a review of the literature of previously completed consumer analysis surveys, and KAP studies), and by mail with European pharmaceutical houses, most of the work will be done by the Contractor sending core teams to the countries to be studied. In the course of the survey the Contractor will collect, analyze, document, evaluate, and present marketing data on *importation, local production, distribution, sales*, and *use*

of all contraceptives sold on the commercial market, *excluding* those requiring medical application (specifically the IUD), *excluding* surgical procedures for the prevention of conception, and *excluding* post-conceptive birth prevention (abortion). In the case of orals, the surveys will include orals when sold with and without medical intervention. (Injectables such as DEPRO PROVERA would be included where applicable.)

In some countries much of the data to be collected under *Part One* are available in varying degrees of completeness and reliability. The Contractor must evaluate the available data, indicating in the final report (explained later) his estimation of the data. Whether the data are available or not, the Contractor will have to send professionals to each of the countries, who will gather marketing information from such sources as: government organizations, drug companies and their detail men, national programs (public and private) where applicable, local importers, local distributors, AID Missions, trade associations, among others. In obtaining *use* data, minimum consumer analysis sample surveys will be conducted. In the case of *use* data, the Contractor will budget only minimum costs for surveys, perhaps in only two countries. To supplement this effort, the Contractor will utilize recent pre-existing use data when available.

In planning field work (Part One) the Contractor will, in each country, work closely with a host country counterpart, which could be a member of his firm's staff in that country, a university department, a professor, or a government employee. The Contractor shall train or assist his host country counterpart in such a way that having left the country, the host counterpart can carry on this work in the future. These efforts must be documented in the final report.

Whenever and wherever possible the Contractor will keep the United Nation's family organizations and field representatives informed of his activities.

Part One: Specific

The Contractor will present in written form an in-depth data presentation, which will answer as many of the following questions as possible for each contraceptive by country, but in any case will cover the major commercial activities of *Importation, Production/Manufacturing, Distribution, Sales, Use.* Suggested questions by major category are:

A. *Importation* What kinds of contraceptives are being imported? From where? Countries? Companies? In what form? Raw materials? Prepackaged? Bulk? By whom? Intended destination? Private sector/national program/private programs? To what extent does government control or restrict imports? What trade policies are important to contraceptive imports? What are import figures over time? What is extent of government reporting system for imports? Is it reliable?

B. *Production/Manufacturing (Local)* What kinds of contraceptives are being manufactured? Over time? In what form? In what quantity? What controls and restrictions apply? How many companies? Are they locally owned or foreign subsidiaries? Does government collect production figures? Are they reliable? How much of indigenous production leaves country by exports? Destination?

C. *Distribution* Is there an identifiable contraceptive distribution network? Where are distribution outlets? Rural? Urban? How many for each? What is size of detail force for major companies? What government controls/restrictions apply to distribution?

Is there a viable distribution system for associated consumer products that could be utilized for contraceptives?

Are there outlets not now selling contraceptives that might logically handle these products?

What is being done to increase handlers' profit? Incentives used or possible?

D. *Sales* What is sales history for each contraceptive? By channel?

What are sales at a point in time? Within a time frame?

What factors account for sales fluctuations? Totally and by district?

What is price level? How is it established? Margins at wholesale and retail level?

How much advertising is involved? General public? Special public?

Are special promotional efforts made?

What accounts for mark-up variations, if any?

What contraceptives require medical intervention?

E. *Use (Consumer Analysis Surveys)*

Proportion of total users who get contraceptives from private sector?

Demographic/social characteristics of users?

What is sales/use by urban rural? Sex/age/parity?

What are continuing estimates?

Does use appear to depend upon easy availability?

Part Two

The Contractor will evaluate the data collected (in Part One) and will provide a cross-country/cross-regional analysis of the data, and present hypotheses dealing with such questions as: What are the market limitations for distribution and sales? What are the immediate and long-run market potentials? It is anticipated that a number of questions will arise in the course of completing Part One, which the Contractor will address in his final report.

Part Three

The Contractor will submit written recommendations or possible plans for future consideration by interested parties such as governments and private firms, which would address the following *kinds of issues*:

The role of the private sector in stimulating contraceptive use.

The role of the government (of the country studied) in stimulating the private sector.

Opportunities for increased private sector sales (possible market stimulation) and bottlenecks to private sector activity.

Innovative approaches to contraceptive marketing, and imaginative new uses of unconventional channels.

Future market activity.

Public and private sector relationships with special attention to those matters that influence use in the commercial sector vis-à-vis the public program.

Contraceptive-related consumer goods distribution systems that might be utilized successfully for contraceptives.

Product improvement or product substitution.

Specialized information programs for the commercial sector.

Special marketing problems that might be associated with prostaglandins.

Part Four

Based on the preceding three parts the Contractor will make written recommendations for a formal marketing program for at least two countries. The Contractor should present material and recommendations that are appropriate in his best professional judgment. He undoubtedly will wish to keep in mind the social/economic/political/cultural/ethnic realities of life. The Contractor will choose countries from the eight (8) countries studied, justifying his choices in the final report.

Exercise 2 (NSF)

The following request for proposal (RFP) has been issued by the Research Applied to National Needs program of the National Science Foundation, a federal funding agency. The evaluation criteria to be used by NSF in evaluating proposals submitted in response to this RFP are also presented.

CONSUMER DEMAND ANALYSIS

Integral to any analysis of solar heating and cooling of buildings should be an analysis of U. S. consumer demand for solar energy systems. There are two aspects of the analysis of consumer demand to be considered: nonmarket (life style factors) and market (prices of alternative energy sources).

With regard to the nonmarket aspects, it would be unwise to design solar heating and cooling systems without concern for consumer preference. Substantial adaptations of solar technology have occurred in Japan, Israel, and Australia, and to a lesser extent in parts of Florida and California. Experience has shown that over a period of time there is a tendency for consumers to switch from the solar energy system to electric or fossil fuel technology. An analysis of the past experience of consumers with solar energy systems is desired. In order to determine the market aspects of this demand, a schedule of consumer demand given alternative sources of energy is also requested. The resultant analysis should yield recommendations to be taken into consideration by designers of buildings to be cooled and heated with solar energy.

CRITERIA OF EVALUATION

The Foundation will select for award those proposals which offer the greatest total value. Although the estimated cost will be considered in determining which proposal offers the greatest value, the primary basis for selection will be the three review factors described below:

1. Problem Comprehension

The quality of the hypotheses integrated into the research design as well as the policy consequences that might follow from the acceptance or rejection of such hypotheses will be part of the basis for the evaluation.

2. Research Design and Methodology

(a) General plan of work

(b) Design of experiments, methods, and procedures

3. Personnel and Management Plan

(a) Organization resources, commitment, flexibility, and experience

(b) Permanent staff qualifications, in particular those of the project manager

(c) Outside consultants and sources

(d) Project management plan

(e) Financial management plan

Approximately equal emphasis will be placed on each of these factors.

Assume you are employed by an organization involved with solar heating and cooling or an organization capable of performing the consumer demand analysis. Prepare a research proposal which your organization would submit to NSF.

Assume that your research has been conducted for you and you must make specific recommendations to marketing management about the question as to whether new product buyers can be identified. As a marketing research director prepare a written report describing how these data can be used by marketing management.

Can New Product Buyers Be Identified?

Edgar A. Pessemier, Philip C. Burger, and Douglas J. Tigert

Insights into the characteristics of buyers and nonbuyers of a new branded detergent are given, which are based on measures obtained before and after the product's introduction.

Primarily because of the paucity of relevant data, few empirical studies have appeared on the characteristics of early, late, and nonbuyers of new products. This article discusses data collected for the "Lafayette Consumer Behavior Research Project" [9]. For the project, a great deal of information was gathered about introduction of a new heavy duty detergent. The branded detergent used was promoted as having a new fluorescent ingredient with unusual brightening power. Data were obtained from diary records and two questionnaires. One questionnaire was given before the product introduction and the other after a seven-month period during which purchase diaries were kept by 265 housewives.

The theoretical basis for this study was largely derived from the literature on adoption and diffusion. Studies by rural sociologists [11], Katz and Lazarsfeld [6], C. W. King [7], Coleman, Katz, and Menzel [3] and others led to the following hypotheses about variables that would discriminate among early, late, and nonbuyers of the new laundry detergent:

1. Early buyers would be more trial-prone toward brands in the product class and be heavier users of the product class (high salience) than late or nonbuyers.
2. Early buyers would actively transmit information about their experience with the brand and class; late buyers would be information receivers.
3. Early, late, and nonbuyers could be identified on the basis of demographic characteristics, mass media exposure factor scores, activity, interest, and opinion factor scores, and several product variables.

SOURCE: Reprinted from the *Journal of Marketing Research*, Vol. IV (November 1967), pp. 349–354. Published by the American Marketing Association.

Because of the sample size (265) subjects could not be assigned to the five classifications described by Rogers [10]: innovators, early adopters, early majority, late majority, and laggards. Only the trial stage of the adoption process was investigated. The time to trial, if any, may be influenced by the level of current satisfaction, the perceived risk of trial as modified by advertising and feedback from earlier buyers, the available stock, and the rate of usage of the product class (subjects who purchase infrequently may fall by chance into the late buyer category). Subjects may develop brand preference leading to adoption after receiving information about the product and after using the product. Nonbuyers may have a poor opinion of the new brand or no opinion. A great many consumer attributes could be related to these elements, for example, the independent variables that will be examined. In addition, laboratory research indicates that experimental data on buyer preferences for existing brands, and possibly for a new brand, may materially aid in predicting brand switching and market behavior for the new brand [8].

DATA AND DEFINITIONS

A buyer of the new detergent was anyone who bought the product at least once in the seven-month period of diary keeping. An early buyer was one who purchased the product in the first 70 days after introduction. All remaining subjects who bought were late buyers. The 70-day period was a cutoff because the number of first-

time buyers per 10-day period reached a peak in the seventh 10-day period.[1] Of the 265 subjects in the sample, 52 were in the early buyer category, 62 the late buyer category, and 151 the nonbuyer category.

Fifty-seven variables (Table 1) were used to examine differences between subjects in the three buyer categories. Each variable was either a "before" or an "after" measure. The before measures were obtained by questionnaire prior to the product introduction and the after measures were gathered from questionnaire at the end of the diary period.

Some comments may clarify the variable groupings. The activity, interest, and opinion factor scores (AIO) and the media factor scores were from two sets of questions. In each case, the response sets were obliquely rotated after principal component factor analysis [12]. The product preference variable (Variable 40) was constructed as follows: Each respondent rated 16 general product characteristics for detergents on a five-point scale, from "not important" to "extremely important." She then rated each of the top ten brands that she knew about on the same set of characteristics. These two ratings were vector multiplied giving a number for each brand defined as brand prefer-

[1] A plot of time to first purchase was made on Weibull probability paper. It indicated a change in the forces influencing first purchase occurred at the 70-day point on the time axis. This result parallels the effect of catastrophic and wearout failures found in the electron tube life-testing investigations of J. H. K. Kao [5].

TABLE 1   *List of Variables Cross-Tabulated against Early, Late, Nonbuyer Classifications*

Socioeconomic variables (before measures)

1. Number of children 18 years and under living in the home
2. Number of rooms in residence
3. Number of different residences lived in during past 15 years
4. Rent or own residence
5. Present credit buying behavior for durables, including automobiles
6. Wife's age
7. Wife's education[a]
8. Wife's employment status
9. Husband's age
10. Number of different employers husband has had since completing formal education[a]
11. Wife's religion
12. Husband's occupation
13. Husband's education
14. Total family income
15. Socioeconomic status score
16. Status consistency score

Trial-proneness variables

17. Certainty about current brand versus other brands (before)[a]
18. Willingness to try known but untried brands (before)[a]
19. Perceived seriousness of product failure for detergents (before)
20. Willingness to shop for preferred brand (before)
21. Feelings about experimenting with new detergents (after)[a]
22. Likelihood of trying new detergents early (after)[a]

Activity, interest, and opinions factor scores (before measures)

23. Health and social conformity
24. Price conscious
25. Compulsive, orderly housekeeper
26. Fashions conscious
27. Careless or irresponsible behavior in personal, financial, and shopping affairs
28. Negative attitudes towards the value of advertising
29. Conservative middle class attitudes, sociable, mature
30. Weight watcher, dieter
31. Risk avoidance
32. Outdoor, casual, activist
33. Nonparticipating sports enthusiast[a]
34. Active information seeker
35. Do-it-yourself homemaker
36. Husband-oriented, interested in husband's activities

Product variables (after measures)

37. Total usage rates for all detergents for period (by total weight purchased)
38. Whether housewife received a free sample of the new detergent[a]
39. For those who received the sample, how much was used[a]
40. New product preference[a]

Informational variables (after measures)

41. Information transmission habits for detergents[a]
42. Information receiving habits for detergents[a]
43. Awareness score for new detergent[a]
44. Advertising slogan recognition score for new detergent[a]
45. Opinion leadership

Media exposure factor scores (before measures)

46. Factor score, cultural, intellectual magazines (*Atlantic Monthly, New York Times,* etc.)
47. Factor score, light reading magazines (*Life, Look, Readers' Digest,* etc.)
48. Factor score, fashion magazines

TABLE 1 *(continued)*

(*Vogue, Mademoiselle, Glamour,* etc.)	51. Store display
˙49. Factor score, homemaker magazines (*Family Circle, Woman's Day,* etc.)	52. Television advertising
	53. Magazine advertising
	54. Friends and relatives
	55. Package label
Judged importance of information sources on new detergents (after measures)	*Social activities* (after measures)
50. Importance of actual trial	56. Membership in church groups
	57. Membership in informal groups

ᵃ Significant at .05 level when cross-classified against the early, late, nonbuyer variable.

ence. Only the preference score for the new detergent was used in this analysis.

The awareness score (Variable 43) resulted from summing individual responses to four questions about the new detergent. One question asked subjects to write down all brands they knew that were not already listed. A second requested names of brands introduced in the area in the past year. A third requested names of brands for which samples had been given in the area in the past year and the fourth, advertising copy points for new brands recently introduced.

The accurate information score was obtained by scoring responses from a list of true-false questions on product characteristics and advertising slogans for several brands. Finally, the opinion leadership measure represented the standard question from the literature: "Would you say you are more likely, about as likely, or less likely than any of your friends to be asked your advice about laundry detergents?"

The purchase data on the new product were taken from diaries for the seven-month period. For each of ten product categories, including detergents, data about date of purchase, price, brand, total weight, deal amount, and place of purchase were collected.

TECHNIQUES OF ANALYSIS

Three kinds of statistical analysis were done. First, the 57 variables in Table 1 were cross-classified against the early, late, and nonbuyers category. Second, the variables that proved significant from the cross-classification were used in a stepwise multiple regression analysis. The regression involved prediction of number of days to first purchase for the subgroup of 114 respondents who had purchased the new detergent at least once in the seven-month period. Finally, the same set of variables was used in a discriminant analysis to try to classify subjects as triers or non-triers.

RESULTS

Cross-Classification

Fourteen variables were significantly ($p < .05$) related to the kind of buyer in the cross-classification analysis. These variables (starred in Table 1) were in four distinct categories: socioeconomic, trial-proneness, product-related, and informational. Though all were significant, only those relating to specific hypotheses are examined. The opinion leadership question, the AIO factor scores on information seeking and risk avoidance, and the media factor scores were conspicuous for their inability to distinguish the kind of buyer. Also, usage rate for the product class did not differentiate among early, late, and nonbuyers.

Table 2 shows the relationship between new product brand preference and kind of buyer. Nonbuyers had the least preference for the new brand, and the early buyers the greatest.[2] Also, 19 percent of the nonbuyers indicated a high preference for the new brand. These subjects could eventually become late buyers of the new product.

Table 3 shows that early buyers were significantly less confident about their past brand purchases than late

[2] Note that the early buyers would have a longer period for evaluating the product and to develop stronger likes or dislikes for this new brand.

TABLE 2   *Degree of New Brand Preference versus Kind of Buyer of New Detergent*

Preference	Early buyer	Late buyer	Non-buyer
High (250–400)	55%	39%	19%
High Medium (200–249)	25	31	21
Low Medium (50–199)	12	12	17
Low (0–49)	8	18	43
Total	100%	100%	100%
Base	52	62	151

TABLE 3   *Feelings about Present Brand of Detergent and Kind of Buyer for New Detergent*

Degree of certainty	Early buyer	Late buyer	Non-buyer
Very certain	17%	31%	48%
Usually certain	67	48	37
Sometimes certain or almost never certain	16	21	15
Total	100%	100%	100%
Base	52	62	151

Question: How certain are you that the brand of heavy duty detergent you are using will work as well as or better than any other brand you know of but have not tried?

buyers, and that late buyers were less confident than nonbuyers, indicating a predisposition by early and late buyers to try new brands.

Table 4 supports the predisposition to try the new brand. When asked about willingness to buy known, but untried brands, early and late buyers indicated a greater willingness than nonbuyers. This result suggests that an advertising campaign aimed at shaking confidence in current brand offerings may be an effective strategy.

Two slightly different questions about innovativeness, reported in Tables 5 and 6, were part of the follow-up questionnaire. Early buyers clearly see themselves as experimenters to a significantly greater degree than late or nonbuyers (Table 5). However, early buyers *did not* perceive themselves as innovators (Table 6). It seems that early buyers view their buying time for new detergents as concurrent with others. That is, there seems to be a perceived differ-

TABLE 4 *Willingness To Try New Brands and Kind of Buyer for New Detergent*

Feelings	Early buyer	Late buyer	Non-buyer
Very anxious or willing to try it	40%	36%	20%
Hesitant about trying it	52	53	49
Very unwilling to try it	8	11	31
Total	100%	100%	100%
Base	52	62	151

Question: When I am shopping and see a brand of heavy duty detergent that I know of but have never used, I am . . .

TABLE 5 *Feelings about Trying New Detergents and Kind of Buyer for New Detergent*

Feelings	Early buyer	Late buyer	Non-buyer
Enjoy experimenting with new detergents	42%	29%	13%
Prefer to wait until others have tried it	33	29	22
Prefer to wait until product has been established for some time	17	27	45
Don't know	8	15	20
Total	100%	100%	100%
Base	52	62	151

Question: (an "after test") Check the one statement that best describes your feelings about trying new detergent products.

TABLE 6   *Trying New Detergents and Kind of Buyer for New Detergent*

Likely to try new detergents	Early buyer	Late buyer	Non-buyer
Earlier than most people	8%	8%	1%
About the same time as most people	54	39	25
Later than most people	27	34	46
Don't know	11	19	28
Total	100%	100%	100%
Base	52	62	151

Question: In general, are you more likely to try new laundry detergents earlier, about the same time, or later than most people?

ence between experimentation and innovation. Other consumers that the early buyers had in mind might include other innovators. Literature on adoption indicates that innovative people with high interest tend to maintain active communication with one another. In this context the hypothesis seems tenable. Finally, in Tables 5 and 6, a significantly greater percentage of nonbuyers are in the "don't know" category.

Table 7 confirms an additional finding of adoption researchers about information transmission and reception. Compared with late and nonbuyers, the early buyers exhibited a higher degree of transmission of product information. However, a greater percentage of the late buyers were information receivers.

Two demographic variables were significant in the cross-classification analysis. Late buyers, compared with early and nonbuyers, had a significantly higher education. The other significant demographic variable, the number of different employers of the husband for the past 15 years, is a partial indicator of mobility. Here 43 percent of the husbands of early buyers had four or more employers; comparable figures for late and nonbuyers were 25 and 19 percent. High mobility might create the capability to easily adjust to new elements in one's environment or might reflect dissatisfaction with present conditions.

The effect of the free sampling campaign is shown in Table 8. Sixty-five percent of all subjects reported receiving a free sample; however, in the late buyer group, 77 percent reported receiving the sample. When only those who received the sample are used as a base for studying the relationship between usage of the sample and kind of buyer, the nonbuyers do not give the sample a fair test. (Instructions on the package told housewives that several washings were needed to fully demonstrate the cumulative effects of the brightening agent in the product. Nonbuyers may have rejected the sample before trying it or after incomplete testing.)

TABLE 7 *Information Transmission and Receiving about Detergents and Kind of Buyer*

Information	Early buyer	Late buyer	Non-buyer
	Kind of buyer—transmitting[a]		
Yes	40%	32%	22%
No	52	65	69
Don't know	8	3	9
Total	100%	100%	100%
Base	52	62	151
	Kind of buyer—receiving[b]		
Yes	29%	43%	27%
No	65	57	65
Don't know	6	—	8
Total	100%	100%	100%
Base	52	62	151

[a] Question: Have you recently been asked your opinion on detergents or have you volunteered any information on detergents to anyone?

[b] Question: Have you recently asked or has anyone volunteered information on detergents to you?

TABLE 8 *Receiving and Using Free Sample and Kind of Buyer*

Free sample	Early buyer	Late buyer	Non-buyer
	Receiving free sample		
Did receive a free sample	67%	77%	59%
Did not receive a free sample	33	23	41
Total	100%	100%	100%
Base	52	62	151
	Using free sample		
Used all of the free sample	100%	98%	73%
Used some of the free sample	—	—	16
Used none of the free sample	—	2	11
Total	100%	100%	100%
Base	35	48	89

Regression Analysis

To further examine differences between triers of the new product, a stepwise multiple regression analysis was done on the early and late buyers. The dependent variable was the number of days to first purchase, and the independent variables were all variables which were significant in the cross-classification analysis as well as several additional variables from Table 1. The results are as follows:

Significant independent variables	Increase in R^2
Number of rooms in the house	7.3%
Total family income	5.7
Number of husband's employers	6.6
Buying on credit	4.4
Feelings about trying known but unused detergents	3.7
Media FS; movie, crime	3.4
New product preference score	1.8
Total	32.9%

The demographic variables dominated the analysis. Early buyers lived in smaller houses, were in higher income groups, had husbands who had worked for more employers, and were less likely to buy large items on credit. In addition, early buyers expressed willingness to try new detergents, were relatively heavier readers of movie-crime magazines, and developed a higher preference for the new product. Remember, on the basis of the cross-classification analysis, early buyers were in relatively lower education groups. Thus, except for the income relationship, early buyers compared with late buyers appear to be typical of the lower socioeconomic classes. No convincing explanation for the income relationship appeared.

Several of the demographic variables, significant in the regression analysis, were not significant in the cross-classification analysis. The cross-classification analysis involved three groups: early, late and nonbuyers whereas the regression analysis treated only early and late buyers. Many variables that were significant in the cross-classification analysis reflected differences between triers and non-triers rather than between early and late buyers. The latter differences are reported in the discussion of the discriminant analysis. Conversely, several demographic variables, significant in the regression analysis, were not significant in the cross-classification analysis because their power to discriminate between early and late buyers was reduced after adding the third group (nonbuyers) to the cross-classification analysis.

Although the stepwise regression analysis explained only 33 percent of the variance in number of days before first purchase, the results are highly significant and suggestive of the market segment at which advertising should be aimed. For those people who made at least one purchase of the new product, one must accept the hypothesis that there were significant differences between the early and late buyers.

Multiple Discriminant Analysis

Also, the data can be examined for differences between triers and non-triers of the product. A two-group discriminant analysis was done on the buyer, nonbuyer classification, using the Cooley and Lohnes [4] program and then the BIMD 07M stepwise discriminant program [1]. The BIMD program was run to examine the multicollinearity among variables in the analysis. The analysis using the Cooley and Lohnes program resulted in eight significant variables not reported here. Table 9 gives the results of the stepwise discriminant analysis resulting in four significant variables, a subset of the eight variables from the Cooley and Lohnes analysis. The stepwise discriminant analysis gave the same "hit and miss" classification as the Cooley and Lohnes program with only four rather than the original eight variables.

The buyer and nonbuyer samples were split into an analysis and validation group, and the results are shown in Table 9. For the validation sample, 72 percent of subjects were correctly classified compared with 54 percent if all subjects had been assigned to the largest group. A 72 percent classification was also achieved for the analysis group of subjects. Early buyers were more aware of the product, had a higher preference, were more willing to try new brands, and scored higher on likelihood of trying new brands early.

CONCLUSIONS

Cross-classification, regression and discriminant analysis of differences between early, late, and nonbuyers for a new brand detergent gave significant results that tended to support several hypotheses on new-product trial. Triers and non-triers of the new detergent were significantly different

TABLE 9 *Stepwise Multiple Discriminant Analysis of Buyers versus Nonbuyers*

Discriminatory variable	F Value contribution
Awareness of the new product (after measure)	50.1[a]
Willingness to try unused brands (before measure)	20.9[a]
Preference for new product (after measure)	10.0[a]
Likelihood of early new brand trial (after measure)	5.0[b]

	Classified as	
Actual category	Buyer	Nonbuyer
Analysis Sample		
Buyer	57	23
Nonbuyer	31	79
Validation Sample		
Buyer	24	10
Nonbuyer	12	29

[a] Significant at .01 level.
[b] Significant at .05 level.

for product specific and trial minded variables. But given that the consumer made at least one purchase, differences between early and late trial tended to relate to socioeconomic factors.

Several important variables differentiating between buyers and nonbuyers may be interesting but impractical because they were measured after purchase. That is, are buyers more aware of the product because they purchased it, or did they purchase it because they were more aware? Similarly, did brand preference develop after buying and using, or vice versa? For some subjects a high awareness and a strong brand preference developed, which might account for the eventual wide market acceptance of the new detergent. Future research should be aimed at measuring brand preference before purchase, maybe by laboratory experiments or test marketing.

How much these findings can be generalized to other product categories or brands in this product category was not tested. The particular brand studied was heavily promoted and also free sampled, undoubtedly contributing to the high product awareness in the community. The free-sample strategy may have added to the heavy level of trial purchases. However, the findings are generally applicable. In particular, it is likely that early and late buyers are qualitatively different and that the variables that most strongly separate these groups will be different from the ones that separate buyers from nonbuyers.

REFERENCES

1. *Biochemical Computer Programs,* Health Sciences Computing Facility, Department of Preventive Medicine and Public Health, School of Medicine, University of California, Los Angeles, September 1965, 587–598.

2. Philip C. Burger, Charles W. King, and Edgar A. Pessemier, "A Large Scale Systems View of Consumer Behavior Research," University of Texas Symposium, *Exploration in Consumer Behavior,* April 1966.

3. James Coleman, Elihu Katz, and Herbert Menzel, "The Diffusion of an Innovation among Physicians," *Sociometry,* 20 (December 1957), 253–270.

4. William W. Cooley and Paul R. Lohnes, *Multivariate Procedures for the Behavioral Sciences,* New York: John Wiley & Sons, Inc., 1962, 116–133.

5. John H. K. Kao, "A Graphic Estimation of the Mixed Weibull Parameters in Life Testing of Electron Tubes," *Technometrics,* 1 (November 1959), 389–407.

6. Elihu Katz and Paul F. Lazarsfeld, *Personal Influence,* Glencoe, Ill.: The Free Press, 1955.

7. Charles W. King, "Adoption and Diffusion Research in Marketing: An Overview," *Science, Technology and Marketing,* fall conference proceedings, American Marketing Association, August 1966, 665–684.

8. ———, Edgar A. Pessemier, *Ex-*

perimental Methods of Analyzing Demand for Branded Consumer Goods with Application to Problems in Marketing Strategy, Pullman, Wash.: Washington State University, June 1963.

9. Richard Teach, and Douglas J. Tigert, *The Consumer Behavior Research Project*, Herman C. Krannert Graduate School of Industrial Administration, Purdue University, 1965.

10. Everett M. Rogers, *Diffusion of Innovations*, Glencoe, Ill.: The Free Press, 1962.

11. Bryce Ryan and Neal C. Gross, "The Diffusion of Hybrid Seed Corn in Two Iowa Communities," *Rural Sociology*, 8 (March 1943), 115–124.

12. Douglas J. Tigert, "Consumer Typologies and Market Behavior," Unpublished doctoral dissertation, Herman C. Krannert Graduate School of Industrial Administration, Purdue University, 1966.

Appendix: Tables

TABLE 1   *Cumulative Normal Distribution**

$$F(x) = \int_{-\infty}^{x} \frac{1}{\sqrt{2\pi}}\, e^{-t^2/2}\, dt$$

x	.00	.01	.02	.03	.04	.05	.06	.07	.08	.09
.0	.5000	.5040	.5080	.5120	.5160	.5199	.5239	.5279	.5319	.5359
.1	.5398	.5438	.5478	.5517	.5557	.5596	.5636	.5675	.5714	.5753
.2	.5793	.5832	.5871	.5910	.5948	.5987	.6026	.6064	.6103	.6141
.3	.6179	.6217	.6255	.6293	.6331	.6368	.6406	.6443	.6480	.6517
.4	.6554	.6591	.6628	.6664	.6700	.6736	.6772	.6808	.6844	.6879
.5	.6915	.6950	.6985	.7019	.7054	.7088	.7123	.7157	.7190	.7224
.6	.7257	.7291	.7324	.7357	.7389	.7422	.7454	.7486	.7517	.7549
.7	.7580	.7611	.7642	.7673	.7704	.7734	.7764	.7794	.7823	.7852
.8	.7881	.7910	.7939	.7967	.7995	.8023	.8051	.8078	.8106	.8133
.9	.8159	.8186	.8212	.8238	.8264	.8289	.8315	.8340	.8365	.8389
1.0	.8413	.8438	.8461	.8485	.8508	.8531	.8554	.8577	.8599	.8621
1.1	.8643	.8665	.8686	.8708	.8729	.8749	.8770	.8790	.8810	.8830
1.2	.8849	.8869	.8888	.8907	.8925	.8944	.8962	.8980	.8997	.9015
1.3	.9032	.9049	.9066	.9082	.9099	.9115	.9131	.9147	.9162	.9177
1.4	.9192	.9207	.9222	.9236	.9251	.9265	.9279	.9292	.9306	.9319
1.5	.9332	.9345	.9357	.9370	.9382	.9394	.9406	.9418	.9429	.9441
1.6	.9452	.9463	.9474	.9484	.9495	.9505	.9515	.9525	.9535	.9545
1.7	.9554	.9564	.9573	.9582	.9591	.9599	.9608	.9616	.9625	.9633
1.8	.9641	.9649	.9656	.9664	.9671	.9678	.9686	.9693	.9699	.9706
1.9	.9713	.9719	.9726	.9732	.9738	.9744	.9750	.9756	.9761	.9767
2.0	.9772	.9778	.9783	.9788	.9793	.9798	.9803	.9808	.9812	.9817
2.1	.9821	.9826	.9830	.9834	.9838	.9842	.9846	.9850	.9854	.9857
2.2	.9861	.9864	.9868	.9871	.9875	.9878	.9881	.9884	.9887	.9890
2.3	.9893	.9896	.9898	.9901	.9904	.9906	.9909	.9911	.9913	.9916
2.4	.9918	.9920	.9922	.9925	.9927	.9929	.9931	.9932	.9934	.9936
2.5	.9938	.9940	.9941	.9943	.9945	.9946	.9948	.9949	.9951	.9952
2.6	.9953	.9955	.9956	.9957	.9959	.9960	.9961	.9962	.9963	.9964
2.7	.9965	.9966	.9967	.9968	.9969	.9970	.9971	.9972	.9973	.9974
2.8	.9974	.9975	.9976	.9977	.9977	.9978	.9979	.9979	.9980	.9981
2.9	.9981	.9982	.9982	.9983	.9984	.9984	.9985	.9985	.9986	.9986
3.0	.9987	.9987	.9987	.9988	.9988	.9989	.9989	.9989	.9990	.9990
3.1	.9990	.9991	.9991	.9991	.9992	.9992	.9992	.9992	.9993	.9993
3.2	.9993	.9993	.9994	.9994	.9994	.9994	.9994	.9995	.9995	.9995
3.3	.9995	.9995	.9995	.9996	.9996	.9996	.9996	.9996	.9996	.9997
3.4	.9997	.9997	.9997	.9997	.9997	.9997	.9997	.9997	.9997	.9998

x	1.282	1.645	1.960	2.326	2.576	3.090	3.291	3.891	4.417
$F(x)$	.90	.95	.975	.99	.995	.999	.9995	.99995	.999995
$2[1 - F(x)]$	.20	.10	.05	.02	.01	.002	.001	.0001	.00001

* From *Introduction to the Theory of Statistics* by A. M. Mood and F. A. Graybill, 2d ed., table II, page 431. Copyright 1963 by McGraw-Hill Book Company. Used with permission of McGraw-Hill Book Company.

TABLE 2 *Cumulative Chi-square Distribution**

$$F(u) = \int_0^u \frac{x^{(n-2)/2} e^{-x/2}\, dx}{2^{n/2}[(n-2)/2]!}$$

n \ F	.005	.010	.025	.050	.100	.250	.500	.750	.900	.950	.975	.990	.955
1	$.0^3393$	$.0^3157$	$.0^3982$	$.0^2393$	.0158	.102	.455	1.32	2.71	3.84	5.02	6.63	7.88
2	.0100	.0201	.0506	.103	.211	.575	1.39	2.77	4.61	5.99	7.38	9.21	10.6
3	.0717	.115	.216	.352	.584	1.21	2.37	4.11	6.25	7.81	9.35	11.3	12.8
4	.207	.297	.484	.711	1.06	1.92	3.36	5.39	7.78	9.49	11.1	13.3	14.9
5	.412	.554	.831	1.15	1.61	2.67	4.35	6.63	9.24	11.1	12.8	15.1	16.7
6	.676	.872	1.24	1.64	2.20	3.45	5.35	7.84	10.6	12.6	14.4	16.8	18.5
7	.989	1.24	1.69	2.17	2.83	4.25	6.35	9.04	12.0	14.1	16.0	18.5	20.3
8	1.34	1.65	2.18	2.73	3.49	5.07	7.34	10.2	13.4	15.5	17.5	20.1	22.0
9	1.73	2.09	2.70	3.33	4.17	5.90	8.34	11.4	14.7	16.9	19.0	21.7	23.6
10	2.16	2.56	3.25	3.94	4.87	6.74	9.34	12.5	16.0	18.3	20.5	23.2	25.2
11	2.60	3.05	3.82	4.57	5.58	7.58	10.3	13.7	17.3	19.7	21.9	24.7	26.8
12	3.07	3.57	4.40	5.23	6.30	8.44	11.3	14.8	18.5	21.0	23.3	26.2	28.3
13	3.57	4.11	5.01	5.89	7.04	9.30	12.3	16.0	19.8	22.4	24.7	27.7	29.8
14	4.07	4.66	5.63	6.57	7.79	10.2	13.3	17.1	21.1	23.7	26.1	29.1	31.3
15	4.60	5.23	6.26	7.26	8.55	11.0	14.3	18.2	22.3	25.0	27.5	30.6	32.8
16	5.14	5.81	6.91	7.96	9.31	11.9	15.3	19.4	23.5	26.3	28.8	32.0	34.3
17	5.70	6.41	7.56	8.67	10.1	12.8	16.3	20.5	24.8	27.6	30.2	33.4	35.7
18	6.26	7.01	8.23	9.39	10.9	13.7	17.3	21.6	26.0	28.9	31.5	34.8	37.2
19	6.84	7.63	8.91	10.1	11.7	14.6	18.3	22.7	27.2	30.1	32.9	36.2	38.6
20	7.43	8.26	9.59	10.9	12.4	15.5	19.3	23.8	28.4	31.4	34.2	37.6	40.0
21	8.03	8.90	10.3	11.6	13.2	16.3	20.3	24.9	29.6	32.7	35.5	38.9	41.4
22	8.64	9.54	11.0	12.3	14.0	17.2	21.3	26.0	30.8	33.9	36.8	40.3	42.8
23	9.26	10.2	11.7	13.1	14.8	18.1	22.3	27.1	32.0	35.2	38.1	41.6	44.2
24	9.89	10.9	12.4	13.8	15.7	19.0	23.3	28.2	33.2	36.4	39.4	43.0	45.6
25	10.5	11.5	13.1	14.6	16.5	19.9	24.3	29.3	34.4	37.7	40.6	44.3	46.9
26	11.2	12.2	13.8	15.4	17.3	20.8	25.3	30.4	35.6	38.9	41.9	45.6	48.3
27	11.8	12.9	14.6	16.2	18.1	21.7	26.3	31.5	36.7	40.1	43.2	47.0	49.6
28	12.5	13.6	15.3	16.9	18.9	22.7	27.3	32.6	37.9	41.3	44.5	48.3	51.0
29	13.1	14.3	16.0	17.7	19.8	23.6	28.3	33.7	39.1	42.6	45.7	49.6	52.3
30	13.8	15.0	16.8	18.5	20.6	24.5	29.3	34.8	40.3	43.8	47.0	50.9	53.7

* This table is abridged from "Tables percentage points of the incomplete beta function and of the chi-square distribution," *Biometrika*, volume 32 (1941). It is here published with the kind permission of the author Catherine M. Thompson, and the editor of *Biometrika*.

TABLE 3 *Cumulative "Student's" Distribution*[*]

$$F(t) = \int_{-\infty}^{t} \frac{\left(\dfrac{n-1}{2}\right)!}{\left(\dfrac{n-2}{2}\right)! \sqrt{\pi n} \left(1 + \dfrac{x^2}{n}\right)^{(n+1)/2}} dx$$

n \ F	.75	.90	.95	.975	.99	.995	.9995
1	1.000	3.078	6.314	12.706	31.821	63.657	636.619
2	.816	1.886	2.920	4.303	6.965	9.925	31.598
3	.765	1.638	2.353	3.182	4.541	5.841	12.941
4	.741	1.533	2.132	2.776	3.747	4.604	8.610
5	.727	1.476	2.015	2.571	3.365	4.032	6.859
6	.718	1.440	1.943	2.447	3.143	3.707	5.959
7	.711	1.415	1.895	2.365	2.998	3.499	5.405
8	.706	1.397	1.860	2.306	2.896	3.355	5.041
9	.703	1.383	1.833	2.262	2.821	3.250	4.781
10	.700	1.372	1.812	2.228	2.764	3.169	4.587
11	.697	1.363	1.796	2.201	2.718	3.106	4.437
12	.695	1.356	1.782	2.179	2.681	3.055	4.318
13	.694	1.350	1.771	2.160	2.650	3.012	4.221
14	.692	1.345	1.761	2.145	2.624	2.977	4.140
15	.691	1.341	1.753	2.131	2.602	2.947	4.073
16	.690	1.337	1.746	2.120	2.583	2.921	4.015
17	.689	1.333	1.740	2.110	2.567	2.898	3.965
18	.688	1.330	1.734	2.101	2.552	2.878	3.922
19	.688	1.328	1.729	2.093	2.539	2.861	3.883
20	.687	1.325	1.725	2.086	2.528	2.845	3.850
21	.686	1.323	1.721	2.080	2.518	2.831	3.819
22	.686	1.321	1.717	2.074	2.508	2.819	3.792
23	.685	1.319	1.714	2.069	2.500	2.807	3.767
24	.685	1.318	1.711	2.064	2.492	2.797	3.745
25	.684	1.316	1.708	2.060	2.485	2.787	3.725
26	.684	1.315	1.706	2.056	2.479	2.779	3.707
27	.684	1.314	1.703	2.052	2.473	2.771	3.690
28	.683	1.313	1.701	2.048	2.467	2.763	3.674
29	.683	1.311	1.699	2.045	2.462	2.756	3.659
30	.683	1.310	1.697	2.042	2.457	2.750	3.646
40	.681	1.303	1.684	2.021	2.423	2.704	3.551
60 ·	.679	1.296	1.671	2.000	2.390	2.660	3.460
120	.677	1.289	1.658	1.980	2.358	2.617	3.373
∞	.674	1.282	1.645	1.960	2.326	2.576	3.291

[*] This table is abridged from the "Statistical Tables" of R. A. Fisher and Frank Yates, published by Oliver & Boyd, Ltd., Edinburgh and London, 1938. It is here published with the kind permission of the authors and their publishers.

709

TABLE 4 *Cumulative F Distribution**

m degrees of freedom in numerator; n in denominator

$$G(F) = \int_0^F \frac{[(m+n-2)/2]!\,m^{m/2}n^{n/2}x^{(m-2)/2}(n+mx)^{-(m+n)/2}}{[(m-2)/2]!\,[(n-2)/2]!}\,dx$$

n	G	1	2	3	4	5	6	7	8	9	10	12	15	20	30	60	120	∞
1	.90	39.9	49.5	53.6	55.8	57.2	58.2	58.9	59.4	59.9	60.2	60.7	61.2	61.7	62.3	62.8	63.1	63.3
	.95	161	200	216	225	230	234	237	239	241	242	244	246	248	250	252	253	254
	.975	648	800	864	900	922	937	948	957	963	969	977	985	993	1000	1010	1010	1020
	.99	4,050	5,000	5,400	5,620	5,760	5,860	5,930	5,980	6,020	6,060	6,110	6,160	6,210	6,260	6,310	6,340	6,370
	.995	16,200	20,000	21,600	22,500	23,100	23,400	23,700	23,900	24,100	24,200	24,400	24,600	24,800	25,000	25,200	25,400	25,500
2	.90	8.53	9.00	9.16	9.24	9.29	9.33	9.35	9.37	9.38	9.39	9.41	9.42	9.44	9.46	9.47	9.48	9.49
	.95	18.5	19.0	19.2	19.2	19.3	19.3	19.4	19.4	19.4	19.4	19.4	19.4	19.5	19.5	19.5	19.5	19.5
	.975	38.5	39.0	39.2	39.2	39.3	39.3	39.4	39.4	39.4	39.4	39.4	39.4	39.4	39.5	39.5	39.5	39.5
	.99	98.5	99.0	99.2	99.2	99.3	99.3	99.4	99.4	99.4	99.4	99.4	99.4	99.4	99.5	99.5	99.5	99.5
	.995	199	199	199	199	199	199	199	199	199	199	199	199	199	199	199	199	199
3	.90	5.54	5.46	5.39	5.34	5.31	5.28	5.27	5.25	5.24	5.23	5.22	5.20	5.18	5.17	5.15	5.14	5.13
	.95	10.1	9.55	9.28	9.12	9.01	8.94	8.89	8.85	8.81	8.79	8.74	8.70	8.66	8.62	8.57	8.55	8.53
	.975	17.4	16.0	15.4	15.1	14.9	14.7	14.6	14.5	14.5	14.4	14.3	14.3	14.2	14.1	14.0	13.9	13.9
	.99	34.1	30.8	29.5	28.7	28.2	27.9	27.7	27.5	27.3	27.2	27.1	26.9	26.7	26.5	26.3	26.2	26.1
	.995	55.6	49.8	47.5	46.2	45.4	44.8	44.4	44.1	43.9	43.7	43.4	43.1	42.8	42.5	42.1	42.0	41.8
4	.90	4.54	4.32	4.19	4.11	4.05	4.01	3.98	3.95	3.93	3.92	3.90	3.87	3.84	3.82	3.79	3.78	3.76
	.95	7.71	6.94	6.59	6.39	6.26	6.16	6.09	6.04	6.00	5.96	5.91	5.86	5.80	5.75	5.69	5.66	5.63
	.975	12.2	10.6	9.98	9.60	9.36	9.20	9.07	8.98	8.90	8.84	8.75	8.66	8.56	8.46	8.36	8.31	8.26
	.99	21.2	18.0	16.7	16.0	15.5	15.2	15.0	14.8	14.7	14.5	14.4	14.2	14.0	13.8	13.7	13.6	13.5
	.995	31.3	26.3	24.3	23.2	22.5	22.0	21.6	21.4	21.1	21.0	20.7	20.4	20.2	19.9	19.6	19.5	19.3
5	.90	4.06	3.78	3.62	3.52	3.45	3.40	3.37	3.34	3.32	3.30	3.27	3.24	3.21	3.17	3.14	3.12	3.11
	.95	6.61	5.79	5.41	5.19	5.05	4.95	4.88	4.82	4.77	4.74	4.68	4.62	4.56	4.50	4.43	4.40	4.37
	.975	10.0	8.43	7.76	7.39	7.15	6.98	6.85	6.76	6.68	6.62	6.52	6.43	6.33	6.23	6.12	6.07	6.02
	.99	16.3	13.3	12.1	11.4	11.0	10.7	10.5	10.3	10.2	10.1	9.89	9.72	9.55	9.38	9.20	9.11	9.02
	.995	22.8	18.3	16.5	15.6	14.9	14.5	14.2	14.0	13.8	13.6	13.4	13.1	12.9	12.7	12.4	12.3	12.1
6	.90	3.78	3.46	3.29	3.18	3.11	3.05	3.01	2.98	2.96	2.94	2.90	2.87	2.84	2.80	2.76	2.74	2.72
	.95	5.99	5.14	4.76	4.53	4.39	4.28	4.21	4.15	4.10	4.06	4.00	3.94	3.87	3.81	3.74	3.70	3.67
	.975	8.81	7.26	6.60	6.23	5.99	5.82	5.70	5.60	5.52	5.46	5.37	5.27	5.17	5.07	4.96	4.90	4.85
	.99	13.7	10.9	9.78	9.15	8.75	8.47	8.26	8.10	7.98	7.87	7.72	7.56	7.40	7.23	7.06	6.97	6.88
	.995	18.6	14.5	12.9	12.0	11.5	11.1	10.8	10.6	10.4	10.2	10.0	9.81	9.59	9.36	9.12	9.00	8.88
7	.90	3.59	3.26	3.07	2.96	2.88	2.83	2.78	2.75	2.72	2.70	2.67	2.63	2.59	2.56	2.51	2.49	2.47
	.95	5.59	4.74	4.35	4.12	3.97	3.87	3.79	3.73	3.68	3.64	3.57	3.51	3.44	3.38	3.30	3.27	3.23
	.975	8.07	6.54	5.89	5.52	5.29	5.12	4.99	4.90	4.82	4.76	4.67	4.57	4.47	4.36	4.25	4.20	4.14
	.99	12.2	9.55	8.45	7.85	7.46	7.19	6.99	6.84	6.72	6.62	6.47	6.31	6.16	5.99	5.82	5.74	5.65
	.995	16.2	12.4	10.9	10.1	9.52	9.16	8.89	8.68	8.51	8.38	8.18	7.97	7.75	7.53	7.31	7.19	7.08
8	.90	3.46	3.11	2.92	2.81	2.73	2.67	2.62	2.59	2.56	2.54	2.50	2.46	2.42	2.38	2.34	2.31	2.29
	.95	5.32	4.46	4.07	3.84	3.69	3.58	3.50	3.44	3.39	3.35	3.28	3.22	3.15	3.08	3.01	2.97	2.93
	.975	7.57	6.06	5.42	5.05	4.82	4.65	4.53	4.43	4.36	4.30	4.20	4.10	4.00	3.89	3.78	3.73	3.67
	.99	11.3	8.65	7.59	7.01	6.63	6.37	6.18	6.03	5.91	5.81	5.67	5.52	5.36	5.20	5.03	4.95	4.86

P	ν	14.7	11.0	9.60	8.81	8.30	7.95	7.69	7.50	7.34	7.21	7.01	6.81	6.61	6.40	6.18	6.06	5.95
.995			3.01	2.81	2.69	2.61	2.55	2.51	2.47	2.44	2.42	2.38	2.34	2.30	2.25	2.21	2.18	2.16
.90	9	3.36	3.01	2.81	2.69	2.61	2.55	2.51	2.47	2.44	2.42	2.38	2.34	2.30	2.25	2.21	2.18	2.16
.95		5.12	4.26	3.86	3.63	3.48	3.37	3.29	3.23	3.18	3.14	3.07	3.01	2.94	2.86	2.79	2.75	2.71
.975		7.21	5.71	5.08	4.72	4.48	4.32	4.20	4.10	4.03	3.96	3.87	3.77	3.67	3.56	3.45	3.39	3.33
.99		10.6	8.02	6.99	6.42	6.06	5.80	5.61	5.47	5.35	5.26	5.11	4.96	4.81	4.65	4.48	4.40	4.31
.995		13.6	10.1	8.72	7.96	7.47	7.13	6.88	6.69	6.54	6.42	6.23	6.03	5.83	5.62	5.41	5.30	5.19
.90	10	3.29	2.92	2.73	2.61	2.52	2.46	2.41	2.38	2.35	2.32	2.28	2.24	2.20	2.15	2.11	2.08	2.06
.95		4.96	4.10	3.71	3.48	3.33	3.22	3.14	3.07	3.02	2.98	2.91	2.84	2.77	2.70	2.62	2.58	2.54
.975		6.94	5.46	4.83	4.47	4.24	4.07	3.95	3.85	3.78	3.72	3.62	3.52	3.42	3.31	3.20	3.14	3.08
.99		10.0	7.56	6.55	5.99	5.64	5.39	5.20	5.06	4.94	4.85	4.71	4.56	4.41	4.25	4.08	4.00	3.91
.995		12.8	9.43	8.08	7.34	6.87	6.54	6.30	6.12	5.97	5.85	5.66	5.47	5.27	5.07	4.86	4.75	4.64
.90	12	3.18	2.81	2.61	2.48	2.39	2.33	2.28	2.24	2.21	2.19	2.15	2.10	2.06	2.01	1.96	1.93	1.90
.95		4.75	3.89	3.49	3.26	3.11	3.00	2.91	2.85	2.80	2.75	2.69	2.62	2.54	2.47	2.38	2.34	2.30
.975		6.55	5.10	4.47	4.12	3.89	3.73	3.61	3.51	3.44	3.37	3.28	3.18	3.07	2.96	2.85	2.79	2.72
.99		9.33	6.93	5.95	5.41	5.06	4.82	4.64	4.50	4.39	4.30	4.16	4.01	3.86	3.70	3.54	3.45	3.36
.995		11.8	8.51	7.23	6.52	6.07	5.76	5.52	5.35	5.20	5.09	4.91	4.72	4.53	4.33	4.12	4.01	3.90
.90	15	3.07	2.70	2.49	2.36	2.27	2.21	2.16	2.12	2.09	2.06	2.02	1.97	1.92	1.87	1.82	1.79	1.76
.95		4.54	3.68	3.29	3.06	2.90	2.79	2.71	2.64	2.59	2.54	2.48	2.40	2.33	2.25	2.16	2.11	2.07
.975		6.20	4.77	4.15	3.80	3.58	3.41	3.29	3.20	3.12	3.06	2.96	2.86	2.76	2.64	2.52	2.46	2.40
.99		8.68	6.36	5.42	4.89	4.56	4.32	4.14	4.00	3.89	3.80	3.67	3.52	3.37	3.21	3.05	2.96	2.87
.995		10.8	7.70	6.48	5.80	5.37	5.07	4.85	4.67	4.54	4.42	4.25	4.07	3.88	3.69	3.48	3.37	3.26
.90	20	2.97	2.59	2.38	2.25	2.16	2.09	2.04	2.00	1.96	1.94	1.89	1.84	1.79	1.74	1.68	1.64	1.61
.95		4.35	3.49	3.10	2.87	2.71	2.60	2.51	2.45	2.39	2.35	2.28	2.20	2.12	2.04	1.95	1.90	1.84
.975		5.87	4.46	3.86	3.51	3.29	3.13	3.01	2.91	2.84	2.77	2.68	2.57	2.46	2.35	2.22	2.16	2.09
.99		8.10	5.85	4.94	4.43	4.10	3.87	3.70	3.56	3.46	3.37	3.23	3.09	2.94	2.78	2.61	2.52	2.42
.995		9.94	6.99	5.82	5.17	4.76	4.47	4.26	4.09	3.96	3.85	3.68	3.50	3.32	3.12	2.92	2.81	2.69
.90	30	2.88	2.49	2.28	2.14	2.05	1.98	1.93	1.88	1.85	1.82	1.77	1.72	1.67	1.61	1.54	1.50	1.46
.95		4.17	3.32	2.92	2.69	2.53	2.42	2.33	2.27	2.21	2.16	2.09	2.01	1.93	1.84	1.74	1.68	1.62
.975		5.57	4.18	3.59	3.25	3.03	2.87	2.75	2.65	2.57	2.51	2.41	2.31	2.20	2.07	1.94	1.87	1.79
.99		7.56	5.39	4.51	4.02	3.70	3.47	3.30	3.17	3.07	2.98	2.84	2.70	2.55	2.39	2.21	2.11	2.01
.995		9.18	6.35	5.24	4.62	4.23	3.95	3.74	3.58	3.45	3.34	3.18	3.01	2.82	2.63	2.42	2.30	2.18
.90	60	2.79	2.39	2.18	2.04	1.95	1.87	1.82	1.77	1.74	1.71	1.66	1.60	1.54	1.48	1.40	1.35	1.29
.95		4.00	3.15	2.76	2.53	2.37	2.25	2.17	2.10	2.04	1.99	1.92	1.84	1.75	1.65	1.53	1.47	1.39
.975		5.29	3.93	3.34	3.01	2.79	2.63	2.51	2.41	2.33	2.27	2.17	2.06	1.94	1.82	1.67	1.58	1.48
.99		7.08	4.98	4.13	3.65	3.34	3.12	2.95	2.82	2.72	2.63	2.50	2.35	2.20	2.03	1.84	1.73	1.60
.995		8.49	5.80	4.73	4.14	3.76	3.49	3.29	3.13	3.01	2.90	2.74	2.57	2.39	2.19	1.96	1.83	1.69
.90	120	2.75	2.35	2.13	1.99	1.90	1.82	1.77	1.72	1.68	1.65	1.60	1.54	1.48	1.41	1.32	1.26	1.19
.95		3.92	3.07	2.68	2.45	2.29	2.18	2.09	2.02	1.96	1.91	1.83	1.75	1.66	1.55	1.43	1.35	1.25
.975		5.15	3.80	3.23	2.89	2.67	2.52	2.39	2.30	2.22	2.16	2.05	1.94	1.82	1.69	1.53	1.43	1.31
.99		6.85	4.79	3.95	3.48	3.17	2.96	2.79	2.66	2.56	2.47	2.34	2.19	2.03	1.86	1.66	1.53	1.38
.995		8.18	5.54	4.50	3.92	3.55	3.28	3.09	2.93	2.81	2.71	2.54	2.37	2.19	1.98	1.75	1.61	1.43
.90	∞	2.71	2.30	2.08	1.94	1.85	1.77	1.72	1.67	1.63	1.60	1.55	1.49	1.42	1.34	1.24	1.17	1.00
.95		3.84	3.00	2.60	2.37	2.21	2.10	2.01	1.94	1.88	1.83	1.75	1.67	1.57	1.46	1.32	1.22	1.00
.975		5.02	3.69	3.12	2.79	2.57	2.41	2.29	2.19	2.11	2.05	1.94	1.83	1.71	1.57	1.39	1.27	1.00
.99		6.63	4.61	3.78	3.32	3.02	2.80	2.64	2.51	2.41	2.32	2.18	2.04	1.88	1.70	1.47	1.32	1.00
.995		7.88	5.30	4.28	3.72	3.35	3.09	2.90	2.74	2.62	2.52	2.36	2.19	2.00	1.79	1.53	1.36	1.00

* This table is abridged from "Tables percentage points of the inverted beta distribution," *Biometrika*, volume 33 (1943). It is here published with the kind permission of the authors Maxine Merrington and Catherine M. Thompson, and the editor of *Biometrika*.

Glossary

Attitude A predisposition to act in a certain way toward certain people or things.

Attitude-scaling test Test that asks the respondent to evaluate a number of statements.

Attribute A means by which a person evaluates an object.

Average See **Mean.**

Bayes Theorem A formula for computing conditional probabilities of an outcome.

Bias A methodical error that occurs in selection of respondents or measurements.

Bias in sampling Any method that causes one element of a population to have a different probability of being selected for a sample from other elements of the population.

Binomial distribution Distribution of the probabilities of getting x successes in n independent trials when there are only two possible outcomes.

Brainstorming Technique to encourage creative thinking in a group situation.

Cardinal measure A measure that contains numbers which are strictly proportional (2 is twice 1).

Carryover effects Effects resulting from the use of one stimulus or manipulation on subsequent experiments.

Causal imageries Conceptualizations of cause-and-effect among two or more variables.

Causal relationship A relationship that satisfies the condition that a variable or group of variables causes changes in another variable.

Cell A segment of a population defined by two or more variables.

Chi-square test A statistical procedure used to test the similarity of two or more percentage relationships.

Client A person or institution who purchases market research services.

Cluster analysis A set of techniques designed to group people into meaningful groups.

Cluster sample Geographically oriented random sample.

Computer package A group of related computer programs.

Concept Certain characteristics of phenomena that can be grouped together. A symbol representing similarities in certain phenomena.

Concurrent validity A subtype of criterion-related validity in which the criterion and the predictor concepts are measured at the same time.

713

Confidence interval Area of the estimated values of the sample within which the true value lies with a predetermined probability (usually 95 percent in social science research).

Construct validity The extent to which an operationalization measures the concept which it purports to measure.

Consumer behavior analysis The application of the behavioral science to decision making among consumers.

Content validity The degree to which an operationalization represents the concept about which generalizations are to be made.

Control Systematic manipulation of some element related to or contained within a system so as to effect a change in one or more elements in that system.

Control group Used in an experimental design to establish a base line against which the effect of an experimentation can be estimated.

Control unit A test unit that is observed during the course of an experimental treatment, but is not subjected to the treatment.

Control validity The degree to which a concept is manipulatable and capable of influencing other variables.

Convergent validity The degree to which two attempts to measure the same concept through maximally different methods are convergent. It is generally represented by the correlation between the two attempts.

Cover story A series of cues that direct a subject's attention from real purpose of research.

Criterion-related validity The degree to which the concept under consideration enables one to predict the value of some other concept which constitutes the criterion.

Culture ". . . that complex whole which includes knowledge, belief, art, law, morals, custom, and any other capabilities and habit acquired by man as a member of society." Edward B. Taylor.

Data bank An organized set of data from various areas from inside and outside the firm.

Debriefing Procedure to explain fully the true purpose of the experiment to the subjects having completed the experimental tasks.

Decision-making process A conscious and human process, involving both individual and social phenomena, based on factual and value premises, which concludes with a choice of one behavioral activity from among one or more alternatives with the intention of moving toward some desired state of affairs.

Degree of freedom (d.f.) In a numerical system it is the number of observations that can be varied without changing the constraints or assumptions associated with that system. The d.f. equals the total number of observations, n, less the number of constraints.

Dependent variable Variable whose value is determined by the value of one or more other variables.

Direct question A question explicitly asked.

Discriminant validity The extent to which a concept differs from other concepts when real differences are present.

Dispersion The spread of observed values in a distribution.

Dynamic model   A model that explicitly includes time.

Error   In verifying hypotheses two kinds of errors must be distinguished. First are errors of type 1: the null hypothesis is rejected in coming to a decision although it is correct. Error of type 2: the null hypothesis is accepted although it is wrong.

Errors   Methodical: improper facts caused by improper data-collection methods. Random: improper estimates of fact resulting from chance and subject to the laws of probability, may result from the fact that the sample is not truly representative of the population from which it was drawn. See also **Bias.**

Estimated value   Statistical measurement of a variable from samples which are transferred to the whole population.

Ethics   Socially accepted and desired practices.

Evaluation apprehension effect   A tendency of the respondent to create a positive evaluation from the interviewer.

Expectancy effects   Biases caused by researcher's (or experimenter's) opinions and expectations regarding the answer to a problem (or a question).

Experimental design   A method of planning experiments in such a way that as far as possible the results are neither affected by random errors nor confused by other factors and, moreover, so that the sampling error can be measured. It refers also to the organization of an experiment (for example, whether one or more measurements is to be made on each subject; whether one or several levels of an independent variable will be used to observe and test a subject).

Experimental treatment   Manipulation of the independent variables being tested.

Experimentation   A process where events occur in a setting at the discretion of the experimenter, and controls are used to identify the sources of variation in subject's response.

Experimenter effect   See **Researcher effect.**

External invalidity   The lack of ability to generalize the results of an experiment to the larger world.

External validity   The extent to which the results of the experiment may be generalized to new contexts, situations, and individuals.

Factor analysis   A technique for finding a set of dimensions latent in a set of variables, with the purpose of reducing a large set of variables to a smaller one.

Field research   Primary research by personal interviews or observations by interviewers on the spot, "in the field."

Field staff   Persons who administer questionnaires in the "field."

Frequency distribution   A table in which the data have been grouped into classes and the number of cases falling into each group is shown.

Function builder   See **Model specifier.**

Guttman attitude scaling   Method of aggregative scaling in which values are ordered by importance.

Halo effect   A tendency for a general opinion or attitude derived from rating an individual as high or low on one item of a test to exert an influence upon the rating of other and separate items, traits, or responses.

Heterogeneous sample   Sample that has many strata or segments.

Homogeneous sample   Sample that has only one segment.

Horizontal diversification strategy   Strategy broadening the line of products offered to present customers through technology unrelated to the company's present products.

Hypothesis   An assertion about the value of the parameter(s) of one or more variables.

Independent variable   Variable whose value is not influenced by the other variables or constants in the equation.

Indirect question   Question whose response is used to implicitly suggest information about the respondent.

Induction   The process by which a marketing researcher forms a theory to explain the observed facts: it involves reasoning or inference from the specific to the general.

Inferential statistics   A body of techniques based on probability theory—the researcher to make estimates, predictions, or judgments about the composition of the larger population on the basis of his sample data and the statistics computed from it.

Information aggregation   The level of detail of information which is stored in a data bank.

Information recency   Time lapse between the occurrence of a given marketing event in the real market and the time it is recorded in the management information system.

Innovation   An idea, practice, or object perceived as new by an individual.

Interaction effect   The effect of one variable on another.

Internal validity   The degree to which one can be sure that an experimental result is produced by some specific factor and not extraneous ones.

Interval estimates   The area in which it is estimated that the true value in the population lies.

Interviewer bias   Systematic error arising as a result of the interviewer influencing the interviewee.

Library   A collection of past research reports, books, and so on, used to formulate future research.

Linear discriminant analysis   Technique that determines differences between populations on the basis of random samples drawn from each of the populations.

Linear regression analysis   A procedure of fitting a line to a given set of data, usually observations on two or more variables.

Loaded questions   Questions containing words or concepts which tend to produce automatic approval or disapproval.

Management access time   Time lapse between the management's request for certain information and the receipt of the desired report or display.

Market development strategy   Strategy to find new classes of customers that can use the company's present products.

Market position of the product   The relative standing of competitive products in a specific market in terms of customer perceptions and/or sales.

Market segmentation strategy   Strategy designed to attract new customers by appealing to differing segments.

Marketing decision variables   Variables that marketing management can manipulate and influence.

Marketing indicator   A measurement of a marketing phenomenon whose movements indicate whether a particular marketing situation is improving or worsening in terms of some goal.

Marketing information system   Tool as well as philosophy of marketing management. Formal system for gathering, cataloging, storing, retrieving, and analyzing market data.

Marketing mix   The total marketing package including product, design, price, promotion, distribution, and service.

Marketing policy problem   A difficulty concerning a general orientation or operating philosophy of marketing management.

Marketing problem   A situation that is perceived by the marketing organization as a source of dissatisfaction for its members and for which preferable alternatives are considered possible.

Maturation effects   Processes within the respondents operating as a function of the passage of time per se. (Not specific to the particular events.) Campbell.

Mean   The sum of all observations divided by the number of observations (the average value).

Media (mass)   The entire communication spectrum which is used to announce, educate, entertain, and promote products and services through mechanical or electrical means.

Media research   Investigation of the structure of the audience reached by a particular advertising medium.

Median   The middle value when all the observations or data values are arranged in order of magnitude.

Mode   The value that occurs most frequently.

Model   A set of causal statements about the factors which are relevant to a given situation.

Model specifier   A series of operations that elicit the hypotheses of the manager.

Motivation   Inner striving condition described as wish, desire, or drive which activates behavior toward a particular goal.

Motivational research   Research on relationship between the underlying motives, desires, emotions, and so on, of the people and their behavior.

Multiple discriminant analysis   Technique for classifying persons into one group or another given certain information.

Multidimensional scaling   A set of techniques for measuring the perception of objects in a multidimensional space.

Multiple regression analysis   Technique for estimating the relationship between one "dependent" variable and a number of "independent" variables.

Multistage sampling   The sampling techniques where one makes several sequential random decisions.

Multivariate analysis   Analysis concerned with the relationship between sets of independent variables.

Mundane realism (prima facie)   Specifically, how well the experimental setting does in fact conform to the real world analog that it purports to depict.

Nominal numbers   A number only represents a word (1 = yes, 2 = no).

Nomological validity   The extent to which predictions based on the concept which an instrument purports to measure are confirmed.

Nonparametric test   A test method that is used when the statistical quantities to be tested are not metric or cardinal.

Nonrandom sample   Sample in which every element does not have a known probability of being selected.

Normal distribution   A bell-shaped function whose values are distributed symmetrically about their mean. It is typical of the distribution of population characteristics in many situations.

Norms   Standardized modes or rules of behavior which establish a range of tolerable activities for the individual in his relationship with other people.

Null hypothesis   The statistical hypothesis that the result of an experiment is due only to chance.

Observational validity   The degree to which a concept is reducible to observations.

Open-ended question   Question that does not provide any explicit choice of alternatives.

Operational research epistemic gap   Lack of correspondence between a theoretical concept and its operationalization.

Operationalization   Empirical expression of a theoretical concept.

Opinion leader   Person who influences the thoughts and behaviors of other individuals through interpersonal communication.

Ordinal number   A number system where values are only relations (2 is only greater than 1).

Panel   A group of people, members of a market population, who are used to provide information on purchase behavior, media response, or product usage.

Parameter   A value that specifies the relationship between a dependent and an independent variable.

Parametric tests   Tests based on the prerequisites of particular distribution functions, such as binomial distribution or normal distribution.

Partially structured interview   See **Unstructured interview.**

Percentage   A ratio of category responses to total responses.

Personality   The configuration of individual characteristics and ways of behaving which determines an individual's unique adjustment to his environment.

Pilot study   A run through the entire experiment, usually with a small number of subjects.

Population   Set of human respondents who form a total group.

Predictive validity   A subtype of criterion-related validity in which the criterion measure is separated in time from the predictor concept.

Price elasticity of demand   The ratio of the proportionate change in price to the proportionate change in quantity bought. It measures the relative change in the amount of a commodity purchased in response to relative changes in its price.

Program director   Marketing research manager.

Projective test   Psychological test method in which the interviewee makes comments about other fictitious persons, and so unconsciously comments on himself by projecting his own unconscious motives.

Proportion   Percentage of a population or sample having a particular characteristic.

Propositions   Sequences of concepts having specified relationships between them.

Question   See **Direct question, Indirect question, Open-ended question.**

Questionnaire   An instrument for collecting data from human subjects.

"Quick-cut" technique   Advertising technique involving the rapid movement from one scene to another.

Random sample   Sample in which every element of the population has a known probability of being selected.

Range   The difference between the highest and the lowest of a group of values.

Recurrent marketing problem   A persistent and visible difficulty concerning a general orientation or operating philosophy of marketing management.

Refashioned marketing problem   A marketing problem of long standing that has been given a new definition.

Reformulation strategy   Strategy concentrated on improving present products to increase sales to customers currently being served by the company.

Replacement strategy   Strategy designed to replace current products with new products having better ingredients or formulations.

Replication   Repetition of an experiment in the same conditions as the original. Technique used to increase the precision of the estimate of experimental error.

Rerecognized marketing problem   A problem that has received new attention but has always been present.

Research budget   Funded limitation for research.

Research design   Specification of methods and procedures for acquiring the information needed.

Research error   The extent to which the research results deviate from the "true" state of the whole population of interest.

Research proposal   A written communication submitted by a researcher to a potential sponsoring agency identifying a problem to be researched, the methodology to be used, and the end result of the research.

Researcher effects   Sources of errors such as expectancy, affecting the researcher.

Resurvey   Redoing a research project.

Role   Expected behavior pattern of a given status or position.

Round tabling   Forging questionnaires.

Sample   A subset of elements from a population. See also **Random sample, Sample size, Nonrandom sample, Heterogeneous sample, Homogeneous sample, Structured sample.**

Sample size   The number of respondents in a sample.

Sampling error   The difference between the results of taking the sample and the actual state of the total population.

Sampling method   Means of obtaining the sample from the population.

Scatter   See **Dispersion.**

Science   The set of activities that concerns studying a system. The performance of studies which are reproducible and being objective in terms of not influencing the results to fit one's own predilections.

Scientific prediction   Forecasting with the help of scientific or technological theories and data.

Segment   A subset of the population which has common values on such variables as age, income, and education.

Semantic differential   A question that compares to extremes of meaning.

Semantic validity   The degree to which a concept has a uniform semantic usage.

Sequential sampling   Drawing a series of samples until one or more predetermined criteria are met.

Shill   A paid informant posing as a research subject who influences other subjects.

Significance test   A device that enables the researcher to reach a statistical decision when interpreting the results of a market survey.

Social class   Category or situation of people with roughly similar status ranking in a particular community or society.

Social marketing   Design implementation and control of programs calculated to influence the acceptability of social ideas and involving considerations of product planning, pricing, communication, distribution, and marketing research.

Standard deviation   A measure of dispersion, mathematically defined as the square root of the variance.

Standardized interview   See **Structured interview.**

Statistical inference   The science of making inferences about populations by examining samples from these populations.

Status   Position occupied by the individual within a group relative to the other members.

Stochastic model   A model that explicitly includes uncertainty (or risk).

Strata   See **Segments.**

Structural interview   Interview where the interviewer is instructed to ask every question precisely as it is worded in the schedule with no additional explanations or interpretations.

Structured sample   Sample in which several strata are logically connected in some way.

Survey   The operation in which the hypotheses are put to test using a questionnaire.

System authority   It refers to the ability of the management information system to make decisions.

Systematic validity   The degree to which a concept enables the integration of previously unconnected concepts and/or the generation of a new conceptual system.

***T* distribution**   A bell-shaped function with its values symmetrically distributed about its mean and which changes shape with sample size or more precisely, with the degrees of freedom.

Technological forecasting   A series of human/computer techniques to forecast changes in technology which are likely in certain time frames.

Test market   A geographically isolated (usually) market used for a marketing experiment.

Test units   Individuals, firms, or markets whose responses to the experimental treatment are being studied or who simply observed during the test period.

Universe   See **Population.**

Unstructured interview   Interview centered around a list of general topics where the interviewer is used only to aid the respondent in the full expression of his thoughts and to encourage communication.

Variability   See **Dispersion.**

Variable   Value that is measurable and subject to change. Any measurable part of the environment.

Variance   Value that indicated how much the individual data values are spread around the mean. Mathematically defined as the average of the squares of the deviations from the mean.

Variation   See **Dispersion.**

Name Index

Aaker, David A., 611
Abell, Peter, 56n
Abelson, Herbert I., 171
Abelson, P., 615n
Abelson, Robert P., 190n, 612, 613
Achenbaum, Alvin A., 242, 246
Ackoff, R. L., 75n
Adler, Lee, 246, 247
Ajzen, I., 244, 246
Alexander, Ralph S., 186n
Alpert, Mark I., 177, 209n, 227–239
Amstutz, A., 538
Anderson, Ira D., 5n
Andreason, Alan R., 145, 208, 209n
Angelmar, Reinhard, 38n
Appel, V., 243, 246
Applewhite, P. B., 189n
Argyris, C., 77
Aronson, E., 247, 264n, 284, 288n, 344n, 350n
Assael, H., 243, 246
Atkin, K., 243, 246
Axelrod, Joel M., 209n

Banks, Seymour, 235, 351n, 354n
Barnett, H. G., 69, 73n
Bass, Frank M., 177n, 209n, 460
Bauer, Raymond A., 191n, 241, 246, 372
Berkowitz, Leonard, 611, 612
Bigman, S. K., 79n
Birdwhistell, R. L., 94n
Bither, Stewart W., 611
Blackwell, Roger D., 148, 151, 154, 169, 173n, 247, 364n, 366n, 368n, 369n, 569
Blalock, A. B., 71n
Blalock, Hubert, 39n, 56n, 71
Blau, Peter, 70

Bogart, Leo, 286n
Bolger, John F., Jr., 231
Borgatta, E. F., 69n
Boring, E. G., 105n
Boring, R. A., 339n
Boruch, R. F., 632n
Bowman, E. H., 385n
Bowman, Russ, 14
Boyd, Harper, 6, 119, 177n, 209n, 366n, 382, 402
Brehm, Jack W., 611
Britt, Stewart H., 366n, 367n
Broadbeck, May, 33n
Brooks, William D., 98n
Brown, Douglas B., 611
Brown, George, 15
Brown, James K., 364n
Brown, L. A., 6
Buckner, Hugh, 186n
Bunge, Mario, 31, 56n, 591
Burger, P. C., 214n, 467, 692–703

Cagley, J. W., 185n
Callom, F. L., 185n, 191n
Campbell, D., 98n, 244, 246, 346n, 348n, 363n, 372, 634
Cannell, Charles F., 264, 284, 288, 296, 307, 308n
Cardozo, Richard N., 185n
Carlsmith, J. M., 344n, 350n, 356n
Carlson, R. O., 626n, 636n
Carmone, F. J., 216, 218n, 475n, 480n
Carroll, J. D., 224
Cayley, Murray A., 177n, 209n
Chang, J. J., 224
Chesler, Mark, 34n
Chu, Godman C., 611
Churchill, Gilbert A., 185n

725

Subject Index

733

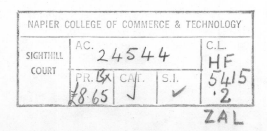